A
History of the Baptists

THOMAS ARMITAGE
1819-1896

A
History of the Baptists:

TRACED BY THEIR

VITAL PRINCIPLES AND PRACTICES,

FROM

THE TIME OF OUR LORD AND SAVIOUR JESUS CHRIST

TO THE YEAR 1886

BY THOMAS ARMITAGE

Volume One

Originally published in New York
in 1890 by Bryan, Taylor & Co.

The Baptist Standard Bearer, Inc.
NUMBER ONE IRON OAKS DRIVE • PARIS, ARKANSAS 72855

Thou hast given a *standard* to them that fear thee;
that it may be displayed because of the truth.
-- Psalm 60:4

*Reprinted
by*

THE BAPTIST STANDARD BEARER, INC.
No. 1 Iron Oaks Drive
Paris, Arkansas 72855
(501) 963-3831

THE WALDENSIAN EMBLEM
lux lucet in tenebris
"The Light Shineth in the Darkness"

ISBN #1-57978-921-8

Thomas Armitage

Thomas Armitage was born in Yorkshire, England, in 1819. He is descended from the old and honored family of the Armitages of that section of Yorkshire, one of whom, Sir John Armitage of Barnsley, was created a baronet by Charles I in 1640. He lost his father at a tender age, and his mother when he was five years old. She was the grand-daughter of the Rev. Thomas Barrat, a Methodist minister. She had great faith in Jesus, and prayed often and confidently for the salvation of her oldest son, Thomas. At her death she gave him her Bible, her chief treasure, which she received as a reward from her teacher in the Sunday School. Her last prayer for him was that he might be converted and become a good minister of the Saviour.

The religious influence of his godly mother never forsook him. While listening to a sermon on the text, "Is it well with thee?" his sins and danger filled him with grief and alarm, and before he left the sanctuary his heart was filled with the love of Christ.

In his sixteenth year he preached his first sermon. His text was, "Come unto me all ye that labor and are heavy laden, and I will give you rest." The truth was blessed to the conversion of three persons. He declined pressing calls to enter the regular ministry of the English Methodist Chruch, but used his gifts as a local preacher for several years.

Like many Englishmen he imbibed republican doctrines, and these brought him in 1838 to New York. He received deacon's orders from Bishop Waugh, and those of an elder from Bishop Morris. He filled many important appointments in the M. E. Church in New York, and when he united with the Baptists he was pastor of the Washington Street church in Albany, one of its most important churches, where the Lord had given him a precious revival and eight y converts. At this period his influence in the M. E. Church was great, and its highest honors were before him. When he was first examined for Methodist ordination, he expressed doubts about the church government of the Methodist body, and about sinless perfection, falling from grace, and their views of the ordinances; but he was the great-grandson of a Methodist minister, his mother was of that communion and he himself had been a preacher in it for years, and his misgivings were regarded as of no moment. In 1839 he witnessed a baptism in Brooklyn by the Rev. S. Ilsley, which made him almost a Baptist, and what remained to be done to effect that end was accomplished by another baptism in Albany, administered by the Rev. Jabez Swan of Connecticut. An extensive examination of the baptismal question confirmed his faith, and placed him without misgiving upon the Baptist platform in everything. Dr. Welsh baptized him into the fellowship of the Pearl Street church, Albany. Soon after a council was called to give him scriptural ordination. Dr. Welsh was moderator; Friend Humphrey, mayor of Albany, and Judge Ira Harris were among its members. A letter of honorable dismissal from the M.E. Church, bearing flattering testimony to his talents and usefulness, was read before the council, and after the usual examination he was set apart to the Christian ministry in the winter of 1848. He was requested to preach in the Norfolk Street church, New York, in the following June. The people were charmed with the stranger, and so was the sickly pastor, the Rev. George Benedict. He was called to succeed their honored minister, who said to Mr. Armitage, "If you refuse this call is will be the most painful act of your life." Mr. Benedict never was in the earthly sanctuary again. Mr. Armitage accepted the invitation, in his twenty-ninth year, July 1, 1848. In 1853-54, 140 persons were baptized, and in 1857, 152, while other years had great blessings.

The first year of his ministry in Norfolk Street the meetinghouse was burned, and another erected. Since that time the church reared a house for God in a more attractive part of the city, which they named the "Fifth Avenue Baptist Church." The property is worth at least $150,000 and it is free from debt. The membership of the church is over 700. In 1853, Mr. Armitage was made a Doctor of Divinity by Georgetown College, Ky. He was then in his thirty-fourth year.

At a meeting held in New York, May 27, 1850, by friends of the Bible, Dr. Armitage offered resolutions which were adopted, and upon which the Bible Union was organized two weeks later, with Dr. S. H. Cone as its president and W. H. Wyckoff, LL.D. as its secretary. In May, 1856, Dr. Armitage became the president of the society. In this extremely difficult position he earned the reputation of being one of the ablest presiding officers in our country. The Bible Union reached its greatest prosperity while he presided over its affairs.

Dr. Armitage is a scholarly man, full of information, with a powerful intellect; one of the greatest preachers in the United States; regarded by many as the foremost man in the American pulpit. We do not wonder that he is so frequently invited to deliver sermons at ordinations, dedications, installations, missionary anniversaries, and to college students. As a great teacher in Israel, the people love to hear him, and their teachers are delighted with the themes and with the herald.

Seventeen years ago a gentleman wrote of Dr. Armitage, "The expression of his face is one of mingled intelligence and kindness. As he converses it is with animation, and his eyes sparkle. His manners are easy, graceful, and cordial. He fascinates strangers and delights friends. He appears before you a polished gentleman, who wins his way to your esteem and affection by his exalted worth." The description has been confirmed by time.

(Taken from the Baptist Encyclopaedia, edited by William Cathcart, 1883, Louis H. Everts, Philadelphia.)

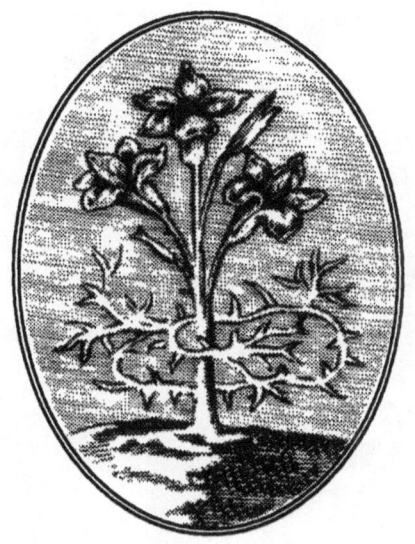

Sicut lilium inter spinas sic amica mea inter filias

On The Cover: We use the symbol of the "lily among the thorns" from Song of Solomon 2:2 to represent the Baptist History Series. The Latin, *Sicut lilium inter spinas sic amica mea inter filias*, translates, "As the lily among thorns, so is my love among the daughters."

PREFACE.

EARLY in the summer of A. D. 1882 the publishers of this work called upon the author to confer on the desirableness of issuing a Baptist history. He laid before them the histories extant by our writers, commending their merits. They said that, after examination of these, whilst each filled a peculiar niche in Baptist history, they were satisfied that a larger and more comprehensive work was demanded by the present public want, and requested him to undertake the task of preparing one.

This request was declined on account of its inherent difficulty and the pressure of a large New York pastorate. He submitted two or three weighty names of those who, in his judgment, were in every way better qualified for the work, among them the late Dr. William R. Williams, and wrote letters of introduction to these several gentlemen. In a few weeks they returned, stating that they had consulted not only those referred to, but other well-known Baptist writers, each of whom suggested that, as the author had devoted years to the examination of the subject, he owed it to his denomination to write and publish thereon.

After fuller consideration he consented to make the attempt, with the distinct understanding that he should be entirely unfettered in regard to the principle on which the work should be written. He saw at a glance that as Baptists are in no way the authors or offspring of an ecclesiastical system, that, therefore, their history cannot be written on the current methods of ecclesiastical history. The attempt to show that any religious body has come down from the Apostles an unchanged people is of itself an assumption of infallibility, and contradicts the facts of history.

Truth only is changeless, and only as any people have held to the truth in its purity and primitive simplicity has the world had an unchanging religion. The truth has been held by individual men and scattered companies, but never in unbroken continuity by any sect as such. Sect after sect has appeared and held it for a time, then has destroyed itself by mixing error with the truth; again, the truth has evinced its divinity by rising afresh in the hands of a newly organized people, to perpetuate its diffusion in the earth.

It is enough to show that what Christ's churches were in the days of the Apostles, that the Baptist churches of to-day find themselves. The truths held by them have never died since Christ gave them, and in the exact proportion that any people have maintained these truths they have been the true Baptists of the world. The writer, therefore, refused to be bound in his investigations by an iron obligation to show a succession of people who have held all the principles, great and small, of any sect now existing—no more and no less.

When Roger Williams left his followers they were in great trepidation lest they had not received baptism in regular succession from the Apostles, as if any body else had. They heard, however, that the Queen of Hungary had a list of regularly baptized descendants from the Apostles, and were half persuaded to send their brother, Thomas Olney, to obtain it at her hands. Still, on the second sober thought, they could not swallow this dose of the essence of popery, and concluded not to make themselves ridiculous. Whereupon Backus solemnly says, that at length they 'concluded such a course was not expedient, but believing that now they were got into the right way, determined to persevere therein.' Thus, once more, wisdom was justified in her children, under the application of the radical anti-Romish principle that the New Testament is the only touch-stone of Christian history. The men who obey it in all things to-day, the men who have obeyed it since it was written, and the men who wrote it, are of one flock, under the one Shepherd, whose holy body John buried beneath the waters of the Jordan.

The author has aimed, so far as in him lay, to command accuracy of statement with a style adapted to the common reader in our churches, thus especially reaching and interesting the young and making the work a reliable reference for all.

A lamentable lack of intelligence exists amongst us in regard to our origin and principles as Baptists. This book is written for the purpose of putting within the reach of all such facts as shall inform them of their religious history and what it cost the fathers of our faith to defend the same.

While cumbrous notes have been dispensed with, yet, for the benefit of those who honestly desire to inform themselves, references upon important points to authorities, mostly Pedobaptists, are given at the close of the volume. For the same reason the work is a defense and an exposition of our distinctive principles, as well as a history. Biography is here combined with history proper, and numerous portraits are given, chiefly of those not now living.

The engravings of the volume, with the exception of the steel-plate of the author, have been executed by the experienced hand of John D. Felter, Esq., whose ability and artistic skill are widely recognized. The letter-press and mechanical finish of the book are all that can be desired, even in this age of elegant printing, and bespeak the public favor for the gentlemanly publishers, who, by their enlarged business generosity, have secured to the reading public this volume in the best style of the printing art.

Whilst the author has noticed at length the rise and progress of the Baptists in the several States of the Union, he has not been able to present, with but few exceptions, the history of local churches and associations. To have attempted this would have extended the work far beyond the prescribed limit, and, owing to the great number of Baptist churches, the result must necessarily have been meager and unsatisfactory.

The author has done his work in all candor, with a sincere regard to the purpose of history and the maintenance of truth. He sends it forth with the prayer that it may fulfil its mission and afford profit to all who peruse its pages. Despite the utmost care to avoid mistakes, it is very likely that some have crept into the text, but on discovery they will be promptly corrected hereafter.

It was desirable to seek the aid of several young scholars, specialists in their departments, who have rendered valuable service by the examination of scarce books and documents, and submitted their own suggestions for consideration. Of these it is specially pleasant to mention:

Rev. W. W. Everts, Jr., of Philadelphia, who has devoted a large portion of his life to the study of ecclesiastical history, and has had rare opportunities, as a student in Germany, to make himself acquainted with the records of the Continental Baptists. He has made his investigations with great care and enthusiasm:

Henry C. Vedder, Esq., a junior editor of the 'Examiner,' and an editor of the 'Baptist Quarterly.' He is especially at home in all that relates to the Baptists in the time of the English Commonwealth, and has shown superior ability in examining that period:

Rev. George E. Horr, Jr., of Charlestown, Mass., who is thoroughly acquainted with the American period of our history, and in his researches has made free use of the libraries at Cambridge and Boston, turning them to most profitable account.

The first two of these gentlemen have also read the proofs of the respective departments to which they have thus contributed.

Rev. J. Spinther James, of Wales, was recommended by Rev. Hugh Jones, late president of the Llangollen College, as quite competent to make investigations in the history of the Welsh Baptists. These he has made and submitted, having had special facilities for information in the library of that institution.

Hon. Horatio Gates Jones, of Philadelphia, consented to prepare a full Baptist bibliography, but a press of legal business has prevented the accomplishment of his work, after devoting much time to the subject.

The portraits of these gentlemen are grouped, and preface the American department. It is but honorable to add, that none of these scholars are to be held responsible for any statement of fact or for any sentiment found in the book; that is entirely assumed by the author.

Hearty and sincere thanks are hereby rendered to Frederick Saunders, Esq., librarian of the Astor Library, for many attentions, especially for the use of Garruci, in photographing ten of the illustrations found in the chapter on Baptismal Pictures; to Dr. George H. Moore, of the Lenox Library, for the use of the great Bunyan collection there; and to Henry E. Lincoln, Esq., of Philadelphia, and Rev. Daniel C. Potter, D.D., of New York, for photographs used.

vi *PREFACE.*

The author owes a debt of gratitude also to T. J. Conant, D.D., LL.D., for his kindness in reading the proof-sheets of the chapters on the Baptism of Jesus and the Apostolic Churches as Models ; to Heman Lincoln, D.D., Professor of Ecclesiastical History at the Newton Theological Seminary, who examined the proofs on the Second and Third Centuries; to Albert H. Newman, D.D., LL.D., Professor of Church History in the Toronto Theological Seminary, who read all the chapters on the Continental Baptists from that on the Waldensians to that on the Netherlands; to Rev. D. McLane Reeves, D.D., of Johnstown, N. Y., who read the chapter on the Waldensians; to Rev. Owen Griffith, editor of the 'Y Wawr,' Utica, N. Y., who read the proof of the chapter on the Welsh Baptists; to Henry S. Burrage, D.D., editor of 'Zion's Advocate,' who examined the two chapters on the Swiss Baptists ; to S. F. Smith, D.D., of Mass., who has aided largely in the chapter on Missions ; to Reuben A. Guild, LL.D., Librarian of Brown University, who read most of the proofs of the chapters on the American Baptists; to J. E. Wells, M.A., of Toronto, who furnished much material for the chapter on the Baptists in British America; and to Rev. J. Wolfenden, of Chicago, Ill., for many facts concerning the Australian Baptists. Each of these scholars made invaluable suggestions, laying both the author and the reader under great obligations.

Acknowledgments of debt are also made to Rev. William Norton, A.M., of Chulmleigh, England, and to Rev. Joseph Angus, D.D., LL.D., Principal of Regents' Park College, London, for the examination of works not easily found in this country. Also to William Cathcart, D.D., of Philadelphia ; Henry G. Weston, D.D., of Crozer Theological Seminary ; to Howard Osgood, D.D., of the Rochester Theological Seminary ; to Ebenezer Dodge, D.D., LL.D., president of Madison University ; to Rev. Frederic Denison, of Providence, R. I.; to Hon. William H. Potter, to Hon. L. M. Lawson, Roger H. Lyon, Esq., and Dr. S. Ayers, of New York ; and to D. Henry Miller, D.D., of Connecticut. The General Index has been prepared by Mr. Henry F. Reddall, of New York. Many other friends have kindly assisted the author in various ways in the preparation of the work, who will please accept his devout thanks ; and last, but not least, those members of the press who have voluntarily spoken so kindly of the work on the inspection of portions of the manuscript personally or by their correspondents.

THOMAS ARMITAGE.

PARSONAGE, No. 2 WEST 46TH ST., NEW YORK,
    January 1, 1887.

INTRODUCTION.

A HISTORY of the Baptists should be understood in its objects and aims; and cleared, in the beginning, of misapprehension and perversion. It is not the history of a nationality, a race, an organization, but of a people, 'traced by their vital principles and gospel practices.' The unity to be exhibited and demonstrated was not brought about by force, by coercion of pains and penalties, by repressive and punitive Acts of Conformity; but by the recognition and adoption of a common authoritative and completed divine standard.

The error of many previous attempts has consisted in the assumption that a Church and Christianity were identical. We have had numerous and voluminous histories of Churches and creeds; and untold abuses have resulted from confounding them with Christ's people, with New Testament doctrines and practices. This *petitio principii* has been the source of much evil. Its hurtful influence has been seen and felt in the arrogant pretensions of these 'Churches,' their alliance with and use of civil authority, the abuses which have come from unrestrained and irresponsible power; and in the revulsion and extreme rebound of persons and communities, when reason and conscience and science and patriotism have exposed the deceptiveness of claims, and the hungering soul has had no satisfying response to its clamors for the bread of life. Many infidels have taken refuge in deism, atheism, agnosticism, because they in their ignorance supposed the 'Church,' as they saw it, to be the embodiment of Christianity, the authorized exponent of Jesus Christ. Much of the ridicule of priestcraft and denial of the inspiration of the Scriptures is directly traceable to the corruption of the clergy, to *autos-da-fé* to the churchly opposition to science and support of political tyranny and kingly wrongs. The genesis of the painful skepticism, so abundant in France, Spain and Italy, one need not search far to find. '*Le Clericalisme, voila l'ennemi*' is the belief of many.

Bossuet advised Catholics, in their controversies with Protestants, to begin with the Church. A Church, in its idea, attributes, organization, membership, officers, ordinances, has been the battle-ground of ecclesiastical and religious dispute; and literature, thought, public opinion, government, manners, worship, have been so much affected and controlled by these disputes, that it is not easy now to bring back a discussion, or confine it, to the real, primal, essential question.

The idea of a New Testament Church is more subjective than objective. A Church is not an *a priori* organization, as innate ideas are *a priori*.

It is not an antecedent agency or instrumentality for the conversion of men. Men are not members by natural birth, by inheritance, by legislative act, by priestly rite. Believers are not made such by the *opus operatum* of Church ordinances. They dwell in Christ and Christ dwells in them by the consciousness of grace imparted. They came together into the primitive Churches by an elective affinity, an inwrought spiritual aptitude and capacity; and constituted a brotherhood of the baptized, a holy fellowship of the redeemed, a community of regenerated men and women, united to one another by the same animating spirit. A New Testament Church, the apostolic model, was a result, a product, an evolution from antecedent facts and principles. The Christ did not constitute a Church in advance of preaching and salvation and baptism, and endow it with powers and functions to execute the great commission. As the apostles and disciples preached, men and women heard, believed, and were baptized. The believers, coming together in local assemblies, were empowered to perform certain acts for edification and usefulness. These simple organizations were in the early days of Christianity the divinely approved Churches. A Church is no more a pre-ordained agency, an exterior antecedent instrumentality for saving men and women than the fruit is a pre-existing agency for propagating its kind. Both are evolutions and necessities in the wisdom and providence of God. From certain elemental principles—the logical and spiritual consequences of regeneration, faith, love and obedience—Churches, with their membership, organizations, officers and ordinances, are evolved.

The evolution is none the less such because scriptural precepts can be produced; for in the sense in which the word is used, these commands are evolutions of the wisdom and grace of God. It is readily seen how too much importance can be attached to forms and organizations and officers. Christ taught truth, promulgated ideas, sowed seed. Character, life, organism, union, followed. Philosophy, politics, science, religion, are valuable not as the outcome of a pre-ordained scheme, but as the product and growth of correlated thought, ideas actualized, principles, abstractions, put into concrete, vitalized forms. Moral and spiritual should precede and dominate the physical as ideas precede form and organism. Whatever is durable, immortal; whatever conduces to man's well-being, to the development of humanity which had its genesis in divine thought, must in its ultimate analysis be traceable to fundamental principles, to eternal verities. Civilization, government, religion, must be imperfect, ephemeral, and fail of their noblest end if not based on an intelligent and cordial adoption of the right, the true, the imperishable. Just in so far as mere expediency controls there will be superficiality, imperfectness, failure. A Christian Church must come from the divine thought and seek the divine end. A Church in the true New Testament idea, so originated and wrought out, presents a perfect ideal, ever stimulating, beckoning onward and upward, never perfectly attained. It exalts God's word, magnifies Christ's work, relies on the Spirit's presence and power, individualizes and honors man, teaches his personal responsibility and privileges, and necessitates his completest moral and mental development. Individualism runs through New Testament Christianity. Right of private judgment in religious matters, the requirement of personal faith and obedience, leads inevitably to civil freedom. Individuality in relation to God and Christ and salvation, the Scriptures and judgment and eternity, conducts by an irresistible sequence to freedom of thought and speech and press to popular government, to unfettered scientific investigation, to universal education. Soul liberty cannot be dissevered from civil freedom. All modern reforms in government, broadening from the few to the many, can be traced to the recognition more or less complete of man's personal relations to God, and to the rejection of sponsors, priests and mediators, in faith and obedience and study. Intense religious activity quickens enterprise in all proper directions. Free thought on grand religious problems awakens thought on other topics. Communion with the King of kings, free and constant and invited access to him, makes one feel that the artificial distinctions of earth are transitory, and that a joint heir with the Christ is superior in freedom and nobleness and possibilities to any sovereign on the throne of the Cæsars.

New Testament Churches in their idea and ends have been perverted. From various causes they have degenerated into human organizations, and have been so assimilated to States and Nations as to be scarcely distinguishable from the kingdoms of this world. The tests or marks of a State would not be inapplicable to 'The Church' as it has acted, or claimed to act. It has been bound into a body politic, has exercised through the medium of a common government independent sovereignty and control over all persons and things within its boundaries, has entered into international relations with other political communities, has represented itself by embassadors and legates, has partitioned continents and oceans, has interfered in successions, has acquired territory, has been known by all the *indicia* of temporal authority. Becoming a secular power, it has claimed equal authority over many distinct kingdoms, exacted from their citizens an allegiance upon oath above that which the municipal law of their own country could impose, claimed Empires as fiefs, exacted oaths of vassalage and collected feudal revenues, absolved sovereigns and subjects from their oaths; claimed for the persons and the property of the officers it employed and the law by which they were to be governed a *status* wholly distinct from that of the subjects of the country where such officers were; stirred up crusades against refractory kings and republics, against schismatical princes, against pagans, against heretics; through the Inquisition ' secured to the ecclesiastical authority the arm of the secular power without any right of inquiry or intervention as a condition of its use, ' and put infidelity to the Church on the same footing as rebellion against the throne. All along through twelve centuries Churches have claimed the right to enter into alliances with civil governments, to direct executive, legislative and judicial action, and to use the power of the State for the execution of their decrees.

The claim of a Church to universal dominion is, like the claim of Spain and Portugal, based on papal grants, to the exclusive navigation, commerce and fisheries of the Atlantic and Pacific Oceans. It is, however, just as reasonable as the pretense that a parish can be set off by metes and bounds, or that a territorial area can be assigned to a particular minister to exercise therein exclusive ecclesiastical and spiritual functions. The assertion of a Church, or of a man, to supremacy over human conscience and judgments, is less defensible than a claim to special occupancy of land and water. Some nations have been driven to renounce, as against another, a right to parts of the ocean; but a man, in the image of the Creator, cannot surrender his inalienable liberty of worship or right of free thought.

The continuity of a Church is not like that of a State. There is little analogy between the two. One cannot by natural birth, by inheritance, by purchase, by the will of the flesh, become a member of the kingdom of Christ. A State may change its form of civil constitution from a monarchy, an aristocracy, to a republic, to any imaginable shape; but it does not lose its personality, nor forfeit its rights, nor become discharged from its obligations. France under President Grevy is the France of Napoleon or Louis Fourteenth. It retains its identity through all mutations. The corporate body succeeds to the rights and obligations of its predecessor. '*Idem enim est populus Romanus, sub regibus, consulibus, imperatoribus.*' It would require a vast stretch of credulity or ignorance to imagine the hierarchies of the present day to be the same as the Churches to which Paul wrote his letters. Conditions of citizenship, descent or alienation of property, distribution of estates, may be changed by human governments; but the conditions of membership in a New Testament Church are unalterable because they are spiritual and God-p'scribed.

Our books contain treaties in reference to intervention by one nation in the internal affairs of another upon the ground of religion, and learned discussions as to the right of law-making departments of government to prescribe, modify, or interpret articles of religious faith. It seems that in England even there is one and the same identical law-giver for Church and State. The Parliament, in the Act of Uniformity of Elizabeth, instituted the Thirty-nine Articles of Religion and put together a Book of Common Prayer. The atrocious cruelties of the religious persecutions, 'the execrable violations of the rights of mankind,' to use the strong denunciation of Sir James Mackintosh, have grown out of the claims of government and Churches to control and punish men's opinions. An Establishment is necessarily and always a usurpation and a wrong. A New Testament Church cannot, by possibility, be in alliance with a State and retain its scripturalness, its conformity with apostolical precept. Capability of such a union is the demonstration of a departure from a primitive model.

A tree is known by its fruits. An Establishment, *ex vi termini*, implies discrimination, irregularity, injustice, an arrogant claim to make Cæsar determine what belongs to God. Things will follow tendencies. Those permanently supported by the government sustain the government and resist concessions of popular liberty. In the time of Henry VIII. marriages in England were regulated by the canon law of Rome, 'grounded often on no higher principle than that of papal caprice;' and when the king's conscience and conduct demanded it, the Church found a semblance of excuse for his lust and tyranny. When Elizabeth was on the throne the Archbishop of Canterbury, to quiet some doubts as to her legitimacy, was ordered to draw up a 'Table of Degrees' which would place her succession on scriptural grounds. The disingenuous adulation of the dedication to King James in the 'Authorized Version' of the Bible is disgraceful to those who signed it.

The ecclesiastical Peers in the House of Lords uniformly and almost as a unit have, to quote from Joseph Hume, 'been the aiders and abettors of every tyranny and oppression which the people have been compelled to endure.' Bills for removing Roman Catholic disabilities, Jewish disabilities, University tests, and to open church-yards to Non-conformist burial services, etc., etc., have found in them steadfast opponents.

Joseph Chamberlain, in 1885, in a public address, put this pertinent inquiry: 'Is it not a singular thing that of all the great movements which have abated the claims of privileges or destroyed the power of tyrants, which have freed the nation or classes from servitude and oppression, or raised the condition of the great mass of the people, there is scarcely one which has owed any thing to the initiative or encouragement of the great ecclesiastical organization which lays claim to exclusive national authority and support?'

This hostility to popular rights and the removal of abuses is the natural consequence of the system of union of Church and State. Since the Reformation there has been much progress in securing the free exercise and enjoyment of religious profession and worship without discrimination or preference. Our Federal and State Constitutions, following the lustrous precedent of Rhode Island, have embodied religious liberty in American organic law; and our example and the undisputed success of voluntaryism are teaching lessons of freedom to the crushed millions of earth. In all civilized countries toleration is practiced. Wearily and painfully the work goes on. Privileges are wrested from reluctant hands, always after stubborn resistance, never once through gracious concession. Even when laws are repealed the social stigma is vigorously applied. 'Have any of the Pharisees believed on Him?' is constantly rung in our ears. Truth will prevail. Sire bequeaths to son freedom's flag, and establishments and endowments must yield to religious equality before the law. It is a delusion to imagine that the final victory has been won. Prerogative and privilege, sanctioned by antiquity and buttressed by wealth and power, will contest every inch. The demands of the pope for the restoration of his temporalities, and his lamentations over his voluntary imprisonment in the Vatican, show that Cardinal Manning spoke *ex cathedra* when he affirmed that the *Unam Sanctam* Decretal and the Syllabus contain the doctrines of Ultramontanism and Christianity. Pius IX., in a letter, August 7, 1873, to William, King of Prussia, claimed that every one who had been baptized belonged in some way or other to the pope. In July, 1884, a Cuban archbishop declared in the Spanish Cortes that 'The rights of the Roman pontiff, including the rights of temporal power over the States, were inalienable and cannot be restricted; and were before and superior to the so-called new rights of cosmopolitan revolution and the barbarous law of force.'

The tenacity with which the Establishment in England and Scotland holds on to its power and perquisites, and the success up to this time in foiling the Liberationists, are proofs that the battle of a thousand years is still to be prolonged.

The 'History of the Baptists' shows the victories of the past and the true principles of the contest if permanent success is to be attained. Justification by personal faith in the Lord Jesus Christ lays the axe at the root of all sacramentalism, sacerdotalism, alliance of Church with State and interference with soul liberty. The entire sufficiency and authority of the inspired word of God, the right of private judgment, the individuality of all religious duties, a converted church-membership and the absolute headship of the Christ, will give success to efforts for a pure Christianity.

Dr. Armitage has exceptional qualifications for writing a history of the Baptists. His birth, education, religious experience, connection with England and the United States, habits of investigation, scholarly tastes and attainments and mental independence, fit him peculiarly for ascertaining hidden facts and pushing principles to their logical conclusion.

J. L. M. CURRY.

CONTENTS.

INTRODUCTORY CHAPTER.

	PAGE
Have we a Visible Succession of Baptist Churches down from the Apostles?	1

NEW TESTAMENT PERIOD.

CHAPTER I.
John the Baptist 13

CHAPTER II.
The Baptism of Jesus 25

CHAPTER III.
The Baptist's Witness to Christ 36

CHAPTER IV.
Christ's Witness to the Baptist 47

CHAPTER V.
The King in Zion—Laws for the New Kingdom 57

CHAPTER VI.
Pentecost and Saul 71

CHAPTER VII.
Saul and Gentile Missions 88

CHAPTER VIII.
Nero and Paul, Peter and John 99

CHAPTER IX.
The Apostolic Churches the Only Model for all Churches 114

CHAPTER X.
The Officers and Ordinances of the Apostolic Church 129

CHAPTER XI.
The Baptist Copy of the Apostolic Churches 148

POST-APOSTOLIC TIMES.

CHAPTER I.
The Second Century 155

CHAPTER II.
The Third Century 172

CHAPTER III.
The Third Century—*Continued* 182

CHAPTER IV.
The Fourth Century 194

CHAPTER V.
The Fifth Century 211

CHAPTER VI.
The Sixth, Seventh, Eighth, and Ninth Centuries 226

CHAPTER VII.
Baptism and Baptisteries in the Middle Ages 243

CHAPTER VIII.
Ancient Baptismal Pictures 256

CHAPTER IX.
The Twelfth Century 276

CHAPTER X.
The Waldensians 294

CHAPTER XI.
The Bohemian Brethren and the Lollards 313

THE ERA OF THE REFORMATION.

CHAPTER I.
The Swiss Baptists 327

CHAPTER II.
The Swiss Baptists—*Continued* 340

CHAPTER III.
The Reformation—Zwickau and Luther 354

CHAPTER IV.
The Reformation—Peasants' War—Mühlhausen and Münster 362

CHAPTER V.
The Reformation—The German Baptists 379

CONTENTS.

CHAPTER VI.
The Reformation—German Baptists—*Continued* 395

CHAPTER VII.
The Reformation—Baptists in the Netherlands.. 407

BAPTISTS OF GREAT BRITAIN.

CHAPTER I.
Immersion in England. 425

CHAPTER II.
Immersion in England—*Continued*—Persecution.. 437

CHAPTER III.
British Baptists—John Smyth—Commonwealth.. 453

CHAPTER IV.
British Baptists—John Bunyan.. 474

CHAPTER V.
British Baptists—John Bunyan—*Continued* 493

CHAPTER VI.
British Baptists—Bunyan's Relations to the Baptists.. 511

CHAPTER VII.
British Baptists—Bunyan's Principles.. 528

CHAPTER VIII.
British Baptists—Commonwealth and the Restoration.. 540

CHAPTER IX.
British Baptists—Liberty of Conscience—Associations—The Stennetts—Irish Baptists...... 555

CHAPTER X.
The Scotch and English Baptists—Missions—Men of Note.. 572

CHAPTER XI.
British Baptists—The Welsh Baptists.. 598

THE AMERICAN BAPTISTS.

CHAPTER I.
The Colonial Period—Pilgrims and Puritans.. 619

CHAPTER II.
Banishment of Roger Williams.. 627

CONTENTS.

CHAPTER III.
Settlement of Rhode Island.. 641

CHAPTER IV.
The Providence and Newport Churches.. 658

CHAPTER V.
Chauncey—Knollys—Miles and the Swansea Church............................. 674

CHAPTER VI.
The Boston Baptists.. 686

CHAPTER VII.
New Centers of Baptist Influence—South Carolina—Maine—Pennsylvania—New Jersey..... 704

CHAPTER VIII.
The Baptists of Virginia... 724

CHAPTER IX.
Baptists of Connecticut and New York....................................... 739

CHAPTER X.
The Baptists of North Carolina, Maryland, New Hampshire, Vermont and Georgia........ 757

CHAPTER XI.
Baptists and the Revolutionary War... 776

CHAPTER XII.
The American Baptists and Constitutional Liberty........................... 796

CHAPTER XIII.
Foreign Missions—Asia and Europe... 814

CHAPTER XIV.
Other Baptist Missions—Foreign and Home.................................... 836

CHAPTER XV.
Preachers—Educators—Authors.. 852

CHAPTER XVI.
Theological Seminaries—Literature—Revivals................................. 872

CHAPTER XVII.
Bible Translation and Bible Societies...................................... 893

CHAPTER XVIII.
Baptists in British America and Australia.................................. 919

TABLE OF STATISTICS.. 943
REFERENCES TO AUTHORITIES QUOTED... 944
APPENDIX.—CONFESSION OF SCHLEITHEIM....................................... 949
GENERAL INDEX.. 953

LIST OF ILLUSTRATIONS.

	PAGE
Abraham's Pool at Hebron	16
Ampulla, The	272
Ancient Baptistery at Aquileia	248
Ancient Church Edifice in Cornwall	226
Ancient Font at St. Martin's, Canterbury	425
Ancient Roman Bath, Vatican Museum	249
Ancient Ship	94
Ancient Stone Font in Cornwall	227
Bainham, James, at St. Paul's	326
Baptism of Jesus facing	25
Baptism at Rheinsberg	423
Baptism in the Thirteenth Century	274
Baptistery at Florence	251
Baptistery at Pisa	243
Baptistery in Catacombs of St. Ponziano facing	265
Baptistery of Bishop Paulinus	255
Baptistery of St. John Lateran	251
Baptizing in the River Ebbw facing	598
Barada River—Damascus in the Distance	86
Barnabas Introducing Paul to Peter	91
Basle on the Rhine	346
Beheading Block, The	342
Brescia	276
Bunyan's Cottage and Forge at Elstow	498
Bunyan's Monument	482
Bunyan's Tomb	481
Burning of Anne Askew and Others at Smithfield facing	448
Burning of Mrs. Elizabeth Gaunt facing	551
Castelluzo, Cave of	311
Christians given to the Lions in the Roman Amphitheater	169
Church, The, as a Ship, on Christ the Fish	257
Cloven Tongues as of Fire	263
Constantine the Great	197
Conversion and Baptism	261
Cup of Alba	272
Fanatical Monk Preaching, A	282

	PAGE
Fifth Mile of the Via Appia, Restored	96
Forbidden Book, The facing	301
Fords of Jordan	82
Interior of Baptistery of Florence	252
Jerusalem from the Mount of Olives	71
Jesus Baptized in the Jordan	259
Jesus Blessing a Child	69
Judson's Translation of the Scriptures Finished	818
Keach's Chapel	549
Keach in the Pillory	548
Mars' Hill	93
Martyrdom of John Badley	323
Monumento ad Arnaldo da Brescia facing	293
Moot House at Elstow	507
Mosaic, Arian Baptistery, Ravenna	270
Mosaic from Baptistery of St. John, Ravenna	266
Mosaic of the Seventh Century	274
Münster	362
Ninth Century Fresco, Basilica of St. Clement.—Cyril Immersing a Convert	241
Old Baptismal Font, St. John on the Pedestal	269
Pass in the Wilderness of Judea	18
Paul Preaching	105
Pool for Ablution—Baba-atel Temple	79
Pool for Religious Ablution—Golden Temple, India	87
Pool of Hezekiah	78
Pool of Siloam	75
Prison on Bedford Bridge, The	477
Pulpit, Baptistery, and Table at Pisa	253
Reputed Spot of Christ's Baptism	29
Roger Williams and the Indians	642
Ruins of Mellifont Baptistery	570
Schaffhausen	340
Solomon's Pools	76
St. Paul's Bay, from the south	95
Successful Gospel Preaching	261
Supposed Immersion of Jesus, A	259

xviii   LIST OF ILLUSTRATIONS.

	PAGE		PAGE
Symbol of the Church as a Ship	258	Waldensian Symbols	295
Symbolic Supper, The	257	Waldshut on the Rhine	327
Tarsus	82	Whipping of John Florence	324
Theater at Ephesus—seen by Paul and John	113	Zoar Street Chapel, Southwark	479
Upper Pool of Gihon	80	Zwickau	354

PORTRAITS.

Anderson, Martin B.	868	Hubmeyer, Balthazar	337
Angus, Joseph	589	Hutchinson, Mrs. Lucy	466
Armitage, Thomas (steel plate)	frontispiece	Ivimey, Joseph	587
Arnold of Brescia	291	James, J. Spinther	facing 619
Backus, Isaac	779	Jenkins, J.	facing 607
Baldwin, Thomas	852	Jessey, Henry	472
Bede, the Venerable	426	Jones, Hon. H. G.	facing 619
Bennett, Alfred	856	Jones, Hugh	617
Booth, Abraham	569	Judson, Ann Hasseltine	817
Boyce, J. P.	facing 872	Kendrick, A. C.	facing 893
Broadus, John A.	869	Kiffin, William	467
Brown, Hugh Stowell	592	Knollys, Hanserd	676
Brown, Joseph E.	773	Leland, John	788
Bunyan, John	474	Maclaren, Alexander	577
Carey, William	579	MacVicar, Malcolm	936
Castle, John H.	934	Manning, James	783
Cathcart, William	870	Menno Simon	410
Colgate, William	913	Milton, John	540
Conant, T. J.	facing 893	Morgan, William	616
Cone, Spencer H.	904	Newman, Albert H.	935
Cramp, J. M.	926	Northrup, G. W.	facing 872
Curry, Rev. J. L. M.	738	Oldcastle, John	324
Dodge, E.	facing 872	Oncken, J. G.	828
Ellis, Robert	616	Osgood, Howard	facing 893
Evans, Christmas	610	Rippon, John	561
Everts, W. W., Jr.	facing 619	Sharp, Daniel	857
Foster, John	590	Smith, Samuel F.	858
Fuller, Andrew	584	Spurgeon, Charles H.	596
Fuller, Richard	760	Stillman, Samuel	780
Gano, Stephen	854	Strong, A. H.	facing 872
Guild, Reuben A.	866	Thomas, Joshua	facing 607
Hackett, H. B.	facing 893	Thomas, M.	facing 607
Haldane, James Alexander	575	Thomas, Timothy	614
Hall, Robert	593	Vedder, H. C.	facing 619
Harris, Joseph	facing 607	Watkins, Joshua	614
Havelock, Henry	591	Weston, H. G.	facing 872
Horr, G. E., Jr.	facing 619	Williams, John	facing 607
Hovey, A.	facing 872	Williams, William R.	859
Howard, John	565		

INTRODUCTORY CHAPTER.

HAVE WE A VISIBLE SUCCESSION OF BAPTIST CHURCHES DOWN FROM THE APOSTLES?

ON the western coast of India, near Goa, and also in the Mediterranean, springs of fresh water, which do not rise to the surface but are run off by the undercurrent, rush out of the strata at the bottom of the sea. But in the Gulf of Xagu, on the southern coast of Cuba, a wonderful fountain of fresh water gurgles up in the open sea; forcing aside its salt waters, it passes off in the surface-current and is lost in the ocean. From this spring navigators often draw their supplies of pure water in the midst of the briny waste. Here nature lends us a forceful type of the fact that there may be a flow of visible succession without purity, and that there may be a continuous purity without a flow of visible succession.

Is an unbroken, visible, and historical succession of independent Gospel Churches down from the apostles, essential to the valid existence of Baptist Churches to-day, as apostolic in every sense of the word? This question suggests another, namely, Of what value could any lineal succession be, as compared with present adherence to apostolic truth? From these two questions a third arises: Whether true lineage from the Apostolic Churches does not rest in present conformity to the apostolic pattern, even though the local church of to-day be self-organized, from material that never came out of any church, provided, that it stands on the apostolicity of the New Testament alone. The simple truth is, that the unity of Christ's kingdom on earth is not found in its visibility, any more than the unity of the solar system is found in that direction, for its largest domain never falls under the inspection of any being but God. So, likewise, the unity of Christianity is not found by any visible tracing through one set of people. It has been enwrapped in all who have followed purely apostolic principles through the ages; and thus the purity of Baptist life is found in the essence of their doctrines and practices by whomsoever enforced. Little perception is required to discover the fallacy of a visible apostolical succession in the ministry, but visible Church succession is precisely as fallacious, and for exactly the same reasons. The Catholic is right in his theory that these two must stand or fall together; hence he assumes, *ipso facto*, that all who are not in this double succession are excluded from the true apostolic line. And many who are not Catholics think that if they fail to unroll a continuous succession of regularly organized churches, they lose their genealogy by a break in the chain, and so fail to prove that they are legitimate Apostolic Churches. Such evidence cannot be traced by any Church on earth, and would be utterly worthless if it could, because the real legitimacy of Christianity must be found in the New Testament, and nowhere else.

The very attempt to trace an unbroken line of persons duly baptized upon their personal trust in Christ, or of ministers ordained by lineal descent from the apostles, or of churches organized upon these principles, and adhering to the New Testament in all things, is in itself an attempt to erect a bulwark of error. Only God can make a new creature; and the effort to trace Christian history from regenerate man to regenerate man, implies that man can impart some power to keep up a succession of individual Christians. Apply the same thought to groups of churches running down through sixty generations, and we have precisely the same result. The idea is the very life of Catholicism. Our only reliable ground in opposition to this system is: That if no trace of conformity to the New Testament could be found in any Church since the end of the first century, a Church established to-day upon the New Testament life and order, would be as truly a historical Church from Christ, as the Church planted by Paul at Ephesus. Robert Robinson has well said: 'Uninterrupted succession is a specious lure, a snare set by sophistry, into which all parties have fallen. And it has happened to spiritual genealogists as it has to others who have traced natural descents, both have woven together twigs of every kind to fill up remote chasms. The doctrine is necessary only to such Churches as regulate their faith and practice by tradition, and for their use it was first invented... Protestants, by the most substantial arguments, have blasted the doctrine of papal succession, and yet these very Protestants have undertaken to make proof of an unbroken series of persons, of their own sentiments, following one another in due order from the apostles to themselves.'[1]

Sanctity is the highest title to legitimacy in the kingdom of God, because holiness, meekness, and self-consecration to Christ are the soul of real Church life; and without this pedigree, antiquity cannot make Church existence even reverent. This sanctity is evinced by the rejection of error and the choice of truth, in all matters which the New Testament has enjoined, either by precept or example. In things of light import, demanding a robust common sense, the noble and courteous spirit of Jesus must be maintained, for personal holiness is the highest test of Christianity in all its historical relations. But this matter of visible Church succession is organically connected with the idea of Church infallibility, rather than of likeness to Christ. The twin doctrines were born of the same parentage, and the one implies the other, for a visible succession must be pure in all its parts, that is, infallible; if it is corrupt in some things, no logical showing can make it perfect. Truth calls us back to the radical view, that any Church which bears the real apostolic stamp is in direct historical descent from the apostles, without relation to any other Church past or present. In defense of this position the following considerations are submitted to all candid minds:

I. That Christ never established a law of Christian primogeniture by which he endowed local churches with the exclusive power of moral regeneration, making it necessary for one church to be the mother of another, in regular succession, and without which they could not be legitimate churches. Those who organized the churches in apostolic times went forth simply with the lines of doctrine and order in their hands, and formed new churches without the authority or even the knowledge of other churches. Some of these men were neither apostles nor pastors, but private Christians. Men are born of God in regeneration and not of the Church. They have no ancestry in regeneration, much less are they the offspring of an organic ancestry. The men who composed the true Churches at Antioch and Rome were 'born from above,' making the Gospel and not the Church the agency by which men are 'begotten of God.' This Church succession figment shifts the primary question of Christian life from the apostolic ground of truth, faith and obedience, to the Romanistic doctrine of persons, and renders an historic series of such persons necessary to administer the ordinances and impart valid Church life. How does inspiration govern this matter? 'Whoso abideth not in the *teaching* of Christ, hath not God; he that abideth in the *teaching*, the same hath both the Father and the Son. If any man cometh to you and bringeth not this *teaching* receive him not.' Pure doctrine, as it is found uncorrupted in the word of God, is the only unbroken line of succession which can be traced in Christianity. God never confided his truth to the personal succession of any body of men; man was not to be trusted with the custody of this precious charge, but the King of the truth has kept the keys of the truth in his own hand. The true Church of Christ has ever been that which has stood upon his person and work.

Whitaker, treating of this blunder of the hierarchy, says, '*Faith*, therefore, is, as it were, the soul of the succession; which, being wanting, a naked succession of persons is a dead body.'[2] Tertullian says, 'If any of the heretics dare to connect themselves with the Apostolic Age, that they may seem to be derived from the Apostles, as existing under them, we may say: Let them, therefore, declare the origin of their Churches, let them exhibit the series of their bishops, as coming down by a continued succession from the beginning, as to show their first bishop to have been some apostle or apostolic man as his predecessor or ordainer, and who continued in the same *faith* with the Apostles. For this is the way in which the Apostolical Churches calculate the series of their bishops.'[3] Ambrose takes the same ground, thus: 'They have not the inheritance, are not the successors of Peter who have not the *faith* of Peter.' Gregory (Nazianzen), in defending the right of Athanasius, to the chair of Alexandria, against his opponent, uses these words: 'This succession of piety ought to be esteemed the true succession, for he who maintains the same *doctrine of faith* is partner in the same chair; but he who defends the contrary doctrine, ought, though in the chair of St. Mark, to be esteemed an adversary to it

This man, indeed, may have a nominal succession, but the other has the very thing itself, the succession in deed and in truth.'

Calvin's view is in harmony with this testimony; he says: 'I deny the succession scheme as a thing entirely without foundation. . . . This question of being successors of the Apostles must be decided by an examination of the doctrines maintained.' Zanchius gives the same view: 'When personal succession, alone, is boasted of, the purity of true Christian *doctrine* having departed, there is no legitimate ministry, seeing that both the Church and the ministry of the Church are bound not to persons, but to the *word of God*.' Bradford, the martyr, truly said of the Church, that she is 'Not tied to succession, but to the word of God.' And Stillingfleet says, with spirit: 'Let succession know its place, and learn to vaile bonnet to the Scriptures. The succession so much pleaded by the writers of the primitive Church was not a succession of persons in apostolic power, but a succession of *apostolic doctrine*.'[4] On this ground it follows, that those who hold to a tangible succession of Baptist Churches down from the Apostolic Age, must prove from the Scriptures that something besides holiness and truth is an essential sign of the Church of God. The whole pseudo-apostolic scheme, from its foundation, was a creation of the hierarchy for the purposes of tyranny. The question of veracity is of vastly more moment in Baptist history than that of antiquity. Veracity accepts all truth without regard to time; gathering it up, and putting it on record exactly as it has been known through the centuries. Historic truth has many parts in harmony with each other, but the hard and fast lines of visible succession are those of a mere system and not those of true history. The Bible is the deep in which the ocean of Gospel truth lies, and all its streams must harmonize with their source, and not with a dreamy, sentimental origin. As it is not a Gospel truth that Christ has lodged the power of spiritual procreation in his Churches, so it is not true that all who come not of any given line of Church stock are alien and illegitimate.

II. OUR LORD NEVER PROMISED AN ORGANIC VISIBILITY TO HIS CHURCH IN PERPETUITY, AMONGST ANY PEOPLE OR IN ANY AGE. He endowed his Church with immortal life when he said: 'The gates of hell (Hades) shall not prevail against it.' But this has nothing to do with the question of a traceable or hidden existence. He gives his pledge that his Church shall not perish, and he has secured to her this stability. The forces of death have proudly dashed themselves against her a thousand times, but despite their rage, she stands firmly built on a 'Rock.' She has been driven into the wilderness again and again, as a helpless woman, to find a home as best she could. Its fastnesses, wastes, dens and caves, have invited her to their secrecy and shelter; but though her members have been driven like chaff before the wind, she has never been destroyed. An army is not overthrown when withdrawn from the field, it is retired only to make it indestructible. A grain of wheat enswathed and hidden in a pyramid for thousands of years grows as fresh as ever when brought back to light and moisture. So Christ signally evinces his watch-care over his

Church when he brings her into a secret retreat for safety, or as John expresses it, into 'her place prepared by God,' that she may be 'nourished for a time,' to come forth stronger than ever. Men have often thought the Church dead, first amongst this people and then that, when she was more alive than ever for her occasional invisibility. At such times her organization has been broken, her ordinances suspended, her officers slain, her members ground to powder; but she has come forth again, not in a new array of the same persons, but in the revival of old truths amongst a new people, to reproduce new and illustrious examples of faithful men. Christianity has been one web through which the golden band of truth has been visible from edge to edge at times, then a mere thread has been seen, then it has been fully covered by the warp. But anon, it has re-appeared as bright as ever, from its long invisibility.

III. CHRIST NEVER PROMISED TO HIS CHURCHES THEIR ABSOLUTE PRESERVATION FROM ERROR. He promised his Spirit to lead his Apostles into all truth, and kept his word faithfully when they wrote and spoke as the Spirit moved them. But when he had finished the inspired rule for their guidance, he did not vouchsafe to keep them pure, *nolens volens*. They might mix error and false doctrine with his truth, and disgrace themselves by corrupting admixtures; but the loss and responsibility were theirs. To have pledged them unmixed purity for all time despite their own self-will was to endow them with infallibility, which is precisely the doctrine of Rome, and a contradiction of all reliable history. Even in the first century there was great defection from the truth, as the Epistles show. Some of them were written, indeed, for the express purposes of correcting error, especially the latter writings of Paul and John. From the second to the fourth century, we find a rapid departure from inspired truth, with many sects, and no churches exactly after the Apostolic order. Some few men, original thinkers who followed no man's teachings, broke loose from the leadership of all. They went independently to the text of Scripture, but stood single-handed, and took with them some error from which they could not free themselves, so that they fell below their own ideal; and the original model was not restored for some length of time. Nay, more than this even is true. Those organic bodies of men who were drawn together into reformed churches, were moved by mixed motives, and in attempting a new order of things, few of them came up to the New Testament standard in all respects. And the failure to reach that standard in all churches has been so marked as to render it vain to look for a visible line of succession, which constitutes the only true Church descent from Apostolic times to ours. Some churches have been faithful to one divine truth and some to another, but none have embodied all the truth, and few individual men now known to us have kept all the requisitions of the Gospel.

This principle of infallibility and Church succession is the central corruption of Rome, and has so polluted her faith that she scarcely holds any truth purely, both in the abstract and the concrete. She believes in the proper Deity of Jesus Christ and of the Holy Spirit,—in the Unity and Trinity of the Godhead,—in the authenticity and inspiration of the Scriptures,—in the doctrines of incarnation and atonement,—and in eternal glory and retribution. But which of these has she not modified and perverted, under the pretense that she is endowed with Catholicity and perpetual visibility, as the rightful Church Apostolic, all her defilement to the contrary? and now she makes her errors her real life. What is true of the hierarchy is equally true, in this respect, of most of the bodies which have protested against and shaken off her chief heresies. They clung to some truths which she trod under foot, but they hugged some of her errors as closely as she hugged them, defended them as stoutly, and often persecuted unto death those who differed with them, even in minor matters.

IV. THE WORLD IS VASTLY MORE INDEBTED TO A LINE OF INDIVIDUAL MEN WHO HAVE CONTENDED FOR THE TRUTH, EACH BY HIMSELF, THAN TO ANY ORGANIC CHURCHES, WHICH CAN BE TRACED BY VISIBLE SUCCESSION FROM THE APOSTLES, UNDER ANY NAME WHATEVER. In religion, as in other departments of life, great movements have almost always centered in one or two isolated individuals, who have become immensely influential, by first turning their eyes upon the needs of their own souls, without human aid, and generally in opposition to all organizations. External influences had little to do in shaping their powers. They were molded above and in advance of their age, and created a new life for all about them, often far outside of their native sphere. First of all they were obliged to escape from and master themselves, then they led their times into a higher and purer godliness. God wrought some grand consummation by them without the aid of any local church, under those uniform laws of truth by which Christ's kingdom has ever been governed. These powerful examples, scattered through the centuries, show that not organic association, but regenerated manhood makes true history, as we might expect from the fact, that the foundation of Gospel obedience is laid in the deep soul-convictions of individual men.

The most marked discoveries and advancements of history have been made, not on the plans of concerted bodies, but by individual minds. Galileo seized the idea of the telescope from a casual glance at a boy holding a tube to his eye; and Newton found the law that binds the universe in a falling apple. So, the few who have been impregnated with holy purposes, saturated through and through with fidelity to Christ, have arisen in imperial strength to vindicate his truth; these are the Alpine peaks that mark the centuries. Their love to Christ held their action responsible to him, and made its final results safe. Religious systems arose out of their personal exertions, but when did a religious system create a new life, after the first century? Baptists are greater debtors to such a train of men than to any train of churches that can be named. This great law of individuality has not escaped the notice of skeptics. Matthew Arnold says, in his Introduction to Literature and Dogma: 'Jesus Christ, as he appears in the Gospels, and for the very reason that he is manifestly above the heads of his reporters there, is, in the jargon of modern philosophy, an absolute; we cannot explain him, cannot get behind him, and above him, cannot command him. He is, therefore, the perfection of our ideal, and it is as an ideal that the divine has its best worth and reality. The unerring and consummate felicity of Jesus, his prepossessingness, his grace and truth, are moreover at the same time the law for right performance on all great men's lines of endeavor, although the Bible deals with the line of conduct only.' Goethe speaks of the person of Christ in the same strain: 'The life of that divine man, whom you allude to, stands in no connection with the general history of the world in his time. It was a private life; his teaching was for individuals. What has publicly befallen vast masses of people, and the minor parts which compose them, belongs to the general history of the world, the religion we have named the first. What inwardly befalls individuals, belongs to the second religion, the philosophical: such a religion was it that Christ taught and practiced so long as he went about on earth.'

This tribute to Christ from such sources may be applied largely to those who have pre-eminently imbibed his spirit, were made what they were by closely following him, and who lived singly to his glory. The distinctive religious life which they introduced into their times was in advance of their day, as his life was in advance of his day. Their progress was slow, like his, because they set up a high mark and suffered for it; their patience and growth drew men to their side, and when they retired, perhaps as martyrs, their aim was reached by the world, so that that which others first scouted became necessary at last to their bliss. Some few such men drew the historic boundary lines, as a few headlands mark the entire sweep of a dim sea-coast. The truths which they insisted upon were changeless, though they were neglected under the reign of ignorance, or the sway of violence. But the king-men were not to blame for the dwarfishness of others. They gave unity to the centuries by keeping the struggle alive for the purity of eternal principles, the idea for which they suffered has interpreted its priceless value by their sufferings. Because the masses of the people were ignorant they were ferocious, for in the Middle Ages men did not seek high principle in troops; as great souls only can prefer a pure religion to one that is corrupt, one that is simple to one that is complicated, one from heaven and unstamped by earthly and grotesque intermixtures. The natural creed of the masses lodges in ceremony, mummery and external sanctity, and simple purity is too great to enlist admiration, when men prefer sophistication. Of course, where such religion is preferred there can be few men of gigantic stature.

Then, it often happens that men of high excellence rise in character far above their creed, for in historic religion creed and character do not always harmonize. When a few men rise above the character of a whole people they rise above the level of their age, and in that case they must pay a large price in suffering for the purpose of blessing their race, a price that but few are able to pay. A great mind of our day avows, 'That in the whole period from the sixth to the tenth century, there were not in all Europe more than three or four men who dared to think for themselves;' and even they were not classed with the creators of their age. They were neither rulers nor statesmen, but quiet and unobserved suggesters, who discovered abuses and pointed out remedies which future times were proud to apply. Chiefly through this order of mind we are to trace the record of Baptist sentiments, but the name 'Baptist' must not mislead us to enlist into our ranks men who would be unworthy of that name to-day, simply because they held some things in common with ourselves. Rather, we must embrace only those who cherished in full, the conception which both the New Testament Baptists and those of the nineteenth century set forth as underlying the entire kingdom of Christ. It is in the embodiment of these principles, whether in individuals or churches, that we are to look for true Baptist history. Because they are imbedded in the Bible we bow to their holy teachings, the antiquity of principles being quite another thing from the antiquity of organizations. As doctrines and practices originated in after times are late and new, we must reverence that antiquity alone which God uttered in the beginning. A system running through ages is an empty boast unless it reproduces the vital, spiritual copy of the first age.

For seventy years the Jews lost the line of the Passover, when Jerusalem lay in heaps and Israel was enslaved in Babylon, but when Hezekiah brought them back and restored the feast, the seventy missing links of festivity came with them. Two generations of their people had died and certain of their tribes were never heard of again, yet their true history as Jews was not broken nor the significancy of the Passover impaired, 'although they had not done it of a long time in such sort as it is written.' The moment that the Temple was rebuilt, its doors opened, and its lamps relit, the old authority of the institution revived. No Jewish household now living can trace its descent to any given tribe which existed at the fall of Jerusalem, A. D. 70. All have been so scattered and intermixed amongst themselves and the Gentiles, that tribal lines are entirely obliterated; yet none will deny that they are the direct descendants of Abraham. The principles above set forth are not those which have been generally adopted in Baptist history. But the writer is persuaded that they are the only true channel through which it can be traced, and by which Baptists can be made a unit with Apostolic Churches, while visible descent and the unbroken succession of churches are not and cannot be a proper test in the matter. We enjoy the right of self-government in the United States by a regular descent of democracy from the Roman Republic, but it is impossible to trace its course by a line of democracies to which our own is the successor. But the two, separated so widely in point of time, are essentially the same in their liberties. Individuals have asserted the rights of man in every country, and bands have struggled to embody them in every government, but who will say that these have not been the true patriots of the world, because a perpetual and visible line of organized republics has not come down to us, side by side with a similar line of despotic governments?

Historical truth applies the same processes to the several streams of natural science. Certain families and tribes are found in vegetable and animal life; that is to say, a given type multiplies itself into groups, sequence being our guide; yet no scientist discards faith in the existence of a type, because he cannot trace its visible sequence, while again and again he finds its outward course strangely resumed. So we speak of a people known as 'Baptists,' who have been substantially of one order of religious faith and practice, and have been made so by one order of religious principle. If crushed at one time, or entirely driven out of sight, others bearing the same Apostolic stamp and force have come forth to fill their places, under other names. A sunbeam is a sunbeam, no matter upon what putrescence it may fall, or with what pollution it may mingle; and by a ray of this character we thread our way from Christ down in ecclesiastical life. But the pretense that any one communion now on earth can trace its way down from the Apostles, in one line of fidelity and purity to New Testament teachings, is to contradict all reliable history. Dr. Abel Stevens says: 'Obscure communities, as the Cathari of the Novatians, the Paulicians, the Albigenses, and the Waldenses, maintained the ancient faith in comparative purity from the beginning of the fourth century down to the Reformation.' These and other sects held one or more distinctive Baptist principles, but none of them were thorough Baptists, through and through. A Baptist church is a congregation, and not a denomination of congregations, and find it in what nook we may, if it can trace its doctrines to the Apostles it is an Apostolic Church. 'A church,' says Dr. Ripley, 'that came into existence yesterday, in strict conformity to the New Testament principles of membership, far away from any long-existing church or company of churches, and therefore unable to trace an outward lineal descent, is a true Church of Christ. . . . While a church so-called, not standing on the Apostolic principles of faith and practice, and yet able to look back through a long line up to time immemorial, may have never belonged to that body of which Christ is the Head.'

The reader of religious history must be as honest as its writer, for the one is as much exposed to bias as the other. Yet, the exact facts which are found by the truthful historian are often condemned unweighed, because they are unpalatable; and true chronicles are often buried under the abuse which they heap upon their subject. For some reason much of this unfairness crops out, with many, whenever the truths of the New Testament are under consideration. Hence a man only honors himself and the vital teachings of the Holy Spirit when he separates himself from all that is superficial in his own methods of examination. Above all people, Baptists should be content to separate their history from all questionable material, and to write and read it in the form in which facts have cast it, its complete touchstone being conformity to the Gospel. Those only have been Baptists who have conformed to this rule, from age to age, without addition or subtraction. Error must eternally remain error, and no antiquity can sanctify it into truth. For all the ends of truth merely venerable custom is weak; yet, if a supreme love of truth does not force it back, it will dominate the mind through the senses, which are captivated by the hoary. As the dykes of Holland repel the approaches of the sea, so Baptists can only reserve the fairest provinces of truth by resisting ancient custom, simply because it is ancient. Ecclesiastical custom is as mutable as its maker, and yet, when an old practice conflicts with the New Testament, many make that practice the true interpretation of God's word without questioning its authority. Although not one jot has been added to the truth since the death of the Apostle John, the bare antiquity of a tradition enshrines it in the faith of many, especially if it came down from one of the so-called 'Fathers.' A late able scholar of Dr. Wayland's illustrated the feeling of many on this subject. He asked whether, if the doctor had lived near the time of Paul, his word would not have been weightier than that of other men. The great tutor replied, 'Yes, provided Paul had said in his writings, "I leave Francis Wayland my interpreter."' And if not, how could he have interpreted an apostle better than any one else, without special inspiration from God? The noblest minds are often crippled by this straining after uninspired antiquity, under the notion that it must touch the divine, without reaching after Christ's infallible ideal, when it stands openly before their eyes.

Baptist historians have always written against great odds. Commonly those who rejected our principles in past ages were filled with bitterness, and destroyed the best sources of exact data in the shape of treatise, narrative and record. The hated party was weak, and the dominant sought its destruction. Often these helpless victims of tyranny were obliged to destroy their own documents, lest discovery should overwhelm them in calamity. We shall see also that while many of the old sects were more or less imbued with Baptist principles, each had its own class of deductions, convictions and practices. In consequence, what was a cherished faith with one was held in contempt by another, and these states of mind became a part of the men themselves. Their different stages of faith were different stages of consciousness; and it came to pass, that to oppose each other fiercely was to attain high fidelity. In the dreary weakness of human nature each man held his own sect virtuous and the other vicious, all the time forgetting that as relative bodies they modified each other, and were largely responsible for each other's conduct. Then, as the Baptists had control of no national government, they could not preserve their records as did others. They managed no legislation or system of civil jurisprudence, and could keep no archives, having no legal officers whose special business it was to store up and keep facts. Necessarily, therefore, what few records they have left are fragmentary, without due continuity of register, and almost barren of vital events. The hand which carried the sword to smite this people, carried also the torch to burn up their books, and their authors were reduced to ashes by the flames of their own literature. The material for building up their chronicles is both crude and scanty. The governing life of a people, and not circumstances alone, gives value to their claim, and so we are thrown back on principle and hard generalization.

If Baptist history be peculiar, it is only because they have been a peculiar people. Their enemies have always accounted them as 'heretics,' whose prime value was to keep a cold world warm by their use as fuel for the stake. Men have never been willing to understand them, because they never would accept them on their own showing, but have insisted on measuring them by other standards than their own. With a great price they obtained their freedom, and their radical individualism made them appear to other men as disturbing and even violent. In turn, almost every man's hand has been against them, and as a people of but one book, they have taken a fixed and sturdy character, which has made them look as if their hand was against every man. What Burke said of Americans, in another line, is true of them in their devotion to the Bible, namely: 'In no country, perhaps, in the world, is the law so general a study.'

We see, then, that Robinson, Crosby, Irving, Orchard, Jones, Backus, Benedict, Cramp, and other Baptist historians, have written under every possible disadvantage. Still, their work shows an instinctive love of the truth for the truth's sake, worthy of such veterans. Their spirituality is elevated, their piety without guile, their devotion to the Gospel ardent, and their historical acumen quite equal to that of other Church historians. In the main, their leading facts and findings have not been proven untrustworthy, and no one has attempted to show that their general conclusions are untenable. Possibly, their chief mistake has lodged in the attempt to find the stray and casual links of a certain order of churches which may, by accommodation, be called Baptist. The design of this work will be, to follow certain truths through the ages, on that radical Protestant principle which professes to discard the Romish claim of catholicity and succession, and so to follow certain truths down to their chief conservators of this time, the Baptists. By this method we can best understand their battles with error and power, their defeats and victories. In general history no writer will be content to seek a succession of kings and courts, of warriors and bloody fields, but he will find truth in the social and civil life of a people, in the march of constitutional freedom, and the phenomena of human elevation.

The best service that can be rendered to the Baptists is, to trace the noiseless energy and native immortality of the doctrines which they hold, after all their conflicts, to the glory of Christ, for it is exactly here that we see their excellency as a people. If it can be shown that their churches are the most like the Apostolic that now exist, and that the elements which make them so have passed successfully through the long struggle, succession from the times of their blessed Lord gives them the noblest history that any people can crave. To procure a servile imitation of merely primitive things has never been the mission of Baptists. Their work has been to promote the living reproduction of New Testament Christians, and so to make the Christlike old, the ever delightfully new. Their perpetually fresh appeal to the Scriptures as the only warrant for their existence at all must not be cut off, in a foolish attempt to turn the weapons of the hierarchy against itself. The sword of the Spirit must still be their only arm of service, offensive and defensive. An appeal to false credentials now would not only cut them off from their old roll of honor, but it would sever them from the use of all that now remains undiscovered and unapplied in the word of God. The distinctive attribute in the kingdom of Christ is life; not an historic life, but a life supernatural, flowing eternally from Christ alone by his living truth.

Such existence does not claim the right of long possession in this soil or that, or through this or that course of time; nor is this the best title by which Baptists can prove their heirship to their fair inheritance. So far from their right to live inhering in organic ancestry by ancient descent, their right to be, in the nineteenth century, comes by their oneness with the truth given by Christ in the first century. Their present possession of that truth, is the testimony to their unity with an endless life, is their only authority for existence at any time, with or without human records, and shuts out all other considerations. The life of all Gospel churches must center in the truth which has come down unscathed from Jesus Christ; we must find it here or nowhere, and there can be no course, extreme or *via media*, which applies the true test of Church life but this. A human figment may serve the ends of Catholicism, but as Baptists are not Romanists, only Christ and Apostolicity as they are found in the Divine Writings can suffice for them. The spirit and outcome of these in their normal form afford the staple for genuine Baptist History.

NEW TESTAMENT PERIOD.

CHAPTER I.

JOHN THE BAPTIST.

WHEN Malachi finished the promissory books, B. C. 397, his vision shot the great gulf between the Old and New Revelations. He had just stated that on the other side 'The Sun of Righteousness should arise with healing in his wings,' and looking 400 years in advance he saw Christ's 'messenger,' his own successor, in a young Judean prophet, and heard him uplift the cry 'Behold your God.' Nearly 4,000 years before Malachi, a four-headed river had flowed from Eden 'to water all the ends of the earth,' and his faith now descried on the banks of the antitypical Jordan, the Master with the messenger, two Godlike forms, each first-born, and cousins' sons. Whom Malachi saw in vision, Matthew met in real flesh and blood, the Baptist 'herald' and the Lord from heaven. The voice, 'Make straight his paths,' is the first sentence in Baptist history. No moral night had been so dark as that athwart which this prophet cast his eye to see the coming 'Day-star.' Only remnants of the old Jewish faith were left, and the national life was fast going forever, with that public patriotism, free thought and outspoken manliness, which had already perished.

At first God gave the Jews the most popular government of all the nations; it treated the personal man with honor and dignity. Though they had no human king or hereditary ruler from time to time, he gave them such a political head as war or peace required, with prerogatives which met present necessity. In time the theocracy gave witness to the unity of God, and its liberties were linked to this vital truth. This theistic doctrine made Jehovah their common Father, they were uncrippled by doubtful negations, untainted with atheism, and the ideal in each man's soul clothed his fellow with the rights of a brother. The radical teaching from which all abiding liberty flows is this: 'Love God with all thy heart, and thy neighbor as thyself.'

During the period between the last prophet and the first evangelist the Assyrian, Persian, and Macedonian empires, with their endless divisions and subdivisions, had culminated in the Roman Empire. This power absorbed into itself the sentiment, humanity, political economies, and religious philosophies of thousands of years, covering the histories of all the great races, Semitic and Indo-European, having welded the whole into a homogeneous mass. It had sprung from an obscure city more than seven centuries B. C., and now embraced the civilized world. The great republic had waged its renowned conflict between plebeians and patricians for constitutional government. The democratic spirit had passed away with its stanchest defender, the regal and republican forms of government having been swallowed up in the imperial under Augustus.

Palestine was but a hundred and eighty miles long, by about half that width. Yet, when John and Jesus came the officers of Rome were every-where, with no jurisprudence left; only appeal to a heathen emperor, under privilege. Three native kings, indeed, divided the old Hebrew patrimony: Antipas, in Galilee; Philip, in Ituria; and Lysanius, in Abilene. Still, over these was Pilate, the sixth procurator in twenty-three years, with the Governor of Syria over him, with Tiberius above all, and each ready to enforce his mandate by the arms of the empire. These tyrants quarreled alternately with each other, in turn issued conflicting commands, fleeced each other in particular, and the Jews universally. One Jewish party flattered and copied the native rulers, another the foreigners, and all were proud to serve as minor officers, if they might wring a crust out of official rapacity. A third party hated and defied the intruders, plotting revolt and sedition, which kept the nation in a seething excitement and its blood ever flowing. Yet, a few men of God never yielded heart or hope. However dark the hour of adversity their lamp was always burning. They waited for the Deliverer to break every yoke. Their fellows, worn-out, grounded arms and died, their eyes glazed with despair. But the love of Jehovah and liberty never forsook these. No matter if the red-handed family of the age held Jacob by the throat, the holy few felt the shadow of the King at the gate. If the iron had entered their soul it was not rusted by heart-tears. The time had come for a new manhood; a new revelation of truth and holiness was needed, fresh in righteousness and true holiness. An age of moral suasion was dawning to work a new character in the personal man. Then, from renewed individuals should come 'the kingdom of heaven' in a regenerate society. Zacharias and Elisabeth, Simeon and Anna, felt their old hearts revive, because another Elijah was at the portal to open the golden age. Groans and strife, tears and blood, had tracked the horrid length of 400 years. At length there came a 'little child' to lead them, with a 'voice' to prepare his way; and when their withered arms pressed the reforming Baptist and his redeeming Lord to their bosoms, the first chapter in Baptist History was begun.

Edward Irving truly says, 'John was the beginning of a new race.' But the words of Jesus better fix his proper place in history: 'Amen, I say unto you, among them that are born of women there has not risen a greater than John the Baptist.' These words alone make him the most remarkable character on the sacred page, save only He who spoke them. Zacharias, his father, was a priest in Israel, Elisabeth, his mother, was a daughter of Aaron. Not only had their priestly ancestry stretched down fifteen centuries, but they were 'filled with the Holy Spirit.' This is said of no other father and mother of our race. They feared that their honorable lineage would soon be blotted out, for they were old and childless. The words, 'Thy prayer is heard,' imply that their empty home had been the subject of petition at God's throne. He had promised them a son, and when he would fulfill his word, it fell to the lot of John's father to pass through the golden gate into the holy place to burn incense: a high and holy privilege which never was repeated by the same priest, as it brought him so near to Jehovah. Already the live coals had been carried in a fire-pan from the altar of burnt-offering, the sweet spices sprinkled thereon, and the floating perfume was on its way to the clouds, when lo! a mysterious form glided into the hallowed place. Gabriel stood by the altar, bright in native benignity, at its 'right side,' too, the side of good omen, and in the attitude of Oriental service. In a moment the temple heard the new revelation, that a son should be born in the home of the man of God.

Gabriel and Michael are the only angels called by name in the Bible. Michael is the judicial messenger, the destroyer, valiant for the Lord of Hosts in terrible warfare. The mission of Gabriel is peace, especially Messianic peace. At the 'evening oblation,' the same hour of incense, he told Daniel that the Prince, Messiah, should come. He brought the same news to Mary, and to the father of John; the three cases ascribe to him the office of Messianic angel. No person but the priest could stand by the altar and live, and fear fell upon Zacharias when he saw that the celestial visitant did not fall dead. Then Gabriel broke the silence of four centuries, and opened the Baptist Age, saying: 'Fear not, thy wife shall bear a son, and his name shall be called John.' The venerable priest staggered through unbelief, and asked for a sign. Gabriel gave it in the very dumbness of the tongue that asked it until the child should be born. He then went forth to the people mute, beckoning, perhaps in an excited manner, but he could not pronounce the usual blessing, and they perceived that some strange thing had happened. He retired to his home at Hebron, or Juttah, near to Hebron, and remained speechless for three fourths of a year.

The 'city Juda,' the Levitical city of Juttah, as shown by Reland and Robinson, is about six miles south of Hebron, in the hill country, seventeen miles south of Jerusalem. Jerusalem stood 2,400 feet above the sea, and Hebron was 200 feet above that. Hebron was the ancient home of Abraham, where his pool still exists, the oldest now known in the world. This city had been given to the children of Aaron, 'with the suburbs thereof round about it,' and was a fitting birthplace of the Baptist, the greatest descendant of Aaron's house. Here David received his crown, and here were the sepulchers of Abraham, Sarah, Isaac, Rebecca, Jacob and Leah. Rabbinical tradition says of this spot, that the morning sacrifice was never offered at the temple till the watchman on its tower saw these uplands ablaze with the newly-breaking morning sun. Zacharias saw this glory despite his speechless state, meanwhile Gabriel's words rang through his soul concerning the coming child. The pledge: 'He shall be great before the Lord,' did not refer to his native wisdom, fidelity or influence, but royally set forth his great office; the great era which he should usher in, the great truths which he should proclaim—and, above all, the new stamp of manhood to be brought in his own person, as a specimen of those whom the new era was to produce. Without rank, or wealth, or power, he was to loom up above the old classes of good men, mighty before God. Consecrated to a greater work than any other man, and opening a greater future than any had foreseen, he was to take a higher type of moral character than any had yet borne. Of a priestly house, he was to offer no sacrifice, but was to preach the first Sacrifice from a princely house. Priesthood needed not the fullness of the Spirit, and seldom possessed it, but in order to establish the new office of preacher, to lead men to salvation, he needed the indwelling Spirit. Nor was the first prophet in four centuries to work a miracle, but simply to proclaim the Christ.

ABRAHAM'S POOL AT HEBRON.

When the cry of the new-born babe had brought music to the quiet home, a dispute arose among the neighbors about his name, some calling him Zacharias. This could not be. No one was named after his own father in the Old Testament. 'Nay,' said his mother, 'he shall be called John,' meaning: 'Bestowed of the Lord.' The neighbors remonstrated, none of his family were known by that name, and they made signs to his father to decide the question, who wrote upon a tablet: 'His name is John!' The child was to begin the world's new sermon, and as it was meet that the Gospel theme which had been pent in his father's soul so long should break forth, the tongue of the dumb was unloosed. With his first gust of voice he cried: 'O, child! thou shalt be called prophet of the Highest, for thou shalt go before the face of the Lord, in order to give knowledge of salvation to his people, in the remission of their sins.' It were worth the dead silence of a life-time to speak these words. Their meaning was so broad, and their music so sweet, that the old priest repeated the word 'salvation' three times before he could stop. 'A horn of salvation,'—'salvation for our enemies,'—'salvation in the remission of sins,' was the astonishing threefold theme on which he practiced his new-found tongue, in the new-found language of truth. Gabriel put a key into his hand to open this mystery, saying: 'Fear not, Zacharias, many of the sons of Israel shall he turn to the Lord their God;' in the converts whom John should make. Nay, he said, that 'the mouth of the holy prophets of old' had spoken of this 'redemption' as if the mystic fingers of dead Malachi were sweeping his old heart that day, till its chords vibrated as those of a harp.' That child had brought the missing link between the two dispensations, had become the veritable bridge-builder, the true Christian pontiff, who spanned the arch from the last outskirt of Judaism to the frontier line of the Gospel. What manner of child was this first Baptist?

The Gospels are silent on John's youth and early manhood, saying: 'That the hand of the Lord was with him,' that he 'Grew and became strong in spirit, and was in the deserts till the day of his manifestation to Israel.' God marked him by special tokens for his great task. While his body grew his soul became mentally and morally mighty till he was ready for his public work. The inspired limner gives simply this bold outline which makes 'the hand of the Lord,' the power of God, the emblem of his force. Gabriel throws light upon his discipline when he imposes the Nazarite's vow, to 'drink neither wine nor strong drink.' Nothing inflaming was to pass his lips or affect his brain. The vow also exempted him from attendance at the feasts, and kept him separate until his 'showing unto Israel.' Samson, Samuel, and John were all Nazarites from birth, severe consecration and denial of luxury being specially needful in the forerunner of him who was separate from sinners. His father's priestly house furnished him with Hebrew Biblical knowledge, and held there under the holy influence of Elisabeth, like Moses in Midian and Elijah in the desert, no rabbin could pervert him, till he was ready to stir the life of Judea to its center, by the Gospel. He is the only man in Scripture, except his Master, of whom no act of sin is recorded. Samson and Samuel were 'sanctified,' set apart to the Lord from their birth, but neither of them was filled with the Holy Spirit, as was the Baptist; one of the train of wonders in his character and mission.

It seems most likely that he left his home and plunged into the wilderness of Judea when he had passed his twentieth year, the time at which young priests were inspected by the Sanhedrin for their office. The 'deserts' which he entered are supposed to be that weary region that stretches over Western Judea, bordering on the Dead Sea, including its desolate basin. It includes Engedi, extending from the Kedron twelve miles south of Jerusalem to the south-western end of the Sea of Death, and in width, from thence to the mountains of Judea. It is not called a 'wilderness' for barrenness of vegetation, like the African sand-wastes. On the contrary, it is a perfect tangle of growth. Lonely and wild, the broom-brush, the stunted cedar, the osher, the rush and the Apple of Sodom, all flourish there, and nomads pasture their cattle with great profit. It is watered by the Kedron and other streams, their course lying dark and deep, in ravines and chasms, where all is grim and ribbed with rock, sometimes to the depth of 1,000 feet below the brow of the cliff.

This region abounds in gorges, crevices and caverns. It is torn by sharp precipices from the heaving of earthquakes, leaving the flint, chalk and limestone rents in every weird aspect. Rills of water gush forth, twisting their way here and there, or falling in cascades over crags and shelves, in haste to sweeten the acrid plain and sullen Sea of Salt. There, the jackal, the wolf, the fox, the panther, the boar, find their lairs and dens. From ridge to ridge, the hoarse scream of the vulture, the raven and eagle, echoes mingled with the pensive song of the thrush, and the drone of the bee, wandering from wild flower to wild flower, yellow and blue, crimson and white. In all its grandeur, this howling wilderness was the chosen home of the first Baptist. Its solemn desolation and wild elements preached to him of God, inured his body to hardship, and turned his soul inward upon itself. The parchment which warmed in his hand stirred him to communion with the Inspiring Spirit, who had invested its sentences with immortality, and proved its truths divine by their appeal to his heart. Life had coursed through the skin on which the text glowed before the knife of slaughter flayed it; and now, the holy *afflatus*, which the sacred penman had infused into its texture, warmed his soul with the beatings of an immortal life. There, he listened to the still, small voice, as did Elijah in sacred Horeb, away from noise and contention, till his spirit waxed strong in God and in the power of his might.

PASS IN THE WILDERNESS OF JUDEA.

In his austerity, this holy recluse wore the coarsest of raiment. The rough camel's hair-cloth, bound to his loins by a band of undressed leather, covered his limbs. Young and full of fire, he stood, the living image of courage, in the garb of the elder prophets. His Nazarite vow had kept his hair unclipped from birth, his diet was locusts, dried, ground, and eaten with wild honey which dripped from the rock, and he cooled his thirst at the spring wherever he roamed in the freedom of the desert. His removal from the uplands of Hebron into this somber desolation was not a mere incident. He must be equipped for his iron mission, as far as hardship could fit him to cope with moral evil. For years, he had been wrestling with the slow openings of his fore-felt work. Self-recognition had come glimpse by glimpse, till new insight had brought him into new sympathy with the Holy One who had sent him. Struggle after struggle had wrought in him an ardent spirituality, which rebukes sin with the quietest authority. Pleading with God day and night, the depravity of his brethren, and the hollowness of their ritual were echoed to his soul from the hollow rocks by his own foot-falls.

Did he pass his time amongst these grots and caverns without studying the word of God? Without the Sacred Parchments brought from his father's house, the gold had become dim and the fine gold changed, he had not been a true Baptist if ignorant of these, to win his countrymen back to Jehovah. We can scarcely doubt, that in the desert these treasures showed him how the rod of Aaron, his great ancestor, should bloom again and his empty pot of manna be refilled. How the Nazarene, then sweating at the carpenter's bench should suddenly come to his Temple, to rekindle the Shekinah in new glory over the mercy-seat. The Law, the Prophets and the Psalms in his retreat, made his heart burn with prophetic fire, for he heard the voices of old Prophets quivering in the air. As night gives brilliancy to the gem, so did his desert gloom bring out lustrous truth from the inspired lore of ages, every line that he unrolled telling a divine story; for every-where he found his Redeeming kinsman of the tribe of Judah, of whose 'Salvation' his father had sung. God would not entrust the education of his greatest prophet to the skill of mortals. In visions of the night when deep sleep fell upon his father's house, fear came upon him and trembling, which made all his bones shake. An image stood before his eyes, spirits passed before his face and he heard a voice. When the breathing Parchment crackled in his hand, the pulsations of a deathless life stirred him, and the Holy Oracle was alive with living images. The flaming sword of Eden waved before him, and the ascending fire of Abel. Enoch, the seventh from Adam, told him that Jesus opened the gate of heaven, when he rose to his home without tasting death. Noah told the Baptist that the ark, wherein eight souls 'were saved through water,' was a type of his coming Captain. That when it rocked over an immersed world in the darkness of its grave, Jesus was the lamp which hung in its window above the gloomy deep. Nay, it was he who gave hues to the first rainbow that spanned the new world, when the eight elect antediluvians pitched their tents again on dry ground, and offered sacrifice under its radiant arch.

John, also, saw Abraham's day in the desert and was glad, when the great forefather assured him that he had seen the coming King, as he looked out from the steeps of Hebron. Isaac avouched to him that he had seen his Star, when he went into the fields at eventide to meditate; and Jacob declared, that at Bethel he saw Jesus standing at the top of the mystic ladder, and on his pillow of stone dreamed in the night watches about the glory of the latter day. David, the son of Jesse, showed the Baptist that his great Son guided his fingers over the Messianic harp, when his throne trembled in raptures, and living anthems flew like angels from the strings. Moses told him of the Rock that followed Israel, which 'Rock was Christ;' and Isaiah, that Jesus was the 'Stem' that blossomed by the house of

Jesse, on the hill-side of Bethlehem. In a word, from the days of Eve, the mother of all living, to those of Mary, the mother of Jesus, the history of the Promised Seed was traced in the desert by the son of Elizabeth. And, yet, a few miles from his dingy retreat, the incarnate God had already been wrapped in swaddling bands and laid in a manger.

All this fitted him for the office to which he was born, armed him with a fidelity which nothing could daunt to grapple with his adulterous generation. Without this strength defeat only awaited him. Being fully clad in celestial panoply, the word of the Lord said to him: 'Go,' and he arose to begin his true Baptist work. He emerged from the desert of the North, and came first upon the well-watered plain of the Jordan. His sandals then pressed the soil of Lot, on which the eye of Moses rested, when he died on Nebo. There the name of John became eternally united with the name of Jesus, the Christ. Whenever an Oriental monarch passed through his realms, a herald went before him, proclaimed his coming, and required his subjects to make the neglected roads passable for their sovereign, by removing all hinderances to his progress. When Semiramis, the Queen of Babylon, marched into Persia, she crossed the Zarcean mountain, but not till its precipices were digged down and its hollows filled up to make her way smooth. We have similar records of Xerxes, Caligula, and Titus, and when Jesus entered upon his kingly course, John, his herald, demanded that all obstructions be removed before him in his march. He cried, 'Prepare the way of the Lord,' that all flesh may see his glory. His progress was not to be that of pomp and pageantry, but that of a nation's repentance. Rugged and wretched as were the moral wastes, he was to make the desolation ring with the demand for 'repentance,' summoning all to surrender to the coming Prince. The valleys must be filled. All debasing affections must be elevated, the downtrodden and the despairing must be lifted up. Mountains must be brought low. The proud and haughty were to be leveled, abased in the dust. The crooked should be made straight. All tortuous policies, winding deceits, and lying frauds of the self-righteous, should be exchanged for simplicity and transparency. The rugged ways must be made smooth. Coarse severity, rough tempers, bitter asperity, hot fanaticism, and stoical hardness must be cast aside, for gentleness and child-like affections. Then, all flesh should see the salvation of God. No lofty shadow was to fling its length before the face of God's Anointed. The 'Voice' cried: 'Prepare the way of the Lord.'

When John left the howling of beasts in the desert, it was to electrify the land by the startling cry 'Repent,' and thenceforth, he frowned on all brutal passion. The whole nation started to its feet and flocked to him, as its center of hope. City, village, and hamlet, poured forth their hardened multitudes to see and hear the new Baptist preacher. The prophecy of Malachi had said: 'Behold, I will send you Elijah the prophet, before the coming of the great and dreadful day of the Lord;' and, as the universal expectation of the Messiah was cherished by the Jews at this time, they looked for the literal accomplishment of this prediction in the return of the Tishbite, as his precursor. The news, therefore, flew through the land that this faithful servant of God who ascended to heaven in the reign of Jehoram, had been borne back to the earth, to break the Roman Scepter, and hurl himself like a thunder-bolt against all tyrants, that he might restore the glory to Israel by enthroning her new king. Every eye longed to see this somber old giant of Carmel and Horeb, and every ear listened for his strange voice; hence, all flocked to the banks of the Jordan whence he ascended, for, said they, the chariots of Israel and the horsemen thereof, had landed him on the very spot where he laid down his mantle and burden 900 years before.

But instead of launching forth denunciation against Roman strangers, John opened an accusative ministry upon his own people. He made not his voice soft and smooth in his ' cry.' He presented a new and striking figure to them, enthusiastic, yet self-poised. Filled with deep conviction of the truth, inspired of God and consecrated to the truth, he had evidently come on no dubious errand, and his aim was worthy of his great work. Under the pressure of a divine influence, he set his face like flint, in downright fearlessness. The scorn of every form of cunning filled his voice, holy indignation at sin flew in every syllable from his lips. His body was free from sanctimonious vestments, and his soul inflamed with zeal; he lifted up the truth, a lambent torch, for his word made dread exposures, and searched men to the core of their being. Without the tears of Jeremiah, the sublimity of Isaiah, or the mystery of Ezekiel, he bravely struck home by rebuke and exhortation and heart-piercing censure. He dealt in no arts of insinuation, no apologies, no indulgence; but upbraided the hollow and pretentious, and shivered their pious self-conceit to atoms, while they gnashed their teeth at him. He was a living man, just sent from the living God, dealing with cardinal verities, in an original and emphatic vigor that stung the cold-hearted, and held the malignant conscience by a remorseless grip. Wicked men saw the majestic flow of holiness in his eye, they felt its nervous vibrations in his abrupt anatomy of character, and were borne down before his impassioned demands for self-loathing. The slothful were startled in their dreams; he held up the self-blinded for their own inspection, in their true colors; he rudely tore off the masks of the false. The hard-hearted saw their guilt staring them in the face, and the reckless were haunted by the ghosts of their murdered mercies from the God of Abraham. Yet, he wielded no weapons of earthly chastisement; he mingled not the blood of sinners with the waters of the Jordan, but he pointed to the uplifted ax, as it gleamed in the terrors of the Lord, about to strike a blow and fell the withered tree.

Strangely enough, instead of repelling the multitude, his fidelity fascinated them. The Spirit of God gave power to his proclamation. This, of itself, made his holy serenity soft and saving. Consciences were aroused, hearts were broken, and the sorrows of the people for sin, re-awakened the ancient sobbings, when their fathers wept, on the death of Moses. A rude and arrogant mind, having so difficult a work to do, would have been harsh in its rebukes, only exciting anger and resentment. But John's words cut to the quick because his affectionate holiness, gravity, sincerity, and good-will made them sharp. He had been so much in retirement with God that he was imbued with his love and compassion. He carried not the mien of an ill-mannered, bold, and self-appointed censor of sin.

True, the great Baptist had brought a fire-brand out of the wilderness which set all the dry stubble in the land ablaze. But with this came confession of sin in lowly simplicity, and sincere reformation of life, which sought expression in the new faith and baptism. Instead of meeting Elijah, descending in the regal state of flame to smite the waters of their great national river and divide them, the young representative of Elijah's God stood there demanding that their buried bodies, and not his rod, should divide the waters in token of death to sin. The alarming cry 'Repent ye' rang up and down the valley of the Jordan. This demand laid bare God's extreme holiness, and their personal guilt against him. The word itself (*metanoia*) means a change of mind or purpose; so that he not only required deep sorrow, or contrition for their wickedness, but such an inward moral disposition as should thereafter obey the will of God. Then they were to bring forth fruits worthy of repentance, so that the outward expression of that disposition should prove the inward change to be radical. He made their immersion in water the exterior method of 'confessing' the reality of an honest, heart-felt reform. Here, then, he required a spiritual revolution, a baptism for the 'remission' or forgiveness of sins, and the implanting of a new principle of life in keeping with the kingdom of heaven at hand.

These requirements, urged with the courteous fidelity of holy conviction and the sacred simplicity of an overawing holiness, led a multitude of wounded and stricken hearts to fly from all legal rites and ceremonial performances, for purification of heart and life, after the evangelical order of Isaiah:

> 'Wash you, make you clean;
> Put away the evil of your doings
> From before mine eyes.'

At a stroke of the pen Matthew draws another vivid picture. Priests, Levites, and doctors in the holy city had donned their robes and bound on their phylacteries and other ecclesiastical trappings for a visit to the great river, that they might pass upon John's commission. Sweeping with pomp and dignity through the gates, they mix with the throng on the slopes of the Jordan, first with a conceited curiosity, and then with a bigoted scowl. But John's keen eye read their character, and he began to ply them with solemn invective. In the desert he had seen the slimy viper gliding through the moss; crafty, malicious, with a powerful spring and a hollow tooth through which it ejected deadly poison. He had seen the brawny forester swing the ax to cut the tap-root of a tree and fell it for burning. And converting these into blunt figures of speech, he allied his visitors with false teachers from the 'old serpent' who could not be trusted for a moment. Like the flat-headed, ash-colored reptile, they had stung the sons of God; and with bitter irony he compares them to the twisting young, ejected from their dam, to hiss, and fight her venomous battles. Scathing them with cold sarcasm, he demands, 'Brood of vipers! have ye come to my baptism? What sent you? The ribbon on your robes is beautifully blue, the phylacteries on your brow are ostentatiously pious, but they cloak corruption. Delude not yourselves with the thought that ye are Abraham's sons. His blood may warm your veins, but ye deny his God, for your souls are dead to his faith. Behold the stones at your feet, and know that from them God is able to raise up sons to Abraham. One word from his mouth will bring from the adamant, truer Jewish hearts and softer than those that beat in you.' He then demanded that if they were sincere they should prove this by bringing forth fruits worthy of repentance. Nor did he change his tone with his simile; for when he dropped the lash of scorpions, he took the edge of the woodman's ax. He could not away with their sanctimonious hair-splittings and religious tamperings, but would hew them down to be cast into the fire.

But other and better classes of the people hailed his ministry with awe, as from God. So powerfully did divine truth move them, that they actually reasoned in their hearts concerning John, whether he himself were not the Christ. How beautifully our Lord Jesus speaks of these, when he would know of the rulers whether John's baptism were from heaven or of men. 'Verily, I say unto you, that the publicans and harlots go into the kingdom of God before you. For John came to you in the way of righteousness, and ye did not believe him; and ye, when ye had seen it, repented not afterward, that ye might believe him.' These Rabbis were in the habit of saying; 'That if the nation would repent but one day, the Messiah would come,' yet, when he came, they themselves were obdurate. And, when publicans, soldiers and others, who were openly sunk in sin, came to the Baptist, convicted of their iniquity, it was with the saving inquiry upon their lips, 'Teacher, what shall we do?' They seemed to look upon their own case as hopeless, but he fortified every man with encouragement at his weak point. He told the publicans, to 'Exact no more than that which is appointed you.' The tax-gatherers, to whom the Romans farmed out the taxation, were extortionate and cruel, for they paid so much to the government and then levied their own rates. He did not blame them for filling the political office, but he charged them to stop all rapacity, so that a new miracle would be found, when men should see an honest publican. His reply was of great breadth, forbidding them to confiscate property by unjust exaction. To the soldiers he replied: 'Do violence to no one, neither accuse any falsely; and be content with your wages.' Josephus shows, that at this very time, Herod Antipas was sending an army against his father-in-law, Aretas, King of Arabia Petræa, who had declared war in consequence of Herod's bad treatment of his daughter. This being true, their route would lie directly through the region where John was preaching and immersing. This historian's full description of John is in perfect accord with the spirit of the above statement. These hearers of the Baptist were men of the bow, the arrow, the sword and the shield; their trade was war. He stood before them the living image of discipline and self-denial, and demanded of them, that they keep the insolent licentiousness and brutality of war in check, and disregard the lying doctrine that might makes right. In prosecuting their hard craft, godless pillage must cease. What lessons of love were these, enforced upon rough, heathen legions by which an unarmed young Baptist preacher tamed the fierceness of military tigers, and remanded desperate warriors back to the camp and field, made by their new faith as harmless as doves. Last of all, he threw the bridle over their license of riot and plunder, to curb them with a double bit. They must commit no robbery upon the conquered, indulge no selfishness, raise no mutiny against their officers to get more pay, but take their three *oboloi* a day; and be content.

Such a scene had never been witnessed on earth, and the most remarkable thing about it was, that so sweeping a ministry provoked no physical resistance. Jewish priests had shed streams of sacrificial blood at the altar for hundreds of years, whenever the nation groaned beneath the heel of its foes. They sighed for the tender mercy of God to rescue them from the hand of their enemy, and guide their feet anew into the way of peace. But now, while they felt the rankling humiliation of a hated race, and their hearts sank as they looked at the broken scepter of their nation, a stern preacher of their own race stings them with rebuke, and demands not sacrifice but repentance. The Ark of the Covenant was no longer there with its Tables of Stone. Urim and Thummim were gone. The glory of Bright Presence had departed forever from the most Holy place. The Golden Candlestick gave no light. Their ensigns were torn, their minstrelsy hushed, their royalty beggared, and their covenant with God broken. Was not this enough? Their hearts sank within them when they remembered the past, in which they were never again to take lot or part, and the hatred of their hearts toward their foes filled them to the brim. Yet, without one word of sympathy for all this, they were warned to flee from coming wrath, to humble themselves under the mighty hand of God, to bury all their old sins with their bodies under the waves of Jordan, and to rise into the New Kingdom; and without a murmur it was done!

BAPTISM OF JESUS.

CHAPTER II.

THE BAPTISM OF JESUS.

THE Evangelist says that Jesus came from Galilee to the Jordan to John, to be immersed by him, 'But John sought to hinder him, saying: I have need to be immersed of thee, and dost thou come to me? And Jesus answering said to him: Suffer it now; for thus it becomes us to fulfill all righteousness. Then he suffered him.' In approaching this august event, the forcible words of Godet attract our attention. He says:[1]

'John and Jesus resemble two stars following each other at a short distance, and both passing through a series of similar circumstances. The announcement of the appearing of the one follows close upon that of the appearing of the other. It is the same with their twin births. This relation repeats itself in the commencement of their respective ministries, and lastly in the catastrophies which terminate their lives. And yet, in the whole course of the career of these two men, there was but one personal meeting—at the baptism of Jesus. After this moment, when one of these stars rapidly crossed the orbit of the other, they separated, each to follow the path that was marked out for him. It is this moment of their actual contact that the Evangelist is about to describe.'

The meeting was worthy of both, but pre-eminently worthy of the Father who directed their steps. The star of the morning was herald to the rising Sun, and then faded away in the fullness of his beams. For thirty years Jesus was secluded in Nazareth, calmly awaiting the ripe day for his public work. Eagerly he watched the shade on the dial, to indicate that his hour had come for release from that holy restraint which held back his consuming zeal. Often he knelt in prayer on the mountain-tops which overlook the plain of Esdraelon, till the sentinel stars took their stations in the sky; and then returned home, silent and pensive, to wait for the dawn of his ministry. When slumber fell upon the carpenter's household, Mary often rehearsed to him the ponderings of her own heart, the mysterious secrets of his birth, and the dealings of God with her cousin in Hebron. The story fell upon the soul of mother and Son as a radiance from heaven, full of sad beauty and divine love; for the dim foreshadings of separation moved their pure hearts to the parental embrace and the good-night kiss, as in other sweet human homes. At last, the moment came when a sacred attraction drew him from the little upland town and dwelling forever; save on one brief visit to the plain old sanctuary, where his young heart had been warmed by the words of the Law.

His journey from Galilee to the Jordan, after the touch of parting with his loved ones, stirred heaven with a deeper interest than the footsteps of man had ever excited, for then he recorded the hallowed resolution: 'Lo, I come to do thy will, O God.' Many a hard-fought battle had soaked the plain which he crossed, with blood; but that day he went forth single-handed to the hardest war that had ever been waged upon this globe. After he had swept the foot of Tabor, at every step he trod on holy ground. And when he reached the western slope of the Jordan, like Jacob, his great ancestor, he crossed the ford that he might lead many pilgrim bands over a darker stream 'to glory.' 'All the people had been baptized,' and he presented himself as the last arrival of that day, because he was not one of the common repenting throng. He had done no sin, neither was guile found in his mouth; hence, remorse never broke his heart. Yet, he numbered himself with the transgressors. At the close of his ministry he was to sleep in a sepulcher wherein never man had laid; and it was meet that in opening his ministry he should be buried in the liquid grave alone, and separate from sinners. Baptism was the door by which he entered upon his work of saving mediation. The Baptist says, that up to this time he 'knew him not,' as if he had not met him before, and yet, he also says, 'I have need to be baptized of thee,' as if he knew him well. This apparent discrepancy has led to large discussion, with this general result; that while John knew him in person as Jesus, he did not know him in Messiahship until Jehovah who sent him to baptize in water said to him, before the baptism of Jesus: 'Upon whom thou shalt see the Spirit descending, and abiding on him, the same is he who baptizes in the Holy Spirit.' But do John's words necessarily imply that he was ignorant, either of the person or Messiahship of Jesus, before his baptism? One great prerogative of the Christ was, that he should baptize men in the Holy Spirit. This fact had not come to John's knowledge till Jehovah gave him the special revelation that One should come to him for baptism, on whom he should see the Spirit 'descending and abiding,' and that he should be the pre-eminent Baptizer, who should baptize in the Holy Spirit. This thought seems to have struck John with deep awe, for he carefully draws a contrast between his own baptism which was 'in water' only, and that of Christ which should be 'in the Holy Spirit' himself. If John did not know him, in the sense of the Baptizer in the Holy Spirit till Jehovah had announced to him the impending token and its signification, then we can well understand why he said: 'I have need to be baptized of thee, and comest thou to me?' The revelation that Jesus should be the Baptizer in the Spirit was special to John: 'He who sent me to baptize in water said this to me.' And, it was said before the Baptism of Jesus, for the visible sign of the descending Spirit crowned the act of his baptism. If this be the sense of John's words, the Fourth Gospel, written A. D. 97 or 98, throws a strong light upon the First, written about A. D. 60.

It would harmonize exactly with the known methods of Divine Providence to suppose that the hand of God had kept them apart till that moment. Jesus had lived in the north and John in the south of the land, and we know of no high purpose which demanded a meeting previously, whilst their separation must silence all suspicion of combination or collusion between the servant and his Lord. Gabriel had put John under the Nazarite's vow from his birth, which exempted him from attendance at the triple annual feasts, so that they had not met in the metropolis. Nor had John gone abroad in search of him. This was not his work. He must wait till God brought them lovingly together. That time of manifestation to Israel would come of itself. John went to the Jordan when he was sent, saying: 'That he might be made manifest to Israel, for this I came baptizing in water.' Like a man 'sent of God,' he was waiting for his Master to show himself fully and promptly, and Jehovah honored his faith by the foretoken agreed upon in the visible descent of the Spirit. Hence, when the solitary stranger joined the throng on the approach of evening, the eagle-eyed Baptist kenned him, and the vision made his whole being quiver with expectation. When David came to the throne in the garb of a young shepherd, the Lord said to Samuel: 'Arise, anoint him, this is he!' And, why should not the Holy Spirit, who had 'prepared' the body of Jesus, and filled the soul of John, say this of David's Son?

With godlike serenity and dignity the Prince of Peace presented himself for baptism. The words of his mouth, the repose of his body, the purity of his face, the soul of his eye, overpowered John with a sense of reverend princeliness. When the stern herald stood face to face with the Son of the Highest his soul was submerged under a rare humility, which extorted the cry: 'I have need to be baptized of thee, and comest thou to me?' Captivated by the dignity of the Candidate, and abashed by his own inferiority, he was helpless as a child before this incarnate God—this shrine of the Holy Spirit. He who had walked rough-shod over all pride, and had leveled all distinctions of human glory, was seized with the conviction of a worthless menial, and as a holy man, was thoroughly daunted when the Lord sought a favor of his own servant. The reasons are apparent. He found the Promised of all promises, the Antitype of all types, the Expected of all ages, standing before him in flesh and blood, and he was startled at the thought of inducting him into the new faith by the new ordinance; for his baptism was administered to the penitent, but the Nazarene was guiltless. 'Suffer it now, for thus it becomes us to fulfill all righteousness.' He defers to John's scruple, and asks for the new baptism, not of right, but on sufferance. What did Jesus mean by these words?

Viewed in any light it seems strange that Christ should have sought baptism as a high privilege which he could not forego, for what could it confer upon him? Augustine beautifully replies, 'To any one who asks this question: Was it needful for the Lord to be born? Was it needful for the Lord to be crucified? Was it needful for the Lord to die? Was it needful for the Lord to be buried? If he undertook for us so great humiliation, might he not also receive baptism? And what profit was there that he received the baptism of a servant? That thou mightest not disdain to receive the baptism of the Lord. Give heed, beloved brethren.'[2] He clearly intended to render obedience to some law of his Father. What law? He had honored every requisition of the Old Covenant by circumcision, obedience to parents, hallowing the Sabbath, temple worship, observance of the feasts, all except in bringing the sin-offerings. For a full generation he had submitted to every claim of Jehovah's law upon him, in every institution and ordinance. But now his Father had established the last test of obedience in the baptism of John, and Jesus, born under God's law, must honor the new divine precept. Jesus himself gave this reason when he accused the Pharisees and lawyers with rejecting 'The counsel of God toward themselves' in not having been baptized by John.[3] The will of God was his only reason for obeying any law; he held it an act of obedience to keep all the Divine appointments. Although not a sinner himself, he impleaded to be treated as a sinner; therefore he humbled himself to receive a sinner's baptism, as well as to submit to a sinner's death. This deep mark of mediatorial sympathy and mystery must have entered largely into his plea, 'Suffer it now.' With great clearness Geikie puts this point: 'Baptism was an ordinance of God required by his prophet as the introduction of the new dispensation. It was a part of "righteousness," that is, it was a part of God's commandments which Jesus came into the world to show us the example of fulfilling, both in the letter and in the spirit.'[4] His baptism was the channel through which the Divine attestation could best be given to his Messianic dignity; and when we consider that he had reached the full maturity of all his human powers of mind and body, this manner of entering upon his public work gave a mutual and public sanction to the mission both of John and Jesus.

Yet, with our Lord's interpretation of his own words before their eyes, men will insist upon it that he was initiated into his sacrificial work by baptism, in imitation of the mere ceremonial ablutions of the Aaronical priesthood. Jesus was not even of Aaron's line as was John, much less of his office, but sprang of the tribe of Judah, of which tribe 'Moses spake nothing concerning priesthood.' Did Jesus receive the vestments, the consecrating oil, or any other priestly insignia? Even when he made his sin-offering, and assumed the Christian High-priesthood, three years after his baptism, he neither assumed the vesture nor breastplate, the censer nor miter of Aaron. Because he was not made a High-priest after the order of Aaron, but after the order of Melchizedec, who knew nothing of sacred oils, ablutions, or vestments. How much better is it than a solemn caricature to set forth the baptism of Jesus as an idle, empty, ritualistic pageant? He came to abolish and cast aside forever the Aaronical priesthood with the economy that it served, and how could he do this by submission to any ceremonial act which they observed? John felt the binding force of Christ's words, when he appealed to the obligations of spotless holiness, and he threw aside his objections in a moment.

With gratitude and grace he yielded and obeyed. He found that his Master was under the same law of obedience as himself, and with holy promptitude he honored the sacred trust which God had put into his own hands, but which no other man had ever yet held. 'Then he suffered him.' O! sublime grandeur — awful honor! And when the great Baptist bowed the immaculate soul and body of Jesus beneath the parting wave, all the useless ceremonies of past ages sank together like lead, to find a grave in the opening waters of the Jordan, and no place has since been found for them.

This traditional spot is fixed in human memory as are points on the Tiber, the Thames, and the Delaware, where great armies have crossed. It is a little east of Jericho, near by the conquest of Joshua, also where David crossed in his flight. Christian pilgrims and scholars have visited it for centuries, Origen in the third, Eusebius in the fourth, Jerome in the fifth, and millions of others down to our day. Its thick willow groves are used as robing rooms, whence Copts and Syrians, Armenians and Greeks, go down into the Jordan and immerse themselves three times in the name of the Trinity. The place so fascinates and subdues the spirit that the visitors of every

REPUTED SPOT OF CHRIST'S BAPTISM.

land and creed, reverently descend into the stream once a year. 'Having been baptized, Jesus went up immediately out of the water; and lo, the heavens were opened to him, and he saw the Spirit of God descending, as a dove, and coming upon him. And lo, a voice out of heaven, saying: This is my beloved Son, in whom I am well pleased.' To this account taken from Matthew, Luke adds: That the heavens were opened while Jesus was '*praying*,' that the Spirit took 'the *bodily* shape' of a dove, and the Baptist says, that he saw the Spirit '*abiding* on him.'

The time of our Lord's baptism may here be examined with profit. Luke says: 'That in the fifteenth year of the reign of Tiberius Cæsar, the word of God came to John, the son of Zacharias, in the wilderness;' at which time he entered on his public ministry. And, again, that Jesus began his ministry when he was about thirty years of age.[5] This last statement has the value of a date in a letter. The fifteenth year of Tiberius dates from the time that he commenced his joint reign with Augustus. 'Reckoning thus, the year 765, from January to January, as the first of Tiberius, the fifteenth is the year 779, from the founding of Rome. Some time, then, in 779, is the beginning of John's ministry to be placed. Allowing that his labors had continued six months before the Lord was baptized, we reach in this way, also, the month of January, 780. There is good reason to believe that in December or January, Jesus was baptized, yet the day of the month is very uncertain.'[6] As John and Jesus were born within six months of each other, in the year 749, Christ's baptism must have occurred somewhere near the above date, as he was then 'about thirty years of age.'

What act performed by John is called baptism? John was his proper name, and the term 'Baptist' added by the inspired writers, is a title of office, as Bloomfield thinks, 'To distinguish him from John the Evangelist.' By this name he was known pre-eminently as the administrator of the religious rite called baptism. That is, according to Liddell and Scott, 'one that dips;' or Donegan, 'one who immerses or submerges.' Dean Stanley says: 'On philological grounds, it is quite correct to translate John the Baptist, by John the Immerser.' (*Nineteenth Century*.) Baptism is a fundamental practice in Christianity, which has run through all its ages. Of baptism, in association with John, Edward Irving says: 'This is the first baptismal service upon record. The new rite of baptism, unknown under the Mosaic dispensation.'[7] Much has been said on the subject of Proselyte Baptism, whereby heathen converts were inducted into the Jewish faith, and so, many have depreciated John's baptism as a mere imitation of an existing rite. But modern scholarship has shown conclusively that the reverse of this is true, and that Proselyte Baptism is, in fact, an imitation of the Christian rite, incorporated into Judaism after the Destruction of Jerusalem, A. D. 70. It is true, that the Jews from early times used various symbolical lustrations as well as the Gentiles, but these were always purely ceremonial, and were never used as a rite by which others were inducted into their faith. Josephus says, that many of these washings amongst the Jews were purely of their own will, without direction from the Lord,[8] and Von Rohden denies that they were 'performed by immersion.' He also points out these fundamental differences: 'The washings enjoined by the Law had for their object purification from ceremonial defilement; but the baptism of John did not: the one rite was performed by the candidates themselves upon their own persons: the other was administered to its recipient by the Baptist himself, or by one of his disciples properly authorized: the former was repeated upon every occasion of renewed defilement; the latter was performed upon the candidate only once for all. The two ceremonies, therefore, were essentially different in their nature and object.'[9] The first witness in favor of Proselyte Baptism is found in the Commentary of the Talmud, which was composed in the fifth century after Christ, and it represents the rite as existing in the first century.[10] But this Commentary is not valid history, it is mere tradition at the most, and does not carry the ceremony back so far as John; nor could it have been known at that time, for had it been, the Jews would have scouted John's baptism, instead of submitting to it, because it would have placed them on a level with the heathen as converts to the new faith. Proselytes to Judaism were divided into *proselytes of the gate, and proselytes of righteousness.* The first class had renounced idolatry, and bound themselves to keep the seven Noachic precepts, against idolatry, profanity, incest, murder, theft, eating blood and things strangled, and permitting a murderer to live. The second class not only renounced heathenism, but became Israelites in every respect excepting birth. Males were admitted into Judaism by circumcision, females by a free-will offering: after Christ, the Jews added baptism for both sexes admitted into their faith.

Dr. Lightfoot thus describes this baptism, as the Jews practiced it in after Christian times: 'As soon as he grew whole of the wound of circumcision, they bring him to baptism, and being placed in the water, they again instruct him in some weightier and in some lighter commands of the law'—then, 'he plunges himself, and comes up, and behold, he is an Israelite in all things. The women place a woman in the waters up to the neck, and two disciples of the wise men standing without, instruct her about some lighter precepts of the law, and some weightier, while she, in the meantime, stands in the waters. And then she plungeth, and they, turning away their faces, go out while she comes up out of the water.'[12] Maimonides gives this circumstantial account also: 'Every person baptized (or dipped, whether he were washed from pollution, or baptized into proselytism) must dip his whole body, now stripped and made naked, at one dipping. And wheresoever in the Law, washing of the body or garments is mentioned, it means nothing else than the washing of the whole body. For if any wash himself all over except the very tip of his little finger, he is still in his uncleanness.'[13] On the same subject, Geikie well says: 'Bathing in Jordan had been a sacred symbol, at least, since the days of Naaman, but immersion by one like John, with strict and humbling confession of sin, sacred vows of amendment, and hope of forgiveness, if they proved lasting, and all this in preparation for the Messiah, was something wholly new in Israel.'[14] In this case, circumcision availed nothing, nor did uncircumcision, but a new creature. Jew and heathen must alike be immersed into the new faith, or they could not be numbered amongst its votaries. This view is presented also by Godet. He says: 'The rite of baptism, which consisted in the plunging of the body more or less completely into water, was not at this period in use among the Jews, neither for the Jews themselves, for whom the law only prescribed lustrations, nor for proselytes from paganism, to whom, according to the testimony of history, baptism was not applied until after the fall of Jerusalem. The very title, *Baptist*, given to John, sufficiently proves that it was he who introduced this rite. This follows, also, from John i, 25, where the deputation from the Sanhedrin asks him by what right he baptizes, if he is neither the Messiah nor one of the prophets, which implies that this rite was introduced by him; and further, from John iii, 26, where the disciples of John make it a charge against Jesus, that he adopted a ceremony of which the institution, and consequently, according to them, the monopoly, belonged to their master.'[15]

It is clear enough, that John did not pick up and use an old, effete institution, and adopt it as the door into the New Age of the great salvation, but that his 'baptism was from heaven,' as directly from God as his commission to preach. The preaching, the baptism, and the man, were all newly sent from God to usher in the Gospel Day.

Prof. Lindsay, of Glasgow, says: 'The connection between the baptism of John and the Jewish baptism of proselytes, of which a great deal has been made, is also founded on assumptions which cannot be proved. This very plausible theory first assumes that proselytes were baptized from the early time of the Jewish Church, although the Old Testament tells us nothing about it, and then supposes that John simply made use of this ordinary rite for the purpose of declaring symbolically that the whole Jewish nation were disfranchised, and had to be readmitted into the spiritual Israel, by means of the same ceremony which gave entrance to members of heathen nations. But the subject of the baptism of proselytes is one of the most hopelessly obscure in the whole round of Jewish antiquities, and can never be safely assumed in any argument, and the general results of investigation seem to prove that the baptism of proselytes was not one of the Jewish ceremonies until long after the coming of Christ, while there is much to suggest that this Jewish rite owes its origin to Christian baptism.'[16] And Herzog writes 'The later origin of proselyte baptism is to be accepted.'[17]

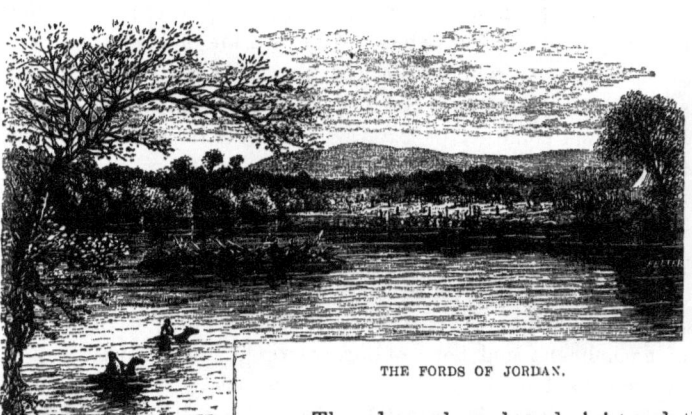

THE FORDS OF JORDAN.

The place where he administered the ordinance demands our attention, namely: the great river of Palestine, the Jordan. Some of the most interesting associations of sacred story cluster around this stream. Israel first knew it when they crossed its channel dry-shod, in their flight from bondage. From that moment it was the silver thread on which the historic memories of the nation were strung, as pearls on a necklace; John and Jesus being the brightest gems that ever shone in the line. It takes its source in about 33° 25′ of north latitude in a fountain near Hâsbeiya, west of Mount Hermon, although Josephus locates its rise in the larger fountains near Cæsarea-Philippi; and then it passes through the lake, or what is called in Josh. xi, 5–7, 'the waters of Merom.' Emerging thence, it flows rapidly through a narrow and rocky ravine, till it empties into the lake of Galilee, and from the southern end thereof it flows through the valley down to the Dead Sea, into which it empties, in lat. 31° 46'. The distance from the lake of Galilee to the Dead Sea is about 56 geographical miles, but the many windings of the channel make about 150 miles between these points. Its width will average, according to Schaff, 'from 60 to 100 feet, and its depth from 5 to 12 feet.' The valley of the Jordan runs from five to six miles in width, and is inclosed by mountains; in many places it is remarkable for its luxuriant fertility. The exact spot where John first used this Divine baptistery cannot now be positively identified. Anciently, it was known as 'Bethabara,' supposed to be about three miles from Jericho, and his second baptismal scene was farther north, being known as 'Enon, near Salim.' Each eminent writer and traveler now fixes upon some picturesque locality, often selected largely on poetical taste; but all conjecture fails to point it out definitely. Some pitch on a line between Gilgal and Jericho, and some still farther north, at the ford where Gideon threw up fortifications against his foes. But as the whole valley was filled with crowds of candidates, from the Salt Sea to the head-waters, it is most likely that he used various places, especially as John, x, 49, speaks of the place where he '*first* baptized.' Frequently, reckless writers rush into random statements, and assert that its depth would not allow of immersion, utterly regardless of all topographical exploration, such as that made by Lieutenant Lynch, of the United States Navy. Yet, Jehovah found it necessary to divide the waters for Israel and Elijah, while Pococke and other explorers estimate its daily discharges into the Dead Sea, to be about 6,000,000 tons of water.[18]

Dr. Schaff ('Through Bible Lands, 1878) speaks thus : 'At the bathing place of the Pilgrims, the traditional site of Christ's baptism, the river is 80 feet broad and 9 feet deep. . . . After the salt bath in the lake of death it was like a bath of regeneration. I immersed myself *ten* times, and felt so comfortable, that I almost imagined I was miraculously delivered from rheumatism. I have plunged into many a river and many a lake, and into the waters of the ocean, but of all the baths, that in the Jordan will linger longest in my memory.'

Was John's baptism a burial in water or not? Candid minds can scarcely doubt what this action was, when they weigh the meaning of the Greek word *baptizo*, the places where he administered it, and all its attendant circumstances. John, as well as all other sacred speakers used words in their commonly accepted sense of their times, and this is as true of this word as of any other. Its sense is easily found. Conant, the great philologist and translator, gives a complete monograph of the root word, in his '*Baptizein*' taken from the best known Greek authors, running from B. C. 500 to the eleventh century A. D.; and, in 168 examples from the Greek literature, covers both the literal or physical, and the tropical or figurative sense of the word. Their whole scope shows that the ground meaning of the word is: 'To immerse, immerge, submerge, to dip, to plunge, to imbathe, to whelm.' A few of these examples, taken from objects already in water, will clearly illustrate its sense:

Pindar, born B. C. 522 years, in likening himself to a cork floating on the top of a net, says: 'When the rest of the tackle is toiling deep in the sea, I, as a cork above the net, am unbaptized (undipped) in the brine.'[19] Aristotle, born B. C. 384, speaking of discoveries made beyond the Pillars of Hercules, says, that the Phenician colonists of Gadira, 'came to certain desert places full of rushes and sea-weed; which, when it is ebb-tide, are not *baptized* (overflowed), but when it is flood-tide are overflowed.'[20] Polybius, born B. C. 205, speaking of the sea-battle between Philip and Attalus, tells of one vessel as 'pierced, and being baptized (immerged) by a hostile ship.[21] Again, in his account of the naval engagement between the Romans and Carthaginians, he accords the greater skill to the latter. 'Now sailing round and now attacking in flank the more advanced of the pursuers, while turning and embarrassed on account of the weight of the ships and the unskillfulness of the crews, they made continued assaults and "*baptized*" (sunk) many of the ships.'[22] Strabo, born B. C. 60, says that about Agrigentum, in Sicily, there are 'Marsh-lakes, having the taste indeed of sea-water, but of a different nature; for even those who cannot swim are not *baptized* (immersed), floating like pieces of wood.'[23] In the same work he speaks of Alexander's army marching on a narrow, flooded beach of the Pamphilian Sea, in these words: 'Alexander happening to be there at the stormy season, and, accustomed to trust for the most part to fortune, set forward before the swell subsided; and they marched the whole day in water; *baptized* (immersed) as far as to the waist.'[24] Diodorus, who wrote about B. C. 60-30, reports the Carthaginian army defeated on the bank of the river Crimissus; and that many of them perished because the stream was swollen: 'The river rushing down with the current increased in violence, *baptized* (submerged) many, and destroyed them attempting to swim through with their armor.'[25] He also describes the annual overflow of the Nile thus: 'Most of the wild land animals are surrounded by the stream and perish, being *baptized* (submerged); but some, escaping to the high grounds, are saved.'[26]

These examples bring us down to John's day and fully sustain the learned Deylingius, when he says of him: 'He received the name *ton Baptiston*, from the office of solemn ablution and immersion, in which he officiated by a divine command. For the word *baptizesthai*, in the usage of Greek authors, signifies immersion and demersion.'[27] Josephus, born A. D. 37, frequently uses this word, and always in the same sense. The following are noteworthy examples: Aristobulus was drowned by his companions in a swimming bath, and in relating the murder he says: 'Continually pressing down and *baptizing* (immersing) him while swimming, as if in sport, they did not desist till they had entirely suffocated him.'[28] He also describes the contest, in his 'Jewish War,' between the Romans and the Jews, on the Sea of Galilee, and says of the Jews: 'They suffered harm before they could inflict any, and were *baptized* (submerged) along with their vessels.... And those of the baptized who raised their heads, either a missile reached, or a vessel overtook.' Again, in describing his own shipwreck, he says: 'Our vessel having been *baptized* (sunk) in the midst of the Adriatic, being about six hundred in number, we swam through the whole night.' Lucian, born about A. D. 135, in a satire on the love of the marvelous, tells of men that he saw running on the sea. They were like himself except that they had cork-feet. He says: 'We wondered, therefore, when we saw them not *baptized*, (immersed) but standing above the waves and traveling on without fear.'[29] Dion Cassius, born 155 A. D., says of the defeated forces at Utica who rushed to their ships and overloaded them, that: some of them were 'thrown down by the jostling, in getting on board the vessels, and others *baptized* (submerged) in the vessels themselves, by their own weight.'[30] In the same work he gives an account of the sea-fight between Marc Antony and Augustus, at Actium, when, near the close of the battle, men escaped from the burning ships. He says: 'others leaping into the sea were drowned, or struck by the enemy were *baptized*, (submerged).'[31]

These citations from classic Greek writers, covering about 700 years, including the Apostolic Age, unite in describing things on which water was poured, or which were partially immersed, as *unbaptized;* while others, which were dipped or plunged in water and overwhelmed, they declare to have been baptized; showing, that when the sacred penmen use the same word to describe the act of John in the Jordan, they use it in the same sense as other Greek authors, namely: to express the act of dipping or immersion.

This cumulative evidence fully justifies Calvin in saying: 'Baptism was administered by John and Christ, by the submersion of the whole body.'[32] Tertullian, the great Latin father, A. D. 200, also says: 'Nor is there any material difference between those whom John dipped in the Jordan, and those whom Peter dipped in the Tiber.'[33] So Lightfoot: 'That the baptism of John was by the immersion of the body, seems evident from those things which are related concerning it; namely, that he baptized in the Jordan, and in Enon, because there was much water, and that Christ being baptized went up out of the water.'[34] MacKnight says the same thing: 'Christ submitted to be baptized, that is, to be buried under the water by John, and to be raised out of it again.'[35] Olshausen agrees with these interpreters, for he says: 'John, also, was baptizing in the neighborhood, because the water there being deep, afforded conveniences for submersion.'[36] De Wette bears the same testimony: 'They were baptized, immersed, submerged. This is the proper meaning of the frequentative form of *bapto*, to immerse.'[37] And Alford, on Matt. iii, 6, says: 'The baptism was administered in the day-time by immersion of the whole person.'

These authorities abundantly show that our Lord, in requiring the first act of obedience on the part of his new disciple, employed a Greek word in common use for expressing the most familiar acts of every-day life. And the testimony of the Septuagint, the Greek version of the Old Testament, completed B. C. 285, harmonizes exactly with this use. When quoting the Hebrew Scriptures, Jesus and his apostles generally used this version. Here the Greek word '*ebaptisato*' is used to translate the Hebrew word '*taval*' (2 Kings v, 14), where the English version also renders it by the word 'dipped,' to express the act of Naaman in the river Jordan. The word '*taval*' is used fifteen times in the Old Testament, and is rendered in our common English version fourteen times by 'dip,' and once (Job ix, 31) by 'plunge.' In Gen. xxxvii, 31, the Jewish scholars who made the Septuagint version rendered '*moluno*' to stain, the effect of dipping, as in dyeing, this being the chief thought which the translator would express. It is also worthy of note that the preposition '*en*' is rendered '*in*' before Jordan in all the commonly received versions of the English New Testament (Matt. iii, 6), namely: in that of Wiclif, 1380; Tyndal, 1534; Cranmer, 1539; Geneva, 1557; Rheims, 1582; and King James, 1611. In the last named '*with*' was afterward substituted for '*in,*' but it is restored by the late Anglo-American revisers, in various passages of the Gospels.

CHAPTER III.

THE BAPTIST'S WITNESS TO CHRIST.

JOHN gave a threefold testimony to Christ. As a prophet, he proclaimed the kingdom of God, through the Messiah; as a preacher, he led the people to preparation for the Messiah; and as a witness, he pointed out Christ in person as the Messiah. The people believed that the Baptist was the veritable Elijah. The Sanhedrin was bound to prevent any false prophet from misleading the people, and in order to subject John to a rigid examination, they sent a deputation of officials from Jerusalem to question him. They asked him: 'Who art thou? The Christ? Elijah? The Prophet?' He answered: 'No.' But his ministry so stirred the people that they found a pledge therein of deliverance from Roman rule, and 'reasoned in their hearts whether he were not the Christ.' The deputation was of the Pharisees, who, stinging under his rebukes, sought to pay him back by entangling him in political difficulties, craftily supposing that they could bring him to account if they could throw his fiery ministry into a false position. Their cunning only succeeded in bringing out the humility and modesty of his character. Bold as a lion before men, he was a timid lamb in the shadow of his Lord, and nonplussed them by saying: 'I am not the Christ, nor Elijah, but simply the voice of a crier.' Unable and unwilling to lead the eager throngs to a contest with their oppressors, he lifted up his voice and proclaimed: 'There stands one in the midst of you, whom ye know not, the latchet of whose sandal I am not worthy to loose.'

Beautiful message-bearer of our God and Saviour. Pure truth, gentle modesty, blushing humility, marked few of his contemporaries; but, while he would not play the rôle of a false Messiah, he longed for the honor of stooping, with suppressed breath and tremulous hands, to do the work of a slave for the true Christ. His glory was to throw himself into the background, to tie the sandals of Jesus when he went abroad, and loose the dusty leathern thong when he returned. His reply rebuked the pride and scorned the vanity of the whole viper-brood. Their haughtiness is censured, and their fawning repelled by the servant of the Son of the Highest prostrate in the dust at his feet. This holy chivalry makes a true man a broken reed in the presence of Jesus, while it tempers his sinews with steel in dealing with men. 'I am not your Messiah—I go before him—he stands among you—he is mightier than I—I am a stranger to his prerogatives—I immerse your bodies in water to symbolize your soul's purification, but he shall overwhelm your souls in the Holy Spirit.' This sharp distinction brought out for the first time the fullness of Christ's Gospel, or as Mark expresses it, here was 'The beginning of the Gospel of Jesus Christ.' This said, and the Baptist delivered from the snare of the fowler, he reasserts himself in new strength. The rulers flattered themselves that they would be the golden grain of Messiah's husbandry, the *élite* wheat that should fill his garner. John mocks that expectation, casts it to the winds, and tells them that Jesus will treat them as the Palestine farmer treats his harvest, when it is cut down, trampled under the hoofs of oxen, torn 'by instruments with teeth,' till the kernel is severed from the 'chaff' and then winnowed that it may be burned. They could never be gathered as the pure grain of the kingdom. Another baptism awaited them, that of repentance in the Jordan, when the Messiah should toss wheat and chaff into the empty air, that the grain might fall back free of refuse, while the wind would take the chaff into quenchless fire. These terrible words express John's cardinal idea of Christ's nature and prerogatives. They attribute to him the scrutiny of motives, the purification of character, and the condemnation of the impenitent; in a word, the prerogatives of God. But this was not all.

The 'next day,' the Baptist saw Jesus and cried: 'Behold the Lamb of God, that takes away the sin of the world! This is he of whom I said: After me comes one who is preferred before me; because he was before me.'[1] 'I have seen and have borne witness that this is the Son of God. I saw the Spirit descending as a dove out of heaven, and it abode upon him.' Here he affirms Christ's pre-existence. John was born six months before Jesus, yet he says 'He was before me.' The Greek terms here, both translated 'before,' express not only pre-eminence in rank and dignity, but priority of time. This enigma was to the startled Jews the first hint given by any New Testament speaker of Christ's personal pre-existence, and unveils him in the Bosom of the Father, before he became flesh. Then follow Christ's attestation by the Holy Spirit,—his mediatorial character and his divine Sonship. And he gave grandeur to his testimony in that he '*cried*,' with vehemence in their avowal. He tells us that the Holy Spirit justified these claims as he set them forth. Indeed, the most remarkable thing in the Baptist's ministry is the prominence which he gives to the doctrine of the Spirit, in its new form.

He introduced the second Person in the Trinity to the world, and held relations to the Third which no man before him had filled. Next to the coming of Christ, his ministry held a place and formed an epoch of the highest possible importance in the history of redemption. It was, in the Gospel sense, the beginning of the Spirit's administration in the personal salvation of men, as it first brings out his separate personality with great clearness. The Dove came from the Father, and on the banks of the Jordan remained upon the Son, making him thenceforth the sole Baptizer in the Holy Spirit, the one source through whom he has since acted in administering salvation to men. All this was directly opposite to the history and tendencies of Judaism, but it identifies John with the very soul of the Gospel as nothing else could. It was not the baptism of Jesus in the Jordan which anointed him for his work, for, says Peter: 'God anointed Jesus of Nazareth with the Holy Spirit and power.' This prodigy of the descending Dove and Christ's inscrutable unction enabled John to say: 'I saw, and bear record that this is the Son of God.' The Spirit made him a witness to the Messiah, when the Lord's anointed was solemnly invested with his divine office. Through the Spirit, the Father dwelt in the Son and the Son in him. Luke gives the splendid piece of information, that when Jesus was 'praying' at his baptism, the heavens were opened. Through the cleft vault his eyes were fixed upon his Father's throne. He penetrated into the fullness of divine light and life, and uttered the first sigh of humanity for that perfect indwelling of God which accomplished redemption. This pledge of his final triumph was given when his body was dripping with the waters of baptism. When he was setting aside all empty institutions his hand knocked at heaven's gate, and by the will of the Father it was opened; for he was well pleased with the obedience of his beloved Son.

How sweetly inspiring is the thought, that the first breath which passed his newly baptized lips asked for the Holy Spirit; who at once was given to him. And not in measure, but without degree; in him 'dwelt the fullness of the Godhead bodily.' To him the Spirit was not given as to the Apostles, through the emblem of unconscious flame in divided sheets, but through the organic and sensitive symbol of life in a hovering dove. From the blue vault, from infinite leagues of ethereal space, came forth a delicate, timorous nature and lit upon the only pure spot on this earth, the Sacred Head, while his locks were yet wet from the tremulous wave. When the guilty earth was baptized in the deluge, a dove flew over the waste of waters and brought the hope of a new world to Noah, in a frail olive-branch rescued from the flood. But the New Testament Dove winged his way to the New Testament Ark, the type of a life-giving energy, which said: 'Behold, I make all things new,' when Jesus came up out of the stream and stood upon the dry land. Here is the seven-fold symbol of chaste purity, peace and hope, for the gentle emblem seems invested with the infinite powers of new birth. The expression: 'The Spirit lighted and abode upon him,' conveys that idea of a hovering motion implied in the Hebrew word by which Moses describes the mode of creation: 'The Spirit was *brooding* over the face of the waters,' as a bird over her young in incubation, imparting vivifying warmth in each shudder passing from the pulse of one animated being to another. The white-winged messenger in corporeal form, from the bosom of the Father, came not on his celestial mission to make Jesus holy, nor to invest him with grace and beauty, but with infinite energy as the Head of an endless race: 'He shall see his seed.'

Prediction had said: 'The Spirit of the Lord shall rest upon him; the Spirit of wisdom and might, and shall make him of quick understanding.' The body of Jesus was his offspring, and his soul-powers were developed by the same Spirit; then, from the moment of his baptism, the Holy Spirit directed his life, his words, and his work. He himself declared : ' The Spirit of the Lord is upon me ; because he anointed me to preach good tidings to the poor ; to proclaim the acceptable year of the Lord.' Nor is this all. From the moment of his baptism 'he began to preach the good news of the kingdom ;' to ' heal the sick ;' to ' cast out demons by the Spirit of God.' He also warned men against 'the blasphemy of the Spirit ;' promised that ' the Spirit should teach them what to say ' in persecution, and breathed upon his disciples, saying : ' Receive ye the Holy Spirit,' and they received him. But, above all, at Pentecost he sent the Spirit to fill his own place on earth. Nor may we suppose that either John or Jesus were not filled with the Spirit in the largest sense simply because John (vii, 39) says : ' The Holy Spirit was not yet [*given*], because Jesus was not yet glorified.' The word ' given ' is not in the Greek text, which simply reads ' was not yet,' the word ' given ' is supplied to complete the sense. Luther says on the passage : ' One must not fall into such senseless thoughts, as to suppose that the Holy Spirit was only created after Christ's resurrection from the dead ; what is written is, " The Holy Spirit was not yet," that is, was not in his office.' Stillingfleet says the Spirit was not yet found in the extraordinary gift of tongues and other miracles. But Jesus tells his disciples that they ' knew him,' that 'he abides with you,' and that his Father would ' give the Holy Spirit to those who ask him.' The Spirit had qualified Old Testament men for extraordinary work, but he was to be poured out on ' *all flesh* ' in Gospel times. The sovereignty, therefore, of the Spirit dwelt in Jesus, by which he raised all men to a high level in the Gospel. This doctrine the Baptist preached.

Hence, with the sight of the descending Spirit he heard the attesting voice of divine Fatherhood and Sonship : ' This is my Son.' That august voice which rent the empty heavens above the Jordan told John of God's complacency in his Son : ' In him I am well pleased.' This voice sank into the inner being of the Baptist, and thrills the hearts of his brethren to-day in all the dialects of the earth. Jehovah has honored no other great institute as he has Christ's baptism, when he used the new rite to mark his inauguration as Head of the Gospel Church. The anointing of his Only Begotten Son by his Holy Spirit, sanctified the new-born ordinance. Therein the Father, Son, and Holy Spirit were revealed, and from that day to this, whenever true Christians visit Christ's baptism, they sing : ' God, even thy God, has anointed thee with the oil of gladness above thy fellows.' There we have the first distinct revelation of the Godhead. There the whole Trinity united in laying the foundation of the Gospel Church, in the name of the Father, and of the Son, and of the Holy Spirit. All true Baptists may point to Christ's Baptism, and say with Augustine to Marcion : ' Go to Jordan and thou shalt see the Trinity.'

The next great cognate truth which John was the first to publish, was Christ's vicarious sacrifice. This he comprehended from the first, although his own Apostles never understood it till after his resurrection. From the beginning, the Baptist proclaimed him as the Sin-bearer. He cried : ' Behold the Lamb of God that taketh away the sin of the world!'[2] These sacrificial words have been descanted upon, probably more than any found in the New Testament, and they seem to have moved all John's being. He had previously given testimony to the abiding of the Spirit with the Son, and now that great truth gave birth to this. The more he saw of Jesus, the more the deep spring of truth welled up within him. His theologic eye was opened at the Jordan, and he soon saw wonderful things in his Master. At first, the Dove, symbolical among birds for the purposes of thank-offering and ceremonial purification, was the extent of his discovery. Now, he proclaims him as the Lamb, of God's choosing, from his own flock, the image of spotlessness and cleansing merit. The Dove spoke of the heavens whence he came, the Lamb spoke of the altar where he takes away the sin of the world. This sublime picture revealed Isaiah's Lamb on his way to slaughter. His language neither expresses an act of the past, nor one of the future, but one which forever continues. The mediatorial work had begun, the morning sacrifice had been offered. In his baptism God had inspected him, had pronounced him well pleasing, had accepted him as his own Sin-victim, and now the sacrificial work was in process : '*Taketh* away the *sin*,' abstractly and concretely, 'of the world.' The Apostles have since elaborated the saving doctrine, with exquisite clearness and power, but they caught their keynote from John, who first announced the astounding revelation. The Evangelist John placed his throbbing temples on the bosom of the Lamb, but not till the Baptist John had told him twice, how pure, and soft, and warm it was. This doctrine won the Evangelist in a moment. When the Baptist told him this he was one of John's disciples, but the moment that John told him of God's Lamb to expiate his sin, he became a follower of Jesus. Since that day the son of Zebedee has been crying with one breath : 'I love him because he first loved me!' and with the next: Behold the Lamb! Behold the Lamb!'

If possible, the Baptist's next testimony to Christ, brought him into greater Gospel fullness still, for he gave it under the severest trial. Two years had passed since he opened his ministry, when his disciples were thrown into a controversy 'with a Jew about purifying.' Then, his disciples said to him : 'Rabbi, he who was with thee beyond the Jordan, to whom thou hast borne witness, behold he baptizes, and all come to him.' This dispute was neither amongst his disciples themselves, nor between the disciples of John and Jesus, about the merits of their baptisms, as some pretend, nor did it concern baptism at all. 'A Jew,' who belonged to neither set of disciples, tried to draw John's disciples into a debate on the question of legal ablutions, for the traditionists were bewitched to torture every body with their petty quibbles, and so this 'Jew' baited John's disciples to set them at variance with the elders, as the Pharisees attacked Christ's disciples for not washing their hands before eating, after the tradition of the elders. Irving forcibly covers this case thus : 'It was not a dispute concerning their relative baptisms I judge from this, that the word is "purifying," not baptism. The word for purifying is never applied either to the baptism of John or of Christ's disciples, or of the Holy Ghost, or any other baptism. The word "baptism" is in one place applied to purifying, as the baptism of cups, pots, and tables; and once in the Hebrews, where it is rendered "the doctrine of baptisms," I think it much better to translate the baptism of doctrine, or the purifying influences of doctrine. But the word "purifying" is never, on the one hand, used for baptism, and on that account cannot be so taken in this place, without violence to every rule of interpretation.' ³

Although this artful attempt failed, John's disciples allowed a spirit of rivalry to enter their bosoms, because Christ's disciples baptized more persons than John. This drew from him new and clearer testimony for Christ. ' Rabbi,' they said, ' he who was with thee beyond the Jordan, to whom thou hast borne witness, behold he immerses, and all come to him.' This clause, ' borne witness,' carries the thought, that John's testimony to Jesus had given dignity to him, and made him John's debtor. The words, ' he was with thee,' imply that they considered Jesus a follower of John, like themselves, and ' he baptizeth' suggests, that they thought he was usurping John's work and high calling. What appeared worse than all to them, he was using the distinction which John had given him to draw John's following to his own standard, and so building up his own name on John's decaying cause; ' all men come to him.' That is, they charge Jesus with building up a rival Baptist sect. It was a keen trial to John to see this distrust and envy of Christ in his own family. His soul was stirred when he saw that his own testimony to the Redeemer's character and work was misunderstood, and with a minute, verbal clearness which he had not used before, he proceeded to silence forever this misleading suspicion in his followers. To this end he gave this noblest reply which ever fell from the lips of mortal; and with these words turned both them and his own work over into the hands of Jesus forever, as his divinely appointed superior.

' John answered and said : A man can receive nothing, except it be given him, from heaven. Ye yourselves bear me witness, that I said, I am not the Christ, but I am sent before him. He that has the bride is the bridegroom. But the friend of the bridegroom, who stands and hears him, rejoices greatly because of the bridegroom's voice. This my joy therefore is made full. He must increase, but I must decrease. He that comes from above is above all; he that is from the earth is of the earth, and speaks of the earth; he that comes from heaven is above all. And what he has seen and heard, that he testifies; and his testimony no one receives. He that received his testimony has set his seal, That God is true. For he whom God sent speaks forth the words of God; for he gives not the Spirit by measure. The Father loves the Son, and HAS GIVEN ALL THINGS INTO HIS HAND. He that believes on the Son has everlasting life, and he that believes not the Son shall not see life, but the wrath of God abides on him.' ⁴

Here John not only points his disciples and all subsequent believers to Christ for ' everlasting life,' but he shows his own exact relation to ' the Son,' as being that of the groomsman to the Bridegroom. As the ' friend of the Bridegroom' he had prepared for the marriage of God's Son, and as his work was now finished, his 'joy was full,' and he retired, leaving the Bride in the care of the Bridegroom. 'He must increase, but I must decrease,' is his prophetic forecast. 'God loves him; and has given all things into his hand.' Then and there, dropping his special commission as a herald, he became the first New Testament preacher of a present trust in Christ for salvation, or of salvation by faith, declaring that he who 'believes not the Son shall not see life, but the wrath of God abides on him.' We have seen, that not only was John the first to preach the pre-existence and divinity of Christ as one who had come 'from above,' and was now 'above all;' to preach Jesus as God's sacrificial victim for sin, his 'Lamb' bearing away the 'sin of the world;'—but on the banks of the same Jordan where he had baptized him, he declares him the Saviour, to whom his own disciples and all other men must now look for salvation from 'the wrath of God.'

No passage in the New Testament more clearly points out the glorious truth that men are saved only by trust in Christ than John's words: 'He that believes on the Son has everlasting life.' And none more powerfully shows that the destiny of man is left in the hand of Christ, than the fearful words: 'He that believes not the Son shall not see life, but the wrath of God abides on him.' There is no possibility of misconstruing John's doctrine of eternal retribution here. Human ingenuity and gloss have tried to explain away all Christ's words on this subject, but the terrible decision of the Baptist's words defy all the attempts of sophistry. From the first, he held that the obdurate rejector of Christ must endure a baptism in 'unquenchable fire.' John spoke of a baptism in the Spirit for the good, but Christ's fire-baptism is always spoken of as destructive, as 'chaff' is consumed by fire. Neander says: 'The Messiah will immerse the souls of believers in the Holy Spirit,' but 'those who refused to be penetrated by the Spirit of the divine life should be destroyed by the fire of the divine judgments.'[5] Von Rohden so understands John's preaching: 'The baptism of fire, then, refers to the destruction of those, who, under the Messianic government, should refuse to receive the baptism of the Holy Spirit, those who should oppose themselves to the reign of the Messiah.'[6] When Luke speaks of the 'promise of the Father' (Acts i, 5), he omits John's words, 'and with fire,' for they couched a threat, not a promise. Even the symbolical tongues which rested upon the Apostles at Pentecost, were not of fire, but only '*like* as of fire.' Hence, in John's last testimony to Christ, he presents not simply the 'Lamb' in his saving aspects, but also in his Leonine administration, and vindicates his honor against the sin of rejecting him.

Throughout, John's testimony to Christ presents his character in a glorious light, by showing, that he is thankful to be distanced in the race, if the glory of Christ be advanced. Bright as a star himself, he is content that his own light should be lost in the noontide glory of the firmament. The prospect of extinction awakened triumph in his breast, that he might be nothing and Jesus all things.

His only grief was, that men received not his testimony. What a wonderful summary of Christian doctrine and consecration he gives. What are the struggles of a patriot for his country, compared with his eager devotion to lay down his life for his Friend, and to see his own glory die in the splendor of his Master? His meridian was past, and his sun was setting, and now when the shadows of night fell upon him, his ecstasy was this: 'He that cometh from heaven is above all.' Beautiful Baptist! The first great New Testament theologian. For thousands of years all study amongst Jews and Gentiles had failed to unveil the doctrines which he brought to light, and all after study has failed to exhaust them. 'More than a prophet,' none have discoursed so grandly on his Redeemer's person, office and love: and what new doctrine has any inspired writer revealed since?

The imprisonment and martyrdom of the Baptist must now be noticed. The faithful son of Zacharias was hated for his fidelity. Herod Antipas, the tetrarch of Galilee, was a son of Herod the Great, and had married a daughter of Aretas, King of Arabia-Petræa, who was to him a faithful wife. Antipas had a half-brother, Herod Philip, not by the same mother, who had married Herodias, the daughter of Aristobulus, still another brother. Herodias, therefore, was granddaughter to Herod the Great and niece to Antipas. But Antipas fell in love with her, persuaded her to abandon her husband, divorced his own wife, and then married her. This woman took her young daughter, Salome, Philip's child, with her; and as the adulterous queen of Antipas, came to the Galilean tetrarchy and shared with him his vice-regal palace, where she reveled in guilty splendor. When the Baptist heard of this disgusting crime it stirred his indignation, and he bluntly rebuked the incestuous paramour in terms as stern as his upbraidings of the scornful Pharisees. As God's messenger he thundered in the ears of Antipas: 'It is not lawful for thee to have thy brother's wife!' Luke adds that he reproved him: 'For all the evils which Herod did;' a long and black list of crimes. For this cause he seized John and threw him into the dismal fortress of Machaerus, the 'Black Castle,' east of the Dead Sea, an outrage instigated by Herodias; for she was angry with him, and fastened on him like some ferocious animal clinging to its prey. She desired, says Mark, to put him to death but could not, for Herod feared John, knowing that he was a just and holy man. The imperiousness of truth which lifted John above the fear of rank and of death, made his person so sacred, that the stony heart of the adulterer was overawed. One glance of purity made the adulterous tyrant writhe in dread fetters. John was unarmed and alone. Herod was compassed by royal guards. Yet John hurled subtile arrows from an invisible quiver, which, piercing the armor of steel, made the king's heart faint.

'It is not *lawful* for thee to have her,' was the metal-point which made John's barb so keen. The Jewish laws had thrown a colossal rampart around the sanctity of marriage, a holiness which the whole Herodian family had set at naught, in one way or another. In the person of Antipas, the Baptist brought that whole household up to the scrutiny of the Bible standard. His terrible appeals were made to the Scriptural law. He threw the whole question back, not on public scandal or the shock of public feeling, but on the supremacy of God's word. There he planted himself firmly in the eloquence of lamentation, protest, and demand. Unwilling to fawn, unable to varnish, he put one finger on the ulcer, and with the other resting on Lev. xviii, 16, he demanded obedience to Divine authority. Whatever the enactments of men might say in the case, the Law of God was the first and last source of his appeal. The craven Sanhedrin knew as well as John that Herod was trampling the law of God under-foot and defying Jehovah's mandate, but all its members sealed their lips to the barefaced disgrace. John frowned upon the triple crime through a 'thus saith the Lord;' and his daring fidelity to Revelation, as the only rule of life, wrote his name at the head of a long roll of Baptist martyrs, who have sealed the Truth with their blood.

At length Herod's birthday dawned, that day in the calendar around which he should have summoned all the years of his life for a sweet song, that Jehovah had sent him into the world an innocent babe. But instead, its celebration wrote this dark entry on his record: 'It were better for him that he had never been born!' Well might he have prayed with Job: 'That day, let not God from above seek for it. Let it not rejoice among the days of the year, nor come into the number of the months, neither let it behold the eyelids of the morning!' But with his birthday came the revelry of a court festival. Instead of sackcloth and ashes for his sins, and the turning over of a new leaf with the merciful anniversary, he gathered his generals and peers around him, took upon him his most hilarious mood, gave reins to his vanity and ostentation, spread his feast and lavished his wine, drowned his fear in the fumes of the cup and the strains of music, and when his brain began to reel under the adulation of nobles and the wassail-bowl, then a revengeful woman turned the day of birth into the night of death.

Wild abandon, wanton voluptuousness, and hot carousal, now ruled the royal banquet, and the call was issued for the pantomimic dance. Herod winced under John's rebukes, yet could bear them. Herodias could not. Her pride would not brook them, and revenge rankled in her heart. Her crafty soul knew that the *ballet dancers* would be asked for when the guests were well flushed with madness, and her dainty foresight had prepared for them a special treat. Vengeance had drawn its bow to the double strain and set its fiery arrow to a true wing, its blistering eye had spied the vulnerable point in the harness and laid its hand to launch the bolt. And, in icy hatred she sent her beautiful young daughter, the future mother of kings, to dance for the company; her rage reminding us of science freezing water in a red-hot capsule. The grace and condescension of Great Herod's granddaughter so charmed the high-bred revelers of Galilee, that the drunken king swore to give her aught she asked, to 'the half of his kingdom.' The courtly throng were all ear for her request. One thought that she would ask for gems to further adorn her handsome person, another knew that she would demand the finest estate in the realm, and a third was sure that she would covet a marriage dower worthy of a princess. Delight intoxicated her, and she rushed to her mother's chamber for instructions. The royal dancer returned with the irony of fate upon her pale lips. Guilty plot and vengeful blood-thirst threw tragedy into the feast; the delicate girl craved the head of John the Baptist on a dish! But she proved her true Herodian blood, when she betrayed haste to stain the escutcheon of her forefathers with a new blot, by the imperative behest that the boon should be delivered then and there. 'I will, that immediately thou give me on a plate, the head of John!' She would carry the ghastly gift to her mother in her own hands, lest the head of a slave be palmed off upon her for John's, and so, her maternal soul should shudder and faint for the shedding of innocent blood.

The thought that John's pulse should cease to beat on the day that his own caught the throb of life from the heart of his mother, sobered the drunken sovereign and brought him to his senses. But for his oath's sake he ended the struggle in his own breast, consented to the horrible demand; the executioner was commissioned. A shrill cry made the dismal dungeon ring, and the gory head of the great preacher lay gasping in the hall of the festal carouse, silenced forever. The sacred pen has left a veil over John's last feeling, his last word, his last act. Was he excited or serene? Did he pray for his murderers or depart in silence? Only this we know, the sword left his trunk bleeding in the prison, and sent his head to the feast. The celestial dreamer would have written: 'I saw a chariot and a couple of horses waiting for Faithful; who, as soon as his adversaries had dispatched him, was taken up into it, and straightway was carried up through the clouds, with sound of trumpet, the nearest way to the Celestial Gate.' Whether the viper uncoiled and stung the bosom of the murderess we have no record. Tradition says, that when the head of the martyr was brought to her and its glazed eyes pierced her, she transfixed the tongue with a bodkin in revenge for its rebukes.

Her shameful deeds, and those of her husband, drove them into obscurity and exile. Not, however, is the veil of revelation entirely drawn over Herod at this point, for Mark tells us, that in beheading John he slew his own peace. When the news reached him that Jesus was working every sort of good and benevolent work amongst the people, the specter of the murdered man stalked through his conscience, and he exclaimed: 'John, whom I beheaded, is risen from the dead.' Go where he would, or do what he might, in slumber or revelry, the stain of the Baptist's blood would not out, and the startling eye-balls of his image haunted him; those eyes through which holy love had gleamed, and heaven's fire had shot. All that was sensitive in him had long been seared as with a hot iron, yet twinges of pain crept through the festering canker in every apparition of this heartless tragedy. This son of him who restored the Temple to beauty and strength, found the sanctuary of his own soul in ruins, and heard everywhere the echoes of a still small voice, mocking the criminal who had broken its pillars and piled up its ruins. His spirit was in mutiny with itself; it wandered in chill, and damp, and dark places, where the shriek of murder made his ears tingle at every turn. His sire had heard the shrill scream of the babes in Bethlehem, and thirsted for the blood of the redeeming Infant, when Rachel aroused from her slumbers in her sepulcher, groaned and wept, and refused to be comforted, because the unrelenting butcher soaked the turf above her in the gore of her offspring. Nor did she resume her sleep of death till the echo of their piercing cry died away in her tomb, and instead thereof, her cold ear caught the songs of her little ones, who had soared from Bethlehem to the skies, singing hosannas to the new-born King; a chant from the first infant martyrs to the child born and the Son given. Then was she quiet; for Jehovah soothed her to rest, saying: 'Refrain thy voice from weeping, and thine eyes from tears: for thy work shall be rewarded, and thy children shall come again from the land of the enemy.' Ah! but there was no such soothing for godless Antipas. The blighted monarch saw nothing but the open door in the world of spirits, through which the headless Baptist had come back to torment him before his time.

This was the sole reward for his heartlessness, his indulgence of a woman more abandoned than himself. His caprice had made him a slave to his paramour's rage, and left him as helpless in her hands as the head of the Baptist on the cruel trencher. Herod's folly had entrapped him so completely, that while his conscience stickled in mock honor to break a rash and forceless oath, he could deliberately perpetrate the blackest crime known to mortals. His example of false shame is the most contemptible in history. Rather than brook the implication that he really was capable of a moral scruple, he went the full length of crime. What a choice; rather than allow a set of drunken men to shoot the lip at an empty, broken word, he would carry the blood of holy innocence in his skirts through life. Did a minister of his court ever look in his face again, without reading his spectral fear of the slain prophet? Clearly enough, after this, the ministry of Jesus himself was to him the 'savor of death unto death.' His heavenly words and Godlike acts were never reported, but Herod saw the dead man clothe himself afresh in all the sanctities of his being; he was 'John risen from the dead!' How could the tormented monarch know any interpreter of benevolence but the contortions of a trunkless head?

CHAPTER IV.

CHRIST'S WITNESS TO THE BAPTIST.

WHEN John knew that his departure was at hand, he lovingly sent two of his disciples to ask whether Jesus were the Messiah, or should they look for another. This act touched the heart of Jesus tenderly. John was not angry with Herod for his imprisonment, nor did he distrust his own mission or that of Christ; but for the sake of his disciples he sent them, that his own testimony might be confirmed, that their convictions might be established, and that now they might cling to Jesus only. Our Lord re-assured them by an appeal to their sense of sight and hearing. 'Go tell John the things that ye see,—the blind, the lame, the deaf are restored, and the dead are raised. Tell him the things that you hear, to the poor the glad tidings are preached.' If he cannot believe the first he must accept this last evidence, for no teacher but one from heaven would begin with the poor. This testimony confirmed their faith, and their Master's witness. When they were gone, Jesus said to the multitude: 'What went ye out into the wilderness to see? A reed shaken with the wind?' He wished them to know, that the rough prophet who dwelt amongst savage beasts, did not quail now that he was in the grasp of the tyrant. Though confined within a dungeon of solid masonry, he was no more like a lithe reed, tossed by every gust, than when he thundered against the sins of the nation. This errand of inquiry, so far from indicating that John quailed, confirmed his integrity, and showed him to be the same self-conscious athlete as ever, just as resolute and firm. 'Went ye out to see a man clothed in soft raiment? They that wear soft clothing are in king's houses.' John was decreasing, but Jesus testified that he was no self-indulgent, easy-going preacher at the court of Galilee, seeking luxury, and fawning to pomp, because he was without that moral fiber, which men call steel. No, this son of the hoary desert was still hardy. Delicate living and gorgeous clothing were in the palace of Antipas, while the fortress of Machaerus was happy in the old austerities. Then Jesus gave his climax: 'Went ye out to see a prophet? Yea, and more than a prophet. Verily I say to you, Among those born of woman there has not risen a greater than John the Baptist. But he who is least in the kingdom of heaven is greater than he.'

A greater than all the prophets is not easily terrified, and Jesus pronounced John greater. No one prophet had prophesied concerning another; but other prophets had foretold John, as 'the messenger who should prepare the way of the Lord.' His character and office had both been predicted. Nay, he had foretold the glory of Christ,—had seen him in his beauty,—had lived contemporary with him,—was his blood-relative,—and had inducted him into his Messianic office. Did Jesus exaggerate when he pronounced John greater than all those born of woman, and more than a prophet? Is this the panegyric of an unguarded enthusiast? Need we say that Jesus weighed his words; and enstamped John's character forever in sentences of embronzed truth? He made the Baptist a very gem of divine reality, sent from his Father's crown-jewel room. Jehovah had filled him with light in the mine, and Herod was bringing it out in the cutting.

How reverentially the Evangelist tells us, that when John looked no longer through his prison bars, 'His disciples came, took up his corpse, and laid it in a tomb;' but he adds significantly, that they 'went and told Jesus.' After their master's body was buried, they found no grave for their griefs but in the warm heart of his Master; and from that moment they transferred their discipleship to his ranks. Then Jesus not only pronounced this holy eulogy: 'He has borne witness to the truth, he was a burning and a shining light;' but he prophesied that posterity should do him justice, 'wisdom must be justified on the part of her children.' Truly, John's character and claims have been justified in his posterity, as history has defended those of no other man. Yet says Jesus: 'He that is least in the kingdom of heaven is greater than he.' These words cannot have reference to John's moral and spiritual character; for none of our Lord's disciples have outstripped him in spirituality 'who was filled with the Holy Spirit, even from his birth.' Clearly, Jesus speaks of his official position, as John's prophetic character is the only point of which he is treating. As crying 'prophets' the lowliest fishermen amongst the disciples formed a great contrast with John. The Baptist's own followers, Andrew and John the Evangelist, outstripped their old master in all his proclaiming privileges. He preached a Saviour who had come to do his work, they preached him crucified, buried, and risen from the dead. Filled as he was with the Spirit, he wrought no mighty works; but the fishermen did the same works that were done by their Master. Stirring as was John's ministry, it was shut up to the narrow home of the Jews, while the Apostles were sent to the ends of the earth In these respects the least of them was greater than he.

Jesus enlarged his witness to John, at this point, by settling the mooted question of his relation to Elijah: 'If ye are willing to receive it, he is the Elijah that should come.' Some think that John's imprisonment made him sad and impatient, and so, that he desired Jesus to come and liberate him by miracle. If this be correct, then the true magnanimity of Christ is seen in rising above John's waning popularity in the nation, to make his dungeon an eternal Temple of Fame. Like as the star of Bethlehem hung a witness to himself over his stable-cradle, so he hung this lamp over gloomy Machaerus in the darkest hour of John's life: 'This is the Elijah that was to come!' Gabriel had said that John should come, 'In the spirit and power of Elijah.' The nation supposed, that when Messiah came the prophet of Carmel would descend in the awful manner of his ascent. But the heavens had not re-opened, nor the whirlwind regathered, nor the chariots flashed down ablaze, to theological Jericho. No retinue of angels had brought back the reverend prophet, to tell with bated breath that he could not remain in mansions above, while his brethren were crushed to the earth. They expected to see him wrap his old mantle about him once more, and with a double portion of his own royal spirit, proclaim the coming Lord God of Elijah. Here, they were sadly mistaken; God's true Elijah was in prison, not in Paradise.

John was not the venerable seer of Horeb, but was like him in spirit and power and character. He is named Elijah for the same reason that Jesus is called 'David,' not to point out that monarch personally, but to declare his kingship. There was a unity of purpose between Elijah and John, betokening the same commission in both. Each bent his energies to the same sacred work of reformation. Both walked with God in the desert, in abstinence and solitude, bound the same rough garment around their sturdy frames, and suddenly broke on the nation asleep in its sins, when its crimes were crying aloud for vengeance. They both reproved the incorrigible, rebuked kings, and warned the land of coming wrath. They silenced religious wranglings, tore men's delusive sophistries to shreds, and demanded new holiness of heart and life. Yet, Jesus pronounced John: 'More than a prophet,' among all that had been born. The Baptist was greater than Elijah. Elijah fled from persecution, John met it face to face. Jezebel terrified Elijah, and hiding in the desert under a clump of broom-sedge, he prayed God to take his life. John bearded power in a palace, and quailed not before brutal Herodias, though the queen demanded his head. And John was greater than Elijah in that he went to heaven, a martyr's wreath upon his brow flecked with his own blood, while Elijah rose to the skies in a chariot of ease.

Our Lord's witness to John was weighty in words, but if possible, his deeds were weightier still. He ratified John's baptism as divine, by submitting to it himself and never seeking any other; then, he adopted it as a part of the Gospel system, unaltered and unalterable with his consent, to the end of time. The Evangelist tells us the mind of Jesus in this matter when he says: 'There was a man sent from God whose name was John. The same came for witness, to bear witness of the light, that through him all might believe.' John says that God, 'Sent me to baptize, in water.' So marked was his authority from the Father to do this, that an inspired Evangelist found it needful to disavow that he was 'The Light' himself, lest men should be confused as to which of them was the Christ. Because John was so directly from God, Jesus not only took his own baptism from his hands, but received John's disciples into his own Apostleship, without administering any other baptism to them.[1] The identity and validity of their baptism he put side by side with his own, not only marking it as from heaven, but pronouncing it, 'The Counsel of God.' He charges guilt upon the Pharisees and lawyers in rejecting that counsel, by refusing baptism at John's hands.² The very purpose for which the Baptist was sent into the world was, 'That through him all might believe' on Christ.³ Paul declares that John said to the people, 'That they should believe on Jesus.' In person, Jesus then stood amongst them; in office, he was 'to come after him,' and accept his work. The phrase 'to come' cannot relate to Christ's birth, for he had already baptized him as a man of thirty, but must relate to his future Messianic reign. John lived, preached and baptized after Christ had entered on his Messianic work, just as much as any of Christ's Apostles did. The Baptist preached repentance in the presence of Jesus, and baptized converts to him for about two years after he had baptized him; for his martyrdom took place but a few months before Christ's crucifixion. John saw his glory, noted his miracles, 'rejoiced in his light,' proclaimed the atonement that he was about to make as God's 'Lamb,' and demanded that all penitents should 'believe on him' who then stood amongst them. Saving that Gospel ministers now preach Christ's redeeming acts as finished, John preached all that we now preach or can preach, the agency of the Holy Spirit in the Gospel Church included.

With these facts on the very face of the four gospels, the question whether John's baptism were Christian or not, is reduced to a dispute about words, which only casts discredit upon Christ's own baptism, as if it had no binding force upon his own churches. Those who reject Christ's personal baptism and that of his Apostles by John, as wanting in some vital Christian element, do so because it was administered before Pentecost. Of course, this not only implies that Christ's baptism and theirs were defective, but that all the baptisms administered by the Apostles before Pentecost were defective, as Christian baptisms! What was the inexplicable mishap in these baptisms, a deficiency which Christ himself did neither detect nor rectify? The Evangelist says, That Jesus 'made,' or discipled the converts whom his disciples baptized.⁴ Also he says, That they were baptized in Christ's presence: 'He tarried with them and baptized.'⁵ Then what had Pentecost to do anyhow with the ratification of the baptisms which he had authorized, as Christian? Under credentials from God, the baptism practiced by John and Jesus was identical at any rate. But neither the Father, the Son, nor the Spirit, added one injunction on baptism after Pentecost. Christ administered both baptism and the Supper before his death, and his Apostles practiced baptism under his own eye. Was this a distinct institute from that which his Father had ordained for John? and from that which followed Pentecost too? In that case, we have three sorts of baptism in the New Testament, one for John, one for Jesus and his Apostles, and still another for all the ages after Pentecost! To say that either of these acts were not Christian in the fullest sense of the word, is to throw endless perplexity about the right obedience of the New Testament converts.

Clearly, there was no vital difference between the manner, the obligation, the object, or the value of baptism, before Pentecost and after. The difference between the first and later baptisms by Christ's Apostles related only to their enlarged field. At first Christ sent them to 'the lost sheep of Israel,' but his post-resurrection commission enlarged their sphere to 'all nations.' Either his Apostles baptized none before his resurrection; which cannot be, for, 'They baptized more disciples than John;' or they baptized without his authority at that time; or else he gave them two separate commissions to baptize, one before his resurrection and one after, and so their first baptisms were defective as compared with their last. If any of their first baptisms were defective, which? and in what respect? The post-resurrection commission of Jesus gave them no indication that the rite was new, nor that it was a re-establishment of the old rite. Both its wording and spirit imply that it was the simple continuance of a rite with which they were familiar, already existing by divine appointment, and now, by the same appointment made outreaching to 'all the world.' He then gave permanent type to the formula, adding the name of the Spirit to his own and to that of the Father, for very obvious reasons. On the authority of the Father, the Christian age and institutions began with the baptism of the Son, its first and primary design being to manifest him to the world. It was adopted and sanctioned by the Son all through his ministry, and enforced on others through his Apostles. The Holy Spirit had ratified it by his descent upon the Son in his baptism, and when the Spirit should fill Christ's place on earth after his ascension, it was but meet that it should thenceforth be administered in the Triune Name.

Can absurdity be more absurd than that which supposes John to have stood in a nondescript dispensation of his own when he baptized Jesus; while Jesus, when he received his baptism, stood in still another dispensation. John's ministry had nothing in common with the economy of Moses, for Jesus himself says that the 'Law was *until* John,' from which time the 'good news of the kingdom is preached, and every man presses into it;' the same kingdom that both John and Jesus preached. And what other kingdom is preached to-day? Christ was never baptized in water but once; and will men say that his baptism was not in the Christian dispensation, simply because he was baptized before he ascended to heaven? For the same reason they may read the Lord's Supper out of the Christian dispensation, for 'the Spirit had not come' on the night of its first celebration. John and Jesus both preached the same 'kingdom of heaven' at the same time, and to the same people, either in the Christian age or out of it, certainly; so that if John's preaching and baptism were neither Mosaic nor Christian, neither could those of Jesus be; as authorized by God to introduce the Gospel, they stand or fall together.

The cases of Apollos and the twelve Ephesians are directly in point here, although out of their chronological order. Apollos (Acts xviii, 24–28) 'knew only the baptism of John;' meaning that he had been baptized by John or one of his followers. The narrative shows that Apollos had found that repentance, faith in

Christ, and personal holiness under John's teaching, which led him to speak and teach 'correctly the things concerning Jesus.' On these he had received baptism, as appears, without knowing every thing concerning Christ historically, for Priscilla and Aquila 'taught him the way of the Lord more perfectly.' Among other things, however, they did not teach him to repudiate his baptism from John, on the ground that there were two sorts of baptism and two sorts of baptizers, and so, that his baptism would not admit him into a post-Pentecost Gospel Church, for before he could be received there, he must seek a new baptism. They simply gave him fuller light 'on the way of the Lord,' as the Apostles had received new light from time to time, and as do all devout souls.

Dr. Brown, Professor of Theology at Aberdeen, treats this case happily, thus:

'He comes to Ephesus already instructed in the way of the Lord, fervent in the spirit, and mighty in the Scriptures, though yet only on the Joannean platform; and what Priscilla and Aquila did for him seems to have been simply to impart to him those facts of the new economy, with which he was unacquainted. And just as those disciples who passed from the ranks of the Baptist to those of Christ needed and received no new baptism, so this already distinguished Christian teacher, having merely received a riper view of those great evangelical truths which he already believed and taught, neither needed nor received rebaptization.'

On his faith and baptism he passed from John's discipleship into the Apostolic Church at Ephesus, was commended to them as a Christian teacher, and became a champion of the faith, 'watering' where Paul 'planted.' Instead of the Church setting aside his baptism from John as defective, in any respect, it was adopted as thoroughly satisfactory in every respect, and that without question. Here we find a full justification for the strong words of Calvin, when he says:

'It is very certain that the ministry of John was precisely the same as that which was afterward committed to the Apostles. For their baptism was not different, though it was administered by different hands; but the sameness of their doctrine shows their baptism to have been the same. John and the Apostles agreed in the same doctrine. Both baptized to repentance, both to remission of sins; both baptized in the name of Christ, from whom repentance and remission of sins proceed. John said of Christ: "Behold the Lamb of God, who taketh away the sin of the world;" thus acknowledging and declaring him to be the sacrifice acceptable to the Father, the procurer of righteousness, and the author of salvation. What could the Apostles add to this confession? Wherefore, let no one be disturbed by the attempts of the ancient writers to distinguish and separate one baptism from the other; for their authority ought not to have weight enough to shake our confidence in the Scripture. . . . But, if any difference be sought for in the Word of God, the only difference that will be found is, that John baptized in the name of him who was to come, the Apostles in the name of him who had already manifested himself.'

Touching the case of the twelve believers whom Paul found at Ephesus (Acts xix, 1-7), we need to bring great candor and docility to its examination; for its interpretation is more difficult, and it has been the subject of much controversy. High sacramentarians have always disparaged John's baptism, in order to exalt their own as the only Christian 'sacrament.' With this in view, the Council of Trent decreed: 'If any one shall say that the baptism of John had the same efficacy as the baptism of Christ, let him be anathema.'[6] On the other hand, Protestants generally, at the Reformation, held that they were essentially the same, for the Apostle does not raise the question concerning the baptism of these 'twelve' with reference to their admission into Christianity; like Apollos, they were Christians already. Paul addresses them as having 'believed,' and Luke calls them 'disciples;' nor were they seeking fellowship with Christians when the Apostle met them; they were already numbered amongst Christians. Liddon says: 'They must have acknowledged a certain relation to Jesus Christ as their Master, or the name "disciple" would not have been given them. Jesus was in some sense their Master; they were his disciples.' Paul's question related to their reception of the miraculous gifts of the Spirit when they exercised faith on Christ, and they limited their answer accordingly: 'We did not so much as hear whether the Holy Spirit was.' Not that they were ignorant of the Spirit's existence. This cannot be the meaning, since the personality and office of the Holy Spirit, in connection with Christ, formed an essential subject of the Baptist's teachings. Literally: 'We did not even hear whether the Holy Spirit was' [given], that is, at the time of their baptism. Calvin says:

'It is not probable that Jews, though they had never been baptized at all, would have been destitute of all knowledge of the Holy Spirit, who is celebrated in so many testimonies of Scripture. . . . I grant that the baptism they had received was the true baptism of John, and the very same with the baptism of Christ, but I deny that they were baptized again. . . . If ignorance vitiate a first baptism, so that it requires to be corrected by a second, the first persons who ought to have been rebaptized were the Apostles themselves, who, for three years after their baptism, had scarcely any knowledge of the least particle of pure doctrine; and among us, what views would be sufficient for the repetition of ablutions as numerous as the errors which are daily corrected in us by the mercy of the Lord.'[7]

This great divine presses his point more strongly still in his Commentary on Acts xix:

'Paul doth not speak in this place of the Spirit of regeneration, but of the special gifts which God gave to others at the beginning of the Gospel. . . . Because the men of old had conceived an opinion that the baptism of John and of Christ were diverse, it was no inconvenient thing for them to be baptized again, who were only prepared with the baptism of John. But that diversity was falsely and wickedly believed, it appeareth by this, in that it was a pledge and token of the same adoption, and of the same newness of life which we have at this day in our baptism, and therefore we do not read that Christ did baptize those again who came from John unto him. Moreover, Christ received baptism in his own flesh, that he might couple himself with us, by that visible sign (Matt. iii, 15). But if that feigned diversity be admitted, this singular benefit shall fall away and perish, that baptism is common to the Son of God and to us, or that we have all one baptism with him. But this opinion needeth no long confutation; because to the end they may parade that these two baptisms be diverse, they must needs show first wherein the one differeth from the other; but the most excellent likelihood answereth to both parts, and also the agreement and conformity of the parts, which causeth us to confess that it is all one baptism. . . . Now the question is, whether it were lawful to repeat the same, and furious men in this our age trusting to this testimony, went about to bring in baptizing again. I deny that the baptism of water was repeated, because the words of Luke import no such thing, save only that they were baptized with the Spirit. . . . And whereas it followeth immediately that when he had laid his hands upon them, the Spirit came, I take it to be added by way of interpretation.'

Then, as in all other cases where baptism in the Spirit occurred, 'they spoke with tongues,' a 'sign' which few believers received; it does not appear that even Apollos possessed this distinction. The same free Spirit which had converted and kept them now bestowed miraculous gifts upon them.

In this transaction Paul did not raise the question of the validity of John's baptism; why should he, more than with his fellow-Apostles themselves? With him the vital point covered only the endowment of the Ephesian believers with miraculous gifts. The question of conversion to Christ is not raised in the narrative; but as these gifts sometimes preceded baptism and sometimes followed it, Paul simply asked whether or not they received them when they 'believed.' Dr. Brown sums up the cases of Apollos and these twelve thus: 'There is no evidence to show that our Lord caused those disciples of John, who came over to him, to be rebaptized; and from John iv, 1, 2, we naturally conclude that they were not. Indeed, had those who first followed Jesus from among the Baptist's disciples required to be rebaptized, the Saviour must have performed the ceremony himself, and such a thing could not fail to be recorded; whereas the reverse is intimated in the passage just quoted.' Hence, it follows that these Ephesians needed not a new water baptism any more than the twelve Apostles. And it is remarkable that in Peter's statement of qualifications needed in the candidate who should fill the place of Judas, was this, namely, that he should have companied with them from the time of John's baptism to Christ's ascension. His intimacy with John and Jesus from the 'beginning' made him eligible. They then made prayer to Jesus the great Heart-Knower to determine who it should be, and he appointed Matthias. But not a word is said about his need of rebaptism either before or after Pentecost, in order to a valid filling of the Apostleship with the eleven. Matthias, Apollos, and the twelve at Ephesus, seem to have held much the same relation both to John and Christ. It seems impossible to determine whether these 'twelve' were rebaptized or not. Calvin best expresses the writer's idea, but such high Baptist authority as Drs. Hackett and Hovey take the opposite view. If they were rebaptized, the reason is not found in any defect in John's baptism as Christian, but in their personal want of the full qualifications for receiving baptism. Dr. Hackett puts this view of the case in these strong words: 'Their prompt reception of the truth would tend to show that the defect in their former baptism related not so much to their positive error as to their ignorance in regard to the proper object of faith.' Such ignorance, however, did not obtain in the cases of the Apostles chosen by Christ, of Matthias (Acts i, 22), nor of Apollos, who received baptism from the same source, and were not rebaptized, their examples showing that baptism before and after Pentecost differs only as noon differs from morning.

In this sketch of John, harbinger, preacher, theologian and martyr, next to his Master, we find the great typical Baptist of all ages. It is more than a blunder to place him on the banks of the Jordan, with his face toward Sinai and Egypt, as a perfect personification of the Mosaic age. His face was turned toward Tabor, Calvary, Olivet, and the New Jerusalem, as, next to his Master, the embodiment of the New Testament. John and Jesus looked only forward, eye to eye. His ministry glided into that of Christ, as a mountain tarn soon loses itself in the deep sea. Frederick Robertson, with his usual scope and beauty, says:

'He left behind him no sect to which he had given his name, but his disciples passed into the service of Christ, and were absorbed in the Christian Church. Words from John had made impressions, and men forgot in after years where the impression first came from; but the day of judgment will not forget. John laid the foundations of a temple and others built upon it. He laid it in a struggle, in martyrdom. It was covered up with the rough masonry below ground; but when we look round on the vast Christian Church, we are looking at the superstructure of John's toil.'[8]

That is narrow and pitiable cant which makes him the mere incarnation of his age. Was he such an embodiment of surface life? The New Testament says that he resisted his age, reformed his age, and overturned its old things that all things might become new. Could the worst age of Judaism produce the holiest man in the Gospels? Yes, as much as the densest darkness can create a quenchless light. The later Judaism produced scribes, Pharisees, hypocrites, but John the Baptist never. He was sent of God to his age, and gave it much, but borrowed nothing. He interpreted it, and tried to save it, and it slaughtered him in recompense. No man in the Bible brought so many new truths from God, truths virgin to the soul of man, and which still stir the best spirits on earth with their freshness. The sure and certain sound which echoes through all lands to-day, as loudly as ever, was his first trumpet-call. His personal piety opens to us his inner life. Tertullian thinks that he brought in a new method of prayer, which led the Apostles to say: 'Lord, teach us to pray, as also John taught his disciples.' Whence came that model prayer: 'Our Father,' etc. Far from being the nondescript which narrow modern interpretation makes him, he was the leader in the great moral upheaval which first demanded personal loyalty to Christ. Pointing out salvation, not by hereditary institutions, or by birds and beasts, he demanded a radical revolution, by the establishment of a new kingdom: 'Not of birth, nor of blood, nor of the will of the flesh, nor of the will of man, but of God.'

The Baptist was not a book, but a voice; not a functionary of the old age, nor yet a representative of the Law and the Prophets. They represented themselves.

As a voice, he was living, strong, clear; and 'Jesus' was the 'Word' that he spoke with all his might. So well did he preach Jesus, that his Lord's lips pronounced him 'A burning and shining lamp,' words which he uttered of none other. So luminously did he preach Christ, that, like a lamp, he threw light on his theme. So fervently did he preach him that his ministry burnt with the pungency of a flame. 'Repent, obey the living King,' he cried, and when God gave his hearers repentance unto life, he immersed their bodies in the Jordan. He focused sin as it appears in the New Testament, in all its odiousness; and in this respect, Jesus had closer affinity with him than with any of his Apostles. And that embassador of Christ in our times, who has the most of John's courage, love for Christ and zeal in pushing the great truths which he preached, does the best service in his Master's work. Such a man is a 'scribe, well instructed in the kingdom of God,' a true antitype of Christ's greatest witness.

Like John, Baptists have found through long centuries, that when they have dared to enforce the whole truth as it is in Jesus, they have commonly sealed their own death-warrants. The first Baptist of his race is not the only man of that race whose fidelity has invoked murder in cold blood. More heads of that household than his have gasped on a lordly dish, things of beauty for crowned heads and delicate princesses to gloat their eyes upon. Standing at the head of the noble army of Baptist martyrs, his tragic fidelity to God has been the standing sign of their own end. No story in history is so sad as his, and none so paints criminal splendor and sacred bravery in their true colors. John sets forth the sterling mission of true Baptists in sterling ideal. He was Jehovah's royal minister and man's hated culprit. Needed not the world a 'kind of first-fruits' in God's messengers for its ferocity, and who could meet the need so well as John? In ante-Gospel times the Lord enrolled a long array of brilliant names in his book of remembrance, and these were his jewels. But in the Lamb's book of life, John heads his list of martyr names. Did the Lamb himself refer to this record, and couple these names with his own slaughter, when he said of John: 'They knew him not, but did to him whatever they would. So also is the Son of Man about to suffer.' John's sun has long since set in Palestine, but his glory lays upon the world from its Dan to its Beersheba. The people could not forget him when his frame moldered under the turf, Jesus could not forget him, his Apostles could not forget him; he lived in their thoughts, a palpable entity. Jesus asked the twelve: 'Whom do men say that I am?' They answered: 'John the Baptist.' No apostle of Christ ever met with a eulogy like that. So Christlike was he as to be taken for the Son of God himself, by the very people who knew them both. And all this was when the God-man addressed them daily, and the headless body of the Baptist rested in the soil which they trod. 'Such honor have not all his saints.'

CHAPTER V.

THE KING IN ZION.—LAWS OF THE NEW KINGDOM.

GENEVA, like Jerusalem, is encircled with mountains, Alp rising on Alp. There is the stretch of the mighty Jura, and towering above all, solemn Mont Blanc. He looks down from azure heights in a purity of awe which breathes the spirit of eternity on all below. Yet his summits and battlements of alabaster are so dwarfed by distance, that several princes of his court are easily mistaken for the king himself. Still the practiced eye cannot be misled. When once the sun kisses his brow and steals down his visage, a pink tint warms him into the radiance of life; then, like an archangel asleep, a smile plays on his face, and each courtier around his chair of state catches the glow of his beatitude. So, when we look back to the blue sky on which the Rock of Ages outlined himself, encompassed with Evangelists and Apostles, we may readily rob Jesus of his majesty and put the Baptist, or Peter, or Paul on the monarch's throne. But when the sunlight of God's glory floods the Sacred Head, at once the man of Tabor looms up, the Sovereign of the group. Then, once more, Joseph's 'eleven' sheaves and 'thirteen' celestial orbs arise and bow to him who is King of kings.

The Baptist put the diadem on the rightful brow, for when the people saw Christ's glory they said: 'All things that John spake of this man were true.' His career glided into the public ministry of Jesus, not making the one the fortuitous after-execution of the other, but as a part of one grand design—a far-sighted method of God's eternal love, for a strange unity covers their history. Their ministries are two voices attuned to one strain, and their key-note is 'the kingdom of God.' Jesus took up the theme where John dropped it, and in a more joyful key. He gave the exact burden of John to his Apostles in their Judean mission : 'As ye go preach, saying, The kingdom of heaven is at hand.' Here is a progressive and Godlike unfolding of the same doctrine, the good news of Christ's reign upon the earth. Kingship here is not a celestial institution, but a moral sovereignty over all earthly institutions, the establishment of a spiritual empire on the earth. Bengel forcibly groups the events from Christ's Baptism to his Ascension, in his treatment of the favorite word Gospel in Mark : 'The *beginning* of the Gospel is in the Baptist, the Gospel in the whole book,' to the Great Commission. The Apostles passed the mutilated body of John stretched on the threshold of Christianity, when sent on their errand of struggle and victory ; and they were inspired to endurance by the fall of the strong, pure, young martyr. Jesus lifted up the standard of Jehovah when it fell from John's hands, and it has never fallen since. He took up the very words of John and gave them eternal meaning, by becoming his own herald at the head of the new kingdom. The unity of the New Testament in all its truths and principles shows but one mind; its forecasting and fullness are all of a piece. Hence, what John preached and practiced has never been superseded, or even suspended, to this day. Because it included the substance of Christian truth, it is still moving on in its progressive completeness. There was no rent in John's garment, and our Lord put into it no new piece of cloth, but only enlarged the same divine web.

Pilate asked Jesus: 'Art thou a king then?' and he honestly told the politic Roman that he was the King of the Truth. 'Thou sayest it because I am a King. To this end I came into the world, that I may bear witness to the truth.' Yet he disavowed that his kingdom was of this world: 'If my kingdom were of this world then would my servants fight. But my kingdom is not of this world.' His countrymen looked for a king in pomp and circumstance, who should come literally in the clouds of heaven. But the kingship of Jesus was to sway its power over the souls of men. Look at his answer to the political question, on the lawfulness of paying the poll-tax to the Romans. He took the coin in which it was paid, bearing the image and inscription of Cæsar Augustus, in such a year, after the conquest of Judea. This proving their subjection, he said: 'Give Cæsar that which belongs to him, and render unto God that which is his.' He made a part of their duty lie in loyalty to their protecting government, and having done this, they must obey God in all things. Here he laid down the great law of his own kingdom, duty to God above all human policy, and a sacred regard for all wholesome human law.

He would form a community for other purposes than those of national existence, but would not interfere with human governments. He would select its subjects, make its officers, enact and enforce its laws, and govern it under the will of God. With the founding of such an empire in view, he needed no assistance from human sources, as other men. His servants would neither fight for supremacy nor ask political Powers to fight for them. His kingdom should conquer by choice and not by force—it should be taken from every stock and race, and held together by love. It should grant no special privileges to any class, or blood, or nation; but, on the contrary, races hostile to each other, speaking different tongues and following different interests, should be compacted into a harmonious whole. No man's courage had dared to take principles as deep and broad as human nature itself, for the corner-stone of human conduct. Self-will, defiance, war and blood-ties had been built upon, but disinterested love never. This was to take men out of one world into another, while they remained in the same. It was to create in man a new feeling, interest and pursuit, a new spirit, principle and end. Here sight was to give place to faith, the visible to the unseen, the selfish to the benevolent, and the circumstantial to the rightful. Citizens in his Commonwealth were to be elevated above the animal; they were to move in a new moral universe, because they loved with a pure heart fervently. They were to make each other strong and good, and were to stimulate all about them to the bravery of blessing. The weak were to be borne up, as the oak bears the ivy that it may become stronger; and the stout were to stand firmly alone with the stout, as the fir and elm stand alone, but keep company with each other.

Jesus distinctly renounced all temporal power. Legal coercion is powerless to command the assent of a soul to his doctrines, or the obedience of a life to his laws. He was the King of souls, to reign over intellect, affection, conscience; and his conquests were to be moral, not physical. His throne must be set up in the willing soul, for here is his palace. The question of tribute was intended to place him between two fires. Either he must declare for Cæsar against the turbulent Jews, or against Cæsar, and so meet the charge of sedition. He refused to be made a king, or to touch civil authority. In the modern sense of the word, there was no Church or State in the Jewish Theocracy. They were one and the same institution, and, therefore, there was no such alliance as we are acquainted with. It knew no distinction between the religious and the political, for Jehovah was its only Deity and Magistrate. Jesus prohibited all civil penalties in his Gospel kingdom, as at variance with its first principles. No man can persecute another on religious questions from a sense of duty to Christ, but only on his own arrogant inclinations. When Peter drew his sword in defense of his persecuted Master, Jesus deprecated his act, and commanded him to put it back into its sheath. Duty to God cannot be an offense against society; therefore, to persecute men for the discharge of that duty, under the directions of moral conviction, is to violate the law of natural morality. And, if under the guise of religion men violate secular authority, they must be punished, not as religionists, but as abettors of civil crime. Offenses against God which are not offenses against man cannot be noticed by a secular tribunal, without trenching on those prerogatives of God which he has delegated to no power on earth. Nor can the kingdom of Christ, by his authority, coerce any temporal power, or interfere in its jurisdiction. The State is the natural channel for reaching all ends contemplated by the State. The very idea of alliance between the Church and the State implies their distinct character primarily, and their native independence of each other. They may form a compact for each other's moral support, but Christ has prohibited the interchange of their original rights as unlawful. Consent or dissent, as before the civil power, are not to be named nor thought of, much less the establishment of religion, or even its toleration. The power to tolerate is the essence of intolerance. It implies disapproval tempered with charitable restraint, to punish independent thought and practice, as if these were wrong in themselves; and that then tolerance were an act of very gracious kindness. But if independence be wrong, then not to punish it is to declare it no offense, and to declare it right is to recognize Christ as the only King in the Gospel kingdom.

All this shows that Jesus did what no man's originality had thought of projecting, namely, the founding of a kingdom on character: on the mental and moral, and not on the material; on inward life, and not on exterior organization. That is to say, he gave man power over himself, so that his self-control should bring all his passions and powers under the law of a sanctified manhood. Until this, men did not know that they were sons of God, or that they were brothers; much less did they know that they could all be kings amongst men. Differing from other legislators he made not the letter of the law his standard of obedience, but his own person, which covered both its letter and spirit. A Christian is to be a representative of Christ in character. He loved all men and nations, and in proportion as they should become true copies of himself, should they become nobler men. He laid his law of citizenship on the plane of selection. Men of high character, judged by this standard, were to be winnowed out from men of low character. He would organize them into communities, having made them worthy of the kingdom of God. Then, under this new code, right character was to be created by new exactions enforced upon the individual man. Truth should be applied under their individual search for truth, without regard to old levels. His law was not traced by the finger of a child on the sand of the sea, but was graven deep on the tablets of his own inner life. Every element in his followers must be substance, as in himself, justice, mercy, purity, self-sacrifice. They must be real men and not images; and the higher their spiritual tone the nearer would they approach to the reality of God's Son. He had come to unveil true character by revealing God to man, full-orbed. He came to show the Father in the express likeness of his person, and to recover man to his paternal government.

Also, he spoke with authority and certainty, because he found these profound laws embodied in himself. The genuine pearl in his hand had been brought up from the depths of his own nature. The fruit was good because the tree was good. Men read the one by the other. The inner recesses of his soul, its secret motives and genuine life, are photographed in his Sermon on the Mount. His sphere of government being the soul, he governs the outer life through its thinking and willing, and through the truth which molds the motives and controls the entire existence. This method of ruling clothes his word with power. When he laid bare a depth of life to which men were strangers, they found it impossible to resist the hidden majesty with which he spoke. His plain forms of expression were the more mysterious in their force, from the fact, that he used no means to captivate men but the invitation, 'Come unto me,' words which sprang from the deepest fountain of his tenderness. His subject-matter is truth from above; but he uses human words to tell of heavenly things, and they sink into the soul. As the great Master of thought and language, he brought Divine volitions from the hush of his Father's guest-chamber, that he might enshrine them first in the temple of his own manhood, and then in the life of his disciples. The signet-ring of God had set his seal to the fact that Jesus was true; for he embodied all that he required in other men, and as their perfect pattern, demanded, that each man should seek a close conformity to himself. He would reconstruct in each a new humanity, and so, man by man, the whole race should become new. This moral and spiritual renewal must amount to a new creation.

Christ differed from Moses, the great lawgiver, in that he penned no law. The law of life was in himself. This makes all his exactions weighty and imperious upon the citizens of the new kingdom. The King himself leads his subjects in the thick of the contest, making himself the text-book of service, and his infectious leadership in danger, the word of command to the front. Character and deeds form the body of laws for the new commonwealth; for his life exposes all dark snares—silences all lurking passions—quickens all health—adorns all beauty—reconciles all contradiction. To each faint disciple his character is a rock of strength; he is the Brother in adversity, the torch of truth, and the incarnation of nobility. He is the ideal God, and yet, in his march, he draws men after him as in the footsteps of an ideal man. To be like him is to be a Christian. This is the profound philosophy which led him to brush aside all theories of life, to live, which threw him into the midst of moral chaos, in order to commit the new life, not to writing, but to the law of actual guardianship. When other men asked, 'What is truth,' he answered: 'I am the Truth.' Any theory that he might have written, even as the King in Zion, could and would have been misrepresented. But when he made his own character, example, and obedience the standard of his law for others, his authority was simply beyond mistake, and living beyond doubt. The law of Moses made no man perfect, because it gave no perfect model of its teachings; but that of Jesus did, because in the true God-philosophy he said: 'Learn of me.'

Yet, he did not destroy the old law, or even set it aside, as if it were a failure, but he proved its success for its own purposes, by fulfilling its demands. Had men chosen to keep it, it had brought them to God. But when Jesus kept it, he showed it to be holy, and just, and good, and then gave himself to be the new law of conformity, and so was made the end of the law by bringing in his own joyful life. By perfect obedience he could calmly, confidently, and perpetually say: 'Thus, and thus it is written,' in a sense far beyond the ordinary ken. It is not a little remarkable that he so often refers to the Law, the Prophets and the Psalms, as illustrated by his acts, his person and spirit, until the Written Word of the Old Testament is enshrined in the Living Word of the New. The Jews honored the letter of their holy books when they counted their words, and so invested them with sacredness. But, how infinitely more he honored them, when he translated their spirit into the oracle of his Living Self, to become the vital Epistle of Moses and David, Isaiah and the Prophets.

Never was the Old Testament understood till the Lamb took the roll and broke its seals. Since then, it is an open book which the wayfaring man may read while he runs. His whole life was pre-written in the volume of the Book, and was then transcribed into him so clearly, that his first biographer caught the picture perfectly, and made his Gospel literally the Gospel of fulfilled prophecy. He traces these predictions in the virgin mother, the place and time of his birth, and in his name, 'Immanuel.' He even listened to Rachel's sobs around the manger, when they gave new anguish to the sad dirge of Jeremiah. And, when the Magi returned to the East, they left a brighter dawn than had ever flushed on the Syrian sky, in the vision of Israel.

What fullness dwells in the words : ' I came down from heaven not to do my own will, but the will of him that sent me.' In this sense, as well as in a higher sense, he lived out of himself in the Father, and the Father lived in him. The law of Jehovah which had been revealed from the beginning in deathless principle and written statute, he reproduced in flesh and blood, and made eternally binding in all its integrity. His soul was radiant with its simple clearness and glowing warmth, and it dominated the whole sweep of his legislation and teachings. Hence, his inflexible reverence for the mind of God, and his august loathing of the nullifying traditions of man. He threw every type of men's antique dictation to the four winds, with a deliberate contempt which brought rank and culture, assumption and pride of lording to a dead stand-still, before the inexorable bar of him who says : ' Thus it is written.' Quietly, he tore up by the roots that conceit of autocrats who deem themselves the licensed law-mongers of humanity, with full power to hawk their venal wares in the market-place against the enstamped commands of God, and to push his Word aside.

Then, Jesus followed that holy veneration which never questioned one jot of inspired truth, with a sacrificial submission which would not gloss a line or haggle with a principle thereof in disobedience. His all-pervading spirituality led him with cheerfulness into death itself, if moral obligation issued the mandate. When his steadfast eye laid bare the path, his willing feet trod therein. His obedience wound its way through type and shadow, the longings of hope and the penetrations of promise, and ended in the Valley of Death. But with mental self-possession and divine calmness, he paid the cost of obedience in pain and hardship. True, in the presence of death itself he became weak as a smitten lamb, and great drops of blood stained his brow, so that, an immaculate angel who had never broken a precept of heaven's law, or felt the faintness of death, appeared to strengthen him. But, when the palm of this soft hand wiped our Lord's temples, the holy touch but changed each clot into a passion-flower of Paradise, and each fleck of gore into a ruby. Then, under the dark olives of Gethsemane, the first Son of man who had ever kept Jehovah's law, wore his own diadem of obedience, which all the cursed thorns of the next day failed to blacken or disgrace.

Having kept the law himself as the Holy of God, his gentleness imposed the same dutiful yoke upon all his fellows, that they might share the satisfactions of his own life and love. Love had drawn him from his Father's throne for them, and now it would lift them up to God, for oneness, and fellowship, and friendship. This pure purpose drew him, at times, into those rythmic bursts of joy which celebrated the return of prodigals, and the adoption of babes into his Father's house. The refrain of this anthem sounded up and down his entire life: 'It is meet that we should be merry and glad, for this our brother was dead and is alive again, was lost and is found.' And, this love he extended to all men, Gentiles as well as Jews. The sweep of his net drew fish of every kind, and the sheep of his flock were housed from every fold. Here again, God's Viceroy is instinct with Jehovah's high benevolence. All power was given into his hands, without the display of thunders and lightnings, and the voice of trumpets, but in the conscious conviction that he represented all that dwelt in the bosom whence he came. With him eternal principles were not only axioms of the Divine mind, but practical ideas. Because they were vitalized with the immortality of God, his invitations were Jehovah's decrees. Purity and love made his whole spiritual code sternly absolute. It is this which makes his influence so visibly distinct, so definitely potent. He never opens his lips but fresh truth distills from them, in apt, keen, loving words. Fichte, who argued that character is simple self-development, thinks, that by the mere purity and elevation of Christ's character, he was carried into that region of eternal morality which men seldom reach. Carlyle, who doubted the Divine in Christ, calls his life a 'perfect ideal Poem,' and says: 'The greatest of all heroes is One whom we do not name here. Let sacred silence meditate that sacred matter.' Renan, who colors the facts of Gospel history by fancy, calls him: 'The incomparable being to whom the universal conscience has decreed the title of The Son of God.' But Bayne, true to the manhood of Christ, with greater boldness still, asks of his miracles: 'Whether from the moral character of Christ, it would, or would not, have been a greater miracle than these, that in asserting himself to wield creative power, he *lied*.'

And, why not? He himself demands: 'Which of you convicts me of sin?' A challenge which is spirit and life. But no man charges home the miracle of falsehood on Jesus Christ—no man throws the name of one vice into his face. The thought that he could lie freezes the blood in all men's veins, as, in itself, a greater miracle than to grind the stars into diamond-dust between two millstones. Serenely, without excitement, and apparently without preparation, he lays his truths before men, in secluded places or public walks, and the more men look at them the more they wonder at their native depth. When mankind first heard them, the haughty became humble, the grasping benevolent, the crafty honest, and the narrow large-hearted. Like himself, his laws were cosmopolitan, lifting the truth indifferently above all national distinctions, and drawing followers to his great soul simply as men, in the free garb of all their social habits. The tones of his call were holy, demanding separation from all unholy society, social and civil; and yet, men's only isolation the one from the other, was to be by a line of holiness. His was to be a Church without blood-relationship, held together by love, common aims and common hopes; the only two qualities necessary for admission being, humanity of birth and divinity of renovation. The two great pillars in his Palace of Truth are love to God and love to man. These he hewed out and polished after a heavenly similitude, for no man had seen them before. They were foundation doctrines, not dogmas. Dogmas are fallible interpretations of infallible truths, and his infallibility excluded dogma alike from his utterances and acts. But while inflexibly absolute, he was the life of all forbearance. He persecuted no man, and allowed not his disciples to persecute. Even when they would resent affronts by force, he rebuked them as ignorant of their own spirit; for that, the Son of Man came not to destroy men's lives, but to save them. He made selfishness, malignity and revenge out of place amongst his devotees.

Persecution runs in the blood of nature. Not only do the wolf and tiger persecute, but all living things, small and great. The sweetest lark that sings in the sky will dive down upon his brother songster and tear him, and the least minnow in the brook will torment his fellow. But Jesus strengthened the last fiber that held the reed together, and revived the last spark in the smoking wick. Yea, and his purpose was to give this gentle pre-eminence to all his redeemed people. True men of God cannot persecute until their heavenly tempers are subdued by their carnal passions. Jesus never raved, but often wept over the erring, for only the Good Shepherd would lay down his life for the sheep, while the hireling steals and kills. Reared amongst bigots his triumph was: 'Whom the Son makes free he is free indeed;' and his Gospel Republic is the first government from Adam which could accord entire independence of thought and act, even in morals. Jesus appeals directly to the convictions of men and allows no man to interfere with those convictions. He rebukes prejudice in his followers, and proposes to draw all men to himself by the exercise of conscience and reason; an exercise as free as the breath of the winds around the Alpine flowers, or as the rays of the morning sun which fly to kiss them in mid-heaven.

When Jesus put the leaven into three measures of meal, the fourth quarter of the globe was undiscovered, and of Asia, Africa, and Europe, he chose Asia, the largest division of the earth then known, as the spot where it was to begin its assimilating process. Palestine lay on the extreme western edge of that huge continent, closely adjacent to Europe and Africa, and almost in the center of the world as it was to be and is now. Asia contains a greater variety of climates than either of the other divisions of the Eastern Hemisphere, united with great advantages, especially in its countless littoral islands, its vast rivers, and endless kinds of products, from its temperate and tropical zones. Its majestic mountain chains and table-lands, the wealth of its soil and its streams emptying into the sea, open it to agriculture, arts, trade and commerce in every direction; and its easy division into large empires fitted it pre-eminently for the spread of dominion by the Great King.

Africa lies almost entirely in the torrid zone, has two great rivers, the Niger and the Nile, with a desert of sand stretching from the Red Sea to the Atlantic, and covering one fifth of the continent. Only its northern part was known to the ancients, and figures in their history. But the Roman Empire, which at that time ruled Europe, civilized and barbarian, had also conquered the greater part of civilized Asia and Africa, holding sway over the world west of the Euphrates. The Jews, whose civilization was most in harmony with Christianity, were scattered almost every-where through the empire, and were very powerful. Egypt was full of them, as well as Rome itself, while in Antioch they formed more than a third of the population. Our Lord intended to take each individual man, however rude or polished, to change his character and habits, to lift him out of vice into purity; and by spiritual forces to bring him under his royal law, until his perfection was marked by a translation out of moral degradation, into the full, free and pure citizenship of his kingdom. All his parables show the smallness of his beginnings, and the secret growth of his reign. A blade of wheat, out of which an endless harvest shall spring,—a grain of mustard-seed, from which outspreading trees shall grow, and five other parables, were employed by him to show the noiseless, gradual, but resistless advance of his Empire. It was to be broad and many-sided, severe in its power and calm in its elevation. Tiny in its beginning, it was to outgrow all rivals, until out of the hidden, its visibility was to be world-wide, because it inclosed the germs of all true life; and its aim was to be a practical universality.

He, himself, was a veritable man, born of a woman. A babe is the weakest thing in nature, yet it is endowed with all the potentialities that man can know. And, contrary to all received religious philosophy, woman's gentle nature and voice were brought under the mysteries of revelation, and her spirit was knit into incomprehensible converse with God to accomplish his holy purpose. Christ appealed to her strongest interests, enforced her noblest duties, and led her by enchanting promises into the great moral revolution, through the surpassing marvel of an incarnate God. By a select imagery, which none but God could invoke, immensity was contracted to a span, and eternity inclosed in an hour; divine power was enwrapped in the softest weakness, and deathless love was hidden in the new-born Babe of an honored woman. This made it meet that man should be intrusted with the spread of his kingdom. Six couples of plain, honest, receptive men were sent forth. They were of various habits and affinities of temperament, called from the lowest strata of society, where the strongest foundations of humanity are laid. He threw them in all the dependence of their lowly origin upon the sympathy and justice of their fellow-men for their daily bread, in return for their toils, and made their only protection the spoken truth.

They were Galilean fishermen too, taken from the only region of Palestine which had not been corrupted by the Rabbis, for these held Galilee accursed and let it alone. Hence they were unsophisticated, simple, and spiritual, but positive and firm, confronting the world in the strength of conviction. This commended them to their brother men. They were the select band of students to whom Jesus had minutely expounded his doctrines, and now, their life-work was to expound them on the house-tops. The radical truths which had pervaded his own mind, were to be saving in their results on others to whom they were sent. The perceptions, constitutional peculiarities, and personal dependence of these choice minds fitted them to influence others, and to reproduce in them what they were themselves. The same laws of condensation which clothe steam, frost and electricity with power, obtain more distinctly in mind, and so, he compressed the mightiest elements of spiritual effectiveness in these few, instead of broad-casting his truths at once before the incohesive multitude. Judged by human standards, they were unfit for their work. But, he saw more than human fitness in sending a handful of rustics from an inland lake, who were willing to die for the truth. Any learned man of that age, priest or layman, if chosen as an Apostle, would have mixed up current notions with the Gospel, in spite of himself, and would have thwarted its design, by corrupting its simplicity. Christ's sensitive nature was often brought into painful contact with the brusqueness of his Apostles, and their coarse janglings jarred upon his lofty fellowships; yet, he could trust their blunt and unfaltering fidelity, unmixed as it was with the vagaries of the times. Firmness of honor was what he wanted, and not polish of manners, in a small, compact band of eye-witnesses. As professionals, their testimony on any point of law, art, or tradition would have been trivial, but as provincials, it was full of plainness and mother-sense; qualities which were helps instead of drawbacks, in declaring matters of fact.

Yet, Jesus appears to have pushed aside all calculating precautions in their choice. There were amongst them three pairs of brothers, two relatives of his own family; and half of them were taken from one town. Men would call this a narrow selection, and an insidious designer would have taken another course. Conscious imposition would have made a great show of candor, by choosing men out of all districts in Palestine, representing all social ranks, that their witness might appear enlarged and impartial; but the sober honesty of the King in Zion rose infinitely above all such coverts for fraud. Having trained their judgment, proved their consciences, and formed their character, he confidently sent them forth. In temperament, the Gospels generally group them in this order: Peter for his hardness, and Andrew his brother for shy and childlike simplicity; then James and John, the sons of Zebedee, for their choleric disposition, being known as 'Sons of Thunder.' The second group is headed by Philip, for his earnest teachableness; Bartholomew, called Nathanael, for his utter want of guile; Thomas for his phlegmatic deliberation, and Matthew for his practical perception and gravity. The third class comprises James, the son of Alpheus, who was marked for his modesty; Lebbæus, whose surname was Thaddeus, for his hearty boldness; Simon Zelotes for his fiery impulse, and Judas the traitor for his frozen heart. They soon showed their peculiarities toned up to their highest plane, for all their powers were consecrated to their work. Their virtues, weaknesses, and gifts fitted them to cope with human nature in each phase, for they represented every possible combination of temper in mankind. Their characters exhibit the bias and bent which mark off all the individualities and relations of life, while in purity, Jesus required them to be every thing that he was.

Happily, when the great Lawgiver laid down the vital principles of his government, he proceeded carefully to specify the terms on which men should be admitted into the new kingdom. Nicodemus was a teacher well versed in all that Judaism demanded, but Jesus showed him that each subject under the Messiah's reign must be thoroughly renovated in the inner man. No one could be eligible till spiritually born again, created anew after the image of Christ himself. As was his wont when he gave great energy to his words, he opens this momentous subject with the double asseveration: 'Verily, verily I say to thee, Except a man be born again, he cannot see the kingdom of God.' The venerable Hebrew understood him to speak of a second physical birth, but Jesus brought him back to the fundamental thought of a birth from above. Its source was to be the Spirit; its nature a transformation of the whole spiritual being. A person born of the flesh is flesh, and will follow all fleshly necessities; but one born of the Spirit is spirit, and is filled with the principles and dispositions which the Holy Spirit only can generate. When Jesus has pressed this truth home to the conviction of Nicodemus, he reiterates: 'Except a man be born of water and the Spirit, he cannot enter into the kingdom of God.'

Many think that our Lord couches baptism under the term '*water*' here, and in proportion as they lay stress upon baptism, as an efficacious ordinance in salvation, they press this point. It is questionable, however, whether he refers to baptism at all, or simply to a concomitant element in natural birth, to show that he intended to enforce a thorough renewal, equivalent to a veritable 'new birth,' which must be of God. This would put 'water' to a purely figurative use as a material element, adding new force to his twofold insistance on an entirely spiritual renovation. He certainly does not speak of two births, one of water and one of the Spirit, but only of one: that of water and the Spirit in conjunction. Campbell says: 'Though our Lord in this account of regeneration, joins water and spirit together, he does not, in contrasting it with natural generation (John iii, 6), mention the water at all, but opposes the Spirit to the flesh.' Nicodemus had full knowledge of John's baptism, for he was a member of the Sanhedrin that questioned John, and but for the special emphasis laid by Jesus upon the birth of the Spirit, he might have fallen into the idea, that without baptism no man can be eternally saved. But Christ's demand for a work of renewal by the Spirit, excludes the fatal error which would save Simon Magus because he was baptized, and reject the repentant thief on the cross because he was not. Rather does Whitby express our Lord's thought: 'Except a man be renewed in his mind, will, and affections by the operations of the Holy Spirit, and so becomes a new creature . . . he cannot see, that is, enjoy, the blessings of the kingdom of God.' Or, as another expresses himself: 'He cannot discern either the signs of the Messiah, or the nature of his government.'[1]

Our Redeemer was equally explicit in pointing out the several steps which a renewed man must take for full enrollment and induction into his kingdom. As preachers, his Apostles were to be 'witnesses' to his death and resurrection, and they were to 'Preach repentance and remission of sins unto all nations.' 'Preach the Gospel to every creature.' 'Disciple all the nations, baptizing them in the name of the Father, and of the Son, and of the Holy Spirit, teaching them to observe all things whatsoever I commanded you.' Here he makes preaching, repentance, faith and baptism, of perpetual obligation. By preaching repentance and the remission of sins, they were to attempt the 'discipling' or conversion of every creature. Then, those who believed on the Saviour were to be baptized into his kingdom, and after that, they were to be instructed in all that related to the Christian life.

The Apostles were not instructed to baptize the nations *en masse*, simply because each person was an integral part of the whole; for, as it has been said with great force: 'It is one thing to make disciples *in* all nations, and another thing to make *all nations* disciples.' They were to baptize those, and those only, who had the above-named qualifications for baptism. Countless millions in the 'nations' would remain unbelievers, blasphemers, atheists, idolaters and debauchees, after every attempt had been made to save them. These were to 'be condemned.' Neither were babes to be baptized simply because they were a part of the nations, till they could be 'discipled.' The word 'disciple' carries with it the idea of instruction, and therefore, here, of gaining converts to Christ, by bringing them over to certain fixed principles and practices. Babes are no more capable of obedience in baptism, than they are of repentance and the forgiveness of sins, or of exercising faith on Christ for salvation. And, what is more and better, they need none of these, so long as they are free from voluntary and personal transgression; for Jesus has procured their salvation without these. When once they reach responsibility and become actual sinners, then they may avail themselves of all these, if they will become believers in Jesus. Mark calls the subjects of baptism 'believers,' and Matthew, 'disciples,' plainly meaning the same persons. Our Lord here excluded infant baptism of design, and the commission cannot be tortured into the support of this injurious practice; thus, we cannot wonder that no case of such baptism is mentioned in the New Testament. On the contrary, such conditions are every-where imposed on those who are baptized, as to unavoidably exclude all who either cannot or do not voluntarily obey Christ's commands. So Jerome interprets this commission: 'They first teach all the nations; then, when they are taught they baptize them in water; for it cannot be that the body should receive the sacrament of baptism, unless the soul have before received the true faith.' And again he adds: 'The order here observed is excellent; he commands the Apostles, first to teach all nations; and after that to dip them with the sacrament of faith; and then to show them how they must behave themselves after their faith and baptism.'

Then, did Jesus make no provision for children in his kingdom of grace and glory? Yes; and the amplest that infinite love could make. He is the only great Teacher who ever pressed them to his bosom, as the subjects of saving care. The Jewish religion protected and accounted them precious. Yet, it subjected its males to a severe and bloody rite, for the purposes of national identity and privilege, without vouchsafing any special revelation as to their future state, when dying in infancy. Roman grossness regarded children as a misfortune, and freely practiced infanticide. The Carthaginians offered them in sacrifice to Saturn. Diodorus Siculus mentions the sacrifice of two hundred of their noblest babes at a time.[2] Molech, the ferocious god of Ammon, did not stand alone, for all the Syrian and Arab tribes had their fire-gods, before whom their little ones were presented as burnt-offerings. But Jesus looked upon these helpless ones as the most fragrant flowers of earth—he longed to silence the wail of their sufferings in these cruel rites, and to perfect praise out of the mouths of babes and sucklings.

To this end, he vouchsafed salvation for all children, before he tasted death on their behalf, enwrapping them in a free redemption, without conditions of any sort. They could bear no yoke, and he put none upon their necks. Parents coveted his love for their offspring and brought their little ones for his 'blessing.' In keeping with the spirit of those times, his disciples would drive them away; a fact, which in itself, shows that they knew nothing about infant baptism. Their parents did not bring them to be baptized, but that he would 'lay his hands upon them and bless them,' as Jacob had blessed the sons of Joseph. As Jacob 'blessed' his grandsons without baptizing them, so these infants were brought to Jesus unbaptized, and were taken away unbaptized, but not for that reason unblessed. He rebuked his disciples, wishing them to understand that he came from heaven to save the babes as well as the parents. Then, he took them in his arms and 'prayed for them' and gave them his blessing, declaring as his words import, that 'to such belongs the kingdom of heaven,' simply through his benediction and love, without conditions of any sort such as try the loyalty of willful and responsible sinners. As their Elder Brother, bone of their bone and flesh of their flesh, he then and there, hung a bright lamp over an infant's head, pledging him salvation while in infancy, without repentance, faith, baptism, the Supper, or any other observance. With this display of Christ's love to little children, it is simply heathenish and horrible to suppose that deceased babes miss heaven, under any circumstances. More than half of

JESUS BLESSING A CHILD.
(From the Catacombs.)

our race, especially in lands where infanticide is practiced, die in infancy; and every true man will rejoice in the Redeemer's plan of saving these precious ones unconditionally. Millions of them pass into the presence of the Great Shepherd whose parents are pagans or infidels, and spurn baptism or never heard of its existence; and it borders on the fiendish to say, that the Christ-loving parent jeopards the salvation of his redeemed babe, because he leaves his salvation to the atoning death and sacrificial love of Jesus, refusing to submit him to a rite which the adorable Lamb of God never imposed upon the unconscious one. In the pre-existence of our Lord, from the death of the first child of Adam's race to the moment of his own birth in Bethlehem, he had been with ransomed children in heaven. When on earth he missed their society, and, to fill their places he drew our little ones to him, for they tenderly reminded him of the Father's house which he had left; hence, in his words and acts he treated them as of 'the kingdom of heaven.' Bishop Taylor beautifully says: 'Why should he be an infant but that infants should receive the crown of their age, the purification of their stained natures, the sanctification of their persons, and the saving of their souls by their infant Lord and Elder Brother.' The kingdom belongs to them by Christ's purchase and gift, without those tests of obedience which try the fidelity of responsible offenders. They had not sinned 'after the similitude of Adam's transgression,' and he gave them his full blessing without conditions, despite their original taint. Then, he warns willful offenders that if they receive not the kingdom of God as little children, they shall not enter therein. While the phrase 'of such' includes others besides those 'brought' to him, it also includes all who are clothed with the child-like spirit. With the love of Christ thus displayed to children, it is simply horrible to suppose that a deceased babe misses of heaven because he was not christened on earth, and because here no one had promised that if he had lived he would have repented and believed for himself. Can any thing so rob our atoning Lord of his glory, in part or in whole, as to suppose that this act affects the child's salvation in the slightest degree? As in Adam he died unconditionally, so in Christ is he unconditionally made alive.

These are some of the great principles and practices laid down by the infallible Lawgiver, for the establishment and government of his kingdom in the earth. God gives us in John the Baptist, the specimen man of holiness. Then comes the King in Zion, revealing the Father in his own person, and making Divine provisions for the regeneration of such men to the end of time. After Jesus had cast this Gospel hope athwart the destinies of our race, he took his seat as Mediator at the right hand of God. There, he has proved the acceptance of his sacrifice and the efficacy of his intercession by sending the Holy Spirit to fill his place on the earth. The Spirit now administers his kingdom under these laws, and gathers pure Churches out of all nations, of men created anew by his energies, in Christ Jesus, and kept in his name, unto life eternal.

JERUSALEM FROM THE MOUNT OF OLIVES.

CHAPTER VI.

PENTECOST AND SAUL.

THE ablest chronologists vary the date of our Lord's ascension from A. D. 29 to 36; possibly the year 33 may be taken as the most satisfactory. Before his death, our Lord had founded his Church, by selecting the Twelve, the Seventy, and many other disciples, by teaching them his doctrines, authorizing them to preach and baptize, and by establishing the Supper. This organic body known as 'the kingdom of God' he also called, 'My Church'—his infant Church truly, but no less his Church, as he was the Christ as much when a Babe in the stable, and a Youth in the Temple, as when a Man on Calvary. His Church was to be endowed with special and plenary powers to increase its constituency, extend its influence and establish new assemblies. Hence, the Church at Jerusalem kept its divine organization perfect by a popular election to fill the place of Judas in the Apostolate, and then waited for the promised reign of the Holy Spirit, to fill the Redeemer's place in the Gospel Church. Ten days after Christ's enthronement at God's right hand, he sent the Spirit to administer the earthly affairs of his Church, to vindicate the mission which he had finished, to sustain his claims against all foes, and in every way to compensate for his own absence. The Spirit manifested himself on the second Jewish feast, Pentecost, which celebrated the ingathering of the wheat harvest and the giving of the Law.

The first work in the ministry of the Spirit, as in that of the Son, was to attest his own mission by miraculous evidences. These, in keeping with his entirely immaterial character, were to be wrought, not alone on the human frame or on sea and firmament, but on mind; on the mental constitution of man and his powers of speech. At once, therefore, he honored himself and 'glorified' Christ, by qualifying his Apostles to obey his commission in preaching the Gospel to all nations. The babble of tongues was the most stubborn obstruction to the universal spread of the Gospel, and Jesus seemed to have made no provision for the removal of this enormous difficulty, but had committed its preaching to the most unlearned of men. They knew their mother tongue so imperfectly that their uncouth provincialisms were betrayed in the accents of their chief orator as a 'Galilean.' With their scanty education they could not have mastered the cosmopolitan grammar of the Pentecostal throng in a life-time. If, then, a linguistic miracle were not wrought by the Spirit, their attempt to preach had been a failure, for there was no visible method by which they could reach the world with the new religion. At that moment there were men in Jerusalem from the remotest regions of the civilized world; who, if they could be made to understand the truth, could take it to the ends of the earth. The wide, geographical circuit including the homes of these men, swept from north-east to south-east, and far north, covering seventeen different languages and dialects. Parthia lay north-west of Persia, a powerful kingdom about six hundred miles long. The Medes had come from an easterly point of the compass, and were of a harsh and rude race. The Elamites had come from an ancient Shemite district, east of Persia Proper. Those from Mesopotamia represented the region between the Tigris and the Euphrates. Idumea, the rugged old territory of Edom, follows the geographical order of Luke, but he breaks from his circle to mention Judea and his own home language. Cappadocia was a stretch of high table-land in the eastern part of Asia Minor. Continuing north, he comes to Pontus, north-east of the Black Sea. Asia, Roman or Proconsular, was washed by the Ægean Sea, on its western shore. Phrygia was in the center of Asia Minor, and Pamphylia, farther south, was touched on the north by the Mediterranean. Egypt was in the north-east of Africa; and the parts of Libya, lay on the African coast, west of Egypt. Luke then ascends from these southern lands, to Rome, in Italy; and last of all mentions the Arabians from the East, and the islanders from Crete, now called Candia.

A very limited unity of tongue had been wrought by the conquests of Alexander, in the free use of the Greek, which had been adopted as the language of traffic and of the Roman court; while in the basin of the Mediterranean it was universally spoken. Jews born in Syria, Egypt, Asia Minor, or Cyrene, spoke it fluently and read their Scriptures therein; and in the great cities of the empire their synagogue services were conducted in the Greek. The 'Twelve' appear, however, to have known little of Greek, and were qualified to preach only in Palestine. In this condition of things, while the young Church waited for miraculous endowment from the Spirit, Peter began to preach Jesus and the resurrection to the mixed throng of Jews and proselytes who had come to the feast. His sermon was full of vigor and simplicity, of bold directness and reasoning, and, as if by instinct, his concise and clear mind flew from facts within his own knowledge to the Sacred Oracles; where he grasped firmly the prophecies of Joel and David, concerning the Messiah. Finding these in exact accord with his own personal knowledge, he centered his appeal upon the reason and conscience of his hearers, and charged the Jewish rulers with the judicial murder of Jesus, as 'lawless ones.' Some of them had joined the motley crowd who had clamored for his blood, and as he proved the guilt of the nation alarm seized them. They saw that their rulers had duped them into one of the worst crimes in their annals, and the echoes of their execrating prayer in Pilate's palace were re-awakened in their ears, 'His blood be on us and on our children.' When they cried in sorrow, 'What must we do?' Peter offered them salvation through the blood of Jesus for the sin of shedding it, and urged them to leave the wicked hierarchy, and enter the new kingdom by faith and baptism.

While Peter was preaching, an infinite energy overwhelmed him and his brethren, subduing every faculty and power of their being. Their imagination, their understanding, their conscience, their memory, their will and affections were all submerged in the Holy Spirit, as a pearl is buried in the sea. Or as Ellicott expresses it, 'The baptism with the Holy Spirit would imply that the souls thus baptized would be *plunged*, as it were, in that creative and informing Spirit which was the source of life and holiness and wisdom.'[1] And immediately there sat upon the heads of these elder sons of Zion a coronation flame, pointed like the human tongue, but divided and forked likewise, not only to indicate vitality and fluency, but also as a fitting emblem of the varied languages which they should speak, as if they were natives of every country, instead of fishermen from an inland lake. This flaming appearance was not fire, as loose interpretation says, but '*like* as of fire.' Its appearance was attended by a loud sound, not of wind, but '*like* a rushing mighty wind,' indicating that the influences of the Spirit kept pace with the holy storm which was sweeping away every linguistic obstruction to the triumph of the Gospel. They were all filled with the Holy Spirit, and began to speak with other tongues, as the Spirit gave them utterance, and every man heard the Gospel in his mother-tongue. The preachers spoke grammatically, for had they expressed themselves improperly, their hearers would have suspected fraud. Instead of this, when they heard their own living languages spoken accurately by unlettered Galileans, they were amazed and demanded what it meant. Those from Asia, Phrygia, and Pamphylia spoke Greek in various idioms. The Parthians,

Medes, Elamites, and Persians used it in provincial forms. The native Jew heard the local dialects of Palestine, which were all Aramaic, though they differed from each other, and the foreign pilgrims the languages of their several nationalities. Many of these languages held affinity to each other, as from a common parent, but others were marked by those great diversities which come of a varied origin. None could account for the phenomenon, and the vulgar refusing to believe in the reign of the Spirit, charged it to the use of new wine; a charge which Peter easily repelled, because it was unlawful for a Jew to break his fast before 'the third hour of the day.' What adds to the interest of the miracle is, that those who could only use the Galilean dialect before Pentecost, as Peter, John, James, and Jude, afterward wrote books of the New Testament in terse and even lucid Greek, as if a fork of the fire-like tongue followed every stroke of their pen.

It is worthy of note that as Jesus entered his office by baptism in water, so the Spirit commenced his administration by baptizing Christ's Apostles into himself. On the head of the inaugurated Lord he descended like a dove to indicate meekness and purity; but he sat as fire upon the heads of the Apostles. Jesus had foretold their intense sufferings by the tropical use of the word baptize, 'Ye shall undergo the baptism that I must undergo,' when he was plunged into deep sorrow. And now, in like manner he fills them with power for their ministry, as he had said, 'Ye shall be baptized in the Holy Spirit not many days hence;' in both cases using the rhetorical figure, according to the solid structure of language, by stating the literal truth in the trope. As Jesus was overwhelmed when he was 'filled with sorrow,' so were his Apostles overwhelmed when they were 'filled with the Spirit.' Every attribute of their nature sank into the Spirit, till his billows passed over them, as Jesus sank when the dark waters of sorrow passed over his soul. They were baptized in the Spirit. Thus the Holy Spirit attested his mission to them, and proved theirs to be from heaven, accrediting their Gospel to the nations. That day, in the midst of the stir, enthusiasm, and triumph of the vindicated fishermen, they so handled the keys of the kingdom, that three thousand men were added to the earlier believers, and the first abundant harvest was reaped in the great Jewish field.

These three thousand were immersed that day, as converts to the faith of Christ. Because the Sacred Record does not give the exact locality where this took place in Jerusalem, nor the number of administrators, some affect to doubt that immersion was administered. With characteristic candor Dean Plumptre says (Acts ii, 41): 'The largeness of the number has been urged as rendering it probable that the baptism was by affusion, not immersion. On the other [hand] (1) immersion had clearly been practiced by John, and was involved in the original meaning of the word, and it is not likely that the rite should have been curtailed of its full proportions at the very outset; (2) the symbolic meaning of the act required immersion in order that it might be clearly manifested, and Rom. vi, 4, and 1 Pet. iii, 21, seem almost of necessity to imply the more complete mode. The pools of Bethesda and Siloam (see John v, 7; ix, 7), or the so-called Fountain of the Virgin, near the temple inclosure, or the bathing places within the Tower of Anthony (Jos., 'Wars,' v. 5, § 8), may well have helped to make the process easy.'

Dr. Döllinger thinks that the baptisms did not take place the same day, but says that it was an 'Immersion of the whole person; which is the only meaning of the New Testament word, a mere pouring or sprinkling was never thought of.' All historians, in treating of Jerusalem, set forth the number and value of its

POOL OF SILOAM.

public baths, and its immense storage of water for public use. In all its calamities by famine and siege, we have no account that it suffered for want of water. Like other cities of antiquity its natural water springs had much to do with the selection of its location. These abounded on the spot and in its vicinity, so that its water-wealth was great when gathered into wells, pools, and reservoirs. As the Jewish capital, it was visited yearly by hundreds of thousands of pilgrims, at the three feasts, so that its religious washings, purifications and ablutions rendered a large supply indispensable, for religious as well as domestic purposes. Josephus tells us that at the Passover alone two hundred head of beasts were sacrificed. All these must be watered and washed as sacrificial victims. He also says, that the sect of the Essenes was numerous there, and that they immersed themselves daily. The

THE VARIOUS POOLS.

Pools of Jerusalem, and those south of Bethlehem, which supplied the city, were numerous, large, and adapted to immersion, all being accessible for that use. The following were their names and dimensions:

NAMES.	LENGTH.	BREADTH.	DEPTH.
	Feet.	Feet.	Feet.
Pool of Bethesda, north of the Temple . . .	360	130	75
Pool of Hezekiah, north of Mount Zion . .	210	144	3 to 4
The King's Pool, now Pool of the Virgin, E. of Jer.	15	6	Not great.
Pool of Siloam, S.-E. of Jerusalem . . .	56	18	19
Upper Gihon, N.-W. "	316	200	18
Lower Gihon, W. "	592	245 to 275	35 to 42
Solomon's Pools—Lower Pool	582	148 to 207	East end 50
" Middle Pool	423	160 to 250	" 39
" Upper Pool	380	229 to 236	" 25

Some of these were excavated out of the earth or limestone rock, and supplied by hidden springs; to others water was conveyed by hewn subterranean passages, waters being brought from the mountains. Hezekiah built a conduit (2 Kings

SOLOMON'S POOLS.

xx, 20), and Solomon built the three enormous pools, five and a half miles from Jerusalem, which brought their waters to the city by an aqueduct, their springs near Bethlehem being enlarged and arched over. The Lower Gihon was formed by two dams (2 Chron. xxxii, 30), and was intact even in the eleventh century. It was used by the Crusaders, and their Norman chronicler calls it a 'lake,' where 'the horses of the city are watered.' Besides these, the brook Nachal-Kidron held a different relation to the Holy City in ancient times to what it holds now. Then, it was a natural water-course (2 Chron. xxxii, 3, 4), and Hezekiah summoned the forces of Israel to seal its fountains, B. C. 713, as a defensive war measure. Sennacherib was besieging Jerusalem, and his army could not subsist without water. 'So they stopped all the fountains and the brook that ran through the midst of the land, saying: Why should the King of Assyria come and find much water?' This upper spring-head, which burst out in the wady north of the city, being closed, rendered the vicinity desolate and embarrassed the besiegers. The wonderful fertility which marked those suburbs in after times, indicates that these fountains were re-opened. Dr. Bonar ('Land of Promise,' p. 169) observes, that this running stream carried off the refuse of the city. The Kidron rises about half a mile from the north-west corner of the city, and its present bed winds round its north and east sides, half inclosing it, and receives the brook Gihon at the north east corner, after which it passes off by a precipitous ravine to the Dead Sea.

Much of the year it is entirely dry, a fact which Dr. Olin and Dean Stanley attribute to the entire absence of wooded lands and forests, but in the rainy season it still swells to a torrent of great impetuosity. This makes the well-known bridge necessary, for at those times the stream cannot be forded; which bridge is seventeen feet above the channel. Modern research renders it probable that the Kidron now flows beneath the ground, and Dr. Barclay thought that he had discovered its course by the noise of hidden running waters. Lieutenant Warren believes that he has discovered a flight of steps, which anciently connected with this current. Be this as it may, all modern exploration justifies Wilson, Tristram, Stanley, and others in the opinion, that Kidron was a large and more constant stream in the days of our Lord than now. Indeed, the officers of the Palestine Exploration Fund say: 'The enormous mass of rubbish now lying in the valley *has displaced the old bed of the stream, shifting it ninety feet to the east, and lifting it forty feet higher than its former position.*'[2] These facts render it highly probable that the Kidron was available for the purposes of immersion in Apostolic times. Thompson says: 'No other city in this part of the world' had such profuse supplies of water. 'Jerusalem was so abundantly supplied with water, that no inconvenience from this source was experienced, even during the many and long sieges which the city sustained.'[3] It is simply absurd to pretend that while a whole nation could find water enough to keep the Jewish feasts three times a year, a little band of three thousand converts could find no water for an act of obedience in following the example and command of Jesus but once in all the ages.

Herod had put all the water-works of Jerusalem in repair, and in our Lord's time they were in full use. The Pools were open to the free use of the public, some of them for public bathing purposes, as is evident from John v, 2-9; ix, 7; Christ's disciples having as free access to them as others. The Jewish priests used to wash the sacrificial animals in Bethesda, and hence it was commonly known as the 'Sheep-pool.' Dr. Carpenter doubts whether the priests themselves washed them there, but says that they were washed there before being delivered for sacrifice.[4] It covered more than an acre of ground, and 30,000 people could bathe in it at once. John speaks of a 'multitude' waiting to bathe there, none questioning their right. The Lower Gihon was alike ample and accessible for the same purpose. Thompson speaks also of the Pool of Hezekiah as 'An immense reservoir, capable of holding water sufficient for half of the city. My guide called it Burket Hamman, and said that the water was used chiefly for baths.'⁵ The descent of steps and the shelving bottom of most of these Pools, adapted them for easy descent into the water at any desired depth. Antoninus, the martyr, who lived in the sixth century, says, that the people constantly bathed in Siloam, as we have seen that they did in Bethesda. Horne, in his 'Introduction,' says : ' It was one of the laws of the Hebrews, that the bath should be used. Lev. xiv, 8, 9. We may, therefore, consider it as probable

THE POOL OF HEZEKIAH.

that public baths, soon after the enactment of this law, were erected in Palestine, of a construction similar to that of those which are so frequently seen at the present day in the East.' These are very numerous, especially in India. Butler, in his 'Land of the Veda' (pp. 27, 28), gives a full account of the ablutions of the devotee in these pools, and tells us that after his ceremonies and prayers, ' He plunges *thrice* into the water, each time repeating the prescribed expiatory texts.' There were many of them, also at Rome, wonderful structures. Agrippa built about a hundred and sixty of them at Rome, and Caracalla supplied marble seats in one bath for sixteen hundred persons, for eighteen hundred could bathe at one time. Diocletian kept 140,000 men for years in building his baths for the public.[6]   The constant influx of strangers at Jerusalem rendered similar arrangements necessary, even to ordinary health and cleanliness. Dean Stanley thus disposes of the question : ' In that age the scene of the transaction was either some deep way-side spring or well, as for the Ethiopian ; or some rushing river, as the Jordan, or some vast reservoir, as at Jericho or Jerusalem ; whither, as in the Baths of Caracalla at Rome, the whole population resorted for swimming or washing.'

As to the time and number of administrators, the case is quite as clear. The 'Twelve,' and the 'Seventy,' made eighty-two administrators of Christ's own selection, who were ready to administer the holy rite, out of the one hundred and twenty disciples present. In baptizing, two minutes for each candidate allows the greatest deliberation in the immersion, and this slowness at Pentecost would have allowed the baptism of three thousand with great ease. In the triumphs of Christianity, this number of baptisms in a day is by no means exceptional. In Ireland, Patrick immersed seven kings and 11,000 of their subjects in a day, according to Farrell's Life of him ; Austin immersed 10,000 in the Swale, April 20, A. D. 598; Remigius immersed Clovis I. and 3,000 of his warriors in a day; and at Velumpilly, in the Madras Presidency, in July, A. D. 1878, 2,222 persons were immersed on the faith in Christ, in about six hours, the ordinance being administered with great solemnity by six administrators.

POOL FOR ABLUTION—BABA-ATEL TEMPLE.

Luke tells us, that after the 3,000 had been added to the original body of believers they 'remained steadfast in the Apostles' doctrine and fellowship, and in breaking of bread and in prayers.' Here he defines every true element in the Apostolic Church, or that can be necessary to any Gospel Church to the end of time. Luke's definition is the best that has ever been given, and in every particular.

They were 'added' when they had given proof of Repentance and Trust in Christ; then they received Baptism, followed by Fellowship, the Lord's Supper, and Public Worship. In treating of the Constitution of a Gospel Church, it will be necessary to speak of the election of deacons at Jerusalem and of other things.

Philip and Stephen, two of the 'Seven' chosen to serve the Church at Jerusalem, now loom up as men of great note and influence; Stephen, especially, being marked by great endowments, both natural and spiritual. At this time, the synagogue was found everywhere as a local institution, and was a greater educator of the Jews than the Temple itself; as the Scriptures were read there on the Sabbath and several other days of the week, expositions were given also, and free disputation had,—practices which kept the public mind awake in search of religious knowledge. The Rabbins mention the extravagant number of 480 synagogues in the holy city.

UPPER POOL OF GIHON.

To these, the inhabitants constantly resorted, and the foreign Jews had established their own there, for the use of their countrymen. Classed with the Asiatic synagogues we find the strangers from Cilicia, to which body it is most likely that Saul of Tarsus was attached. Acts vi, 9. The natural supposition is, that Stephen and Saul first met there in warm dispute, for Stephen defended the Gospel against the frequenters of these synagogues, and being unable to answer him, false witnesses charged him with defaming the Temple and the law. On this plea he was dragged before the Sanhedrin, where he delivered his matchless defense, equaled only in grasp, eloquence, and logic by the after addresses of the young Cilician himself. But its effect was to enrage the council and the people; and against all forms of law he was dragged out of the city and stoned. While suffering without the gate he offered the very prayer presented by Jesus with his last breath: 'Lord, lay not this sin to their charge;' and there stood by a young man named Saul, who was consenting to his death. Heaven only knows the quiverings which this plea stirred in that young breast, quiverings which were never quieted till Jesus gave him rest. Two quenchless flames burst forth at that moment, a great persecution which scattered the Church at Jerusalem, and an intense missionary enthusiasm. Stubborn prejudice against the Gentiles had restrained the Jewish Christians from taking the Gospel to the ends of the earth, until Stephen saw Jesus standing at the right hand of God, his first revelation since he entered the heavens years ago, and the ecstatic vision inspired his people to obedience. Jesus looked down and saw Stephen suffering where he had suffered, for the same soil was drinking up the blood of his servant, and when he heard the cry: 'Lord Jesus, receive my spirit,' Jesus remembered the softness of his Father's bosom when he sent forth the same plea. Then he arose from his throne, for as the Head he felt Stephen's pain, and eagerly sheltered him on his breast, safe from the stony shower. The martyr's pale cheek glowed with life and love, when his Master's arms welcomed the first Baptist Deacon safely across the Vale of Death. This is the only time that we read of Jesus 'standing' at the right hand of God, touched in immortal friendship, by the first horrors of martyrdom.

But as Jesus welcomed Stephen's spirit through the heavenly gate, his eye fell upon the young Tarsian standing by the garments of his murderers, and from that hour Saul was made, as he expressed it himself, the 'slave of Jesus Christ.' On the soil which was dyed purple with the blood of the murdered officer of Christ's Church, there sprang up the first blade in the harvest of Christian missions. Saul became furious for a time, but Stephen's prayer had lodged in his bloodthirsty soul like a barbed arrow, and electing love in heaven had ordained him the Apostle to the Gentiles. Four-and-twenty years afterward, when a similar mob sought to kill him in this same Jerusalem, the old scene rose before him in all its freshness, and extorted from him the touching cry: 'When the blood of thy witness, Stephen, was shed, I myself was standing by, and consenting and keeping the garments of those who slew him.' Acts xxii. 20.

The picture which Luke draws of the infuriated Saul is frightful: 'He made havoc of the Church, and breathed out threatenings and slaughter against the disciples.' Maddened first by the barbs in his heart, and more enraged with the blood which he had already tasted, his hot breath became slaughter, like that of the panting tiger. And yet, Stephen's triumphant fortitude and faith had recalled him to his better self. But this neither staggered nor softened his obstinate hatred of the Nazarene. He says that he was 'so exceeding *mad*' that he gave 'his voice,' or vote, against the saints and persecuted them unto death. Misgiving made his brutality more ferocious at the first, but the horrors of remorse came afterward. It were impossible for a man of his sensitive nature to remain unmoved by the manly reasonings and sublime love of young Stephen. They not only haunted him as a saintly specter, but so long as he resented them they goaded him. So long as he writhed in a hot frenzy, the blood from Stephen's temples only flecked the foam of his own mouth, so that he sought relief in new outrages. He hunted the harmless flock of Christ from city to city, staining his sword with their innocent blood. In reality, however, he had long been at school under a combination of such teachers as infinite wisdom only could command. In preparing for the new brotherhood, he was to be qualified for a work many-sided and greater than had yet fallen to the lot of any man, and it called for an education which none other had received. Why did Jesus need a thirteenth Apostle? or why had he not chosen that number at the first? The new emergency called for a new man. The Twelve had been faithful to the Jews, but they had neglected the Gentiles, so that when the new crisis arose there was no missionary ready to enter the great centers of Greek and Roman life for Christ.

Little is known of Saul's parents, except that they were Jews, of the tribe of Benjamin and of the Pharisaic sect. His father, however, was a Roman citizen, as his son was 'free-born,' a fact giving higher rank to the family than the Jews generally held. They evinced some decision in naming their son after the heroic king of their own tribe, whose pride and suicidal death had dishonored his fame for ages. Saul was born at Tarsus, the capital of Cilicia, in Asia Minor, probably about seven

TARSUS.

years after the birth of Christ. This was no mean city in population, influence, or history. It was founded, B. C. 820; was captured by the younger Cyrus, 401; again by Alexander the Great, 333, and stood loyal to Cæsar against Pompey, B. C. 47. Its schools abounded in number and superiority, so that it was a seat of great learning. In rhetoric, philosophy, philology and science, it disputed pre-eminence with Alexandria and Athens, and many of its scholars were famous. It was, also, a free city, situated on the navigable river Cydnus, which emptied into the Mediterranean, then the central sea of the world. It had large commercial dealings with Europe, especially Italy, which gave it considerable political strength. The forests of Tarsus made it a great timber market, and it manufactured large quantities of coarse, black hair-cloth, clipped from the countless goats of the forests. This was woven for the covering of tents and other rough uses. Saul was a maker of this fabric, a trade which called for little skill, and gave but a scant reward, leaving him free to think of the wandering races whom his cloth would cover. But Tarsus was a thoroughly pagan city, as bad, morally, as it well could be. Its population was chiefly of the Greek and Aramaic races, and its language a dialect of Phœnicia. In this seething mass of superstition, dishonesty and immorality, Saul spent his childhood and early youth, when his senses were the most quick, and his soul the most impressible; and his after life reveals the deep impression which his observations left upon him. So powerfully were his convictions moulded touching the abominations of a city given to idolatry, that the drift of his feeling differed from that of his compeers of Galilee. His native city showed him next to nothing of the landscape and the imagery of nature, but as he elbowed his way through throngs in its narrow streets, he studied pagan man as man. This early study ran in the lines of passion, law, self-discipline and self-degradation, as he saw them before his eyes. This gave him a widely different knowledge of the masses of humanity from that of the Twelve, and made him a profounder student of pagan philosophy and its practical results, than he could have been had he spent his life in studying its theory, though versed in its minutest axioms. It even affected his methods of speech, for as a rule, his metaphors and symbols were borrowed from metropolitan life;—architecture, military garrisons, movements of troops in fortified cities, and the games which drew excited crowds from their gates.

This was the school for the examination of idolatry, and in the lives of the gods, and their devotees. Saul read these lessons there. His knowledge of the tongue, customs, manners, spirit and practices of the pagans, qualified him to approach and understand the enormous majority of our race, as few Jews then living understood them. It is thought that he never mastered the Greek elementally, as his style is not after the classic models, his rhetoric being defective and his figures harsh and mixed. Possibly, any tutor of Tarsus would have ridiculed his Syriac peculiarities and Hebraisms, and Aristotle might have scouted his logic. But was it needful for an Apostle to be a finished Grecian in order to beard godless Greek wickedness? He had to handle its moral side rather than its metaphysics and mysteries. He must be able to unsheath the sword of the Spirit, and strike home in easy and natural strokes, without first mastering foreign tactics. His first necessity was a perfect freedom from prejudice against the Gentiles, and a tender love for them, with ability to address them fluently and forcefully. Perhaps it was impossible for a native Palestinian to overcome entirely the national antipathy against the Gentiles which imbued his whole people. Saving sympathy with the Gentile masses must come by feeling the power of their mental acuteness, as well as the foulness of their depravity. The Twelve knew little of this by actual contact, and Saul did not come to understand it in a day. He was allied to the heathen by first breathing life in their midst, by loving them as natives of his mother-land, and by tenderness for them as his own countrymen. Having met them first in the gates of death, he could throw open to them the gates of life, with a free and firm hand. Personal knowledge of the immunities and realities of Roman citizenship, of the charms of Greek intellect and its religious blight; and at the same time, an intimacy with the deepest tone of Hebrew reverence and legalism were indispensable in an Apostle to the Gentiles. Natural affection under the compelling love of God, must bind him to Roman, Greek and Jew, without a perpetual fight with his prejudices, in order to save them all. These met in Saul, as in no other man of whom we have knowledge. Even the feet of Jesus had never trodden Greek soil, nor was he a Roman citizen, but the vassal of a captured province, under Roman law, or he could not have been the Man of Calvary.

Saul also needed a thorough Hebrew training, which should subject all his other knowledge to his religious convictions. For this purpose he went to Jerusalem, possibly when about thirteen years of age, to be educated by Gamaliel, the great Hebrew preceptor. Jewish custom kept him at home until he was five years old, where as a child-student he was taught only the Scriptures as a 'Son of the law,' until he was sent to school at six. At ten, he took up the study of the oral law, and if he was to be a Rabbi, he entered the school of some great master at thirteen, as a 'Son of the Commandment,' that is, a student of the traditions of the fathers. While Jesus, therefore, under less than a score of years was sweating at the carpenter's bench, without the privilege of 'letters;' Saul, a youth of thirteen, was in hard training for his service in a school of the highest order, and less than seventy-five English miles from him. Day by day the Carpenter bent to his work, and pensively read his sacrificial end in the very fiber of the wood which his edge-tools laid bare; but the young tent-cloth maker was in the lecture-room at Jerusalem, poring over the hero-Messiah in the Hebrew Parchments, certain that he was near at hand, not to build thrones as a mechanic, but to sit upon them as a monarch.

The Jews had but seven great educators, to whom they gave the title of Rabban. Saul's tutor was of the most liberal order, in broad contrast with Shammai, of the hard and harsh school. No Rabbi then living was so well qualified to form Saul's character; for Gamaliel was humane, tolerant, high-minded, and for a Pharisee broad, so large that he permitted the use of pagan literature to his pupils. In this great school all Hebrew scholarship was interwoven into Saul's life. His manhood tells us, that as a boy he was impetuous and unselfish, with a strong will, a vigorous intellect, and of deep emotion. From these would spring felicity of manners, lofty aspirations, rigid simplicity of habit and firmness of opinion; the very qualities which make the best and worst of men, according to the motives which control them. He was devoted to pure ethics and religious ideals, but the Rabbinical process of interpretation surfeited his spirit with an ultra scrupulosity for the letter of Scripture, in fact, made him a thorough Talmudist. No man could walk easily in the web which those teachings spread for his feet. They split up the commands and prohibitions of Moses into 613 separate enactments; putting casuistry for conscience, and a petty, hair-splitting piety for honest obedience to God. They made men do more than God required, by turning a short corner on the enactment, although they cheated it by failing to do half of what it demanded. In all acts of microscopic piety the sieve was so fine that the tiniest gnat on the wing was caught and held firmly; but in graver matters, like mercy, justice and truth, its meshes passed a camel without touching hump or hoof. Tables, plates, pots, cups and ceremonial vessels of all sorts, were rinsed, scoured and scrubbed to thinness. When a Sadducee saw a Pharisee in a heavy sweat while rubbing the golden lamp-stand in the Temple, he solemnly suggested that the sun might bear a scouring now and then. When a few widows' houses were to be devoured, pious greed filled its maw with serene composure; but if an unfortunate hen laid an egg on the Sabbath, that raised the serious gastronomic question whether or not it could be eaten, on which point Hillel and Shammai came to heavy Pickwickian blows. Whether Partlet had broken the Sabbath was a dispute which could not so easily be settled; but the demand that a man let his light shine was easily met; for a serio-comic Pharisee would at once don his robes, carefully arrange its fringes and tassels, and make a long prayer at the street-corner, and so one street was all ablaze with piety at any rate, if the rest of the city were left in midnight gloom.

It was needful that Saul should be thoroughly versed in all the trifling questions of this sort, that he might perfectly understand the Jewish piety of his day, and how to deal with its empty claims; his summary disposal of them afterward indicates his early training therein, and his power in enforcing their opposites. Hard study of this traditional literature exposed to him its whole inner life and legal hardness. Free from the sensual, for a time he was stubbornly wedded to a narrow formalism, which made him a daring zealot for every jot of Pharisaic precision, even to intolerance. After he left the school of Gamaliel, we first meet him, a 'young man' possibly of thirty, standing relentlessly over the mangled body of Stephen. His keen, far-reaching eye saw that unless the Nazarene heresy were crushed at once, it must be fatal to the ancient faith, and his zeal to crush it kept pace with his quick intellectual caliber. He determined to lead in this crusade, a fanatic as to the tradition of his fathers, and obtained letters of authority from Theophilus, the High-Priest, and chief of the Sanhedrin; search-warrants legalizing his frosty exasperation to leave no home safe against his sharp inquisition. Hearing that Christ's disciples had gathered a flock in Damascus, he caught new fire and flew to their slaughter. That city was 140 miles north-east of Jerusalem, a five-or-six-days' journey, but he determined to drag men and women that weary distance to punish them. Had his power equaled his hate, his hot breath had flashed like lightning to slay every Christian in the great Syrian city. But to reach this cage of unclean birds, he must speed his way across the Jordan, over the hills of Bashan, through the burning lands of Ituræa, and past the brow of Hermon. He seems never to have met Jesus in his Jerusalem ministry, yet he had often trodden in his foot-prints, in walking its streets, climbing the Temple hill, or passing its gates.

Now, he swept the same road which Jesus had taken when he came from Nazareth, passing Bethel to Jericho, and on to Bethabara, where John baptized. Thence he forced his way up to blue Galilee, where Jesus trod the wave, opened the eyes of the blind, and unstopped deaf ears, as adder-like as Saul's.

Onward he pressed, league after league, over ground which the sandals of our Lord had made holy. On his right Gilead loomed up in majesty, on his left Tabor and Hermon, but he saw no glory of Transfiguration. He saw not a foot-mark of the Lamb of God in the way, and heard no lingering echoes of his voice amongst the cedars and spurs of Lebanon. As he crossed the limped Pharpar and reached those plains of Paradise watered by many fountains and the golden Abana, a world of beauty and bloom thirty miles long, olive-yards and vineyards, rich fields and fig-

RIVER BARADA—DAMASCUS IN THE DISTANCE.

orchards stretched before him. Every hue of Syrian sunshine was reflected from their glossy foliage and fruit. The grape hung in festoons, the apricot bent the tree, the peach and pomegranate, the prune and walnut adorned every rod. They rose and fell in turn over plain and declivity, but neither to tempt his appetite nor to quench his thirst. He heard nothing but the mutterings of death in the leaves of the trees, and thirsted only for a stronger cup, the wine of which was red, drawn from the veins of saints, till its fumes should make him drunk and reel. And what was it to him that the distant domes and towers spoke of the ancient city and its founder, the grandson of Shem; what that it was a way-mark to Abraham on the road to Canaan, 1,900 years back; or that Elisha broke into tears before its walls for the woes brought upon Israel by Hazael, in slaying men and women in cold blood there, as Saul himself would do? What cared he that David had captured Damascus for Judea 1,000 years ago? He was not seeking the relics of antiquity, but the divine pulse that had just begun to beat in the new-born Syrian Church. The glaring sky quivered with molten heat; but his fiery spirit made it hotter. It was high-noon, just when his victims were at midday prayers, imploring mercy on their enemies; and the mad zealot had gone far enough. A word from Christ threw the gate of heaven open, and the sun in the firmament turned pale. The Friend of Stephen had patiently watched the splendid fanatic, and stepped from his throne to forbid his trampling one saint under foot in that Gentile city. Jerusalem had stained its hoary old ashes with the blood of the Man of Sorrows and his servant Stephen, and not one drop should stain the streets of Damascus that day, to rob the Holy City of its gory notoriety.

When the shower of stones fell upon Stephen, Jesus felt the pangs, and now the voice of double tenderness demanded: 'Saul, Saul, why persecutest thou me?' Stephen's Saviour told Saul that he was 'apprehended,' made a prisoner of love, and that it was the part of an infuriated ox to resist and drive the goads deeper into his own flesh. Thus fettered and stricken blind, Saul fell to the ground, praying: 'Lord, what wilt thou have me to do?' For the first time the guilt of his old life burst upon him, and he saw himself the 'chief of sinners.' Blind to outside life, he looked within now, where an unseen world burst upon his consciousness. When the Risen One stood before him in the path of vision, and called himself 'Jesus,' a holy fear crept over his flesh and spirit, a touch of new life changed the universe to him. He asked not what his companions in crime would say, — whether the authorities at Jerusalem would wreak their vengeance upon him for his breach of faith as an apostate,—but only what the hated Nazarene wished him to do! In a moment, his violence is softened into inquiry, his fanaticism into submission, his tyranny into manliness. In the twinkling of an eye he becomes a prodigy of saving grace; a brother of all mankind emerges from the ringleader of persecutors, a thirteenth Apostle comes to the birth: 'Born out of due time.'

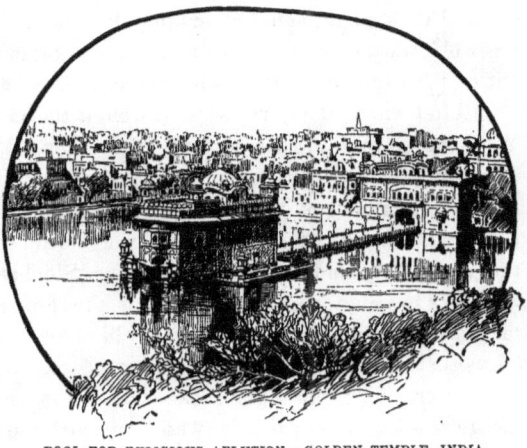

POOL FOR RELIGIOUS ABLUTION—GOLDEN TEMPLE, INDIA.

CHAPTER VII.

PAUL AND GENTILE MISSIONS.

SAUL'S cavalcade is dispersed and he is led stricken and helpless, that his head may weep in a dark place while his eyes are sealed. Did ever man question his crest-fallen soul like this man, in the home of Ananias? The talk that he hears is all new, and the strange hymns which float under its roof awaken hidden thoughts in the secret chambers of his spirit. The disciples who waited for his prisons and chains, hear that he is the blind subject of Christian hospitality. Yesterday he fell before the gate a ruined sinner, but rose a consecrated saint—fell a butcher of the saints, rose a champion Apostle. Yesterday morning he was a vulture sailing over the prey on which he gloated; to-day, he is a gentle dove covered with silver, and feathers of yellow gold. Outside the gate, he was a prowling wolf; in the home of Ananias, a trembling lamb; for the slayer of women came out of the baptistery with his heart breaking for all human woe.

After three days, news ran through the city that he was at the synagogue. Why was he there? Let us see. It is thronged, and crowds gather at its doors. Floods of eloquent truth flow from a strange voice, and sound out a strange Name in the holy oratory of the synagogue. This reasoning is not after the dialectics of Gamaliel, it is like Stephen's, as clear, as warm, as conclusive. The old apology of that martyr haunts him; Saul is wielding Stephen's old logic with mighty power. He dares to say, that the Crucified is the Son of God! Perhaps his mind's eye sees the face of the martyr shining like the face of an angel in the heaven of heavens. Or does the ghost of the murdered man make his penitence eloquent? No matter. The synagogue rocks with excitement. In the first stupor of surprise, the Jews ask: 'Is not this he who destroyed the Galileans? This is not the fierce man of Tarsus. He could not frame such thoughts, would not talk so wildly.' Yet, he grows warmer, bolder, broader. He cites the Sacred Rolls from Genesis to Malachi to prove that Jesus is the Christ. Blank astonishment seizes the Jews; they gather in knots to consult, and are half-paralyzed. Their surprise gives place to indignation. Why do they not drag him forth, cast him out, put him to death? But he moves on and on like a torrent, clearer and stronger than ever; until he comes to tell of his own rescue from perdition. As he gives his story, new and holy fire makes him tremble from head to foot in the realities of one who is saved, when he cries to the surging crowd: 'I was a blasphemer, and a persecutor, and overbearing; but I obtained mercy, that in me first Jesus Christ might show forth all long-suffering, for a pattern to them who shall hereafter believe on him to life everlasting.'

The account which he writes of his early Christian life, in his Epistle to the Galatians, shows that he now spent three years in Arabia; which, by Jewish reckoning, might mean one whole year with a part of two others. A veil is thrown over this Arabian visit. Whether the name designates the peninsula of Sinai, bounded by Egypt and the upper part of the Red Sea, or the desert north of this, or the desert of Petraea or all these together, is not known. Most likely the word 'Arabia' has a somewhat local meaning, which covers Sinai and the regions adjacent. Arabian Jews had heard the Gospel from Peter at Pentecost, and, possibly, having been converted, had returned to their own country. The original inhabitants of these wild districts were descendants of Ishmael, whose religion degenerated into a sort of fetich idolatry, and amongst these Arabs, Saul was to outgrow his cold bigotry and narrow traditions into a broad messenger of grace to all orders of Gentiles. He tells us, that in going there he neither consulted his own inclinations nor the wishes of others, but cheerfully took the burden laid upon him by Christ. This was the great crisis of his life, and he must be severed from all controlling human influences until he passed it safely. At the birthplace of the Old Covenant, which burned with fire, he must study the ministry of death, that he might better preach the life of the New Covenant. Up to this point in his history, his great strength lay in the fact, that he owned himself without reserve, for in his intense hate his imperious will had been the regnant center of his being. In Arabia he must put himself entirely under the will of another. As a strong man, he held the new truth without wavering, free from those petty suspicions which torment the weak. For him to take liberties with the truth would be disloyalty, but thorough exploration of all its parts would give its whole empire a unity, which must correct his distortions of the moral law, and tutor him for the invincible preaching of the Gospel. In this way he could perfect his character, and prepare for action on a large scale; being first a debtor to the Jew and the Greek, the polished and the barbarian. But in order to repay the whole race, he must go first to Arabia.

Had he gone back to Jerusalem to consult with the elder Apostles, their prejudices against taking the Gospel to the Gentiles might have chilled him, or it might appear that he had received authority from them. But Jesus kept him apart by sending him to those solitary granite mountains where Moses, the head of the law, and Elijah, the head of the prophets, were educated for their work, and where isolation brought him under the absolute dictation of his Lord. For three years Christ had instructed the Twelve personally, and Saul, the new Apostle, must go for the same length of time, to these crags, cliffs and wastes, for schooling around the frowning mount, under Christ's exclusive teaching. He had now rejected his former interpretation of Moses, and so at Sinai he must learn anew what the Lawgiver meant, as quoted by Stephen: 'A Prophet will God raise up to you, him shall ye hear.' He could better learn this on the holy ground which had quaked in blackness and tempest. Saul should study the Gospel where the Law was given, and obtain full knowledge of the blood of sprinkling where God had ordained that there can be no remission of sin without blood-shedding. When calmed, instructed, and strengthened under the shade of Sinai, he would be ready to ascend Calvary. The trumpet resounding around the legal mount, should teach him how to press another trumpet to his lips and proclaim the voice of other words, with a self-conscious joy which should exult in the cry: 'Thanks be to God who makes us to triumph in every place.'

At the end of his Arabian life he returned to Damascus, where he was assailed by his foes, who were maddened against him; and he fled for safety to Jerusalem. His preaching forced the Jews to re-examine their own faith, and they plotted his assassination at the opening of his Apostolic career. His Christian brethren kept him secret until night, and when the streets and walls of the city were under close guard, they let him down in a net, or rope-basket, from a window in the wall, opening into a house inside the city. Stealing from the eyes of men whom he fain would bless, for the first time the world's Apostle fled for his life. When lowered into the outer darkness, as into a well, he grasped the rope, but he could hear his own heart beat; and what thoughts trooped through his soul at that sad moment! He came to that city to lash by the wrists Christ's disciples in gangs, and now fled to a rope for his own deliverance, that he might preach that Christ to all. Then, he would cage all the saints in prison, to kill them; but now, how gladly he cramps himself into a basket to save his own life that he may make more disciples. Isaiah's figure presents him to us as 'a wild bull caught in a net' at last; and, possibly, the hands that drop him to the ground are those which he intended to enchain. He groped his way through the dark, with only a star here and there to shed a ray on his path, as if poetic justice reminded him by contrast of his noon-tide persecution. He trod upon his own dark plots at every step, and no chapter in his history would so stir our hearts as the record of his thoughts when he repassed the spot where Christ smote him to the earth. Did he look into the heavens now to see them re-open? O! what would he have given then for one more glimpse of the Son of man! And how wakeful was the ear of his heart, to catch one whisper of his voice. He tells us himself (Gal. i, 18) that he desired to see Peter. For what? He has concealed his heart musings. But for once, he wanted to look the honest boatman in the face; to catch the wondrous story of redemption from a fresh memory and a full heart. His soul-musings must have been wonderful as he made his way back through Palestine. On reaching 'The Place of Stoning,' hard by the Damascus gate of Jerusalem, where he first breathed out threatening and slaughter, what were his thoughts? Did he pick up a stone there, to see if it still bore the stain of Stephen's blood? Did he bury his face in his 'cloak' and sob, where he had watched the clothes of those who stoned Stephen? That had been Paul-like.

Saul came back to the Holy City another man. He longed to nestle in the warm love of those whom he had hated, and sought to join them. Three years had proved his conversion thorough, and he made not for the home of his old tutor, nor did he seek for Onkelos, the coming author of the Targum, who had sat at his side in the great school as Gamaliel's pupil. But he went directly to the disciples of Jesus. The Jews had once reposed confidence in him and promised him a brilliant

BARNABAS INTRODUCING PAUL TO PETER.

future, now they had turned their backs upon him, and he met a cold reception amongst the Christians. They suspected him. Luke says: 'All were afraid of him, not believing that he was a disciple.' He had been so furious against them that his name was odious, and they feared to be entrapped in some horrible plot. In this atmosphere of distrust, the delicate love and heroic courage of that choice spirit, Barnabas, took him by the hand, led him to the Apostles, and told them all the particulars of his conversion. They saw that his vision was no creation of his brain, and that the words of Jesus to him were no note of his imagination, but that in truth he had become a follower of Jesus. Barnabas silenced the fears of the brethren, and Saul was welcomed by Peter and James, our Lord's brother, whom he now met for the first time. The new Apostle began at once to build up the faith where he had sought its destruction, until the Grecian Jews threatened his life. This latter fact shows how thoroughly his three years' study of Christian truth had subordinated his Jewish attainments to the service of Christ. Saul had never met the Son of Mary in the metropolis, but their eyes had looked upon the same men, and now their feet had passed the same streets on the same errand of love, and their hearts had become the treasury of the same truths.

Saul remained in Jerusalem only fifteen days (Gal. i, 19); and then his brethren saved his life a second time, by sending him to Tarsus, where, most likely, he established the churches in Cilicia. Meanwhile, persecution had driven certain disciples to Antioch, which was now to become a great center for the spread of the Gospel, to which work the Apostle should devote the best thirty years of his life. For this work Christ had educated this great workman. Eighty years were spent by Moses in his education, forty in the academies of Egypt, and forty in the desert of Horeb, for a third forty years' work, in making a nation from a mob of slaves. Jesus spent thirty years in preparing for the work of three, and it was meet that his greatest Apostle should spend the same length of time in preparing to lead the Gentile world to the foot of his cross. Some of the disciples who first visited Antioch were from the Island of Cyprus, the very hot-bed of worship offered to Venus; others were of Cyrene, a Greek city on the African coast between Carthage and Egypt. These first preached to the Jews in Antioch, then turned to the Gentiles and a great number believed. Acts xi, 21. Here the first battle for Christ with unmixed paganism was waged, and the first purely Gentile Church was formed entirely outside of all Judaizing influences. This event shaped the future of Christianity, proving that 'The field is the world.' It is remarkable that this Church was founded without the aid of an Apostle, by converted Hellenist Jews, who had not heard the parable of the sower; for Barnabas and another Cypriot convert had built up this first Gentile Church in the great Syrian capital. These very irregular and disorderly proceedings amongst the primitive Baptists have greatly shocked certain prelatical parties. But they must bear up under the affliction in some way, for at last it will certainly appear that a simple, immersed Evangelist, confirmed the first Church ever called 'Christian.' Nay, so great was the ingathering that Barnabas was compelled to go from Antioch to Tarsus, in search of Saul to help him in the great harvest-field. Antioch was all inquiry; and the broad nature of Barnabas saw that the issue must be met by a man of wide conceptions, earnest convictions, and liberal sympathies; a man with full knowledge of human nature, cool, courageous, cosmopolitan; dead, as far as possible, to crude and timid preferences for race and nationality; who, in earnest and without doubt, could clearly and sharply define the new faith. Hence, he passed by all the conservative Baptists at Jerusalem, and made no mistake in bringing the radical young Tarsian to be captain of the Lord's Gentile host.

Antioch had a population of about 500,000, being inferior only to Rome and Alexandria. But, as the third city in the empire it vied with these in magnificence, state, luxury, wealth, art and brilliant culture, being called the 'Queen of the East.' Yet, it was the home of every thing vile. Rénan, the skeptic, names it, 'The capital of all lies, and the sink of every description of infamy.' It knew nothing of truth or purity, it was unbridled in its debaucheries, atheistic in its philosophy, and vulgar in its pleasures and worship. Its wit was sharp and its squibs scurrilous, which accounts for the derisive nickname coined there, 'Christians;' and the sights

MARS HILL.

perpetrated at its shrines were ribald, nay, shocking beyond degree. This was the battle-field chosen by Jesus for the first real clash of arms between his Gospel and the Gentile gods, and Saul was his chosen missionary. However small the company of disciples within its walls at this time, with this Apostle as their leader, Antioch soon planted all the Asiatic churches, and became the world's pulpit for the cross. Even then it gave promise of the day when Ignatius was to pass its gates to seal the truth with his blood, in the Roman amphitheater. Chrysostom was to be born there, to tell the story of the risen King in Constantinople; and there 100,000 men were to bind the sacred name of derision to their hearts; and above all, there Bible theology and Gospel songs were to be framed for the inspiration of our race. From the day that Saul entered Antioch, the faith of Christ cut every leading-string which bound it to Mosaism, and this city became the birth-home of a pure Christian nobility, into which all bloods and races were fused, in the name of Jesus. That was a strange cry which this embassador raised in Antioch, when he called her satirists and wits, her rhetoricians and military men, her quacks and necromancers, her buffoons and dancing girls, to 'Behold the Lamb.' But he continued in this toil for 'a whole year,' and a 'great multitude believed.' A famine occurred in Judea in the fourth year of Claudius, and collections were taken up in Antioch and other Gentile churches for the relief of the Jewish Christians at Jerusalem. These contributions were sent by the hands of Barnabas and Saul, A. D. 45; this was the Apostle's second visit after his conversion, and in the same year he returned to Antioch; from thence he, Barnabas, and John Mark, went forth on the Apostle's First Great Missionary Expedition.

When Columbus left the harbor of Palos with two small caravels, no such moral results hung in the balance as those which impended when Barnabas and Saul left all that was dear to them in Antioch. They must first go to Seleucia, the sea-port of Antioch, fourteen miles west, and five miles north of the mouth of the river Orontes, to take ship for the Island of Cyprus, for from that black-sand beach the ark of the world must be launched. The Mediterranean had now become the highway of civilization, ideas and empire, as well as of commerce; and they sailed about a hundred miles, when they landed at Salamis, on the island where Christ wrought signs and wonders by the Gospel. Here, the great Apostle dropped the name of Saul, and was known thereafter only as Paul or Paulus. Some think that the Roman name was assumed to conciliate Gentile prejudice, but more likely this had been his Roman name from childhood, while amongst the Hebrews he had been known as Saul. From that time the sacred story changes, Paul taking higher rank. He is no longer second to Barnabas, as at Antioch, but he takes precedence, and now we read of 'Paul and Barnabas,' not only the order of names being reversed, but Barnabas falls into the background and Paul becomes the great figure on the glowing canvas, by land and sea.

No story could be more enchanting or instructive than that of following Paul through his three great missionary tours, but this our limits forbid. Nothing in history is so enriched, excepting the life of Jesus. It is an inspired panorama. The account covers so many lands, tongues, climates and civilizations that it opens the ancient world to us. His various methods of travel, his many companions, the endless phases in which he met every possible development of Judaism and paganism, his devious styles of preaching, his orders of controversy, the unfoldings of old truths and the revelation of new, his nameless sufferings and successes, are themes pregnant with importance, and every temptation presses to their full treatment. But self-denial imposes silence here, as well as upon his numerous Church organizations, especially those to whom he addressed his wonderful Epistles, as the Galatians, the

ANCIENT SHIP.

Philippians, the Thessalonians, the Corinthians, the Ephesians and others; together with their contents and the circumstances which called them into existence. All this, with much more, must be omitted, until we meet him on a cold, murky November morning, at the close of his great voyage and shipwreck. His wonderful life's work was substantially done when he stood shivering with that wretched group of two hundred and seventy-six souls, on that tongue of land now known as St. Paul's Bay, on Malta. Bruised, shelterless and haggard, they stood near the headland where 'two seas met,' in a more significant sense than is indicated by currents and shoals on a dangerous sea-coast. There, while huddled together in a pelting rain, and drenched in sea-water, Paul and his party, hungry and benumbed

ST. PAUL'S BAY, FROM THE SOUTH.

with cold, gathered a heap of brush and made a fire. But a chilled viper had been unwittingly thrown with the sticks into the blaze. Blistered with heat, the reptile darted out in anger and fastened its poisonous fangs on Paul's hand. He coolly shook it off again into the fire and remained unhurt: a fit type of the victory which awaited him at Rome, where God would shortly beat down Satan under his feet. On reaching Puteoli, in Italy, the news of his arrival quickly flew to Rome, a distance of a hundred and forty miles which he must travel in chains over the immortal Appian Way. And yet, no conqueror in triumph, no Emperor in purple, had ever passed over this pavement, on whom such tremendous results hung in Roman destiny. When forty miles from Rome they came to Appii Forum, at the end of the canal which ran through the Pontine Marshes. There they were met and welcomed by a company of disciples from the Eternal City. A few miles farther on, a second group of Roman brethren met and greeted them, at the Three Taverns, where the road from Actium came into the main road, and where multitudes of travelers met.

When the Apostle saw that he had a home in the hearts of so many whom he had never before seen in the flesh, he 'thanked God and took courage.' The thought that he must enter Rome, a mass of two millions of people from all lands, a prisoner, unknown and nearly alone, may have dampened and even stifled his companionable soul with a sense of that unutterable loneliness which is never so deeply felt as in a crowd. But when the great city burst upon his sight from the Alban Hills, and he found a band of faithful, redeemed souls, on his right and on

FIFTH MILE OF THE VIA APPIA RESTORED.

his left, the old Jerusalem-Philippian-Ephesian fire glowed anew in his brave spirit, and in a moment he was strong to preach the Gospel at Rome also. Thus, in the month of March, in the seventh year of Nero's reign, and the sixty-second of that Christ, whose he was and whom he served, the immortal tent-maker passed through the Carpenian Gate, to save the Eternal City.

That day Julius delivered his precious charge to Burrus Afranius, the Prefect of the Prætorian Guard, a humane and honest officer, who made his report to the imperial court. The illustrious prisoner, however, was permitted to dwell by himself in his own hired house, within the limits of the Prætorian quarter, still linked to his guard by his humiliating chain. He had been in Rome but three days when he sought a conference with the principal officers of the seven synagogues there, before whom he desired to lay his case for consultation. They assured him that they had received no communication concerning him from Jerusalem, although they knew that his sect was in bad repute every where. Yet, they assembled on an appointed day to hear him expound its doctrines in his own lodgings: a practice which he continued for two whole years, for the benefit of all who wished to hear him. It is clear also, from his Epistles of the Imprisonment, that he met with much success in preaching the Gospel in Rome; some of his converts being found in Cæsar's household. It is not now easy to determine the exact district to which his person was limited, as the Prætorian camp was outside the walls, at some distance short of the Fourth Mile-stone. The Prætorium was the head-quarters of the Roman military governor, and the camp so called at Rome, was created by Tiberius, before whose time the troops were lodged in different parts of the city.

The direct Scripture narrative concerning Paul's career closes with his arrival at Rome, and the statement that he remained there 'two years.' But the various allusions and references made in his Epistles of the Imprisonment indicate that he was released A. D. 63-64, and that after this he traveled through Asia Minor, Crete, Macedonia, Greece; and many think that he visited Spain, and some, that he planted Christianity in Britain. The fair inference is, that he returned to Rome voluntarily, as we have no hint of the time and place of his arrest, nor of any charge against him. That he finally endured martyrdom there is clear; some think as early as A. D. 64, while others put the date as late as A. D. 68. When a prisoner, he was comforted by the presence of Luke, Timothy, Aristarchus of Thessalonica, and Epaphras, a Colossian; also by Mark, the cousin of Barnabas, and Tychicus, of Asia. It is difficult to account for the long delay of his first hearing before the Emperor. But these two years were not lost; as he expresses it, they turned out 'for the furtherance of the Gospel.' The charges sent by Festus were, most likely, lost in the shipwreck; and if so, much time would be consumed in waiting for a duplicate copy from Cæsarea. The slowness of his accusers to appear against him, because of the known weakness of their case, was disheartening to him, as well as the long delays in the course of Roman law at its fastest pace; meanwhile, false brethren were studiously adding affliction to his bonds, by persecuting his converts, and he was betrayed by some of his friends.

We may as well dismiss the legend of horrors in the Mamertine Prison, as one of those fictions which will not bear the light of history. His sufferings sank deeper than the shudderings of the body in a dark and wet dungeon, whose walls were great blocks of tufa anchored together by clamps of iron, and where every limb was chilled for want of his 'cloak.' We know that he was sick in person, and that he was ill-treated by Tigellinus, the wretch who followed Burrus, as Chief Prætorian Prefect. How many sighs he heaved in secret before God we never can know, till we read the stains on the immortal page which Jehovah keeps. But no voice in history brings down to us such a touch of melancholy as we hear in the cry: 'At my first answer no man stood with me, but all men forsook me.' Some think that while a prisoner he had influenced such men as Linus, who was to be the pastor at Rome, Prudeus, the son of a senator, and Claudia, a British senator. One almost wishes that this opinion may not be correct, as no citizen of Rome had the courage to stand by him. In his Roman captivity he looked back upon the past, and, at least, found himself Christ-like in this, that just as all the Apostles fled from Jesus in his peril, so his chief Apostle was left to provide for his own safety. They abandoned an old and grey-headed man to captivity and martyrdom, in an ungenerous and dastardly manner, instead of defending him as eager and staunch friends. Still, we are scarcely surprised at their fear, when exile and sword threatened them, for the Roman Christians suffered ruthless persecution. Yet, Paul proved his largest liberty by his chains. The world had been riveted in breathless attention, while he crossed its mountains and seas, crying with the Baptist: 'Behold the Lamb of God!' Even in his captivity all was animation. His prison-home gives us glimpses of his fortitude, heroism, and true leadership as a champion of the truth. Fetters weigh him down, and the sword, half-drawn from its sheath, gleams before him, and with a rude soldier chained to his arm, he keeps his pen busy for Christ. In an important sense he did more for Christ when in bonds than when in full liberty. Luther was a prisoner at the Wartburg, till he could give Germany a popular Bible; Bunyan passed twelve years in his 'den' at Bedford, till he could set all ages dreaming of heaven; and it was meet that Paul should illuminate and confirm the faith of churches to be formed in all lands while time lasts. Unable to go from land to land, his pen gave the world the Epistles of the Imprisonment, the Letters to the Philippians and the Colossians, with his queen Epistle to the Ephesians; also, those to Philemon, to Timothy, and to Titus. It is scarcely too much to say, that while a prisoner he did more for the unborn centuries, than all the rest of his life did for that in which he lived; for under his Master, he erected a new world of moral thought, language and life for the human race.

These peerless letters have hourly instructed the ignorant, strengthened the weak, and consoled the comfortless for eighteen hundred years. They are so few in number, and so small in bulk, that a child can handle them, yet so simple in structure that a peasant can make them his own. They have created a world-wide literature, which puts the scholarship of the world under tribute, for they still produce the profoundest thought ever known to man. For beauty and fragrance, they are so many 'beds of spices;' for fullness and wealth, so many exhaustless mines. Mankind stands a debtor at the door of Paul's prison-house, whence he gave out these holy sheets, and will never be able to pay its debt to their high culture and mighty inspiration.

CHAPTER VIII.

NERO AND PAUL, PETER AND JOHN.

THE persecutions of the Primitive Christians did not spring from pure hatred or tyranny on the part of the Roman authorities. When we attribute them to mere blood-thirst we miss the real contest between Christ and Paganism, and his great conquest over its noblest forms. Contrary to the old Greek and Oriental faiths, Rome blended its religious with its political existence, as one of its institutions, for the rulers held, that the oath could not be binding, that there could be no public credit, and no administration of justice, without reverence for the deities. Hence, the laws were generally enforced in the coolest manner, and without passion, in defense of the national life. Plutarch made religion the necessary basis of civil government, and Polybius extolled Roman piety for the security that it gave to the State. Even the Greeks had held the rejecter of all gods as a bad citizen, Plato made him a criminal, Draco punished him with death, and Aristotle would have but one established worship. Tully thought that the gods inspired Roman wisdom when it relegated religion to the control of the rulers, so that it became a science in civil jurisprudence, and a prop to the public safety. On this ground, Augustus required each senator to worship some god before he took his seat in the Senate. Hence, also, the rulers endowed the priesthood, and lavished gifts upon the gods, as on the accession of Caligula, which was celebrated by offering 100,000 sacrifices.

Still, religious tolerance was the steady policy of Rome from time immemorial. Niebuhr says, that 'the whole life of the constitution depended on it.'[1] It was allowed, however, only on respect for some god, rejection of all of them being treason to the Empire. Universal conquest had allied it with the whole family of deities who had presided over its arms, and had consolidated its law and religion into a unit. Each city and country had its divinity, of whose honor it was jealous, and its devotees had hot controversies about their favorite gods. The capital invited all deities, and those of the provinces had been freely translated thither, which made Rome a huge pantheon for the idols of the world. War had destroyed many temples, which were rebuilt in great splendor, and every oracle of country and town was crowded with worshipers. As Christians worshiped none of them, they were a disquieting element in the government, and were treated as atheists; therefore, Christianity was contrary to law. A man's conscience belonged to the State as much as his limbs, and the crime of the Christians was, that they would think for themselves. Celsus said: 'Knowledge is an evil; it causes men to lose their soundness of mind;

they perish through wisdom.' Moreover, pagan influence was sustained by the military service, and as Christians would not enlist, their faith was not national, and they were accounted enemies of the State, rebellious, obstinate, for which Statecraft put them to the sword. They would not drink in honor of the Emperor's birthday, which proved them unsocial and haters of society,—they treated the gods with contempt, which proved their ignorance,—they publicly adored an invisible God, which proved them guilty of sedition,—and when adoration of Christ was forbidden they worshiped him privately, which proved them secret plotters against the government. Their reasoning could not be answered, but they could be hated. Whatever they did was legally wrong, the law demanded their condemnation, and the calmest officer was the most cruel in exacting absolute obedience. As guilds, clubs, or associations, they could select a patron divinity, but he must take some visible form, or they must be treated as godless.

Paganism was stronger under the Empire than ever before, and the number of gods was increased rather than diminished. No place was without its deity. The exchange, the home, the work-shop, the palace, the wood and the wheat-field had its divinity, its humiliation and its festival. A woman in social life was not respected who did not bring gifts to some sacred image, or fane, or faun. At her betrothal, her marriage, the birth of her children, the death of any in her household, she was equally devout. Uhlhorn says: 'There was the goddess Lucina, who watched over the birth of a child; Candelifera, in whose honor at such a time candles are lighted; Rumina, who attended its nursing; Nundina, who was invoked on the ninth day when the name was given; Potina and Educa, who accustomed it to food and drink. The day when the child first stepped upon the ground was consecrated to Statina; Abeona taught it to walk; Farinus to lisp; Locutinus to talk; Cunina averted from it the evil enchantments lying in the cradle.' Then there was the god of the soil, the door, the stable, the ship, the prison and even of the brothel. Every thing in turn had its sacred side. Hill and dale, day and night, seed-time and harvest, summer and winter, equally demanded a sacrifice from prince and peasant, so that in some places there were more gods than men.

This politico-religious trend accounts for the craze which frenzied the popular mind in the deification of the Emperors. At Athens, the philosophic spirit of the Greek still animated a subjugated people, but at Ephesus, the center of Asiatic Greek culture and Roman imperial rule, we see paganism in its true light as an adjunct to the government. Thus, the sphere of divinity could be reached with ease from the Oriental *cultus*, where the deeds of the heroic and illustrious won the popular assent to deification. We contemn the thought that any man can rest a vital faith in his fellow, as God. But when the Senate decreed Cæsar a divinity, and erected temples to his honor during his life-time, the wish of the people gave validity to the decree, because they looked upon him as the author of all their temporal power, political peace, and unbroken sway over the nations. The soldier worshiped the Emperor from motives of patriotism, the freedman because he had conferred liberty upon his class, the statesman as the source of his promotion, and the provincial as the guardian of his security. Cæsar-worship took deep root in the soil of self-interest and gratitude, while the deified Emperor bestowed fresh privileges upon his adoring subjects, centralizing the public interests, and binding all closer to his person and prerogatives. He, therefore, gave general unity to the common faith, for the whole Empire found in him the center of its universal bliss, the Emperor-god being its veritable PONTIFEX MAXIMUS. The necessary result was, that a crime against this deity was a crime against the State, which could not long be brooked, but put the life of each dissenter in peril. The essence of paganism was rite, and not faith, so that the priest presided at the ceremony which the magistrate enforced. This made the struggle sharp between the princes of this world and the Lord of souls. The Gospel claimed divine origin, it branded paganism as human or infernal, to be cast aside, while it was enthroned in the heart; there could, therefore, be no end to such a struggle until the stronger overthrew the weaker.

Still another thing. There was an awakening of new ideas, a strong undercurrent of skepticism mixed with all this pagan cult, for its traditions were derided as well as doubted. Amongst the intellectual classes, its legends were mocked, its gods sneered at, and its fables ridiculed. Menander sacrificed to the gods, but said that they did not 'care for him.' Others derided their pretensions, made sport of their prongless tridents, and either laughed at the whiz of their thunder-bolts, or defied them as myths, without existence *per se*. Yet those who treated them with contempt were made obedient by fanatical fear, superstition working in them slavish hypocrisy. In the Senate itself Cæsar boldly proclaimed himself an unbeliever; but he never felt safe in his chariot without repeating a magical talismanic word. Augustus rejected the gods, yet all the day long he was afraid, if he put his shoe on the wrong foot in the morning; and Pliny, a practical atheist, pinned his faith to absurd charms. Indeed, when general confidence in paganism failed, it was carefully fostered for State purposes. This consideration made its poets sing, its politicians plan, its priests minister, and its Emperors chant its liturgies on their knees. No goddess could find her vestals amongst virgins of high birth, but took these venerated persons from the freed women, chiefly of the lower ranks, and the Emperor increased their rights, to make their office the more attractive. Of course, the aristocracy clung to the old faith for State purposes. It was the law of the land, its ceremonies were easily complied with, and it was sternly enforced by imperial example and authority. The consequence was, that when this policy was adopted by the Julian line, it was made stronger than ever, as the Gospel begun its attacks upon the system; that the new faith should not stand in the wisdom of men, but in the power of God.

With these facts in view we easily understand the *animus* of persecution on the part of those Emperors, who sincerely and conscientiously served the gods themselves, and it is quite as clear, how the ambitious, the cruel, and the malignant sought every occasion to gratify their caprice under the show of patriotism, even when it was purely wanton. The first noted example of this sort meets us in Nero. Seneca, his tutor in philosophy, says: That he was a clement sovereign when he ascended the throne; others regarded him as the best prince since Augustus; and Trajan speaks of his reign as dignified during his first five years, but bad during the last eight. He was the last of the Julian family, born A. D. 37, and the Cæsars died in him, A. D. 68. His father, Domitius, was thoroughly evil, and his mother, Agrippina, has no equal in history for plot and infamy. That language could scarcely be unmeasured which wrote her down a Jezebel, a Cleopatra, and a Lucrezia Borgia, all in one. First, she was the niece of the Emperor Claudius, then his fourth wife, then she poisoned him. He had adopted Nero, her own son and his step-son, into the imperial family, and immediately she began to plot against his own son, Britannicus, the rightful heir to the throne. By a series of bold and unscrupulous intrigues, she finally stole the purple for Nero, and then attempted to murder him, because she could not control his reign.

When young, he was extremely beautiful in person, early displaying a taste for art, in painting and sculpture, as well as for poetry, music, and the drama. At seventeen he became Emperor, and died at thirty. Monstrous as was his mother, he soon became his own masterpiece, and rose to be the prime monster of the world. He never developed the first attribute of a statesman, nor showed the slightest sign of humanity, nor blessed his empire by one noble deed; but lived only to display a frenzy of passion and a guilty splendor. His ill-regulated mind was the slave of his selfish whims, and daily incubated brood after brood of groundless suspicions and jealousies. He married Octavia, the daughter of Claudius, then divorced and murdered her. After this he poisoned Britannicus, whom he had robbed of the purple, and failing to drown his own mother, had her assassinated with a dagger. Having begun a career of blood, he killed his first two wives, and slew noble after noble, without end. A man must be polluted with crime through and through to become an adroit 'inventor of evil things,' yet this was his pre-eminence. When Poppea, a beautiful but worthless Jewess, became his wife, and was about to become a mother, he kicked her to death. In order to attract him by her fair appearance, she bathed daily in milk taken from five hundred she asses, and these beasts she shod with gold and silver shoes. With her husband, she paraded her vices in the most public and shameless manner.

This was the man to whom the holy Paul was obliged to appeal, from the fury of 'God's High-priest,' when he sought to worship Christ in peace. No record is left of the time or place of his trial before Nero, but as the Emperors never relinquished the power of life and death in such cases, it is every way likely that he stood before him as a prisoner. Paul gives a mere hint of such a meeting when he notes his 'first answer;' and says, that Jesus 'stood at his side,' when all men abandoned him. He exults, also, that he 'was delivered out of the mouth of the lion,' as if he referred to Nero's ferocity, while he praises Christ for his freedom.

Behold the two men! They had not one thing in common, either in person, character, or relation. Paul was so advanced in years that he calls himself 'the aged;' diminutive in body, 'weak in presence,' defective in sight, 'contemptible in speech,' and prematurely worn-out by labors, hardships, and sufferings. The blood of a simple Jewish artisan ran in his veins; his hands were horny with honest work, and fettered in irons; his body disfigured with scars, his head loaded with curses, and his life hunted, penniless and friendless. Nero was a young man, not more than six-and-twenty. The blood of the last Cæsar tingled in his veins, the adulation of the world lay at his feet, and the sovereignty of the globe stood behind him. Legion after legion, half a million of men in arms, waited to do his bidding. Six millions of people thronged his capital, and twenty-five millions formed his empire, ready to lavish upon him all that treasure and power could demand. His jeweled hand grasped such a scepter as the world had never seen before, and which had been held in the palm of Augustus and Tiberius, of Caligula and Claudius. But his young face, furrowed deep by the keenness of human passion, was unable to blush, for his heart took hue from a bottomless pit of depravity, whose smoke ascended for ever and ever.

The chain which cut into Paul's wrist that day, has long since fretted itself into fine dust; but he held the truth in righteousness, and by its power he wielded that pen which still stirs the heart of the world, and makes the pulse beat strongly in millions of unmanacled arms. But canker had seized Nero's heart. Like a honeycombed petrifaction, it was eaten through and through. His brow was wreathed in a diadem, or adorned in laurel; but his soul beneath was a dark vault, where demons had jostled out each relic of manhood, and then clenched the gate against its return, with steel bolts and bars which no charm could draw. He threw the saints to lions, tigers, and hyenas, till hoof and jaw were satiated; then, dripping red with the blood of God's elect, they haunted him while he slept. Paul's heart had broken, when the tears of elders fell upon his neck. But Nero's soul was a sea of ice, in which a spark of love could not live. Paul stood, a ripened and mellowed spirit ready to be borne home on angels' bosoms; Nero sat, a juvenile, nondescript compound of vulgarity and hate; who had not felt a new sensation of devilishness for years.

There they stood, Paul and Nero; the foulest and the purest of men. The one a deity of paganism, the other a disciple of the Good Shepherd; each represented his own universe; each embodied the elements of his own system, as if the struggle between them was reduced to a personal combat, and symbolized in the two men. A temple of the Holy Spirit without a spot of impurity from pavement to topstone would image forth Paul, but Nero must throw Rome into flames to find the true image of himself. Miles of embers and ashes, more black and ill-shapen than the statues, temples, and palaces of his calcined capital might picture him, every arch broken, every pillar fallen, every altar crumbled. Rome was swept by its calamitous fire, July 19, A. D. 64. It began in the eastern part of the city, and burned on before an east wind for six days, then died out for want of fuel, when a second fire broke out in the western part, and a west wind took what the first had not reached. Six districts out of fourteen were entirely destroyed, and four were seriously damaged, leaving but four intact. The most memorable monuments of antiquity were swept away. The city was thrown into a panic, when the belief seized it that Nero was the incendiary, that ruffians had applied the torch at his command, and that he had simply amused himself on the tower of his palace by enacting the 'Destruction of Troy,' in the light of the conflagration. Then, wild rage threatened not only his throne but his life. History has made it clear that he was at Actium, between thirty and forty miles from Rome, when the fire began, but suggests that absence was a cover for his plot, for the pagan writers, generally, lay the crime at his door. He hastened to the city, and distributed money in the smoking streets, to allay the excitement. The Christians interpreted the fire as a divine judgment on the city, and Tacitus accuses them of lighting the flame. But he also charged them with being so fanatical a sect, that they 'hated the human race,' and so must be suppressed at all risk. We can depend but little on his authority in this matter. Nero pretended to deal with them as incendiaries, to transfer the odium from himself; but the people believed him guilty of using them as a screen to hide his face from the fire. At times the Jews had been turbulent, and the government had suppressed them; and now he found in their fellow-sect a convenient scape-goat, on the charge that they sought the overthrow of the national faith and existence, by burning the capital.

He issued edicts against them, condemning them to death, but still the people held him guilty of the crime. Many were seized as victims, were enwrapped in oil or pitch; Rome was invited to the imperial gardens, and crowds gloated their eyes on the poor wretches who were burnt, while Nero played the clown as a charioteer in a horse-race. Others were crucified, possibly in contempt of Christ's death, were wrapped in the skins of beasts and torn to pieces by dogs, or impaled, death being let loose upon them in every form. The fury of the people was drawn from himself and allayed for a time, but reacting pity soon demanded that the brutal slaughter should stop. To replenish his coffers and rebuild Rome he confiscated the estates of many nobles, which led to a conspiracy against him; but he plunged deeper and deeper into depravity and buffoonery, till all classes became disgusted, especially the provincial armies and the Greeks. To appease them he rebuilt Rome in a new style of architecture, leaving the image of voluptuous Greece upon its face, by thousands of ornaments and statues stolen from that country. He built for himself his Golden House, covering a large part of the burnt district, appropriating enormous inclosures for gardens, galleries, baths, bridges, and fish-ponds; until he convinced Rome that he had burned the city to make room for this world of mansions. Gloom settled upon the popular temper and revolt followed. This made him desperate, and in his mad efforts to retain his grasp of power he swung from the flatteries of hope to the remorse of despair, exposing the nakedness of his character, until he drew upon him the contempt of the Empire. Like a lunatic he went to Greece to conciliate it by becoming a petty actor, in a cracked voice publicly rehearsing doggerel, accompanied by clownish contortions. This he repeated in the theater, circus, and games of Rome; at one time, before 200,000 of the rabble, in the Circus Maximus. Then he boasted that at last he was 'lodged as a man,' and not as a beast, in his new Golden House, until the mob surged against its gates; when rending his vestments and tearing his hair he cried: 'I have neither friend nor foe left.' After this he played the craven, and would have taken poison, had not the casket in which he kept it been stolen.

Pale with fear and rage, he took horse by night and fled four miles without the walls, hiding himself in the house of one of his freedmen. Here his spirit was shattered, he gratefully accepted a cup of water and a crust, and a few hours brought his death-warrant; for the Senate decreed him an enemy to the State, and sentenced him to death 'in the ancient way.' He asked what this phrase meant, and when told that he must be stripped bare, his neck fastened in the forked limb of a tree, and his body beaten with rods, a horrible terror seized him. He then took a pair of daggers from his bosom, and finding that their edge was keen, he could not force himself to pierce his marble heart. Soon he heard the tramp of horses, but before the avenger clutched him, he bade his slave force the blade home. The Roman guard caught his eye, and another moment had put him in their power; but the imperial monster was dead. His body was

PAUL PREACHING.

burnt on the spot and his ashes left with his minions, as if to ratify the imprecating curse of his mother, who fell before her murderer crying: 'Strike the womb which bore a monster.'

The great Apostle had passed away before Nero, but how differently from this mass of royal leprosy. As his head was laid on the block, he saw a glittering crown awaiting him. Nero pitied the world that could not prize him and wished to kill himself, yet dared not do the world that one act of justice; but Paul went singing, 'I am now ready to be offered.' Nero took his wreath of thorns, Paul bowed his head to receive his crown of glory from the 'Righteous Judge.' And while all that was left of the Emperor was a heap of smoldering ashes without a sepulcher, the monument of the great Apostle is found in the regenerated and baptized communities which he established for all lands and all time.

At this point it may be desirable to speak of the other Apostles, especially of Peter and John, and of the principles and practices which they laid down. At Chartres, a great artist has given his insignia of the Twelve Apostles, in a series of enamels found in the Church of St. Peter. He represents Andrew with a cross, shaped like the letter X, John with a cup, Peter with keys, and Paul with a sword, as an armed soldier of Christ. Whatever may be the merit of this artistic legend in other cases, it truly indicates Paul's bold calling, that he might please Him who had chosen him to be a soldier. Yet, his brethren also fulfilled their mission boldly and faithfully. According to the best authority at command, Peter, James, and John labored principally amongst the Jews, scattered abroad in all nations. From the first, these unwittingly became the protectors of the Christians, whom they persecuted. We have seen that Palestine stood in the center of the then known world. The highways which held Asia and Africa together touched the Holy Land, and commerce found its course flowing through Philistia and Phœnicia. On the south, Arabia led to the Gulf of Elath, the east opened to the Euphrates, the Persian Gulf, and all Southern Asia. For centuries the Jews had dispersed themselves over all these lands. In the time of Christ they numbered 80,000 in Rome, in Egypt they formed an eighth of the population, and they had penetrated west not only to Germany and Spain, but to Britain. They partook of the new life around them, but retained their individuality. Yet, they became somewhat weaned from their old Temple ritual, their synagogues infused a democratic spirit into their religion, and they came to depend less upon sacerdotalism, and more upon the study and interpretation of their Sacred Books. True, they still paid the Temple tax, sent sacrifices to its altars, and occasionally visited Jerusalem; but their synagogues and Scriptures were herald missionaries of the Gospel amongst all pagan peoples.

Besides this, they became the great money dealers and wheat factors of the world. In fiscal transactions they so far outwitted the Roman knights, the bankers of the day, that complaints were made to the Emperor that they drained Asia Minor of its money; and in Egypt they nearly held a monopoly in breadstuffs. Juvenal said, 'The Jews sell every thing;' and Strabo, 'It is not easy to find a place in the habitable world which has not received this race, and is not possessed by it.' Roman law specially exempted them from military duty and certain taxes, and left them free to enjoy their religion. They traveled without hinderance, were wealthy, and formed communities of great influence in universal society; although hated every-where for their exclusive faith, they were every-where felt and feared. For purity of morals their lives were unique, and in great contrast with the pagans; for what was sacred to the one, the other detested. They looked upon the Gentiles as 'dogs,' and the dogs held them in contempt. As a chosen race, they thought themselves superior, and because they looked for universal dominion by their Messiah, the Romans scouted them as ridiculous dreamers. In A. D. 19, public indignation compelled Tiberius to recruit his army from the Jews in Rome; yet, Seneca, who was then living, says, that 'The vanquished have given laws to the victors;' not an unusual thing. Of course, their synagogues were so many meeting places for inquiry amongst those who were weary of the gods, influential people in every city embraced Judaism, and many women of the highest Roman families became proselytes. One step more led them to the Gospel.

For a long time the Romans looked upon the Christians as a mere sect of the Jews, and gave them the same privileges. Hence, Judaism, like a gnarled and sturdy oak, while it shaded the young sprout at its foot and refused it the sun, shielded it from storms until it could stand defiantly alone. A well-known bird lays its eggs in the nest of another, and its offspring is raised with the strange brood, and thus the Gospel was nourished under the wing of Judaism; which in this manner prepared the way of the Apostles. In their great missionary circuits they were much like the planets, making their course singly, with occasional conjunctions, but very infrequent. Peter, for example, is not mentioned in the Acts after the fifteenth chapter, leaving the impression that when he had used 'The Keys' at Pentecost, and in the house of Cornelius, his special work was done. We know but little of his missionary life, excepting through his Epistles and an occasional reference to him in those of Paul; so that, when tradition undertakes to complete his biography, we must take its statements with great caution. The Scripture outline of him is extremely Oriental, and no incident is more thoroughly so than that given by Luke in describing his visit to the house of Mary, after his release from prison. In true Eastern style he knocks two or three times and then waits to listen, when one from within asks 'Who?' without opening the door. Standing outside he answers, 'I—open.' Then his name is demanded, which he gives, but continues knocking, according to usage, till the servant-maid, Rhoda, ran to her mistress and reported, leaving the door unopened still. She knew his voice, 'and told how Peter stood before the gate.' This, and other peculiarities, marked him in his entire ministry. He had been specially fitted for an Apostle to the circumcision, for having lived on the Jewish side of the middle wall of partition, he knew only that side of the world. He was warm, courageous, practical; but was not naturally endowed with that genius, reflective faculty, and profound sagacity, which of the twain made Paul a 'new man.' He was confined to a narrower sphere, and showed greater reluctance to abandon Jewish ordinances, although he triumphed over this at last, and did a great work for Christ amongst the Twelve Tribes.

But his personal intimacy with Jesus is sweetly visible all through his life, for he speaks of him with great vividness as an 'eye-witness' of his ministry. His great Apostolic heart seems to throb in its full integrity when he says: 'We did eat and drink with him;' 'Whom having not seen ye love;' a 'Witness of the sufferings of Christ.' Then, his quenchless love for his nation is visible in his perpetual reference to her institutions and symbols, which he freely borrows to set forth the Christian Church. She is 'the chosen generation, the royal priesthood, the peculiar people.' With this feeling in his heart he long remained in Judea and about the western coast of Palestine; but love for them drew him farther East, to the 'scattered strangers' in Asia. 'The Church that is in Babylon salutes you,' which word we take in its literal sense, as we accept the names of other cities from which Epistles were sent. For centuries Babylon had been a great Eastern center for Jews, and under Parthian tolerance Peter could labor there with impunity. The Churches in that region date back to a very early period, which leaves little doubt that he was their founder. This accounts for the presence of Mark and Sylvanus with him in that capital. After Paul's Second Missionary Journey we hear no more of Sylvanus, but when Paul was first imprisoned in Rome, he tells the Colossians that Mark was about to visit them (Col. iv, 10), and afterward he speaks of him as with Timothy at Ephesus (2 Tim. iv, 11); this being the period when Peter wrote his first Epistle, and accounts for Mark's presence with him in Babylon.

At the best, Peter's closing years are lost in gloomy traditions and floating romance, created to endow him with a supremacy above his brethren, which he never claimed, which Christ never bestowed, and which never belonged to him. Probably Luke suddenly quenched his historical lamp, as a protection to him when State persecution arose, to leave his whereabouts and doings in darkness. For when Christian records and correspondence intended for Christian eyes, only came to public light under 'informers,' the most innocent matter compromised the best of men. Even the writers of the first three Gospels observe a marked reticence of Peter's name in recording that 'a disciple' cut off the ear of Malchus, in Gethsemane. Only John tells us that it was Peter, and not he till the impetuous Apostle was safe in heaven, and the High-priest's palace empty of the man who owned the ear as well as of his master. Had Luke put on record where each Apostle was, and what he was doing, he would only have discovered them to the malignity of their foes, when one unguarded word would have drawn more brutal cruelties upon their heads. Their lives, therefore, float on the wings of fiction, and we do injustice to ourselves and to them when we rely on this or that legend to set forth their labors and death; an imposition upon our credulity for an unworthy end.

All fables to the contrary, it is more than questionable whether Peter ever saw Rome. The claim that he introduced the Gospel there, labored for some time in company with Paul, and suffered martyrdom in that city with him, cannot be sustained by one word from the New Testament, or any thing like reliable history. At Pentecost, 'strangers of Rome, Jews and proselytes' heard Peter preach. These were native-born Jews, converts from the pagans to the Jewish faith, and visitors at the feast; so that there is no great stretch of probability in supposing that they took Christianity back with them to Rome, and won their families and friends to Christ on their return. Every religion of the East was found in the capital, and it is likely, in the nature of things, that Christianity made its way there earlier than to many of the provinces. It is not known who introduced the Gospel into Rome. As at Antioch, some simple disciple, not an Apostle, seems to have secured this honor. Probably it was there as early as A. D. 51, for a well-established Church is found by Paul at Puteoli, the port of Rome, A. D. 60–62. Paul addressed his Epistle to the Church in Rome A. D., 58, in which many passages show, that it had been constituted of both Jews and Gentiles, especially of Greeks, whose names are given in the salutations as persons well-known in that Church. In this Epistle Paul makes no allusion to Peter, a negative which could scarcely have occurred if he had either established or fostered that Church. Even if Hippolytus had not shown, that long after Peter's death it retained its democratic character and simplicity, there is nothing in this Epistle which hints that Peter was ever the pastor of Rome, much less that his supremacy dignified it in any way. Eusebius states the tradition that he went there A. D. 42, and remained twenty-five years; but this is in direct contradiction of Luke, who shows that he lived in Jerusalem A. D. 44 (Acts xii), and labored in Cæsarea and Antioch A. D. 48–50. Acts x. Peter himself punctured the bubble on which this figment of supremacy rests, when he gave express testimony to Christ as the Corner-stone, saying: 'Other foundation can no man lay than that is laid, which is CHRIST JESUS.' Too well did Peter remember that he was cursing, swearing, and falsifying his Lord on the day that Jesus gave himself for his Church, to convince himself that he was the fit material upon which to build a stable and spotless Church. Nor does the Council at Jerusalem yield this picture any support. Peter spoke in that assembly, but he neither called it together, nor presided over its deliberations, nor took its voice, nor gave its decision, nor assumed superiority over his brethren in any respect.

When Peter asked our Lord at the Supper Table, 'Whither goest thou?' Jesus answered, 'Whither I go thou canst not follow me *now*, but thou shalt follow me afterward;' evidently alluding to his own crucifixion and Peter's. Again Jesus prophesied Peter's crucifixion in the words: 'When thou shalt be old, thou shalt stretch forth thy hands, and another shall gird thee, and lead thee whither thou wouldest not. This he spoke signifying by what manner of death he should glorify God;' and it settles the mode of Peter's death, but the time and place are not alluded to in the New Testament. Fable fixes them at Rome, under Nero, and many great names have subscribed to it, as well as to the notion, that at his own request he was executed with his head downward, as a sign of his humiliation for denying Christ. This part of the story probably arises from the fact, that Roman soldiers nailed their victims to the cross in any attitude which derision inspired. The object of all these fictions is apparent; they are created to exalt the see of Rome above all other Churches.

The New Testament gives us but few facts concerning the Apostle John and his missionary toils, after the third chapter of the Acts. In the immediate morning of Christianity he stands forth with great prominence; and when all the other Apostles had finished their work his sun bursts forth anew, after an obscurity of about forty years, to gild the setting century with a peculiar splendor. While Peter was doing his great work in the beginning, and Paul his, in the middle of this period, God did strangely hide the venerable John, and only brought him to light again after the fall of Jerusalem. Jesus had foretold John's long life in the word: 'If I will that he tarry till I come, what is that to thee?' Not alluding to his coming at the end of time, as the silly legend of the 'Wandering Jew' interprets his words, but to his visitation in the overthrow of the Jewish capital and nation, A. D. 70. Paul speaks of John as 'a pillar' in the Church at Jerusalem, when himself and Barnabas held their interview there with the Apostles. Tradition locates John's labors chiefly in Parthia and Ephesus, and his Epistles indicate that his mind was engrossed in the study of those Gnostic errors which began to infest the Churches on the foundation doctrines of the Gospel. His writings suggest many reasons why these years were spent in reverent thought and less activity than those of his brethren, a serenity which educated and mellowed him for a special calling when theirs was fulfilled. When our Lord hung upon the cross he confided his mother, as a special trust, to the keeping of John, and fidelity to this trust may have confined his early labors to Palestine and the Hebrews. John xix, 26, 27. Still, the Apocalypse clearly connects him with missionary toil in Asia Minor. His long experience, ripe age, and close walk with God, qualified him to gather up and more fully organize what the zeal of Peter and Paul had produced, and to give a calm solidity to the kingdom of Christ. He was compelled to combat errorists in the Churches after Paul's death, but although they treated him malignantly, he well filled Paul's place in defending the truth. The extraordinary gifts appear to have passed away, and we are left to infer what new light the Spirit threw upon the organization of the Churches through John.

Jesus breathed his personal life into the first movements of the Gospel; and, for his great resemblance to Christ, John was reserved as the last of the Apostles, to bring out perfectly Christ's deepest teachings. In their first love, the Churches were not ripe for this calm result, and John was to close the august age as the other Apostles could not have done. The methods of each were necessary to the full establishment of the truth, but even John needed a new vision from God, in order to qualify it for its sublime destinies. Hence, he soars and sings of Christ's triumphs in the Apocalypse, of his perfect humanity in his Epistles, and of his glorious deity in the Fourth Gospel. John is called 'the divine,' however, not with the modern idea of a theologian, but as a true Theologus, who gives unclouded and sublime testimony to Christ as the 'Word of God.' His writings imply that persecution drove him from Ephesus to Patmos, some think under Domitian, but more likely under Nero. The place indicates his arrest in Asia, as Patmos is one of the group of scattered islands in the south-east part of the Ægean Sea. This prison of the illustrious exile was about thirty miles in circumference, and very sterile. It was rough, overhung with cliffs, full of fissures and caverns, and here and there dotted with a scrubby olive, cypress or palm; a fitting scene for the revelation which he received. When the ship which left him in this awful solitude had sunk below the horizon, the sad silence in his soul was broken by the cry of his perishing brethren who were being put to death, and he looked for every new billow to bring some brother Apostle safely to this dreary rock. Night and day, the splash of the waves, the scream of the eagle, the howl of the winds, were the only sounds which he heard, save the echo of his own foot-fall and the throb of his own heart, as he rested in some den which the sea had scooped out for his home. Did he dream of Jesus there? Did the hard rock remind him by contrast of Christ's soft bosom? Was he wakened in his ease by the blast of trumpets; alone, yet not alone? Possibly, the 'seven golden lamps' flamed in his prison, a Man in shining garments stood before him, girt not with a 'towel,' but with 'a golden girdle;' and his countenance 'as the sun shining in his strength.' John 'fell at his feet as dead.' He had seen that face before, when purple with blows and stained with blood, and when he bade him go and '*speak* the words of this life.' He had also known Tabor, and so, when Jesus 'laid his right hand upon' him, and bid him take the *pen*, he was endued with new power to 'write' his glory.

That touch clothed the Apostle with new energy, a new literature flooded his mind, a new dialect moved his hand, and on the withered palm, or plaintain, his *stylus* traced a new story. Had the sea emptied its abyss and thrown all its gems on the shore, had the heavens hung all their lights over the black isle, had all history thrown its allegory before him, these had formed one mass of dazzling poverty when likened to the wondrous things written in the prophecy of this Book. What new veracities swell his sentences, what new realities enlarge his soul. He introduces the era of martyrdom, and builds the stage for the drama of redemption, and Rome, the first figure that reels over it, drunk with the blood of the saints. Then come thunders, and lightnings, and wrath. Mad prophets follow, and corrupt sorcerers, and horrid blasphemers. A scroll of registered woes is unrolled. Then a hallowed urn empties its fire, when whirlwinds roar through the orifice of heaven, and the bottomless pit is emptied. After this the rattling of chains is heard in his grot, and Satan is bound. Figures, dark and dreadful, fly before a volley of curses, for a cluster of falling stars lights them to their native hell. The most solemn imagery flits in cavalcade before the eye of the holy seer. A black horse and a balance,—a red horse and a sword,—a pale horse and a specter,—a white horse,—'and he who sat on him had a bow, and a crown was given to him, and he went forth conquering and to conquer.' Above all, the black cloud of imperial persecution is spanned with a rainbow, on which light from the cross began to glow; for the Conqueror rode past a blood-besprinkled altar, and a procession of burning ones came forth, in white robes, with palms in their hands. These were led by the 'faithful martyr Antipas,' and Patmos was enshrined in glory. Then there broke forth a chorus all around the ribbed island, like the sound of the Ægean lashing it in a storm, saying: 'The kingdom of this world is become our Lord's, and his Christ's; and he shall reign for ever and ever!'

This revelation of Christ's glory to John was meet. When young, he was the only Apostle who clung to his Master's cross on Calvary, and because he was willing to lose his life he saved it. He was the only one of the Twelve who died a natural death, bathed in glory while putting many crowns on that Saviour's head on whose bosom he had rested his own, more than half a century before. It was meet that this disciple of the Baptist, who first met Jesus by the baptismal waters in the valley of the Jordan, should be the last Apostle of the Lamb to proclaim him on his throne in the New Jerusalem. He had no clearer perceptions at the first that Jesus was pre-existent, having come from the bosom of the Father, than had his brethren. But when error attacked Christ's person, both in his flesh and deity, the beautiful old saint came to his Master's defense, not as Peter, with a sword in dark Gethsemane, but with his more powerful pen, in his living Epistles and Gospel. The fullest revelation was given when the Church needed it the most. Probably he was the youngest of all the Apostles at the time of his conversion, and as he outlived them all by a quarter of a century, he had seen the Gospel in all its phases. Now, his tremulous hands were the only ones left to 'handle the Word of Life.' When young, he was a son of thunder, full of fire and narrow prejudices; but now he had become meek as his Master, and broad as his Gospel.

Amongst the many traditions concerning him, this is in such harmony with his character as to seem probable. It is reported, that when extreme age and infirmity rendered him unable to preach or even to stand, he still retained all his powers of love. So, he was frequently brought to the Church at Ephesus, when he would spread out his hands in its gatherings and say: 'Little children, love one another. Keep yourselves from idols.' The time and circumstances of his death are unknown, but the date is conjectured at from A. D. 98 to 100. During his life the Gospel had extended over large portions of Europe, Asia, and Africa; but the missionary spirit was hindered, for Christianity was compelled to don its armor for a conflict with the errors which arose in its own bosom, for which the Apostles prepared many antidotes before they fell asleep.

John wrote his three Epistles after he had seen Christianity in all its struggles and stages of development. Through the first century the Churches had been reaping the great harvest of revealed truth. As the disciple of the Baptist, he was among the first to put in the sickle, and now he was spared to bind up its last sheaf. The winsome trait of his old age is seen in one of the last acts in life, when simple, gracious love prompted him to send an inspired Epistle to an Elect Lady; for now it

IN AGE AND FEEBLENESS EXTREME. 113

was needful that the women who filled the baptized Churches should be recognized 'in the truth,' for 'the truth's sake.' Paul had sent four sacred books to individual men, but from Moses down no sacred writer had addressed one to a woman. In youth the natural vehemence of John had earned for him the appellation, Son of Thunder. The unlovely heat of his spirit had prompted him to ask his Master whether he should not call for fire from heaven to consume a Samaritan village which had rejected his message, when the rebuke of Jesus told him that he was ignorant of his own spirit. Possibly he inherited this fiery ambition from Salome, his honored mother, who wished her two sons to sit as prime ministers at the right and left of the Messiah, on a political throne. But John had learned more heavenly

THEATER AT EPHESUS—SEEN BY PAUL AND JOHN.

lessons on Jesus' bosom, at his cross and tomb. Then, he had sheltered Mary, the revered mother of Jesus, under his own roof, and had been as a 'nursing father' to the Ephesian Church. All these, under the influence of the Holy Spirit, had mellowed him and qualified him to write in hallowed strains to an Elect Lady for her confirmation in the New Commandment, 'which we heard from the beginning.'

Tradition assigns the labors of Matthew (Levi) to Ethiopia, and different parts of Asia; Philip to Phrygia, in Asia Minor; Thomas to Parthia; Andrew to Syria, Thrace, and Achaia; Thaddeus to Persia or Arabia; Bartholomew (Nathanael) is said to have labored in India; Simon (Zelotes) in Egypt and Lydia; and Matthias in Ethiopia. But of this there is not reliable evidence; the record of their life and death, aside from the New Testament account, numbers the band of glorious worthies with the hidden ones of our Lord.

CHAPTER IX.

THE APOSTOLIC CHURCHES THE ONLY MODEL FOR ALL CHURCHES.

WE now come to the task of setting forth the great principles on which the Christian Churches stood at the close of the Apostolic Age; for these are to be copied as the exact model to the end of time. Our chief work is to find what this model was; as the inner and divine life of those Churches molded their entire organization. When we have determined this standard, we may easily see how far it has been followed or abandoned by succeeding Churches. Many misconceptions arise in Church history from the failure to stop at this point, and to thoroughly weigh the divine history of the Churches before proceeding to consider the human. It is lamentable to witness the haste and light treatment with which this age is passed over, as if the New Testament history were but the starting-point in the great story, to be disposed of as casually as possible; whereas, it is the end of all controversy in the matter of Church life.

In this way the course of Church history is inverted, and the human record is made to falsify and cover up the divine. The true historian must fix his eye steadfastly at the beginning of his work, upon the New Testament pattern, and never remove it; because it is the only guide to truth in every age, and the only authority of ultimate appeal. An exact likeness, therefore, of the Apostolic Churches should be sought at the outset, as the test to which every position and fact in the whole investigation must be brought back and tried. We never can be wrong in following the pattern found in the Constitution of the Apostolic Churches; for here we find an impervious shield for the true ecclesiastical rights of all Christian men. If we make the Apostolic Churches the mere stepping-stone to the investigation, instead of finding in them the standard of all true fact, how can we measure our way through the centuries, or exhibit their wide differences, without confounding all their real distinctions? Hatch goes to the root of this matter when he says: 'The virtue of a canonist is the vice of a historian. Historical science, like all science, is the making of distinctions; and its primary distinctions are those of time and space. . . . The history of Christianity covers more than three fourths of the whole period of the recorded history of the Western World. It goes back, year by year, decade by decade, century by century, for more than fifty generations. If we compare what we are and what we believe, the institutions under which we live, the literature which we prize, the ideas for which we contend in this present year, with the beliefs, the institutions, the literature, the prevalent ideas of a hundred years ago, we shall begin to realize the difference between one century and another of these eighteen centuries of Christian history. The special difficulty of studying any such period of history arises from the fact that the centuries which are remote from our own, seem, in the long perspective, to be almost indistinguishable. . . . Between the third century and the fourth, for example, or between the fourth and the fifth, there seems to all but scholars who have trod the ground, to be a hardly appreciable difference. If a writer quotes in the same breath Eusebius and Sozomen, or St. Hilary of Poitiers and St. Leo the Great, he seems to many persons to be quoting coeval or nearly coeval authorities. And yet, in fact, between each of these authorities there is an interval of a hundred years of life and movement, of great religious controversies, of important ecclesiastical changes. The point is not merely one of accuracy of date; it is rather that usages and events have at one time as compared with another a widely varying significance. For different centuries have been marked in ecclesiastical as in social history by great differences in the drift and tendency of ideas.'[1]

For these reasons, if for none other, we must bring every event in whatever century, every drift, tendency and change, of whatever character, back to the law and the testimony of the New Testament, and must measure it by the life and letter of the Apostolic Churches, or we shall run the risk of substituting the vile for the precious and the spurious for the genuine, in Christian history. The foundation principles then, that we find in these divine organizations, are these, namely:

I. THAT THE WORD OF GOD WAS THEIR ONLY RULE OF FAITH AND PRACTICE. During the last half of the first century, this rule was perfected by the completion of the New Testament. From A. D. 52 to the close of the century, each Epistle was received as authority by the Church or person to whom it was sent; and copies were used by interchange amongst the Churches, until their contents became generally known, and took rank with the Old Testament. Of necessity, the remoter Churches did not possess all the books, and some might not have reached them until they were collected in one canon. All their doctrine and practice were gained either from the Old Testament, from the direct influences of the Holy Spirit orally, or by these new books. The first century presents Christianity in its fullness and freshness, its variety and unity; and all its revelations ceased with the death of the Apostle John. After the order of nature, the New Testament gave the Apostolic Churches no systematic formula of doctrine, but left a happy liberty in its expression which reached the truth in other ways. It was centuries afterward before any thing was known of scientific theology; so that millions of souls came to the full truth as it is in Jesus without this. A systematic theology has been helpful to many thinkers, while others have been hindered thereby in reaching Christ personally, because they could see only so much of him as was discernible through the system, which was largely a net-work of human propositions. Perhaps, this is unavoidable, as human interpretations constantly change; but the Apostolic Churches were founded on primary truth, as it is found, and ever will be found, in the Inspired Text.

Words without Bible knowledge have so often darkened New Testament counsels, that it is wonderful that men have discovered Christ at all as a living Saviour, by the teaching of many modern Churches. But often, a true heart takes men farther Christ-ward than even a true head; and so Bible truth is ever proving its divinity by doing this great saving work. But still, wherever a human standard is set up in place of the Scriptures, it is always more jealously preserved than the teachings of revelation. A fanatic who corrupts the word of God is more heartily fellowshiped by many modern Churches, than he who opposes human decrees and inventions against the Scripture; while he who insists upon obedience to their authority, excites the greatest possible odium, because, to do this wounds the pride of man. Men pay a great price for saying, that the right to legislate for Christian Churches belongs to Christ alone. Yet, he has given his law in the Bible, and every form of Church life that is not in accordance with that law, directly sets it aside. So then, in a very important sense, it partakes of disloyalty to say that Christ has not made sufficient provision for his Churches in the Scriptures, in every thing that affects their well-being.

We have seen that the only appeal made to authority by the founders of the Apostolic Churches was, to the truth as it is found in the Old Testament, the teachings and acts of Christ, and the direct inspirations of the Holy Spirit. In the Epistle to the Hebrews alone, there are thirty-four quotations from the Old Testament, while in that to the Romans there are forty-eight. Christ and his Apostles always appeal directly to the Law, the Prophets, and the Psalms, and to their co-relative sentiments, facts and precedents, where they are applicable; and where they are not applicable, a new revelation was granted. They always cite the Old Testament as the direct word of God, or of the Holy Spirit, by such forms of speech as these: 'It is written,' 'God says,' or 'Isaiah,' or 'Moses saith.' The Apostolic Churches were never allowed to fall into the dangerous popular notions of modern times, namely: That all religious teaching is simply an opinion, which happens to be held differently by certain bodies of men. Such an assumption makes mere Church doctrine a powerful weapon, and gives life to all that falls under the sacramental system; which itself is based upon human dogma and patristic belief. This makes the Church and not the Bible the standard of faith and obedience; and men come to be satisfied with the substitution after this form: 'We believe the whole revealed dogma as taught by the Apostles—as committed by them to the Church—and as declared by the Church to us.' And, it follows, of course, that the Scriptures were intended to prove doctrine, but not to teach it, for that the Church is to teach it through its creeds and formulas. This doctrine shifts the whole standard of authority from the Bible to antiquity, makes antiquity the true exponent of Christianity, and forbids all appeal from its traditions to divine authority. Thus, tradition nullifies the law of Christ, by making it a dream, a sentiment and finally a mockery.

The very reverse of this was the law in the Apostolic Churches. In the hands of this human, mystical and sacramental principle, sacraments become the expression of great truths in human language; and the doctrine is fostered that material phenomena become the instrument of communicating unseen things, to which the mind of man is unequal; as if water could purge away the pollutions of sin, or bread and wine could give eternal life, and so nature becomes a parable, and revelation an allegory. The inevitable consequence is, a Church armed with awfully mysterious sacraments and rites as channels of saving grace, and with a narrow religious teaching founded on the will of the Church, as she chooses to define it from time to time. After that, of course, the Rule of Faith is found in the Catholic teaching of the early centuries—in the decrees of councils—and in sanctioned usages. At this point, the right of private judgment is entirely cut off, because a new power has been created on earth which is competent to push aside the individual right to reason and judge about the demands of Divine Truth, as its facts and exactions assert themselves. That right once yielded, the Church claims to judge infallibly for all men on all religious questions; and it must be obeyed without a word. Independency of mind being thus destroyed, paralysis of the intellect follows, the courage of the soul dies with its liberty, discussion becomes dangerous; and so, all must submit and be silent, as it is safe to yield to absolute authority where one dare not dissent. The final consequence is, that it becomes a crime to claim the personal right to obey that truth which rests on the sole authority of the Inspired Word.

Yet, this fact is perfectly clear, namely: That the New Testament contains all that entered into the faith and practice of the Apostolic Churches. Whether it contains little or much, it covers all that they had, and all that we have, which has any claim on the Churches of Christ. It is the only revealed record of Christian truth. It is stamped with the divine character, and it utterly excludes every species of authority from uninspired sources. Its authority stands out alone, and will allow of no parallel or supplementary authority whatever, however venerable. The most revered antiquity stands on purely human ground, without any thing in common with the New Testament, when that antiquity is not in the Holy Book. The age of a custom is one thing, its nature is another. The question of time merely has nothing to do with authority. When the line is drawn between the close of inspiration and all after-time, what follows stands upon another and a lower level, and can be no authority whatever. Even the Roman Catholic body admits this, in the claim that inspiration is still needful and is continued in her deliberations and decisions; hence, that they are of equal value with the New Testament. The purest and best of the ancient fathers, being outside of the finality of Bible inspiration, are outside forever; and, for the purposes of authority are no nearer to the fountain of truth than are the investigators of our day. As witnesses to the facts which occurred in their own times, they are to be prized, as truthful men who deposed to facts, but nothing more; for then as now the demand was inexorable, 'To the law and to the testimony.' Wherever the fathers deflect from this standard, their testimony is of no more nor less value than that of other uninspired men.

II. IN THE APOSTOLIC AGE, THE CHURCH WAS A LOCAL BODY; AND EACH CHURCH WAS ENTIRELY INDEPENDENT OF EVERY OTHER CHURCH. The simple term *'Ecclesia'* designates one congregation, or organized assembly, and no more, this being its literal and primal meaning. Our Lord himself designated such a society by the Aramaic word *ghiedto*, meaning a congregation; answering to the Greek *'Ecclesia,'* which is translated by it in the Aramaic version of the Old and New Testaments. These words are exactly equivalent in meaning.[2] The Septuagint renders the Hebrew word for congregation by the word *'Ecclesia,'* where it designates three specific bodies: 1. A whole people collectively. Ezra ii, 64, 'The whole *congregation* together was forty-two thousand three hundred and three-score.' 2. A general assembly of the people. 'A very great congregation.' Neh. v, 7. 'In the day of the assembly.' Deut. ix, 10. 3. A company of persons associated for religious purposes. 1 Sam. xix, 20. 'Company of the prophets.' Psa. lxviii, 26. 'In companies they bless God.' Joel ii, 16. 'Sanctify the congregation;' 'Solemn assembly.' Lev. xxiii, 36, and elsewhere, is the translation of a different word. This word *'Ecclesia'* was borrowed from the Greek translation and naturalized into Christianity. Jesus and his Apostles used it with the strictest regard to its etymology, and if we would catch their meaning in its use, we must interpret it by its primitive sense. Its contemporary use in common secular life answered exactly to its sacred use. When Jesus first used it to characterize an association of Christian believers, all sorts of voluntary societies were common throughout the Roman Empire, in the form of clubs and guilds, for trade, sports, finance, literature and mutual help; all of which were known as the 'Ecclesia' of those times. Whether secular bodies existed in Palestine in our Lord's day, under this name, is not known, but the synagogues were known by this title. Amongst the Greco-Romans, however, the large number and importance of secular bodies called *'Ecclesia,'* demanded special governmental legislation, defining their powers and limits, as a guard to the public weal. After a time the Roman authorities came so to understand the primary constitution of the Christian congregations, as to bring them under the general law which regulated all other voluntary associations.[3]

When our Lord appropriated this secular word to a sacred body, he threw no sacred meaning into the term itself, but retained it in its common application. The popular *'Ecclesia,'* in a free Greek city, was formed of those who were selected or called out, under the laws of citizenship for the transaction of public business. These qualified voters were convoked by the common criers, and formed the legal assembly for deliberation and decision in civic affairs, and their solemn decisions were binding. Of all the Greek terms which designate a calm and deliberative convocation, this was the most appropriate to characterize a body of Christians, charged by their Master with concerns of vast moment. Other words would have carried with them the idea of a crowd, of a show, or of a purely governmental assembly, such as the Senate; having other elements than that merely of a properly organized assembly. Certain passages of the New Testament have been wrested by the necessity of a hierarchy, to mean that all separate Christian congregations are grouped as an aggregate under the sense of this word. Christ is said to have founded his *'Ecclesia'* upon a rock, to be its Head, and to give it pastors and teachers; but this interpretation is foreign to the scope of the word, and loses sight entirely of the purely tropical sense couched in such passages. The trope must be expressed in exact accord with the literal sense from which it is borrowed. When Stephen speaks of the *'Ecclesia'* in the wilderness, the term evidently means the whole people assembled at the Tabernacle, as the commonwealth was not many assemblies, but only one gathered in the male population. So, when the New Testament speaks of the entire Christian community as one 'Ecclesia,' it simply uses a common *synecdoche*, by which the whole is put for a part or a part for the whole, as the case may be; the *genus* is put here for many individuals.

Consequently, when Jesus is called the Founder, the Head, the Redeemer of his *'Ecclesia,'* it is clearly meant, that what he is to one Christian congregation he is to all such congregations, the same severally and collectively. Exactly the same collective figure is used of a single Christian assembly, which is made up of many individuals. It 'is one body,' putting the one for the many, because each congregation is 'the flock,' the 'family,' the 'household' of Christ, and what is true of each such assembly is equally true of all. It follows, then, that the New Testament nowhere speaks of the 'Universal,' 'Catholic,' or 'Invisible Church,' as indicating a merely ideal existence, separate from a real and local body. There can be no distinction between the Church and the members who constitute the Church. Such a generalization is a mere ideality, incapable of organization under laws, doctrines, ordinances, and discipline. No man can be a member of such a body, because it can assume no responsibility either to God or man; it can have no representation, and no man can be a member of an assembly which it is impossible to represent. Everywhere, the Scripture *'Ecclesia'* is a tangible body, numbering so many by count, properly local and organized, and each congregation is as absolutely a Church as if there were not another on earth. But as there are more than one, and each is his 'body,' his 'flock;' his 'Church' is made up of every congregation, because he is equally the 'Head' and 'Shepherd' in each. The same thought which impels Paul to say, that believers 'are members of each other,' leads him to say of himself, personally, the same thing that he says of every Christian congregation: 'He loved *me*, and gave himself for *me*.' So, he says to the several Hebrew Christian congregations: 'Ye are come to a full assembly, to the *Ecclesia* of the first-born whose names are enrolled in heaven.' It is difficult to divest the mind of the merely human and modern thought, that aggregated congregations only form the body of which Jesus is the Head; but when this is done successfully, immediately the primitive idea of one congregation attaches to the term Church. A local organization fully expresses the meaning of the word *Ecclesia*, wherever it is found in Holy Writ.

In harmony with this thought, as Jesus and his Apostles expressed it, the Apostolic congregations are always spoken of in the New Testament as so many separate Churches; and groups of such congregations are designated as, the Churches in Asia, Achaia, or Macedonia, in the plural number. Our English word Church is from the Saxon *kirik*, changing the *c* hard to *ch;* and this word, as the Scotch use it, is from the Greek *kuriou oikos*, 'house of the Lord.' Even the word Church, then, uncorrupted, is not a term which expresses a sensibility or a figment, but a material substance; that is, an assembly of rational beings among whom God dwells.

As to government, no man can properly say that Christ laid down no definite laws for the government of his Churches, simply because he did not give those laws a prescriptive form. Oneness of faith and practice worked out the same results in all those Churches, and these are recorded in the New Testament as matters of fact. In conserving true Christian principles they needed no more than this in attaining their status, and what more do we need in reaching ours? Christ's positive law was written in these facts, just as the law of redemption is written in the facts of his birth, life, death and resurrection. In both cases, the facts embody his law for every age. In their vital regeneration as believing souls, and in their uniform organization, he gave the law of their constitution, to be kept, as changeless in the united body as the saving life was to be preserved in the individual member. He established his doctrines on divine principles, without the formula of a creed, and in like manner, the Holy Spirit instituted the order and discipline of the Churches on divine principles, without a code of formal precepts. In the framing of doctrines, the converting of members and the constitution of Churches, he followed the same order. The model of the New Testament Church is found in what he made it, in every portion of the total. A skilled naturalist takes the separate limbs and joints of a fossil, and by these, will give us its entire structure and functions, until we have an outline of the perfect organism. So, by carefully following the unfoldings of the New Testament, any man may trace the entire order of the New Testament Churches, as they reached completion from the hand of their Author and Finisher. They were the work of Christ, wrought through the Apostles, and not the product of Apostolic plans. Thus, as disconnected stars hanging over a dark sea show the doubting mariner his course, so the books of the New Testament, by their conjoint rays, give us a unity of truth as our guide in the matter of Church government.

The right of the Churches in the Apostolic Age to manage all their internal affairs, arose primarily from the fact that each congregation was perfect in itself for all the purposes of its own Church life. Whatever fraternal sympathy and fellowship it might crave, it was in itself the visible Church of Christ, and complete for all the ends of a visible Church. Of course, this Apostolic idea is at variance with all the popular notions of Church life as it exists to-day; but it is no less Apostolic on that account. Well does Dr. Carson remark, 'As to a visible Universal Church, it exists nowhere but in the ideas of polemical writers and the absurd distinctions of scholastic divinity.'[4] An invisible Church is a purely indefinite and mythical idea. How can we 'hear' the voice of an impalpable body of men? The New Testament never speaks of all Christians in all localities, as if they belonged to one outward and visible Church, which forms one corporate body. This is a pure myth existing only in the imagination. But the Apostolic Churches were local bodies that could be found and known and governed; and the wording of the New Testament is very minute on this point. Hence, these local Churches are never designated as the Church of God of this or that district, province or nation, but the Church 'in,' or 'at' such and such a place. Moreover, the Churches in all localities were organized after the same order; and there is no recorded instance of any one of them which was denied the right to regulate all its affairs.

Not only was *Ecclesia* a word in common use, as has been shown, to express a civil assembly, or association, as these were formed in all cities and circles, but it expressed a special cult, and often took a religious cast amongst the pagans. Ulhorn says: 'The burial clubs, the guilds of artisans, merchants, working men of various sorts, all of which gained increasing importance to society during the Empire, bore at the same time a religious tone. Each had some god or other as a patron, and was instituted in part for his worship. His image and altar stood in their place of assembly, and every meeting began with a sacrifice.'[5] We clearly see, then, that when the divine Founder of the Apostolic Churches incorporated this word *Ecclesia* into Christianity, he intended the usual sense of the word to limit its application in its new sphere to a local body of men. The only invisible Church that exists is embodied in the visible, local, and self-governing Church.

The Romish figment of an impersonal and invisible Church never existed until the fourth century, when it was created in order to bring the local Churches under the yoke of an irresponsible and arbitrary power, at the utter sacrifice of those divine rights, with which Christ, the rightful Head, had endowed the local Churches. The local Church was the only Church known to the Apostles themselves, the only body which they ever addressed, and which they knew collectively as the 'Churches scattered abroad.' The Church at Rome was made up of those who lived there, who were 'beloved of God, called to be saints'—that at Corinth of 'them that are sanctified in Christ Jesus'—and the Church at Ephesus 'of the faithful in Christ Jesus,' who lived there. Even those who attended worship with those Churches, but were not numbered with the believers, had nothing to do with their government. Only those who were born of God, and met in any one place for all the purposes of a Church under obedience to Christ's law, were the Christian Church in that place. There may have been more than one Church in a given city; but there is nothing in the New Testament to show, that one central body in that city governed all its Churches, if there was more than one.

The power of discipline being lodged in the local Church, all its members took part in its enforcement. The Corinthian case of incest is markedly in point here. 1 Cor. v, 4, requires the whole Church to meet and put the offender away, 'when ye are gathered together,' under the unseen headship of Jesus Christ. And when the offender repented and was readmitted to fellowship, the same sovereign tribunal which pronounced his sentence, pardoned and restored him. 2 Cor. ii, 6. The words which express the rights of these Churches, harmonize with the principles on which they were formed. The Epistles are not addressed to their officers, but to the Churches themselves, and none of these letters either deny the right of self-government to the Churches, or instruct another class or body to regard itself as higher than the Churches; but every thing was to be done by their will. The Churches held the supreme place in all things, each being expected to rectify its own evils; and no outside power is appealed to, to do this, nor is the local Church itself referred to others for their supervision. There was nothing that partook in the slightest degree of an Apostolic hierarchy, and no one Church ranked above another in control. Each Church was a society, a family, a republic in itself, forming a perfect sovereignty for the ends of self-government. Every foundation principle was laid down indeed by the precepts or example of Christ and the Holy Spirit, or by the Apostles, and nothing could be enforced without this sanction. So then, no legislative power was given to them, but only the power of administration. In minor and secondary matters, such judgment and prudence might be followed as were in harmony with the principles of Christ's law, but these were not to be enforced as obligatory, binding, or indispensable. They settled every question affecting their own welfare by an appeal to the truth, and without appeal to any other authority. It could not be that these powers were left anywhere but inviolably in the local Church, in which, by reason of its purely local character, no sacerdotal element could exist. There was no external bond of central unity between the Churches, which made them dependent in the slightest degree upon each other. They never met in a general association, synod, or assembly of any sort up to the close of the first century, though they might have consulted with each other if they had chosen to do so; exactly as the Church at Antioch consulted with the Church at Jerusalem, purely for fraternal purposes. But, on the contrary, they each followed the law of perfect liberty, holding one another in sisterly reverence, having a common faith, cherishing a common love, and knowing no other constraint than to keep the law of Christ, each amongst themselves.

III. EACH OF THE APOSTOLIC CHURCHES ELECTED ITS OWN PASTORS DIRECTLY, IN THE EXERCISE OF THEIR FREE SUFFRAGE. This they did by stretching forth their hands as the sign by which they cast their vote, as many deliberative bodies now cast their vote by the uplifted hand. This was the power of ordination, which was lodged in the local Church, which ordination consisted in their election. In the Apostolic Churches ordination did in no way consist in the laying on of hands; for the appointment of a man to the pastoral office was his ordination, with or without this. The laying on of hands was often connected with the setting of any one apart for office, or for a special service, but not always, in either of these cases. Our Lord 'ordained' his Apostles, but not by the laying on of hands. He observed this form when he healed the sick and blessed little children, because both these acts couched a special benediction. For the same reason it accompanied the bestowment of supernatural gifts, as when Peter and John laid their hands on the Samaritan believers, and they received the Holy Spirit (Acts viii, 17), and as when Timothy received the same 'gift given through prophesy, with the laying on of the hands of the eldership.' 1 Tim. iv, 14. So Paul, who had long been an Apostle, and had preached the Gospel abundantly, received the laying on of hands at Antioch, not to induct him into the Gospel ministry, but into a special missionary work on a special missionary journey. Acts xiii, 2, 3. Dr. Hacket says on this passage: 'Paul was already a minister and an Apostle (see Gal. i, 1, *seq*.), and by this service he and Barnabas were now merely set apart for the accomplishment of a specific work. They were summoned to a renewed and more systematic prosecution of the enterprise of converting the heathen.'

Again, sometimes the laying on of hands was attended by prayer, and sometimes it was not. But in time it became subject to abuses in common with other apostolic practices, some of which have continued unto this day. It became, in post-apostolic times, an efficacious accompaniment of baptism, of the Supper, of the restoration of the excommunicated, and of the ordained to the work of the ministry. In fact, it was perverted—made a superstitious and sacerdotal act; and Cyprian did not scruple to say of the baptized what the hierarchy now says of ordination: 'Receive the Holy Ghost through our prayer, and the laying on of our hands.' When hands were laid on deacons and elders, or on men set apart for any special work, it was the *sign* of their appointment only.

In the election of a pastor, the whole Church united in prayer for the blessing of God upon the man whom they had chosen to serve them; and the laying on of hands by the presbytery of the local Church publicly attested their suffrages. The elders or bishops of another local Church had no right to interfere in the matter.[6] The man selected was a member of the Church in which he was to exercise oversight. But so far from the laying on of hands indicating that the work to which the Church had called him was perpetual and changeless, he might cease to be the pastor of that Church at any time, and his election and the act of the Church in his case left him where they found him.

The fullest, clearest and most reliable account known to the writer, setting forth this whole matter, is from the pen of the learned Dr. Gill, and may be profitably quoted here:

'Epaphras, a faithful minister of Christ for the Church at Colosse, is said to be one of you, a member of that Church, Col. i, 7, and iv, 12; one that is not a member of a Church cannot be a pastor of it. . . . As every civil society has a right to choose, appoint and ordain their own officers, as all cities and towns corporate their mayors or provosts, aldermen, burgesses, etc., so Churches, which are religious societies, have a right to choose and ordain their own officers, and which are ordained, αυτοις, *for them*, and for them *only ;* that is, for each particular Church, and not another. Acts xiv, 23. The election and call of them, with their acceptance, is ordination. The essence of ordination lies in the voluntary choice and call of the people, and in the voluntary acceptance of that call by the person chosen and called; for this affair must be by mutual consent and argument, which joins them together as pastor and people. And this is done among themselves; and public ordination, so called, is no other than a declaration of that. Election and ordination are spoken of as the same; the latter is expressed by the former. . . . Paul and Barnabas are said to *ordain elders in every city* (Acts xiv, 23), or to choose them; that is, they gave orders and directions to every Church, as to the choice of elders over them; for persons sometimes are said to do that which they give orders and directions for doing, as Moses and Solomon with respect to building the tabernacle and temple, though done by others; and Moses particularly is said to choose the judges. Exod. xviii, 25. The choice being made under his direction and guidance.' [7]

Gill further says of elections in the Apostolic Churches:

'This choice and ordination in primitive times was made two ways: by casting lots and by giving votes, signified by stretching out of hands. . . . Ordinary officers, as elders and pastors of Churches, were chosen and ordained by the votes of the people, expressed by stretching out their hands; thus it is said of the Apostles, Acts xiv, 23. *When they had ordained them elders in every Church*, χειροτονεῖν, by taking the suffrages and votes of the members of the Churches, shown by the stretching out of their hands, as the word signifies, and which they directed them to, and upon it declared the elders duly elected and ordained.'

But he explicitly denies that there was any imposition of hands used at the ordination of elders or pastors in apostolic times, in these words:

'No instance can be given of hands being laid on any ordinary minister, pastor or elder at his ordination; nor, indeed, of hands being laid on any, upon whatsoever account, but by extraordinary persons; nor by them upon any ministers, but extraordinary ones; and even then not at and for the ordination of them.' [8]

He also claims that whatever 'gift' was bestowed upon Timothy, no 'office' was bestowed upon him either by the laying on of the hands of Paul or of the presbytery, but that the whole proceeding was extraordinary. He further deprecates the practice as 'needless' at the present day, and as a 'weakness.' This, however, he gives as a mere opinion, in view of the abuses to which the imposition of hands has been subjected, and not as an authoritative utterance based on the requirements of Scripture. In keeping with these views, however, the English Baptists have never held councils, nor, as a custom, used the imposition of hands for the ordination of men to the ministry, but have left the whole matter in the hands of the Church which calls a man to this work; a prerogative which Christ lodged in that Church, and which all the Churches on earth cannot remove. The ordinary Church may invite sister Churches to advise her, and assist her in the matter, or she may dispense with this as she pleases. But when once her sister Churches avow that there is something defective in the ordination if they and their elders or presbyters are not called in to assist, on the pretense that men are ordained for a 'denomination,' and not for an individual Church; they introduce a new element into the Gospel system, and deliberately rob a Gospel Church of her inalienable rights. If hands must be laid upon a pastor when he is first chosen to serve a Church, it is infinitely better to repeat that act every time that he changes his pastorate, than that outside Churches should interfere with the Gospel rights of a sister Church under the pretense of fraternity. Once violate this principle in the genius of the Gospel, as neighboring pastors and Churches, and we depart therefrom, as much as any priest, primate, or pope whatever, and become partakers of their sin. According, then, to the New Testament, the right to ordain pastors is given by Christ to the individual Church which calls them severally, with or without a council as she pleases; and to resist her right in this matter is to resist a divine ordinance; to arrogate a prerogative which would disgrace any honest pope, while it honored his disgraceful office. Leave Christ's Churches where he left them; to their own Master they stand or fall. It were better that we never hold another council while the world stands, than that such a body should tyrannize over a sister Church by pretending that it can set any man apart to the work of the Gospel ministry, even if a Church should pretend to delegate its power to such a body; a thing which it cannot do by any permission or example of the New Testament.

IV. THE APOSTOLIC CHURCHES WERE ACTIVELY INDEPENDENT OF THE STATE. We have seen that Jesus laid the corner-stone of religious freedom in liberty of conscience, so that in the voluntary service of God his followers should not be vassals to human dominion. That he alone should be obeyed in all matters of faith and practice, is the spring from which all their other liberties flow. In this law he set forth his great doctrine of the majesty of the soul, when left to the sway of intelligence and responsibility. He treated a man as a man, and all men stood before him on a common level; hence, he addressed each man personally, inviting him to voluntary discipleship, through his own reason and conscience, making himself the absolute King of willing subjects. Then, his inspired Apostles carefully guarded this holy principle of soul-liberty by requiring implicit obedience to him, and enforcing among his followers all the relations of brotherly democracy. All intrusion between these they condemned as foreign and oppressive. They, therefore, neither asked permission of human governments to preach and form Churches, nor would they desist from doing so at their command. Christ being their only religious Sovereign, they neither sought favor nor feared blame from the State; every man must be fully persuaded in his own mind, and give his account to God. M. Guizot clearly expresses the Apostolic idea when he says:

'We can conceive that a man can abandon to an external authority the direction of his material interests and his temporal destiny. But when it extends to the conscience, the thought, and the internal existence, to the abdication of self-government, to the delivering one's self to a foreign power, it is truly a moral suicide, a servitude, a hundred-fold worse than that of the body, or than that of the soil.[9]

Neander, in applying this principle laid down by the great civilian, lodges the right to soul-liberty in 'the peculiar nature of the higher life that belongs to all true Christians.' This is but Christ's doctrine: 'Ye must be born again,' words which demand that the whole mental and moral nature, with the passions, be consecrated to him. Here, our Lord lifts the religion of the individual soul above all organization, whether in Church or State; the existence of the Church itself being dependent upon the vital, spiritual life of the individual Christian. As Head of the Church, therefore, Jesus retained all judicial power in his hands and is its only Lawgiver, taking no account of the pains and penalties of civil law; for the civil power in religious matter ends where the law of conscience begins. As Jesus himself was all that he required his followers to be, both toward God and man, so he made duty to God throw light on duty toward man. With him, personal conviction said, 'Render to God the things that are God's;' and after that, 'Render to Cæsar the things that are Cæsar's.' That is, obedience to his Father was the first obligation, and having perfectly met that, Rome, by her highest local authority, pronounced him spotless: 'I find no fault in this man.' His disciples were to make duty to God their calm, staying power, without any civil or ex-cathedra utterances; and then obedience to the State would cheerfully follow, for in the nature of things the most God-fearing man is the truest citizen.

We have already seen that in matters of faith, all forms of paganism led the State to trample upon the rights of conscience at will; so that at the coming of Christ the whole world was educated in this false theory of civil government. Such Statecraft cared nothing for the individual, but only for the State, in its arbitrary and conventional claims. Cicero maintained those claims when he said: 'No man has a right to have particular gods, not recognized by the law of the State.' But Christ threw himself into direct opposition to all such tyranny, by uplifting the natural rights of man God-ward; and the Apostles sustained this teaching when they introduced a new issue with the law, in the face of the current civilization. They demanded the right to worship without molestation, and if need be, contrary to the mandates of the law; nay, and to invite all men to do so. Somehow the State has always been troubled with what it had no concern. Free religious inquiry has always disturbed its equanimity, and on that subject it has far transcended its real functions. Jesus never invoked its aid to enforce his religion, and never hinted that it had the power to decree opinions, or to frame and propagate creeds. He left it to attend to its own material and political affairs, to keep its hands off his religion altogether; but on the other hand, he enjoined obedience to its rightful powers, and interfered in no way with its proper governmental rights. Both he and his Apostles recognized the Roman Empire, in all that related to the fundamental idea of civil government. They submitted to it, and supported it in all that concerned its civil well-being. All that they asked, was a free and open field for the proclamation of Christian doctrine in every civilization, and that it might adjust itself every where to its natural surroundings. But that the Churches should be put under its control, was not left an open question. Because the pagan faith had made itself an engine of the State to coerce men by State forces, and in its turn built up all sorts of State policy he said: 'My kingdom is not of this world.'

Why should kings, rulers, and magistrates hold in their hands the government of the Church of Christ? Are not they to obey the Gospel personally, and to be subject to its saving influences, the same as all other sinners? and when they are converted to him, are they not to stand on a parity with all other converted men? But as to having a voice in the control of Christ's Church when they are not holy men, or above other holy men when they become regenerate, the idea is preposterous in the extreme. Civil rulers have generally sought to obtain ascendency in his Church as a tool in their secular aims; and where they could not so use it, they have commonly looked upon it with jealousy. The potentates of the earth, with few exceptions, have not recognized such a thing as a soul, a conscience, a man; but only a body and a sword, which placed society under abject domination. Hence, it never did matter what the civilization of the State might be, the moment it interfered with Christianity it became narrow and bigoted, and held in contempt all who dissented from its dictates. In the nature of things, every form of governmental religion is intolerant and persecuting, and disgraces itself when it prescribes any form of faith for its citizens. In Europe and Asia, both before Christ and since, State religions have always cursed all lands with mobs, and massacres, and wars of the most bloody character. Paganism knew the kingdoms of this world and none other. The fact that Christ gave birth to a perfect individuality in each man, and to a personal responsibility for its use, forever separated pagan oneness of religion and legislation. A man is born into the State without choice; but if he worships sincerely he worships voluntarily; to bind the Church to the State is to destroy the true nature of both. The first act of Christian martyrdom drew a line beyond which despotism could not pass. It slew the enslaved body, but left the native freedom of the soul untouched.

Neander says of the Church: 'The form of a State cannot be thought of in connection with this kingdom. It is a community whose whole principle of life is love. Outward law, forms of judicature, administration of justice, all essential to the organization of a State, can have no place in the perfect kingdom of Christ.' Then, to unite 'the body of Christ,' as Paul calls the Church, to the State, as an integral part thereof, is to convert these communities into monstrosities, for each is a unit of itself, having its own generic character, and it cannot brook an arbitrary unity with a foreign body. Bellarmine may reckon temporal power, pomp and glory amongst the evidences of the true Church, but Christ and his Apostles did not; and wherever the Churches have been forced into alliance with the State, the union has been the cause of departure from the faith, in the Churches themselves. Always, the State has either dragged the Church down to its own level, or the Church has insisted on governing the State, as in the Middle Ages. This struggle for freedom between Christ's kingdom and the civil power has gone on through eighteen centuries. Reason, endurance and truth require the contest to continue, till the ideal of Christ in government is wrought out, and the double usurpation is banished from the earth, namely: The interference of the Church in temporals, and of the State in spirituals. The State has introduced sacerdotalism into the Church as a political policy, and the Church has introduced ritualistic sacramentarianism into the State for the ends of temporal aggrandizement, in the place of saving grace and holy living. Thus, out of a Christian democracy this union evolves first an aristocracy, and then a hierarchy, for the enforcement of a sacramental salvation by the secular power. The true Gospel has always flourished the most where men have been the freest; where no artificial lines have been drawn between man and man, class and class; and where no fetter of party, State, or race has been applied, but where all have stood on a religious equality.

Now, Jesus left his simple-hearted Churches in that purely organic state which his Apostles had given them. Their faith was to center in him and his benevolent purposes, without reliance on national revenues or political weapons. Eloquence and art, philosophy and legislation, were in battle array against them; yet they must plant his banner in all lands by invading their cherished interests and destroying their established practices, their only weapon being Love. This was to make arid deserts blossom like the rose. No tear, thereafter, should fall unseen by the eye of love, and no sigh expire but on its ear. An ideal cross, borrowed from the sign of felony, was to be their insignia, a meritorious doctrinal cross, outlined against the blackness of darkness itself. By this sign they were to conquer obstinacy and unbelief, as it would supersede all old modes of thought, bring in a new morality, create new intellect and goodness, and revolutionize society. The cross was to be the new scepter over human spirits, and the Crucified should say: 'Behold, I make all things new!'

CHAPTER X.

THE OFFICERS AND ORDINANCES OF THE APOSTOLIC CHURCH.

THE first office to be considered is that of the DEACON. This word is the English of the Greek *diaconos*, and means a servant; literally, to pursue after, to hasten by speed in service. The cardinals are regarded as the servants, or deacons of the Pope, a fact which accounts for their strange costume, worn in imitation of the ancient errand-man. His hat has a broad brim to shade the eyes from the sun, with long strings to tie under the chin in windy weather; and the end of his cloak is tucked under his girdle so that the limbs may be free for speed. The outside pressure of persecution at Jerusalem, and the burden of deep poverty, called for great sagacity and fidelity in the Christian leaders. Both Christ and his Apostles were poor, so that his servants had been trained to mutual dependence, and the use of a common treasury during his ministry had thrown a new light upon poverty, and given a new religion to the poor. Thus, when thousands of the same class came into the infant Church, their dependence seemed crippling. At this time the whole empire was poor, and the endurance of Christianity was thoroughly tried. The financial world had become exhausted, by disruption and war, luxury and waste, and society was demoralized by the neglect of agriculture in large tracts of country. A few were wealthy, but taxation was oppressive and the poor were very poor. All great cities were deeply in debt, having borrowed large sums of money to build those massive structures whose ruins are now the wonder of the world. On these loans they paid exorbitant interest, which left them bankrupt and filled the land with paupers. Rome itself had 44,000 wretched lodging-houses and other apartments where squalor abounded, to 1,780 decent habitations; and Cicero, who died B. C. 43, reports that city in his time as having only 2,000 proprietors out of 1,200,000 inhabitants.[1]

But no province of the Empire was so impoverished as Palestine. It had always been an agricultural country, without manufactures or commerce. Now, its most enterprising people were scattered over the world for the purposes of trade, it had passed through a long succession of wars and reverses, and the extortionate tribute which Rome had wrung out of its fibers had reduced it to abject poverty. The site of its capital was chosen for its strong natural fortifications, but when it proved vulnerable it was left as the central sanctuary and seat of theology, without wealth to give it attraction, for more than once it was helped by outside charity. Still, to all foreign Jews it was the monument of holy memories, and the object of life-long hope. The visits of the wealthy at the feasts furnished it with some supplies, but all Jews returned to its holy places and privileges for the solace of their souls, when deep poverty overtook them, especially widows and orphans who had laid the bones of their dead in strange soil. The 'chief joy' of these was to gather together what little they had, and hasten to die within the shadow of its hallowed walls, even if they slept in 'the place to bury strangers in.' Yet these classes were not always welcome; even the doctors of the law, who treated all women lightly, refused religious teaching to women. This state of things accounts for the great poverty which Christianity found in Jerusalem, and gives new weight to Christ's saying: 'The poor ye have always with you.' Sometimes pagan rulers and corporations were moved with pity to the extremely poor; but here is a new thing in the earth, in the form of a new religion which made benevolence its ideal. Its Founder had been born in a stable, had spent his life in deep poverty, had been buried in another man's tomb; and now he had made men members one of another, had created a new virtue in the heart toward the weak, and had elevated men to thrift by sympathy. The poor, therefore, embraced the Gospel as a fresh source of strength; it made them rich in bread as well as in faith, and consumed the partition-walls between the poor and rich in the flames of brotherly love. Instead of demanding hecatombs of beasts at the hands of widow and orphan, it tendered them 'one sacrifice for sin,' offered forever, and made the outcast and famishing its altar of sacrifice. Such love led those who had worldly goods to give to the poor, and bound the members of the new faith in a oneness which made all things common. Yet they neither abandoned the rights of ownership in private property, as Peter's questions to Ananias show, nor adopted a communist life, such as would pauperize the members of the Church.

A mere glance reveals the difficulty of the twelve in dealing with this state of affairs; they spread a free table daily for such as needed the bounty of the Church, for as yet they had no division of labor with others, and out of this common meal served to the multitude the deacon's office arose. The Church at Jerusalem was composed entirely of Jews and proselytes from paganism to the Jewish faith, some natives, some foreign born. Those born in Palestine spoke the Aramaic and read the Scriptures in the Hebrew; hence they were called Hebrews. Those born in other lands read and spoke the Greek or Hellenic (from Hellas, in Thessaly, the cradle of the Greeks), and were called Hellenists. These were held in disrepute by the native Jews, and were treated as inferiors because they mixed with the Gentiles. They had seen more of the world than the Hebrews, were less hampered by the rigid and official orthodoxy of Jerusalem, and were more cosmopolitan and less aristocratic in their feelings toward others. These phases of human nature brought jealousies into the fraternity, and as the Hellenist widows were the most numerous, they necessarily called for a larger share of the bounty. So the more strict brethren took it into their heads that their poor were 'overlooked,' and with the true instinct of modern Baptist grumblers, they began to fill the Church with complaints that the distribution of bread was not even and fair. The adjustment of this business so diverted the attention of the Apostles and consumed their time, that they asked the Church to select seven men from their own ranks, who should 'help,' 'wait' and 'serve,' at the provision-tables, and they would confirm the popular choice. They also laid down clearly the qualifications for the work. They must be 'of good report, full of the Holy Spirit and wisdom;' discreet, having the confidence of the people; being marked for consecration, integrity, sound judgment, and impartiality; all this, although their duties were purely material, or, as Jerome expresses it, they were 'attendants on tables and widows.' 'The seven' were selected, but we are not to infer that they were all Hellenists because they bore Greek names, as the Jews commonly took such names, which renders it likely that impartiality ruled, and that they were taken equally from both factions, with one 'proselyte' to keep the balance even. Poor human nature always tells the same story.

Yet those chosen to this service are not called '*deacons*,' but simply the 'seven,' to distinguish them from the 'twelve.' We meet this word first in the New Testament in the Epistle to the Philippians, and some think that the office was borrowed from the almoners of the synagogue. Dr. Lightfoot, the present Bishop of Durham, pronounces it 'a baseless though a very common assumption, that the Christian diaconate was copied from the arrangements of the synagogue.' The duties of the Levite in the temple, and the office of the Chusan in the synagogue, were of an entirely different character from those of the deacon. The Levite took care of the temple sacrifices, removed the blood, offal and ashes of the altar, served as door-keeper at the gates, and aided in the chorus of the psalmody. The duties of the Chusan were of the same order, so far as care for the synagogue went, and aid in the services allowed. But the only work of the deacon was to serve at the table in the daily meal and relieve the poor, a labor which called for another class of qualifications from those of these Jewish officers. In that dishonest and licentious age such a delicate trust as that held by the deacon required rare spirituality and spotless character, keen insight of human nature, large patience and singular tact in dealing with the suffering, as well as a broad and intelligent sympathy. In a word, his sacred duties called for the 'Holy Spirit and wisdom,' special graces which neither Levite nor Chusan needed for their work.

The fact is most marked that those officers at a heathen feast, whose duty it was to serve the portions of food which were eaten, were called the '*deacons*.' One officer slew the victims; another offered them in sacrifice or cooked them; then this third officer served the flesh to the devotees.[2] This fact is very suggestive, as showing the unpretentiousness of the office and title, and may account for the sacerdotal air which superstition has thrown around the diaconate in some communions. This election created a new office in the Church, but not a new order in the ministry, as that term is now technically used. Alford warns his readers (on Acts vi) 'Not to imagine that we have here the institution of an ecclesiastical order so named'—*deacons*. In modern parlance they were 'laymen' before their election, and they remained so after. The reason given for the creation of their office was, that the Apostles might be relieved from those duties which interfered with their full 'ministry of the Word.' One set of ministers was not created to help another to do the same work, but duties that were not ministerial or pastoral were separated from those that were, and given into other hands. So that the deaconship was not probationary to the eldership, nor have we any evidence that in the first century any deacon became an elder. Neither did their office prevent their doing other Christian work, for we find Philip the first witness for Christ in Samaria. But he did not publish the good news by virtue of his office as a deacon, any more than Stephen was martyred as a deacon. Bishop Taylor has abundantly shown, in his 'Liberty of Prophesying,' that in the Apostolic Churches each believer of the brotherhood had the right to proclaim the Gospel as well as the pastors. The work of spreading it by preaching was left to each one as a question of capacity and not of office. Even the private worshipers amongst the Jews had the right of public speaking in the synagogue, as we see by the freedom of our Lord and his Apostles there, for they were not officers in that assembly. So it was in the Christian congregations; and, of course, the office of a deacon did not deprive him of the right to teach in common with his brethren. Luke tells us that the persecution at Jerusalem scattered the Church there 'except the Apostles,' and that the 'scattered,' the whole lay membership of that Church, preached the Word. So the deaconship did not shut up a deacon to the service of tables only; he might do missionary work, by right of his personal regeneration, and attend to his office, also. Did the Apostle Paul act improperly when he carried the collection of the Grecian Churches to Jerusalem, because he was not officially a deacon? Thus a deacon might engage in other religious labor besides that imposed by his office.

The instructions given to the deacon in the Epistles, show the functions of his office to have been the same in the latter period of the Apostolic Age that they were when the office was created; and it nowhere appears that they exercised the pastoral or ministerial office. Even in matters relating to the relief of the poor they were not supreme. When Paul and Barnabas brought relief to the poor saints at Jerusalem, they delivered the gift to the 'elders' and not to the deacons: and no deacons assisted in the call, deliberations, or decisions of the advisory Council at Jerusalem. Paul's associations there were all with the elders and not the deacons of the Church, showing that the deacons held no rank in the pastoral office. Thirty years after their office was formed, he instructs them, and enjoins precisely those qualifications for filling it, which were needed in one whose business it was to go from house to house dispensing alms, and none other. In his Epistle to the Corinthians, A. D. 57, he calls them 'helps;' in that to the Romans, 'the ministration;' and in his letter to Timothy, he lays special stress upon their holding 'the faith in a good conscience,' as men free from vices, especially the sins of greed and gossiping, not even mentioning that they should be 'apt to teach;' which would be a strange omission if teaching were a special part of their office, as a subordinate order in the pastoral ministry. In his Epistle to Titus, about A. D. 66, he does not mention the deacons at all, although he says much to 'elders,' of their appointment, work and qualifications; showing again that he did not rank deacons in the pastoral office, nor were they so ranked in that age. In the third century, when there were forty-six elders in the congregation at Rome, there were only seven deacons; and the Council of Neo-Cæsarea, A. D. 314–325, decreed that no Church should have above seven. Origen says, that 'The deacons dispense the Church's money to the poor;' and in non-Episcopal Churches this office remains substantially uncorrupted to our times.

THE DEACONESS, in the Apostolic Churches did much the same work as the deacon. Grotius says: 'In Judea the deacons could administer freely to the females,' but amongst the Greeks and farther East, the enforced seclusion of women deprived them largely of the public administrations of men; this was the case, to a certain extent, amongst the Romans also. But all through the Oriental nations men were excluded from the apartments of females, contrary to that social freedom which marks western civilization. In all the spheres of life, woman suffered a degradation to which we are strangers, and Christianity purposing to lift her up, provided for her the deaconess, to bless her own sex in her own peculiar way, publicly and privately. Phœbe is the first known to us who filled that honorable office, and Paul passes a high encomium upon her, 'she succored many.' There was abundant room for these valuable helpers as the Churches were then constituted, amongst the rich and poor, women of reputation and the debased slave-women. The deaconess possessed high qualifications, being 'grave, sober, faithful, and not slanderous.' Her sacred duties demanded devotion, approved character and ability, requiring her to be kind, intelligent, courteous, and to follow 'every good work.' Eight years after Paul had spoken so gratefully of Phœbe, he gives full instruction as to these qualifications. These honorable women were chosen from matrons or widows well advanced in life, and many of our best interpreters think that Paul describes them in 1 Tim. v, 9, 10: 'Let not one be enrolled as a widow under threescore years old, having been the wife of one husband; well reported of for good works; if she brought up children, if she lodged strangers, if she washed the feet of the saints [in hospitality], if she relieved the afflicted, if she diligently followed every good work.' We have reason to believe that many of these 'elect' ladies brought great honor to the faith, for Pliny, in his famous letter to the Emperor Trajan, A. D. 110–111, says, that he had just examined 'two women-servants who are called ministers,' deaconesses; by which, he means that he had tortured them, as was common when Christian women suffered persecution for Christ.

The order of deaconess continued in the Latin Church down to about the sixth century, and in the Greek to the twelfth; and was discontinued, principally because the diaconate became a priestly office which women could not fill; nuns then took the place of deaconesses. Anciently they were ordained by form as well as by vote, and the work known as the 'Apostolic Constitutions,' written about A. D. 300, contains this beautiful prayer used at their ordination: 'Eternal God, Father of our Lord Jesus Christ, Creator of man and of woman; thou who didst fill with thy Spirit, Miriam, Deborah, Hannah, and Huldah: thou who didst vouchsafe to a woman the birth of thy only begotten Son: . . . look down now upon this, thy handmaid, and bestow on her the Holy Spirit, that she may worthily perform the work permitted to her to thy honor, and to the glory of Christ.' So long as the immersion of adult females remained in the Churches, the deaconess waited upon them in baptism; but, says Archbishop Kenrick: 'This class of females having ceased, from a variety of causes, it became expedient to abstain from the immersion of females;' and he adds the reason, 'it is certain that the applicant entered the font in a state of entire nudity.'[3] According to 'Hanbury's Memorials,' the Congregationalists of England and Holland restored the office to some extent, in the seventeenth century, and the Moravians continue it to this time. Also the Broadmead Baptist Church, at Bristol, England, two centuries ago, adopted the full Apostolic model, by selecting a plurality of elders, with deacons and deaconesses, making the duties of the latter, the care of the sick and the poor.

The shepherds or pastors of the Apostolic Churches were known as PRESBYTERS, or ELDERS, from *presbuteroi;* and as Bishops, or overseers, from *episkopoi.* This fact should stand in its own order of New Testament time; for if we take it out of its historical surroundings and throw it backward or forward into another century, it will lose its distinctive value. Dean Alford says, with clear chronological truth: 'In those days titles sprung out of realities and were not merely hierarchical classifications.' In such a question as this, chronology is the stoutest logic. We must, therefore, consider and restrict these titles to their primitive sense, as best defining the office which they represent. They are entirely synonymous in the New Testament, and the nature of the office which they represent, is to be drawn from their acknowledged meaning.

Pastors appeared in all these Churches very early after their organization, and the Hebrew Christians called them presbyters (elders) while the Gentile Churches called them bishops (overseers), the terms being interchangeable. The leaders or rulers of the synagogue were called presbyters, but they were not prototypes of the Christian presbyters, for there was next to nothing in common between the two. The synagogue could in no sense become the pattern of the Christian congregation, which was constituted for a different purpose, and demanded that freer and more independent form, which was in harmony with the genius of Christ's more generous teaching.

Neander says:

'It may be disputed whether the Apostles designed from the first, that believers should form a society exactly on the model of the synagogue. The social element of both had something of similarity, enough to warrant the use of the current word presbyter in the ancient sense of leadership; this being the sense in which both civil and sacred rulers had long been known in Israel, and by which the members of the Sanhedrin were then known.'[4]

So, then, every one knew what parties were referred to in the Christian congregation when its 'elders' were spoken of. But the Gentiles, who were not familiar with the peculiarity of Jewish titles and institutions, could not so well come to a knowledge of this spiritual office by the use of the word, when standing alone and unexplained. To them, the term elder expressed age, but little of fitness or rank. Another term was in use amongst the Greeks which exactly expressed the duties of the Christian presbyter, namely, the word *episkopoi*, overseer. With them, this was purely a civil and secular name, which was used in private associations, or in municipal and magisterial bodies. The superintendents of finance, of workmen, the inspectors of bread and produce, and the overseers of public affairs generally, were designated by this term. In fact, all persons who had oversight of affairs, either public or private, were known as bishops. For this reason the same class of men who were known as elders in the Jewish-Christian Churches, were called bishops, or overseers, in the Gentile Churches.

Thus Bishop Lightfoot, after speaking of the presbyters, asks:

'What must be said of the term bishop? It has been shown that in the Apostolic writings the two are merely different designations of the same office. How and where was this second name originated? To the officers of Gentile Churches is the term applied, as a synonym for presbyter. At Philippi, in Asia Minor, in Crete, the presbyter is so called. In the next generation the title is employed in a letter written by the Greek Church of Rome to the Greek Church at Corinth. Thus the word would seem to be especially Hellenic. Beyond this we are left to conjecture. But if we may assume that the directors of religious and social clubs amongst the heathen are commonly so called, it would naturally occur, if not to the Gentile Christians themselves, at all events to their heathen associates, as a fit designation for the presiding members of the new society. The infant Church of Christ which appeared to the Jew as a synagogue, would be regarded by the heathen as a confraternity.'[5]

The duties of the bishop-elders were, to feed and rule the flock of Christ as shepherds, by guidance, instruction, and watch-care. Paul first uses the word bishop at Miletus, when he charges the presbyters of the Church at Ephesus to take heed to the flock over which the Holy Spirit had made them bishops. Here he two names are used interchangeably as descriptive of the same thing. On this point Neander remarks:

'That the name also of episcopus was altogether synonymous with that of presbyter, is clearly collected from the passages of Scripture where both appellations are interchanged (Acts xx; compare verse 17 with verse 28; Titus i, 5-7), as well as from those where the mention of the office of deacon follows immediately after that of "*episcopoi*," so that a third class of officers could not lie between the two. Phil. i, 1 ; 1 Tim. iii, 1–8. This *interchange* of the two appellations is a proof of their *entire coincidence*.' 6

As to the kind of rule which these bishops exercised, it was executive only, and for the purpose of moral up-building, in submission to the truth which they taught, and not for the exercise of lordship. So far from its being an exercise of personal power, they were held responsible to the local Church which they served for their conduct as stewards. Neander says again : ' They were not destined to be unlimited monarchs, but rulers and guides in an ecclesiastical *republic*, and to conduct every thing in conjunction with the Church assembled together, as the servants and not the masters of which they were to act.' 7 The congregation having first taken them from the common ranks by their own democratic action, as Athens invested its officers with governing powers in olden times, they were responsible to the body which created them for the exercise of their powers.

All sorts of false pretentions have been hung upon the word ' bishop,' as used by the writers of the New Testament. But Phil. i, 1 ; Acts xx, 17 ; and James v, 14, set forth the fact that there were several bishops in the same congregation, an idea which will not harmonize with the assumption that a bishop ranks above an elder, or even a body of elders. Then, 1 Peter v, 1, 2, solemnly charges the 'elder' to use well his episcopal functions. Even as late as Jerome A. D. 331–370, this oneness of office was generally admitted in the Churches, for he says : ' The elder is identical with the bishop, and before parties had so multiplied under diabolical influence, the Churches were governed (meaning each Church) by a council of elders.'

Nor were the so-called ' powers' of Timothy and Titus in any sense those of the modern prelate. They were merely the functions of missionary evangelists. These holy men were sent to establish feeble Churches already planted, and to organize new ones, as the same class of men to-day who labor without prelatical authority. Neither did James assume authority at Jerusalem after the form of a modern diocesan. He simply attained greater influence than other pastors by his all-absorbing consecration to God, and to the feeding of his flock, as a holy pastor over that single congregation. In association with his fellow-elders in that body, he sacredly guarded its interests as a brotherhood. Persecution was perpetually breaking up this and other Churches, and was one of the things which made this plurality of elders in the same congregation necessary. The first blow was generally aimed at the elders, as the official heads of these communities. Some of them were cut down, others were obliged to flee for their lives, and at the best the Churches were broken into groups, especially in large cities, so that they must be ministered to, when, where, and as they could. When the elders did meet together for consultation, either in time of peace or in persecution, some one must preside over their conferences; and he who did so, acted simply as the peer of his brethren, without authority over them; for while he was a bishop each one of his brethren was the same. This, James did at Jerusalem, no more and no less.

Again, what was known as the presbytery in the Apostolic Churches was not made up of a body of elders, or pastors from the various local Churches, for 'Scripture presbytery,' as Dr. Carson says, 'is the eldership, or plurality of elders in a particular congregation.'⁸ There is absolutely nothing in the New Testament which gives those who rule in one Church any authority in another; and more, no Church is mentioned as having but one bishop or elder. These had no power out of their own congregation, and no such distinction exists even there as pastoral elders and ruling elders.

Both Dr. Geo. Campbell and Neander have clearly shown that the elders in one Church were all rulers, for the liberty, edification, and usefulness of the body, and that no class or distinction existed amongst them. Had there been two classes, their qualifications had differed with their duties, and so they would have been designated by different names. No elders are spoken of who do not rule, who are not pastors, but all pastors are known as elders. We read of 'all the elders at Jerusalem,' of 'elders for *each* Church' (not an elder), as at Derby, Lystra, Antioch, and other places. At Lystra Paul met with Timothy, and most likely it was there that 'The hands of the presbytery' were laid upon him. Not the hands of presbyters from various local Churches; but, in the language of Dr. Samuel Davidson:

'The elders set over a single Congregational Church.'⁹ The phrase, 'The presbytery,' as the phrase, 'the lawyer,' 'the statesman,' in the classification of men, means every presbytery, in the classification of the body of elders in the several Churches. Carson says, that the word denotes: 'A certain kind of plurality of elders. It represents *stated association*. The accidental or occasional meeting of the elders of a number of Churches, would be a meeting of the elders, not of the presbytery. The word denotes both the plurality and the union. The senate is not even a plurality of senators. . . . It is taken for granted in this kind of expression, that it is a definite, well-known body of men acting in association. As there is no such association among the elders of different Churches, it must be the elders of one Church.¹⁰ Neander corroborates this view, thus: 'It is certain that every Church was governed by a union of the elders, or overseers, chosen from among themselves, and we find among them no individual distinguished above the rest, who presided as a *primus inter pares*, first among equals.'

But, above all absurd positions, is that which makes the bishop of modern times the successor of the Apostles. When they died they appointed none to fill their places, for their office was peculiar and connected only with the planting of Christianity, by upholding Christ's teachings and requirements; their mission being confirmed by the special gifts of the Holy Spirit. All this was indispensable until the standard of faith and practice was settled in the inspired Books; they themselves, for the time being, filling the place of those writings, as the chosen organ of the Spirit. Then, they were the only authoritative guides for the Gospel Churches, by whom the will of Christ was communicated. Through their tongue and pen the Spirit gave his directions and decisions, and they are now exactly what the Churches of their age recognized them; the New Testament supplied their place as the channel through which the Spirit now speaks to the Churches.

Those who would foist diocesan episcopacy upon the New Testament Churches, think that they find their stronghold in the phrase 'angel of the Church' (*angelos*), which is simply a messenger. In Matt. xi, 10, Jehovah himself calls John the Baptist, 'my angel' (messenger), and in turn, John calls his own messengers to Christ, 'angels.' Luke xviii, 18-24. But were these prototypes of modern prelates? Even Paul's thorn in the flesh is called by himself an 'angel,' 'a messenger of Satan.' 2 Cor. xii, 7. So, the seven letters to the Churches, Rev. ii, iii, imply that the angel of the Churches was some person sent from each of them on a temporary mission, and chosen by the Church itself for that mission. Each of the Churches had its separate messenger; there was not one angel only for the seven, after the order of modern episcopacy. A cause must be hard pressed, to lay violent hands upon this part of the Apocalypse in support of such an innovation.

Patmos, where the Apostle John wrote this book, was not far from the seven Churches of Asia, and it was natural that the holy prisoner should request each one of them to send some faithful messenger who should receive from him, personally, what message he had from Christ to send to them severally. The Apostle Paul sent his Epistles to the Churches in the same way, for each messenger who carried them, was then capable of proving that they were not forgeries. And, now, this was the only means left at the command of John for sending Christ's revelations to the Churches, by trustworthy hands. Is it surprising, then, that Jesus should instruct his imprisoned servant, to write this and that message to this and that Church, and to entrust the message to these individual messengers? The trust which the Saviour himself confided to them, entitled them to be called 'seven stars,' each bearing new light to one of the seven Churches of which they themselves were the 'seven lamp stands' set for the illumination of all around them. These Churches were not to be deprived of necessary light because John was a prisoner; but Jesus would prove to them by these seven epistles, that he still held them as stars in his right hand, and had not turned over their keeping to a sevenfold episcopacy, but maintained for each of them a separate message, to be brought to them by seven faithful messengers, as seven separate congregations, who, despite their faults, were still dear to their Sovereign Lord.

BAPTISM was the first ordinance of the Apostolic Churches. Our Lord stamped this institution with a marked and reverend dignity, putting higher honor upon it than on any act in Christianity, by making it the only institution to be enforced in the august names of Father, Son, and Holy Spirit. Neither the preaching of the Gospel, the administration of the Supper, nor any other transaction has this high sanction from his lips, because none of them hold the same solemn relation to the

Trinity which this holds. He did more than merely command baptism to be administered by the authority of the Trinity; as Dr. Dwight puts the formula, 'Not *in* but *into* the name' of the Trinity. Of course, not into the essence of the Godhead, but the baptized are publicly introduced into the family of God, and are entitled in a special manner to the name of God; or, as Dr. Trollope better expresses the sense: 'By this solemn act we are devoted to the faith, worship, and obedience of these three, as Creator, Redeemer, and Sanctifier.' The conception of divine dignity which Christ threw into baptism, led the Apostolic Churches to see the proper place which it holds in the Gospel system, and to shape their polity accordingly. Their conduct contrasts strikingly with that modern fanaticism which pushes it out of the place given to it by Christ, either by making it the source of moral regeneration, or by depreciating it as an optional rite or form. Our only safety is in brushing away the fog which this abuse has thrown about it, and in going boldly back to examine and practice it, as we find it in the New Testament.

Jesus declared it to be from heaven; he doubly honored its appointment by his Father, by obediently submitting to it on the opening of his own ministry, and by enjoining it on others to the end of time. It was the first institution in his mind when he himself began to preach; and the last that he pressed upon those whom he left to preach, when he charged them on the 'mountain in Galilee,' as he spoke his last command in his resurrection body. As John Henry Newman says: 'Friends do not ask for literal commands, but from their knowledge of the speaker they understand his half-words, and from love to him they anticipate his wishes.' Here is not even the reverend 'half-word,' it is his last command that all believing men should be baptized upon their faith. As the Captain of salvation he gave this military mandate, 'Follow me!' and made the law doubly positive by his own example. It was this simple, heart-felt sincerity in obeying him which led a noted saint to say: 'Wherever I have seen the print of his shoe on earth, there I have coveted to set my foot, too.' The Apostolic Churches associated those primal exercises of the heart—repentance, forgiveness of sin, and regeneration of soul—with baptism; these were the preparation for baptism, which exhibited the new religious state into which their members were brought. Hence, says Dr. Jacob: 'It was evident from the first that Christian baptism, though in its outward form one single act, represented no single, isolated state of feeling—but a spiritual transaction carried on in the spirit and conscience, and then declaring itself externally. . . . Consequently, the fact that persons had been baptized is in the New Testament often referred to, both as indicating their privileged position, and as reminding them of their serious obligation to live in a manner not unworthy of it.'[11] This exactly accords with the inspired teaching. 'Through *grace* ye are all the children of God, for as many of you as were baptized into Christ, put on Christ.' Gal. iii, 27. 'Buried with him in your baptism in which ye were also raised up with him, *through faith* in the operation of God.' Col. ii, 12. Men who professed faith and were baptized were regarded by those Churches as true believers, until their conduct proved the contrary. Peter teaches the same doctrine when he says that 'baptism is not the putting away of the filth of the flesh,' the mere cleansing of the body; it goes deeper and signifies the inward state of the baptized, which must correspond with the outward appearance; by 'the answer of a good conscience toward God.' What a terrible rebuke is this to the ignorant notion that if your own conscience approves of your baptism, you have all the baptism that you need. No, the Apostle insists that the purity of your conscience as a saved man must correspond to the profession which you make when you are buried with Christ in baptism. Thus, Jerome understood the New Testament, and says: 'First they taught all nations, then immerse those that are taught, in water; for it cannot be that the body should receive the sacrament of baptism unless the soul has before received the truth of faith.' [12]

In the last edition of Herzog's 'Encyclopædia' (*Art. Taufe*) these words are used: 'Every-where in the New Testament the presupposition is, that only those who believe are to be baptized. That in the New Testament no direct trace of infant baptism is found may be regarded as settled. Efforts to prove its presence suffer from the lack of presupposing what is to be proved.'

Although Liddon makes baptism the instrument of regeneration, perhaps no modern writer so lucidly sets forth its relation to regeneration as he, and his forceful clearness will justify the following long quotation:

> 'Regeneration thus implies a double process, one destructive, the other constructive; by it the old life is killed, and the new life forthwith bursts into existence. This double process is effected by the sacramental incorporation of the baptized, first with Christ crucified and dead, and then with Christ rising from the dead to life; although the language of the Apostle distinctly intimates that a continued share in the resurrection-life depends upon the co-operation of the will of the Christian. But the moral realities of the Christian life, to which the grace of baptism originally introduces the Christian, correspond with, and are effects of, Christ's death and resurrection. Regarded historically, these events belong to the irrevocable past. But for us Christians the crucifixion and the resurrection are not mere past events of history; they are energizing facts from which no lapse of centuries can sever us; they are perpetuated to the end of time within the Kingdom of the Redemption. The Christian is, to the end of time, crucified with Christ; he dies with Christ; he is buried with Christ; he rises with Christ; he lives with Christ. He is not merely made to sit together in heavenly places as being in Christ Jesus, he is a member of his Body, as out of his Flesh and out of his Bones. And of this profound incorporation baptism is the original instrument. The very form of the sacrament of regeneration, as it was administered to the adult multitudes who in the early days of the Church pressed for admittance into her communion, harmonizes with the spiritual results which it effects. As the neophyte is plunged beneath the waters, so the old nature is slain and buried with Christ. As Christ, crucified and entombed, rises with resistless might from the grave which can no longer hold him, so, to the eye of faith, the Christian is raised from the bath of regeneration radiant with a new and supernatural life. His gaze is to be fixed henceforth on Christ, who, being raised from the dead, dieth no more.' [13]

This high doctrinal significance of baptism was constantly kept in mind in the Apostolic Churches, when they buried the bodies of believers in the waters of seas, rivers, and other convenient places, and it could not be set forth in any other way. It would be wearisome to quote critics, historians, theologians, and the highest authorities in exposition to sustain this position, still a few may not be amiss.

Dr. Cave says of ancient immersion:

'By the persons being put into water was lively represented the putting off of the sins of the flesh, and being washed from the filth and pollution of them; by his abode under it, which was a kind of burial into water, his entering into a state of death and mortification, like as Christ remained for some time under the state or power of death . . . and then by his *emersion*, or rising up out of the water, was signified his entry upon a new course of life, differing from that which he lived before.' [14]

Dean Goulburn voices the higher scholarship on this subject in these words:

'There can be no doubt that baptism, when administered in the pristine and most correct form, is a divinely constituted emblem of bodily resurrection. . . . Animation having been for one instant suspended beneath the water, a type this of the interruption of man's energies by death, the body is lifted up again into the air by way of expressing emblematically, the new birth of resurrection.' [15]

The entire Greek Church, which at present numbers about 70,000,000 of communicants, and whose custom it has always been to immerse, thus strongly expresses itself in its great standard, the 'PEDALION,' a folio of 484 pages, and sent forth under the authority of the Patriarch and Holy Synod, on pp. 29–33:

'The distinctive character of the institution of baptism, then, is immersion (*baptisma*), which cannot be omitted without destroying the mysterious meaning of the sacrament, and without contradicting, at the same time, the etymological signification of the word which serves to designate it. The Western (Roman) Church, therefore, has separated from the imitation of Jesus Christ: she has caused all the sublimity of the external sign to disappear; in short, she is guilty of an abuse of words, and of ideas in practicing baptism by aspersion, the mere announcement of which is a laughable contradiction.'

With equal decision, but in milder terms, the Dean of Norwich complains that the substitution of sprinkling for immersion has utterly obscured 'the emblematical significance of the rite, and renders unintelligible to all but the educated, the Apostle's association of burial and resurrection, with the ordinance.' Those who are not Baptists find fault on this subject more bitterly than they do. A treatise authorized by the patriarchs of Jerusalem, Constantinople, and Alexandria, declares in Chapter vii, that the attempt to prove that the ancients sprinkled, is merely an attempt to palm off 'lies.' Chapter xix attempts to show 'that sprinkling being satanical, is opposed to Divine Baptism;' and Chapter xxxiv decides, 'That sprinkling is a Heretical Dogma.' Moses Stuart, the great scholar of our own country, says: 'I cannot see how it is possible for any *candid* man who examines the subject to deny this,' namely: that Apostolic Baptism was immersion. But Dr. Paine, Professor of Ecclesiastical History in the Theological Seminary at Bangor, when charged by some of his brethren with Baptist sentiments, because he teaches that immersion prevailed in all Churches from the Apostles down, replies with great spirit:

'As to the question of fact, the testimony is ample and decisive. No matter of Church history is clearer. The evidence is all one way, and all Church historians of any repute agree in accepting it. We cannot claim even originality in teaching it in a Congregational seminary; and we really feel guilty of a kind of anachronism in writing an article to insist upon it. It is a point on which ancient, mediæval and modern historians alike, Catholics and Protestants, Lutherans and Calvinists, have no controversy; and the simple reason for this uniformity is, that the statements of the early Fathers are so clear, and the light shed upon these statements from the early customs of the Church is so conclusive, that no historian who cares for his reputation would dare to deny it, and no historian who is worthy of the name would wish to. There are some historical questions concerning the early Church on which the most learned writers disagree . . . . but on this one of the early practice of immersion, the most distinguished antiquarians,—such as Bingham, Augusti, Coleman, Smith, and historians such as Mosheim, Giesler, Hase, Neander, Millman, Schaff and Alzog (Catholic) hold a common language. . . . Any scholar who denies that immersion was the baptism of the Christian Church for thirteen centuries, betrays utter ignorance or sectarian blindness.' [16]

Herzog says: 'Baptism was always performed by immersion in flowing water.' [17]

So the learned Schaff, on Rom. vi, 3: 'The meaning of *baptizo* in this passage is undoubtedly *immerse*, and the whole force and beauty of the illustration lies in this very allusion to the act of immersion and emersion.' [18]

The following extract from Coleman's 'Antiquities' very accurately expresses what all agree to:

'In the primitive Church, immersion was undeniably the common mode of baptism. The utmost that can be said of sprinkling at that early period is that it was in case of necessity, permitted as an exception to a general rule. This fact is so well established that it is needless to adduce authorities in proof of it.

THE SUBJECTS OF BAPTISM in the Apostolic Churches, were those who repented of sin, and confessed their faith in Christ for salvation; none else were admitted, hence, infant baptism was unknown amongst them, either by precept or example, nor have we any definition of the relation of infants to the Church, or any provision for their discipline. In itself baptism was the confession of reliance on Christ, having no reference to parental faith, or federal relationship. The infinite difference between the Theocracy and the Christian Church, measured the wide stretch between circumcision and baptism. Admission into the first was by birthright without choice, the subject being 'born of blood and of the will of man.' Men entered the second, by bowing the heart and will to Christ, by the personal abandonment of sin for his sake, and by personal choice of him as their Saviour. Christ was a member of the Jewish nation, but when he reached manhood, he was baptized on his own volition as an obedient Son. No question of federal holiness was involved here. Mary had taken him to the Temple to be circumcised, but she never brought him to John to be baptized. But why not, if infant baptism takes the place of circumcision? and why did he carefully avoid making infant baptism an institute in his kingdom, when one sentence from his lips would have established it forever?

Singularly enough the baptism of believers is practiced by all Christians, who practice baptism at all, because Jesus positively commanded that it should be; yet some who practice infant baptism do so because Christ did *not* command it, but was silent on the subject. One of our first scholars and historians says:

'True, the New Testament contains no express command to baptize infants; such a command would not agree with the *free spirit* of the Gospel. Nor was there any compulsory or general infant baptism before the union of Church and State. Constantine, the first Christian emperor, delayed his baptism till his death-bed (as many now delay their repentance); and even after Constantine there were examples of eminent teachers, as Gregory Nazianzen, Augustin, Chrysostom, who were not baptized in early manhood, although they had Christian mothers. But still less does the New Testament *forbid* infant baptism, as it might be expected to do in view of the universal custom of the Jews to admit their children by circumcision on the eighth day after birth, into the fellowship of the old covenant.' [19]

A guileless investigator of historic truth will naturally ask here, 1. If 'the free spirit of the Gospel' would not have agreed with an express command from Christ to baptize infants, how does their baptism *without* his commands agree with that 'free spirit?' 2. Gospel baptism was for 'all nations,' 'all the world,' without regard to Jew or Gentile as such, what then, had natural 'birth' to do with the question, in any way? Jews and Gentiles were admitted to baptism on the same terms, and millions of Gentiles were baptized, but only a few thousand Jews. In fact, the baptized Churches refused to know men either as Jew or Gentile, because in Christ Jesus there is no race. The Gentiles had nothing to do with circumcision, as the ordinance of a covenant in which they had never had and never were to have a part. Was baptism substituted for circumcision to accommodate them, when they had no natural interest in either? The Jews needed no such change. Any one of them, old or young, male or female, could accept the Redeemer on choice, by passing out of the Old Covenant into the New with him through baptism, by simply asking the privilege. Infant baptism could not be a substitute for circumcision with the Gentiles, and the Jews could have both if they wished, as in the cases of Paul and Timothy. Then what had circumcision to do with the question anyway, when baptism affected only 'a new creature?' 3. As to New Testament silence on the subject of infant baptism: Did the Apostolic Christians understand that whatever Jesus did not forbid they were in duty bound to incorporate into the Christian system? Then, any rite, service or practice, superstition or dogma whatever, might have been introduced, unless expressly forbidden. This casts all the bulwarks of purity to the four winds, and is the essence of Romanism. Where does the New Testament '*forbid*' infant communion, the elevation and adoration of the cup, the limit of its use to the clergy, the use of holy water, the priestly miter and dress, the sign of the cross, and the conduct of worship in Latin; the use of salt, oil, honey and saliva in baptism, the baptism of bells, a college of cardinals, archbishops, auricular confession, the pope's infallibility, nay, the pope himself, with a thousand other mummeries *ad nauseam?*

If it is a canon in Christianity that silence gives consent, and consent imposes duty, then it is not only our duty to baptize our children, whether the 'Christian mothers' of Chrysostom and Augustine baptized theirs or not, but to do many other things which 'his holiness' curses us for not doing. Luther honestly said: 'It cannot be proved by the Sacred Scriptures that infant baptism was instituted by Christ, or begun by the first Christians after the Apostles.' So, when Carlstadt asked him: 'Where has Christ commanded us to elevate the host?' he answered, 'Where has he *forbidden* it?' As if this absurd answer rendered his act a whit the less a trifling with Christ's will in either case. The Constitution of the United States contains no express command to establish a monarchy and elect a king, 'still less' does it '*forbid*' this; therefore any faction is at liberty to establish a kingdom and elect a sovereign! Such work would probably be deemed 'treason' under our positive political institutions, but somehow the same silence affecting an institution of Christ is used to impel to superserviceable loyalty.

Our Lord instructed his Apostles whom to baptize, and on what conditions, and they went no further. God commanded Abraham to circumcise 'his seed,' but he did not practice the rite upon other men's children, because he was not forbidden to do so. Baptism is met with in the New Testament, only in association with a certain set of persons, sentiments and virtues. The baptized are characterized as 'elect,' 'saints,' 'disciples,' 'believers,' and their state of mind as that of 'faith,' 'obedience,' 'remission of sin,' 'following after holiness,' and 'enduring hardness as good soldiers of Jesus Christ;' names which cannot be given to, and things which cannot be said of, infants.

Besides, the universal testimony of Church history says that they were not infants, but refers the whole question of infant baptism to empty inferential usage. Bunsen writes: 'It was utterly unknown in the early Church, not only down to the end of the second, but indeed to the middle of the third, century.'[20] Hahn of Breslau testifies, that 'Neither in the Scriptures, nor during the first hundred and fifty years, is a sure example of infant baptism to be found; and we must concede that the numerous opposers of it cannot be contradicted on Gospel ground.'[21] Curcellaeus declares that, 'The baptism of infants, in the first centuries after Christ, was altogether unknown; but in the third and fourth was allowed by some few. In the fifth and following ages it was generally received. The custom of baptizing infants did not begin before the third age after Christ was born. In the former ages no traces of it appear, and it was introduced without the command of Christ.'[22] These testimonies might be multiplied at length, but only a few of great weight may be added. Dr. Jacob says:

'Notwithstanding all that has been written by learned men upon this subject, it remains indisputable that infant baptism is not mentioned in the New Testament. No instance of it is recorded there; no allusion is made to its effects; no directions are given for its administration. However reasonably we may be convinced that we find in the Christian Scriptures "the fundamental idea from which infant baptism was afterward developed," and by which it may now be justified, it ought to be distinctly acknowledged that it is not an Apostolic ordinance. Like modern Episcopacy, it is an ecclesiastical institution legitimately deduced by *Church* authority from Apostolic principles; but not Apostolic in its actual existence.'[23]

The Bishop of Salisbury, recently deceased, says:

'I most candidly and broadly state my conviction that there is not one passage nor one word in Scripture which directly proves it—not one word, the undeniable and logical power of which can be adduced to prove, in any way of fact, that in the Scripture age infants were baptized, or of the doctrine that they ought to be baptized. Nor, I believe, is there any such direct statement to be found in any writings of the Fathers of the Church before the latter end of the second century.'

Beck has well summed up the constituency of an Apostolic Church thus:

'They are baptized on the strength of personal faith, and pass from the old union with the world into the new associations. It is not baptism in itself, therefore, which makes the Church, it is faith which qualifies both for faith and for the Church. This faith through which a man, of his own free-will, unites himself with God's salvation in Christ leads to baptism; in which God unites himself to men for their salvation, for the forgiveness of their sins and the gift of the Spirit. And such baptized persons form the Church which is, therefore, styled "The multitude of them that believed."'[24]

Because, then, there is no authority for its practice from Christ or his Apostles, it falls to the ground. Of what weight is it that it be a tenet of 'deduction,' 'inference,' 'Church authority' or any other authority; no matter what the pretense may be? In that case it is of purely human origin, manufactured for some end which the oracles of God did not contemplate, and is an act of empty will-worship, for which a man can give no solid account to Christ. The late Archbishop Hughes saw this point clearly, and said, in his 'Doctrinal Catechism:' 'It does not appear from Scripture that even one infant was ever baptized; therefore, Protestants should reject, on their own principle, infant baptism as an unscriptural usage.' But Professor Lange, of Jena, a weightier authority still, says: 'Would the Protestant Church fulfill and attain to its final destiny, the baptism of infants must of necessity be abolished. It has sunk down to a mere formality, without any religious meaning for the child; and stands in direct contradiction to the fundamental doctrines of the Reformers, on the advantage and use of the sacraments. It cannot from any point of view be justified by the Holy Scriptures.'[25]

There are three cases of household baptism mentioned in the New Testament, but the language of each record strongly sustains the above testimony. In the household of Lydia (Acts xvi, 40), those who were baptized with her are called 'brethren,' and are 'exhorted' by Paul. In the jailer's household (Acts xvi, 31–34), Paul 'spoke the word of the Lord to *all* that were in his house,' and they all 'believed in God and rejoiced.' And of the household of Stephanas (1 Cor. xvi, 15), which Paul baptized, he says that they 'addicted themselves to the ministry of the saints.' These are things which no infant can do, and prove that in each case they first heard the Gospel, and then were baptized upon their personal faith in the Lord Jesus. The second ordinance of the New Testament Churches was:

THE LORD'S SUPPER. Its design was purely commemorative of Christ's death. Our Lord instituted it on the night before he was offered. He gave broken bread to his disciples, to represent his body as it should be mangled the next day by crucifixion; then they each drank of the cup, which represented the shedding of his blood for the remission of sins. All his disciples present partook of these, and he made the commemoration perpetual, saying, 'This do in remembrance of me.' Here is the simple and beautiful ordinance about which his followers have wrangled for centuries in the most shameful manner. Human manipulations have made it an 'awful mystery,' a 'dreadful sacrament,' or oath, and even a base idolatry, put in the place of Christ himself. With many who reject the Romish teaching of the Supper, an accretion of ideas and applications are associated with it, which amount to bald superstitions. We hear devout and enlightened Protestants calling it 'the food of the soul,' a 'banquet of flesh and blood,' an 'eating of Christ's flesh and blood,' and the like nonsense. Some even pervert such passages as this by applying them to the Supper: 'If ye eat not my flesh and drink not my blood ye have not eternal life,' whereas Jesus spoke these words a year and a half before the Supper was established; and if they bear upon it at all, they imply that eternal life itself can be had by taking bread and wine at the table. Others, in some way, which nobody knows any thing about, find a real presence of Christ at the Table, as they find him in no other religious observance, and so they insist upon it that the saints have fellowship with him and with each other there, such as they can have nowhere else, and in no other way. Hence, without intending it, contempt is brought upon the Bible teaching that Christ himself and not bread is the food of the soul, that the atonement brings salvation and not the act which commemorates it, in the use of bread and wine. Christ is the only bond of vital union, and the only test of fellowship amongst saints, and not a material ordinance. If fellowship amongst Christians is purchased by sitting with each other at the same table, their love is bought at a very light cost. Oneness with Christ himself, the brotherhood of regeneration by the Holy Spirit, mutual burden-bearing and mutual watch-care, formed the visible bond of fellowship in the Apostolic Churches. This sort of unity cost them something, it ecclesiastical history where the Supper has held any single congregation together for a day. Churches of all names who celebrate it constantly, live in open contention year by year. The love of Judas for John was cramped into a close corner when they sat at the same table, and ate the sop from the same dish. If Christians are not one on a much higher plane than that of eating and drinking the Supper with each other, their true unity is a hopeless business. In fact, as if to prove the perfect emptiness of this pretension, in some Protestant communions, the Supper itself has been the subject of hot dispute, the chief bone of contention from century to century. The greatest bitterness has been indulged, and anathemas have been bandied about, *pro* and *con*, with a freedom which has marked no other form of discussion, and by men, too, who regularly meet at the same table.

About a quarter of a century after Christ's death, the Corinthian Church had corrupted the Supper by the introduction of startling abuses. 1 Cor. xi. They associated the love-feast therewith, and indulged in gluttony and drunkenness. Christ corrected these abuses by a new revelation through Paul, and gave a second definition of the design of the Supper, in exposition of the first. 'As often as ye eat this bread and drink this cup, ye *proclaim* the Lord's death till he come.' Paul 'received of the Lord,' that he intended the Supper as a memorial, preaching institution, whereby the redeemed Church, known as the 'Ye' meeting in 'one place,' preached Christ's death. The Primitive Churches, then, threw no superstitious mystery about it, ascribed to it no semi-saving efficacy, accompanied it with no popish mortification, self-humiliations, super-solemnities, distempered enchantments, or pious legerdemain. To them it was a 'feast' of artless thanksgiving, kept with the 'leaven of sincerity and truth,' for the preaching of a sacrificial Redeemer. The bread and wine were common, like any other bread and wine, and Christ was present with them by his Spirit as in prayer, praise, and other acts of worship, no more sacredly and no less. The converts who had been baptized met together on 'the first day of the week,' and Justin Martyr, A. D. 150, says: 'It is not lawful for any to partake, but such as believe the things that are taught by us to be true, and have been baptized.' There were no such things as 'different denominations' amongst them. Some congregations had factions amongst them, which are called 'sects,' but no sect of Churches was distinguished from other sects of Churches by a different order of faith and practice. In this respect they walked under the same rule, were all immersed believers, and were in perfect accord in their Gospel practice. When men are willing to return to the Gospel order of regeneration and baptism, their own obedience to Christ Jesus will remove all controversy on these subjects by restoring things to the Gospel *status;* and then there must of necessity be again: 'One Lord, one faith, one baptism,' and one Table. But until then there never can be; and what is more, there never ought to be, except on this Apostolic Church principle.

CHAPTER XI.

THE BAPTIST COPY OF THE APOSTOLIC CHURCHES.

FROM the fall of Jerusalem, A. D. 70, to the end of the century, great changes occurred in the Roman Empire, some of which seriously affected the Christian Churches. Domitian occupied the throne from 81 to 96, and like all tyrants, he was weak, cruel, despotic. He exhausted the finances of the empire by lavish expenditures, and laid a heavy tax upon the Jews. He also banished literary men and philosophers from Rome, and persecuted the Christians as 'Atheists,' because they worshiped an unseen God, without visible representation, figure, symbol, image or altar. Besides this, the emperor claimed divine worship for himself, as much as had Caligula before him. He every-where polluted the temples with his statues, and we are told that endless sacrifices were offered at his altars. His decrees began with the words: '*Dominus et Deus noster*' (our Lord and God) commands this and that, and whoever spoke of him otherwise was subject to the charge of treason. Some Jews, to evade the tax, denied their nationality, and as the Christians were classed with Jews, strict examination was made of their persons and rites. Because they refused to pay him the profane worship which he demanded, he was inflamed with rage. The doctrine of the second advent of Christ was confused with the Jewish belief in a coming Messiah, and this kept him on the alert with suspicion, lest a political rival should make him trouble. Hence, great numbers of Christians suffered the confiscation of their goods, others were put to death or exiled, and the 'gloomy atheists' who escaped, were treated by society as impious persons. Happily, his wrath was launched against them late in his reign, or the persecution would have reached a level of severity with that of Nero. His successor, Nerva, A. D. 96-98, was more just and humane, revoked the edict of Domitian, recalled the banished from the mines and the Islands of the Mediterranean, and in fact, forbade the further persecution of Jews or Christians. Then, Christianity came near to the Cæsars and even reached the royal family. Flavius Clement was cousin to Domitian, high in office and in the regard of the people; and there seems to be good evidence that he and his wife, Domatelli, became Christians, with others in the highest ranks of society.

At the close of the First Century, Christianity stands in its ideal beauty, fresh from Christ, full of new life given by the Holy Spirit, and in the pure mold which inspired Apostles had formed, without one defect from the touch of human governments. It looked like a frail craft tossed on a stormy sea, though freighted with all the wealth of heaven. It was the first beam from the Morning Star, making its way out of infinite solitudes as fleetly and softly as the Dove of Jordan. Jesus had come in the Augustan Age, had uttered every word which man needed to hear, and finished every deed needed for his salvation. Yet, his new scepter, swayed over the human spirit, was never to be broken. He came to make life higher, poetry broader, history brighter, and religion sublimer; an art, which should lift the vulgar into the ideal, and perfect praise out of low human passions. When the heavens closed on our ascended Lord, his Apostles went forth to the great uplifting movement amongst slaves, and the poorest of the common people. By a natural but sure process they laid its foundations in their confidence, toil and blood, and built from this basis to the top-stone of society. The century opened with the cries of the Bethlehem Babe, and closed with the Man of Sorrows on his throne, in the heaven of heavens. To the far East he had become the Day-spring, to the far West the Rising Sun. Warlike people and pastoral, polite and barbarian, had begun to feel his power, from Rome to the far-off shores of the Empire, which were washed by every sea. Those Apostles who had stood with him on the mountain in Galilee, had done their work, and were now enthroned with him. Their names, yet unrecorded in the annals of the Empire, were written in the Lamb's Book of Life forever.

Having thus found the model of the New Testament Church, the question is forced upon us: Whether or not this pattern is retained in any of the Churches of the present day? Without casting ungenerous reflections upon any Christian body whatever, it may be said that as to substance and form, the most accurate resemblance to this picture of the Apostolic Churches, is now found in the Baptist Churches of Europe and America. Dr. Duncan reports: 'That when Gesenius, the great German Hebraist and Biblical critic, first learned what Baptist Churches were, he exclaimed: 'How exactly like the Primitive Churches!''[1] So Ypeig, late Professor of Theology in the University of Groningen, and Dermout, Chaplain to the King of Holland, who, together, prepared a History of the Netherland's Reformed Church for that government, have the same principles in view when they say:

'We have now seen that the Baptists who in former times were called Anabaptists, and at a later period Mennonites, were originally Waldenses, who, in the history of the Church, even from the most ancient times, have received such a well-deserved homage. On this account the Baptists may be considered, as of old, the only religious community which has continued from the times of the Apostles; as a Christian Society which has kept pure through all ages the evangelical doctrines of religion. The uncorrupted inward and outward condition of the Baptist community affords proof of the truth contested by the Romish Church, of the great necessity of a reformation of religion such as that which took place in the sixteenth century, and also a refutation of the erroneous notion of the Roman Catholics that their denomination is the most ancient.'[2]

The late Dr. Oncken assured the writer that in forming a new Church at Hamburg, A. D. 1834, the constituent members first resolved that they would shut themselves up entirely to the Apostolic model, as found in the New Testament.

They, therefore, devoted themselves for some time to prayer and the exclusive study of that Book as an inspired Church Manual; and on comparing the result, to their surprise, they found themselves compelled to form a Church in accord with the Baptist Churches in England and America. Yet, there is nothing strange in this; the New Testament is ever the same, and it is but natural that when the devout mind is left free from all standards but this, with the determination to follow it in the most simple-hearted manner, it should produce the same stamp of New Testament Churches every-where and always.

In what, then, do the Baptist Churches of to-day differ from other ecclesiastical bodies? Only in retaining certain peculiarities of the New Testament Churches which others have laid aside. And in what do Baptist peculiarities consist? The fundamental difference between them and others lies much deeper than the question of Baptism, either as regards the act itself or its subjects. The distinction is much broader, deeper and more radical. There was no need for serious protest against the Romish hierarchy, for example, on the subject of immersion, down to the thirteenth century, for that was her settled custom to that time; while it is still the custom of the Greek Church. The living and underlying principles of Baptist Churches, relate to the sovereign and absolute headship of Christ in his Churches; to the exclusive authority of the Scriptures, as containing his law for their direction in all things; to the supernatural regeneration of each Christian forming the Churches; and to the liberty and responsibility to God, of each individual conscience. Here we find the great staple of Baptist life and history, and all other questions are subordinate, growing out of these. Aside from these peculiarities, Baptists stand side by side with many denominations of Christians in the present age, and heartily hail the present state of divinity, as set forth in the clear and vigorous teachings of the Reformed Churches. These are our precious treasure, in common with the holy inheritance of other God-fearing men, and we cling to them with gratitude, as in the main, the embodiment of New Testament truth.

It must ever be kept in mind, that the whole body of Baptists have never put forth an authorized expression of their principles and practices in the form of a creed. Some few of their Churches have never made a formal declaration of their faith aside from the Bible; while in the main, each separate Church expresses what it thinks the Scriptures require of it as a Church, in a 'Declaration of Faith.' There is a substantial agreement in the entire fraternity of our Churches, which it is not difficult to set forth. In common with other orthodox Christians, so called, we believe the doctrines of the Divine Unity and Trinity; of Christ's incarnation and proper Deity; of man's fall and helplessness, and his redemption by the vicarious sacrifice of our Lord Jesus Christ; of the Personality and Deity of the Holy Spirit, and his plenary inspiration of the Holy Scriptures; of free justification by Christ's mediatorial work; of sanctification by the inwrought agency of the Holy Spirit; of holy living on earth after God's commandments; of a future resurrection of the body, and the day of judgment; and of a state of eternal rewards and punishments in another world. Of course, as in all other bodies of Christians, controversies exist amongst ourselves touching the various modifications of these doctrines; enough, at least, to show that there is and must be diversity of view, where the divine right of interpretation is exercised amongst thoughtful men. The distinguishing principles of Baptists, then, may be stated thus:

I. THAT THE INSPIRED SCRIPTURES CONTAIN THE FULL AND SUPREME AUTHORITY OF CHRIST IN ALL THAT RELATES TO CHRISTIAN FAITH AND PRACTICE, WHETHER IN DOCTRINE, ORDINANCE, THE ORDERING OF A HOLY LIFE, OR IN THE ADMINISTERING OF CHURCH GOVERNMENT. These alone must be followed; and all legislation, canon, creed or decree, springing from tradition, ecclesiastical authority, or usage of antiquity, not enjoined in the Scriptures, is to be resisted and rejected, from whatever source it may spring, either inside the local Church or outside, as intolerable in the faith and practice of the Churches. We find a wide difference between a simple confession or declaration of what the Bible teaches, and an authoritative creed. A creed is an imperative test which must be enforced in the interests of absolute uniformity; and this is the exact position of Rome. She reasons thus: 'Divine truth is one; therefore, true believers cannot differ in their subscription to the truth. But they do differ; therefore, in difference there is heresy. Now, heresy must be kept out of the Church; therefore, make a creed to keep it out. Who, then, has the sole right to make a creed? Of course, only the Church.' Thus, the Bible is interpreted by creed-making, and its teachings to the individual man are vetoed, because he is compelled to accept the interpretation in the creed. Creeds tell men what they shall find in the Bible if they consult it, and if they find not that, they shall find nothing. For the time being, what the majority condemns is heresy, and the heretical minority must be punished until they become the majority. Yet, no creed can be made a full and perfect unity; nothing can be that unity but the Divine Testimony, and that must be personally consulted, man by man. He must be bold, indeed, who tries to unify God's word by drawing up a creed, either to supplement it or push it aside. God crystallized his own Oracles as a perfect and changeless creed forever; and when man takes it into his head that he can improve its formulation, he betrays his conceit by perpetually giving us new creeds, in which he appeals to the Bible for their support, provided, that we will read the Sacred Text through his colored glass. But because the Bible has never been outgrown as the one standard, and cannot be creedified in brief; the Baptist holds the substitution of any authoritative creed as the first step in apostasy. Another distinctive principle with Baptists is:

II. THAT A CHRISTIAN CHURCH MUST BE MADE UP ONLY OF PERSONS WHO ARE MORALLY REGENERATED; AND THAT IT IS NOT A SIMPLE VOLUNTARY ASSOCIATION, BUT A BODY OF MEN CALLED OUT OF THE WORLD ABOUT THEM, BY CHRIST'S SPECIAL AUTHORITY, TO BE A PEOPLE PECULIAR TO HIMSELF. The regeneration of each man in Christ's Church must be wrought by the Holy Spirit, he must be baptized upon his own choice, and covenant to maintain the order of the Gospel in its purity. We hold that the fundamental decession from Apostolic teaching, which has created scandal, shame, and division amongst Christians, lodges in that ritualistic grace which has scorned a soul-renovation wrought by the Spirit of God, as a piece of fanaticism, and has put this fable in the place of the Spirit's saving work. This legerdemain has been foisted in under that shadowy figment called catholicity, and outward ordinances have been made the channel of saving efficacy in place of 'a new creature in Christ Jesus.' With us spiritual regeneration is the moot-point against all heresies, for on this all cognate points have turned in every century. Jorg says of Dr. Lange, that he declared publicly in 1854: 'It was not opposition to infant baptism, but Church order and fellowship that is the culminating essence of all Baptists, in the past and present.'[3] Sacramental salvation has been the seed from which every distortion of Apostolic Christianity has sprung. Baptists have stood, and still stand, in stout and holy protest against the abominable doctrine that baptism and the Lord's Supper are saving institutions; and they demand that before any man shall put his hand to either of these, he shall be renovated by the Spirit of God, through faith in his Son, and then he shall be entitled to them because he is regenerate, his regeneration having made this both his duty and privilege.

This radical principle compels them to reject infant baptism, because in the nature of the case the infant cannot be a witness to Christ, as the salt of the earth and the light of the world. Baptism puts the infant into a most questionable position. It cannot bring him into any covenanted relation to Christ which did not exist before. Unbaptized, he was not a member of Christ's Church at all, and his baptism does not so make him a member thereof, as to put him under its responsibilities, or call him to its duties, or make him answerable to its discipline, or require him to honor its brotherhood. Though baptized, he is not allowed to come to the Lord's Table, because he cannot 'discern the Lord's body;' but he was compelled to be baptized, whether he could discern the Lord's baptism or not. If he had died unbaptized, he would have been numbered amongst the saints in heaven without repentance, faith or any other religious act; but if he grows up to manhood after his baptism, he must be converted before he is fitted even for the Church on earth. What, then, has his baptism done for him either in this world or that which is to come? No satisfactory and logical answer can be given to this question but that given by the pope, namely: That his baptism is his regeneration *de facto*. It admits him into the Church on earth with all its privileges so long as he lives; and it delivers him from a horrible *limbus infantum*, if he dies in infancy, and secures salvation for him, die when he may. The rejection of infant baptism by Baptists is not a mere whim or narrow prejudice, but in their judgment this institution vitiates the purity of Christ's Church, as is seen in all the State Churches of Europe, where the law makes the whole population members of the Church through this rite. It attaches an importance to baptism which does not belong to it, and so perverts the design of the Gospel ordinance, by exalting it entirely above its proper place; and it places the innocent child in a nondescript position to which he is a stranger in the Gospel; thus there can be no natural place for it in the Church of Christ. The very object of a Gospel Church is the promotion of mutual growth in truth, purity, and love; the advancement of Christ's cause on earth, and the salvation of the Christless; to none of which ends a babe can contribute. Then, as Baptist Churches are pure democracies, they cannot deprive a child of the right to choose Christ for himself, for in them all are equal; each member having his own vote in all that concerns their well-being, a responsibility which a child cannot assume. Thus we consider that a Church made up of unregenerate members takes the second step in apostasy. One more distinctive principle of Baptists is:

III. THAT THEY MAINTAIN BAPTISM AND THE LORD'S SUPPER AFTER THE APOSTOLIC APPOINTMENT BOTH AS IT REGARDS THEIR RELATIONS TO THEMSELVES AS ORDINANCES, AND TO OTHER GREAT GOSPEL TEACHINGS. We use neither of them as a charm, or spiritual amulet to serve the ends of superstition in the supposition that the first can wash away sin, or that the other exerts any moral efficacy on the soul. All the waters of the sea cannot wash away a moral stain from man, nor can all the bread and wine brought from the harvest-fields and vineyards of earth strengthen his immortal soul. We think that the supper should only be celebrated when and where the purpose of its celebration can be properly served. Hence, we take the elements only when the local Church is met 'in one place' as a body, and shun the popish custom of carrying them to the room of the sick, as if they contained salvation, or some magical influence. Christ personally is the healing medicine of the afflicted Christian, and not bread and wine. We, therefore, hold that every idea of sacramental grace is a piece of superstition, to be sacredly discarded. Sacramentarianism is the third step in apostasy. The last distinctive principle of Baptists is:

IV. THAT THEY EARNESTLY OPPOSE ALL CONNECTION OF THE CHURCH WITH THE STATE, AND ALL DISTINCTIONS MADE BY THE STATE AMONGST ITS CITIZENS, ON THE GROUND OF RELIGION. They protest that the State has nothing to do with the control of religion; but that it must give unrestricted religious freedom to all, as their sacred and natural right in the exercise of a free conscience. All true soul-liberty arises in that purity of conscience, which, unbound itself, leaves all other consciences free. Our idea is, that as the untrammeled conscience is the inalienable right of man, he can be made accountable only to God for its exercise. Hence, when any human power proscribes or persecutes man, by putting him under pains or penalties for following his convictions of duty in obeying God, such interference is an usurpation. When a man follows these convictions, he is entitled to the honest respect and love of all; and he is bound to extend the same rights to others which he claims for himself. Nay, fidelity to manhood and to God requires us to contend, and if need be to suffer, for this, as the right of others, and to treat those who differ from us in religious opinion and practice, with the respect and love which sacredly honors our own immunities. This holy principle lays the ax at the root of all legal proscription and persecution. The persecution of one Christian by another is the coolest wickedness that can be perpetrated, because it hides under the color of law; and when so-called Christian States inflict martyrdom, they simply inflict cold-blooded murder. Men who kill others against law, generally do so under the impulses of irregular passion. But those who legally put men to death because they cannot conform to their religion, lift up red hands as their only rightful claim to Christian discipleship; for they have methodized homicide under the pretense of a holy regularity. They make piety toward God preside with prayers at the blood-shedding of redeemed men. This State-murder has been steadily dealt out to Baptists by every dominant sect of religion, with scarcely an exception, after allying itself with the State; while our people have insisted on their right to the free exercise of their own faith, and to the freedom of all other men to serve God on their own volition, without dictation from any man.

According to the estimate of Sharon Turner there were at the close of the first century already about 500,000 Christians in the world, and the Scriptures show that they cherished the sacred principles here set forth. These doctrines are still as fresh as ever, and are as soundly reproduced in the Baptists of the nineteenth century as in those of the first. It will now be our business to show how and where they have lived in the intervening centuries, when not an Apostle was left to expound or defend them, but only the Word of God in which they abide, and must live forever. Yet, the question is constantly arising why all Christians do not earnestly strive to go back to the pattern of the Apostolic Churches? Beck forcefully answers this inquiry thus:

'It is quietly assumed that the original arrangements of the Church were only possible at that time, and that in later ages they have become impracticable and unsuitable. People have got into the habit of regarding this Scriptural pattern as an ideal that cannot be carried out in practice. But why can we not realize it? Is the cause to be found in the fanatical character of the first period of Christianity, or does it lie in the fact, that the latter progress has proved untrue to the ideal to which the First Age remained true? The latter is the case. The Scriptural Church constitution takes for granted, a society which grows and develops from within by the free faith of those who compose it, and which separates itself from the rest of the community. If doctrine and sacrament must be founded on the divine word, in order to represent and promote true Christianity, this is no less essential also for the constitution and discipline of the Church. The two things cannot be separated, as the history of the great Churches shows, without entailing increasing evil and injury on the Church. The union between doctrine and constitution must take place in accordance with what the divine word represents to have been the rule and the practice from the beginning. This is the only right way to improvement.'[4]

POST-APOSTOLIC TIMES.

CHAPTER I.

SECOND CENTURY.

IT is estimated that at the opening of this century, from two to three hundred Churches had been gathered, some of them thousands of miles apart. When the Apostles died, their authority died with them and they lived only in their writings. Their office did not allow of perpetuation, for they were the chosen witnesses of Christ's life and work, and could not bequeath their oral testimony to others. When these orphaned flocks were left alone in all their humanness, their only directory was the Book by which the Apostles had transmitted their witness and revelations, under the infallible inspiration of the Holy Spirit. No miraculous agency was needed to supplement their writings, and the Awful Volume finished, their twelve thrones were left vacant. Woe to him who makes the Bible a foot-stool to climb into their empty seats. For the first time man was left on common ground, with the choice of making the unmixed authority of that book his guide to Christ, or of committing his soul to the lead of uninspired men. This fact alone put the Gospel to its severest test, and made the second century a most solemn period, as Christians had no alternative but to follow the New Book. How, then, did they bear themselves toward the Sacred Oracles?

Eusebius says, that they 'Vied with each other in the preaching of Christ, and in the distribution of the Scriptures.' The Epistle to the Thessalonians was written about twenty years after the crucifixion, and the last of the New Covenant books within fifty years thereafter. Probably Paul's Epistles were first collected into one volume; but within half a century after the death of John, the four Gospels were publicly read in the Churches of Syria, Asia Minor, Italy and Gaul, and all the New Testament books were collected by about A. D. 150. The first translation appears to have been the Syriac, called Peshito (literal), for its fidelity, rendered most faithfully into the common language of the Holy Land. Some think that our Lord's exact language is better preserved in this version than in the Greek manuscripts themselves. J. Winchelaus, who devoted much research to its history, says that it preserves the letter of sacred Scripture truly, and Michaelis pronounces it 'The very best translation of the New Testament that I have ever read.' It throws a strong light upon the act of baptism in that age. The word which expresses that act is *amad*, which the Syriac lexicons define by 'immerse.' Bernstein uses these words: 'He was dipped, immersed: he dipped or plunged himself into something.' Michaelis declares, that this is the Syriac word which Jesus would use for baptism, in the vernacular language which he spoke. This version was read in the Christian assemblies, with the originals, and where they could not be understood by the people, interpreters rendered them into their mother tongue on the spot. In this age a Latin version was also made, which came into general use immediately. Woide ascribes the translation of the *Sahidic*, the dialect of Upper Egypt, and the *Coptic*, that of Lower Egypt, to this period. In the Latin, the word *baptizo* was rendered by the word *tingo*, to dip, or immerse; in the Sahidic it was transferred, evidently, because as a Greek term it was well understood in Upper Egypt; and in the Coptic it was translated by the word *omas*, to immerse or plunge. Latin versions were soon multiplied. Augustine says: 'Those who have translated the Bible into Greek can be numbered, but not so the Latin versions; for in the first ages of the Church, whoever got hold of a Greek Codex, ventured to translate it into Latin.' He also decides that the ancient Italic is the most literal of the Latin versions. Irenæus, too, speaks of many barbarous tribes who had 'salvation in their hearts without ink or paper;' alluding to the fact that the unlearned heard the Scriptures read in their own tongue in the public assemblies. These early Baptists decided all questions of doctrine by an appeal to their Sacred Books; being very jealous of forged books, which abounded very early. Tertullian tells us where some of the inspired autographs could be found at that time. 'The very images,' he says, 'of their voice and person are now recited and exhibited. Do you live in Achaia? There is Corinth. Are you not far from Macedonia? You have Philippi and Thessalonica. Are you nigh unto Asia? There is Ephesus. Or, if you border upon Italy, there is Rome.'[1] And as late as the fourth century, Peter of Alexandria said, that: The Gospel of John, written with his own hand, was still preserved and venerated in the Church at Ephesus. Before Christ, spurious Jewish writings purporting to be genuine, appeared; and an attempt was made to incorporate some of these manufactures with certain apochryphal gospels, into the Christian Scriptures, in order to incorporate Jewish notions and pagan philosophy into Christianity. These false lights misled many of the primitive Christians, and have had a shameful influence in shaping current Christian history.

Then, a pernicious tradition began to inject itself into the teaching of the Churches. By tradition is meant, from *traditio*, that which is delivered orally, and is left unwritten, passing by word of mouth from one to another. Of these, Eusebius first, and Jortin in modern times, call Papias 'the father.' He died A. D. 163, leaving a collection of random, hearsay discourses and sayings of Jesus and his Apostles, called 'Oracles of the Lord.' He tells us that this was made up of first-hand evidence only, and that he preferred oral testimony to written; hence, he details many ridiculous things, showing that he was fond of gathering up floating stories.

He says that he made inquiry of the Elders, 'What did Andrew or Peter, Thomas or Philip, or James, say?' Yet, it is doubtful whether he had seen any of them. He had a great dislike for Paul, which Jortin excuses, on the ground that he was 'a simpleton,' and which reconciles us to the loss of his writings, beyond a few fragments. But this turbid stream of tradition widened and deepened, notwithstanding Irenæus says, that the Christians came to salvation: 'By the will of God delivered to us in writing, to be the foundation and pillar of our faith.'

These Churches were full of missionary energy. The iron republic had first given place to the pen of the lettered empire, and that in turn had opened the way for the conquering cross; for by A. D. 180 the Gospel had reached all its provinces from Britain to the Tigris, and from the Danube to the Libyan Desert, in many cases including the learned and rich. Justin Martyr wrote that there was no race, Greek or barbarian, that either wandered in wagons or dwelt in tents, which did not offer praise to the Crucified. And Tertullian said, in his Apology to the Emperor: 'We are but of yesterday, yet we have filled your empire, your cities, your islands, your castles, your corporate towns, your assemblies, your very camps, your tribes, your companies, your palace, your senate, your forum; your temples alone are left to you. So great are our numbers, that we might successfully contend with you in open warfare; but were we only to withdraw ourselves from you, and to remove by common consent to some remote corner of the globe, our mere secession would be sufficient to accomplish your destruction, and to avenge our cause. You would be left without subjects to govern, and would tremble at the solitude and silence around you,—at the awful stillness of a dead world.' When Pliny governed Bythnia under Trajan, in the beginning of this period, he complained that 'The sacrifices of the gods were neglected and the temples deserted,' so enthusiastic were the Christians. Their risen Saviour awakened every power of their nature, and they caught his sublime benevolence and self-sacrificing spirit, each regenerated man toiling for him. Their individual names have almost all faded from the pages of history. Of all who lived contemporary with the Apostles and used the pen in the service of Christ we have but six, half the number of their noble chiefs. These are called the Apostolic Fathers, namely: Barnabas, Clement of Rome, Hermas, Ignatius, Polycarp and Papias, of whom the last is doubtful. It would be most interesting to trace the biography of this group of old Baptists, but space will not allow.

A word only may be indulged concerning several of them. CLEMENT was pastor at Rome A. D. 91–100. He was a man of great administrative ability, and his Epistle to the Corinthians has come down to us. For a long time this was read aloud in the Churches. The Church at Corinth, being divided and in trouble, sought advice of her sister Church at Rome, which answered through its pastor, without command, authority, or fatherly curse. The Church at Rome places herself on a perfect equality with the Church at Corinth, thus: 'The Church of God which sojourns at Rome, to the Church of God which sojourns at Corinth.' Even thus early the Corinthian Baptist Church had learned how to abuse its own chosen pastors, and this firm-handed old elder says : ' It is, beloved, exceedingly disgraceful that such a thing should be heard of, as that the most steadfast and ancient Church of the Corinthians should, on account of one or two persons, engage in sedition against its presbyters.' The letter exhorts them to 'do as it is written,' saying: ' Ye knew full well the Holy Scriptures, and have thoroughly searched the Oracles of God.' HERMAS wrote the ' Shepherd,' and Moberly ranks him with the laymen of his time. His book is disfigured with snatches of fantastic poetry and is full of visions, parables and commands. Being very popular in its day and full of similitudes, it has been called the ' Pilgrim's Progress' of the second century, not much to the honor of either of the Baptist dreamers. Jerome calls it 'childish,' and Tertullian ' apocryphal ;' to say the least, it is a singular production. IGNATIUS was a brave and noble character, but his name has been shamefully abused, in the attempt to palm upon him a series of deliberately forged epistles, to make him the representative of an episcopal hierarchy. Trajan demanded that he should sacrifice to the gods, when the venerable pastor of Antioch replied, that he carried God with him, for he carried Christ within his breast. The emperor demanded : ' Dost thou not think we have the gods within us ?' He replied, that there was but one God, Jesus Christ. Trajan asked if he meant the Crucified One, when he answered that he did. He was put in chains, sentenced to be devoured by beasts, and sent, under a guard of ten soldiers, to Rome, where he was torn to pieces in the Flavian amphitheater, amid the shouts of 80,000 spectators.

POLYCARP is supposed to have been the pastor at Smyrna in the days of the Apostle John, and was the veriest Christian patriarch. But in his Epistle to the Philippians, which was long read in the Churches of Asia, he draws a great distinction between himself and the Apostles, and apologizes for writing to a Church which had received an Epistle from Paul. A great plague ravaged the East in the reign of Marcus Aurelius, and popular clamor demanded Polycarp as an atoning victim to the gods; at the age of ninety years he suffered martyrdom, A. D. 166, 167. He had retired to the country, but one of his servants betrayed him. When he approached the city the chief magistrate took him into his chariot, asking him : 'What harm is there in saying Lord Cæsar, and sacrificing ?' This, he said, he could not do, when he was cast violently from the chariot, and lamed one foot in the fall. He limped into the stadium, where the crowd cried for his blood ; and he believed that he heard a voice commanding, ' Polycarp, play the man !' He was ordered to swear by the fortunes of Cæsar, and cry, ' Away with the Atheists,' the proconsul offering him liberty if he would revile Christ. The answer of the simple-hearted old Baptist was : ' Eighty and six years have I served him, and he never did me any wrong ; how, then, can I blaspheme my King and Saviour ?' The proconsul cried : ' I have wild beasts at hand, to them I will cast thee, except thou repent.'

'Call them,' answered the holy man. 'Thou despisest the wild beasts; I will have thee consumed by fire.' Again he replied, 'Why dost thou tarry? bring forth what thou wilt.' The herald was commanded to cry three times, 'Polycarp has confessed himself a Christian!' At once the multitude gave a shout of fury, and called for a lion to be let loose; but the magistrate said: 'Let him be burned!' A pile of fagots was brought, the elder loosed his girdle, laid aside his outer garments, and when about to be nailed to the stake begged: 'Leave me, I pray, unfastened. He who gives me strength to bear the fire, will hold me to the pile.' They simply tied him with cords; when looking up to heaven, he said: 'O, Lord God Almighty! I give thee thanks that thou hast counted me worthy, this day and this hour, to have a part in the number of thy martyrs, in the cup of thy Christ.' The flames were kindled, but they arched over him and would not touch him; seeing which an executioner plunged a dagger into his body, and he ascended to his Lord.

At this time, the whole body of laymen were as much alive to Christ as their pastors, and Bingham tells us of two young men who were taken captive into India, and established Churches there; also of a Christian young woman who brought the king and queen of the Iberians to Christ, and through them the nation. Christians gave their money for Christ as well as their toil. Marcion brought his whole fortune, between $7,000 and $8,000, in our currency, and gave it to the common fund, when he united with the congregation at Rome. Lucian, the cynic philosopher, says contemptuously: 'These poor creatures are firmly persuaded they shall one day enjoy eternal life. . . . They despise, therefore, all earthly possessions, and look upon them as common.' The most lowly in the Churches took an active part in the post-Apostolic synods in Palestine, Pontius, Gaul, and Rome, of which Eusebius gives an account, and exerted great influence in these bodies. And all the Churches maintained their independency, after the original model. Neander says, that every Church was governed by a union of elders, 'chosen from among themselves.' The Churches were so many loving families of spiritual disciples, maintaining their liberty against all ambitious pretensions from without. Mosheim shows, that they were not 'joined together by association, confederacy, or any other bonds but those of charity. Each Christian assembly was a little state governed by its own laws, which were either enacted, or at least approved, by the society.' Sometimes, when they sought advice of each other, they met for consultation, but these assemblies were simply advisory. Theophilus, pastor at Antioch, A. D. 180, compares the Churches to so many islands, as a strong figure of their independence. But toward the close of the century those of Greece and Asia began to meet in the capital of the province, in the spring and autumn, and to frame canons for general observance, till by degrees these ecclesiastical islands formed one confederated continent. Not intending to create a new governing power, they lost their equality and independency through their own fault. Tertullian held, that 'three persons' might compose a Church; and that if necessity arose any Christian might administer the ordinances; an opinion which Bishop Kaye excuses, because: 'All the Apostolic Churches were independent of each other, and equal in rank and authority.' No general council was held or known in this century.

After the first blaze of enthusiasm the love of many waxed cold, their religion became nominal, not a few relapsed into heathenism, and corruption began to creep into both doctrine and practice. With this change unnecessary and offensive practices were introduced, some being borrowed from the pagans, as the washing of hands and putting off the cloak before prayer. The practice of turning to the east in prayer was borrowed from the old sun-worship, and made emblematical of Christ. They also stretched their hands in prayer, in imitation of Christ's outstretched arms on the cross; and they came to abuse the Apostolic kiss after prayer, by ostentation. Clement of Alexandria rebuked this, thus: 'Love is not tested by a kiss, but by friendly feeling; there are those who make the Church re-echo with their kiss, but there is no love underneath.' Several useless ceremonies were added to baptism, amongst them the use of the sign of the cross, intended as a simple emblem of the Christian faith, but which, by A. D. 200, had become an idle habit in general use. Tertullian says: 'On getting up or going to bed, or putting on their clothes or their shoes, or walking out or sitting down, at table or at the bath; in short, in every act or movement, they made the sign of the cross upon the forehead.'[2] They also began to confine baptism to the festivals of Easter and Pentecost,—to anoint the candidate with oil after immersing him in water,—and to give him milk and honey after his baptism, to symbolize, that now he must live on the 'milk of the Word.'

But the most destructive error which crept in, was that of making baptism the channel of regeneration. Before this, it was generally spoken of as 'regeneration,' meaning, as the Scriptures teach, that the regenerated man, by baptism, put himself visibly under the new obligations which regeneration imposed. Now, they began to make it a 'seal,' which bound the man to Christ with the effect of an oath; and they called it an 'illumination,' confounding it with the light of the truth which it followed, and which sprang only from the Holy Spirit. This germ grew, and in time came to overshade the work of the Spirit on the heart, and threw the doctrine of a superhuman regeneration of the soul into the background. As to the act of baptism itself, there was no change in this age. All ecclesiastical writers agree with Venema that: 'Without controversy baptism, in the primitive Church, was administered by immersion into water, and not by sprinkling. . . . Concerning immersion, the words and phrases that are used sufficiently testify, and that it was performed in a river, a pool or a fountain.' The literature of that period compels this testimony. Barnabas, A. D. 119: 'Happy are they, who, trusting in the cross, go down into the water full of sins and pollutions, but come up again bringing forth fruit, having in the Spirit hope in Jesus.' Justin Martyr, A. D. 139, describes the baptized as those 'who receive the bath in the water.' Hermas, about A. D. 150, says, that they go down into the water devoted to death, and come up assigned to life; and that the Apostles 'went down into the water with them, and came up again.'³

Tertullian, A. D. 160–240, wrote the first work on baptism in the Christian era (*De Baptismo*), and opens his treatise with this enthusiastic exclamation: 'O! fortunate sacrament of our water.' He wrote in Latin, using the terms '*tingo*,' '*mergo*,' '*immergo*,' and '*mergito*,' with their connecting words, about fifty times, making the sense 'to immerse,' in each case. He compares the baptized to the earth emerging from the flood of Noah, 'to one emerging from the bath after the old sins, the dove of the Holy Spirit bringing the peace of God, flies, sent from heaven, where the Church is a figurative ark.' Of Christ's commission he says: 'The law of dipping was imposed, and the form prescribed, "teach the nations, immersing them into the name of the Father, and of the Son, and of the Holy Spirit. . . . and so, after that, all believing were immersed."' Semler has proved that he quoted from a Latin version and not from the Greek. In his ardor he lectured those who denied the need of water baptism, thus: 'You act naturally, for you are serpents, and serpents love deserts and avoid water; but we, like fishes, are born in the water, and are safe in continuing in it, that is, in the practice of immersion.' In his work, De Corona (c. iii), he takes pains to describe a baptism as it was practiced in his day: 'A little before we enter the water, in the presence of the congregation, and under the hand of the president, we make a solemn profession that we renounce the devil, his pomp, and his angels. Upon this, we are thrice immersed, making a somewhat ampler pledge than the Lord has appointed in the Gospel. When we come up out of the water, there is given to us a mixture of milk and honey, and we refrain from the daily bath for a week.' The 'ampler pledge,' refers to triune immersions instead of the one dipping; and abstinence from the common 'bath for a week,' arose from the superstition that they might wash off the baptismal water and oil.

After closely scanning all the evidence, Coleman concludes: 'In the second century it had become customary to immerse three times, at the mention of the several names of the Godhead.'⁴ Guericke, Neander, Reuss, Kurtz, Weiss, Schaff, Döllinger, Pressensé, Farrar, Carr, Conybeare and Howson, Stanley, and many other historians, not Baptists, unite in like testimony. Stanley sums up the evidence in these words:

'There can be no question that the original form of baptism—the very meaning of the word—was complete immersion in the deep baptismal waters; and that, for the first four centuries, any other form was either unknown, or regarded, unless in the case of dangerous illness, as an exceptional, almost a monstrous, case. To this form the Eastern Church still rigidly adheres; and the most illustrious and venerable portion of it, that of the Byzantine Empire, absolutely repudiates and ignores any other mode of administration as essentially invalid. The Latin Church, on the other hand, doubtless in deference to the requirements of a northern climate, to the changes of manners, to the convenience of custom, has wholly altered the mode, preferring, as it would fairly say, mercy to sacrifice; and (with the two exceptions of the Cathedral of Milan, and the sect of the Baptists) a few drops of water are now the Western *substitute for the three-fold plunge* into the rushing rivers, or the wide baptisteries of the East.'[5]

There was no baptism of babes in this century. Barlow, Bishop of Lincoln, quite startled the world when he said, in his letter to Tombes, that he believed there was not 'any just evidence for it, for about two hundred years after Christ.' Menzell calls it 'an abuse, and a departure from the original form of the sacrament.' Lange, in his 'History of Protestantism,' alleges that: 'The baptism of new-born infants was altogether unknown to primitive Christianity.' The writers of the second age imply the same thing when they speak of the baptized. Justin Martyr says, they are 'convinced,' 'believe the Gospel to be true,' pray and 'fast for their former sins;' Hermas, that they 'trust in the cross;' Irenæus, that they are 'cleansed of their old transgressions;' and Tertullian declares, 'We are not washed in order that we may cease from sinning, but because we have ceased, because we have already been washed in heart. . . . The divine grace, that is, the forgiveness of sins, remains unimpaired for those who are to be baptized; but then they must perform their part, so as to become capable of receiving it.'

After Neander had gone over the whole ground, he says, that baptism was not admissible at that time:

'Without the conscious participation of the person baptized, and his own individual faith. . . . We have every reason for holding infant baptism to be no Apostolic institution, and that it was something foreign at that first stage of Christian development. At first, baptism necessarily marked a distinct era in life, when a person passed over from a different religious stand-point, to Christianity; when the regeneration, sealed by baptism, presented itself as a principle of moral transformation, in opposition to the earlier development.'[6] In meeting the pretense that infant baptism sprang from Apostolic tradition, he answers: 'That such a tradition should first be recognized in the third century is evidence rather against, than for, its Apostolic origin. For it was an age when a strong inclination prevailed to derive from the Apostles every ordinance which was considered of special importance, and when, moreover, so many walls had been thrown up between it and Apostolic times, hindering the freedom of prospect.'[7]

But although Christians knew nothing of infant baptism, the compassion of Jesus for children had greatly ameliorated their condition amongst the heathen. Uhlhorn says:

'To children, also, the Gospel first gave their rights. They, too, in antiquity were beyond the pale of laws. A father could dispose of his children at will. If he did not wish to rear them, he could abandon or kill them. The law of the Twelve Tables expressly awarded to him this right. Plato and Aristotle approved of parents abandoning weak and sickly children, whom they were unable to support, or who could not be of use to the State. Whoever picked up a child that had been deserted could dispose of it, and treat it as a slave. The father's power over his children was limitless; life and death were at his disposal. Christianity, on the contrary, taught parents that their children were a gift from God, a pledge intrusted to them, for which they were responsible to him. . . . The exposition of children was looked upon by Christians as plainly unlawful, and was regarded and treated as murder.'[8]

The same learned author quotes from Cæcilius, a Roman jurist, who flourished about A. D. 161, the horrid slander which charged them with eating children and drinking their blood. 'An infant covered over with meal, that it may deceive the unwary, is placed before the neophytes. This infant is slain by the young pupil, with dark and secret wounds, he being urged on as if to harmless blows on the surface of the meal. Thirstily,—O horror!—they lick up its blood; eagerly they divide its limbs; by this victim they are pledged together; with this consciousness of wickedness they are covenanted by mutual violence.'

This savage accusation of the Christians became universal amongst the pagans, and the Christian fathers earnestly repelled it in their Apologies. Justin Martyr sent his noble defense to the Senate, A. D. 140–150, and eloquently protests against this infamous falsehood. 'If we were to kill one another,' said he, 'we should be the causes, as far as in us lay, that no more persons should be brought into the world, and taught or instructed in the Christian religion and of putting an end to human kind.' Tertullian demands, with great spirit, that this terrible charge be made good. Biblias, a godly woman, was tortured by the authorities, to extort from her a confession that Christians ate their children, but exclaimed at the door of death: 'How can we eat infants? We, to whom it is not lawful to eat the blood of beasts!' Had infant baptism been known amongst the Christians, they would naturally have cited the fact in proof, that so far from slaughtering their children, they were baptized and stood on a level with themselves in their churches, and so, that they could not feed upon their fellow-members. Instead of this, they take the higher ground, that their Redeemer, whom they were bound to obey, loved their children most tenderly, and had provided for their salvation without reference to any conditions on their part.

Moved by this high conception of Christ's compassion, the gentle Irenæus brings out their view in bold contrast with the brutality of the pagans about them, when he says of Christ:

'Being thirty years old when he came to be baptized, and then possessing the full age of a Master, he came to Jerusalem so that he might be properly acknowledged by all as a Master. For he did not seem one thing while he was another, as those affirm who describe him as being man only in appearance; but what he was, that he also appeared to be. Being a Master, therefore, he possessed the age of a Master, *not despising or evading any condition of humanity*, not setting aside as to himself that law which he had appointed for the human race; but sanctifying every age, by that period corresponding to it which belonged to himself. For he came to *save all* through means of himself—all I say who, through him, are born again to God—infants, and children, and boys, and youths, and old men. He, therefore, passed through every age, becoming an infant for infants, thus sanctifying infants; a child for children, thus sanctifying those who are of this age, being at the same time made to them an example of piety, righteousness and submission; a youth for youths, becoming an example to youths, and thus sanctifying them for the Lord. So likewise he was an old man for old men, that he might be a perfect Master for all, not merely as respects the setting forth of the truth, but also as regards age, sanctifying at the same time the aged also, and becoming an example to them likewise.'⁹

This plea, that Jesus as a 'Master,' by authority, and by passing through all the stages of life himself, wrought out the salvation of 'the human race,' ranks Irenæus side by side with Justin and Tertullian, in rebutting the slanders of the pagans, by showing, as Venema says on this passage: 'That Christ, passing through all the ages of man, intended to signify by his own example, that he came to save men of every age, and also to sanctify or save infants. I conclude, therefore, that Pedobaptism cannot be certainly proved to have been practiced before the time of Tertullian.'¹⁰ In the writings of Tertullian we have the first recorded thought on the subject of infant baptism, and that, in the form of resistance to a proposed innovation. He stood in a trying position. Those who were resisting the encroachments of ritualism upon the original spirit of baptism, had taken in substance the ground held by the 'Friends' of to-day, namely: that only the Spirit and not water was needed. Quintilla preached this doctrine at Carthage, and with her stood several small bodies, according to Backhouse and Tylor, the Aseodrutae, the Seleucians, and Hermians. Others began to insist that no person who had reached intelligence could be saved without baptism, die at what age he might. These demanded that minors be allowed baptism, on condition that they '*ask*' it, and produce *sponsors*, who will be responsible for their conduct while they remain minors.¹¹ Tertullian resisted both these doctrines; and the last named, on the twofold consideration, that it would be a rash measure, because an innovation upon an established Christian ordinance; and because it would be contrary to Roman law in the province of Carthage. On the scriptural ground of objection, he cites the cases of the eunuch and Paul, who were believers, and knew themselves to be vessels of mercy, and so knew what they asked for before they were baptized. He contends, therefore, that it is: 'Most expedient to defer baptism, and to regulate the administration of it according to the condition, the disposition and the age of the person to be baptized, and especially in the case of little ones,' whom he calls '*parvulos*.'

He also objects to sponsors, demanding: 'What necessity is there to expose sponsors to danger;' since they cannot guarantee that the little one is, or will be, spiritually minded. 'Let them come,' says he, 'while they are growing up, let them come and *learn*, and let them be instructed when they come, and when they understand Christianity, let them confess themselves Christians. Why should that innocent age hasten to the remission of sins?' This leads him, as an astute lawyer, to the legal question of suretyship. He says: 'People act more cautiously in secular affairs; they do not commit the care of divine things to such as are not intrusted with temporal things.' The empire knew of no such suretyship in the religion of the gods, the faith of the realm, although it did in secular affairs; and what right had Christians to add to their burdens by meddling with a question that might bring them into direct conflict with an established legal relation? The Roman law made the father the guardian of the child; but when the parent was dead, it permitted the child two guardians during his minority. A tutor cared for his person and education, which included his religion, and a curator managed his estate. But the Christian Churches, being prohibited in the empire, could not be known in law as corporate bodies; and so, the baptism into them of minors (*infantuli*), under sponsorship, would create an illegal guardian; which act would, of course, bring new and needless trouble upon the Churches. He says: 'Death may incapacitate them for fulfilling their engagements.' But if not, with two sets of guardians, one over the morals and the other over the person of the legal minor, the sponsor would be in perpetual danger, hence he asks: 'What necessity is there to expose sponsors to danger?'

Afterward, these minors became members of the Church at Carthage, for Victor states, that when Eugenius was pastor of that Church, A. D. 480, its *infant readers*, whom we should call choir-boys, 'rejoiced in the Lord, and suffered persecution with the rest of their brethren.' That Tertullian uses the word *parvulus*, 'a little one,' to mean a minor at law, is indisputable. If, then, the immersion of babes was the custom of his time, why did this able father raise all this objection and discussion? 'Such as understand the importance of baptism,' he urges, 'are more afraid of presumption than procrastination; and faith alone secures salvation.' A minor who asked for baptism must ask for it on his own responsibility, and so the Church would be as discreet in this matter as the State was in secular things. The value of these facts, as evidence, is: 1. That about the end of the second century we find the first recorded instance of a proposition to admit legal infants, not babes, into the Christian Churches by baptism. 2. That such infants were to 'ask for baptism.' 3. That the proposal was sternly resisted as an innovation on established Gospel custom, and on legal grounds. 4. That there is no assumption here, of a right to the ordinance, even by one who was able to 'ask' for it and also produce sponsors for his conduct; but that the request was pressed as such and opposed. 5. That such evidence is fatal to the presumption that babes were baptized in the Christian Churches at that time.

It is clear enough that Tertullian never abandoned this position, because afterward, he united with those falsely charged with being averse to baptism in water. The Christians of this century had not yet come to the horrible dogma, that unbaptized babes are damned after death. They were anxious to bring all mankind to Christ as soon as possible, but were not yet ready to force their Master upon irresponsible ones, who knew not who he was, nor what he taught. They are truly represented by Schleiermacher, who says: 'The Roman Apostolical practice thoroughly agrees in demanding beforehand a beginning of faith and repentance, as all traces of infant baptism that men have wished to find in the New Testament, must first be put into it; it is, in view of the lack of definite information, difficult to explain how this departure from the original institution, could have originated and established itself so widely.'[12] This is in exact accord with Justin Martyr's account of baptism in his Second Apology, p. 93: 'We were born without our will, but we are not to remain children of necessity and ignorance, but in baptism are to have choice, knowledge, etc. . . . This we learned from the Apostles.' The biographer of Justin well said, 'Of infant baptism he knows nothing.'

As to the Lord's Supper, the writers of this century use ambiguous language, invent new terms, and set forth new ideas concerning it, not found in the New Testament. They still call the elements bread and wine after consecration as well as before; and signs of Christ, 'representing his body and blood,' his 'image,' and 'figure.' Yet, they speak of the Supper as an 'offering,' a 'sacrifice,' of the Table as an 'altar,' and of the administrator as a 'priest.' They also use many other florid words, which have led to corrupt uses in sanctioning the figments of real presence, consubstantiation, and transubstantiation. As yet, they had not fallen into the doctrine that the elements were Christ's literal flesh and blood; but they did hold that these were mystically in the bread and wine. Great efforts have been made to explain away their words, which opened a streamlet of error that has deluged nearly all Christendom, with the notion that the Supper is something more than what the New Testament makes it, a simple memorial. Concerning this ordinance, they introduced a vain system of allegory, between which scheme and transubstantiation there was no logical stopping place, and, in consequence of which, various superstitions were introduced. Even Tertullian feared, lest a crumb of the bread or a drop of the wine should fall to the ground. The custom arose of sending a morsel of the consecrated bread to the absent, lest they lose the blessings which it might impart. It was also used as a protecting charm, and taken to sea in ships for their protection, as if it were no longer common bread; it must be eaten fasting, which, Neander thinks, gave rise finally to the taking of one element in the Supper. Justin Martyr speaks of the wine being mixed with water, partly because the Passover wine was so mixed, partly to symbolize the water and the blood which flowed from the side of Christ on the cross, and partly in token of their union with him. As at the Passover, any one might preside at the table, although the presbyter generally presided. And Justin says, that it was not lawful for any one to partake: 'But such as believe the things that are taught by us to be true, and that have bathed in the bath for the remission of sins.'[13]

A great crisis in the history of soul liberty was brought on in this century. As the purity of Christian life was more and more felt, paganism became more violent, fierce and fanatical. Gospel contrast with the gross and sensual soon made it evident, that the new religion must force its own way or die. The new issue which it had raised in the world was primary, relating to the rights of conscience in matters of faith.

Most of the Christians were poor, and many were slaves who could not command their time, so they denied themselves of sleep, and met at each other's houses in the night. In using the pure but figurative language of their faith, they spoke of 'passing from death to life,' of being 'one in Christ,' of Christ being 'formed in them the hope of glory,' and of 'eating his flesh and drinking his blood' by faith; forms of speech which were seized upon and distorted in the most diabolical manner, exposing them to popular hate. They were pure, meek, loyal men; but all religions were tolerated except that of love, a religion best fitted for torture, wild beasts and flame. Nor could it be otherwise, when Rome herself was a goddess, with the Emperor for high-priest. Sometimes the most odious of the emperors in morals persecuted the Christians the least, as they cared little for the gods or religion. Mosheim pronounces Heliogabalus, 'The most infamous of all princes, and, perhaps, the most odious of all mortals,' yet, he says, 'he showed no marks of bitterness or aversion to the disciples of Christ.' Nero and Domitian were moved by caprice and cruelty largely, but as a rule, those most severe in their morals and devout in their spirit, were the sternest persecutors, because they were purely conscientious. Dean Milman ranks Marcus Aurelius as the rival of 'Christians, in his contempt of the follies of life;' Gibbon calls him a model Emperor, and Guizot couples him with Louis IX. of France, for sincerity and violence. The opposite of the selfish, sensual and reckless emperors, he was ultra-conscientious, even to blood-thirst. Called the 'Philosopher,' he made blood flow freely throughout his bitter reign; but when Commodus, his son, took the purple, he staunched every Christian artery which his father had opened. To this purer class of emperors Christ was unknown and must, in the nature of things, overturn the old politico-religious government, if he should prevail, and they believed that they were best discharging their duty to the State by protecting the pagan faith.

Yet, the Christians did not intend to overthrow the empire, nor did they complain of their political condition. Some of the great jurists of the age held noble sentiments on the primal rights of man. Under the Antonines, the greatest of them all, Ulpian, said: 'According to natural law, all men are born free; in civil law, it is true, slaves are treated as having no rights; not so, however, by natural law, for by this all men are equal.' All that the Christians demanded was, the right to worship God under the laws of nature. When the Proconsul reasoned with Achatius, that he who lives under the Roman laws should love the princes, he answered, 'By whom is the Emperor more loved than by Christians?' 'Good,' rejoined the governor, 'prove your obedience by sacrificing to his honor.' 'Nay,' said the martyr, 'I pray for my Emperor. But a sacrifice, neither he should require nor me pay. Who can offer divine honor to a man?' For this he died, being unwilling to serve the gods by command of the State, the monarch ranking as its chief deity. The Christians never revolted; they obeyed all other laws, they paid for the support of government, and proved their political allegiance at every point; while the laws on religion were enforced against them by special imperial acts and under military power. The younger Pliny shows, that the Roman authorities suspected their love-feasts of being secret unions for political mischief, and they were denounced as such in the edicts. When he was Proconsul of Bithynia, under Trajan, A. D. 106, 107, he tells Cæsar, that he put the question to each suspected person, 'Are you a Christian?' If they would cast a bit of incense on an altar they were discharged; if not, he executed them. This, Trajan approved, under the laws against 'illegal superstition,' and issued his edict against the guilds and clubs, which included the Christians, under the head of secret societies; but after a bloody persecution, an inquiry was made into the real conduct of Christians, and a broad distinction was discovered between their civil and religious conduct. Pliny reports that, though they worshiped Christ, 'they bound themselves by an oath against crime,' and he saw a clear line between their political reverence for the Emperor and their refusal to adore him as god. This ended the persecution, till it was renewed under Hadrian, A. D. 117–138.

It is not necessary to follow the course of the several persecutions, nor to detail the terrible barbarities which were inflicted upon the Christians in the many provinces of the empire; let it suffice to say, that no such bloodshed had ever been known. The homes of Christians in the east and west were plundered; they were driven from the baths and streets to the lists, were dragged from dens and crypts; slaves were forced to charge their masters with cannibalism, incest and every kind of crime; and children were tortured to extort a criminating word against their Christian parents. Wherever a handful of them met for worship, brother after brother was taken from his home to death, and the few who escaped looked at the vacant places which were left. Then they drew a little nearer to each other, not knowing who would ascend in the fiery chariot before the little Church should meet again. They were burned with hot irons, tossed in nets by wild bulls, thrown to ravenous beasts in the arena, and their bones denied burial. Delicate and weak women passed through tortures unheard of, without complaint. An iron chair was devised, made red hot, and the martyrs fastened in it for the delight of the amphitheater. The public appetite was sharpened to all sorts of horrors, and yet these children of God met their fate with a holy heroism that was not only enthusiastic but ecstatic. The inspiring case of Justin, and many others, must be passed, that a few words may be indulged concerning the remakable case of Blandina, who was martyred at Lyons, A. D. 177.

She was a poor slave-girl, fifteen years of age, who was put to every torture, that her Christian mistress might be implicated. She was kept in a loathsome dungeon, and brought into the amphitheater every day to see the agonies of her companions as they were roasted in the iron chair, or torn to pieces by lions. Her spirit was clothed with superhuman endurance, for although racked from morning till night, so that her tormentors were obliged to relieve each other for rest, her constancy vanquished their patience, her only answer being: 'I am a Christian, no wickedness is done by us.' Then they took her into the circus and suspended her on a cross, within reach of the wild beasts, to frighten her fellow-confessors. The multitude howled for her life and a lion was let loose upon the poor child, but not a quiver passed over

CHRISTIANS GIVEN TO THE LIONS IN THE ROMAN AMPHITHEATER.

her frame. She looked into its mouth and smiled like a queen, and the monster did not touch her. Only a century before this, the first slave-girl was converted to Christ, at Philippi, and now her ennobled sister cast holy defiance at the empire, and serenely looked Europe in the face. Her calm soul told this great Power, that at last the weak were endowed with the omnipotence of the Gospel. Her intrepid spirit showed, for the first time, how Jesus could lift a worm into the empire of a human conscience; and could rebuke cruelty in the mute eloquence of love. The brightest page in the history of Rome was written that day, in the beams of that child's hope. Taken down from the cross she was removed to her dungeon, but finally brought back into the arena for execution. Her slender frame was a rare victim for the savage populace, and they gloated on her. But she flinched not, more than the angel in Gethsemane before the swords and staves of the Passover mob. She stepped as lightly as if she were going to a banquet. She was first scourged, then scorched in the hot chair, and at last cast before a furious bull, which tossed her madly. Even then a sharp blade was needful to take the lingering throb of life; and when her body was burnt to ashes it was cast into the Rhone. From that day, this harmless child-slave has been with her redeeming Master in Paradise.

It is clear that this new doctrine of soul-liberty now possessed the whole body of Christians. Before Christ, the only right of the governed was to obey authority backed by force; now his disciples not only comprehended the new right, but resolved to die for its maintenance, if needful. The religious institutions of the Jews were left to them undisturbed by the Romans; yet, they resented Roman intolerance on the question of national independence. Few of the Christians being of Jewish origin, their birth, as pagan citizens, had invested them with the civil rights of their fellows, their contests, therefore, were narrowed down to religious issues. Justin Martyr, who was educated a pagan philosopher, said, in his first Apology to the rulers: 'We worship God alone, but, with this exception, we joyfully obey you; we acknowledge you as our princes and governors, and we ask of you that to the sovereign power with which you are invested, may be added the wisdom to make a right use of it.'[14] Here, was no unreason of fanaticism, nor claim of religious obstinacy, as the emperors supposed, but simply the recognition of a natural and inalienable right in humanity. Nor did Justin make this demand on the first Antonine without effect. Marcus admitted that Pius, his predecessor, had decreed that Christians: 'Should not be subject to any harm, unless they were found to have committed acts injurious to the welfare of the Roman Empire.' But for himself he held this as the law governing religion, namely: 'The end of reasonable beings is to conform to whatever is imposed by the reason and law of the most ancient and honorable city and government.'[15] Here he seemed to defer to 'reason' as well as law, but Athenagoras, in his Apology, openly charged him with partiality and inconsistency in applying law. He urges upon the Emperor's attention these considerations:

'The subjects of your vast empire, most noble sovereign, differ in customs and laws. No imperial decree, no menace held forth by you, prevents them from freely following the usages of their ancestors, even though those usages be ridiculous. The Egyptians may adore cats, crocodiles, serpents and dogs. You and the laws pronounce the man impious who acknowledges no god, and you admit that every man ought to worship the god of his choice, in order that he may be deterred from evil by the fear of the divinity. Why, then, make exception in the sole case of the Christians? Why are they excluded from that universal peace, which the world enjoys under your rule?'[16]

The Roman laws allowed all conquered nations to retain their own religion, but as the Christians had never been a nation, they felt themselves, at least, entitled to the sacred rights yielded to captives. If a pagan had the abstract right to dispose of his own soul in harmony with his own convictions, though not a citizen, how much more those who were free born? They, therefore, held persecution immoral,—treason against free souls. They refused to be stripped of their humanity, because to rob themselves of peace with God and with their honest convictions, was treason against God,—to which they would not yield for a moment. Under this solemn persuasion, the Christian Apologies warned the emperors, again and again, that God would punish them for their daring oppressions, which despised the life that God had given man, and rifled him of his grandest attribute. Justin boldly says to the Emperor:

'You, who are every where proclaimed the pious,—the guardian of justice,—the friend of truth,—your acts shall show whether you merit these titles. My design is neither to flatter you by this letter, nor to obtain any favor. . . . Your duty, as dictated by reason, is to investigate our cause, and to act as good judges. You will then be inexcusable before God, if you act not justly when you have once known the truth. . . . After all, princes who prefer an idle opinion to the truth, use a power only like that of robbers in lonely places. . . . If this doctrine appears to you true, and founded on reason, pay heed to it. If contrariwise, treat it as a thing of no value; but do not treat as enemies, nor condemn to death, men who have done you no wrong; for we declare to you that you will not escape the judgment of God if you persist in injustice.'

He even goes the length of expressing the belief, that the moral triumphs of the Gospel may render the State itself unnecessary, and rates imperial intolerance as more worthy of the hangman than of virtuous princes. In a word, he demands religious liberty in the name of eternal justice, urging the Emperor to lay the matter before the people, saying: 'Is there need to appeal to any other judge than conscience?' And Tertullian was just as bold. 'Religion,' he affirms, 'forbids to constrain any to be religious; she would have consent and not constraint. Man has the natural right to worship what he thinks best. . . . Let one worship God, another Jupiter; let one raise his suppliant hands to heaven, another to the altar of Fides. See to it whether this does not deserve the name of irreligion, to wish to take away the freedom of religion, and to forbid a choice of gods, so that I may not worship whom I will, but be compelled to worship whom I do not will. No one, not even a human being, will desire to be worshiped by one against his will.'[17] In citing Christ's words on duty to Cæsar, he asks: 'What, then, is due to Cæsar? . . . Cæsar's image is on the money, therefore, the money may be fairly claimed by him; God's image is upon man, and he has an equal claim upon his own. Give, therefore, your money to Cæsar, and yourselves to God. If all is Cæsar's, what will remain for God?'[18] Thus, the post-Apostolic Baptists stirred the second century with the strife for soul-liberty.

CHAPTER II.

THE THIRD CENTURY.

IN this period, the Emperors were more lenient toward the Christians, from various motives, sometimes because they paid a heavy tax for peace. Tertullian denounced this practice as a bribe. Alexander Severus, 222–235, was tolerant, perhaps through the influence of Julia, his mother, a friend of Origen. He put busts of Christ and Abraham in his private chapel, with the words engraved on the wall: 'As ye would that men should do to you, do ye also to them.' He was the first Emperor who entertained Christian pastors at court, and the first places of Christian worship were built in his reign; yet, down to this time no Christian bodies had been legalized, except as burial societies. He would have enrolled Christ amongst the gods and built him a temple, but the soothsayers prophesied, that all men would become Christians, and the other temples would be closed if he did this. Under his favor to the Christians, many pliable philosophers united with them, some pastors took civil office. The laws against Christians were unrepealed, and Ulpian collected them into a Digest, ready for use, in his book on the duties of a Proconsul. As Christianity relapsed into security, it began to mix with paganism and weakened. Maximus, the Thracian, resented the leniency of his predecessor and burned the church buildings; but Philip, 238–244, favored Christianity so much, that he was denounced as a Christian. Decius, however, 249–251, determined to restore the old faith, and began a general persecution of the sternest character.

He aimed at the full, legal suppression of Christianity, and the government put forth its whole strength accordingly. The terror of this persecution had scarcely been equaled before. Limborch fully indorses the alarming picture drawn by Dr. Chandler, in his 'History of Persecutions,' when he says of those who would not blaspheme Christ and offer incense to the gods, that: 'They were publicly whipped, drawn by the heels through the streets of cities, racked till every bone of their body was disjointed, had their teeth beat out; their noses, hands and ears cut off; sharp-pointed spears run under their nails, were tortured with melted lead thrown on their naked bodies, had their eyes dug out, their limbs cut off, were condemned to the mines, ground between stones, stoned to death, burnt alive, thrown headlong from the high buildings, beheaded, smothered in burning lime-kilns, run through the body with sharp spears; destroyed with hunger, thirst and cold; thrown to the wild beasts, broiled on gridirons with slow fires, cast by heaps into the sea, crucified, scraped to death with sharp shells, torn to pieces by the boughs of trees, and, in a word, destroyed by all the various methods that the most diabolical subtlety and malice could devise.'

Pride, ease and ambition had entered the Churches, discipline was relapsed, and terror seized them when the sword awoke, and many apostatized. These were called *traditors*, meaning those who revealed hidden copies of Scripture to be collected and burnt. Decius threw the whole strength of the Empire into the persecution, which was terrible beyond description, and such immense numbers 'lapsed,' that fiery controversies rent the Churches when they returned, on the question of their restoration. Cyprian bewailed this state of things as a punishment 'for our sins,' saying: 'Our principal study is to get money and estates; we follow after pride; we are at leisure with nothing but emulation and quarreling, and have neglected the simplicity of faith. We have renounced this world in words only, and not in deed. Every one studies to please himself and to displease others.' Eusebius draws a darker picture still, and writes:

'Through too much liberty, they grew negligent and slothful, envying and reproaching one another; waging, as it were, civil war among themselves, bishops quarreling with bishops, and the people divided into factions. Hypocrisy and deceit were grown to the highest pitch of wickedness. They were become so insensible as not so much as to think of appeasing the Divine anger; but like Atheists they thought the world destitute of any providential government and care, and thus added one crime to another. The bishops themselves had thrown off all concern about religion; were perpetually contending with one another; and did nothing but quarrel with and threaten and envy and hate one another; they were full of ambition, and tyrannically used their power.'[1]

Decius, as a reforming statesman, intended to turn this state of things to his interests, declaring, that he would rather have a second Emperor at his side than a priest at Rome, a remark which shows the trend of Christian feeling at that time.

But extremes meet here, as elsewhere. While so many abjured Christ, thousands presented themselves to the civil power, almost with fanaticism, demanding the martyr's crown. The persecution continued under Gallus and Valerian, A. D. 251-260, until Gallienus proclaimed the first edicts of toleration in the Empire, recalled the exiles, and made Christianity an acknowledged religion in 261. This peace continued under Claudius; but his successor, Aurelian, hated the Christians and issued another edict against them. He was assassinated, however, before it was executed; Tacitus, his successor, revoked it, and the Churches had rest, until the last general persecution under Diocletian, A. D. 303. Then Christianity revived, illustrating the words of Tertullian, uttered long before: 'Our number increases the more you destroy us. The blood of the Christians is their seed.' Amongst the many illustrative cases which exhibit the fortitude of the martyrs is that of Laurentius, a deacon, of whom the magistrate demanded the money of the Church, for the poor. This iron-nerved old Baptist said, most cheerfully, that the Church had valuable treasures, asking the court to send horses and wagons for them, and give him three days to produce them. His request was granted, and when the day arrived, he brought loads of widows and the poor, saying: 'These are the treasures of the Church.' For this, they roasted him alive on a gridiron; but so resolutely did he bear his sufferings, that he told the executioner: 'This side of my body is roasted enough, now turn it and roast the other; and then, if thou wilt, devour it.' Persecution ceased in the West, A. D. 307.

A brief sketch of TERTULLIAN may aid in throwing light upon the Montanists, who held some peculiarities in common with modern Baptists. He was the greatest of the Latin fathers, except Augustine, being pre-eminently the father of his day and class, A. D. 160–240. He was born at Carthage, North Africa, where his father was a Roman Proconsul, and carefully educated his son to be a lawyer. Little is known of Tertullian's conversion, which is generally supposed to have dated about 190. He possessed a powerful mind, was an original but violent thinker, earnest in his convictions, intense in his enthusiasm, and destitute of fear; his fire and independence made him worthy of his Punic blood and Roman training. As forceful with the pen as Tacitus, he was too brief, warm and vigorous to be his equal, either in lucidity or elegance; but he was the most eloquent advocate of the early Churches. He was strong and acute, with a powerful imagination, a quick and vivacious mind; his style was learned but not rhetorical, nor was it always harmonious; yet, his severe, angular fruitfulness presented the truth in a new dress, and made him fascinating, because he was austere in his piety and spotless in his purity. Early in his Christian career, he became deeply moved at the indifference which had fallen on the Churches; and the fear that they were relapsing into paganism, stirred his sanctified genius to a keen and dexterous activity. When he became pastor of the Church in his native city, he threw all his might into the battle with paganism, Judaism, and heretical Christianity. As he exceeded all his contemporaries in intelligence, vigor and sturdy character, his opponents soon looked upon him as stern and censorious. Believing that the Churches had drifted from their primitive state, his puritanical zeal dealt tremendous blows in every direction. His opponents feared him, for he exposed all the baseness of heathenism, and protested against all looseness in Christianity. In his Apology to the rulers, his stirring letter to Scapula, the Prefect of Africa, and his more popular appeal to the people, he heaped scorn and contempt on the ancient gods in a style peculiar to himself; and few did more to overthrow the godless system of Polytheism.

About A. D. 200, he became a Montanist, amongst which sect he ranked as the leader, and at Carthage first launched his famous work on Baptism against Quintilla, who held that faith saves without baptism. He insisted that Christ 'imposed the law of immersion,' and that Paul submitted to it, 'as the only thing' then wanting in him; and as a dispute had arisen in his day about the need of going to the Jordan for baptism, he gave this decision: 'There is no difference whether one is washed in the sea or in a pool, in a river or in a fountain, in a lake or in a canal;

nor is there any difference between those whom John dipped in the Jordan, and those whom Peter dipped in the Tiber.'

The MONTANISTS, with whom he identified himself, sprang from Montanus, a native of Phrygia. He was orthodox in his views, except on the doctrine of the 'Holy Catholic Church,' as it began to be held at that time. Some, however, attribute to him a tinge of the doctrine of Sabellius, which affected his later followers. He taught a gradual unfolding of revelation, and looked for further communications of the Spirit than those given in the New Testament; yet, Cardinal Newman thinks that: 'The very foundation of Montanism is development, not in doctrine, but in discipline and conduct.' Certainly, he introduced no new doctrine, but held to the continued inspiration of the Spirit until the coming of Christ, which he thought near at hand. He labored hard to rekindle the love of many who had waxed cold, and to restore the spirituality of the Churches; but was so extremely rigid in the matter of fasting and other acts of self-denial, that he caught the ascetic side of religion in its demands for a pure life. In his aim to restore Christians to their normal Gospel condition, he associated their decline with the lack of special revelations given to individuals, which should supplement the New Testament, and thought himself commissioned of God to bring them back to this high standard of perfection. This dangerous doctrine led him into ecstasies, which he mistook for new revelations, and which have been unjustly ascribed to deception. Hence, the Montanists called themselves 'spirituals,' to mark themselves from lax Christians, whom they denominated 'carnal;' not only because they demanded a pure life, but also because they sought a thoroughly spiritual religion, unmixed with the perversions of philosophy. Montanus taught that men should not flee from persecution, and insisted on the rebaptism of the 'lapsed;' not because they had been improperly baptized in the first place, but because they had denied Christ, and on re-professing him, ought to be baptized afresh. For this cause only, were they called 'Anabaptists.'

The one prime-idea held by the Montanists in common with Baptists, and in distinction to the Churches of the third century was, that membership in the Churches should be confined to purely regenerate persons; and that a spiritual life and discipline should be maintained without any affiliation with the authority of the State. Exterior Church organization and the efficacy of ordinances did not meet their ideal of Gospel Church existence, without the indwelling Spirit of Christ, not in the bishops alone, but in all Christians. For this reason, Montanus was charged with assuming to be the Holy Spirit himself; which was simply a slander. His mistake lay in pushing the doctrine of the indwelling Spirit so far, as to claim that men and women are as directly under the special inspiration of the Spirit as were the Apostles themselves. For this reason, also, he claimed exact equality amongst them in all respects, and women as well as men were pastors in the Montanist Churches. Woman was held in light esteem both in Church and State in his time, and so, this doctrine was specially odious. History has not yet relieved the Montanists of the distortion and obloquy which long held them as enemies of Christ; while, in fact, they honestly, but in some respects erroneously, labored to restore that Christ likeness to the Churches which had so largely departed. Roman ideas of aggrandizement had corrupted their ideal, and now they greatly varied from the model which Christ had left.

Like many reformers, their aim at high spirituality soon led them to exalt routine observances in little things, into matters of the gravest importance, and to erect new standards of conduct. Seeking great consecration to God, they became thoroughly legal. They excluded themselves from society, were harsh in their treatment of weak and erring Christians; instead of cherishing the forgiving spirit of Christ toward the 'lapsed,' they were bitter against them, with that bitterness which is often the chief sin of high sanctity. Sin after baptism was regarded by them as almost unpardonable, second marriages were wicked in the extreme, matter itself was an unmixed evil; and the world, being as bad as it well could be, was ripe for destruction. In consequence, they were decided Pre-Millenarians. They believed in the literal reign of Christ upon the earth, and longed for his coming, that he might hold his people separate by the final overthrow of sin and sinners, and then his saints would reign with him here in his glory. They regarded every new persecutor on the imperial throne as the Antichrist of the Apocalypse; and made so much of that book, that the Alogians thought it a Montanist forgery.[2] They hoped by preaching these things to purify the Churches, without founding a new sect, and for a time, things tended in that direction. Many returned, in part, to the Apostolic ideal, and in hopeful minds there was promise of recovering a purely spiritual membership.

Their doctrines took deep and wide root in Africa and Gaul, and even the Church at Rome was more than inclined to adopt them, but hesitated. The set of the tide toward worldly conformity and aggrandizement was too strong, however, for this reaction, and the reform largely failed; yet that Church was slow to condemn this honest attempt of the reformers. About A. D. 192, her pastor branded them, but the Council of Nicæa did not put them under the ban. The local Council of Laodicea did, however; and the General Council of Constantinople, A. D. 381, required converts from Montanism to be immersed anew, and treated in all respects as converts from paganism, before their re-admission into the Catholic Church.

They had no controversy with the Catholics on the subject of trine immersion, for it was not in dispute, but was practiced by both parties. As to the immersion of unconscious babes, we have nothing which distinctly sets forth their views, because it was not yet practiced by any party. It was just beginning to appear in this century, as a necessary measure of salvation from original sin by sacramental grace. 'As a matter of history, it must be admitted by candid students, that a false conception of the Church and the sacraments was the direct cause of a change in the Apostolic order, and of the admission of infants to baptism and the Supper, designed only for adults. The same cause induced both changes, and for centuries infant communion co-existed with infant baptism.'³ Both the opposition of Tertullian, and the open denial of the Montanists that baptism is the channel of grace, renders it unlikely that they adopted this practice. They insisted so radically on the efficacy of the Holy Spirit in regeneration, that to have immersed unconscious babes would have nullified their basic doctrine of the direct agency of the Spirit, and have thwarted their attempts at reform, in the most practical manner. As to the independency of their Churches, the facts, that they maintained a separate Church life, and that women filled the pastorate in some of their congregations, under the direction, as they thought, of the Holy Spirit, indicate that they believed this direction was given through the local body when choosing pastors; and also, that their 'superintendents' were but the 'presidents' of Justin Martyr, and the 'elders' of the New Testament.

With the other perversions of the faith, there came the Gnostic heresy, substituting knowledge for faith. The term Gnostic (*man of knowledge*) first denoted the initiated into a secret science unknown to the vulgar. It revolved around the origin of all things, and Tertullian denounced it vehemently. Montanism was looking for the end of all things, and he cried: 'Away with all attempts to produce a motley Christianity, compounded of Stoicism, Platonism, and dialectics.' Gnosticism produced two extreme classes of men, fantastical visionaries, noted for formal asceticism, and those who fell into indulgence and licentiousness. Montanism meant to protest against both, specially resisting pagan worldliness. Many Christians traded with the temples as workmen in constructing them, carving their statues, selling them frankincense and sacrifices. 'Nay,' says Tertullian, 'idol makers are chosen into the ecclesiastical order.' Others served as officers or private soldiers under the heathen standard, all of which the Montanists resisted, so that Harnack calls them 'The old believers, the elder legitimate party, that demanded the preservation of the original Christianity, and the return to Apostolical simplicity and purity.'

About A. D. 281, the NOVATIANS arose. They differed with the Montanists concerning the Spirit's inspiration, while they held much in common. They were charged by the Catholics rather with schism than heresy, as rigid discipline separated them, not doctrine. The case of Novatian is the first recorded instance of departure from immersion in baptism, and the first instance of clinic baptism; that is, baptism of those who were believed to be dying. When a catechumen, he was supposed to lie at the point of death, and asked baptism in order to save his soul, but could not be three times immersed, as was the practice. Yet, something must be done, and that in a hurry; so, while stretched on his bed, water was poured all around his person, in an outline inclosing his whole body; then, it was poured all over him till he was drenched, making perfusion as near an immersion as possible. If he died, this was to stand for baptism, saving him by a narrow escape; but if he lived, his baptism was to be considered defective. Cornelius, the Bishop of Rome at that time, was an obstinate immersionist, and wrote to Fabius, the Bishop of Antioch, concerning Novatian, thus: 'Relieved by exorcists, he fell into an obstinate disease, and being supposed about to die, he having been poured around, on the bed where he lay, received [saving grace]; if, indeed, it be proper to say [it].' Eusebius does not express the object of the verb, but Crusé translates the rest of the passage thus: ' If, indeed, it be proper to say that one like him did receive baptism.' [4] Vales states, that clinics who recovered, were required by the rule to go to the bishop, 'to supply what was wanting in that baptism.' But failing to do this, Novatian insisted on entering the ministry, which persistence shook the nerves of Cornelius beyond endurance; yet, as Novatian was a remarkably talented man, he was made a presbyter without trine immersion.

Cave excuses this in the kindest manner, calling Novatian's 'A less solemn and perfect kind of baptism, partly because it was done not by immersion. . . . Persons are supposed at such a time to desire it chiefly out of a fear of death, and many times when not thoroughly masters of their understandings. For which reasons, persons so baptized (if they recovered) are by the fathers of the Neo-Cæsarean Council rendered ordinarily incapable of being admitted to the degree of presbyters in the Church. . . . They reckoned that no man could be saved without being baptized, and cared not much in cases of necessity, so they had it, how they came by it.'[5] His reference is to Canon xii, which decrees, that no person baptized in time of sickness should be ordained a presbyter, 'because his faith was not voluntary.' Cornelius would not let them pass muster, even if they 'were masters of their understandings;' but Chrysostom was a more notional immersionist still, and gave his reasons at length for doubting the salvation of such men at all! In general, the fathers sneered at these sick-bed baptisms, and named such professors, 'Clinics,' and not Christians, a levity which Cyprian solemnly rebuked, as implying their conversion in a fright. He says that it is a 'nickname which some have thought fit to fix upon those who have thus' been perfused upon their beds. [6]

The NOVATIANS demanded pure Churches which enforced strict discipline, and so were called Puritans. They refused to receive the 'lapsed' back into the Churches, and because they held the Catholics corrupt in receiving them, they re-immersed all who came to them from the Catholics. For this reason alone they were called ' Anabaptists,' although they denied that this was rebaptism, holding the first immersion null and void, because it had been received from corrupt Churches. Martyrs were held in such high honor at this time, that this dignity was sought with a furor. Merit was ascribed to them, in virtue of which they went so far as to give to other Christians, papers, in token of pardoned sin, a practice which it was necessary to prohibit, because it became so dangerous. The Novatians soon became a very powerful body, spread through the Empire, as Kurtz shows; and their Churches flourished for centuries, exerting a purifying and healthful influence. Adam Clarke states that one grave charge against them was: 'That they did not pay due reverence to the martyrs, nor allow that there was any virtue in their relics;' which he pronounces a decisive mark of their 'good sense and genuine piety,' in keeping with their lives, which 'were in general simple and holy.' Lardner thinks: 'It is impossible to calculate the benefits of their services to mankind.'

We have no reliable data on which to state their views on the baptism of babes, beyond the fact, that as infant baptism had not become a general custom when they arose, there was no need to form a sect in opposition thereto. Then, these several facts indicate that they had no sympathy with the few who began to favor this innovation, namely: That Novatian, their founder, was an adult at the time of his illness and so-called baptism; that the difficulty of obtaining pardon of sin after baptism made men defer it as long as possible in this age; and further, that we have no record of one martyr, confessor, writer or member, in any Church being baptized as a babe, for the first two hundred and fifty years of Christianity. On the contrary, it is recorded that the two Clements, Justin, Athanagoras, Theophilus, Tertullian, Cyprian and a nameless host were baptized after reaching full manhood, and on their faith in Christ. When Novatian was a presbyter at Rome, infant baptism had not found its way there. More than a century after his day, Boniface, the Bishop of that Church, is found addressing Augustine on the question, asking his counsel, and expressing grave doubts on the subject, inasmuch as a child could not believe in Christ, and no one could warrant that he would believe thereafter.[7] Socrates says, that Novatian was martyred A. D. 253–260.

This century was marked by the introduction of a centralized Church government, largely to the destruction of Congregationalism; and by a crystallization of the ideas and pretensions of Episcopacy. As to the first of these, Neander clearly shows, how a crude notion arose concerning the inward unity of a universal but unseen Church, and the outward unity of a Church dependent on outward forms. Out of this speculative idea came the purpose to form one great organic body, which should take the place of the Church-family idea, as Christ founded it on the social nature of man. The first step was to depress the individuality of the Church in this or that home locality, supplanting it with the Church of the district; then, of course, would follow that of the nation and of the world. Cyprian carried this thought to its sound, logical conclusion, in his remarkable book on the 'Unity of the Church' (*De Unitate Ecclesia*), written about the middle of this period, amid the confusion with which this innovation had to contend. The term 'Catholic Church' is first found in the Epistle of the Church at Smyrna, in which Polycarp prays for the godly throughout the world under that name, and Tertullian uses it for the same purpose. But the organic Catholic Church itself arose out of the ambitious scheme to sap the foundations of Congregational liberty, and to crush heretics. We read such folly as this from the pen of Cyprian: 'That man cannot have God for his Father, who has not the Church for his mother. . . . Where there is no Church, sins cannot be put away.' He is also the father of that far-fetched and thread-bare 'coat' argument, in which so many complacently wrap themselves, till they split it between the shoulders. He says of our Lord's 'seamless vest,' 'This coat possessed a unity which came down from the top, that is, from heaven, and which was not to be rent. He who parts and divides the Church cannot have Christ's garment.' As if Christ's Church is Christ's coat in any sense, and as if his woolen raiment, woven on some family loom in Palestine, and raffled for by soldiers at the foot of the cross, could be forced to do duty as the symbol of his ransomed body, the Church. There is not the slightest hint in the Bible that the bodily dress of Christ was the embodiment of any thing but its own threads, much less that it was made by him a holy symbol of his redeemed people. Yet, those who are shaking in their shoes all the time about some figment which they call the 'sin of schism,' but which they are careful never to define, are perpetually quoting Cyprian's nonsense, as if it were unanswerable Bible truth.

Again, Cyprian says: 'There is no salvation to any except in the Church;' which to him was true, by the dimensions of the Church as he measured it, which measurement, happily, differs several cubits from the enlarged fullness in which Jesus comprehends all who love and obey him, 'in sincerity and truth.' Cyprian also held that there was no true baptism outside of the Catholic ranks, and so, he rebaptized all heretics and schismatics who came to him, while Stephen contended that if the due forms had been observed in baptizing them, they should be re-admitted simply by the laying on of hands.

As to the prerogatives of Episcopacy, the hierarchy was not established at once. Like all other perversions of great principles and institutions, the decadence was gradual, almost imperceptible, until the change became thorough and radical. When the 'priest' had taken the place of the teacher, and the 'Church' the place of the diffused congregations, then the 'Church' alone could confer salvation by its priesthood, ordinances and discipline; for the whole power of the 'Church' was merged into the clergy. New forms produced new laws and new offices. Division in the Churches had opened the way for one pagan practice after another in government, as well as doctrine, until the spirit of old Roman imperialism gradually formed a priestly hierarchy. What Westcott calls 'the local and dogmatic ideas of Catholicity' remained in germ, and were latent till new circumstances broke the force of public opinion. One emergency followed another in breaking up the system of separate Church action, and compelling the Churches to conform to one regime. Then the ecclesiastical form of the sin of schism was cautiously created as a bugbear, its seeds being planted in the restriction of free thought. Imperialism became the bulwark of Episcopacy, which, at first, operated gently; for after district prelacy was established, each district being independent for a time of all others, managed its own affairs by its provincial synod. The public mind had been educated to this form of government in civil affairs. This policy had failed in the Greek republic, and had been lost in her wider dominion; but when Rome conquered all States, its ideal of government was centered in one irresponsible will, and sought its golden age there. In like manner, these simple Christian communities passed step by step into the hands of their ambitious brethren, who sought to imperialize the Churches. The bent of the Roman Church was to adopt the policy of the Roman State, and to swallow up all these artless families into itself. The necessary result was, that the primitive sense of personal union with Christ was sunk into incorporation with the general Church, to be connected with which was salvation. After this, every thing savored of episcopal prerogative.

Nothing of this was known in the Apostolic Churches, for there no particular man was distinguished as a priest, much less as a high-priest of priests. Bishop Lightfoot says, in his 'Christian Ministry:' 'The sacerdotal title is never once conferred upon them. The only priests under the Gospel, designated as such in the New Testament, are the saints, the members of the Christian brotherhood. As individuals, all Christians are alike. . . . The highest gift of the Spirit conveyed no sacerdotal right which was not enjoyed by the humblest member of the Christian community.' Yet, the men of the third century reasoned, that as paganism had found strength in a centralized government, Christianity could not cope with it without using the same forces. Hence, in substance, if not in form, the rule of the Galilean Peasant was thrown aside, and the image of the Emperor put in his place by an Episcopacy, first to charm and then to govern. After that, a technical sense was attached to the term 'bishop' which never fell from Apostolic lips, the corruption of the term springing from the corruption of the office. The first grade of departure is found in the mutual consultation of the elders, as equals, concerning the welfare of a few Churches in their vicinity. Then, one of them began to exercise lordship over the other, till, in the opening of this age, the city elders assumed rank and authority over their suburban brethren, who were but common country folk. Because Rome was the mighty capital and the Church there strong, this Church early betrayed that feeling. Besides, the smaller Churches were often quite dependent upon those out of which they came, cherishing great love for them, and so were led by their influence. Roman society daily familiarized men with all grades and successions of power, and it required constant resistance to keep the Churches in their Christ-like simplicity of government.

The credulity of Cyprian, as to the almost miraculous effects of the ordinances, and the divine authority of Episcopacy, strengthened these tendencies in Africa, where he acted in a childish manner. In a letter to Pupianus he says: 'The bishop is in the Church, and the Church in the bishop; and if any one be not with the bishop, he is not in the Church.' Neander thus expresses himself most freely: 'A candid consideration cannot fail to see in Cyprian, a man animated with true love to the Redeemer and to his Church. It is undeniable that he was honestly devoted as a faithful shepherd to his flock, and that it was his desire to use his episcopal authority for the maintenance of order and discipline. But it is also certain that . . . he was not watchful enough against self-will and pride. The very point he contended for, the supremacy of the episcopate, proved the rock whereon at times he made shipwreck.'[8]

CHAPTER III.

THE THIRD CENTURY.—*Continued.*

THE four men who figured most largely in this century were Tertullian, who labored for the purity of the Churches; Origen, who blended philosophy with revelation; Cyprian, who struggled for episcopal authority; and Hippolytus, who as stoutly resisted clerical wickedness. We may speak more fully of the last.

HIPPOLYTUS, A. D. 198-239, was Bishop, probably of the Church at Portus, at the mouth of the Tiber, and spent the most of his life in and about Rome. He was one of the greatest men of his age, 'a name,' says Cardinal Newman, 'which a breath of ecclesiastical censure has never even dimmed. . . . A man without any slur upon his character or conduct, and who stands, in point of orthodoxy, range of subject and ability, in the very front rank of theologians, in the ante-Nicene times.'[1] Chrysostom calls him: 'A most holy doctor, and a man of sweetness and charity.' For twenty years he was active in the affairs of the Church at Rome, but was in no way under its authority, being elected bishop by his own flock, without episcopal consecration. He openly and boldly opposed the bishops of the capital in all their pretensions, exposing their gross iniquities. He refused all communion with the Church at Rome, calling it a 'school,' not a church, and laid bare the immoralities and crimes of its pastors, in what had been a scurrilous manner, had it not been true. A. D. 199-218, Zephyrinus was its pastor, whom he denounces as ignorant, corrupt and bribed to connive at the error of Noetus, namely, that Christ was the Father, and so that the Father was crucified, denying the proper personality of the Son. When Hippolytus exposed his error, he confessed his sin.

Callixtus was pastor at Rome from 219 to 223. He was originally a slave, nurtured in cunning, falsehood and vice. Having stolen money, he was sentenced first to the treadmill, and then to the mines in Sardinia, on the following proceedings: His master, a devout Christian of Cæsar's household, trusted him with large amounts of money for banking purposes. This business Callixtus followed in the Piscina, a public fish-market, one of the quarters of Rome, celebrated for its large financial transactions. His master's influence was so great that many Christians, widows and others, intrusted their deposits with the slave as with the master himself. But he soon made away with these, and fled for the sea. Being pursued and captured in the harbor of Portus, after an attempt at suicide by drowning, he was brought back to Rome and sent to the treadmill. He claimed that various persons held money to his credit; many kind-hearted Christians pleaded with his master to release him, and he yielded to their entreaties. The knave, knowing that he could not escape, invited death by disturbing a Jewish synagogue while at worship; but instead of killing him outright, they dragged him before the Prefect of the city. The Jews charged him with disturbing their worship, contrary to Roman law. Then his master appeared and charged him with theft and an attempt to provoke death, denying that he was a Christian. This led to his banishment to the pestilential mines, in Sardinia. By fraudulent means he obtained his release and returned to Rome. Then Zephyrinus procured him the appointment over the cemetery in the Via Appia. While filling this place he flattered his patron, by duplicity and artifice secured his influence for promotion after his own death, and at the death of Zephyrinus he actually became the Bishop of Rome! Even without the Sardicean decree, this act would justify Dollinger in saying of the papacy that it was 'a forgery in its very outset, and based upon an audacious falsification of history.'[2]

Once seated in the episcopal chair, he began the prosecution of every evil work. Hippolytus states that, 'He was the first to invent the device of conniving at sensual indulgences, saying, "That all had their sins forgiven by himself. . . . This man promulgated as a dogma that if a bishop should commit any sin, even if it were a sin unto death, he ought not to be deposed."' He also admitted immoral persons to the Supper, quoting from the Parable of the Tares: 'Let both grow together till the harvest;' justifying himself from the fact that clean and unclean beasts were quietly housed together in Noah's ark. Of course, under his fostering care the most atrocious crime and iniquity grew rapidly, and profligacy ran riot in the Church at Rome. But when he came to sanction the union of any Christian maiden of good family with a pagan husband of rank, even without the form of marriage, Hippolytus, astounded at such licentiousness, exclaims, in disgust: 'Behold into how great iniquity that lawless wretch has proceeded! . . . And yet, after all these enormities, these men are lost to all sense of shame, and presume to call themselves a Catholic Church! . . . These things the most admirable Callixtus contrived, not making any distinction, as to with whom it is fit to communicate, but offering communion indiscriminately to all.' He also adds that 'During the pontificate of this Callixtus, for the first time, second baptism was presumptuously attempted by them.' With all this profligacy Callixtus was very zealous to promote true orthodoxy. And in proof of this, he excommunicated the Sabellians as heterodox. But Hippolytus says: 'He acted thus from apprehension of me, and imagined that he could in this manner obliterate the charge against him among the Churches, as if he did not entertain strange opinions. He was then an impostor and knave, and in process of time hurried many away with him.' For elsewhere he charges that Callixtus was a 'fellow-champion of these wicked tenets' with Zephyrinus, and that the two made many converts; he tells us, too, that he had sternly confuted and opposed them, but that, after a time, they would 'wallow again in the same mire.' In this way he molded his predecessor, an 'illiterate,' 'uninformed and corrupt man,' and seduced him by illicit demands to do whatever he wished, then used him to create disturbance in the Churches; but was careful to keep the good-will of all factions himself, duping them into the belief that he held the same doctrines that they did.

Hippolytus says: 'And we, becoming aware of his sentiments, did not give place to him, and withstood him for the truth's sake.' The plural 'we' shows that he held himself to be an equal of Callixtus in the Churches, and was independent of his government, considering himself more a successor of the Apostles than the Roman bishop, who not only made a schism amongst the Churches about Rome, but established a heretical school of his own. Hippolytus despised the episcopal assumptions at Rome, not only denying the supremacy of that bishop, but exposing his heresy and scandalous life, and resisting him at every step. He looked upon priestly assumption as an innovation and a source of scandalous immorality, and plainly shows that an elder in the Church of God was not an autocrat, or a sacrificial mediator in the eyes of this great and good man, who had been 'elected' a bishop by his own congregation. The history of the third century never could have been read or written, if his *Philosophoumena* had not been discovered in the convent of Mount Athos in 1842. But by its light we come to understand how this courageous and uncompromising friend of moral purity and fervent piety came to possess the undying honor which he has won; and which made 'his name and person,' as Cardinal Newman says, 'so warmly cherished by popes of the fourth, fifth and sixth centuries.' It is supposed that he suffered martyrdom by drowning in the Tiber, A. D. 235–239.

One of the most remarkable things about this century is, that it originated the great baptismal controversy, which, in one form or another, has been kept alive in the great Christian bodies ever since, and is as rife to-day as ever. At that time it related to those who had 'lapsed' from the faith, and there were three parties to this controversy. One, would not restore them on any condition; a second, would take them back without much restriction; and a third, led by Cyprian, would re-admit them after due repentance. Then, about the middle of the century, the immersion of babes began to creep into the Churches, under the new sacerdotal order of things. Toward the close of the second century, Celsus had charged the Christians with initiating the 'mere child' into their Churches, while the pagans initiated only 'intelligent' persons. The qualifying word 'mere,' indicates that he wished to throw the reflection upon them, that children who were little more than babes were taken into their fellowship. This insinuation Origen repelled, in his Contra Celsum, as a false accusation and a calumny. His words are: 'In reply to these accusations, we say, . . . We exhort sinners to come to the instruction that teaches them not to sin, and the unintelligent to come to that which produces in them understanding, and *the little children* to rise in elevation of thought to the man. . . . When those of the exhorted that make progress show that they have been cleansed by the Word, and, as much as possible, have lived a better life, then we invite them to be initiated amongst us.' However young, then, the 'mere child' might be, Origen says that they did not admit him until he had been 'exhorted,' 'cleansed by the Word,' had begun to live 'a better life,' and then he was initiated only on invitation—'we invite them.' All these conditions might be found in 'little children,' as in the case of Jonathan Edwards, who believed that he was converted at four years of age; but they could not refer to unconscious babes.

Origen seems but to have related his own experience here, as there is no evidence that his holy father, Leonides, had him immersed when a babe, more than that Monica, the consecrated mother of Augustine, had her babe immersed. But like an honest and God-fearing Baptist, Origen's father thoroughly educated his son in the Holy Scriptures, leading him to commit many passages to memory. The child's mind was deep, quiet and inquisitive. He often asked questions about the inner meaning of texts, and God greatly honored his training. His father loved him most tenderly, and constantly consecrated him to God in prayer, that the little one might be led to Jesus, a willing sacrifice. Prayer was answered; his boy early gave himself to Christ; and when the lad was asleep, his father would uncover his bosom and devoutly kiss it as the temple of the Holy Spirit. In the persecution under Severus, when this beautiful youth was but seventeen, his father was thrown into prison for being a Christian, was stripped of his property and left penniless. Then his son honored his hallowed love. The father's head fell under the ax for Christ, and Origen resolved that he would die with his father. But one martyr's crown for that home was enough for that day, and the father stooped to receive it alone. His godly mother found entreaty and remonstrance vain to keep her son back from the joint-sacrifice, and thwarted his purpose by hiding his clothes. Then, cleaving to her and her six other children, in abject poverty, he sent this letter to his father at the point of martyrdom: 'See thou dost not change thy mind for our sake!' and the head of Leonides fell at the block with these grand words of his child ringing in his ears and thrilling his heart. Origen was well able to repel the falsehood of Celsus, by showing that only children who believed in Jesus and loved him with all their soul were baptized. And, it is more than probable, that he drew his inspiration from the memory of his early childhood, when his father 'exhorted' him, brought him to the 'Word to be cleansed,' and 'invited him to be initiated amongst us.' Thus, when Leonides was with his Saviour, his son was answering his own description of a godly child rising 'in elevation of thought to the man,' in Christ Jesus.

This order of things accords exactly with the statement of Baron Bunsen, the translator of the manuscript of Hippolytus, found in 1842. He says: 'Pedobaptism, in the modern sense, meaning thereby the baptism of new-born infants, with the vicarious promises of parents, or other sponsors, was utterly unknown to the early Church, not only down to the end of the second century, but, indeed, to the middle of the third.' This, he derives from Hippolytus himself, in these words: 'We, in our days, never defended the baptism of children, which in my day had not begun to be practiced in some regions, unless it were as an exception and innovation. The baptism of infants we do not know.' He was born in the last half of the second century, and died in about A. D. 240; this gives the period meant by 'my day.' The 'some regions' where infant baptism had not begun to be practiced except as an 'innovation,' must have included Rome and adjacent parts of Italy; for there he spent the greater part of his life, and it must be of that locality that he speaks, saying : ' *we* never defended the baptism of children,' 'the baptism of infants *we* do not know.' His words imply, however, that in 'some' other 'regions' it had begun to be practiced. Its twin doctrine, that all who died unbaptized must be eternally lost, had, however, begun to take root quite generally, and from that time became more and more prevalent; until Gregory of Nazianzus, Ambrose and Augustine, came to contend stoutly that all infants who died unbaptized were eternally lost. This horrible libel on the Lamb of God was chosen, by these builders, as the chief stone in the corner for infant baptism.

We must now look at the other 'regions' where the baptism of babes began to be practiced, and mention some things in association with the incoming 'innovation.' In Africa, helpless infants were inhumanly sacrificed to the hideous gods, at this time. Fidus, a generous-hearted country pastor, who labored in this dark province, wrote to Cyprian, at Carthage, to know whether new-born babes might be baptized. If they could, of course, this would save them, whether they died or not, and would be an act of divine grace of special efficacy, where the cruel heathen stole them to offer in sacrifice. Cyprian's heart was as tender as that of his country brother, and he wanted all the children's souls saved, of course. But the proposition staggered him, and he dared not venture to trust his own judgment in so new and serious a case. It happened that a council of sixty-six pastors was in session at Carthage at the time, A. D. 252, called to consider various Church matters, but especially the subject of rebaptizing those who had received heretical baptism. In his perplexity he submitted the question of Fidus to these brethren; a thing which he need not have done, had it been customary to baptize babes from the Apostles down. Tertullian had been pastor of the Church of which Cyprian was now pastor, twenty years before this, and had baptized legal minors into its fellowship, but not babes. Cyprian's course and the decision of the council show that it was a new question to them all, for it decided that they *might* be baptized when eight days old, but was careful not to insist that they must be; further showing that this was a different sort of children's baptism from that which the Church had previously practiced under the pastorate of Tertullian.

It is to the transactions of this provincial synod in North Africa that Grotius refers, when he says of infant baptism : 'You will not find in any of the councils a more ancient mention of this custom than in the Council of Carthage.' So, Bunsen, also (iii, p. 204), says: 'In consequence of this alteration and complete subversion of its main features, brought about principally by the Africans of the third century, and completed by Augustine, these natural elements have been, in the course of nearly fifteen centuries, most tragically decomposed, and nothing is now remaining elsewhere but ruins. In the East, people adhere to immersion, although this symbol of man voluntarily and consciously making a vow of the sacrifice of self, lost all meaning in the immersion of a new-born babe.' The 'natural elements,' the abandonment of which he is deploring in this passage, he calls: 'Instruction, examination, the vow and initiation,' as the four great Christian elements in beginning the life of a disciple. Neander gives the same account of the matter: 'The error became more firmly established, that without external baptism no one could be delivered from inherent guilt, could be saved from the everlasting punishment that threatened him, or raised to eternal life; and as the notion of a magical influence, or charm, connected with the sacraments, continually gained ground, the theory was finally evolved in the unconditional necessity of infant baptism. About the middle of the third century this theory was already generally admitted in the North African Church. The only question that remained was whether the child ought to be baptized immediately after its birth, or not till eight days after, as in the case of the rite of circumcision.' (Ch. Hist., I, p. 313.)

This was not a learned body, for that part of the Christian Church was the least critical in its knowledge of the Scriptures; but it was much too wise to introduce this innovation on the silence of the New Testament. Therefore, as that said nothing on the question, they shrewdly passed over it to the Old, and introduced the new rite under the shield of circumcision. The pagans also had something in sympathy with this, though hardly borrowed from the same source. Planti and other ancient writers state that in Greece babes were purified by lustral waters and sacrifices long before infant baptism was established. This occurred on the fifth day after birth, and on the seventh they were named. Amongst the Romans, for female babes, the eighth day was chosen for the same ceremony, and the ninth for males. When this had been done at their own homes, the babe was taken to the temple and initiated into paganism in the presence of the gods.[3] Thus infant baptism made the door into the Church of Christ as wide as that of the Jewish and pagan faiths together. The African council could not comfortably introduce circumcision into Christianity, nor could they lustrate children by water and animal sacrifices; but they could conciliate the prejudices of Jews by making circumcision a precedent, and those of the heathen by lustrating babes by water without animal offerings. Their chief trouble was to keep those unreasonable Christians quiet who could find no authority from Christ for this superstitious innovation. For these they invented the doctrine of Apostolic tradition, which they lugged in through the 'holy kiss.' Even tender-hearted Fidus squirmed a trifle there. He could not give the usual brotherly kiss to the new-born infant, as it was unclean for some time after its birth. Cyprian, who, despite all his high-church air and strut, had as sisterly and soft a heart in his bosom as ever beat, easily settled that question for him by saying:

'Every thing that lies in our power must be done that no soul may be lost. . . . As to what you say, that the child in its first days of its birth is not clean to the touch, and that each of us would shrink from kissing such an object, even this, in our opinion, ought to present no obstacles to the bestowment of heavenly grace; for it is written, "To the pure all things are pure," and none of us ought to revolt at that which God has condescended to create. Although the child is but just born, yet it is no such object that any one ought to demur at kissing it, to impart the divine grace and salutation of peace.'

Some think this letter of Cyprian's spurious, and possibly . is reputation would not suffer if it were. Fidus disappears from the century, and all direct records of infant baptism with him, for the innovation made poor headway, and babes were not generally baptized until the fifth century. And when it was adopted, public opinion, formed on the practice of baptizing believers only, compelled it to take faith with it from some quarter; and so it borrowed that from the sponsor, making him believe for the babe by proxy, a direct tribute to the common sense of those who resisted the invention. Sponsors had long existed in law for civil purposes, in protecting youth during their legal minority. But now they were put to sacred uses, believing for the child when he could not believe for himself, and standing ready to help him to believe afterward. Taking this scheme throughout, for making Christians of dear little folks who knew nothing about it, it was quite an able achievement. But what it did for the Church in after centuries, must be told, to its shame and sorrow, thanks, not to the lands where Jesus and his Apostles had preached, but to Proconsular Africa; for with this came in a legion of other superstitions, not the least of which was the power on the part of the priesthood to consecrate holy oil, the 'mystic ointment' for the exorcism of the devil from the water, and from the candidate who was immersed therein. This brought regenerating efficacy to both, and the laying on of the priest's hands brought the Holy Spirit after baptism. Once wrenched from its native bearings, the simple and unpretentious New Testament baptism was first made a saving institution, and then the stalking-horse for the whole pack of vain novelties. For example, the angels were supposed to exercise a special ministry in baptism, and so, to represent them, a 'Baptismal Angel' was appointed to preside at every baptism.[4] He was known as *Angelus Baptismi Arbiter*, was regarded as the harbinger of the Spirit—what the Baptist was to Christ—his office being to prepare the soul of the candidate for the spirit of baptism.[5] The idea was borrowed from the angel who troubled the waters of Bethesda. With this came in exorcism, by breathing in the face of the candidate, for the expelling of the evil spirit and the inbreathing of the good. Tertullian tells us that the consecrated oil, which was poured upon the water in the form of the cross, before it became the baptismal grave, drove the devil out of that element. At this time the Gnostic idea, that the material world was largely under the dominion of evil spirits, had mixed itself with the Christian faith. Demons ruled the flight of birds, presided over the winds and waves, and it was necessary to drive them out of the waters by some sort of charm or amulet, before the saints were immersed in them. They haunted these waters as sprites and nymphs, but they fled when the sacred oil was poured thereon in the shape of a cross. We shall meet this again when we come to look at the pictures of the Catacombs.

The simple and unwelcome fact is, that the pagans threw an air of great mystery and sacred grandeur around their rites, which filled the wondering spectators with awe, and the Christians were weak enough to catch the infection, until they became filled with the fatal delusion that the holy oil acted as a cabalistic talisman on the waters, for it wrought a change in the element as such. In his sermon on the 'Passione' (p. 62), Pope Leo (440-461) gives this doctrine in full bloom, for he tells us: 'That baptism makes a change not only in the water, but in the man that receives it; thereby he receives Christ and Christ receives him; he is not the same after baptism as before, but the body of him that is regenerated is made the flesh of him that is crucified.' And why not, when Gregory of Nyssa contends that the oil thrown on the water not only changes its nature, but actually transmutes it into a divine and ineffable power, which Cyril of Alexandria calls 'transelementation.' But Cyprian follows with this stronger statement still: 'The water must be sanctified by the priest, that he may have power by baptism to wash away the sins of men.'[6] Baptism was made a sacerdotal act, and unction was necessary before it could be performed at all, for this made it the organ of the Holy Spirit! The whole Council of Carthage followed Cyprian's declaration: 'The water is sanctified by the prayer of the priest to wash away sin.' This superstition spread with amazing rapidity, until men discovered the most marvelous lights and other visions on the baptismal water, as if, indeed, it had become the crystal sea of the New Jerusalem itself.

It is not easy to determine when trine immersion was introduced, but at this time it appears to have been the universal custom. Baptism itself had become a 'mystery,' a name worthy of the semi-heathen institution which men had made it; and after baptism the candidate wore a white linen robe for eight days, as an emblem of the pure life which he was to live thereafter. Down to this time it had been the right of laymen to baptize, as Tertullian says: 'Even laymen have the right, for what is equally received can be equally given.' But now confirmation became necessary to perfect the act, and under the notion of the exclusive spirituality of the bishops, legislation confined it to the priesthood, so called.

Not only were the waters of baptism invested with this mystic air, but also the elements of the Supper. About this time the first thought appears that any change took place in the bread and wine by their consecration. They were common things and of little value before the priestly benediction worked the wonder of changing them into the very nature of God. This pretense stood on an exact level with paganism, in sacrifical importance. The heathen believed that the very substance of their deities was insinuated into the sacrificial victim, and became one with the person who ate thereof.[7] Their idea was that this assimilated them to the gods;

hence, the sacrifice was a great 'mystery.' Paganized Christianity adopted the same thought, and so they modified the original ordinances of Christ, until it was hard to find a vestige of his simple teachings in either of them. This new system of Eleusinianism wrapped up the plain truth in wild vagaries, which have perverted most of Christendom to this day. Many see the blot, but cannot efface it because of its antiquity. It insults man's senses, but his reverence for the hoary cares not to wipe it out; and yet, true antiquity goes back beyond the youth of the third century to the age of Jesus and his Apostles, at whose feet Cyprian and the fathers should fall, on a level with all other poor and uninspired sinners, instead of being allowed to send Christianity down the centuries on masquerade.

Hippolytus tells us of one Marcus, who played all sorts of tricks both with Baptism and the Supper, under this religious jugglery. He pretended to give the people a mixture of purple, or blood-red color, which bestowed ineffable grace from God; and taught that men who received this cup were beyond the reach of danger if they sinned, because it had made them perfect. To these he administered a second baptism, called redemption, attended by the laying on of hands and the whispering of some knavish gibberish into their ears, a process which admitted them into the higher mysteries.[8] These fanatics ranked with Elxai, who taught his followers to set a high value on water as a divinity, and to swear by it, as well as by salt, and the wind.[9] He laid great stress on baptism, to which he attributes, *ex opere operato*, the forgiveness of sins; and it must be frequently repeated, as marked sins are committed. He not only exhorts such sinners to be baptized afresh, 'together with your garments;' but Hippolytus gives us one of his rubrics, in which he entreats a person bitten by a mad dog to cure hydrophobia by this specific. He must ' Run with all his garments on into a river or running brook, where is a deep place, to call upon God and make vows as in baptism, and washing there, he will be delivered.'

However, to the honor of these third century Christians, they held fast to the logical consistency which would not allow Baptism to be severed from the Supper. Hence, when the babe had been immersed they administered to him the elements of bread and wine to render his salvation doubly sure. Bingham speaks of the known practice and custom in the ancient Church, of giving the eucharist to infants, which, he says, continued in the Church for several ages. It is frequently mentioned by Cyprian, Austin, Innocentius, and Gennadius, writers, from the third to the fifth century. Maldonat confesses it was in the Church for six hundred years. And some of the authorities just now alleged, prove it to have continued two or three ages more, and to have been the common practice beyond the time of Charles the Great. Again he says: 'It is evident, that the communion itself was given to infants, and that immediately from the time of their baptism.'[10] Herzog fully corroborates these facts. In his account of 'dispensing the elements to actual babes,' he says: 'The first trace of this custom is found in Cyprian (third century), who, in his treatise *On the Lapsed*, represents infants as saying on the day of judgment,

"We have not forsaken the Lord's bread and cup." (*De lapsis*, c. ix.) And in the same book he tells a striking story, how an infant refused the cup, and, when the deacon forced some of the wine down her throat, she was seized with vomiting. The explanation was, that the child, unknown to her parents, had previously, while under the care of her nurse, eaten bread soaked in wine, which had been poured out at an idolatrous ceremony. (*De lapsis*, c. xxv.)

Bingham further testifies that: 'The Greek Church to-day, and also the Nestorians, Jacobites, Armenians and Maronites, persist in the practice, using, generally, only the wine, and giving it either by the spoon or by the finger.'[11] This practice was born, and very properly, in the same North Africa which created the trine immersion of babes. Dean Stanley, also, says: 'The Oriental Churches, in conformity with ancient usage, still administer the eucharist to infants. In the Coptic Church it may even happen that an infant is the only recipient.' And he gives this reason for the practice: 'which, as far as antiquity is concerned, might insist on unconditional retention,' namely: 'A literal application to the eucharist of the text representing the bread of life, in the sixth chapter of St. John, naturally followed on a literal application to baptism of the text respecting the second birth in the third chapter; and the actual participation in the elements of both sacraments came to be regarded as equally necessary for the salvation of every human being.'[12]

The literal interpretation of the third chapter calls for the literal interpretation of the sixth to-day, for the one is no more necessary to the salvation of the babe than the other. If baptism is to be forced upon him in order to save him, so also should the Supper be; but if it is a mockery of the design of the ordinances to give him the one, it is a greater mockery to withhold the other, and to deny him the rights of membership in the Church, after initiating him into its fellowship. If there is divine authority for one there is for the other, and both should be observed. But if there is not divine authority for either, both should be laid aside.

A stout contest began in the third century between tradition and the supreme authority of Scripture. Some bowed to the absolute mandates of the Bible, allowing no compromise; while others reduced it to a book of divination, by introducing bibliomancy, or the 'sacred lots.' They casually opened the book, and by the first passage that came to hand predicted the future. Tertullian refused to dispute with the heretics out of the Scriptures, because they rejected their authority in part. Yet, when they sustain his position, he quotes them; but when they do not serve him, he appeals to custom and tradition, as in his Corona (p. 337): 'If thou requirest a law in the Scripture for it, thou shalt find none. Tradition must be pleaded as originating it, custom as confirming it, and faith in observing it.' On the contrary, Hippolytus condemns all errors opposed to the Scriptures, and binds every article of his faith to their teaching. Speaking of Carpocrates and other heretics, he says, that they brand their disciples 'in the posterior parts of the lobe of the right ear,' a practice at which he was rather apt himself, figuratively.

Early in the century Origen had procured a faithful edition of the Septuagint, Lucien a second, and Hesychius a third. Copies of all the Scriptures so abounded that, A. D. 294, Pamphilus had founded what may be called the first Bible Circulating Library, and made numerous copies with his own hands to give away. In their writings at this time, the fathers quote the Scriptures copiously; Origen, alone, making 5,765 quotations from the New Testament. Libraries were founded at Alexandria, Cæsarea and other places, and the Sacred Books were put in the church edifices, for all who could to read in their own tongue; besides which there were readers and interpreters in all the congregations.[13] The Churches proved themselves less and less worthy of this heritage. They quarreled with each other like termagants, spent their energies in pious hair-splitting, and were reckless in the extreme. Things were fast setting into a hierarchy, and the Churches were soon brought under thrall to aspiring officers. But, for a long time, powerful voices were raised to arouse the people against this. Even at Rome there was a struggle for Church independency; as Hippolytus says, that when Noetus, the pastor there, was tried for blasphemous utterances, it was '*before the Church;*' but where the spirit of independence went, its form soon followed, and blind submission or 'schism' was the only alternative. Origen wrote a letter to Philip and Severa, urging the freedom of religious opinion; the dominant 'Catholic' party began to tyrannize over others, in the interests of uniformity. The empire of Zenobia, Queen of Palmyra, which tolerated all religions, arose in 267; but Paul, the pastor of Antioch, who held civil office under this remarkable woman, put forth doctrines which other pastors condemned, and when Zenobia succumbed before the hosts of Aurelian, those pastors made a formal appeal to the conqueror to expel Paul from his pastorate. This is the first case on record, where Christians threw aside the dignity of their manhood to seek the aid of the civil power in settling their squabbles, in enforcing Christian doctrine. The emperor, with more regard to decency in the case, left it to the decision of an assembly of pastors at Rome. Victor was the first bishop of Rome who carried all measures with a high hand, in behalf of the claims of that Church. He was a busy, hot-headed mischief-maker, who stirred up discord on every trivial matter to carry a point; and before long a strong government was developed in the politics of Christianity. The Clementine and Ignatian forgeries followed, to sustain prelatical authority, in which some scoundrel puts the following into the mouth of Ignatius: 'We ought to look unto the bishop as unto the Lord himself. . . . Let all reverence the deacons as the command of Jesus Christ, and the bishop as Jesus Christ, being the Son of the Father; and the presbyters as the sanhedrin of God, and college of the Apostles. Without these it is not called a Church.'[14] 'What the bishop approves of, that is also well-pleasing to God, that whatever is done may be infallible and sure.' 'The Spirit proclaimed, saying thus: Do nothing without the bishop.' 'He who honors the bishop is honored by God, he who does any thing without the privity of the bishop, worships the devil.'[15] Cave attributes the Recognitions to Bardesenes, but Justin does not think that 'he could have been the author of so many shameless lies.' [16]

Thus, by the close of the third century we have the absurdity of Baptism regenerating the soul, and the Supper feeding it, an episcopacy with which is lodged eternal life, a 'Catholic Church,' outside of which all are heretics, and no salvation out of the Church. For this, Cyprian, a converted pagan, rhetorician and bishop of Carthage, is more to blame than any other man. Pupianus, like a simpleton, took it into his head to 'inquire carefully into our character,' says Cyprian. But in his reply to that callow brother, the gentle bishop reads him this sweet lecture: 'What presumption! What arrogance! What pride it is, to call the prelates and priests to account! The bees have their queen; the armies have their generals; and they preserve their loyalty; the robbers obey their captains with humble obsequiousness! How much more upright, and how much better are the unreasonable and dumb animals, and the bloody robbers, and swords and weapons, than you are. There the ruler is acknowledged and feared, whom not a divine mandate has set up, but whom the reprobate rout have appointed of themselves.' He then warns him that as one who calls his brother 'Fool' is in danger of hell fire, he is in greater peril who inveighs against 'priests.' [17]

Well may Isaac Taylor say in his Primitive Christianity: 'The first three (centuries) of the Christian history, comprise a sample of every form and variety of intellectual or moral observation of which human nature is at all susceptible, under the influence of religious excitement. No great ingenuity, therefore, can be needed in watching any modern form of error or extravagance, with its like, to be produced from the museum of antique specimens.' And he deprecates the abject slavery of so prostrating 'our understandings before the phantom, venerable antiquity, as to be inflamed with the desire of inducing the Christian world to imitate what really asks for apology and extenuation.' [18]

CHAPTER IV.

THE FOURTH CENTURY.

NEAR Geneva the Rhone flows in swift but calm majesty at the foot of those Alps, which are more majestic than itself. There its waters are a dark blue and beautifully crystal, as they flow from a cool azure lake far up in the region of alternate snow and sunshine. The river Avre comes rushing down from those horrid valleys where the glaciers grow and grind, striking the Rhone at almost right angles. It is a little, furious, brawling, muddy stream worthy of its fountain; it scowls like the brow of a dark villain rushing from his den, and launches its dirty current into the sheet of light. The Rhone, as the daughter of purity, shrinks from its defilement and glides on in disdain, refusing all amalgamation. Long they move on side by side in the same channel, parted by a deep-drawn line between them, but without one spot on the mountain maiden. Thus repelled, the Avre sinks to quiet, softened into decency by the sun-lit side of the Rhone, which melts, first into pity then into compassion. And why? At every rock the impudent intruder breaks into foam and then lulls into murmurs, as if it were pleading for tolerance, till quietly the larger stream consents to absorb the less, eddy by eddy, and so at last it is overcome by importunity and embraces what it first spurned. From that hour the glory of the Rhone is gone, a few leagues below the two are one, and in their turbid dishonor they rush down together as one polluted stream. This is but a faint image of the River of Life, mingled with the tide of pagan philosophy, which **have come** down to us confluent from the opening of the fourth century.

It would require a volume to trace the corruption of Christianity with Platonism, for we have this heresy in germ in the Apostolic Churches long before the Gnostics injected it into the truth at Alexandria, as the exalters and defenders of knowledge against faith. Paul found it creeping in at Crete, Colosse and Ephesus. The ideas of Pythagorus had prepared its way in Crete, Ephesus was the center of all pretentious philosophy, and Colosse was full of Phrygian pantheism entwined with the mysteries of Pan, Cybele and Bacchus. All these were dexterously interwoven into Christianity by Simon Magus, the real father of Christianized Gnosticism; others fostered it, and Manes led it to full manhood by the end of the third century. Paul saw its drift and warned Timothy against the opposition of 'knowledge falsely so called.' At first it was simple, without system or great power, never arraying itself openly against the truth; hence, its danger lay not in the violence of its attacks, but in its secret aggressions. Hippolytus calls it a 'hydra,' which had been pushing its way in the dark for many years; but no error matched it in efficiency. In his time it had corrupted between thirty and forty sects and subsects, who differed amongst themselves, all holding principles contrary to the simple faith of Christ and putting it under the control of Oriental paganism. The Gnosis of Alexandria is not easily defined; for it was a compound of monotheism, materialism, pantheism and spiritualism, taken from the heart of Platonism and the reasoning of Aristotle, with an admixture of native Egyptian thought. It professed to be the essence of intelligence, and so won the learned by its liberal speculations, the rationalist by its mastery of all logic, the superstitious by its many mysteries and the ignorant by its pretense, that it explained every thing. The Greek philosophy was too narrow for its tastes, and the teachings of Jesus too practical for its uses, so it made sad havoc of Homer's pure literature and Christ's plain revelations. It refused to take any thing in the proper and natural meaning of its words, and its allegory distorted every thing by the attempt to transfigure its simplicity. Hippolytus says that the whole system reminded him of Thales, who, 'Looking toward heaven, alleging that he was carefully examining supernal objects, fell into a well; and a certain maid, Thratta, remarked of him derisively that while intent on beholding things in heaven, he did not know what was at his feet.'

At the opening of the fourth century none of the Churches were entirely free from this corrupt leaven. It affected their doctrine and practice, had created an aristocracy in their ministry, pushed aside the letter of Scripture in sublimating its interpretation in relation to the person of God, of Christ, good and evil, incarnation and atonement; and had left but little in the Gospel unchanged, either in theory or experience. Almost all the African fathers had gone after it, and it had produced swarms of monastic orders in Greece, Gaul and Italy. Worse than this, it had destroyed the common bond of brotherhood between the rich and poor; and because of its pomp, ceremony, symbol, mystery and liturgical worship, it had found that favor with the nobles which exalted Christ's religion into an awful sacredness, and well nigh made the Church a secret society, which now cared little to up-lift the slave, the poor and the downtrodden. This explains why Christianity took the shape that it did in its final struggle with paganism. Having corrupted itself and become weak, the steps were easy to popular influence, and the unity of the temporal with the spiritual power. For forty years the law of Gallienus had recognized the Christians as a legal community. They had become numerous and influential. In the great cities they had large and costly temples furnished with vessels of gold and silver; their faith was much the rising fashion; the army, the civil service, the court, were filled with Christians, and the old Christ-likeness had nearly gone. A century had passed since the Antonines; the Empire was fast breaking up of its own heterogeneous elements; and one more attempt was made to recast it on the old faith and a more absolute model, if possible, by two Emperors after the Oriental fashion. Now we have the last bitter persecution, for the modified Christian faith was supplanting heathenism faster than had the simple Gospel. This persecution burst forth Feb. 23, 303, at Nicomedia, where the Imperial Palace was then located. Because the Scriptures were regarded as the source of all Christian aggression, the aim of the persecutors was to destroy every copy, and the cry passed up and down the empire: 'Burn their Testaments!' This Bible burning was firmly resisted, and at Carthage, Mensurius the bishop removed all copies from the sanctuary, putting worthless MSS. in their place. Afterward he was accused of betraying the Bible, a charge never sustained. Many gave up the sacred book willingly to be burnt in the market-places, and were expelled from the Churches, while others preferred death to this treachery. An African magistrate demanded that Felix should give up his Bible for burning, when he answered that he would rather be burnt himself. He was loaded with chains, sent to Italy and beheaded. In Sicily Euplius was seized with the Gospels in his hand and put on the rack. When asked, 'Why do you keep the Scriptures forbidden by the Emperor?' he answered: 'Because I am a Christian. Life eternal is in them; he that gives them up loses life eternal.' The Gospels were hung about his neck when led to execution and he was beheaded. At Ælia, in Palestine, Valens, an aged deacon, proved his love for the Scriptures by committing large portions of them to memory, and repeating them with accuracy. John, a blind Egyptian, did the same with such perfection that he could repeat the whole of the books of Moses, the Prophets and the Apostles.[1] Hot irons were thrust into the sockets of his eyes.

This persecution lasted ten years, and was severer than all that had gone before. But it acted like fire on incense, in drawing out the finest and richest essences in Christian character. One day, when it was beginning to abate, the Emperor's bed-chamber was found in flames. Diocletian was stricken with terror, and suspecting his Christian servants, he put them to torture and stood by to extort their confessions. Two weeks later a second fire occurred in the same room. He was more enraged than ever, and made closer inquisition for blood in the palace. Several servants were put to death, and the Empress and his daughter, who were Christians, were compelled to sacrifice to the gods. No language can describe the brutality of this persecution under Diocletian, Galerius and Maximian, whom Lactantius calls 'three ravenous wild beasts.' It is estimated that 17,000 suffered death in one month, that 144,000 were martyred in Egypt alone; and of the banished, and those condemned to the public works, no less than 700,000 died. In some provinces scarcely a Christian was left. So great was the triumph against Christianity that it was commemorated by striking off a gold coin. On one side was the head of Diocletian, crowned with laurel, and on the reverse, Jupiter, brandishing a thunder-bolt, and trampling upon the genius of Christianity—a human figure with feet of serpents. This Dance of Death was revived, however, under one Emperor after another, until Constantine conquered Rome, A. D. 312. At that time he reigned over the Western Empire only, but in 323, after the battle of Chalcedon, he became sole Emperor of the Roman world. He published an edict concerning Christians in 312, at Rome, but this document is lost. In 313 another, issued at Milan, gave toleration to all religions, and restored the confiscated property of Christians; he also gave large sums of money to rebuild their places of worship. But in 324 he inflicted a blow upon the Christian system from which it has not yet recovered, by making it the religion of the State. Between 315 and 323 he had sent forth five edicts admitting Christians to offices of state, civil and military; had taken measures to emancipate Christian slaves; had exempted the clergy from municipal burdens, and had made Sunday a legal day of rest from public work. But in 325 he attempted to settle the disputes in the Church by presiding at the first General Council which ever was held, that of Nicæa, in which Arianism was condemned, the unity of the Catholic party proclaimed, and the last step taken to establish the union between Church and State.

This great historical character has been the subject of malignant depreciation or extravagant laudation, according to the point of view from which he has been seen. Like all other great men, he took type from the character of his times, and the truth will make him human, without magnifying his virtues or blackening his weaknesses. He was born of a Christian

CONSTANTINE THE GREAT.

mother, who must have been troubled with Baptist notions, for she never had him christened. His disposition was naturally mild and tolerant; and his father, who was not a Christian, being moved by clemency toward Christians, had probably influenced him in the same direction, as well as the counsel and example of his mother. In his early manhood he worshiped at the shrine of the gods, but after the removal of the government to Constantinople he forbade pagan worship in that city, and leveled its temples throughout the Empire. Having renounced that religion himself, he persecuted the unconverted pagan for his constancy therein. He is said to have seen the cross in the sky, but possibly his Christianity had borne a higher character had he discovered love for the true cross of Christ in his soul; crosses in the firmament are of rather light moral worth. Unfortunately, it was years after this traditional vision that his nominal Christianity allowed him to kill his son, his second wife and others of his family. Full of ambition and passionate resentment, it would require considerably more to-day than a sky miracle, a sword in the hand, and a conquering army at the Malvian Bridge to give him membership 'in good standing' in the Baptist Church recently established at Rome. It is said that the cross in the heavens was attended with the inscription: 'By this sign conquer!' What, and whom? His own sin? His own soul? It seems not. But rather Maxentius and Rome and a throne. At the beginning Jesus had made himself king in Zion, to disallow all imperialism there; and did he now rise from his throne to hang his cross of peace an ensign of blood in the firmament, and to indicate that he turned over his universal lordship to an unregenerated heathen? This cross story needs thorough revision.

Common sense and the after life of Constantine rather say, that he kenned this cross in the clouds with the eye of a politician and statesman. The 'eagle' soared high that day, but he saw the beam of the cross soaring above the head of the Roman bird. Clear-headed and far-sighted, he read the meaning of that noiseless agency, which had quietly struggled for three hundred years to open a new history in the world. Other eyes besides his were turned in the same direction. The men clothed in purple had blindly sacrificed nameless thousands of their purest, wisest and most patriotic subjects to dumb idols. The gods had kept the Empire in a perpetual broil, and had often murdered his predecessors, before the crown had made a dint upon their brows. Constantine was not so blind to the real cross that he needed a miraculous phantom in the skies to interpret for him the signs of the times. He was cool, ambitious, practical; and knew what the principles of patient integrity must do in a new government, which, through the cross, had well nigh overthrown all the powers of the old government. The new idea of Calvary had awakened a new enthusiasm in man, had created a new order of patriotism, and he saw that the Via Dolorosa had become the Roman highway to unity, elevation, solidity. Long after this he came to embrace Jesus in person; for as age came and life was about to close, he sought and received baptism at the hands of Eusebius, the Bishop of Nicomedia, in the baptistery of the church known as Martyrium Christi. He expressed the hope ' To have been made partaker of the salutary grace in the river Jordan;' but his violent illness cut off that hope, and left him unable to take the long journey to the sacred river. He died on the 23d of May, A. D. 337, in great peace, at the age of sixty-four, about one month after his immersion. He had delayed this act of obedience to Christ under the absurd notion of his times, that baptism would cleanse away the sins of a life-time at once. Before his immersion he laid aside his purple robes and never donned them again; but from that day wore the white garment of newly immersed believers, until he exchanged it for the shroud in death.[2]

Spain, in the Western Empire, felt little of the Diocletian persecution which convulsed the eastern division, and how did the Spanish Christians use their exemption from suffering? Chiefly in the attempt to consolidate the new system of

THE SYNOD OF ELVIRA.

corporate unity, in place of the isolation of Apostolic Church independency. With this end in view, we find nineteen bishops, twenty-six presbyters and many deacons, holding the Council of Elvira (Eleberis) in the retired district of Bætica, under the lead of Hosius, the great Bishop of Cordova. He was a man of genius and power, born to rule. At Nicæa he took the second seat, Constantine filling the first, but at Elvira, A. D. 305-306, he was the guiding spirit. His prime idea was to put Christianity on a surer footing, by first consolidating it into a catholic body, and then uniting it closer to the national life. This synod was professedly called to restore order in the Churches of Spain, by deciding what to do with those who had 'lapsed' from the faith, and to settle other questions of morality and discipline. Its tone and temper were supposed to be in sympathy with Novatian; but Hosius adroitly turned it, not to reconcile the Churches one to another, but to unite the Church with the State. Afterward he was very influential in the private councils of Constantine, and served as his diplomatic agent on many occasions.

Under the frame-work of the new policy, this Spanish Convention of independent assemblies was to issue a general code of decrees which should bind them by concert of action, as if they were one congregation. In this way an organic union could reach the 'heretics' and 'rural' pastors, could bring them under subjection to the bishops of large cities; and so at one stroke they could keep the Church pure and strong. This was Spanish Catholicity in its infancy. Then, if one nation might have a Church, why not each nation, and if each, why could not all nations form one general Church? This proposed purification of the Church suited the Novatians exactly, but they did not dream that they were weaving meshes for their own feet in this Synod. With all the simplicity of their hearts they united in the XXIVth decree, which demanded that a man who had been baptized in one province should not enter the ministry in another, a long step toward a diocesan system. Heresy was put also on the same basis with deadly sin, and wrong in the laity was to be condoned with a leniency which did not apply to pastors. This claimed pre-eminent sanctity for the clergy, and conciliated the people to the innovation. The special privileges to the people, however, were attended with larger distinctions of rank amongst the clergy, and the bishop began to assume new functions over his brethren. Others might baptize, but in every case the convert must be brought to the bishop to be confirmed. The XLIId article enjoined two years of probation before a catechumen could be baptized. Non-communion at the Lord's Table became a retributive act, making exclusion therefrom penal, and men were excommunicated for a given time, from one to ten years. Christ intended his ordinances as a trowel to build up the Churches, they used them as a sword to cut them down in arbitrary retribution. First they made baptism a magical rite to save from sin, then they withheld it as a penance for sins committed, as in the case of Constantine, who had long been a catechumen. The Supper had been the first festival of joy to the convert on entering the Church; now its refusal to him was to shut the gate of heaven in his face forever, even in some cases when he was penitent. This Synod decreed that any one who, after faith in the baptism of salvation, shall fall into idolatry, or falsely accuse a bishop, priest or deacon, 'shall not receive communion even to death.' This is what is meant by the Church 'arming itself with sacraments!' And so the Lord's ordinance of thanksgiving and commemoration of the sacrifice of Jesus, 'armed' the Church to punish any one who was absent from the Church for three Sundays with the penalty of denial to the Supper itself.

The whole trend of the Synod was to make the ministry an aristocracy, by building up sacerdotalism; and to this end it was considerate of the dead, while it was harsh toward the living. The XXXIVth article provided that, 'Tapers shall not be lighted in the cemetery during the day, for the spirits of the saints must not be disquieted.' Great homage was paid to the martyrs. One good thing was done, however. Baptism had been attended with gifts and offerings from the candidate, a practice which had grown into a regular tax exacted of all who were immersed. The XLVIIIth article forbade this tax, also the custom of washing his feet after the anointing with oil.

During the reign of Constantine the Empire was rocked by theological contest, his Christian subjects being divided by bitter animosity; the Arian division raged in the East, the Donatist in the West. He saw that this must be healed, for political reasons, if for no other. The DONATIST agitation arose in North Africa, A. D. 311, in what are now known as the Barbary States; but it centered in Carthage, Numidia and the Mauritanias. Its field covered nearly seven degrees of north latitude, immense centers of commerce and influence, soils and climates; marking a stretch of land nearly 2,000 miles long by about 300 wide, reaching from Egypt to the Atlantic, and fringing the Atlas mountains, the Mediterranean and the desert. The Punic wars had raged there under Hannibal and Africanus, and the contestants inherited all that was brave and fiery in Phœnicia, Carthage and Utica. Still warm with this enterprising blood, such a people were not likely to surrender their Church independency, and take the yoke of the Councils of the Catholic Church without a struggle. Constantine's hands were full. Besides, a deep sigh had long filled the Christian atmosphere for a return to Gospel simplicity, and the late persecution opened the way for its free expression. In this region the inner independency of the Churches had been more firmly maintained than in many other places, and the late encroachments upon it had aroused the Churches to a determined defense. Merivale says of the Donatists: 'They represented the broad principle of the Montanists and the Novatians, that the true Church of Christ *is the assembly* of really pious persons only, and admits of no merely nominal membership.' They dreaded any form of un-Christian membership which eats out the spiritual fellowship of a Gospel Church.

This is more strictly true of their later history, after they had entirely shaken off the Catholic notion that unity is of more consequence than purity, and so that a spiritual regeneration was the prime qualification for membership in the Churches of Christ. They had come to charge the Catholic with being a fallen Church, because it had become lax in its morals, tolerating open and notorious sin, and regarding visible unity as a higher attribute of Church-life than personal purity. Yet notwithstanding this, Parmenian, one of their greatest writers, preached baptismal regeneration as strongly as any of the men of his times.

Jerome, Augustine and others class the Donatists with the Novatians, as to general aim and purpose, and Augustine sneers at them as 'spotless saints.' Kurtz represents them as holding that Church and State should stand apart, and Walsh asserts that Constantine had condemned them in his decrees, before they appealed to him for the trial of their case.[3] But still the fact stands, that in their controversy with the Catholics they sought his decision. There has been much dispute about their views of infant baptism, and many affirm that they were anti-pedobaptists, notably amongst these Guy de Bres, who said: 'That they demanded that baptized infants ought to be baptized again as adults.[4] Although this controversy was not general at this time, yet as it was somewhat rife in Africa, it is quite likely that they took this position, as they took their rise there; and Augustine's letters against them imply the same. They certainly rebaptized those who came to them from other communions, but Dr. Owen thinks only because the impurity of other Churches rendered their baptism null; while Long says that they refused to baptize infants.[5] It is commonly conceded that Augustine wrote a separate work against them on infant baptism, which has not come down to us. If he did, the fair inference would be that they rejected that doctrine.

Still, as is usual with all true reformers, they were reluctant to break up old ties, and a petty, party strife must needs bring on a collision between them and their opponents. Mensurius, Bishop of Carthage, manfully opposed the mania which led thousands to court martyrdom in order to take the martyr's crown; because he thought it savored more of suicide than of enforced sacrifice for Christ. But he died in 311, and Cæcilianus, who was of the same opinion, was elected to fill his place, with which election a majority were dissatisfied. Others were displeased because he had been ordained by Felix, who was charged with giving up the Bible to be burnt, and a division took place in the Church. The retiring party first elected Majorinus their bishop, who soon died, and after him Donatus of Casæ Nigræ (that is, of the Black Huts). This party increased greatly, and was read out of the Catholic body, Constantine taking sides against them. At this point they fell into the great and strange blunder of appealing to the Emperor to redress their grievances. Nothing could have been more stupid or inconsistent. They were struggling for a pure Church against the laxness of the Catholic party, the head of which party was himself unbaptized and a semi-heathen; asking him to make the Church at Carthage and elsewhere pure by the exercise of his political power! The proposition itself put the knife to the throat of their own principles, by tendering an alliance of the Church with the State, in disregard of its Gospel constitution. Nor can this folly be extenuated; they knew enough to seek a pure Church for Christ, and should have sought that blessing according to his known will. Nominally they held to the entire separation of the Church from the State, and that persecution for religious opinion was an oppression of a free conscience; yet, when they fell into disputes with their opponents they were the first to appeal to the civil authority to settle them.

Here, then, with all the goodness, zeal and manliness of the Donatists, they had the folly to invoke the secular power to settle a purely religious dispute between Christians. Yet it is but just to say that, so far as is known, this is an isolated act in their history, and not one of a number in the same line. Bitterly they repented of their folly. Their 'appeal to Cæsar' was sent in a sealed package of papers, in a leather bag, inscribed : 'Statement of the Catholic Church, presented by those in communion with Majorinus, in proof of the crimes of Cæcilian.' Their petition closed with the words :

'We address ourselves to you, most excellent Prince, because you are of a righteous parentage, and the son of a father who did not persecute us, as did his colleagues the other Emperors. Since, therefore, the regions of Gaul have not fallen into the sin of surrendering the Scriptures, and, since there are disputes between us and other prelates of Africa, we supplicate your Piety, that our cause may be submitted to judges chosen from Gaul.' [6]

Under the old faith, as Pontifex Maximus, the Emperor was the judge in all religious affairs, and so his 'Piety' was now ready to oblige them, and he called a Council at Rome, October, A. D. 313, of over thirty bishops, who decided against the Donatists. They asked him for a second hearing, and he called the Council of Arles, 314, composed of more than two hundred bishops from Gaul, Brittany, Germany, Spain and Africa. In his letter to this body he says that they should not have called on him to judge in such difficulties, and charged them with 'Acting like the heathen in calling upon him to settle their religious disputes.' When writing of the same Council to Celsus, Vicar of Africa, he says that he felt strictly bound to fulfill 'the duties of a prince, and extirpate all the errors which the rashness of man has introduced, and to establish union and concord amongst the faithful.' But in his letter to the Prefect Ablavius he puts his duty in a stronger light, thus : 'I do not believe that it is permitted us to tolerate these divisions and disputes, which may draw down the wrath of God, not only upon the Commonwealth, but also upon myself, whom his divine will has charged with the care and management of all things upon earth.'

The Council of Arles decided against the Donatists, when they suddenly awoke to their mistake in staining one of the cardinal truths in Church liberty; for the Emperor enforced the decision with the secular arm. Accounting the Donatists enemies of the State, he deprived them of their churches, confiscated their property, and banished their bishops or pastors, of whom Mosheim says that they had four hundred in North Africa, which number precludes the idea that they were either of the metropolitan or diocesan order. The Donatists defied his authority, but with ill consistency, and he sent an armed force to Africa to subdue them. This was the first Christian blood ever shed in a disgraceful contest amongst themselves; yet Constantine piously tells Celsus that he was laboring that 'the true religion may be embraced by all the world.'[7] Afterward he undertook to settle the Arian controversy, which Jortin describes, as 'the occasion of innumerable lies, slanders, forgeries, pretended miracles, banishments and murders,' and 'of many false and partial histories.' In order to end this contest, Constantine assembled the Council of Nicæa, a city of Bithynia, near Constantinople, May 20, A. D. 325. The number of bishops present is put down at from 250 to 320; and Dean Stanley says that each bishop was allowed two presbyters and three slaves as his retinue. The Emperor, who was fond of prodigality and display, brought them together and maintained them in state at his own expense. Great interest was excited, from the fact that he was the first Roman prince who had publicly consorted with the Christians, and so scholars, philosophers and men of rank flocked in from all directions. Christianity had but just emerged from the blood and wreck of persecution, and such a body of veteran confessors had never met together before. They came from all parts of Asia Minor, Syria, Palestine, Phœnicia and Arabia, one coming from Persia, and one even from Gothia. They presented a stirring appearance when assembled in the imperial palace, most of them bearing some mark of suffering for Christ. They had been tortured, maimed, scarified, and some of them were blind. Hot irons had plowed furrows upon some of them, some had an arm cut off; one of the Asian bishops had lost the use of both his hands by burning, and another from Upper Egypt had his right eye dug out. As Christian warriors they needed but the entry of the Captain of their salvation, with the wounds of the spines, the spikes and the spear, to make their sacramental congress perfect. Then had they cast themselves at his feet to kiss the sacred prints, each in holy love exclaiming: 'My Lord and my God!' and he had breathed upon them his holier salaam: 'Peace be unto you!'

Alas for them, with all their fortitude, the simplicity of the Upper Room, the 'piece of broiled fish and the honey-comb,' had given place to royal apparel, princely fare and 'king's houses;' but there was no Son of Man returning fresh from Edom. They sat waiting in solemn silence; but a new Head of the Church came in, and they rose to do him reverence. He was of majestic height and bearing, wrapped in royal purple, with a golden fillet on his head and without a thorn-scar on his temples. He had not redeemed the Church with his blood, he had not stained his raiment in the sacrificial wine-press. His flushed face and downcast eyes were reflected back in the gems of his vesture; the sword of nations and the shepherd's crook lay at his side; but where was the Good Shepherd who laid down his life for the sheep? This is Cæsar, and not 'another King, one Jesus!' When seated in the golden chair placed for him in their midst, he gave a sign, and each bishop, according to his rank, sat down in his presence. How are the mighty fallen! Their lawful sovereign and good friend was hailed as their Head, and they waited for his image and 'superscription' to attest their orthodoxy; for the first time the old Baptist Churches of the world are found crouching at a monarch's feet! Farewell, soul-liberty, hie thee to the wilderness for a time! This body sat until the 25th of July, and the Emperor presided over its Councils most of the time, aided now and then by Hosius. Constantine addressed it graciously, listened to and took part in its debates, led it to its decisions, and confirmed its decrees. He closed the sessions with a great banquet on his birthday, and loaded its members with imperial gifts. He even embraced Paphnutius, kissing the empty socket from which his eye had been torn, and exhorted all the bishops to prayers for himself, his family and the Empire; then he bade them farewell!

After the Council, Constantine became bitter toward the Arians, although he finally became an Arian himself. He banished Arius and ordered his works to be burnt, threatening with death all who kept them, and all who rejected the findings of the Council came under its anathema, the civil power enforcing uniformity where it could not be commanded by reason. The Emperor issued an edict against all dissenters, saying: 'Know ye, Moravians, Valentinians, Marcionites, Paulians and Cataphrygians (that is, various Gnostic and Montanist sects), that your doctrine is but vain and false. O ye enemies of truth, authors and counselors of death, ye spread abroad lies, oppress the innocent, and hide from the faithful the light of truth.' Then he forbids their meetings in private or public, orders their places of worship pulled down, and their property confiscated to the 'Catholic Church.' Eusebius, of Cæsarea, was delighted with this edict, and berated the heretics as 'hypocrites, caterpillars and locusts.' The Arians and others suffered frightfully, and the pagans stood astonished; for while they had various sects amongst themselves, they never persecuted each other to enforce uniformity. After A. D. 330 Rome and Constantinople became the highest sacerdotal seats, with boundaries answering to those of the Empire, and the will of the court held the scales of orthodoxy and heterodoxy; all who differed with the dictates of the Emperor and his party were guilty of 'heresy and schism.'

The condition of things at that moment is well set forth by Niebuhr in the following words: 'The religion which he had in his head must have been a strange compound indeed. The man who had on his coins the inscription, "Sol invictus," who worshiped pagan deities, consulted the auspices (diviners), and indulged in a number of pagan superstitions, and interfered in the Council of Nice, must have been a repulsive phenomenon, and was certainly not a Christian. He was a superstitious man, and mixed up his Christian religion with all kinds of absurd superstitions and opinions; when, therefore, certain Oriental writers call him equal to an Apostle, they know not what they are saying; and to speak of him as a saint is a profanation of the word.'[8] Thus that fantastic mixture of Judaism, heathenism and Christianity, then called the 'Catholic Church,' became one compact Roman system, held together by bonds within and pressure without, exalted into a tremendous mystery of rite and pomp—a very trampling tyranny. The Carpenter of Nazareth was to be no longer strong in his own weakness, but was to be made mighty by the paralysis inflicted through an imperial, half-pagan autocrat!

It is scarcely necessary here to state how soon every sort of superstition and heathen ceremony was mixed with this State Christianity. The bones of Stephen were found by a revelation from Gamaliel, Paul's teacher, after they had rested for three centuries. Many made pilgrimages to his shrine at Jerusalem and were wonderfully healed, while others made wonderful sums of money out of the exhibition of these relics. The bodies of Luke and Andrew were discovered, and removed to a great temple which the Emperor had built in Constantinople. The remains of Joseph of Arimathea were recovered, and large portions of stone and earth removed from his tomb for miraculous uses. Most wonderful of all, Helena, Constantine's mother, found the real cross of Christ, not that which her son saw in the sky, but that on which Jesus suffered; and although it had been buried for three centuries, the wood was as sound as the heart of oak! This proved an immense treasure. It not only wrought miracles, but although countless pieces were taken all over the world, it grew no less; at any rate that is what Tillemont says. It was a sad oversight that Constantine did not build a war-ship out of its wood for blowing heretics to atoms. Besides all this, it is estimated that by the end of the fourth century 27,000 monks and nuns were found in Egypt alone, most of whom were piously austere, ignorant and lazy.

These, and many other things are stated by numerous writers of the hierarchy, with pride and even with triumph, and we cannot but honor their frankness. So far from attempting to disguise these things by pious lying, it is their delight to make them known, with others just as disgraceful. Take, for example, Cardinal Baronius, who says with delicious openness: 'It is allowable for the Church to transfer to pious uses those ceremonies which the pagans employed impiously to superstitious worship, after they have been purified by consecration; for the devil is the more mortified to see those things turned to the service of Jesus Christ, which were instituted for his own.' Polidore Virgil says: 'The Church has borrowed several customs from the religion of the Romans and other heathens; but that they have improved them and put them to a better use.'[9] And Guillaume du Choul sums up the whole case in these words: 'If we examine narrowly we shall discover that several institutions of our religion have been transferred from the Egyptian and other Gentile ceremonies. Such as the tunics and surplices, the crowns or tonsures, of our priests, bowing round the altar; the sacrificial pomp, church-music, adorations, prayers, supplications, processions, litanies and several other things which our priests use in their mysteries; offering up to our only God, Jesus Christ, what the ignorance of the

Gentiles, with their false religion and foolish presumption, offered to their false deities and to mortal men of their own deifying.'[10] Even Eusebius, in the life-time of Constantine, reports that: 'This Emperor, to make the Christian religion more plausible to the Gentiles, adopted into it the exterior ornaments which they used in their religion.'

These corruptions were lamented and resisted by brave and earnest men, but with slight success; partly because they themselves held some palpable error, and because they were assailed with calumny and resentment. Amongst these was Aerius, a presbyter, A. D. 355, who maintained that the New Testament makes a presbyter a bishop, condemned prayers for the dead, rejected all fasts ordained by the Church and attempted to restore Apostolic discipline. He had many followers. 'For some time his party, the Aërians,' says Herzog, 'assembled in the open fields, in forests and among the mountains; but, persecuted from all sides, it soon melted away.'[11] The bitterness of the writers of those times shows that these bare-faced perversions were met by formidable resistance; but ingenuity circumvented these struggles, cursed and branded the men and crushed out their measures. A remarkable case of this sort is found in the manner in which Jerome trampled upon Jovinian and Vigilantus. His injustice comes to the face of his own reports, through exaggerated noise and vulgar abuse. Jovinian was one of the best-known heretics in the last half of this period. He was thoroughly versed in the Scriptures, and wrote stoutly against voluntary martyrdom, fasting and monkery. He also contended that all baptized believers have morally the same calling, dignity, grace and blessedness. So great was his influence, that a Synod was held at Rome, A. D. 390, at which he was condemned, and a second followed at Milan, 395. He held the vital principle of regeneration by the Spirit of God, the perseverance of the saints, and denied the perpetual virginity of Mary. It is believed that he was scourged at Rome, and banished for holding conventicles. So far as we can judge from his writings quoted by Jerome, he held, in substance, the same views as those of Luther.

Vigilantus was born in Gaul, and ordained a presbyter A. D. 395. He went to Palestine, thinking that he would find things there, in the cradle of Christianity, much after the Apostolic order. Instead of this he was disgusted, as Luther was afterward at Rome, and returned. Then, he and Jerome fell into controversy. He attacked the worship of the martyrs and of relics as a lapse into paganism; making an attack, also, upon the claim of superior sanctity in clergymen, monasteries, celibacy and the vows of poverty. To these two we may add a' most noble advocate of liberty of conscience in Lactantius. He was the tutor of Crispus, the son of Constantine, as well as the historian of the Diocletian persecution, and, according to Milman, the adviser of the Emperor in questions of legislation. From full conviction, he became a Christian in early life, and stoutly defended religious freedom. He says:

'To defend religion by bloodshed, torture and crime, is not to defend, but to pollute and profane it. For nothing is so much a matter of free-will as religion, in which if the mind of the worshiper is disinclined, religion is at once taken away and ceases to exist. The right way to defend religion is by patient endurance unto death, through which the keeping of the faith is pleasing to God, and adds nothing to the truth.'[12]

Besides these, we have Helvidius, who lived at Rome in the latter part of the century. He and Jovinian were the first who dared to attack the doctrine of Mary's perpetual virginity; and he also assailed nunnery and other evils. After Jerome had written bitterly against Vigilantus in his sixty-first letter, he attempted to answer Helvidius, under great excitement. He did them great injustice by that most cowardly thing which a man can do, namely: to misrepresent his opponent, and so cut off his appeal to an unbiased posterity. The pen of Jerome was rendered very offensive by his grinding tyranny and crabbed temper. No matter how wrong he was, he could not brook contradiction. In these cases, it were simply mild to call his composition venom; for no man can read his replies to the simple and inoffensive words which he quotes from Vigilantus without disgust. He pretends to call it 'sacrilege,' either to hear or repeat what his opponent says. He then calls him a 'Jew,' a 'Samaritan' and a 'madman, disgorging a filthy surfeit.' He said that his tongue was only fit to be cut out—he had a 'fetid mouth, fraught with a putrid stench, against the relics and ashes of the martyrs.' He denounces him as a 'dog,' a 'maniac,' a 'monster,' an 'ass,' a 'fool,' a 'glutton,' a 'servant of the devil,' and a 'useless vessel which shall be shivered by the *iron rod* of Apostolic authority,' with a few other names quite as gentle and saintly. Jovinian received the same treatment from this delectable doctor. This reformer had said that there was no difference of *merit* between the married and the unmarried. This made Jerome's pious indignation boil over, and he calls the statement a 'savage howling of ferocious wolves, scaring the flock;' with other characteristic sayings of a slightly acid sort. Possibly, an interpretation of this animus is given in the 'Retractationes' of Augustine when he laments the Jovinian heresy, which had so far prevailed at Rome, that several nuns, whose honor was spotless, had been led away into the error of matrimony.

One marked feature which relieves the tendencies of this age is the vigor with which the Scriptures were multiplied. Few had ever possessed complete copies of them, and these were now rare, the late Bible-burnings having made a famine of the word of God; it was, therefore, in great demand, and great efforts were made to meet that demand. Diligent search was made for copies that had escaped destruction, and transcripts of them were multiplied. Constantine instructed Eusebius to have fifty copies of the Sacred Writings beautifully engrossed on parchment 'by artificial transcribers of books, most skilful in the art of accurate and fair writing, which (copies) must be very legible and easily portable, in order to their being used.' He also dispatched letters to his civil officers in various provinces, to see that every thing necessary was provided for this work, and supplied two public carriages to convey them to him at Constantinople, at his expense. This order was immediately executed, and the fifty copies were sent to him 'in volumes magnificently adorned.' [13] He also established a library in the imperial city, into which he gathered nearly seven thousand volumes, chiefly of Christian books. This grew to a hundred thousand in the days of the younger Theodosius, most of which were destroyed by the Emperor Leo III. Tischendorf conjectures that the Sinaitic MS., which he discovered in the Monastery of St. Katharine, on Mount Sinai, A. D. 1854–59, might have formed 'One of the fifty copies of the Bible which, in the year 331, the Emperor Constantine ordered to be executed for Constantinople.' [14]

The people had no power to resist the decisions of Councils, now enforced by the Emperor; and their free use of the Scriptures may have greatly pacified them to bear more patiently the many innovations which had crept into the Church. Possibly with this in view, the Council of Nicæa ordained that 'No Christian should be without the Scriptures,'—that of Antioch, A. D. 341, that those who stayed at public worship only to hear the Scriptures read, without partaking of the eucharist, should be excommunicated; and that of Laodicea, A. D. 343–381, 'That the Gospels, with the other Scriptures, ought to be read on the Sabbath day.' The monks of those days were diligent students of the Scriptures; for Chrysostom not only exhorts 'the servant, the rustic and the widow,' to read them, but he asks, 'Are the Scriptures to be read only by monks?' And the common people used them freely, even the women and children hanging the Gospels about their necks, a fact proving that something more is needful to a pure Christianity than free access to the Bible. A Bible possessed but neglected, or used and distorted, leads to the same result in substance; on the principle understood and adopted by Julian the Apostate, when he forbade Christian educators to teach Gentile learning: 'Lest, being furnished with our armor, they make war upon us with our own weapons.'

This century was likewise very active in the revision and circulation of the Scriptures in several languages. Jerome, the crabbed monk of whom we have already spoken, devoted his life chiefly to the revision of the already existing Latin versions, known as the Ante-Hieronymian, that is, those made before his time, as the word denotes. This most learned of all the Latin fathers, A. D. 331–420, undertook his work at the request of Damasus, the Bishop of Rome. Much of the Old Testament he translated from the original Hebrew, but his revision of the New was based upon the old Latin version known as the Itala, compared with the Greek text. His work is now known as the Vulgate, or current Latin text of the Bible, and is declared by the Papal Constitution to be 'authentic, and unquestioned, in all private discussion, reading, preaching and explanation.' By 'authentic,' here, is meant authoritative, and Sixtus V. threatened to excommunicate all who should vary from that text. Yet, the Vulgate as we have it to-day is not the unchanged text that Jerome left, for some of its renderings have been corrupted and made to fit into certain dogmas, as Fulke has shown in countless instances in his 'Confutation of the Rhemish Testament.' Whether these were made by Pope Sixtus, or by Clement VIII., it is not easy to decide, as both of them changed Jerome's version. Clement charged that the edition of Sixtus swarmed with errors, and made two thousand changes therefrom. But Jerome himself introduced, or at least sanctioned the system of Latinizing Greek words by introducing them into the Latin Bible; the obvious effect of which was to render his version obscure, or, as the historian, Fuller, says, his translation 'needed to be translated over again.' And of the Vulgate as rendered in the Rhemish New Testament, the same writer quaintly says: 'They could no longer blindfold the laity from the Scriptures, resolved to fit them with false spectacles.' [15]

But Jerome said of his own version, that he had 'Corrected only those errors which seemed to change the sense, and had permitted the rest to remain;' and that he had used for the purpose 'Greek copies which did not much differ from the usual Latin reading.' Amongst many Greek words which he transferred instead of translating them, was the family of words relating to baptism, making them cluster around the verb '*baptizo*;' so that, those who knew the Latin only, could not possibly tell what those words meant. This new-coined method of keeping back the meaning of God's commands has debauched the consciences of translators, and perverted many versions from Jerome's time to our own, by copying his pernicious example, and refusing to translate the exact sense of these words into the mother-tongues of those for whom their translations have been made. And what has rendered this practice the more blameworthy has been, the common pretense, either that these words were too holy to be translated, that their meaning was immaterial, that it was indefinite, or that they were incapable of translation, for want of proper equivalents in the tongues in which these versions were made. The soul of a translator who attempts to pull that sort of wool over the eyes of honest folk, would suffer no injury by a very literal rendering from the Greek, of Rev. xxi, 8, especially if he made it when alone on his knees before God. Possibly, Cartwright and Fulke had some such thought in mind when they said of the Rhemish Testament: 'That, compared with the authentical Greek text, it is, in many places, ridiculous, *insincere*, *untrue*; and, consequently, of no authority.' This conduct of Jerome in forming the Vulgate, justly brought upon him the censure of Baillet, when he says: 'It is agreed that Jerome may be the greatest saint of all translators, but that he is not the most exact. He hath taken liberties which the laws of translation will not admit, and his adversary, Rufinus, fails not to charge him with it.' [16]

But this was not the character of all the versions made in the fourth century. For example, the 'Gothic,' by Ulphilas, is pronounced by scholars to be very faithful and accurate. This able and devout bishop of the Goths had induced his countrymen to become Christians, and they reposed boundless confidence in him, saying that whatever he did was well done. He was of Cappadocian ancestry, but was a native Goth; still, as his people had no written dialect, he found it necessary to construct a language for them, and first framed an alphabet of the Gothic language from the Greek, Latin and Runic characters, suited to his work. Into this he made a translation of the Old and New Testaments, excepting the Books of Kings and Chronicles; and tradition says, that these were omitted lest they should increase the fierce passions of his people for war. The relics which are left of his version are amongst the most valuable of antiquity, as it was made from the Greek text. These fragments cover the larger part of the New Testament, and he translates the verb *baptizo* by the word '*daupjan*,' which means to dip. Tregelles thinks this to have been the vernacular Bible of a great part of Europe in the fifth and sixth centuries. Ulphilas lived A. D. 311–381, and after the ninth century his translation was lost until the sixteenth, when the Gospels were recovered; in the nineteenth, his Epistles of Paul were found. German scholars find the Gothic of this version superior to the German language, of which it is the parent, in richness and dignity of expression, as well as harmony and purity of tone.

The Ethiopic version, mentioned by Chrysostom in his second homily on John's Gospel, was made in the ancient and vernacular tongue of Abyssinia, but by whom is not known. It is commonly referred to Frumentius, who first preached Christianity in that country; but at the best this is only tradition. It is generally ascribed to this century, and is regarded as the oldest monument of Ethiopic literature. Dillman declares it to be 'very faithful; being for the most part a verbal rendering of the Greek, and yet readable and fluent, and in the Old Testament often hitting the ideas and words of the Hebrew in a surprising manner.' It also renders the word which defines the act of baptism by '*tamaka*,' to dip.

A number of different creeds are found in this century, but they did not by any means push the Bible aside. Basil is a fair example of his brethren in his love for scriptural truth who, when Valens, the Emperor, promised him promotion if he would embrace Arianism, replied: 'That such fair promises were fit only to entice children, but that he was taught and nourished by the Holy Scriptures, and was ready rather to suffer a thousand deaths, than to suffer one syllable or iota of the Scriptures to be altered.' Then the Emperor fell into a rage, and threatened him with death; to which Basil answered, that 'If he put him to death, it was only to set him at liberty.' The prince then sat down to write an edict for his banishment, but at last tore up the paper and cast it from him; the great divine was left to labor and die in peace.

CHAPTER V.

THE FIFTH CENTURY.

DURING this period the unity of the Roman Empire was broken, and it was divided into the Eastern and Western Empires; after which followed the migration of the barbarous Northern peoples. Then the Western Empire fell to pieces, and new nations sprang up out of the barbarian forests. The Church also was rent by controversies of every kind, chiefly those concerning the person and work of our Lord. This age is marked by the total eclipse of true justifying faith and the simple method of Gospel salvation. A dramatic salvation pushed it entirely aside, and our Lord's beautiful ordinance of baptism was used to push him aside, to take his place as the great remedy for sin. The absurd doctrine of baptismal regeneration had long been growing; but from this time it not only changed the whole current of Christianity for centuries, but corrupted its foundation truths.

True, a few individuals still held saving faith in Christ as a precedent to baptism. Athanasius declared, A. D. 360, that 'Our Lord did not slightly command to baptize, for first of all he said, "teach, and then baptize;" that true faith might come by teaching, and baptism be perfected by faith.' So Jerome of Dalmatia, 378: 'It cannot be that the body shall receive the sacrament of baptism unless the soul have before received the true faith.' In the same year Basil urges: 'One must first believe and then be sealed with baptism. Faith must needs precede and go before. None are to be baptized but the catechumens and those who are duly instructed in the faith.' Several others taught the same thing, but for a long time there had been a strange admixture of error with this doctrine. In the last half of the second century even clear-headed Hippolytus had said of the baptized man, that he 'Goes down with faith into the bath of regeneration, . . . comes up from baptism bright as the sun, flashing with the rays of righteousness; but greatest of all, he comes up a son of God.' The Council of Nicæa had actually decreed that he who goes down into the waters of baptism is 'obnoxious to sins;' but he ascends free from their slavery, 'a son of God, an heir, yea co-heir with Christ.' And the Christian writers of the fifth century generally speak of baptism as intrinsically holy, 'ineffable' and 'astounding' in its results. Chrysostom preaches this dangerous heresy on the subject: "Although a man should be foul with every vice, the blackest that can be named; yet should he fall into the baptismal pool, he ascends from the divine waters purer than the beams of noon. . . . As a spark thrown into the ocean is instantly extinguished, so is sin, be it what it may, extinguished when the man is thrown into the laver of regeneration.' Then he solemnly exhorts those who are deferring baptism to make haste and be thus regenerated, as they were liable, in his judgment, to eternal torment; for he calls trine immersion 'The pool of regeneration and justification.'[1]

But some of the writers of that age went even beyond this extreme, insisting that immersion in baptism wrought miracles on the body as well as grace in the soul. Socrates, the Christian historian, tells of a Jew, at Constantinople, who had been bedridden for years with the palsy; after trying all sorts of physicians he resolved to receive baptism, was brought to Atticus the bishop, on a bed, and when dipped in the water was perfectly cured.[2] This was even worse than paganism. Ovid, the old Roman poet, had ridiculed the idea that lustrations in water washed away sin:

'O, easy fools, to think that a whole flood
Of water e'er can purge the stain of blood!'

Yet Christians clung to this heathen thought, and incorporated it into Christianity. Blondus tells us that at Rome, Mercury's Well purified from perjury and lying. But Ovid laughed at Peleus, who had murdered his brother Phocus, and thought himself absolved because Acastus had lustrated him in river water. A twin thought was perfected by the Christians of the fifth period, namely, that sin committed after baptism was unpardonable, without the severest penance; hence baptism was delayed as near to the hour of death as possible. Gratus was so troubled by this question that he asked the Council of Carthage, A.D. 348, whether a man so sinning did not need a second baptism. This notion wrought such mischief that as few as possible came to baptism; and many sought to bring this state of things to an end. For this reason even Chrysostom pressed that men should follow this duty for duty's sake—as sudden death might cut off the opportunity for baptism; then its neglecters would be lost, and those who were baptized at the last would only shine in heaven as stars, whereas, had this duty been done earlier they would have been like suns. Gibbon says on this subject:

'The sacrament of baptism was supposed to contain a full and absolute expiation of sin; and the soul was instantly restored to its original purity and entitled to the promise of eternal salvation. Among the proselytes to Christianity there were many who judged it imprudent to precipitate a salutary rite which could not be repeated; to throw away an inestimable privilege which could never be recovered. By the delay of their baptism they could venture freely to indulge their passions in the enjoyment of the world, while they still retained in their hands the means of a sure and easy absolution.'

He attributes the conduct of Constantine to this presumption in pursuing his ambition 'through the dark and bloody paths of war and policy;' and charges that:

'As he gradually advanced in the knowledge of truth, he proportionably declined in the practice of virtue, and the same year of his reign in which he convened the Council of Nice was polluted with the execution, or rather murder, of his eldest son. . . . The bishops, whom he summoned to his last illness in the palace of Nicomedia, were edified by the fervor with which he requested and received the sacrament of baptism, by the solemn protestation that the remainder of his life should be worthy of a disciple of Christ, and by his humble refusal to wear the imperial purple after he had been clothed in the white garment of a neophyte. The example and reputation of Constantine seemed to countenance the delay of baptism. Further tyrants were encouraged to believe that the innocent blood which they might shed in a long reign would instantly be washed away in the waters of regeneration, and the abuse of religion dangerously undermined the foundations of moral virtue.' ³

This 'abuse' of the Gospel mocked at the need of a holy life, made an ordinance a mere party watch-word at heaven's gate, and crushed out the spirit of Christ in a candidate for baptism. It became a mere talisman around which men could rally, and in the name of which Christians could persecute their brethren with inhumanity; plots, counterplots, broils, murders, ambitions and briberies, all reveled in a baptized barbarism; while gentleness, justice, purity and brotherly love well-nigh disappeared. The century opened with an intolerant bitterness on the part of the orthodox toward all who differed with them, not only in opinion, but in forms of expression. All dissent must seal its lips or bite the dust. At the close of the fourth, 'heresy' became a capital offense, punishable with death in some cases, under Theodosius, A. D. 379–395. His edict enforced uniformity of belief against all who differed with 'Catholics.' Their places of worship were confiscated for the use of 'Catholics,' they could neither bequeath nor inherit property, they were forbidden to dispute on religion, some of their ordained ministers were fined ten pounds weight of gold, others were banished, and the 'elect' of the Manicheans were sentenced to death as enemies of the State. The civil arm enforced the acts of Church discipline, orthodoxy was made the form of all public acts and offices, and when the balance trembled on any religious topic in controversy, the Emperor threw in the sword for settlement. The last toleration of religious differences was enjoyed under Julian the apostate, A. D. 362, if we except the brief eight months of Jovian in 363; but in 415 Honorius issued an edict forbidding the Donatists to assemble, on pain of death. This was the result of a great debate held at Carthage, 411, between 279 Donatist and 280 Catholic bishops. This edict was not executed to the extreme, but it silenced every opposing tongue. Gibbon tells us that 300 of the Donatist bishops and thousands of their ministers were stripped of their property, banished to the islands, or obliged to hide themselves in the wilds of Africa. Many persons of rank in schismatic assemblies paid ruinous fines, and obstinacy was unpardonable. Of course there was much earnest remonstrance and resistance, and the more far-seeing Catholics were seized with alarm, for if the religion of the majority or that of the Emperor changed, their free action was at an end.

Moved by these fears, the Council of Antioch, A. D. 371, forbade appeals to Emperors in matters of purely ecclesiastical authority, without the consent of the bishop. Augustine led in the debate against the Donatists at Carthage, and afterward advocated forcible means for reclaiming them, under cover of Christ's words, 'Compel them to come in.' But in earlier life, when he was a Manichean himself, he thought it wrong to punish heretics. Petilian, his Donatist opponent, urged strongly that there should be no compulsion, or interference of the civil power in matters of religion. Violence however triumphed as usual, and Theodosius II. commanded all books which did not conform to the Council of Nicæa to be destroyed, and those who concealed them to be put to death. Still, persecution not only followed all dissenting Christians, but the pagans were slain for their paganism. True, the Emperors were yet as much the head of the pagan faith as of the Christian; but they issued decree after decree prohibiting sacrifices to the gods under extreme penalties. The despotism of Theodosius treated his heathen subjects and Christian opponents alike. On the ground of a moral regeneration Christ demanded love for all men; but when this heathenish system of baptismal regeneration supplanted the need of purity of heart, Christians inflicted the same tragedy of horrors upon the defenseless pagans whom they were sent to convert, that the unconverted heathen had inflicted on them. Thus a heathenized baptism belied the gentleness of Jesus in the most atrocious way; and its ravenous thirst for blood pawned his royal crown to deck the brow of hate. When the persecuting demon took possession, Christ's rebuke, 'Ye know not what spirit ye are of,' was forgotten.

At this time the assumptions of the Emperors and the ambitions of the clergy had sunk the rights of the people in the dust, both in State and Church. The congregations had no longer the right to select their own pastors, much less to govern their internal affairs. By canons xii, xiii, of the Council of Laodicea, A. D. 360, the appointment of bishops in villages and other country places was forbidden, and the 'multitude' deprived of all voice in the election of the clergy, all power being now centered in the metropolitan bishop. Jerome was compelled to draw the contrast with former times. He says, in his 'Commentary on Titus.' i, 1: 'Among the ancients, presbyters and bishops were the very same; but by little and little, in order that the plants of dissension might be plucked up, the whole management was intrusted to one individual. As the presbyters, therefore, know that they are subjected to him who was their president by the custom of their Church; so the bishops know that they are greater than their presbyters, more by custom than by the principle of any appointment of Christ.' Cardinal Manning gives us the fully developed doctrine which has grown out of that 'custom,' in the claim of present infallibility for the clergy. He says:

'The pastoral authority, or the episcopate, together with the priesthood and the other orders, constitute an organized body divinely ordained to guard the deposit of the faith. The voice of that body, not so many individuals, but as a body, is the voice of the Holy Ghost. The pastoral ministry as a body cannot err, because the Holy Spirit, who is indissolubly united to the mystical body, is eminently and above all united to the hierarchy and body of its pastors. The episcopate united to its center is, in all ages, divinely sustained and divinely assisted to perpetuate and to enunciate the original revelation.'⁴

These high prerogatives on the part of the bishops made them worse and worse, till they took leave, not only of simple manners and pure doctrine, but of good sense. They gave themselves up to dissipation and voluptuousness, vied with princes in splendor and affected the rank of courts. Martin, of Tours, claimed superior dignity to the Emperor, the Bishop of Rome supremacy over all Church dignitaries, and the Bishop of Constantinople cursed him for claiming his right. Then the Bishop of Jerusalem entered the field, claiming that as his Church was founded first and by the Apostles themselves, he was the most venerable and his authority unquestionable. But the Emperor Valentinian III., A. D. 445, made Leo I. of Rome the rightful ruler of the whole Western Church. The Emperors, however, impiously claimed high honor. They were addressed as the 'Supreme Master,' 'Everlasting King,' your 'Eternity' and your 'Godship.' Many of the bishops were grossly ignorant, for several of those who attended the Councils of Ephesus and Chalcedon, in this century, were unable to write, and attested the decrees in this form : 'I, such a one, have subscribed by the hand of ——; or such a bishop having said that he could not write, I, whose name is underwritten have subscribed for him.' This ignorance excited ambition for the speedy enlargement of the Church by infamous means. Gibbon says: 'The salvation of the common people was purchased at an easy rate, if it be true that in one year twelve thousand men were baptized at Rome, besides a proportionable number of women and children; and that a white garment, with twenty pieces of gold, had been promised by the Emperor to every convert.'⁵ He cites many grave authorities for the truth of this statement. But that process was both too slow and expensive, and Augustine set the fires of purgatory in full blaze, to awaken the people from their apathy. Clement, of Alexandria, first broached the doctrine of purgatory, in the third century. Cyprian had great trouble about those who had become martyrs before baptism, but concluded that as they were immersed in overwhelming sufferings they might be saved. But Augustine thought that the dead must be saved either by water in this world, or fire in the next. The case of the thief on the cross perplexed him sorely. He could not have gone to purgatory, for Jesus said that he would take him to Paradise; and as he suffered for his crimes, suffering could not save him. But as there is no record of his baptism before his crucifixion, Augustine found some relief in the thought, that no one knew that he had not been baptized beforehand! Hare bitterly laments Augustine's 'morbid tendency' to 'twist and warp the simplest facts, to wrench and distort the plainest declarations of Scripture, and to hatch and scrape together the most sophistical arguments and the most fantastical hypotheses, rather than to submit to what makes against some favorite notion or fancy. Yet, Augustine knew the truth here; he had known it thirty years before, when he wrote his earlier work.'⁶ Still as these twistings found for him a way to save men who sinned after baptism, by taking them through purgatory proper; so babes could now be baptized, and yet be saved if they fell into after sin.

This discovery made Augustine bold to take an advanced step for infant baptism. He held (Serm. 294) that unbaptized infants were consigned to eternal fire, though their damnation would be 'the lightest of all;' and began to terrify the world with this horrible dogma. The word '*limbus*,' or 'fringe,' was used by him to indicate the outskirts of hell; but he held that dead babes unbaptized were punished by exclusion from heaven, and by positive pain in this new found *limbus infantium* of his. In that case, infant baptism met a prime necessity for the babes if they did not die, and purgatory another at the close of life, if they sinned after baptism. At this point another motive came in. Orthodox baptism administered to babes would rescue them from Arianism and fill the ranks of the Church by natural birth, and so the sentimental superstition was established. The most eloquent preachers of this day vainly exhorted adults to seek baptism so long as they thought that severe penance could atone for sin after baptism; but a future purgation by fire gave a new phase to the question and rendered the baptism of babes absolutely necessary. Out of this new departure of infant salvation by baptism some fresh and perplexing questions arose. For example: the Council of Neo-Cæsarea, 314-325, answered the curious question, Whether a mother being immersed shortly before the birth of her babe, secured thereby the baptism of her unborn little one? They gravely decided that in this case the mother 'communicates nothing to the child, because in the profession, every one's own resolution is declared.' In treating of this decision, Grotius cites two great commentators upon the canon: Balsamon, who thinks that the child could not be baptized because it was neither 'enlightened,' nor had 'any choice of the divine baptism;' and Zonaras, who decides that the babe had 'no need of baptism' until it was born. Grotius himself concludes that the Council could not think the infant baptized with its mother, as 'A child was not wont to be baptized, but upon its own will and profession.'

In the fourth century, the baptism of a babe outside of Africa was much more common than before; but in order to silence all opposition, the Council of Carthage, A. D. 397, decreed (can. ii) 'an anathema against such as deny that children ought to be baptized as soon as they are born.'[7] Then, according to Bishop Taylor, the Council of Milevium, 416, decreed: 'Whoever denies that new-born infants are to be baptized, to the taking away of original sin—let him be anathema.'[8] The first injunction of infant baptism by Church authority was at Carthage, in 397; the second at Milevium, 416; and this last African decree, being confirmed by Innocent I., was the first indorsement of the innovation by authority at Rome. But the great fight which Augustine made on the subject, marks it as an African movement from the first, and shows that it provoked resistance at every step, until his brave contest enforced it on the fifth century. Winer, the learned German, sums up the whole case thus in his Lectures: 'Originally, only adults were baptized; but at the end of the second century in Africa, and in the third, generally, infant baptism was introduced; and in the fourth century it was theologically maintained by Augustine.' This great critic thus explains the fact that Augustine, A. D. 353–430, was the first theologian who maintained a place for it in Christian theology, and attempted to indicate its theological bearings on the whole Christian system. He presided at the Council of Milevium, and was bound to defend the ground which its ninety-two members had taken. Having collected his brethren and pronounced a curse upon those who denied that immersed babes were washed from moral pollution thereby, he was forced to defend the error. And so this great mind went from one error into another, until he became the champion of ecclesiasticism, sacerdotalism and sacramentarianism, all distorted into monstrous proportions.

Augustine was beset, on the other hand, by Pelagianism, which denied original sin; and hence, to him, the need of baptizing babes. Pelagius contended that they were as pure as the light, and the wide prevalence of this faith terribly aroused Augustine. The companion of Pelagius, Cælestus, an Irish layman, assigned newborn babes to Adam's moral condition before his fall; and the two went together first to Rome and then to Africa. At Carthage, Aurelius the bishop summoned the Irish brother before a synod as a heretic, on the charge that he denied original sin, in that babes had need of remission; and so their baptism was unnecessary because it implied their sanctification in Christ. He was condemned, went under censure to Sicily, A. D. 412, and was condemned again by Zosimus the Roman bishop. He then repaired to Constantinople, 420, but returning to Rome was finally expelled. Augustine thought infant baptism a great bulwark against Pelagianism and an evidence of depravity.

We find another remarkable fact. Down to this time there was no provision for the baptism of babes in the liturgies, but now it began to appear. From an early period questions had been put to those who voluntarily assumed baptism. Ambrose, A. D. 340–397, put these: '"Dost thou believe in God, the Father Almighty?" Thou hast said, "I believe." And you have been immersed. Secondly, you were asked, "Dost thou believe in Jesus Christ our Lord?" and you said, "I believe," and you were immersed. Thirdly, thou wast asked, "Dost thou believe in the Holy Ghost?" and thou said, "I believe." Then you were immersed the third time.' Right here Augustine met another grave difficulty. This formula must now be forced into use for babes in some way, as he wished the immersed babe to stand in Christianity exactly where the adult stood. Because the child could not answer for himself, the sponsor must answer for him. Or, as Dr. Jacob better expresses it, 'As the adult by his own mouth professed the faith which he had, the infant was, by the mouth of another, to express the faith which he had not.' This the doctor calls 'an ecclesiastical fiction, to exhibit an identity which did not exist.' Sponsors had existed for some time for every young person who made a voluntary confession of faith. But Augustine is the first to assume that the sponsors of babes took upon themselves the child's Christian responsibilities, by answering the baptismal questions in place of the babe; and so that in case of the babe's death before reaching responsibility, God would receive their answers as the confession of the child. Therefore, in Augustine's day, the questions were first put to the sponsors: 'Does this child believe in God? Does he turn to God?' etc. They replied, 'He does!' But Boniface I. asked Augustine directly: 'How can it be said with truth that an infant believes and repents and so forth, when it has no thought or sense about such things?' Augustine replied: 'The infant is said to believe because he receives the sacrament of faith and conversion. As the sacrament of the body of Christ is in a certain manner called his body, so the sacrament of faith is called faith; and he who has this sacrament, therefore, has faith; and consequently an infant coming to be baptized may be said to have faith or to believe, because these questions and answers are a part of the celebration of the sacrament of the celebration of faith.'[9] This answer, if it was intended to mean any thing, must mean that the infant believes because he is baptized, and therefore he was baptized.

This constructive faith of proxy made sad havoc of justification by faith; and yet it exhibits Augustine's conception that without faith baptism is invalid, and for that reason that the baptism of babes was a troublesome thing to manage. Faith of some sort must be had; and as the child had none of any order, somebody must believe for the two, although the babe had no hand in the arrangement. Innocent had approved infant baptism at Rome, but it grew very slowly there, for Boniface and others would keep on asking these inconvenient questions about the practice; so that it was not till A. D. 604 that Gregory, the Roman bishop, formed a liturgy for its celebration. It says:

'The font being blessed, and he holding the infant by whom it is to be taken up, let the priest inquire thus: "What is thy name?" (*Answer.*) "Dost thou believe in God, the Father Almighty, creator of heaven and earth?" (*Answer*) "I believe." "And in Jesus Christ, his only Son our Lord, who was born and suffered?" (*Answer*) "I believe." "Dost thou also believe in the Holy Spirit, the holy Catholic Church, the remission of sins, the resurrection of the body?" (*Answer*) "I believe." Then let the priest baptize with a trine immersion, once only invoking the holy Trinity, saying: "I baptize thee in the name of the Father (*and let him immerse once*), and of the Son (*and let him immerse a second time*), and of the Holy Spirit" (*and let him immerse a third time*).'

But the law of the State soon made it compulsory on parents to bring their children to baptism; resist it as they might, the legal demand left them no choice in the matter. Dr. Schaff says that compulsory infant baptism was 'unknown in the ante-Nicene age,' and pronounces it 'a profanation of the sacred event, and one of the evils of the union of Church and State, against which Baptists have a right to protest.'[10]

A notable fact to be observed here is that, after all this stir, Augustine himself was not immersed until he came to manhood. We have noticed elsewhere that

CHRISTIAN MOTHERS OPPOSE INFANT BAPTISM. 219

Monica, his mother, was one of the holiest women in Christian history. She trained his mind, having entered him as a catechumen when he was an infant, but carefully abstained from presenting him for baptism until he chose himself to be a disciple of the Lord. When young he fell dangerously ill, and earnestly desired baptism, but it was 'deferred, lest he should incur the deeper guilt of after sin.'[11] His early life had been very wicked, as his 'Confessions' show. Then, after all his maternal training, before his baptism he spent six months near Milan in receiving Christian instruction; and, strangely enough, was baptized with his own son, who was born of a concubine, and who had now reached the age of fourteen years. Ambrose did not immerse Augustine until he had reached the age of two and thirty years. And he was not alone amongst the fathers in this respect. Ephrem, of Edessa, the greatest hymnist of his age, is supposed to have been born of parents who were martyred for Christ; he was educated by Bishop Jacob at Nisibis, but was not baptized until eighteen years of age. Bishop Liberius did not immerse Jerome till about his twentieth year, although his father was a Christian. The father of Gregory Nazianzen was a bishop, and Norma, his mother, was a saintly woman. She devoted her child to God by prayer, as all true Baptist mothers do; but he was not baptized until he gave his own heart to Christ, when he was thirty years old. His own brother, Cæsarius, physician to the Emperor at Constantinople and a devout Christian, was not baptized till near his death. The ancestors of Basil, of Cappadocia, had been followers of Christ for generations, and Emmelia, his mother, was eminent for godliness; yet he was not baptized till after his conversion when he had reached his twenty-seventh year. Chrysostom had Christian parents, too; and Anthusa, his mother, was so noted for her talents and consecration to Christ, that Libanius, the pagan scholar, said of her: 'Ah! what women there are amongst the Christians!' Still her eloquent son did not receive baptism until he had become a distinguished teacher of rhetoric. Then he studied for three years under Bishop Meletius, at Antioch, and was baptized upon his confession of Christ at the age of thirty.

If our blessed Lord instituted the baptism of infants when he prayed for them and blessed them, it is passing strange that with one consent the holy parents of these great men willfully neglected the baptism of their children, in open disregard of his love and law. The godly parents of these great lights in Christianity deliberately deprived their sons of their rights in the kingdom of God, if Christ required them to bring their offspring to baptism as babes. No women outside of New Testament times rank side by side in sanctity with three of these mothers; and how much better is it than a base slander on them to say that they were remiss in the first duty of Christian motherhood if Jesus required not the baptism of their babes at their hands? No writer of their day has left a rebuke of their sad negligence. Yet thousands of otherwise well-informed Christians in our day almost shudder in holy horror because Baptist fathers and mothers will persist in giving their offspring to

Christ by prayer, by godly example and by Bible instruction, but will not rob them of the right to put on Christ by their own personal obedience—the holy right of making their own good confession of their Redeemer before many witnesses. That is to say, they affect to be scandalized because Baptist fathers and mothers treat their children now exactly as the parents of Ephrem, Jerome, Gregory, Cæsarius, Basil, Chrysostom and Augustine treated their sons. The simple fact is, that the illustrious godliness of these parents knew nothing about the immersion of babes as a Bible duty, and could not trifle with an ordinance of their God and King by so perverting Gospel baptism as to force it on their children. And if these most Christ-like of all Christ's disciples abstained from the baptism of babes on principle, until the Church began to teach the superstition that infants who die unbaptized are damned, what likelihood is there that the unnamed and now unknown thousands of less godly people practiced this pretended apostolic rite, which Augustine so thoroughly clouded by its admixture with the doctrine of salvation through the faith of proxy?

The act of baptism remained the same as it had been, the immersion of the body three times in water, and this amongst the orthodox and heterodox alike; excepting the sect known as Eunomians, of whom Theodoret and Epiphanius had complained in the previous century, because they immersed only the upper part of the body with the head downward. 'These,' says Cathcart, 'were the only men among all the heretics of the ancient Church, that rejected this way of baptizing, by a total immersion in ordinary cases.'[12] This Arian sect used but an immersion of the upper part of the body, as far as the breast. But Cyril, of Jerusalem, says of the orthodox: 'Ye were led by the hand to the sacred font of the divine baptism, as Christ from the cross to the prepared tomb. And each was asked, if he believes in the name of the Father, and of the Son, and of the Holy Spirit. And ye professed the sacred profession, and sank down thrice into the water and came up again.' Basil asks: 'Where the tradition is taken from to immerse a man three times, and answers, that it is not a private or secret one, but of the Apostles. Jerome said: 'We are thrice dipped in the water, that the mystery of the Trinity may appear but one.' Augustine states that this way of baptizing opened a twofold mystery. Trine immersion was not only a symbol of the Trinity, but a 'type' of our Lord's resurrection on the third day. He says, also: 'Three times did we submerge your heads in the sacred fountain.' And Chrysostom tells us that 'three immersions give but one baptism.' Dupin, writes: 'They plunged those three times whom they baptized.' Maitland adds: 'The immersion was required to be threefold, or trine;' and so Bingham, with many others.

Yet, this well-attested historical practice of *three* immersions has no support in the Scriptures, but, as Dr. Conant says: 'Is clearly contrary to the words of the command. Had trine immersion been intended, the words would have been in the names of the Father, etc., or in the name of the Father, in the name of the Son, and so forth.' Jerome classes it with 'many other things which are by tradition observed in the Church, and which have no authority of Scripture for them, but the consent of the whole world,' which, he thought, gave the force of a precept, 'as in the font of baptism to plunge the head thrice under water.'

Further, this innovation now linked to it the repulsive custom of immersing the candidates in a state of entire nudity. Dr. Wall expresses his belief that they thought this better represented the putting off of the old man, also the nakedness of Christ on the cross; but in addition to this, they came to regard baptism as a purifying of the body from all moral taint, so that if the water did not pass over every part of the body, leprous spots might be left. But whatever the motive for this misguided zeal, as Cave says: 'They were brought to the font and were first stripped of their garments, intimating their putting off the old man which is corrupt, with his deceitful lusts.'[13] Dean Stanley gives this exact account of the observance:

'There was but one hour for the ceremony; it was midnight. The torches flared through the dark hall as the troops of converts flocked in. The baptistery consisted of an inner and an outer chamber. In the outer chamber stood the candidates for baptism, stripped to their shirts; and turning to the west, as the region of sunset, they stretched forth their hands through the dimly-lit chamber, as in a defiant attitude toward the Evil Spirit of Darkness, and speaking to him by name, said, "I renounce thee, Satan, and all thy works, and all thy pomp, and all thy service." Then they turned, like a regiment, facing right around to the east, and repeated in a form more or less long, the belief in the Father, the Son and the Spirit, which has grown up into the so-called Apostles' Creed of the West, and the so-called Nicene Creed of the East. They then advanced into the inner chamber. Before them yawned the deep pool, or reservoir, and standing by, the deacon or deaconess, as the case might be, to arrange that all should be done with decency. The whole troop undressed completely, as if for a bath, and stood up naked before the bishop, who put to each the questions, to which the answer was returned in a loud and distinct voice, as of those who knew what they had undertaken. They then plunged into the water. Both before and after the immersion, their bare limbs were rubbed with oil from head to foot; then were they clothed in white gowns, and received, as token of the kindly feeling of their new brotherhood, the kiss of peace and a taste of honey and milk; and they expressed their new faith by using for the first time the Lord's Prayer.'[14]

This picture of pious savagery drawn by the delicate hand of her Majesty's late chaplain at Westminster, will greatly edify those who recoil from the shocking indecency of modern Baptists, who modestly immerse believers in full apparel, because the portrait is that of those canonized saints whom the foes of the Baptists so much admire. Then, it smacks so zestfully of the delectable doings of the Men of Munster, the apt and docile scholars of these fathers, as to deprive decent Baptists of sainthood entirely. But for the re-assurance of all parties, good Brenner, the great Catholic, says: 'If all this at present seems improper, the noble simplicity and innocence of the early Christians took no offense at it. They had but one thought about the matter, which was the importance and sacredness of the "mysteries." They looked at every thing of the natural order in the same sacred light.'[15] And even

St. Otho, Bishop of Bamberg, tells us most solemnly that 'Nothing indecent, nothing shameful; in short, nothing at all that could be disliked by any one,' took place, and that 'no honest persons abstracted themselves from baptism in consequence of shame.' Indeed, why should they, when this was the highest fashion of the times? for Simeon Metaphrastes states that the Emperor Constantine was entirely nude when immersed; and so was Jobia, daughter of Sapor, the King of Persia. Besides, Augustine enforces the practice with this religious consideration: 'Naked we were born, naked we go to the washing, and naked we go to the gate of heaven;' while Cyril addresses the newly immersed thus: 'As soon as you approached, you took off your clothing and so were naked. O, admirable thing! Naked you have been in the sight of all and you did not shame yourself.'

Clovis, the King of the Franks, was immersed after this fashion, December 25, A. D. 496, by Remigius, the Bishop of Rheims, in the cathedral baptistery of that city. His case is a most interesting one and calls for narration. The Confederacy of the Alemanni on the Middle Rhine was a rival of the Frank Confederacy on the Lower Rhine, and Clovis was chosen as the commander-in-chief to repel the invasion of their territory. He was a bold, brave and desperate warrior. He met the foe in fierce encounter at Zülpich, about twenty miles south-west of Cologne, and the battle threatened to go against him. He, therefore, called upon his gods for help, but in vain. His wife, Clotilda, a Burgundian princess who was a Christian, had made every effort to convert him; but while he permitted his two sons to be baptized, he doubted the power of Christ unless he interposed specially in his behalf. Yet, he joined her in prayer to Christ, and vowed to become a Christian if he won a victory. Gregory, of Tours, gives the following as his prayer:

'The army of Clovis began to rush to sure destruction; but he seeing this, pained at the heart, moved to tears and with eyes lifted up to the heavens, said: "O, Jesus Christ, whom Clotilda declares to be the Son of the living God, thou who art said to give help to the struggling and victory to those hoping in thee; devoted to thee, I entreat the glory of thy assistance; and if thou wilt indulge me with victory over these enemies, and I shall have full experience of that valor which the people dedicated to thy name proclaim that they have put to the proof, I shall believe upon thee, and I shall be baptized in thy name. For I have called upon my gods, and they have been far from helping me; from which consideration I believe that the gods who do not come to those obeying them are invested with no power. Now, I call upon thee, and I desire to believe upon thee, only let me not be overthrown by my adversaries." And when he said these things, the Alemanni began to seek flight; and when they perceived that their king was killed, they put themselves under the authority of Clovis, saying, "We entreat that no more people may be killed; we are thine."'

Gregory adds that the queen then sent for the bishop to show him the way of salvation, and the king raised the difficulty that his people would not permit him to forsake his gods. On consulting them, however, they shouted, 'We are prepared to follow the immortal God.' Then, Remigius ordered the baptistery prepared, and the whole city flocked to the cathedral, or more properly to the 'temple of baptism' adjoining. The king walked through the streets under painted canvas, adorned with white curtains, and the baptismal building was lighted by wax tapers, and filled with what he claims to have been a celestial perfume, an odor of Paradise. As the monarch entered this splendor, and the sweetest music floated to his ear, he asked the bishop if this was the kingdom of heaven of which he had heard, and was answered, 'No! but it is the beginning of the way thither.' The baptistery in which Clovis was immersed was a large tank, or pool, which tradition has removed to Paris, where it is now found in the Bibliothèque Nationale. It is seven feet long, two and a half feet deep, about the same in width, and is of polished porphyry. Alcuin gives substantially the same account, representing the eagerness of the king to be 'Washed in the living fountain of Catholic baptism, for the remission of sins and for the hope of eternal life. He led the eager king to the fountain of life, and when he came he washed him in the fountain of eternal salvation. So, the king was baptized with his nobles and people, who rejoiced to receive the sacrament of the healing bath, divine grace having been previously given them.' Before the bishop immersed him he said: 'Meekly bow thy neck, Sicambrian; worship that which thou hast burnt, burn that which thou hast worshiped.' Three thousand of his warriors and large numbers of his subjects were baptized with him, amongst them his two sisters. Hincmar says that the throng which pressed to baptism was so great, that the priest could not press through with the consecrated oil, 'hence, in a wonderful manner another oil appeared.' Avitus, Bishop of Vienne, wrote him a letter, saluting him 'as one born out of the water;' immersed in what Gregory calls 'a fresh fountain.' Thus, the founder of the French nation made confession of the orthodox faith, and was thrice immersed. At that time he was the only orthodox monarch in Europe, the others being Arians, for which reason he was called the 'Eldest Son of the Church.' His subsequent moral inconsistencies show more martial enthusiasm in his conversion than sacrificial cross-bearing; an epitome of his whole life being condensed into his exclamation when he first heard of Christ's crucifixion: 'Had I been there with my brave Franks, I would have avenged his wrongs.'

This century is marked by many translations of the Scriptures. Theodoret, a Syrian bishop, says: 'The Hebrew Scriptures are not only translated into the language of the Grecians, but also of the Romans, the Indians, Persians, Armenians, Scythians, Sarmatians, Egyptians; and, in a word, into all the languages that are used by any nation.' Mesrobe, a devout Christian Minister of State to the King of Armenia, translated them into the Armenian at this time. He formed an alphabet of thirty-six letters in order to do his work; and made his version first from the Syriac, and then from a Greek manuscript which was sent to him from the Council of Ephesus, A. D. 431. On account of its exact and elegant simplicity, it is called the 'Queen of Versions.' He uses the word '*mogredil*' to express baptism, a word which signifies immerse.

This age created those wonderful, illuminated biblical manuscripts, written, in many cases, on red, violet or dark purple parchment, often in letters of gold or silver, with illustrated borders and capitals. Many of them were brilliant beyond description, bound in ivory and studded with gems. The Emperor Theodosius devoted himself to the study of the Bible, and with his own hand produced a copy of the Gospels in letters of gold, formed by a chemical solution of that metal. It was also in this century that Patrick instructed the Irish in the use of the Roman letters.

Clement, of Alexandria, had warned Christians against the authority of antiquity and tradition, and saw no cure, therefore, but the 'written word.' He said that he alone was right: 'Who pursuing this course from year to year, in converse with and conformity to the Scriptures, keeps to the rule of the Apostolic and ecclesiastical purity, according to the Gospel and those established truths which, as given by the Lord, by the law and the prophets, whoever seeks shall find.' Instead of following this counsel, however, tradition came in like a flood. Even Chrysostom taught: 'It is clear that they (the Apostles) did not deliver all things by their epistles, but communicated many things without writing; and these, too, demand our assent of faith; it is tradition, make no further inquiry.'[16] Epiphanius, of Salamis, declares as roundly: 'Tradition is necessary; all things cannot be learned from the Scriptures. The Apostles left some things in writing, others by tradition.'[17] On this ground, every absurd practice was justified. Basil puts such questions as these: 'We sign with the sign of the cross. Who has taught this in Scripture? We consecrate the water of baptism and the oil of unction, as well as him who receives baptism. From what Scripture? Is it not from private and secret tradition? Moreover, the anointing with oil, what passage of Scripture teaches this? Now a man is thrice immersed. From whence is it derived or delivered? Also the rest of what is done in baptism: as to renounce Satan and his angels. From what Scripture have we it? Is not this from private and secret tradition?'[18]

Chrysostom talks similar inane nonsense of the Supper. He tells us of 'The dreadful and mystic Table.' 'The Lamb for thee is slaughtered, the priest for thee contends, the spiritual fire from the sacred table ascends, the cherubim holding their stations round about, while the seraphim hovering around, and the six-winged veiling their faces, while for thee the incorporeal orders along with the priest intercede.' . . . 'Not as bread shouldst thou look at that, neither esteem that as wine, for not like other aliment do these descend into the draught.' . . . 'Think not that ye receive the divine body, as from the hand of man; but rather as was the fire from the tongs of the very seraphim given to Isaiah.'[19]

Think of cherubim veiling their faces, lest they catch a glimpse of bread and wine! No wonder that Tully, when ridiculing the heathen notion of the times, asks, 'Was any man ever so mad as to take that which he feeds upon, for a god?'[20] We can suppose that the angels shudder when men say that they eat the body, soul and divinity of Jesus Christ, and when they say that bread and wine, if dropped into the mouth of the dying and the dead works a miracle, as the Christians did at this time. Gregory Nazianzen, declares that when his sister Gorgonia was suffering from a severe malady she flew to the 'altar,' and holding it fast obtained an instant cure, by rubbing her body with a few crumbs and drops of the elements. Evagrius reports that it was the custom at Constantinople, for the school-boys to eat what remained of the consecrated bread after the Supper. The son of a Jewish glass-blower, in wrath threw another boy into a glowing furnace, but a woman in a purple robe was with him in the flames, pouring water on the coals, and his mother pulled him out unhurt. The fourth canon of the Church of Hippo decreed that: 'The eucharist should not be put into the mouth of the dead. For it was said by our Lord, "Take ye and eat." But corpses cannot receive or eat.' Ferrandus, a deacon of Carthage, was sorely tried because a black slave was taken with a violent fever and baptized before death, while unconscious. The deacon wrote to Fulgentius, Bishop of Ruspe, to know whether he was saved without the Supper. He thought that possibly he might be. In this he differed from Gelasius I., Bishop of Rome, who said: 'Jesus Christ, with his heavenly voice, pronounces, "Except ye eat my flesh and drink my blood, ye have no life in you." We see no exception made, nor has any one dared to say, that an infant without this sacrament of salvation can be brought into eternal life. But without this life he will no doubt be in everlasting death.' In a word, the Supper had long been the subject of sad abuses. The third Council of Carthage, A. D. 397, was obliged to check these, and forbid the custom of giving the bread and wine to the dead, or of burying them with the dead, as was often practiced. By the close of the sixth century, there was no end to the ridiculous virtues claimed for these elements, many fanatics declaring that they had raised the dead.[21] John Moschus, of Jerusalem, has the effrontery to tell this 'lying wonder' of a certain pillar-saint, namely: 'That he threw these elements into a boiling hot caldron, when lo! immediately it was cold, while the bread and wine remained dry and safe!'

CHAPTER VI.

THE SIXTH, SEVENTH, EIGHTH AND NINTH CENTURIES.

THE period stretching from the fifth to the fifteenth century is often spoken of as the Middle Ages, and the first half of that time as the Dark Ages; because of feudal and papal violence, the universal reign of injustice and the torpor of the intellect. Innocent and Leo had long struggled to bring Christendom under the supremacy of the Roman See. This, Gregory the Great succeeded in doing. At

ANCIENT CHURCH EDIFICE IN CORNWALL.

the close of the seventh age, Alexandria and Antioch were captured by the Saracens, with great suffering to the Churches, while the Eastern Empire was fast declining and the Roman pontiffs were left without rivals.

As yet, we have said nothing of the introduction of the Gospel into the British Isles, and as the sixth century marks their Christian history very strongly, it will be proper to advert to the subject here. These islands were scarcely known to Rome, when her heavy hand was laid upon them under Julius Cæsar. The classic nations and all the seats of ancient government lay to the far East; but these were at the extreme of the wild and barbarous West. When Plautius landed his four legions on the coast of Kent and took firm possession of them, Claudius, his master, followed, as if to enlarge the empire, but really to promote the spread of the Gospel, which was to redeem those dark lands from cruel superstition. By A. D. 180, Christianity appears to have reached every province of this colossal realm, from the Danube to Ethiopia and the Libyan Desert, and from the Tigris to Britain. It is not certain when the Gospel reached Britain however; although Bishops Bull, Burgess and Newton contend that it was introduced by one of the Apostles. Gildas thinks that it was before the defeat of the British forces under Boadicea, in 61; Bull and Newton, that a Church existed there before one was formed in Rome. Pagitt unites in this opinion, calling the Church at Rome not only a sister of the British, but 'a younger sister, too.' Matthew Paris fixes the date at about 167; Mosheim, in the reign of Marcus Aurelius, 161–180, being disposed to think that its missionaries took refuge there from France when persecution raged at Lyons and Vienna, 177; and Neander, at the close of the second century, and not from Rome but from the East.

Several of these writers place too much dependence on the statements of Clement Romanus, Irenæus and Eusebius, who speak with a flourish of the Gospel going to 'the end of the West' at that early date. Gibbon contributes to this idea by saying, that the highways 'opened an easy passage to the missionaries as well as the legions from Italy to the extremity of Spain and Britain.' But Tertullian boasts of Christ's reign in his day: 'Among people whom the Roman arms have never yet subdued. . . . In the farthest extremities in Spain and Gaul and Britain;' and he names one or more of the British converts. Several writers of the second century make the same statement to persons high in the State; which, if they were exaggerated, would have defeated their purpose, by provoking official contradiction. But whatever the date of its introduction

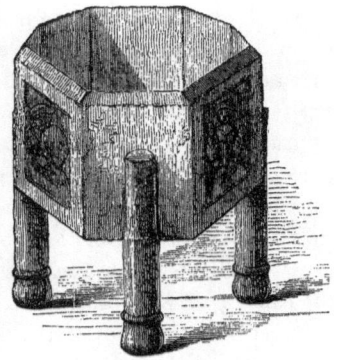

ANCIENT STONE FONT IN CORNWALL.

may have been, we have many evidences that it has never been entirely rooted out since, although the Anglo-Saxons by the middle of the fifth century invaded Britain, destroyed the Christian places of assembly, slew their pastors, burned the Scriptures, and drove the few ancient British Christians who were left into Cornwall, Wales and Cumberland, where in part they still retained a footing. About fifty years ago Mr. Mitchell, the antiquarian, disentombed a church building at St. Pieran, on the sand near Truro, Cornwall, which is supposed to have been built before Austin visited Britain, and to have disappeared in the twelfth century, when several parishes on the north-west coast were buried in the sand. The preceding cuts represent this building and the stone font found there. Of course, idolatry was re-established wherever Christianity was driven out. Two salient points rise out of this early history, namely: Were these British Christians altogether uncorrupted from the simplicity of the Gospel before Pope Gregory sent Austin to Britain, A. D. 596 ? and, Is there any foundation for the oft-repeated assertion that the Welsh people, especially, have never bowed the knee to Rome? It seems impossible to determine the first of these questions, as the general conviction amongst reliable authorities is, that the true Church history of this people and time has never been written, and cannot be with the material now at command. What doctrines they held, what ordinances they practiced, and what was the form of their Church government, are all undetermined questions. But it is at least reasonable to suppose, that owing to their political affinities with Rome during the first four centuries, Christianity took much the same general character in Britain that it did in other western parts of the empire. We know this as a well-established fact, that when the civil and ecclesiastical powers blended at Rome, the corrupt leaven permeated Christianity elsewhere; and in all likelihood this is true of Britain.

Under the theory of uninterrupted Apostolical succession, the Church of England claims to be a continuation of this ancient British Church. This is clearly a modern invention, to serve her clergy as a bridge over which they may trace their line back into the immediate post-Apostolic Church, without dragging the cumbrous chain through all the quagmires of the Church of Rome. The scheme is indeed ingenious, and it is claimed that the Bishops of London and York were both alive, yet in exile, when Austin came to Britain; but the whole plan lacks the evidence of truth, and wears the air of fancy. The swarm of monks which he found at Bangor, Isycoed, Flintshire, N. Wales; also at Bangor on Carrickfergus Bay, Ireland, founded A. D. 530, and in Iona, an island of the Hebrides, shows that these Christians who are said never to have bowed the knee to Rome had fallen into the same errors of faith and practice, in some things at least, with others. When we bring the baptism of King Lucius, St. German and Lupus, with their mission and miracles, together with the lives of the Cambro-British saints, such as David, Beuno, Winefrede and others, into the 'Ancient Christian History of Britain,' we move in the fog of legend and point to Rome as their true source, as surely as the needle points to the pole.

Gregory sent Austin and his forty monks to Britain to restore what the Saxons had destroyed. Of course, he expected to find some remnants of the old Christianity; but his chief design was to convert the idolatrous Angles, Saxons and Jutes, who had wrought the havoc. There were few better or wiser men in his day than Gregory, although as a bigot he was very overbearing. And was he ignorant of the fact, that Columba, the Irish nobleman, known as the 'Apostle of the Highlands,' had established his great monastery in Scotland, and called his followers the 'Servants of God,' *Keldees?* It is of this great school that Dr. Johnson says, it was the 'Luminary of the Caledonian regions, where savage clans and roving barbarians derived the benefits of knowledge and the blessings of religion.' Then, there were many other monks, as at Derry and Durrow, making in all at least from five to seven thousand, and so the conversion of the Saxons was promising. Probably both these considerations excited the zeal of the pope, despite that pleasant story of the Angle youths whom he met in the market-place at Rome. For Bertha, daughter of the King of Paris, had become queen to Ethelbert, King of Kent, one of the seven Anglo-Saxon kings of Britain. She had almost persuaded her husband to embrace Christianity. Thus, Gregory sent Austin, a Roman monk, on this mission of converting the king and, if possible, all Britain, and of placing it under the sway of Rome. He began his work on the island of Thanet, where the king welcomed him, and he then proceeded to Canterbury. The king was baptized A. D. 597, after which he made Austin archbishop of that See, at which place he built his cathedral, 602.

But, in the looseness of the times, Austin had been instructed to adapt the ceremonies of Christianity to the usages of the idolaters, that they might not be shocked by too great a change. And this was done. Bede tells us, that there was often an altar for the sacrifices of paganism and one for Christianity in the same temple; and Procopius his contemporary adds, that some who had embraced Christianity continued to offer human sacrifices. The old British Christians, however, sternly opposed the pretensions of Austin, who assumed great pomp and arrogance; spending more of his time in reducing them to conformity to what he called 'the unity of the Catholic Church,' than in converting the heathen. Up to that time, the Christians of what are now England, Ireland and Scotland had been free from the direct jurisdiction of Rome, and had maintained their ancient rites and customs. Thus, Austin charged them, saying: 'You act in many particulars contrary to our custom, or rather the custom of the universal Church; and yet, if you will comply with me in these three points, namely: to keep Easter at the due time; to administer baptism, by which we are again born to God, according to the custom of the holy Roman Apostolic Church; and jointly with us preach the word of God to the English nation, we will readily tolerate all the other things you do, though contrary to our customs.' This proposition was made at a conference held with the leaders of the British Christians at Chester. But Leland says that they disputed with him with great ability, and refused either to accept him as their archbishop, or the pope as their master, or to change their customs. On the contrary, Dinoth of Bangor said: That they owed love and charity to all Christians, the Bishop of Rome with the rest, 'But other obedience to the pope we know not.' He then censured the pope for usurpation, and asked Austin to restore his unjust and tyrannical power into the hands whence it came. Whereupon Austin threatened them with war and death, for he was filled with indignation.

They refused to observe Easter at the same time with the Romish communion, because they did not believe that the pope celebrated it at the proper time. They refused to preach to the Saxons, because they had driven them from their homes, had persecuted them cruelly, and now sought to make them vassals; and they saw no fitness in exposing themselves anew to their wrath, on the bare request of a stranger who was preaching to them himself. As to the second particular, regarding baptism according to the custom of Rome, it is not easy to determine exactly what he demanded. Some think that he required them to adopt all the ceremonies which the Catholics had added to that ordinance; and others, that he exacted of them the practice of infant baptism. While, perhaps, this point cannot now be fully determined, several things seem to imply that he covered both considerations, and especially the latter. We have no record showing that infant baptism was practiced in Britain at that time, while there are hints that it was; but in view of the great simplicity of these British Christians, it is at least fair to suppose that it was not well and fully established, so that many still doubted its propriety. Geoffry characterized them as 'Sound in the faith, and pure in the worship, order and discipline, of Christ, as it was delivered to them from the Apostles and evangelists.' This statement, however, does not throw so much light on the subject as the following facts, namely:

1. That in 597, according to Bede, Austin 'desired the solution of some doubts that occurred to him,' and sent a letter to Pope Gregory by the hands of Laurentius and Peter the monk, asking for their solution. His eighth question, in part, was this: 'Also, after how many days the infant born may be baptized, lest he be prevented by death?' To which the pope answers: that the child may be baptized, 'The very hour it is born, is no way *prohibited;* because, as the grace of the holy mystery is to be with much discretion provided for the living and understanding, so it is to be without any delay offered to the dying; lest, while a further time is sought to confer the mystery of redemption, a small delay intervening, the person to be redeemed is dead and gone.' This was in harmony with what he had decreed not long before Austin put his question: 'Let all young children be baptized as they ought to be, according to the tradition of the fathers.' 2. But the conference with the British Christians, at which he demanded that they should 'administer baptism according to the custom of Rome,' was not held till A. D. 602, about five years after he had asked Gregory to solve his doubts on this question. 3. If Austin himself, even when he had been ordained 'Archbishop of the English nation,' had doubts on the question as to how many days old a babe should be before he could receive baptism, the pope's answer throws light upon his meaning in the phrase, 'by which we are again born to God,' and more than hints that the Britons neither believed this nor acted accordingly. 5. Disinterested writers, some of them ancient, understand this to have been the subject in dispute. Thierry, in his account of the matter, says of these British Christians, that they refused to believe in the 'damnation of infants dying without baptism,' which is the very point that the pope argues.[1] Fabian represents Austin as demanding, 'That ye give Christendom to children,' that is, that they admit children into Christianity, according to the custom

of the Roman Church. 6. And as if to show the resistance which infant baptism met with, Lingard tells us, that as early as the days of the grandson of Ethelbert of Kent: 'Persuaded of the necessity of baptism by the instructions of his teachers, the legislators of Wessex placed all new-born infants under the protection of the law, and *by the fear of punishment* stimulated the diligence of the parents. The delay of a month subjected them to the penalty of thirty shillings; and if, after that period, the child died without having received the sacred rite, nothing less than the forfeiture of their property could expiate the offense.' ² All this marks the hard struggle which ensued in enforcing infant baptism even upon the converts whom Austin made from the Saxons, and bears strongly upon the second point in his three requisitions.

Austin told the British Christians that if they would yield these three points, he 'would readily tolerate all the *other things*' which they did 'contrary to our customs.' ³ What these were does not appear. But they treated his toleration with contempt, for Geoffrey of Monmouth says that they 'reckoned their faith and religion as nothing, and would no more communicate with the Angles than with dogs.' He then says, that when the King of Kent saw 'That the Britons disdained subjection to Austin, and despised his preaching,' he stirred up Ethelfrid, the King of Northumbria; a great army was raised, they marched against Bangor, A. D. 613, and slew these patriots who stood for religious freedom in their own country. Some writers place the number of the monks and priests who were slain as low as two hundred, while others put them as high as twelve hundred. And one such contest followed another until, before the end of the eighth century, all the Churches of Wales had submitted to the pope's authority. The 'Liber Landavensis' and other trustworthy documents bear abundant proof of their rapid and thorough fall. But that consummation was not reached until the sword, the purse and the pen, of the Saxon, the Dane and the Norman, had all been devoted to the task with untiring energy.

This period is made immortal by that stupendous mental and moral revolution which was effected by Mohammed, a native of Arabia, A. D. 569–632. But a degenerate Christianity had carefully prepared his way, so that every thing was ready for the introduction and spread of his new system. It is difficult to find one body of Christians who, at this time, had not departed in a large measure from the primitive simplicity of Christianity. Metaphysical jargon had taken the place of its doctrines and almost buried its truths. Its holy spirituality had nearly expired in fierce contentions, either about matters of no vital consequence or those which never can be settled. The original beauty of its institutions had been frightfully remodeled, and an intolerable weight of ceremonies had ridiculed its pure and unpretending rites out of existence. With obscure exceptions, Christians had become a by-word and a hissing in Arabia, and in the East generally. They had given themselves up to legends, to the adoration of relics, of images, saints and angels, of Mary-worship, and other ridiculous and extravagant things. These, together with salvation by baptism, the seeking of soul-food by eating the Supper, the forcing of babes into the communion of the Church and their participancy in the Supper, purgatory, ecclesiastical pomp and corruption finished the work; so that Gregory the Great himself likened the Church to a ship, rotten and leaky, hourly looking for wreck. She had become thoroughly indolent, contentious and faithless to her trust, and was ready to be led away with any new doctrine.

Learning was nearly extinct, or was shut up in the cells of monks. Many of those bishops of whose lordliness we hear so much could neither read nor write, and their lives were given to the most odious forms of iniquity. The Church was full of spurious Gospels and other writings; and stood out before the world in bitter strifes and absurd distractions, parading an empty pride which proved to men the need of a new faith and threatened her entire overthrow east of the Bosphorus. The condition of Arabia, social, political, religious, threw powerful influences in favor of a new religion. The Arabians were pre-eminently ignorant, and no one faith prevailed strongly over another, so that no great bond held them together. They were not even united under one civil government, but under several which were at enmity with each other—a condition exactly adapted to combine them under one rapturous book and one bloody sword. Mecca, the birthplace of Mohammed, was also a singular center of religious sects, Jewish, Christian and Pagan; and he saw the weakening effect of their hostilities, especially in the divisions and hatreds of those who professed the same creeds. In the times of Roman persecution the Jews had flocked there for security, and all sorts of Christians had fled for the same protection, where they could cherish and broach their own views without fear. Of course, in this promiscuous interblending, all kinds of errors mixed themselves with truth, until there came a general decay of first principles. The epoch was specially turbulent. New kingdoms were springing up out of the vast wrecks of the Empire and in their seething jealousies Arabia, which was rising into importance, only required a leader to make her formidable. In a word, he would be a great artist, whose pen could draw a picture so black as to exaggerate the fearful state of things in this age of usurpation, fraud and error, which inflicted its due penalty in a dark and endless variety of evils.

Mohammed was highly gifted by nature. He was graceful in person and manners, rising superior to many of his countrymen in his genius, and highly enthusiastic. In very early life his powerful mind grasped the great influence of religion over mankind, an idea which drew him into deep religious contemplation, and rendered him affable to the weak and deferential to the powerful. What his original notions were in framing a new religion, whether enthusiasm or hypocrisy predominated, is a secret left with God. But for years he affected an almost total exclusion from the world, and was ready to burst upon it with his new revelations just after the Emperor Phocas had conferred upon Gregory the Great the title of

Universal Pastor. Phocas had murdered his predecessor, Maurice, in order to take the crown, and he desired to prop up his throne by the support of the Church. Gregory had passed through a long, fiery contest for this supremacy in the Church, and so he sanctioned the usurper and received his reward. But dying at that juncture, Boniface took the title, A. D. 606, while the Arabian prophet really opened his public mission in 609—a remarkable coincidence. The many sects of his own home opened to him a wide field for his joint-political and religious experiment. The first idea which seized his mind was that the doctrine of the Unity of God was in danger of being lost. This one great truth was common to Jews, Christians and Arabs. But pagan polytheists amongst them contradicted this doctrine; and by gratuitous assertion he accused the Jews of holding a plurality of gods by believing in Ezra as the son of God; and accused the Christians of the same in the doctrine of the Trinity. By this artifice he made himself the apostle of the tenet of the Divine Unity, and used it to prove his own legation from God.

In that gloomy cave at Mount Hara, near Mecca, he made this fundamental article of the Old and New Testament the corner-stone of his new system. He was shut up to the alternative of framing an entirely new religion, or of grafting new notions of his own into the credibility of those already existing. In this laboratory, therefore, he tampered with Christianity and Judaism, mixing certain elements of these weighty and ancient faiths with a curious compound of pagan superstitions. The admixture under his weird alchemy came forth an eclectic faith from genuine, spurious and apocryphal writings, the Bible, the pagan traditions and the reveries of the Talmud. What did not suit his purpose he threw aside, and studiously accommodated his teachings to the preconceptions of all sects, yet directly imitating none. For the Jew he recognized the divine authority of Moses; for the Christian the divine mission of Jesus; and for the pagan he tolerated all his imposing ceremonies. He opened his mission with tact and sagacity, showing that he read the popular mind. He appealed directly to the prejudices and prepossessions of his countrymen; declaring himself a delegate from God to supplement what Moses and Christ had left unfinished, by improving their work, supplying their deficiencies, closing forever the book of prophecy and thus clothing the new revelation with an air of progress. His sagacious penetration employed all these in the best way to promote his ambition. His largest elements, therefore, were taken from Moses and Christ, as he depended on them for his vivifying principle to be cast into the dull and inert mass, and to give it plausibility and consistency. This was his passport both to Jewish and Christian confidence, and shows his superior skill to use the most powerful auxiliaries in his politic cause. Then he bent the sword around the motley mass to bind it together. This laid bare his design on the State, while the Koran interpreted his purpose on the Church. This singular piece of composition, the Koran, is thrown together in the most desultory manner, after the general order of Eastern writing. Yet it possesses great copiousness; it is full of natural, vivid imagery, is elegant in cadence, and wealthy in rhythm. Indeed, the Mussulman is proud of what he calls its inimitable sublimity, and avows that for this reason it cannot be translated out of the Arabic into any other tongue.

The Arabians were also proud of their descent from Ishmael, and the antiquity of their temple, which, Mohammed told them, angels had built for Abraham, after the pattern of that built for Adam in Paradise, and that Ishmael and Abraham both worshiped there. Hence, he was sent to save his countrymen from that idolatry which adored the stars which floated over its venerable walls. But he appealed only to their pride, their blind prejudices and quenchless passions. He gave them a political religion on a level with their sensual lives. There was no mystery in it for their reason to grapple with or for their faith to fathom, no discipline to keep their depraved appetites in check, no pride to be mortified and no sacrifices imposed for the blessing of others. Then he threw into it the martial element. There were new laurels to conquer, new fields of slaughter for fierceness and rapine to flood and new provinces to possess. In order to fire their zeal he declared the divine patience exhausted, and that every monument of idolatry must be destroyed by the sword. Thus all things favored his plan, and the Church was to reap the terrible harvest which she had sown. Yet there was not light enough left to penetrate the bosom of his odious system; not piety enough to exhibit a Christian superiority to the imposition. In fact, he urged it upon his countrymen as a better practical religion than any that then existed, and there was little in the spirit or conscience of the so-called Christian Church to contradict him.

PAULICIAN history has come to us mainly through the persecutors of the Paulicians, and it scarcely has its parallel for calumny in the annals of the centuries. They have always been coupled with the Manichæans, and nothing has been too base to say of them. Bossuet and Bowers have distinguished themselves in this calumny, but Bowers has been effectually answered by the learned Lardner. With his characteristic narrowness of all whom he dislikes, Bossuet says of them: 'This so hidden a sect, so abominable, so full of seduction, of superstition and hypocrisy, notwithstanding imperial laws which condemned its followers to death, yet maintained and diffused itself.'[4] This is his usual style of treating the sober facts of history, hence so collected a pen as Buckle's charges him with an 'audacious attempt to degrade history,' as 'a painful exhibition of a great genius cramped,' who could 'willingly submit to a prostration of judgment, and could display a blind credulity, of which in our day even the feeblest minds would be ashamed.' Fénelon was a lovely spirit and almost adored Bossuet, meeting in return little but taunt and scorn. In his noble book defending Madame Guyon, he had ventured to differ in opinion with him on a single point, whereupon Bossuet arrogantly sent a charge of heresy to Rome in 1697 against his gentle fellow-bishop. True, Louis XIV. had trusted him with great responsibilities, but the good man was compelled to sign a recantation on pain of death—an act which Bishop Burnet treats with contempt.[5] Mosheim esteems him as lightly as Buckle as a historian, saying: 'This writer certainly did not go to the sources, and being influenced by party zeal, he was willing to make mistakes.'[6] Neither Jortin nor Fleury trust him where points of orthodoxy or Church authority are concerned.

The older writers cherished a singular inveteracy against the Manichæans as if they were fiends incarnate. Eusebius denounces Manes as a 'barbarian,' a 'madman,' 'diabolical and furious,' and otherwise speaks so unguardedly that the discreet Lardner says of the great historian in this case, he 'appears out of humor and scarce master of himself.' Without doubt, the system of Manes was abstruse, intricate and subtile, therefore it must be examined with the more care. It was a piece of mystic theology and cold-blooded reasoning which brought the theories of the Gnostic to a point of logical extravagance, and mingled the doctrines of the Magi with those of Christ. It allied with it little superstition, but aiming at the profoundest philosophy, it was as cold as ice; this alone put it beyond the grasp of a fiery spirit like Bossuet, and he confounded the Paulicians with the Manichæans, principally because he implicitly trusted their two enemies, Photius and Siculus, the authors who have sent their names down from the ninth century on a tide of acrid invective. Arnold of Germany, Beausobre and Lardner have honored themselves and the subject with sedate investigation and judicial candor, and have set right many of the inconsistencies and contradictions of Photius and Siculus. Let us examine the competency of these two witnesses. Who were they and to what did they testify?

Photius possessed great ability, but he was an interested party in his own evidence, and we may fairly question how far he is entitled to absolute credence. As Patriarch of Constantinople, no one was more interested than he in crushing the Paulicians. He was a layman, a great diplomat, and headed one of the most scandalous dissensions of his times. In five days he hurried himself through the five necessary orders, to become Patriarch on the sixth day, thrusting himself into the place of Ignatius, son of Michael I., a man of blameless character, who was deposed because he refused the put the Empress out of the way of plotting Bardas by forcing her into a nunnery. But Pope Nicolas I., by the advice of a synod held at Rome, deposed Photius as an usurper, A. D. 862. In turn, Photius excommunicated the pope, but Gass says that another synod deposed Photius in 867 as 'a liar, adulterer, parricide and heretic.' He was restored to the patriarchate on the death of Ignatius, but was degraded and banished by the Emperor Leo in 886 for political intrigue and embezzlement of the public money. This is the chief witness on whose word the Paulicians are condemned.

Peter Siculus is not so well-known; but he was a nobleman under Basil when that emperor drifted into a war with the Paulicians. He was sent to Fabrica, a Paulician town, to negotiate an exchange of prisoners, remaining there from seven to nine months under restraint, within an enemy's lines by sufferance. After this, he pretends to write their history as a sect. But they were split up into several sects, and how could he learn the history of them all in that place and time? They were scattered, according to Gibbon, 'through all the regions of Pontus and Cappadocia,' and made up of 'the remnant of the Gnostic sects,' with many converted Catholics, and 'those of the religion of Zoroaster.' This was the training he received for writing a history of the Paulicians, under the absurd notion that they were followers of Manes. Gass remarks that Photius wrote his book before A.D. 867, and Siculus wrote his after 868, the latter having a 'curious resemblance' to the former, from which Siculus 'borrowed.' Gibbon charges him with 'much prejudice and passion' in defining 'the six capital errors of the Paulicians.' Now, on common legal principles, what is the value of these two witnesses? Had they full knowledge of the subject to which they deposed? Were they disinterested and unbiased? And did their testimony harmonize? On the first of these questions we have scant knowledge. As to the second, no more partial witnesses could be chosen, one being patriarch of that religion which the Paulicians opposed, the other embassador to a prince who was seeking their lives. And as to the third, their testimony conflicts in many points, and bears the marks of ill-will. They openly take the place of accusers rather than of witnesses, and treat them as enemies whom they would destroy. Photius makes no attempt to disguise his hatred, but bluntly titles his book 'against' them. Then, Siculus is so violent in his denunciation that he spends his strength and space in scorning what they denied, rather than in stating what they held, his deepest grievance being, that they rejected so much that he avowed. The whole animus of their design and drift is seen in their unblushing effort to stigmatize them as Manichæans.

The Paulicians themselves certainly should have known what they were, and both these witnesses explicitly state that they repelled this charge with great spirit. But what difference did that make with these maligners? So long as they could befoul their fame by that odious brand, they pinned the charge to them as if it were true. Gibbon states that the Paulicians disclaimed 'the theology of Manes, and the authors of the kindred heresies, and the thirty generations, or æons, which had been created by the fruitful fancy of Valentine. The Paulicians sincerely condemned the memory and the opinions of the Manichæan sect, and complained of the injustice which impressed that invidious name on the simple votaries of St. Paul and of Christ.'⁷ All through, these witnesses judged them by a false standard of their own raising, while the Paulicians are allowed no counter evidence nor cross-examination, nothing but denial and protest. Photius pretended fair play when he took up his pen to write '*Contra* Manichæos' in one book, without telling what they did believe; and then, on a false assumption, followed that by three others to confute them as though they were disciples of Manes. Mosheim protests against such a bare-faced abuse when he says of the Paulicians: 'They declared their abhorrence of Manes and his doctrine, and it is certain that they were not genuine Manichæans, although they might hold some doctrines bearing a resemblance to those of that sect.⁸

There were different classes of Manichæans as well as Paulicians, but Photius and Siculus lump them *en masse* and convict themselves again and again of misrepresentation in matters of public notoriety. They were much like Augustine, who for nine years had been a zealous Manichæan, and whose loudest complaint against them afterward was that they laughed at Catholic credulity and mocked at its authority, setting up reason against these, as well they might. Photius and Siculus weaken themselves by that silence which shows that they did not tell the whole truth, as well as renders it doubtful whether they told nothing but the truth. We find such contradictions as these in their testimony. They admit that Constantine, the leader of the Paulicians, received the New Testament as his inspired guide, and cited it to prove his tenets, and then charge him with claiming to speak by the Holy Spirit. They fail to charge him with teaching any new doctrine, but allege that he pretended to speak by the Holy Spirit, and then charge him with borrowing his doctrines from the Scythian, Pythagoras, and other pagan teachers! They contemn him for professing to be the very power of God, but fail to show that he ever attempted miracles! They ridicule the Paulicians as an aristocratic organization, then sneer at them because they gave the Scriptures to every body, because they had no priests, and because, instead of listening to the ravings of their inspired leader, they read the Scriptures publicly! They charge them with dissolute lives, with gluttony and obscenity at their festivals; and in the same breath tell us that they studiously married, drank no wine and ate no flesh! They taught that they might eat fruit, herbs, bread, but neither eggs nor fish. In other things they discredit their whole testimony under the ordinary rules which govern evidence.

So far as we know the true history of the Paulicians is this. They first appeared about A.D. 660, and on this wise. Constantine, a young Armenian and a Manichæan, sheltered a Christian deacon who was flying from Mohammedan captivity in Syria. Grateful for his hospitality, the deacon gave him a copy of the Four Gospels and Paul's Epistles. These the youth prized as a new treasure from God. Gibbon says:

'These books became the measure of his studies and the rule of his faith; and the Catholics, who dispute his interpretation, acknowledge that his text was genuine and sincere. But he attached himself with peculiar devotion to the writings and character of St. Paul. The name of the Paulicians is derived by their enemies from some unknown and domestic teacher; but I am confident that they gloried in their affinity to the Apostle to the Gentiles. . . . . In the Gospels and the Epistles of St. Paul, his faithful follower investigated the creed of primitive Christianity; and, whatever may be the success, a Protestant reader will applaud the spirit of the inquiry.'

He then affirms that the Paulicians respected the Old Testament, the Epistles of Peter and the teachings of Manes.

It is hard to obtain their full creed. Siculus blesses 'the divine and orthodox Emperors,' because they committed their books to the flames, 'and if any person be found to have secreted them, he was to be put to death, and his goods confiscated.' Beausobre states that they agreed but little with the Manichæans, gave the Scriptures to all, even women, and treated the worship of crosses, images, relics and Mary with contempt. Like the Friends, they had no order of clergy or pastors, but held their assemblies as a universal priesthood, having no councils, synods or association; or, as Gibbon expresses it, their 'teachers were distinguished only by their scriptural names, by the modest title of fellow-pilgrims, by the austerity of their lives, their zeal or knowledge, and the credit of some extraordinary gifts of the Holy Spirit. But they were incapable of desiring, or at least obtaining, the wealth and honors of the Catholic prelacy; such anti-Christian pride they bitterly censured, and even the rank of elder or presbyter was condemned.' They rejected the perpetual virginity of Mary, but believed that she gave birth to the body of Jesus precisely as its form came from heaven. For these reasons they could not live in the Greek Church, nor could they be Manichæans, believing and practicing as they did, neither were they Baptists.

In regard to Baptism and the Supper, Neander says that they rejected 'The outward celebration of the sacraments;' and Gibbon, that 'In the practice, or at least in the theory of the sacraments, the Paulicians were inclined to abolish all visible objects of worship, and the words of the Gospel were, in their judgment, the baptism and communion of the faithful.' By which is clearly meant, that they neither used the elements of water in baptism, nor of bread and wine in the Supper. They believed in a baptism known as the Consolamentum or baptism of the Spirit, which they administered by laying a copy of the Gospels on the head of the candidate, accompanied with prayer. As to the Supper, they fed on Christ only by faith in the heart, regarding this as the spirit of the institution. In a word, on the ordinances they were in substance Quakers. In this, again, they differed from the Manichæans, who both administered water baptism and the Supper, in the use of the proper elements, as is seen in the dispute of Felix with Augustine, and the accusations against them of Leo the Great; though Beausobre surmises that they used water instead of wine at the Supper, because of their known abstinence from wine. The simple fact appears to be, that they became so thoroughly disgusted with all the ceremonies and nonsense which the Catholics threw about baptism, making it regeneration *de facto*, and with the ridiculous abomination of transubstantiation, that they rejected both, by swinging to the other extreme. And no wonder. Clearly enough, they were Reformed Manichæans, who were disgusted with the rubbishly teachings of the times all around, and were groping their way back to primitive truth as best they could, with the little light that they possessed. They were terribly troubled with Gnosticism and Oriental Magism, as were most of the Christians of their day, and were filled with all sorts of speculations as to the nature of God, the origin of matter, its relations to moral and physical evil; and so were poor specimens of Christians any way, when measured after the full order of the Gospel. But the Christian world at that time afforded nothing better. Dr. Semler accords them more correct ideas of godliness, worship and Church government than the Catholics of that time, and these virtues drew upon them more persecution from the hierarchy than their doctrinal views. Besides, as we shall see hereafter, the germ of a great movement in the right direction was lodged in them, which, finally, led to the most gratifying results.

As best they could, they were trying to get at the Bible and to follow its light. Wolff, the Editor of 'Photius,' speaks of them as mightily affecting Apostolical things, because they changed their surnames to scriptural names, as Timothy, Titus and Sylvanus, and called themselves 'Christians,' as if Catholics were Roman and heathen; they also designated their Churches by New Testament titles, as Ephesians, Colossians, and the like. All this was of little account, but the future showed that this love of the Bible grew with them, for Siculus tells us of the manner in which Sergius one of their most successful defenders was converted to their views, about 810. A Paulician woman asked him: 'Why do you not read the holy Gospels?' He replied, 'It is not lawful for us laymen, but only for the priests.' She pressed him to the privilege, declaring that God desired all to be saved, and showed him his right to the Scriptures, as a good Quakeress or Baptist woman might; and being converted, he stirred Western Asia for more than a generation and brought nameless thousands to Christ.

It may be well to say, in closing, that some think the conversion of young Constantine a mere revival of this sect. Mosheim finds its origin in two brothers, Paul and John, natives of Samasoto, and Photius in another Paul, who lived under the reign of Justinian II. Several state that this sect had been treated with great rigor in a number of imperial edicts, and had almost disappeared when Constantine revived it, only to be treated with greater barbarities. Be this as it may, he preached his doctrines with all his might for seven-and-twenty years, and they spread wide and fast, shaking the whole of Asia Minor, reaching to the Euphrates. Such vast numbers of Catholics were converted, that the Emperor sent Simeon, one of his officers, with a military force to Cibossa, to bring the guilty preacher to justice. Gibbon touchingly describes the scene, when he says: 'By a refinement of cruelty, they placed the unfortunate man before a line of his disciples, who were commanded, as the price of their pardon and the proof of their repentance, to massacre their spiritual father. They turned aside from the impious office; the stones dropped from their filial hands, and of the whole number, only one executioner could be found, a new David, as he is styled by the Catholics, who boldly overthrew the giant of heresy. This apostate, Justus by name, again deceived and betrayed his unsuspecting brethren, and a new conformity to the acts of St. Paul may be found in the conversion of Simeon; like the Apostle, he embraced the doctrine which he had been sent to persecute, renouncing his honors and fortunes, and acquired amongst the Paulicians the fame of a missionary and a martyr.'

But, as is usual in such cases, the word of God grew more and more, and so prevailed. Such a change came over the spirit of the Eastern Church itself that Leo Isauricus the Emperor issued an edict, A. D. 726, prohibiting the worship of images; and in 754 his son called a council of three hundred and thirty-eight bishops, who condemned not only their worship but their use. The result was that the Churches were cleared of images, and pictures of the crucifixion only were left, the images being publicly burned. The Roman Pontiff resented this, and civil war followed, with all sorts of complications between the rulers, both of Church and State. Under the Emperor Nicephorus their religious liberty and privileges had been restored. But persecution broke out afresh under Michael Caropalatus and Leo the Armenian. Then their endurance failed. They rebelled, slew the tyrannical Bishop of Neo-Cesaræa, with the Emperor, magistrates and judges, and took refuge with the Saracens. But one persecution followed another until the Paulicians allied themselves with the Mussulmans to save their people from total extermination. The Empress Theodora issued a fresh edict against them, and between A. D. 832 and 846 one hundred thousand of them were put to death in the most barbarous manner. Infuriated with their persecutors, they took up arms in self-defense, and the contest continued in one shape or another until, in 973, large numbers of them were transported to Philippopolis, south of the Balkan mountains, in what is now called Bulgaria. For more than a century the Paulicians stood with unshaken fortitude, which the sword was unable to suppress. Like men, they defended their rights to home, religion and liberty under the holy sanctions of rebellion against intolerable tyranny. And now they were accorded full religious freedom in their transportation, on condition that they would guard the borders against the pagans. But the conflict between them and the Greeks continued till the twelfth century. Alexius Comnenus put forth some kind efforts to reclaim them, but failed, and they finally took refuge in Europe, where we shall meet them again amongst the Albigenses. Anna Comnena tells the sad story in her great historical work.[9] God wrought mighty things through the Paulicians.

In the sixth century, the Philoxemian (Syraic) version of the New Testament was produced by the Bishop of Hierapolis, who was a thorough opponent of image worship. He was denounced as a Manichæan, and the Emperor Justin banished him into Thrace, where his enemies murdered him. In translating the word *baptizo* he used the word 'amad,' immerse, as it was used in the Peshito. Mar Abba translated the Old Testament into Syriac about the same time. The Arabic version was made in the seventh century, and employs two words for this purpose, '*amada*' and '*tsabagha*,' both of which give the sense of immerse and are used interchangeably in the version. It may be noted here, that this period originated the practice of obliterating the manuscript text of Scripture from the face of vellum or parchment by some chemical process, by boiling, or the use of quick-lime. As this was done for gain in sale, the Council of Trullo, in canon lxviii, forbade the practice on pain of excommunication.

In the gloom of the eighth century the word of God shone here and there as in a dark place. The Persic Version, as now known, came into existence, rendering the words relating to baptism by the terms *shustan, shuyidan,* or *wash.* But in its influence upon modern Christianity, we have the much more important translation of the four Gospels into the Anglo-Saxon. The Saxons from Northern Germany and the Angles from Denmark, who emigrated to Britain A. D. 449, spoke dialects of the same language, which in process of time blended and became known as the Anglo-Saxon in England; for the Angles gave their own name to their new home, Engle-land. This work was executed by that great Saxon, the Venerable Bede, who almost with

NINTH CENTURY FRESCO, BASILICA ST. CLEMENT CYRIL IMMERSING A CONVERT.

his last breath dictated to his amanuensis the closing words of John's Gospel. Lewis mentions a very ancient version of the four Gospels in the old Saxon, said to be made by one Alfred a priest as early as the year 680, but it is lost. Two days before Bede's death he was taken suddenly ill; he breathed with great difficulty and his feet began to swell. He understood what this meant, and dictated all the day long, saying: 'Make haste, I know not how long I shall hold out; my Maker may take me away very soon.' His scribe remarked, 'There is but one chapter more.' The man of God replied, 'It is easy; take your pen, dip it in ink and write as fast as you can.' He did so, and coming to the end of the chapter, said: 'Master, but one sentence is wanting.' 'Write it quickly,' said the dying translator. 'It is done,' cried the amanuensis.' 'Thou hast well said the truth,' rejoined the gasping bishop, 'it is finished. Hold my head with thy hands; let me sit on the holy spot where I have so often prayed, and I will invoke my Father.' When placed on the pavement of his cell, he sung 'Glory be to the Father, and to the Son, and to the Holy Spirit.' And as the word 'Spirit' dropped from his lips he breathed his soul into the bosom of Jesus before the ink on the last chapter of John was fairly dry.

He rendered his work faithfully. The words used by him to express the Christian ordinance of baptism were *dyppan, fullian;* that is, dip, cleanse. There are three MSS. copies of the Saxon Gospels, and in cases which relate to this rite, *depan, dyppan* and *fullian* are used, the last word meaning to *whiten;* probably having reference to the idea of regeneration, as the effect of the dipping. There is no

17

possibility of mistaking what he means when he uses '*dyppan*' as the translation of *baptizo* in Matt. iii, 11, and xxviii, 19; for, in describing the rite as Jesus received it in the depths of Jordan, he says, of that spot in the eighth century: 'In the place where our Lord was baptized stands a wooden cross as high as a man's neck, and sometimes covered by the water. From it to the farther, that is, the eastern, bank, is a sling's cast; and on the nearer bank is a large monastery of St. John the Baptist, standing on a rising ground, and famous for a very handsome church, from which they descend to the cross by a bridge supported on arches, to offer up their prayers. In the farther part of the river is a quadrangular church, supported on four stone arches, covered with burnt tiles, where our Lord's clothes are said to have been kept while he was baptized.' [10]

The ninth century gave Alfred to England, a prince who ranked with Charlemagne in ability, but was much his superior in gentleness and godliness. Under the influence of Alcuin his instructor, the great Emperor unwittingly prepared the Saxons whom he had conquered, and thus made Germany—the fruitful soil in which Baptist principles afterward flourished. Alfred, stimulated by the affection of Judith his step-mother, first acquired a thirst for knowledge and then a love for Christ. He gave the English the right of trial by jury, and said of them: 'It is just that they should ever remain free as their own thoughts.' But his great love for them is seen in his Christ-like design to give them the Bible in their mother tongue. The old Chronicle of Ely says that he succeeded in doing this, but this is doubted; it is more likely that William of Malmesbury gives the exact fact when he tells us that Alfred began a translation of the Psalms with his own hands, but left it unfinished, for he died at fifty-two. Still, Boston of Bury states that 'he translated the whole of the Testament into the English tongue.' Spelman thinks the same, and that he had commenced the Psalms when death stopped his work. It is clear, however, that he did one or both these forms of work, and was the first layman who made such an attempt.

CHAPTER VII.

BAPTISM AND BAPTISTERIES IN THE MIDDLE AGES.

THE Emperor Justin crushed out the last right of conscience in the matter of baptism in the sixth century, by making it a special subject of civil legislation. He issued an edict commanding all unbaptized parents to present themselves and their children for baptism at once. Leo III. issued another edict, A. D. 723, demanding the forcible baptism of the Jews and Montanists. Toward the close of the sixth century the baptism of infants was turned to gain, in the shape of fees paid for its administration; but the charges soon became so enormous that the poor could not pay them, yet, lest their children should die unsaved, the frightened parents strained every nerve to get them baptized. A few, and but a few, opposed these outrages. Stokes mentions Adrianus, a pastor at Corinth, who not only refused to baptize infants, but cast his influence against the practice; for which Gregory accused him to John of Larissa of the crime of turning young children away from baptism and suffering them to be lost.[1]

As showing the religious greed of the times, it may be said here in passing, that both in France and Spain the sale of bishoprics became common in these centuries. The refinement and hospitality of the clergy may be in-

THE BAPTISTERY AT PISA.

ferred from the fact that A. D. 585 the Council of Macon decreed that bishops should not keep mastiffs to worry beggars. Many of these bishops, whose haughtiness was unendurable, could neither read nor write and their lives were given up to the most odious forms of iniquity. In 653 the Council of Toledo forbade the ordination of those who could not read the psalms and hymns used in the public service, with the ritual in baptism. In Britain the canon of Edgar required the priests 'To take care of their churches, and apply exclusively to their sacred duties;

and not to indulge in idle speech, or idle deeds, or excessive drinking; nor to let dogs come within their church inclosure, nor more swine than a man might govern.' Besides this, the grave Council of Prague censured those of the higher clergy who whipped the inferior ministers, or compelled them to carry the bishop upon their shoulders. And as if these barbarities were not enough, in the seventh century the wine of the Supper was mixed with ink and the pen dipped therein, when a contract or covenant was signed. Such signatures were peculiarly holy, especially when made in the sign of the cross. When bishops wished to throw uncommon venom and gall into their curses and excommunications, they called for the consecrated cup, which was intended to commemorate the love of Christ, and dipped the pen in this fluid to strike the superstitious with double horror. Such absurdities readily prepare our minds for the many perversions to which baptism was subjected during the same period.

Infant baptism had about as severe a struggle to force itself upon the faith of men as had transubstantiation. In the fourth century we find Gregory of Constantinople obliged to defend it and publicly censuring parents who delayed it for their children. In his fortieth oration and in the pulpit of his cathedral, when preaching to many who did not believe in the absurdity, he said:

'But, say some, what is your opinion of infants who are not capable of judging either of the grace of baptism, or of the damage sustained by the want of it; shall we baptize them, too? By all means, if there be any apparent danger. For it were better they be sanctified without their knowing it, than that they should die without being sealed and initiated. As for others, I give my opinion that when they are three years of age, or thereabouts (for then they are able to hear and answer some of the mystical words, and although they do not fully understand, they may receive impressions), they may be sanctified both soul and body by the great mystery of initiation.'

He gives this as 'my opinion;' and the value of his opinion is seen in its entire absence of reference to Bible authority, and in the fact that he was trying hard to drive Baptist notions out of 'some' of his hearers, who raised troublesome questions on the subject. His embarrassment can best be understood when we take into account that this primate of all Greece was born when his father was a bishop, and yet was not baptized himself at 'three,' but only at thirty years of age. Nay, his own Emperor, Theodosius, who was very likely one of his hearers, had just been baptized at the age of thirty-four or five years. Nectarius, who succeeded him as bishop in the same diocese and pulpit, was not baptized at all until after his election to fill Gregory's place. All his surroundings made it a most interesting occasion for a controversial sermon on infant baptism from this great pedobaptist oracle.

Yet the Penny Cyclopedia says that some of the fathers of the fifth century did 'not scruple, in spite of edicts and decrees, to condemn the practice of baptizing infants, as a deviation from Scripture and the early custom of the Church.' In 858–882 infant baptism had become almost universal, to the exclusion of believer's baptism, excepting in mission fields where new peoples were converted. Indeed, to deny infant baptism was considered, both by the ignorant and the learned, as the denial of infant salvation, and all dissidents were hated accordingly. Possibly it was on this ground that a synod of British prelates, held near Clonesho in 747, decreed that the clergy should take no money for baptizing infants. Charlemagne made baptism a political institution, and compelled the conquered Saxons to be baptized under pain of death. After this, political baptism and political Christianity soon became nearly universal. In 826 his son Lewis was asked to restore Harald, a petty king of Jutland, to his throne; he consented on condition that he would be baptized, and so Harald and his brother were baptized at Mentz. After that two priests accompanied him to his own country and baptized his subjects. Hence Christ's simple institution was converted into a piece of political craft, a machine of State. Even good Alfred made it a condition of peace that the conquered Danes should be baptized; and Hume tells us that 'Guthrun and his army had no aversion to the proposal; and without much instruction, or argument, or conference, they were all admitted to baptism. The king answering for Guthrun at the font, gave him the name of Athelstan, and received him as his adopted son.' Thierry adds that the Dane promised Alfred that if he would desist from pursuing him, he and his army would be baptized and retire to East Anglia in peace; and Alfred, A. D. 879, not being strong enough to carry on the war, accepted the proposal. So this historian says that 'Guthrun and the other pagan captains swore by a bracelet consecrated to their own gods to receive baptism faithfully.' It may be well to remember that this beautiful arrangement was not made by Jesus and John at the Jordan, but by an English king and a pagan Dane, in the ninth century. Ridpath, speaking of this enforced treaty-baptism, says that to the Danes it 'was no more than a plunge in the water. Sweyn himself had already received the rite at the hand of the zealous priests, anxious for the welfare of his barbaric soul. One of the other leaders made a boast that he *had been washed twenty times*.[2]'

We have another case quite as interesting, in connection with Norway and Iceland, which is detailed in the Encyclopædia Britannica, Art. 'Infant baptism,' by T. M. Lindsay, D.D., Professor of Divinity and Church History in the Free Church College, Glasgow. He shows that infant baptism, as a pagan civil rite, existed for civil purposes in these two countries long before the introduction of Christianity. It was connected with the savage custom of exposing infants who were not to be brought up; much after the order of things in Africa. The Doctor says:

'The newly-born infant was presented to the father, who was to decide whether the child was to be reared or not; if he decided to rear it, then water was poured over the child and the father gave it a name; if it was to be exposed, then the ceremony was not gone through. If the child was exposed by any one after the ceremony had been gone through, it was a case of murder; whereas it was not thought a crime if the child was made away with before water had been poured over it and it had been named. The same people, after the introduction of Christianity, turned this into a Christian rite called *skéro.*' Then the Doctor remarks that the analogy between the two 'lies in the use of water, the bestowal of the name, and the entrance into civil life through the rite.'

This thorough and frank scholar might also have added the difference in the form of using the water between the ancient pagan rite and the so-called Christian rite of these centuries; for Christianity was introduced into Norway in the tenth and eleventh centuries, and its baptism was very different from that of the Apostolic age. However, if the ancient Norwegians and Icelanders had immersed their babes it would have made no difference, as Herzog says that 'the people remained pagan at heart long after they had officially become Christians.'[3] Well did Baronius speak of this as a 'monstrous age' for many other reasons; but what could be more 'monstrous' than the enactment of Charlemagne, that all infants should be baptized before they were a year old, a nobleman being fined for neglect 120 shillings, a gentleman 60, and others 30. In those days a sheep, was bought for a shilling; so that a poor man must sacrifice a flock of 30 sheep and a nobleman 120, if he neglected to bring his babe to this Christian State-fold.[4] The Northumbrian law, A. D. 950, was in substance the same: 'Let every infant be baptized within nine days, upon pain of six *ores;* and if the infant die a pagan within nine days, let his parents make satisfaction to God without any earthly mulct; if after he is nine days old, let them pay twelve *ores* to the priest besides.' Whether the fine paid to the priest would rescue the deceased little pagan from its *limbus infantium* does not appear. It is difficult to determine, at this distance of time, what the basis of 'satisfaction to God' might be, as between a babe of seven, nine and ten days; but there must have been some difference, as Ælfric understood the matter, when he addressed the priesthood about A. D. 759, saying: 'Ye should give the Eucharist to children when they are baptized, and let them be brought to mass that they may receive it, all the seven days that they are unwashed.' Evidently these teachers were not troubled at all about the question of consciousness on the part of the child in either of the ordinances; for about 960 Pope John XIII. baptized a bell in the Lateran, and named it John the Baptist; still the bell understood the matter quite as well as the babe.

The very enactment of these penalties, proves the existence of dissent from the custom of infant baptism in all the ranks of society, and in all places where they were imposed. Labbe and Cossart tell us that in 1022 ten priests at Orleans, France, were found who rejected the doctrine that baptism washes away sin, and that the real body and blood of Christ exist in the bread and wine. The king and queen and many bishops flew to the spot in alarm, accused, tried and burnt these holy men at once; the gentle queen keeping guard at the door of the cathedral where the proceedings were held, and in a most lady-like manner knocking out the eye of her own confessor, who was amongst those consigned to the flames.[5] There was no necessity for protest against the method of baptism even in these dark centuries for Cardinal Pullus, in the twelfth century, describes it thus: 'Whilst the candidate for baptism in water is immersed, the death of Christ is suggested; whilst immersed and covered with water, the burial of Christ is shown forth; whilst he is raised from the waters, the resurrection of Christ is proclaimed.'[6] But infant baptism was opposed at every step. Dr. Allix speaks of a people in Turin and Milan who vehemently condemned it as an error, and the Bishop of Vercelli sorely complained of them in 945. Dupin quotes Dachery as authority for saying that the canons of the cathedral in Orleans, mentioned above, suffered for their views of infant baptism. 'They maintained that baptism did not remove original sin,' which was the plea commonly used in its favor, in behalf of infants. Milner and Hawies tell us of Gundulphus, the leader of a people who were brought to trouble for the same views. 'They particularly objected to the baptism of infants, because they were altogether incapable of understanding or confessing the truth.'[7] When Gerard, the Bishop of Cambray and Arras, cited Gundulphus to appear before a synod in St. Mary's, at Arras, A. D. 1025, he seems to have become nearly wild on the subject. The same charge of heresy was brought against Berengarius by the Bishop of Leige, and also by the Bishop of Aversa; and Archbishop Usher thinks that 'Several of the Berengarian sect had spread his doctrine in several of the Belgic countries, who upon examination did say that baptism did not profit children to salvation.'

A very warm controversy arose in the sixth century on the subject of trine baptism. Pope Pelagius complains of the Eunomians: 'That they baptize in the name of Christ alone and by a single immersion.' He avows that Christ requires baptism 'by trine immersion,' and in the name of the Trinity. Pope Gregory, too, enforces this order in his 'Sacramentary:' 'Let the priest baptize with a triple immersion, with only one invocation of the Holy Trinity.' When the Spanish bishops explained to him that they had begun to practice single immersion because the Arians, who also immersed three times, taught that a second in the name of the Son, and a third in the name of the Spirit, indicated their inferior condition to the Father; he modified his order, under the idea that one immersion best expressed the equality of each person in the Trinity. Leander, Bishop of Seville, sought the pope's counsel in the matter, who, in a letter, replies: 'Concerning the three immersions in baptism, you have judged very truly already, that different customs do not prejudice the holy Church whilst the unity of the faith remains entire.' So he assents to the use of one immersion, lest the 'heretics' interpret the three immersions 'as a division of the Godhead;' at any rate so far as Spain was concerned. 'Yet this judgment of Pope Gregory did not satisfy all men in the Spanish Church; for many still kept to the old way of baptizing by three immersions, notwithstanding this fear of symbolizing with the Arians. Therefore, some time after, about 633, the fourth Council of Toledo which was a general council of all Spain, was forced to make another decree to determine this matter and settle the peace of the Church.

While some priests baptized with three immersions, and the others with but one, a schism was raised endangering the unity of the faith; for the contending parties carried the matter so high as to pretend that they who were baptized in a way contrary to their own were not baptized at all.'[8] The council sided with the pope, yet it was a long time before trine immersion was abandoned.

BAPTISTERIES.—As these centuries were peculiarly distinguished for their great baptisteries, we shall consider these striking examples of Baptismal Archæology in this place. The valuable remains of antiquity are found not only in books, but in ruins, coins, vases, sculpture and other works of art. The fact that Augustus Cæsar changed Rome from brick to marble throws great light upon the true sources of Roman history; as it shows the trend of the Roman mind not only in the material, but in its measurement, shape, cost and use. Inscriptions also are found with other signs on the natural rocks, on tombs, metal plates, tablets of fine clay, pillars of temples and palaces. Some of these have continued for thousands of years, and are readers to us of ancient history, especially that of Egypt, Assyria, Persia, Greece and Rome. This is especially true when they are intended as monuments of human transactions and events. In this way the Baptistery is the monument of Christian baptism.

To Jesus and his Apostles, the foundations of the Temple, its towers and fortresses, were relics of the stone age of Israel. As our Lord habitually walked to and fro in its porches and cloisters, these relics filled him with sacred thought; and his unlettered disciples asking for the import of this sacred Archæology, exclaimed: 'Master, see what manner of stones and what buildings are here?' In like manner, these ancient baptisteries call us back to the true baptismal age, its literature and primitive teaching, as these were understood by their builders. These antiquarian remains challenge our reverence for Christian truth, and every lover thereof will take pleasure in these historic stones, will walk about them to tell their number and honor their dust. His love of the truth endows them with a voice; they cease to be dead architecture and become living teachers. Such sacred remains calmly rectify the mistakes of the present; for in that case, the simplicity of the child corrects the sophistication of the man. They teach us that present truth-lovers do not stand alone in their generation, but that the years of ancient times call us back, to our profit. Old centuries as by magic draw us back, and old generations rehearse the truth as it lives in venerable art and antiquity. These throw the inward spirit of the past into the

ANCIENT BAPTISTERY AT AQUILEJA.

present outward form and become the frame-work for new thought; and through their imagery the living past and the living present are brought into the equipoise of a sublime truth. They help us to put new meaning into old words and acts; so that instead of casting the old away, it is continued, found to be eternal and exactly harmonious.

The baptisterium amongst the ancient Romans was simply a place of bathing, which Rugler calls the 'swimming-tank of the ancients;' and its construction is well illustrated by the discoveries at Pompeii, especially in one of the lesser baths of white marble, which Gell describes as of a circular form eighteen feet six inches in diameter. With them, as with us, a bath in the ordinary sense of the word was the immersion of the body in a medium different from the ordinary one of atmospheric air, which medium was usually common water in some form. The Romans practiced warm more than cold bathing, and wherever they found hot springs they converted them into baths. The 'warm' water spoken of in the recently discovered 'Teaching of the Apostles,' leaves the implication that the public baths were used for baptism. The baths of Caracalla contained 1,600 marble seats around the inner sides, for the use of bathers; and those of Diocletian, 3,200; these buildings being open to the public, and the price for

ANCIENT ROMAN BATH. VATICAN MUSEUM.

bathing being only about half a cent of our money. Of course, primarily, these baths were constructed without regard to the Christian rite, but in all probability they suggested the form of Christian baptisteries. Wallcott says in his 'Sacred Archæology:' 'The early Christians were baptized in water by the road-side (Acts viii, 36–38); or in a river (Acts xvi, 13–15); or in a prison (Acts xvi, 33); or in a spring, or at sea; or in private houses (Acts ix, 18; x, 47, 48); or in any place.' At Rome there was an early baptistery in the house of Cyriacus, in the Pontificate of Marcellus, A. D. 308–310, according to the same authority. Down to the middle of the second century no place was specially set apart for the rite, for at that time the Christians had no places of worship. But by the end of the third century they had not only sanctuaries of their own, but also special buildings devoted to the uses of baptism, as those spoken of by Eusebius, at Tyre. Haydn's 'Dictionary of Dates' says: That in the 'reign of Constantine, 319, baptisteries were built, and baptism was performed by dipping the person all over.' Hope says that the early Christians 'Always practiced baptism by immersion, and out of the church (edifice); consequently they wanted a building for the purpose of baptism, as much as for that of worship.' [9]

The earliest Christian baptistery known is in the Catacomb of Calixtus at Rome, and was used in the times of the pagan persecutions. Parker says that this catacomb was a burying-place as early as the first century, although its earliest inscription is A. D. 268–279. This secret, subterranean relic is a small chamber, containing a cistern, or as it is called, 'a well,' a fountain; and is about four feet deep, supplied by a small stream on the left side, with steps down into it, as Parker says, 'for baptism by immersion.' When the first Christian sanctuaries were reared, baptisteries were also erected as distinct buildings; but often the baptistery preceded the Church edifice itself and was the point about which the place of general assembly arose. In such cases the baptistery was built on a large scale for receiving a great number of people, and it stood near to the church building to which it belonged. Generally the form of the baptistery was hexagonal, but some were circular and all had a lare *piscina*, or reservoir, in the middle. They were also called '*illuminatoria*,' because there the converts were instructed or illuminated before baptism. The baptistery was not introduced into the church edifice until the sixth century, and then only into the porch or entrance, to indicate that immersion was the door into the Church itself; but this practice did not become common until the ninth century. Yet Clovis was immersed in a church edifice in the latter part of the fifth century.

We have distinct accounts of about sixty of these structures in Italy alone; in the generality of Italian cities one large baptistery sufficed for all the churches of that city. These commonly adjoined the cathedral, as at Pisa and Florence, but in Rome itself most of the churches were supplied with baptisteries; for mention is made of the building or repairing of five different baptisteries in that city, between A. D. 772–816. Pope Leo III. rebuilt that of the Apostle Andrew, a circular building and enlarged its 'fons,' because the place was too small for the people who came for baptism. In distinction from all others this building became known as 'The Baptistery;' and as its size increased it grew into a meeting-place for religious assemblies, even for ecclesiastical councils. In each baptistery there was a table for the Supper as well as a reservoir for the immersions; and Martene tells us that until about the eleventh century the Supper was administered there to all who were immersed. Immersion was the necessity which called these structures into existence. Rahn says that their 'origin' was 'dependent' on the old custom of having a great baptismal occasion, and of the rite of immersion; otherwise a bowl in the hand would have met every purpose, as now, in all cases where immersion is not practiced. The 'Encyclopædia Britannica' truly says, Art. 'Baptistery:' 'Christianity made such progress that infant baptism became the rule, and as soon as immersion gave place to sprinkling, the ancient baptisteries were no longer necessary.' Then the size of the font was reduced, and as immersion was pushed aside the bowl sufficed. Gailhabaud in his celebrated work on architecture covers this point:

'At the origin of the new religion baptism was to be administered by immersion. We desire to especially note a locality marked by the cemetery of St. Pontianno. There one sees a kind of large basin, filled with water, and hollowed out of the soil at a depth quite convenient to receive quite a number of neophites.' But when the Church in most of Europe ceased to 'recognize the inopportuneness of immersion and replaced it by pouring,—ever since that time it has established, in place of the reservoir made below the soil and filled with water for immersing the neophites, the font of stone. This marks in the history of religion and of the liturgy a very noticeable change in the administration of baptism.'[10]

BAPTISTERY OF ST. JOHN (LATERAN).

In the nineteenth century, where Christians have turned their backs upon the old ordinance and substituted another, they build no such edifices at an enormous cost; but the primitive Christians looked upon burial in water as obedience to Christ, and their antiquated baptisteries stand as solemn witnesses against the popish innovation. Prior to the tenth century, Easter, Pentecost and the Epiphany were the ordinary times employed for baptism, when great numbers of the candidates and their friends assembled; rendering it needful that the baptisteries be spacious and separate from the church buildings, which were always crowded by the general worshipers.

BAPTISTERY AT FLORENCE.

The most celebrated of the baptisteries now remaining are found at Rome, Florence and Pisa; the most ancient being that of St. John of Lateran, at Rome, fourth century. This building is octagonal, being about 75 feet in diameter and is extremely splendid. The *piscina*, or bath, is octangular, of green basalt, about 25 feet in diameter and from 3 to 4 feet deep. It was constructed by Sixtus III., who died A. D. 440; and, according to De Bussiere, 'has served as a model for all those' erected in the principal Italian cities. On the ceiling of one of its chapels is an old mosaic of the Baptist immersing in the Jordan, possibly of the fifth century. It is seldom used for baptism, yet to this day such Jews and pagans as accept the Roman faith are immersed there on Easter Eve. On the shape of these baptisteries Audsley makes these curious remarks, in his 'Dictionary of Architecture:' 'For more than one reason the octagon appears to have been adopted in preference to the circle. It was the one which presented the least difficulty of construction, especially when the classic entablature was retained; it was also from very early times held as the emblem of regeneration. The square, from the original idea of the earth's shape, was accepted as the emblem of the world; the octagon was adopted by the Christians as that of perfection, consequent upon the confession of the faith, and the new birth in baptism; and the circle as the emblem of eternity or everlasting life.' [11]

INTERIOR OF BAPTISTERY OF FLORENCE.

The most magnificent baptistery now in existence is that of Florence. It has a diameter of about 100 feet, its gallery is supported by 16 granite columns, and its vault is decorated by the richest mosaics. Its bronze doors are marvels of beauty in bass-relief, and fifty years were spent in preparing them. This structure was originally the cathedral of the city, built about the middle of the seventh century. The old font stood in the center; but when Philip de Medici was immersed in it his father to the great disgust of Florence, had it destroyed, for the same reason that Peter I., of Russia, broke the drinking-cup of Luther after drinking from it himself, namely, that it should never be used again. The locality of the font is still seen, however, as that part of the floor is plainly paved, while the rest is laid in beautiful patterns of black and white marble. The present font was erected A. D. 1658, to supply the place of that which was destroyed A. D. 1577.

The baptistery of Pisa is known to the entire world for its splendor. It has a diameter of 116 feet, and its pear-shaped dome towers 160 feet high, supported by most costly columns and arches. It was commenced A. D. 1153, and its cost was so great that it long remained unfinished, until the citizens levied a rate upon themselves for its completion. Its walls are eight feet thick, it has a basement, a main and an attic story. The font is described by Webb as an octagonal bath 'for adult baptism.' The building was begun by Diotisalvi, but the work was not prosecuted until 1278, nor completed till about the opening of the fourteenth century. Credulous people of the nineteenth century would have us believe that all this taste, toil and cost was had for the purpose of pouring a handful of water upon the head! The accompanying cut of the interior as it stands to-day gives the ancient ideal of Gospel order: 1. The pulpit, from which the candidate for baptism is exhorted to faith on Christ. 2. The basin or font in which he is immersed. It is octagonal, being 14 feet in diameter and 4 feet deep, and is supplied with water by a tube.

PULPIT, BAPTISTERY AND TABLE AT PISA.

3. The Lord's Table, where he took the Supper after his immersion.

The largest baptistery ever built was that of St. Sophia at Constantinople. At one time it served as the residence of the Emperor Basiliscus, and a great ecclesiastical council was held within its walls. Three thousand people once assembled in the baptistery at Antioch at one time, to be baptized; but the baptistery of St. Sophia was greater even than that at Antioch.

Mention may be made of the great baptistery at Aix, which was constructed A. D. 1101; of that of Verona, A. D. 1116; and of that of Parma, with its three matchless gates, said to have been pronounced by Angelo as worthy of being the gates of Paradise. The same praise is claimed for those of Florence, and yet it is questionable whether he said this of either of them. The Parma baptistery was begun A.D. 1196, and completed 1281. Its great marble font, 8 feet wide and 4 feet deep, is cut out of one yellowish-red block and stands in the middle of the floor, bearing date A. D. 1299. The records of the Church at Parma contain an official report of its uses, sent to the pope and bearing date November 21, 1578, saying that this sacred font was consecrated to baptism 'per immersionem.'[12]   The baptistery at Verona contains a basin of marble 28 feet in circumference, hewn out of a single block of porphyry, and is four and one half feet deep. The baptistery of Pistoia is especially interesting, and differs from most of those described. It was built A. D. 1337. The font is of white marble and is square. Standing near to the western entrance is a beautiful black and white marble pulpit, from which sermons were preached, to show that the people must hear and believe before they could pass into its waters. Its square pool is 10 feet in diameter and 4 feet deep. The baptistery at Milan is peculiar, and differs from all others. As if to convey the Scriptural idea of burial, it is in the shape of the ancient sarcophagus. Its material is porphyry, being 6 feet 8 inches long and 24 inches deep. Dean Stanley refers to this baptistery in the words: ' With the two exceptions of the cathedral of Milan and the sect of the Baptists, a few drops of water are now the Western substitute for the threefold plunge into the rushing rivers or the wide baptisteries of the East.'[13]

Great Britain furnishes a beautiful example of a natural but historic baptistery which must be noted here. Dr. Cathcart presents it in this graphic description:

'About eleven miles from the Cheviot Hills, which separate England from Scotland, and about the same distance from Alnwick Castle—the well-known residence of the Dukes of Northumberland—and two miles from the village of Harbottle, there is a remarkable fountain. It issues forth from the top of a slight elevation, or little hill. It has at present as its basin a cavity about 34 feet long, 20 feet wide, and 2 feet deep. By placing a board over a small opening at one end its depth can be considerably increased. A stream flows from it, which forms a little creek. . . . The spring is a place of public resort for the population for many miles around, and for numerous strangers, on account of its early baptismal associations. . . . An ancient statue, as large as life, lay prostrate in the fountain for ages, probably from the period when the monasteries were destroyed, in the time of Henry VIII. This statue, when the writer saw it, was leaning against a tree at the fountain. It was, most likely, the statue of Paulinus. It was called "the bishop." Its drapery, the action of the atmosphere upon the stone of which it is made, and its general appearance, show that it was set up at a very remote period, perhaps two or three centuries after Paulinus baptized the Northumbrian multitude in the fountain.'[14]

This fountain is commonly known as ' Our Lady's Well,' after the Virgin, and is one of the natural baptisteries where Paulinus administered Christian immersion. The Vicar of Harbottle has caused a crucifix to be erected in the center, with the following inscription: 'In this place Paulinus the bishop baptized three thousand Northumbrians, Easter, 627.' This accords exactly with the statement of Camden, who describes Harbottle as ' on the Coquet River, near to which is Holystone, where it is said that Paulinus, when the Church of the English was first planted, baptized many thousands of men.' A convent lies in ruins at Holystone, close by, which was probably raised as a monument to the holy spot and its waters. Camden lived in the last half of the sixteenth century, when the tradition was all aglow; and the clerical son of Oxford reared this cross as late as 1869.

As to the Supper, the doctrine of transubstantiation crystallized in those centuries, and apparently in an incidental way. In 787 the Council of Nice alleged that the bread and wine of the Supper were not images of Christ, but his very body and blood. This brought the great controversy to a head, and giants on both sides drew their swords. Amongst these Ratram wrote a powerful treatise against transubstantiation, 863, which centuries afterward convinced Ridley of his error on

BAPTISTERY OF BISHOP PAULINUS.

the subject; then Ridley lent it to Cranmer, in whom it wrought a similar change. John Scotus, the Roger Bacon of his day, wrote a stronger work, 875, which lived for about two centuries. Many Councils denounced, and that of Rome, 1059, condemned it to be burnt. Berengarius, 998–1088, followed with heavy blows. Bigotry wrecked itself upon these men in every shape, but their doctrines spread through Germany, Italy, France and Britain; for as fires never burn out controversies, more than winds blow out stars, the dispute went on to the Reformation and is as firm and fresh to-day as ever.

CHAPTER VIII.

ANCIENT BAPTISMAL PICTURES.

THESE have come down to us chiefly in frescoes, mosaics and bass-reliefs. Baptism itself symbolizes thought as it lies in the divine mind, so that the human eye catches the truth of which it is the symbol. Art in these pictures marks the ordinance as it existed in the life-time of the artist, and only to this extent are they of historical value. The co-existing literature of his times, however, must show the purpose of his treatment, and interpret its forms in his absence. In fact we are so dependent on this literature, that where a separate history of the picture is not preserved, only the contemporary writings of its day can give us its age. The pictures, therefore, even in the rudest state of the art are in no case purely realistic, but symbolical also. Dean Stanley pronounces those of the Catacombs, 'mis-shapen, rude and stiff,' which is seen at a glance. Most of them have been restored several times and also altered; so that, as Parker remarks, to this extent they have lost their historic value, especially by changes of shape and color, though the general design is unchanged. He says: 'A work which has been restored becomes the work of the hands that restore it.' Their age and damp situation has rendered their restoration necessary, and in the case of the Callixtine frescoes he ascribes this work to Leo III., 795; and that of Ponziano to Nicholas I., 858–867. Even the great fresco of the Supper by Da Vinci, at Milan, though upon a perfectly dry wall and scarcely four hundred years old, is fast fading out. Parker states that the St. Ponziano has not been restored 'over carefully,' and that 'The rather rash outline of the Baptist's right arm and shoulder are drawn over a far more careful and correct figure.' Also: 'The stiffness of the restoration, white eyes and heavy, incorrect outline, point to a late date.'

Early Christian art at the best was deficient in all respects, and its broad, symbolic ideal must ever be remembered in seeking its historic bearings. The earlier companion pictures on the Supper made by the same hands in the same places strongly attest this. The table is spread, a company is gathered around it, but with one exception no wine is on the table. There is a small supply of bread in some cases, in others abundance, but in all there is much *fish!* A fresco in the Crypt of St. Cornelius presents a mysterious fish swimming in water, with a basket on its back containing the bread and wine of the Supper. Yet this strange conceit is in keeping with the ancient play upon the Greek letters of our Lord's technical name ΙΧΘΥΣ, that is, 'The Fish.' This is a very ancient anagram amongst Chris-

SYMBOLIC PICTURES. 257

tians. Almost all the fathers, Greek and Latin, call him 'The Fish,' the 'Heavenly Ichthus;' and so they made the fish an emblem of both Baptism and the Supper, to set forth the truths which these express. This figure was early engraved upon the rings of Christians by the advice of Clement of Alexandria, 194, possibly because the heathen could not detect its meaning. He says: 'Let the dove and the fish . . . be

NO. 1.—THE SYMBOLIC SUPPER.

signs unto you;' and Augustine calls Christ the Fish, 'Because he descended alive into the depths of this mortal life as into the abyss of waters.' An inscription of the fourth or fifth century found at Autun, France, exhorts the baptized to 'Eat, drink, holding Ichthus in thy hand. Faith brought to us and set before us food, a Fish from a divine font, great and pure, which she took in her hands and gave to her friends, that they should always eat thereof, holding goodly wine, giving with bread a mingled drink.' Yet the ancient Christians never celebrated the Supper by the use of fish. Here, then, while we have the realistic table, we have the mystic symbol of fish thereon—possibly intended by the painter to keep before the mind Christ's presence with his disciples, when he broke bread and ate fish with them on the evening after his resurrection. A more singular use of a fish is found in the Catacombs, where a ship is carried on its back through the water—evidently intended to represent the Church being carried through the stormy sea of life by firmly resting on Christ, 'The Fish.' The helmsman also is Christ, the Dove on the poop is the

NO. 2.—THE CHURCH AS A SHIP ON CHRIST THE FISH.

18

Holy Spirit, and the Dove on the mast represents the heavenly peace which Jesus is giving both to Peter and the ship.

Hippolytus glows when speaking of the Church as a ship, tossed by storms but never wrecked, because Christ is with her. He makes the cross her mast, his word her rudder, his precepts her anchor, the sea her laver of regeneration. The Spirit breathes into her sails to waft her to her heavenly port, and he gives her an abundant entrance into her desired haven. In the above rude gem from the Catacombs two Apostles are rowing, and a third, Peter, is stretching his hand to Christ in prayer as he meets Jesus on the wave, to save him from sinking. But in the following we have the idea of Hippolytus, where the storm-fiend is endeavoring to wreck the Church by persecution. In the distance is a man swept away by the same waves which dash over the vessel, to represent the children of this world being drowned in the billows of perdition. But with Christ on the deck and the Almighty hand reached forth from above, the cross-ribbed flag rises high in the bow above the threatening sea. Although the rudder is swept away, the outstretched hands of Jesus direct her course in the gale.

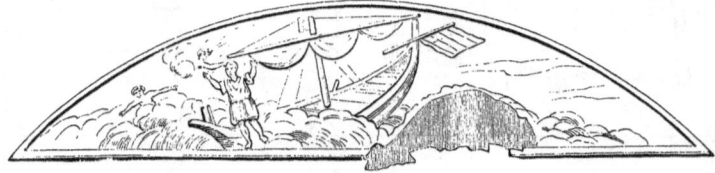

NO. 3.—SYMBOL OF THE CHURCH AS A SHIP.

These purely symbolical pictures from the Catacombs may help us to understand their Baptismal Pictures, where we have a large admixture of the real and the symbolic. No. 4 is from the Crypt of St. Lucina at Rome, and is described by Father Garrucci. Its date is in dispute, but it is the oldest painting of Christ's baptism known. Many high authorities assign it to the close of the second or the opening of the third century, amongst them De Rossi. The Saviour is leaving the Jordan after his immersion, and John takes him by the hand to welcome him to the bank. Neither the head of John nor that of Christ is adorned by the nimbus, which was not adopted into Christian art from pagan art to indicate sanctity and authority till the fifth century. But the leaf in the mouth of the dove, which denotes the Holy Spirit, indicates that he brings a message of peace from heaven in honor of Christ's baptism. A passage from Tertullian throws light upon this figure: 'As after the waters of the deluge, in which the old iniquity was purged away, as after that baptism (so to call it) of the old world, a dove sent out of the ark and returning with the olive-leaf was the herald to announce to the earth peace and the cessation of the wrath of heaven; so, by a similar disposition with reference to matters spiritual, the Dove of the Holy Spirit sent from heaven flies to the earth, to our flesh, as it comes out of the bath of regeneration after its old sins, and brings to us the peace of God.' (De. Bap., c. vii.)

NO. 4.—JESUS BAPTIZED IN THE JORDAN.

No. 5 presents a youth ankle-deep in water, the administrator holding a roll in one hand, and resting the other on the candidate's head to plunge him in the water. The roll in his left hand indicates his authority or commission to baptize, as one 'sent

NO. 5.—A SUPPOSED IMMERSION OF JESUS.

from God;' and also shows that the painter had John in his 'mind's eye,' even if he fell into a double anachronism first as to the extreme youth of Christ, and then in substituting the Roman toga for the Jewish tunic; showing both his Roman taste and the poverty of his artistic genius by copying the drapery of his every-day life. The Ursian Mosaic at Ravenna clothes John in a robe of similar fullness in which the folds hang differently, the toga being capable of endless adjustments as seen in classic statuary. But is this painting from 'the Chamber of the Sacraments,' in the Catacomb of Callixtus, a baptism of Christ? The Arian Mosaic of St. Maria, in Cosmedin, is intended for Christ without doubt, in which he looks almost boyish, as also in this fresco. The ablest writers call attention to this fact, as according with the general methods which treat of him in all departments of early Christian art. Didron, in his great work on 'Christian Iconography,' treats at large upon the juvenility of Christ's figure in all early Christian art, but especially of this curious feature in the earliest Catacomb pictures, which constantly represent him as a youth from twelve to fifteen. He remarks: 'That the figure of Christ, which had at first been youthful, becomes older from century to century, in proportion as the age of Christianity itself progresses. That of the Virgin, on the contrary, becomes more youthful with every succeeding century.' P. 249. This method came neither from mistake nor ignorance; but was chosen as the best mode known to express the meek, lowly and teachable in Jesus. Lord Lindsay says: 'He is represented as an abstraction; as the genius, so to speak, of Christianity; a beardless youth, to signify the everlasting prime of eternity.' The nude figure stands in the water only slightly above the ankles; but his undress, as well as the expanse of the water, are in themselves symbols of his immersion without regard to the depth of the sheet; for why should the artist place him in water at all, especially unclothed, in order to pour water on his head? The youth is standing at his full height, and Garrucci writes of this picture: 'The candidate has only his feet in the water. The water, then, in which one must be immersed, is not, in fact, literally represented, but indicated by sign.' (VI, v, p. 95.)

Nos. 6 and 7 from the Catacomb of Callixtus relate to the same subject; 6 being taken from Garrucci, and 7 from De Rossi. They are symbolical and strikingly illustrate the painter's conception of baptism. These frescoes are on separate walls of the same crypt, and Prof. Mommsen treating them as one continuous picture, says with great clearness:

'We see on the first wall a man striking the rock with his staff; from the spring thus opened a fisherman catches a fish on a hook. Farther on the same spring serves as a baptismal font, out of which the man baptizes the boy standing before him, laying his hand on his head. Without doubt, Christ is here conceived of as the rock, as in the Epistle to the Corinthians: "They drank of that spiritual rock that followed them, and that rock was Christ;" and the man who strikes the rock is more likely Peter, who is often designated the new Moses, than Moses himself. It is not necessary to speak of the fisherman, Peter, who was called to be a fisher of men.' Here we have that favorite symbol of the fathers, which applies the figure of the fish to Christians as well as to Christ, as Tertullian: 'We smaller fishes, after the example of our Fish, are born in the waters;' and of Melito, second century, 'fishes are the holy ones of God.' Hilary, Augustine and Optatus in the fourth century do the same, the latter calling the baptismal waters '*piscina*,' a fish-pond. By introducing the angler into the picture, the idea is conveyed that another conversion has taken place, and so the newly-immersed candidate is another fish caught, a disciple of Christ drawn out of the waters of baptism which flow from Christ the smitten rock; a purely allegorical idea in exact keeping with the religious literature of the times in which the painter lived.

NO. 6.—SUCCESSFUL GOSPEL PREACHING.

NO. 7.—CONVERSION AND BAPTISM.

Here are clearly three distinct and purely allegorical ideas: a wide expanse of baptismal water issuing from a rock and shown to be 'living' water from the fact that it contains large fish; a Gospel minister represented by the fisherman with his hook and line, first acting as a 'fisher of men' and then baptizing the disciple drawn to Christ; after that comes the perfected baptism in the 'laying on of the hand' when the process of conversion is finished and attested. What, then, are we to understand by the profuse, fire-like jets which fall around the candidate as he stands in the water nearly up to the knees? With a singular infatuation this fresco has been eagerly seized upon as the one drawing of antiquity proving the modern doctrine of affusion with water as baptism, either added to immersion or substituted for it; but used chiefly to justify this substitution, directly in the face of all Church history and literature, for the first thousand years after Christ. Clearly his body has just been raised from the water, and this spray shoots above the head of the candidate to the height of about one-fourth of his person, then falls on one side to a line with his thigh and on the other down to the water. It is the only picture of an ancient baptism in which such a spray is found; and the question to be determined is, whether the artist intended it as a symbol or a realism, while much else in the scene is allegory. It cannot be mistaken for a nimbus nor yet for an aureole, although it compasses the whole person excepting a part of one leg. Certainly the law of gravitation determines that it cannot be intended for water dripping from the body after immersion, for it flies upward more than the length of the head and neck together above the head. Nor can it be water or oil, or any other liquid whatever falling from the baptizer's hand or from a vessel, as his hand rests flatly and firmly on the youth's head. Affusion or aspersion of water are entirely out of the question here, because the spray has no natural or apparent source. Neither the sense of sight nor a stretch of the imagination can call it water without showing where it comes from. Let any man try a thousand times to produce such a fillet of water around any one without the use of the uplifted hand, or of some vessel from which it is poured, and he must fail as often as he tries. More than this, the curves have not the appearance of water. The lines start up from the middle of the head in an arched, forked, wing-like form, which cannot be produced with water excepting when dashed upward in a body and with great force. The strokes of the pointed lines above the head, the flamboyant curve as of flame and its arching over the shoulders at so great a distance from them, do not harmonize with the specific gravity of falling water. But they look more like jets of flame projected upward and outward by the natural force of fire, and they convey the conception which the ancient artists expressed of 'cloven tongues, like as of fire.' No. 8, taken from the Catacombs and photographed from Garrucci (vol. iii, pl. 140, No. 1), expresses the same symbolical idea in association with the resting of cleft flames upon the heads of the Apostles at Pentecost.

The artist has introduced the Virgin Mary in the center of the Apostolic group, possibly because she is mentioned with the 'Twelve,' Acts i, 14; and also to express his idea of her superiority to them, by taking the place of her Son at their head, a notion in keeping with the errors of his day. The 'cloven' or divided appearance of the fire, as well as its flashing form, indicates the same idea in these two painters of different dates. The blaze-like curve in No. 7 suggests that the author intended that fresco to express his idea of the figurative and supernatural baptism of fire in union with baptism in water—a thought in perfect harmony with the religious literature of his times. We have innumerable instances in which the Fathers speak of such a baptism in association with the baptism of water. Tertullian tells us that the Valentinians added this fire baptism to their water baptism. Smith's 'Dictionary of Antiquities' not only treats of a sect who maintained the true baptism to be that of the Spirit and fire, but speaks of a treatise in which 'we read of some who, by what means is not known, produced an appearance of fire on the baptismal water, in order to complete what they thought necessary for Christian baptism.'[1] A tradition existed on this subject from Justin Martyr downward. In his dialogue with Trypho the Jew, he says that 'When Jesus descended into the water, a fire was also

NO. 8.—CLOVEN TONGUES, AS OF FIRE.

kindled in Jordan.' The Ebionite Gospel reports that after Christ's baptism: 'Immediately a great light shone around upon the place.' In commenting upon these passages, Dr. Lardner remarks: 'This account, therefore, of the fire in the river Jordan seems to be only a story which Justin had received by tradition.' Drs. Cave and Grabe, as well as Lardner, think this tradition an inference drawn from the evangelical account of the opening heavens.[2] Add to this the avowal of John concerning the baptism of fire not many days hence, and it is easy to see how the traditional fiery baptism associated itself with the primitive water baptism in many minds. Ephrem, the great hymnist of the Syrian Church, fourth century, speaking of Christ's baptism says: 'Behold the fire and the Spirit, in the river in which thou wast baptized.' Is it any more strange that an ancient painter should embody this emblematic idea in a picture, than that so grave a Father as Justin should incorporate it into his controversy with the noted Jew? Surely, there was more common sense in doing either, than in the late attempt to force this fresco into the service of aspersion by making it an annex and interpreter of 'The Teaching of the Twelve Apostles.'

That work requires men to be baptized in 'running water. But if thou hast not running water, baptize in other water; and if thou canst not in cold, then in *warm*. But if thou hast neither, pour water upon the head.' Here, however, the administrator has both running water and an abundance of it; and, therefore, to pour water upon the head would be in direct opposition to the above injunction. A wide stream of 'living water' is presented, big enough to produce a fish, in length one third of the candidate's full stature; and so the baptizer is supposed to be following the instruction in the exceptional case by pouring water on the head, and that miraculously too, without the aid of any vessel or the use of either of his hands! Here is a pedobaptist miracle in resurrection from the Catacombs for enlightening the nineteenth century. Even Smith's 'Dictionary' forces this Callixtine fresco to bear testimony to affusion in baptism as an ancient practice, and cites as a parallel case, that 'one common mode of bathing among the ancients was the pouring of water from vessels over the body, as we may see in ancient vase paintings.' That water was so used in the ordinary spray or shower-bath is clear enough; but what has that to do with this picture? Here is not the representation of the usual bath, but of a Christian baptism. Besides, when the 'vase paintings' picture affusion in the common bath, they show the vessel from which the falling water flows, which is the very thing that this painting does not show. It cannot be enlisted into this modern service without the greatest violence to the literature of the earlier ages. Chrysostom understood the baptism of fire metaphorically, for the gifts and graces of the Spirit; while Cyril of Jerusalem understood it realistically, as seen in the form of cloven tongues at Pentecost.[3] The resemblance to fiery horns rising above the head of the baptized in No. 7, and the forked flames above the heads of the Twelve in No. 8, are clearly intended to represent the same symbolical ideal, by similar arching, cleft and aspiring curves. But the affusion of water is inadmissible until it can be shown where it comes from, and how it ascends far above the head in this cleft and arching way without visible agency or projecting force.

No. 9 is a more important painting, found over the baptistery in the Catacomb of St. Ponziano, which is ascribed by Boldetti to the fifth or sixth century, but by Parker to the ninth. It is over an arched recess, at the bottom of which is a well or fountain, said to have been used for baptism by the early Christians in the times

NO. 9.—BAPTISTERY IN CATACOMB OF ST. PONZIANO.

of persecution. In the upper part Christ is represented as standing up to the waist in the Jordan. The Holy Dove with rays from his beak is over his head, fish are swimming in the water, and a hart or stag is looking intently into the stream. John is standing on the bank reaching forward with his hand on Christ's head. Another figure stands on the opposite side in a white garment; the three figures have the nimbus. The lower part of the representation is under the arch; on the wall is a jeweled cross with the A and Ω hanging from its arms to indicate that Christ is the Beginning and the Ending of faith, and the two candlesticks standing upon them are designed to set forth the Divine and human nature of our Lord. The symbolism here is on a large scale, for the artist evidently intended not only to give us an ideal baptismal scene in the immersion of Jesus, but to associate with it such a body of divinity as would show the great doctrines on which baptism rests, and its necessary outcome from them; so that the emblematic and the realistic are copiously blended. The jeweled cross is very significant, being set with gems, leaves and flowers. This the ancients called The Cross of Glory, while they called the plain wood The Cross of Shame, to mark the degradation to which the Baptized Crucified submitted for our sins. The two flames from the candlesticks on the transverse beam are designed to show the wealth and fullness of illumination which the atonement throws upon baptism, and the light needed by those who are buried beneath its waters. Then, the cross itself descends into the water to exhibit the connection of the atonement by Christ's death with the ordinance. The clear and still fountain beneath is the believer's liquid grave, where he is to be buried 'into the likeness of Christ's death.'

Portions of the upper picture are purely imaginative, as the angel on the right shore from Christ resting on a cloud and holding our Lord's robe. Then, the hart looking earnestly into the water symbolizes the thirst of the believing soul for the waters of baptism. This idea is probably borrowed from Jerome's comment on the first verse of Psalm xlii: 'As the hart pants after the water-brooks, so does my soul pant for thee, O God.' The nimbus thrown around the head of John, Jesus and the angel, and the luminous irradiancy around the Holy Dove, distinguish them as sacred personages. Thus, in this remarkable picture, the immersion of Jesus and the deep baptistery provided for those who cling to his cross are but members of a great system of truth which the artist intended to preach; his primary purpose being to show forth Christ's redeeming work and the results flowing from it by faith and obedience, as seen in baptismal burial and resurrection with him. The baptistery is supplied by a natural spring, and is, according to Ricci, from four to five feet deep; Canon Venable says, with a descent of ten steps. Since writing the above, Dr. Dodge calls attention to Bellermann's description of a baptistery in the Catacombs at Naples: 'There is a niche in the wall under the middle door, eight feet high, five and a half feet broad, in which one still sees a cross with four equal arms painted red, and a Greek inscription, which means "Jesus Christ conquers."

According to a tradition, there was once before this niche a great baptismal basin, deeply embedded in the earth, so that one could look on this place as the baptistery of a subterranean Church.' P. 81. It seems that the cross was a baptismal one, like that which we see in the Pontian Cemetery. The inscription is remarkable. Rev. St. John Tyrwhitt in his work on 'Christian Art and Symbolism' says: 'The earliest crosses, as that called the Lateran, are baptismal crosses. . . . The cross is in its first use the symbol of baptism into the Lord's death, or death with him.' P. 124.

No. 10 presents the same symbolic style. It is the noted Ursian Mosaic, taken from the Baptistery of St. John at Ravenna, supposed to have been built by Ursus, A. D. 390–396, but the mosaic which adorns its high dome is referred to 450. Its three most striking symbols are the lettering at the left of Christ's shoulder; the anointing of Jesus by John with oil or myrrh from a vessel; and the river-god. Our Lord stands up to the waist in the waters of the Jordan, with the nimbus and Holy Dove over his head. John's right hand holds the 'ampulla,' or anointing cup, over Christ's head, but his left hand grasps a jeweled cross. His left knee is bent forward and sustains what looks like a cruet or flask, in shape much like the Oriental bottle made of skin. This object partly obscuring John's knee, the cross and Christ's right arm, suggest the source from whence he has drawn the oil for the anointing. This however, only provided it is not a defect in the mosaic, which is possible. Garruci names no blemish here in his description of the picture, while he speaks of one in the lettering 'Iord,' which was originally 'Iordann.' This medallion realistically confines the subject to the immersion of Jesus in the sacred river; but the artist adds the symbols in harmony with the practice of baptism in his own times. Lundy's comment is, that John 'applies the *unction* with a small shell.' [4]

NO. 10.—MOSAIC, FROM BAPTISTERY OF ST. JOHN, RAVENNA.

At what time the custom of anointing the baptized with oil originated is not known. Jortin thinks that it was unknown to Justin Martyr, A. D. 103–168, as he does not hint at it in describing the rite of baptism. But Justin refers to it in another place, saying: 'If Mary anointed the Lord with myrrh before his burial, and we celebrate the symbols of his sufferings and resurrection in baptism, how is it that we first, indeed, anoint with oil, and then celebrating the aforesaid symbols in the pool, afterward anoint with myrrh?'[5] The general custom of anointing in baptism probably came in a little later, when the wealthy began to embrace Christianity, for Tertullian says much of this unction. We may see the reason for its adoption, for every-where in the Roman Empire the free use of oil was deemed necessary to the completion of a common bath. The Christians found many fanciful reasons for the introduction of this practice in baptism. God anointed Jesus with the Holy Spirit at his baptism—the very name 'Christ' signifies the anointed; Mary anointed his body before his burial, with much more in that line; and so according to the best authorities they gave many reasons for this 'chrism,' as they called it, both before and after baptism. Anointing betokened prosperity and happiness, and so they likened the Spirit to oil and his grace to unction; and after baptism they poured olive oil upon the head, thus, as they said, anointing their converts with the 'oil of gladness above their fellows,' in token of their consecration to a holy life. Tertullian writes:

'We are, acccording to ancient custom, thoroughly anointed with a blessed unction, as the priests were wont to be anointed with oil from a horn. And the unction running down our flesh profits us spiritually in the same way as the act of baptism, itself carnal, because we are plunged in water, has a spiritual effect in delivering us from our sins. Then the hand is laid on us, inviting the Holy Spirit, through the words of benediction, and over our cleansed and blessed bodies, freely descends from the Father that most Holy Spirit.'[6]

They found many other reasons for this practice. In the Grecian games, the wrestlers and runners anointed themselves plentifully before they began their contests. When their frame and joints were pervaded with oil, it was supposed to give them a quick agility of action and an easy grace of movement, and so added to their chances of success. As Paul referred to the laws of these contests, 'so run I, so fight I,' they borrowed a figure from the same, and applied it to the Christian athlete, when beginning his race and combat in baptism. Ambrose, of Cahors, the supposed author of 'De Sacramentis,' says to the immersed: 'Thou didst enter. . . . Thou was anointed as the athlete of Christ.'[7] Dr. Cave, quoting Cyril, remarks:

'They were cut off from the wild olive and were engrafted into Christ, the true olive-tree, and made partakers of his fruits and benefits, or else to show that now they were become champions for Christ and had entered upon a state of conflict, wherein they must strive and contend with all the snares of the world, as the athlete of old were anointed against their solemn games, that they might be more expedite, and that their antagonists might take less hold upon them. Or rather, probably, to denote their being admitted to the great privileges of Christianity, a chosen generation, a royal priesthood, a holy nation (as the Apostle styles Christians), offices of which anointing was an ancient symbol, both of being designated to them and interested in them; and this account Tertullian favors, he tells us 'tis derived from the ancient, that is, Jewish discipline, where the priests were wont to be anointed for the priesthood : for some such purpose they thought it fit that a Christian should be anointed as a spiritual king and priest, and that no time was more proper for it than at his baptism, when the name of Christ was confessed upon him.'[8]

This unction figured largely in the ecclesiastical controversies and legislation of after centuries; and as early as the fourth, a contest arose whether it should precede or follow baptism. Tertullian's statements show that it followed baptism, and most of the Fathers contended lustily for the same order, Augustine being amongst the most earnest. Bunsen says that 'The unction followed immediately after the immersion.' This question fanned the love for anointing into a mania, until Rabanus, Archbishop of Mentz, A. D. 788–856, actually exalted it into a separate 'sacrament.' He did this by doubling each ordinance; and so he called the bread and wine two, and the 'chrisma' another, apart from the immersion; four in all.[9] Dr. Cave, citing Cyril again, says (p. 324) that the person baptized:

' " Was anointed the second time, as S. Cyril tells us; and, indeed, whatever becomes of the unction that was before, 'tis certain that that which Tertullian speaks of as a part of the ancient discipline, was after the person was baptized." The anointing took place both before and after the immersion; and the whole service was finished by binding a white linen cloth, called the "*chrismale*," around the head of the immersed, to retain the oil upon the head for a week afterward.'[10]

The author of the Ursian Mosaic evidently wished to portray the anointing of Jesus in connection with his baptism; but unable to depict the invisible unction of the Holy Spirit, he meets the necessity by putting the ordinary baptismal unction into the hand of John. It entered not his mind to emit a stream from the beak of a dove, so the best agent that his art could supply was the anointing cup in John's hand. Hence he is pouring on the oil above the nimbus and beneath the head of the Dove, to indicate his authority from God to place his hand between the second and the third persons in the Trinity, to the honor of God's anointed Son. This act directly connects the artist's conception of the river-god with the effect of the anointing. When he did this work the universal teaching was that great virtue lodged in the baptismal oil, in fact, that it was miracle-working in its effects. Cyril, of Jerusalem, tells us that the holy oil in baptism destroyed all traces of sin and drove out the evil one; and Pacian insists that 'the baptismal water washes away sin, the chrism gives the Holy Spirit, and so the regeneration is complete.'[11] Not the least of these effects is seen in expelling all demons and evil spirits from the water by the oil. In conformity with this idea, the artist has introduced the emblematic figure of the river-god, according to the ancient form. He has ascended from the stream, with a leafy calamus or reed in his hand and a wreath on his brow, in token of dominion over that river. He is alarmed, is looking away from the holy anointing and bends forward, as if making for the shore to depart from a scene of such sanctity. No. 11 gives us an ancient Roman bath, as is seen by the elegant heathen bass-relief upon it, which had been consecrated to Christian use by placing upon the oil pedestal an image of John the Baptist, who is invoked to serve as its patron saint.

In the baptistery known as that of Constantine, adjoining the Church of St. John of Lateran, at Rome, special provision was made for this service of unction. The circular basin of this building is three feet deep and twenty-five in diameter. Both Anastasius and Damasus, in their lives of Sylvester, say that in their time it was lined within and without by 3,008 pounds weight of silver; and 'in the middle of the basin stood a column of porphyry, bearing on its top a golden phial full of ointment,' to be poured upon the heads of the newly-immersed

NO. 11.—OLD BAPTISMAL FONT, ST JOHN ON THE PEDESTAL.

ones. Hence the mosaic under consideration steps forth to confirm the literature of many centuries, which in its turn reflects light back upon Christian archæology. The attempt, then, to force this picture into the service of modern affusion does the greatest possible violence to all the circumstances of the case, and to the unbroken testimony of the ages. In the absence of color in a piece of sculpture or painting where liquid is poured forth, the circumstances and positive testimony taken together must determine what that liquid is. And in all these cases these pictures unite in showing it to be oil and not water. Common sense alone suggests, nay, even common decency, that no one would take another to a stream of water, strip him naked and lead him down into it up to the waist, for the purpose of pouring water on the head from the hand or a shell or a vessel, either before or after the honest immersion of that head in the same element, much less without such immersion at all. At any rate, those who pour water on the head now and call it baptism are extremely careful not to go through such a series of useless acts to reach that end. If the primitive Christians did, they were not so wise as the moderns. But when they tell us that oil was poured upon the head in baptism, 'as the priests were wont to be anointed with oil from a horn,' as Tertullian expresses it, we cannot only see the reason for all these steps, but for their full expression in ancient Christian art.

This absurd claim renders itself simply ridiculous, in the attempt to show that because clinics or sick persons in bed had water poured upon them, which act passed for baptism, any example of this can establish a universal rule. Jesus was not a clinic at any time, much less when John baptized him; nor were clinics taken to the Jordan and placed in its waters up to the waist, that a cup of water might be poured upon their heads. This picture treats of the baptism of Jesus; and it was just as natural that the painter should invoke the use of oil, the universal custom of his day amongst Christians in baptism, to represent the anointing of the Holy Spirit, as that he should use the cross, the flask and the river-god. But what sane artist would think of making John lead our Redeemer nude into the Jordan to pour a cup of water on his head? He would be deemed as fit for the lunatic asylum as the coming painter who shall represent a current infant baptism in this year of grace 1886 by drawing John in the Jordan with a naked babe in his arms, dropping a particle of water on its brow from a cup, with a flask of water on his shoulder.

No. 12 is found in the dome of the Arian baptistery at Ravenna, and is known as St. Maria in Cosmedin. It is given by Father Garrucci and bears date a century later than figure 10, namely, A. D. 553. Here again, our Redeemer is presented above the loins in the waters of the Jordan; which river is made a winding trench, with a typical resemblance to the actual course of that sacred stream, as if the artist had visited the spot. The Holy Dove has descended directly above the head of Christ and hovers there, emitting a stream of unction from his beak which actually unites him with the person of our Lord. The Baptist is clothed in a camel's skin, holding a bent reed in his left hand, while his right rests upon Christ's head.

NO. 12.—MOSAIC, ARIAN BAPTISTERY, RAVENNA.

At the right of Jesus is the river-god again, a seated figure with long hair and horns; instead of the wreath on his head we have the leafy calamus in his hand to indicate his royalty; his lower limbs are wrapped in an ample robe and an urn stands at his side. Abbé Crossnier points to the horns and urn as emblems of his deity; and his left hand raised in astonishment seems to express wonder and alarm for the holiness of the scene, but especially has the heavenly unction startled him. Here we see what a century had done for the mosaic art. By this time the later artist had devised a better method of symbolical representation, so that he disposes entirely of John's intervening cup between the Spirit and the Son, to express the anointing; and brings the Dove and the Lord into immediate union by a realistic flood from the mouth of the Dove, to set forth the divine unction. This is in exact accord with what

Smith says of another ancient practice. In article 'Dove' he observes: 'A golden or silver dove was often suspended above the font in early times. These sometimes contained the anointing oil used in baptism.' . . . 'Doves of the precious metals, emblematic of the Holy Spirit, were also suspended above the font in early churches.' . . . 'One of the charges brought against Severus by the clergy of Antioch at the Council of Constantinople, A. D. 536, was that he removed and appropriated to his own use the gold and silver doves hanging over the sacred fonts.'[12] But the ampulla was more frequently in other shapes than that of the dove.

With all these facts staring us in the face, men have the temerity to tell us that in one of these mosaics John is pouring out water on the head of Jesus, and in the other the Holy Dove is pouring out—well, they do not exactly know what, but something that teaches the doctrine of affusion in Christian baptism! What do they mean by this? Do they mean any thing, soberly and definitely? Can they mean that the artists in these mosaics intended to teach that the water baptism of John administered to Jesus was incomplete, until the Baptist in the first case and the Spirit in the second superadded a water affusion likewise? Will they give us one example, in the Bible or out of it, in which it has ever entered the mind of man that the Holy Dove has poured water upon any man to complete his water baptism or to supersede his immersion? Certainly not. But this artist clearly did intend, by a too literal and realistic manner, to attempt the reduction of an invisible anointing of Jesus of Nazareth to the physical eye, and hence this stream from the mouth of the dove. The design in both cases is unmistakable. In the Ursian Mosaic the oil descends from John's vessel to depict an anointing of the Spirit by the use of oil without a stream from the Dove, and in the Arian Mosaic the Dove gives forth his own anointing essence; consequently the literal oil is dispensed with, showing that in both cases unction is set forth and not water. If the reader will examine No. 8, he will see that the artist of the Pentecostal scene, intended to present Mary as receiving the Spirit's anointing in the same way precisely. The divided flame rests upon her head as upon each of the Apostles, but in addition the Dove emits a stream from his beak, exactly like that in the Arian Mosaic. Did the artist intend to convey the thought that the Spirit was aspersing Mary with water in baptism? And yet there is the same reason for saying this, that there is for saying that the Arian artist intended the mosaic to carry the idea that the Holy Spirit emitted a stream of water upon her Son in baptism. No, we say with Lundy, in his 'Monumental Christianity:' 'The Dove is pouring down the Divine afflatus from his beak on the head of our Lord.'

No. 13 is a fragment of glass from a broken cup found in the Esquiline, and known by the name on its face. It depicts a newly baptized girl. Those who have examined it say that when held to the light its transparency reveals her figure, with her knee raised and bent and her right arm extended, as if preparing to leave the baptistery. A priest with a halo around his head stands at her side, in a priestly robe. Directly above her is an inverted globular vessel, universally known in ecclesiastical parlance as the 'ampulla.' It is hung in a garland and a liquid flows copiously from it upon the girl's head. This vessel takes this name, says 'Smith's Dictionary of Christian Antiquities' (Art. 'Ampulla'), 'probably from its swelling out in every direction' .... 'A globular vessel for holding liquid;' in fact, the very vessel used in the old Roman bath and at the ancient baptistery for the purpose of anointing. A hand rests upon the girl's head, and a dove hovers above her bearing a branch of seven stems, to indicate the seven graces of the Spirit which are now hers; the dove itself being a messenger of peace, as in the Saviour's baptism (see No. 4). Every item in this frag-

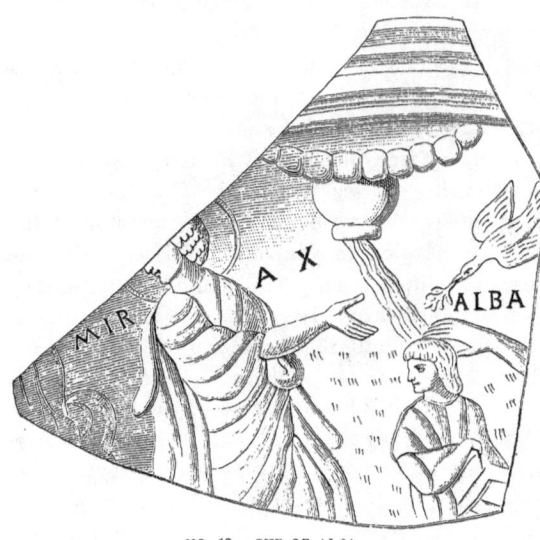

NO. 13.—CUP OF ALBA.

ment is full of symbol. The white clothing indicates the girl's future purity, chastity and faith; the ampulla is hung in a garland to denote that the occasion of the baptism is festive; it hangs near the bright, opening heavens without visible support; the dove is descending to show that she is a favorite, 'beloved' of God; and she stands in the deep water to denote her immersion. We are chiefly concerned, however, with the inverted ampulla, its contents and their use in ancient baptism. The accompanying cut, No. 14, is taken from the article 'Bath' ('Encyc. Britannica'), and is the same vessel found in the cup of Alba. It was in common use amongst the ancient Christians at the altar, for it contained the wine as well as the oil. When John III. ordered the Lateran Church at Rome to supply altar-plate for the Oratory of the Martyrs, with other pieces, he required the ampulla. Yet as 'Smith's Dictionary' says:

NO. 14. THE AMPULLA.

'More commonly the word denotes a vessel used for holding consecrated oil or chrism. Optatus Milevitanus tells us that an "ampulla chrismatis," thrown from a window by the Donatists, remained unbroken. . . . By far the most renowned ampulla of this kind is that which is said to have been brought by a dove from heaven at the baptism of Clovis, and which was used at the coronation of the Frank kings. Hincmar, in the service which he drew up for Charles the Bold (840), speaks of this heaven-descended chrism whence that which he himself used was derived, as if of a thing well-known. Flodoard (10th century) tells us that at the baptism of Clovis, the clerk who bore the chrism was prevented by the crowd from reaching his proper station; and that when the moment for unction arrived, St. Remi raised his eyes to heaven and prayed, when a white dove suddenly flew upon the rostrum, bearing an ampulla filled with chrism from heaven.'[13]

This vessel was often of gold, silver or other metal, and was hung over the font as well as the altar, as in this Cup of Alba. The knowledge of these facts sets aside the unnatural and forced notion, that the ancient Christians took candidates into deep water for the purpose of pouring a little on their heads in lieu of immersion; and that against their own testimony to the contrary for thirteen hundred years. With this glass fragment before his eyes, a man's common sense should tell him that no necessity could call for hanging an inverted vase in this style over the head of a baptized person in order to pour from it a little water on the head, while she stands in very deep water, and the baptizing priest stands at her side empty-handed. His dress and nimbus show him to be a sacred person, while his attitude and outstretched hand express reverence at this falling unction. We have, indeed, records of Church theatricals in the Dark Ages, but few are so ridiculous as this perfusion would be. Such a play would not be good pantomime, but the most senseless of dumb shows, and withal very full of machinery. While unction was no part of baptism as Christ ordained it, but was, as Bingham says, 'an appendage to baptism,' yet it came to be regarded as an essential part of baptism; and the author of the 'Constitutions' insists that the anointing must be had with oil, or ointment, in order to participation in the Holy Spirit, on the part of the immersed.

A word must be added, as to the laying on of the hand in all these pictures. The imposition of the hand is as old as the race, its significance resting on the purpose—that of healing, mediation, investiture in office or blessing. Here it relates to immersion, and of this one act it is symbolic. Generally these pictures present their finished subject, without the order in which one act consecutively followed another in making up the whole. The several parts are to be taken in their natural succession, as the painter has given us his finished ideal. In no other way could he give his subject in repose. He cannot well give it at an unfinished stage of the baptism, as at the moment of burial or when buried or when rising. Therefore, the hand is laid on the head either before the candidate is bowed forward for immersion or when it is raised afterward. In these pictures we have both. Tertullian's remark clears up the whole matter. He says: 'A man having been let down in water and dipped between a few words rises again. . . . Then the hand is laid on us, invoking and inviting the Holy Spirit through the Benediction.'[14]

The accompanying cuts give additional force to this fact. That from St. Mark's, No. 15, is unmistakable, and is evidently intended to give the whole significance of our baptism as well as the facts of our Lord's baptism. We have John's ax laid at the root of the trees, and the generation of Christ's immersed followers represented by the fish and the new-born convert with him in the waters; both symbolical of the newly born to God, whatever their actual age. A man of eighty just brought to Christ is what Paul calls a 'new-born babe;' and in the person of a convert in the water, at the foot of the angel who is about to cover him with a robe, we have precisely the idea of Tertullian: 'We smaller fishes, after the example of our Fish, are *born* in the waters.' No. 16 is found on the northern gate of the Baptistery of Parma, a bass-relief sculpture intended to represent the baptism of Christ, as is seen by the nimbus around the head of the immersed. The waters of the Jordan are thrown up into a heap, after the style of art in the Middle Ages, this picture being attributed to the thirteenth century.

NO. 15.—MOSAIC OF 7TH CENT., ST. MARK'S, ROME.

NO. 16.—BAPTISM IN 13TH CENTURY.

In seven out of the eight pictures used here, where the baptized are standing in the water, the hand of the baptizer is laid upon the head; the only exception being that of St. John, Ravenna, where John is anointing our Lord. Even in the Arian Mosaic, where the Dove is anointing Christ, John's hand is laid on his head to indicate the finished immersion. But the highest authorities on these works of Christian art tell us, that the hand on the head of the person in the water is the sign of immersion. Beltrasni, of Ravenna, says of John's hand on Christ's head in the Arian Mosaic: 'The priest placed his hand fully upon the head of the candidate while in the water; and thus by three immersions and rapid emersions the baptism was complete.'[15] Bottari states that 'The hand is placed on the head to indicate immersion.'[16] The 'Apostolic Constitutions' require 'The priest to lay his hand upon the head of the candidate, dipping him three times.' Garrucci in his history of 'Christian Art' says: 'That the laying on of the hand was customary and of special moment in immersion.'[17] Cardinal Colonna writes: 'The Catechumens, without clothing, descended into the water of the baptistery, and were there immersed three times; the priest accompanying the act with his hand, and invoking at each immersion the name of one of the persons of the Holy Trinity.'[18] And De Rossi warns us that 'We ought not to confound the imposition of the right hand with which the ministrant accompanies the immersion of the candidate with what the bishop does in the case of the neophyte, as he emerges from the water, and is clothed in white at the confirmation.' [19] Thus, these and other adepts, not one of them Baptists, bring daylight from the Catacombs, bearing voluntary and unbiased witness against their own practice as aspersionists.

There are many more early pictures of baptism besides these, amongst them a notable one of a king and queen in a baptistery, each wearing a royal crown, supposed to represent their majesties of Lombardy, immersed about A. D. 590. All, however, bear the same line of interpretation, and all the reliable authorities declare that their interpretation is found in immersion. Then these two things are quite as remarkable in confirmation of its correctness, namely : 1. That in none of the Catacomb pictures is John found pouring any thing on Christ's head, as his anointing was ascribed to God directly. We have the earliest instance of this in the Ravennian Mosaic of A. D. 450, when oil was universally used upon the baptized. 2. We have no case in the Catacombs of any one dipping a babe in water, or of one holding a babe in the arms, pouring or sprinkling water upon him. All are adults, and all are standing their full height in the water ; while we have many inscriptions to deceased infants and some pictures of children, amongst them that of Jesus blessing children, given in this work. But in no case is there the least sign of water in connection with them suggesting baptism. Even where our Lord blesses the child, they both stand on dry land, the little one at his side. This silence, under all the circumstances, is suggestive without the weight of historical testimony ; and as a negative, it hints broadly in confirmation of its opposite positive.

It is believed that while the foregoing suggestions are not intended to be interpretations of the pictures given, they are in harmony with the teaching and practice of the earlier centuries, as their literature shows abundantly. That this teaching and practice varied from New Testament injunction and example is not to the point. The crude and even ridiculous notions embodied in these pictures were seriously entertained by those who executed them, and they all go to show that the practice of those ages was in harmony with that of the Baptists of our own times, in so far as that the radical idea of baptism was that of the burial of the body in water. None of the archæologists, historians or interpreters here cited are Baptists, but chiefly they are Catholics and antiquarians of great note, who have given the result of their researches simply as antiquarians and not as biblical critics or theologians. Their testimony bears every mark of candor and is entitled to great weight.

BRESCIA.

CHAPTER IX.

THE TWELFTH CENTURY.

THIS was the iron age, in which the Church slept her iron sleep. Yet it was a cardinal era, as when the first spike of light darts across an arctic sky to break the night and herald the revolutionary day. Stagnation awoke the soul of the age by its very oppression, and it half resolved to be free. The Crusades had opened the sluices of vice, ecclesiasticism sat drunk on the throne of night, and the Archbishop of Narbonne said that 'St. Peter's boat was sinking.' At this moment Abelard caught the breaking dawn. He represented the free thought which the Crusaders had brought back with them, and helped to loosen the bands of tradition by pointing out the contradictions of the Fathers; ridiculing the current notion that Christ's death was a ransom paid to the devil, and warmly rebuking immorality in peasant, priest, prelate and prince. Admiring youth thronged the presence of this brilliant philosopher, whether in the wilderness of Troyes or the University of Paris. His severity and originality stirred the opposition of the dull, the narrow-minded and the vile, and Bernard accused him of heresy. Bernard himself bewailed the depravity of the priests, but still was a captive to the superstitions of the age. Some of the popes honestly sought to reform the Catholic Church, while Gregory VII. abolished the sale of holy offices and checked concubinage in the clergy.

Another new idea of the times was to encourage the rise of great cities. They became independent friends of light and supported better government. Those of Northern Italy and Southern France drew to them various Oriental sects, many of them 'pure' men, compared with those generally seen; prominent amongst these were Catharists from Bulgaria and Thrace. These strangers brought with them many false doctrines, but they rejected popular vices, the authority of pope and bishop, and studied the New Testament. The fairest civilization of the Middle Ages arose where they flourished. In a certain and important sense Abelard, Bernard and Gregory, with the Crusaders and Cathari, all worked together. And contrary to popular supposition, Tanchelyn was helping them by preaching in the streets of Antwerp and Utrecht, while Peter of Bruis was drawing men to Christ between the Rhone and the Alps. These two were as heartily hated by the priests as they were beloved by the people, and such was the influence of the man of God in Holland that for twelve years the mass had not been celebrated in many places where he preached. Tanchelyn went to Rome with much the same result as Luther, four centuries later. On his return he was imprisoned at Cologne by order of the archbishop, but by the aid of a smith, a disciple, he escaped. Afterward he was slain by a treacherous priest. He held that the Bible is the only guide, Christ the only head of the Church, with no mass and no infant baptism. These doctrines survived him, were preached by his successor, Everwacher, and the after susceptibility of the Netherlands to Baptist principles has some connection with his early sowing. The several sects of the Cathari hold a close affinity to our subject, and we must now present a cursory view of this interesting people.

The CATHARI ('the pure') have been the subjects of much confusion in ecclesiastical history, largely in consequence of classing many and widely different sects under that general name, both amongst ancient and modern writers, whether Catholic or Protestant. The latter have been too ready to hail all dissidents from Rome by that name as welcome simply because they were dissenters, the Catholics as cheerfully consigning all these to anathema for the same reason, with but little distinction. In truth, with few exceptions, all have dealt in this wholesale distribution, instead of examining each sect and candidly assigning it to its true place in the long list of sects, which have been so designated. For the purposes of general description, Schmidt designates the Cathari as 'a dualistic sect which originated in Eastern Europe, independently of the Manichæans and Paulicians, but from the same source—an intermingling of European and Asiatic ideas.' He thinks that they originated in Bulgaria, from whence they spread into Thrace, where they were known as Bogomiles, then into Dalmatia and Slavonia, till merchants brought the heresy to Italy, and the Crusaders to France; and so Flanders, Sicily and other countries became thoroughly infected therewith. But the sects into which the Cathari soon split became almost too numerous to mention here, each one of them retaining more or less of the original leaven; but some being popularly so known while they had nothing whatever in common with the original system, which was very pernicious. To call them all Cathari in that sense, therefore, is a simple slander pinned upon them by their foes.

The generally received opinions amongst them were far enough removed from the Gospel, running all the way from absolute dualism, with its fantastic mythology and its wild fancy, up to a semi-gospel standard of morality and even spirituality, if intense asceticism can be so called. They were decidedly anticlerical, and yet their organization was strictly aristocratic, having one order of teaching for the masses and another for the privileged; all being known respectively as '*auditores*,' '*credentes*' and '*electi*.' Their views of Christ led them to deny his incarnation and resurrection; they denied the necessity of baptism proper, substituting for it the imposition of hands, which they held to be the true spiritual baptism; they also refused to eat all kinds of procreated food, and discouraged, if they did not disallow, marriage. But at the same time they considered relics, images, crosses and even material sanctuaries as odious and the work of Satan, because men had come to adore them.

The BOGOMILES were a branch of the Cathari. Herzog thinks that they took their name from a Bulgarian Bishop of the tenth century, that they were an offshoot from the Paulicians, and says that they abounded in the Bulgarian city of Philippopolis. They were condemned as heretics and suffered great persecution. Basil, one of their leaders, was burnt in Constantinople in 1118, before the gates of St. Sophia. The Paulicians of Bulgaria furnished the Cathari of Southern France. Gibbon thinks that they found their way there either by passing up the Danube into Germany or through Venice in the channels of commerce, or through the imperial garrisons sent by the Greek Emperor into Italy. But come as they might, we find them at Orleans A. D. 1025, in the Netherlands 1035 and in Turin 1051. About half a century later banishment from their own country drove them in great numbers to the west, and they appeared plentifully at Treves and Soissons, in Champagne and Flanders. Their teachings soon attracted the attention of the priests, the peasantry, and even the nobles. Their followers became so numerous as to demand condemnation by the Council of Toulouse, 1119, and that of Tours, 1163. But despite excommunications and curses, they so grew that in 1167 they held a council of their own and openly formulated their faith and ecclesiastical order, which they stoutly held, against both the Roman hierarchy and the secular power for almost a century. Another branch of the Cathari is found in

The ALBIGENSES. They arose in Southern France early in the eleventh century and were first known as Publicani; but at last took their name from the city of Albi, the center of the Albigeois district. They were first called Albigenses by Stephen Borbone, 1225. It is difficult to get at their exact tenets and practices, but they were generally numbered with the Cathari, and had many things in common with other sects so known. They rejected the Romish Church, and esteemed the New Testament above all its traditions and ceremonies. They did not take oaths, nor believe in baptismal regeneration; but they were ascetic and pure in their lives; they also exalted celibacy. They increased so rapidly that they drove the Catholic priests from their churches, of which they took possession, forming schools and congregations of their own. They made the Catholic Church an object of contempt, the nobility heading the movement, and they also formed their own synod; four different Catholic Councils condemned them, but all to no purpose. Bernard tried to reclaim them, and various disputations were had with them; but in 1180 Cardinal Henry commenced a crusade against them with the sword. Much carnage followed. One crusade succeeded another. Innocent III. offered the prelates and nobles all the blessings of the Church for the use of their sword and the possessions of the heretics as an additional reward. Their own prince, Count Raymond VI., was compelled to slaughter his subjects, and the pope summoned the King of Northern France with all his nobles to the same bloody work. Half a million of men were gathered, four Archbishops joined the invaders with twelve Bishops and countless nobles. Towns were sacked, seven castles surrendered to the pope, and five hundred villages, cities and fortresses fell.

Barons, knights, counts and soldiery flocked like eagles to the prey from all directions. Their superstition was fed by the promise of two years' remission of penance, and all the indulgences granted to the invaders of the Holy Sepulcher; and their cupidity was fired by the tender of the goods and lands of the heretics, as well as the right to reduce them to Mohammedan slavery. They followed the lead of Arnaud, the legate of the Holy See, bearing the cross and pilgrims' staves, from the adjacent countries, French, German, Flemish, Norman. They first attacked Beziers, which was strongly fortified and garrisoned; but it was taken by storm and thirty thousand were slain. Seven thousand had taken refuge in the Church of St. Magdalene, and the monk Peter tells us with the most ferocious coldness that they 'killed women and children, old men, young men, priests, all without distinction.' There were many Catholics in the town, and the 'Holy Legate' was asked how these should be spared, when he commanded: 'Kill them all, God will know his own!' Lest a heretic should escape they piled all in an indiscriminate heap, and the Chronicle of St. Denis gives the whole number as sixty thousand. After Beziers had fallen, July 22, 1209, Carcassone was invested. There Count Roger, the nephew of Raymond, was inveigled under the pretense of safe-conduct and a treating for peace out of the city into the enemies' camp and by treachery was made a prisoner as a heretic. When his men found their captain gone they retreated by a private passage, the great city fell, and its captain died in a dungeon, as the pope expresses it, 'miserably slain at the last.' The French barons agreed that any fortress which refused to surrender on demand, but resisted, should when captured find every man put to the sword in cold blood by the cross-bearers, that horror might appall every heart in the land. Their own historian says: 'They could not have dealt worse with them than they did; they massacred them all, even those who had taken refuge in the cathedral; nothing could save them, nor cross, nor crucifix, nor altars. The scoundrels killed the priests, the women, the infants, not one, I believe, escaped.' Eight hundred nobles were either hanged or hewn to pieces, and four hundred heretics were burnt in one pile.

The story of this murdered people for about half a century is heart-sickening in the extreme. They held many errors of the head, but no prince ever ruled over grander subjects. They were far advanced in refinement, and were high-toned in morality. Their record is the brightest, briefest and bloodiest in the annals of pious, persecuting deviltry. It begins in the middle of the twelfth century, and was blotted out before the middle of the thirteenth. It is a short, swift stream of gore mingling with their mountain torrents, but more romantic than their Alps. If the eternal snow and ice had not turned these eternally pale, the frozen steel of St. Dominic had chilled them forever, when the pravity of his infernal machine made them witnesses of a rushing destruction, without parallel in human villainy.

Amongst the Cathari, however, we find a BAPTIST BODY at Cologne and Bonn. Whence they came we are not informed; but they appeared in 1146, and Evervine gives a full account of them in writing to Bernard, of whom he seeks aid in their suppression. He says that they had been recently discovered, and that two of them had openly opposed the Catholic clergy and laity in their assembly; the archbishop and nobles being present. The 'heretics' asked for a day of disputation, when re-enforced by certain of their number they would maintain their doctrines from Christ and the Apostles; and unless they were properly answered they would rather die than give up their principles. Upon this they were seized and burnt to death. Evervin expresses his astonishment that they endured the torment of the stake not only with patience, but with joy; and asks how these members of Satan could suffer with such constancy and courage as were seldom found amongst the most godly. He then describes their heresy.

They professed to be the true Church, because they followed Christ and patterned after the Apostles; they sought no secular gain or earthly property, but were the poor in Christ, while the Roman Church made itself rich. They accounted themselves as sheep amongst wolves, fleeing from city to city, enduring persecution with the ancient martyrs, although they were living laborious, holy and self-denying lives. They charged their persecutors with being false apostles, with adulterating the word of God, with self-seeking, and the pope with corrupting the Apostle Peter's chair. He says: 'They do not hold the baptism of infants, alleging that passage of the Gospel, "He that believeth and is baptized shall be saved."' They rejected the intercession of saints, and they called all observances in the Church which Christ had not established superstitions. They denied the doctrine of purgatorial fire after death, and believed that when men die they go immediately to heaven or to hell. He therefore beseeches the 'holy father' to direct his pen against 'these wild beasts,' and to help him to 'resist these monsters.' He then says, some of them 'Tell us that they had great numbers of their persuasion scattered almost every-where, and that amongst them were many of our clergy and monks. And as for those who were burnt, they in the defense they made for themselves told us that this heresy had been concealed from the time of the martyrs—and that it had existed in Greece and other countries.' All this he evidently believed. But Manichæism had not been 'concealed from the time of the martyrs;' for his predecessors had openly contended with it every-where. This heresy was a discovery of another sort to the provost of Steinfeld.

This letter aroused Bernard, who opened his batteries upon the 'wild beasts' in his 'Sermons on Solomon's Song.' He is especially bitter toward them because they despised infant baptism; is virulent because they refused to take oaths and observed secrecy in their Christian rites; and lays several serious things to their charge, although he professes to know but little about them. And then his little knowledge of them obliges him to bless whom he would fain curse; for he says: 'If you ask them of their faith, nothing can be more Christian; if you observe their conversation, nothing can be more blameless; and what they speak they prove by deeds. You may see a man for the testimony of his faith frequent the church, honor the elders, offer his gift, make his confession, receive the sacrament. What more like a Christian? As to life and manners, he circumvents no man, over-reaches no man, and does violence to no man. He fasts much and eats not the bread of idleness, but works with his hands for his support. The whole body, indeed, are rustic and illiterate, and all whom I have known of this sect are very ignorant.' And so he 'marveled,' as others in the Apostolic times had at the same things.

'This sect,' says Herzog, 'lived on in the regions along the Rhine, especially in Cologne and Bonn.' But it was terribly persecuted. . . . In 1163 several of them were burnt, after the Canon Echbert had tried in vain to convert them. This monk was sent to preach to death all who had escaped the stake. His sermons survive to this day, and in their dedication to Reginald Archbishop of Cologne he rehearses his disputes with 'these monsters,' and tells many things which he had learned about them, in part by torture and the threat of death. But his statements do not hold together. He evinces confusion, if not bewilderment, in his attempt to understand their tenets. Like most of the Catholic witnesses, he fell into the temptation of tracing this particular heresy to some of the old and proscribed 'heretics,' which carried disgrace with it, and so challenged the hatred of men and covered the new 'heretics' with obloquy. Hence, in his thirteen sermons, he labors hard to fasten upon them the faith and practices of the Manichæans; for with most of his brethren, he was afflicted with Manichæism on the brain whenever he scented heresy. He construes their observance of the Supper into a 'mere evasion,' and takes the word of an apostate from them, who says that they denied the birth of Christ, his proper human flesh and his real death and resurrection; teaching that all these were but a simulation. He would have us believe that they renounced water baptism altogether, substituting therefor the Consolamentum; and then takes particular pains to tell us that their principal reason for denying baptism to infants, was found in their incapacity to receive it, and so, that it should be deferred till they came to the exercise of faith. He adds, that they were divided into several sects, yet he classes them all with Cathari, 'a sort of people' whom he pronounces 'very pernicious to the Catholic faith, which, like moths, they corrupt and destroy.' Gieseler shows that they rejected infant baptism, because baptism should be administered only to believers.[1] This zealous monk betrays the entire animus of his denunciation of these Cologne Baptists, when he says of them that they sustained their positions by the authority of Scripture. 'They are armed with the words of the Holy Scripture which in any way seem to favor their sentiments, and with those who know how to defend

A FANATICAL MONK PREACHING.

their errors, and to oppose the Catholic truth; though in reality they are wholly ignorant of the true meaning couched in those words, and which cannot be discovered without great judgment.'

In 1231 Konrad of Marburg, a fanatical Dominican monk, led a terrible persecution against this sect, and little is heard of them in Germany afterward. It is very likely that the band of thirty martyrs, of whom Milner, Dr. Henry and William of Newbury speak, were of this body. They tell us that in 1159 thirty men and women who spoke German reached England, and for their religious principles and practices were arraigned before a Council of clergy at Oxford. They were found guilty of incorrigible heresy, and Henry II. ordered their foreheads branded with a red-hot iron; they were to be whipped through the streets of the city, their clothes to be cut off at their girdles, and then to be turned into the open fields, all persons being forbidden to give them shelter or relief. This was in the depth of winter, and every one of them perished with hunger and cold. These appear to have been the first heretics deliberately murdered in England, for what Newbury calls 'detesting holy baptism' as practiced by Rome. The dates and general facts suggest these as the victims of German persecution, for Echbert says of the Cologne Baptists: 'They are increased in great multitudes throughout all countries, to the great danger of the Church, for their words eat like a canker, and, like a flying leprosy, run every way, infecting the precious members of Christ. These in our Germany we call Cathari; in Flanders they call them Piphles; in French, Tisserands, from the art of weaving, because numbers of them are of that occupation.'

The term Cathari has also been applied to another thoroughly Baptist sect, which arose in the very dawn of the century: the PETROBRUSIANS. Their leader was the great reformer, Peter of Bruis. In order to prevent confusion, it may be well here to define what is meant by the term 'Baptist,' when used to characterize one of these historical bodies. A Pedobaptist is one who baptizes babes. An Antipedobaptist is one who rejects the baptism of babes. But this does not of necessity make him a Baptist; for the Paulicians, Cathari, Albigenses, and in fact the modern Quakers, all cast infant baptism aside, but administered no baptism at all. Hence all these have rejected the baptism of babes as a matter of course, but we cannot, for that reason, number them with Baptists. An 'Anabaptist' is one who baptizes again for any reason. The Novatians and Donatists were 'Anabaptists,' and reimmersed those who came to them from the Catholics. At the same time the Catholics were 'Anabaptists,' when they reimmersed those who came to them from what they called the heretical bodies. They were therefore Pedobaptists and 'Anabaptists' at the same time. But a Baptist proper, in modern parlance, is one who rejects the baptism of babes under all circumstances, and who immerses none but those who personally confess Christ under any circumstances; and those who are thus properly immersed upon their faith in Christ, we have a right to claim in history as Baptists to that extent, but no further.

For this reason we cannot honestly claim several of the Cathari sects as Baptists, simply because volumes might be filled with reliable evidence to show that they hated infant baptism with downright hatred. They opposed it with all their might and even ridiculed it as an unmeaning ceremony, which they classed with images, prayer for the dead, purgatory and such other gear. Often, indeed, they were obliged to have their babes immersed by the Roman priests, because the civil as well as the ecclesiastical law of the land in which they lived laid them under grievous penalties for refusing. But as a moral institution they treated it with contempt, as thousands who are not Baptists now do. Yet what were their views of the immersion of believers in water? Many of them knew but little about it; they had never seen a believer immersed. The baptism of babes enforced by the civil power had well-nigh driven it from nominal Christian countries, made so by the strong clutch of law. They could not be immersed if they would, as believers; for this was unlawful. Deprived of this right, the civil and ecclesiastical law drove them into Quakerism, in counting the believer the subject of a higher baptism, as they called it, in the Consolamentum. And what was that? Ermengard describes it thus:

'When they wish to impart the Consolamentum to any man or woman, he that is called Greater and ordained, having washed his hands and holding in his hands the book of the Gospels, admonishes him or them who come to receive the Consolamentum that they place their entire faith in that Consolamentum. And so, placing the book on their heads, they repeat the Lord's Prayer seven times, and then the Gospel of St. John, beginning with the words, "In the beginning," and going as far as the passage which reads, " Grace and truth through Jesus Christ." Thus is the Consolamentum completed. Do you ask by what persons it is administered? We answer, by those among them who are called the ordained. But if none such be present, there be those who among them are called the Consolati (by them), it is administered, and if there be no men present, even women may administer it to the sick. They believe that by it the remission of every sin and the cleansing of every stain is accomplished, without any satisfactory penance whatever, if they die immediately after. They say even that no one, save he who has received that Consolamentum from the Consolati, can by any work, not even by martyrdom, nor if he keep himself as much as possible from all sins and faults, reach the heavenly kingdom. And they believe this also, that if he who administers the Consolamentum should have fallen into any of the sins they call criminal, as, for example, to eat an egg, or fish, or cheese, or to slay a bird, or any animal save reptiles, or even into any of the sins the Roman Church calls criminal, then the Consolamentum does the recipients no good. Nay, they hold the recipient should again have it administered by another, if he desires to be saved.'

This account is abundantly sustained by indisputable evidence. And this so-called 'spiritual baptism' was administered because they cast aside material water as 'evil' or 'corrupt,' while the Romish Church immersed therein. How can we count such people as Baptists, whatever their views of infant baptism may have been? So far as the question of baptizing babes was concerned, they were Antipedobaptists; and so far as immersion in water was concerned, the Romanists were better Baptists than they.

In the Petrobrusians we find a sect of Baptists for which no apology is needed. Peter of Bruis seized the entire Biblical presentation of baptism, and forced its teaching home upon the conscience and the life, by rejecting the immersion of babes and insisting on the immersion of all believers in Christ, without any admixture of Catharistic nonsense. He was a converted priest, it is believed a pupil of Abelard, brought to the Saviour's feet by reading the Bible. There he saw the difference between the Christianity of his day and of that of the Apostles; and he resolved to devote his life to the restoration of Gospel Christianity, and began his work as early as A. D. 1104. He threw tradition to the winds with the double sense of Scripture, and took its literal interpretation. With this went the doctrine of transubstantiation, holding the Supper as a merely historical and monumental act. He held the Church to be made up of regenerated people only, counted the bishops and priests as he knew them, mere frauds; and cast aside all the ceremonial mummeries of the Romish hierarchy. He would not adore images, offer prayer to or for the dead, nor do penance. He laughed at the stupidity which holds that a child is regenerated when baptized, that he can be a member of Christ's flock when he knows nothing of Christ as a Shepherd, and demanded that all who came to his churches should be immersed in water on their own act of faith. He had no controversy on the subject of immersion with the Romish priests, for they practiced nothing else as the custom of their Church in his day, nor for a century afterward; therefore no separate Baptist body was needed for that reason. His great offense was that he reimmersed those whom they had immersed as babes when they became disciples of Christ and were regenerated by the Spirit of God.

The chief testimony that we have of him is from Peter the Venerable, the Abbot of Clugny, and a brief passage from Abelard. This Peter, his deadly opponent, gave a full account of his doctrines and tried to crush him; but, singularly enough, never breathed a syllable against his practice of immersing, for that was Peter's own practice, only its subjects were babes. The venerable monk, 'Maxima Biblioth.' (xxii, 1035), defines the views of the Petrobrusians precisely as would an able Baptist of to-day, and attempts to answer them with the exact stock arguments of 1886. He says: 'The first article of the heretics denies that children below the age of reason can be saved by the baptism of Christ; and affirms that another's faith can do those no good who cannot yet exercise faith of their own, since, according to them, it is not another's but one's own faith which, together with baptism, saves, because the Lord said, "Whosoever believeth and is baptized shall be saved."' He makes them say in another place, 'It is an idle and vain thing to plunge candidates in water at any age, when ye can, indeed, after a human manner, wash the flesh from impurities, but can by no means purify the soul from sins. But we await an age capable of faith, and after a man is prepared to acknowledge God as his and believe in him, we do not, as you slander us, *re*baptize, but baptize him; for no one is to be called baptized who is not washed with the baptism wherewith sins are washed away.'

The Abbot stood side by side with Bernard in his Biblical scholarship and mental force. They were the leading defenders of the Catholic faith in France, and threw themselves into the gap with all their might to defend her against these simple Gospel Baptists. Instead of bowing to our Lord's words as an obedient disciple, Peter indulged in this absurd reasoning: 'Has the whole world been so blinded and hitherto involved in such darkness, that to open their eyes and break up the long night it should, after so many fathers, martyrs, popes and heads of all the Churches, have to wait so long for you, and choose Peter of Bruis and Henry, his disciple, as exceedingly recent apostles, to correct the long error? If this be true, it is manifest how great an absurdity follows. For then all Gaul, Spain, Germany, Italy, yea, all Europe, since for three hundred years, yea for near five hundred years, has had no one baptized save in infancy, has had no Christian. But if it has had no Christian, then it has had no Church. If no Church, then no Christ; if no Christ, then assuredly they have all perished.' It seems never to have entered his head that Christ was before and above all the fathers, popes and heads of the Churches; and that, therefore, they must all obey him and take the consequences of their own disobedience, be they what they might, rather than nullify his law.

The Petrobrusians were a thoroughly antisacerdotal sect, whose hatred of tyranny threw off the Roman yoke of the twelfth century; a democratic body, in distinction from the aristocratic organizations both of the Catholics and the Albigenses. It appears from the assembly of the latter body, at Lombers, that they had a pope who had come from far-off Bulgaria, and who carefully defined the bounds of their various Catharist bishoprics. In that assembly also they had warm contests; and the names of those are given who were exalted to episcopal functions by the forms of the Consolamentum. We have seen that their numbers were very great as a people, but the members of the Electi were comparatively few. Reiner, who had spent seventeen years amongst them, tells us that 'the Credentes were innumerable,' but that the Electi of both sexes did not exceed four thousand. This form of aristocracy well suited the feudal cast of society in that day, and may explain, in part, why the rationalistic nobles and the hierarchical priesthood so readily became Cathari. But the Petrobrusians were of the common people, who sought the Saviour by simple directness and not through any saving intervention. They demanded the words of Christ in the New Testament for every thing, and not the traditions of an inner and favored few. With a quaint tinge of chagrin, something after the fox-and-grapes order, Peter the venerable abbot hints that his brother, Peter of Bruis, refused to immerse infants because he was too lazy to perform the rite; as if it were easier to dip overgrown peasants in the Rhone than tiny babes in the fonts. He thought, also, that his beloved Baptist brother burned the crosses because it was easier to do that than to worship them; and that he rejected masses because he was hardly paid enough for saying them.

The Petrobrusians were thoroughly and deeply anti-Catholic in all that conflicted with the Gospel. While they were Puritanical they were not ascetic. They abolished all fasts and penances for sin because Christ only can forgive sin, and this he does on a sinner's trust in his merits. They held marriage as a high and honorable relation, not only for Christians generally, but for the priests. They denied that the person of Christ could be made a sacrifice on the altar, that the chair of the pope is the chair of Peter, and that one bishop had power to consecrate another. They made void the priesthood of Rome, condemned its sacraments as superstitious, and demanded that baptism be administered only to believers. With them a Church did not mean an architectural structure, but a regenerated congregation, nor had consecrated places any charm for them; for God could hear them as well in the marketplace as in the temple, and loved them as much in a barn as before an altar. Their success filled the Romish communion with alarm. Peter of Bruis was little superior in learning to Peter of the Gospel; but, like his great predecessor, he was sincere, earnest and eloquent, and the Lord wrought mightily by his hand. Multitudes flocked in all directions to hear him as a man specially sent of God to bring glad tidings of great joy. Soon his word turned the dioceses of Arles, Embrun, Die and Gap upside down. In their enthusiasm the people burned their images and crucifixes, some Catholic places of worship were overturned, and many monks and priests were handled very severely. On a certain Good Friday the crowd brought all their wooden crosses and made a bonfire of them, at which they roasted and ate meat. Their venerable adversary thus describes their work:

'The people are *re*-baptized, the churches profaned, the altars overthrown, the crosses burned, flesh is eaten, even on the day of our Lord's passion, priests are whipped, monks are imprisoned, and by terror and torture they are compelled to marry wives.' If this were true, the whipping and imprisonment of these helpless Romanists is very un-Baptistic; and as to the question of compulsory marriages, the abbot probably drew slightly on his imagination, as none but the priests themselves had the legal power to celebrate marriage; to say nothing of taking their wives under the pressure of Baptist ringleaders whom they banished, and who were obliged to fly to Narbonne and Toulouse for their lives. In these places Peter bravely preached for twenty years, and with great success. Besides, his doctrine spread not only through Provence and Dauphiné, but much farther to the east. At last, however, in 1126, while he was preaching at St. Gilles, he was suddenly arrested by a violent mob and burned at the stake, his eloquent tongue being silenced in the midst of his triumphs.

But the death of Peter was not the end of his cause. Labbe calls him 'the parent of heretics,' for almost all who were thus branded after his day trod in his steps; and especially all Baptist 'heretics.' Even the candid and celebrated Dr. Wall says: 'I take this Peter Bruis (or Bruce, perhaps, his name was) and Henry to be the first antipedobaptist preachers that ever set up a Church or society of men holding that opinion against infant baptism, and rebaptizing such as had been baptized in infancy.'[2] When, like Elijah, God took Peter to heaven in a fiery chariot, he had Elisha ready to catch his falling mantle, in the person of Henry of Lausanne; or, as Cluniacensis much prefers to put it, he was followed by Henry, 'the heir of Bruis's wickedness.' This petulant author imagined that Peter's principles had died with him, and like a simpleton writes: 'I should have thought that it had been those craggy Alps, and rocks covered with continual snow, that had bred that savage temper in the inhabitants, and that your land, being unlike to all other lands, had yielded a sort of people unlike to all others.'

But he soon perceived his mistake. No doubt the sublime aspects of the Alps, like all mountainous regions, were well adapted to start free inquiry in the unfettered mind, and to inspire those distinct tones of religion which stimulate it to advanced thought. Their deep foundations excite to logical deduction, and their broad stretch invites the reasoning powers to throw off all that hampers and hoodwinks them by vulgar submission to antiquated authority. Their very lines and curves, cut gracefully against the blue sky, invite manhood out of itself to talk with God in strains of wonder, poetry and sublimity; until a loving awe for him steals over the spirit, as his sunshine bathes the brow of the peak, and the soul is drawn under the winning dominance of adoration and love. There a man feels both his littleness and his freedom, the pain of being hemmed in by obstruction, the stinging smart of dictation, and the terrible delight of rising upward if he can take no other direction. Like the eagle which sails above his hut, his soul dares to rise into grand and dreadful sensations where his spirit feels the majesty of its own wing; his eye scrutinizes the relations of the man in the valley to the mountains around him, and to the God above him, and he resolves to soar into a freedom as wide and high as the liberty of his own nature. Such a mountaineer is not easily tethered to bogs in the Roman Campagna, nor to the vale of the sluggish Tiber; but he soars to the sources of the dashing cascades, to read his greatness and that of his fellow-men in the wide-open volume at the footstool of Jehovah's throne.

Such a bold soul had Christ been preparing in Henry, the next brave Baptist of the Swiss valleys. He had formerly been a monk of Clugny and had joined himself to his master, Peter of Bruis, in the midst of his toils; and thus had caught his spirit and been imbued with his principles. Our venerable abbot kindly tells us that Henry added some errors of his own to those of Peter, a noble tribute to his progressive mind; but he fails to tell us what they were. Most likely he pushed the attributes of a zealous Reformer a little further against current abuses. Already he had reached the degree of deacon in the Catholic communion, when his fiery eloquence in exposing the wickedness of the clergy cut him off from further hearing amongst them. He then made common cause with Peter, as Melancthon did with Luther and Whitefield with Wesley. The Abbot of Clugny denounces him as an 'apostate, who had returned to the vomit of the flesh and the world, a black monk was he.' He was a man of letters; but his peculiar attraction lay in his contempt for the applauded traditions of the Fathers and in his appeal to the neglected Bible. In Neander's 'Life of Bernard' he says of Henry:

'He had all the attributes to deeply impress the people, great dignity in personal appearance, a fiery eye, a thundering voice, a lively step, a speech that rushed forth impetuously as it flowed from his heart, and Bible passages were always at hand to support his addresses. Soon was spread abroad the report of his holy life and his learning. Young and old, men and women, hastened to him to confess their sins, and said they had never seen a man of such severity and friendliness whose words could move a heart of iron to repentance, whose life should be a model for all monks and priests.' [3]

He appeared in the garb of a penitent, his long beard hanging upon his breast, his feet bare even in winter, a staff in his hand; a very young John the Baptist, in a living voice. In drawing his picture, an enemy speaks of 'his face, through the quickness of his eyes,' as 'like a perilous sea; tall of body, quick of gait, gliding in his walk, quick of speech, of a terrible voice, a youth in age, none more splendid than he in dress.'

In 1116 this lithe, young Baptist apostle of the Alps drew near to the thriving city of Mans, and sent two of his disciples within the gates to obtain permission of Hildebert the bishop to preach in his diocese. This prelate was a disciple of Berengarius, and so looked with favor on Henry's efforts to purify the Church. He was about to depart for Rome, but instructed his archdeacon to treat Henry kindly and allow him to preach. The fame of his piety had reached the city before him, and the people believed that he possessed a prophetic gift. He entered Mans, and while the bishop was visiting Rome the people received him with delight; the priests of the lower order sat at his feet, almost bathing them with tears, while most of the higher clergy protested against him and stood aloof. A platform or pulpit was specially erected for him, from which he might address the people. He made marriage a chief matter in his sermons. He would free it from unnatural restrictions, would celebrate it in early life and make it indissoluble. He would not accept the repentance of an unchaste woman until she had burned her hair and her garments in public. He condemned extravagant attire and marriage for money. 'Indeed,' says his enemy, 'he was marvelously eloquent,' a remark which couches his matter as well as his manner. While the priests wept over his exposure of their corruptions, the people were enraged at the priests. They refused to sell any thing to them, threatened their servants with violence, and their safety was secured only by the shield of public authority. The clergy came to dispute with Henry, but the people handled them roughly and they fled for safety. Chagrined at their defeat, they united in a letter forbidding him to preach, but the people protected him and he went on boldly.

When the bishop returned the people treated his religious acts with contempt and said: 'We do not want your benedictions. You may bless the dirt. We have a father and a priest who surpasses you in dignity, holy living and understanding. Your clergy avoid him as if he were a blasphemer, because with the spirit of a prophet he is uncovering their vices, and out of the Holy Scriptures is condemning their errors and excesses.' The bishop had an interview with Henry, but dared not tolerate the stanch reformer any longer. Henry, therefore, retired to Poitiers and other southern provinces of France, where he continued to labor with great success, in some cases whole congregations leaving the Catholics and joining his standard. The people gave him a ready hearing, for the Catharists and Peter had prepared his way. He had met Peter in the Diocese of Narbonne and received from him the direction of the rising sect. Ten years after the martyrdom of Peter he labored in the regions of Gascony, in the south-west of France, and made a deep impression. In 1134, however, he was arrested by the Bishop of Arles and brought before the Council of Pisa, held by Innocent II., and condemned to confinement in the monastery of Clairvaux, of which Bernard, the chief opposer of the Petrobrusians, was abbot. He soon escaped, however, and was found preaching in Toulouse and the mountain regions round about under the protection of Ildephons, a powerful noble who had become his disciple. His ministry was so influential that Bernard, in his tour of visitation, found 'churches without congregations, the people without priests, the priests without due honor, the mass and other sacraments neglected, and the fast days unobserved.' He complains that 'the way of the children of Christians is closed, the grace of baptism is refused them, and they are hindered from coming to heaven; although the Saviour, with fatherly love, calls them, saying, "Suffer little children to come unto me."' The venerable abbot looked upon their baptism as salvation, and to him their exclusion from the immersion which he administered was exclusion from Paradise. The loving Lamb of God had redeemed them; but because Bernard could not hear his voice calling them through the baptistery of a corrupt Church, he was tormented with the thought that surely they must perish. To be sure, that Church was powerless to admit them into heaven by its blessing, or to shut them out by its curse. So he, with his brethren, put them to the sword, with their parents; and all the time, while the blood of innocents was following its keen edge, Jesus was rising from his throne to receive their panting spirits to his bosom as fast as they were slain. Bernard was fretting his soul with the thought that they were 'forbidden to come' because they were not brought through his appointed way, so he made their shrill wail echo up and down the Alpine valleys, while they passed through the darker vale of death to him who redeemed his little ones with his own precious blood.

At the time when the land swarmed with Henry's followers, Pope Eugenius III. determined to suppress him and his work, and for this purpose employed Bernard, Cardinal Alberic and others. Bernard held a phenomenal influence over the masses on account of his pure life and reputed miracles; and crowds flocked to hear him preach as if he were an angel of God. He proposed at once to prove the divinity of his mission by miracles. 'Let this be a proof,' said he, 'that our doctrine is true and that of the heretics false, if your sick are healed by eating the bread which I have blessed.' But he could not always hold the people. At Vividefolium they left the church, and when he followed and addressed them in the street they interrupted him with Scripture passages until his voice was drowned. On his return he wrote a letter, in which he congratulated himself on gaining something by his labors, but urged the people to finish the work of extermination which he had begun. 'Follow and seize them, and determine not to rest until the sects have been driven out of your territory, for it is not safe to sleep in the vicinity of serpents.' Under such instructions the bishops succeeded in recapturing Henry, when the Pope's legate cited him and his disciples to answer at his tribunal. His followers fled, and in 1148 Henry was brought before the Council of Rheims, at which Pope Eugenius III. presided. He was condemned as a heretic to perpetual confinement and hard fare in a neighboring monastery, where he soon died. But the work which Peter and he had done was so great that when they were dead it survived them. We have seen that Tanchelyn had planted the same seed in Cologne which they had planted in France; and we are reaping the harvest to-day.

One of the great movements of the century brings before us the immortal Italian, ARNOLD. He was born at Brescia, in the North of Italy, about A. D. 1105, and was an educated monk, a disciple of Abelard; having listened to his lectures, with a crowd of other young men, in his school of the 'Paraclete' and been indelibly impressed thereby. God had endowed him with rare gifts. He possessed great fervor, purity and serenity, with a remarkable flow of eloquence; these he united to most graceful and attractive manners and charming conversational powers.

ARNOLD, OF BRESCIA.

As a preacher, he filled Lombardy with resistance to the pride and pretensions of the priesthood. He was the purest, most severe and bold personification of republican democracy, both laical and ecclesiastical, of the century. At that time Feudalism had wrought such desolation that there was a reaction in Italian aspirations to resist empire and the papacy. These were the two grand Italian ideals of his day, and he determined upon the resurrection of the Roman commonwealth and the destruction of the temporal power of the pope. Under the stirring appeals of his deep convictions and impassioned eloquence the popular cry was raised: 'The people and liberty,' and he became as much its incarnation as Mazzini and Garibaldi in modern times. As the apostle of religious liberty, he contended for a full dissolution of the union between Church and State, and fired the cities to seek perfect freedom from both pope and empire by establishing a republic. As a patriot, he looked upon these civil enemies only with contempt, and summoned Italy to shake them off. As a Christian, he was an antisacramentarian, desiring to bring the Church back to the New Testament standard; or, as Gibbon expresses it, he boldly threw himself upon the declaration of Christ, 'My kingdom is not of this world.' He would not use the sword, but maintained his cause by moral sentiment; and yet formed the daring plan of planting the standard of civil and religious liberty in the city of Rome itself, for the purpose of restoring the old rights of the Senate and the people. His pure morals and child-like sense of justice started the whole land.

From about 1130 he preached with such power that by 1139 the Lateran Council sentenced him to banishment; and to escape death he fled to the Swiss Canton of Zurich. Amongst the mountains of Switzerland he found shelter with many Lombards who had fled from the hatred of their own countrymen. In Zurich he boldly maintained 'that every city should constitute an independent state, in whose government no bishop ought to have the right to interfere, that the Church should not own any secular dominion, and that the priests should be satisfied to enjoy the tithes of nature, remaining excluded from every temporal authority.' He was not allowed, however, to remain quietly in his asylum, but was driven from place to place with a price upon his head. At last, goaded principally by Bernard and the pope, he determined to attack Rome boldly and openly; and did so with great effect. In the public streets he proclaimed to the multitude that the sword and scepter are intrusted to the civil magistrate; that abbots, bishops and the popes must renounce their State or their salvation; and that all their temporal honors are unlawful. The Romans rose in a body to assert their inalienable rights as citizens and Christians, to confine the pope to spiritual matters, to put his ecclesiastics under the civil power, and to establish a laical government with the Senate at its head. Rome was thrown into insurrection; all Europe felt his power, and the eyes of Christendom were turned to the Eternal City. After a desperate contest against three several popes, which cost Lucian his life, a new constitution was framed and the sanction of Adrian IV. was demanded to its provisions. The pope fled for his life, his temporal power was abolished and a new government was established in 1143, which maintained the struggle with varying fortunes for about ten years. The violence of the people, however, prevented final success. They rose in insurrection, demolished the houses and seized the property of the papal party, while Arnold was conservative and touched nothing. Nevertheless, his holy apostolate planted the seeds of that republicanism which controls the Italy, Switzerland and France of to-day.

Bernard seems to have hated him with a singular intensity, and called him a conspirator against Jesus Christ. Pope Eugenius III. put Rome under interdict (1154), an act which deprived it of all its religious privileges; the Emperor Barbarossa marched against it with a large army, and after a contest of about eleven years this daring reformer was obliged to surrender. In 1155 he was hanged, his body burned to ashes and his dust thrown into the Tiber, lest the people should

MONUMENTO AD ARNALDO DA BRESCIA.

collect and venerate it as a precious relic. Thus perished this great patriot and martyr to the holy doctrine of soul-liberty. But Italy will ever hold his name in hallowed remembrance. Down to A. D. 1861 a simple slab commemorated his noble deeds, then a modest statue took its place. But in 1864-65 the Communal and Provincial Councils of Brescia each voted a sum of 30,000 lire (Ital.) for a splendid monument to his honor. The city of Zurich made a large contribution, and from other sources, the sum soon amounted to 150,000 lire (Ital.), about $30,000. The ablest artists of Northern Italy competed for the prize model, which was awarded to M. Tabacchi. The base is done after the design of the great architect, Tagliaferri, who has succeeded admirably in reproducing the old Lombard style of architecture of Arnold's time. It is of various colored marbles hewn from the rocks of Brescia. The statue and the four bass-reliefs were cast in the artistic foundery of Nelli of Rome. The statue itself is of bronze and is four meters (13 feet 4 inches) high. Arnold is represented in a preaching attitude; his gigantic figure being that of a monk in a long robe with most graceful folds. His long, nervous arms extend from the wide sleeves, his wonderful face is serene, but inspired for address; and the simplicity of the whole conception is worthy of the greatness of the man. The first alto-relievo represents him expounding his doctrines to the Brescians, holding in his hand the Book of Truth; in the second he is on trial, defending himself before his judges against the accusations of his foes; in the third he stands preaching in the Forum, surrounded by shields, broken columns and capitals, among which is also the Arch of Titus; the fourth presents him on the scaffold with his hands tied behind his back, the judge at his side about to read his sentence, and a funeral pile ready for lighting behind him. The scene is terrible, but he stands in calm majesty, his eyes steadily fixed before him. This beautiful work of art was dedicated to him as the forerunner of Italian liberty in the nineteenth century, and was officially unveiled at Brescia August 14, 1882. Most eloquent orations were delivered, while redeemed Italy looked on, by the patriot Rosa and Zanardelli, ' Minister of Grace and Justice' for that year.

Although the great distinctive feature in which Arnold most sympathized with Baptists relates to his unbending opposition to any union whatever of Church and State, he appears to have symbolized with them in some other respects. Dr. Wall says that the Lateran Council of 1139 condemned him for rejecting infant baptism, and he thinks that he was 'a follower of Bruis' in this respect.[4] If so, then the Council which condemned the Petrobrusians condemned him. Bernard accuses him and his followers of deriding infant baptism. Evervine not only complains of the same thing, but says that they administered baptism only to believers. Gibbon also states that Arnold's 'ideas of baptism and the Eucharist were loosely censured; but a political heresy was the source of his fame and his misfortunes.'

CHAPTER X.

THE WALDENSIANS.

THE cut on page 295 embodies the several Waldensian symbols, and portrays at a glance their struggles and triumphs. The first is a candle lighted in the night, with the motto: 'Light Shines in Darkness.' The flame is enkindled by one of the seven stars, which is fed by light from above. The second is a burning bush unconsumed, to show that their fiery persecutions left them undestroyed. The third is a lily growing amongst thorns, yet unchoked and rising above them—the sign of delicate weakness calmly rejoicing over annoying difficulties. The fourth is the anvil of truth, beaten by the hammers of its foes; Church and State, foreign and home enemies try to split it, but break their own hammers. The fifth is the serene Waldensian, standing bolt upright; he despises the bishop's miter, crook and crosier, with the pope's tiara and rosary, and tramples them under foot.

Walter Mapes, an Englishman of the twelfth century and a favorite of Henry II., was sent on a mission to the papal court, and first met the Waldensians at the Lateran Council, A. D. 1179. He calls them 'Valdesii, from their primate, Waldo,' Peter Waldo, whose name answers closely to the English name Wood. There is fair ground for the belief that an Evangelical people lived in the isolated Cottian Alps before the twelfth century, but the evidence is too scanty and fragmentary to be used with confidence for historical purposes. Some Waldensian writers think that they can trace their origin back to the days of Constantine and even to the Apostles, but Dieckhoff and Herzog have shown that this claim will not bear critical investigation. The ablest modern historians do not find them beyond the great reformer Waldo, an ideal figure of whom, in merchant's dress, now stands in the great Luther monument at Worms.

This man of God was born at Vaux, in Dauphiné, on the Rhone, and became a rich merchant at Lyons, where he lived in a street known for generations after his banishment as 'Cursed Street.' The sudden death of a friend, who fell by his side at a feast, led him to consecrate himself to Christ, A. D. 1160. While his heart was touched by pondering upon the vanity of earthly things, he joined a crowd in the street who were listening to the song of a troubadour, whose theme was the blessed death of St. Alexis. He first took the singer home with him, and then visited a learned divine to ask more about the way to heaven, who replied: 'There are many roads to heaven.' But Peter asked him, 'Which is the surest?' and was answered, 'If thou wilt be perfect, go sell all that thou hast and give to the poor.'

That day he made the Gospel his only rule and literally obeyed the injunction. He paid his creditors, gave his house, field and vineyard to his wife, provided for his daughters, and then spent three days in the week relieving the wants of the poor in the public square. Many thought him insane, but he said: 'I am not mad, as you suppose, I am avenging myself of my enemies (his wealth), who have reduced me to such servitude as made me more mindful of them than of God.'

He also put his money to a use uncommon in those days. He employed Stephen of Ansa and Bernard Ydross to translate the Gospels from the Latin Vulgate of Jerome into the Romance dialect for the common people, as well as the most inspiring passages from the Christian Fathers. Then, filled with the love of Christ, he took preaching tours and sent his converts on the same errand. These three acts were prophetic of the whole Waldensian career: the voluntary poverty of its preachers; the free use of the Bible; the right of laymen to preach the Gospel. No other layman except William the Conqueror, Peter's contemporary, had ventured on such work, and no sect had yet commenced its existence with a popular translation of the New Testament; a bold step which soon aroused opposition.

WALDENSIAN SYMBOLS.

Peter did not at first call in question any doctrine of the Romish communion, nor did he contemplate separation from it, his simple purpose being to win men to a holy life. Hence, he and his followers were not treated as 'heretics;' but the Bishop of Lyons demanded why they preached and expounded the Scriptures without Church authority? They replied, according to Stephen of Borbone: 'We ought to obey God rather than man. Christ commanded his disciples to preach.' They said but little at this time about the superstitions and corruptions of the Catholics. This they left to the fidelity of those in that communion, who, like themselves, wished to see the spiritual life of that body revived. Amongst these, Peter Vidal said: 'The pope and his false doctors have put the Holy Church in such distress, that God himself is incensed at it. Thanks to their sins and follies, the heretics have arisen; for when they give the example of iniquity, it is hard to find any who will abstain.' And Pierre Cardinal exclaimed: ' The priests grasp on every hand, and are reckless of the sorrow they cause. The whole world is theirs, they make themselves its masters. Usurpers toward some, generous toward others, they employ indulgences and use deceit, they give absolutions and they make good cheer. Now they have recourse to prayers, and now pursue their ends by murders. Some they seduce with God, the rest with the devil.' The crime of Waldo and his followers was that they were 'schismatics,' because they established a new apostolate, and usurped the office of preaching without papal authority. The real trouble was that the common people would listen no longer to the greedy, lazy and immoral priests, who addressed them in an unknown tongue and ground them down with tithes. These self-sacrificing, new teachers brought them the Gospel in their mother dialect, claimed no authority over them, preached Bible truth without money or price, and recommended the whole by godly lives. Whether they intended to undermine the hierarchy or not, the priesthood saw the peril, took the alarm, and plied its ecclesiastical authority to save its existence.

Unable to persuade and powerless to compel them to stop, the Bishop excommunicated them A. D. 1176 for preaching without his authority. Instead of accepting this excision, they appealed for redress to Pope Alexander III., and because he wanted them to remain in the Church he laid the matter before the Lateran Council at Rome in 1179. He praised Peter for his vow of poverty, embraced him, and would have permitted him to preach, provided that he maintained the faith of the Fathers Ambrose, Augustine, Gregory and Jerome. For this forbearance Waldo was indebted to Cardinal Pulha; and thus encouraged he sent two of his disciples to the council to secure fuller recognition, as he was not satisfied with the right of preaching himself. The pope turned these over to Walter Mapes for examination, who says of them: 'There were brought to me the two Waldenses, who seemed to be the chief of their sect, to dispute with me, and shut my mouth as one who spoke evil. I confess I sat in fear lest in so great a Council the privilege of speaking might be denied me, seeing that it was at the request of sinners.' But he soon overcame his fear, with good zest began to make light of the simple preachers, and even ridiculed them before the Council because they avowed that Christ had sent them to preach and clothed them with power by the Holy Spirit. He, however, betrayed trepidation, for he said: 'If we let them in, we shall be driven forth ourselves.' They were virtually condemned, for they were granted permission to preach only on condition that the local priest requested it, a thing that he was slow to ask. The reason given for this prohibition was: 'That the Roman Church cannot endure your preaching.' This enforced silence made them all the bolder: 'Did not Christ send us?' said they, 'why should his Church hinder us?' And they went every-where preaching the Word.

This, of course, could not be endured, and in 1183–84 a special council was held at Verona by Pope Lucius III., in the presence of the Emperor Barbarossa, 'to bind in the chain of perpetual anathema those who presumed to preach, publicly or privately, without the authority of the bishop.' Though excommunicated, they were held as less perverse than other disowned ones, their sentence stating that they presumed to preach without any 'authority received either from the Apostolic See or from the bishops of their respective dioceses.' This ban did not class them with the Catharists, with whom they had no part; and often when the priests had controversies with these, they appealed to the Waldensians with their ready store of Scriptural truth to help them. Even as late as 1190 the Archbishop of Narbonne held a colloquy with them to win them back. Their first great contest, then, concerned the right of lay preaching and not doctrine. Pope Innocent, their great enemy, expressly says, long afterward, that they 'would usurp the office of preaching' as an innovation. On the ground of doctrine, they were not obnoxious to Rome at that time. Yet when Lucius anathematized them they were obliged to fly in every direction. Waldo, with one band of his disciples, fled to the rugged fastnesses of the Cottian Alps, the dividing line between Dauphiné in Southern France and Piedmont in Northern Italy. These first settled in Dauphiné, on the French side, but soon crossed the border to the Italian. They labored, however, in both fields, and the great body of the people soon embraced their doctrines.

Piedmont had five valleys, but the mountain tract on the southern side had only three. In these gorges, caverns, passes and dizzy peaks, their descendants still survive, after a period of seven hundred years. Their first real settlements were in the thinly populated and half cultivated valleys of Angrogna and San Martino, where the Romans erected an arch, calling it the 'Gate of Italy.' The house of the Count Lucerna, the ruler of the land, had on its escutcheon the words: 'The light shines in darkness,' which became the Waldensian motto. Their greatest triumphs were in Italy, in the Duchy of Savoy, on the eastern slopes of the Cottians; and their secondary were on the western, under the scepter of France. This Count may have favored the new settlers, but the Benedictine monks, who had a monastery and lands in Savoy, were greatly alarmed at the inroad of this flock of emigrants. In time, however, the Dukes of Savoy assailed them, but the Kings of France were too much engaged to trouble these godly mountaineers, and so they found refuge under one government when the other persecuted them, flight being their only safeguard. For this reason, in part, the history of the Italian Waldensians is far more complicated than that of the French, and more full of adventure by invasion, defense, defeat, suffering and triumph. For a time their very obscurity protected them against the curses of Rome. After a while Waldo turned to the North, but his ferocious persecutors drove him into Bohemia, where it seems likely that, as an old man, he finished his work in peace and fell asleep in Jesus.

The anathema of Lucian, A. D. 1183–84, was followed in 1192 by a demand from the Bishop of Turin that all who found a Waldensian should bring him to his court bound with fetters to be punished, and his successor followed in his steps. But constant persecution sharpened their appetite for the truth and they soon began to fall into so-called 'heresy.' Gradually they claimed the right of private judgment in the interpretation of the Scriptures, and came to oppose some doctrines and practices of the Church of Rome touching the power of the clergy, the sacraments and ecclesiastical authority. They resented the yoke of the pope and the bishops; asserted the right of laymen, and even of women, to preach; avowed that the wickedness of the priest neutralized the effect of the ordinances; declared that confession might be made to a good layman, and that absolution from him was effective. They, also, like the Catharists, denied the oblation of the mass, all oaths, war, begging and capital punishment; while a few of them went so far as to deny infant baptism. It is of this class that Du Pin says, they regarded 'The washings of infants' as 'of no avail to them; the sureties do not understand what they say to the priest.'

Persecution soon scattered small bodies of them in every direction. Individuals wandered where they could, and little companies took refuge in various countries, soon becoming the founders of small communities—who, for convenience, we may call the WALDENSIANS OF THE DISPERSION. Sometimes these bands merged into other sects, or they grew up a separate people, constantly developing new views; and at last they became much more radical protestants against Rome than the original Romance Waldensians. Failure to make this distinction clear, and even sharp, will lead us to confound one Waldensian sect with another, and to mix their doctrines and practices in a medley of confusion; for scarcely two sections of them believed and practiced the same things throughout. Nor did any one class of Waldensians hold the same doctrines and follow the same rites at all times. When we lose sight of these changes and variations we fall both into confusion and contradiction concerning this whole people. Those of the Dispersion had so increased to the West as far as Spain, in 1192, that Alphonso, King of Aragon, issued a decree expelling them from his realm, and they were treated nowhere else with greater severity. Edict after edict, the last generally the worst, drove them out. The wrath of God and the charge of treason were launched upon all who shielded a Waldensian, gave him food, heard him preach, or treated him kindly. The king commanded: 'Let this our edict be read on the Sabbath by the clergy in all cities, forts and villages of our kingdom, and be enforced by our vicars, bailiffs and judges. Any person, noble or not, who shall find a Waldensian anywhere in our kingdom, after three days' notice has been given to leave, may injure him in any way, that will not mutilate his body or take his life, without fear of punishment, but rather with the assurance of receiving our favor. We grant the Waldensians till All Saints' Day to leave or begin to leave the land, or expose themselves to the risk of being plundered and scourged.' In the face of this edict, which was renewed by Alphonso's son, Peter II., the Waldensians continued to spread even as far as Seville. Peter's son, James I., 1227, at Pope Gregory's request, established an Inquisition which caused the flight of many into Castile. They were tracked to its valleys, thrust into prison and severely punished; but not one yielded, and the king himself carried wood to the pile and set fire to the martyrs. Thereafter any one who heard the Waldensians preach, knelt with them in prayer, gave them a kiss or called them 'good men,' was suspected and punished. [1]

Another body of the Dispersed Waldensians was found at Metz, in Northern France, as early as 1199, when the bishop of that city informed Pope Innocent III. of the trouble which they made him. He sought the pope's advice in the matter, telling him that both in the city and diocese a large number of laymen and women were reading the Bible in the Gallic tongue and preaching from place to place. Some of them had come from Montpellier, bringing translations with them which they used in secret assemblies. When the parish priests undertook to correct these things they spurned their interference, telling them plainly that the Bible was better than any thing that they could give them. The pope's reply against the little flock said, that 'Although the desire to understand the Scriptures and edify one another out of them is not blamable, but rather commendable; still, he could not favor the secrecy of their meetings.' He warned them against Pharisaic pride, and threatened them with discipline if they would not hear his fatherly exhortations. But the 'heretics' went on with their Bible teachings; and a delegation of abbots came from Rome, A. D. 1200, who dispersed the assemblies, burned the Bibles and, according to the Chronicles of Albericus, 'extirpated the sect.' In order to stop these Christ-like proceedings of the Waldensians, the fourth Lateran Council, A. D. 1215, and the Council of Toulouse, 1229, forbade laymen to read the Bible either in the language of the people or in the Latin, and the Council of Tarragona, 1242, bound the prohibition on the clergy also.

The Waldensians of the Dispersion became established in various cities, as Geneva, Aquileia, with others in Switzerland and Italy; and, in fact, they stretched all the way from Aragon to Milan and Florence, and dotted Lower Germany. The Bishop of Turin was greatly disturbed by some of them about 1209. He had been a Benedictine Abbot, and took advantage of the passage of the Emperor Otto IV., on his way to be crowned at Rome, to secure the right of expelling the Waldensians who were 'sowing tares in his diocese,' and of expurgating every thing that contradicted the Catholic faith. But the Counts of Lucerna befriended them and secured the free exercise of their religion, in the treaty made with the Duke of Savoy, in 1233. This protected them for many years.

In 1212 a congregation of five hundred Waldensians was discovered at Strasburg. At first the bishop of that city sought to reason them out of their position against the Catholic faith; but such was their ready use of Scripture that disputations always inured to their advantage. Then he proclaimed that all of them who would not forsake their errors should be put to death by fire without delay. Many recanted, surrendered their books, and reported to him that they had three chief centers and three leaders—in Milan, in Bohemia, and on the ground in Strasburg. These leaders, they said, were not clothed with authority like the pope, but owed their influence to the personal confidence reposed in them by their brethren. One of their chief duties was to collect money for the poor. Eighty persons in all, amongst whom were twenty-three women and twelve preachers, would not surrender their faith. John, the Strasburg leader, answered in the name of all. His appeal to Scripture could not be overthrown, and when his persecutors would apply the test of red-hot iron to see if he were sent of God, he replied: 'Thou shalt not tempt the Lord thy God.' 'Ah, he does not want to burn his fingers,' scornfully cried the monks. 'I have the word of God,' he answered, 'and for that I would not only burn my fingers but my whole body.' All who stood with him were put to death. Before their execution they were charged with all sorts of heresy, to which John replied from the Scriptures, moving the by-standers to tears. And when the final demand was made: 'Will you maintain your belief?' he replied, 'Yes, we will.' They were then led, amid the cries of kindred and friends, to the church-yard, where a broad and deep ditch had been dug. Into this they were driven, wood was piled around them and they perished in the flames. To this day men tremble when the 'Heretics' Ditch' is pointed out in Strasburg. [2]

We find another body of Dispersed Waldensians, A. D. 1231, in the provinces of the Danube. They were subjected to a terrible persecution for three years by bloody Conrad of Marburg. An extended account of others is preserved in a 'Chronicle of 1260,' by an anonymous writer. They lived in the diocese of Passau, which was embraced in the Duchy of Austria. He gives the names of forty-two towns and villages in the diocese, some of them upon the Danube and others close to the borders of Bohemia, where Waldensian congregations were found. The Jesuit Gretser, in editing this report, omits the honest explanations which it gives for the spread of the Dispersed Waldensians. The manuscript lays it to the impure life of the priests, to the conversion of the sacraments into gain, to the multiplication of masses, to the prurient use of the confessional and to pretended miracles; such as, tears of blood flowing from a picture, the lighting of a lamp from heaven, the exaltation of false relics as those of angels, the sweat of Christ, and passing off the bones of oxen as those

THE FORBIDDEN BOOK.

of saints. Great fault is also found with the adoration of the pope as God upon earth, greater than men and equal to angels, infallible and sinless. An additional cause for public favor was found in the Waldensians themselves; for the author says that they were content in poverty, avoided lying, profanity and theft, and were diligent in business. They were shoemakers, weavers and other artisans; temperate in eating and drinking, and they led godly lives. Their converts were made by the Bible and religious books. They went as peddlers to a cottage or a nobleman's castle, offering fabrics or jewelry for sale; and when asked if they had anything else, they answered: 'Yes, great rarities; I have one precious stone through which you can see God, and another that kindles love to him in the heart.' With that these peddlers brought out the precious roll of Holy Writ. Whittier, our gentle Quaker poet, has beautifully pictured these heavenly, traveling Waldensian merchantmen with goodly pearls, thus:

> 'O, lady fair, I have yet a gem, which a purer luster flings
> Than the diamond flash of the jeweled crown on the lofty brow of kings;
> A wonderful pearl of exceeding price, whose virtue shall not decay,
> Whose light shall be as a spell to thee and a blessing on thy way.'
> The cloud went off from the pilgrim's brow as a small, meager book,
> Unchased with gold or gem of cost, from his folding robe he took.
> 'Here, lady fair, is the pearl of price, may it prove as much to thee.
> Nay, keep thy gold, I ask it not, for the word of God is free.'

Still another reason for their increase is found in that they were loyal to their prince and country. About this time a violent contest between Pope Innocent IV. and the Emperor Frederick II. compelled every Austrian to choose between his civil and his ecclesiastical allegiance. As Bishop Rudiger took sides with the Emperor and smote the papal legate with his fist, love for the pope was turned into hate in many hearts. In these political convulsions, when the Inquisition and the pope were set at naught, every papal interdict brought a Waldensian jubilee and the sect spread rapidly. Frederick the Warlike, Duke of Austria, who died in 1246, unlike the Emperor, had shown favor to the Catholics by laying violent hands on the Waldensians.

But no class of the Dispersed Waldensians call for more important notice than those of Lombardy. Those who settled in and about Milan were known as the 'Poor Italians,' and were a mixture with dissenters already on the ground. Our interest in them is increased from the fact that many of the Waldensians of Lombardy were really the followers of Arnold of Brescia, of whom we have spoken. For as the followers of Waldo were scattered abroad after his death, so the Arnoldists were driven every-where after the martyrdom of their leader. These, with the 'Humble Men,' so called, of Lombardy, multiplied 'like fishes,' and grew in favor with the magistrates of Milan, who gave them a piece of ground for a meeting-house, and allowed them to rebuild it after the archbishop had destroyed their first structure. Those who were merged into this body were numbered with the Waldensians of Lombardy. In 1877 Preger published at Munich what is possibly the oldest Waldensian document extant, which throws some light on them. It gives a colloquy between six delegates of the original Romance and as many of the Lombard Waldensians. These held a conference on their general affairs at Bergamo, May, 1218; and this account thereof was sent a few years afterward by the Lombardy brethren to the party in Germany.

All classes of Waldensians held some things in common amongst themselves, also with the Petrobrusians and with certain of the Catharists. Yet generally they are confounded with each other, for they are all supposed to have been alike; and so we fail to reach their differences. For example, the Council of Toulouse and the second and third Lateran Councils launched decrees against those who rejected infant baptism, Catharists and others, some suppose including the Waldensians. But that of Toulouse, 1119, and the second Lateran, 1139, were held before the Waldensians existed; as according to all modern history they originated with Peter Waldo in 1160. Again, the third Lateran, 1179, as well as these preceding councils, condemned the Cathari, but not the Waldensians. Dr. Wall thinks that the Baptists of Cologne, 1092, came from Dauphiné, where Peter of Bruis had preached; and if he is correct, then they were numbered with the Cathari and condemned by the same councils. Mistakes have arisen touching the views of the Romance Waldensians on infant baptism, from wrong translations and uses of the 'Antichrist,' the 'Noble Lesson,' the 'Minor Catechism,' and the 'Twelfth Article' with the forged date of 1120. If they opposed infant baptism it is unaccountable that their literature, running through four centuries, gives no formal argument against it, and no accompanying demand for the baptism of believers only. And further, their enemy Pope Innocent in his letter No. 143 says, 'That the Waldenses err in the faith, or depart from sound doctrine, thou hast not expressed to us.' Yet at that moment no departure from the faith of the Catholics was more frightful than the doctrine that infants would be saved if they died unbaptized; and they enforced this doctrine by the most terrible decrees of their councils, but not by name, against the Waldensians. On the other side, too, this subject is full of perplexity. For if the Romance Waldensians actually practiced infant baptism from the first, it is very singular that they have left no argument for its authority, no trace of its defense, and no ritual for its observance, in all their early literature, while they positively rejected the Consolamentum.

When we attempt to supplement their own testimony by that of their contemporaries, we unfortunately find little to relieve this perplexity. Almost all Roman Catholic writers agree with Cardinal Hosius, who says: 'The Waldenses rejected infant baptism.' Addis and Arnold declare of them: 'As to baptism, they said that the washing of infants was of no avail to them.'[3] This impression is deepened by the fact that Farel, Œcolampadius and others, at the time of the Reformation, made strenuous efforts to convince the Waldensians of Eastern

Dauphiné and Savoy of the righteousness of infant baptism; as if the more zealous of them still rejected that doctrine. Dr. Keller thinks that they commonly practiced adult baptism and allowed their children to be baptized, saying: 'Since the Waldenses have always fundamentally (on fundamental principles) held fast to baptism on faith, where they neglected it they did so under the pressure of the constrained position in which they found themselves.'[4] Certain it is that their enemies, to whom we are indebted for the earliest account of their faith and practice, use strong language on this subject. But they fail to tell us clearly of what Waldensian branch they speak, while sometimes the fair inference is that they speak of the Romance and at other times of the Dispersed bodies, as those of the Rhine and other parts of Germany. Take the following examples:

I. Ermengard, about A. D. 1192, says: 'They pretend that this sacrament cannot be conferred except upon those who demand it with their own lips; hence they infer the other error, that baptism does not profit infants who receive it.'[5]

II. Alanus, who died A. D. 1203, appears to include the Waldensians amongst those who reject infant baptism, and yet it is not positive that he does; although he is writing against them. He represents those whom he denounces as saying that 'baptism avails nothing before years of discretion are reached. Infants are not profited by it, because they do not believe. Hence a candidate is usually asked whether he believes in God, the Father Omnipotent. Baptism profits an unbeliever as little as it does an infant. Why should those be baptized who cannot be instructed?'[6]

III. Stephen of Borbone says, A. D. 1225: 'One argument of their error is, that baptism does not profit little children to their salvation, who have neither the motive nor the act of faith, as it is said in the latter part of Mark, he who will not believe will be condemned.'[7]

IV. Pseudo Reinerius, A. D. 1230–1250: 'Concerning baptism, they say, the Catechism is of no value. Again, that the washing that is given to infants is of no value. Again, that the sponsors do not understand what they answer to the priest. They do not regard compaternity' (*i. e.*, the relation of sponsors).[8]

V. Moneta, the Dominican, who wrote before A. D., 1240: 'They maintain the nullity of the baptism of infants, and affirm that no one can be saved before attaining the age of reason.'[9] Hahn, in quoting Moneta, makes him say: 'These heretics charge that the Roman Catholic Church baptizes first and teaches afterward, while the Church of Christ taught at first before baptizing; also, that Christ and his Apostles never baptized any one without faith and reason.'

VI. One of the Austrian Inquisitors, A. D. 1260: 'Concerning baptism, some err in saying that little children are not saved by baptism, for the Lord says, he that believeth and is baptized shall be saved. Now, a child does not yet believe, consequently is not saved.' (By baptism, he must mean.) 'Some of them baptize over again, others lay on hands without baptism.'[10]

VII. David of Augsburg, A. D. 1256–1272: 'They say that a man is then truly, for the first time, baptized, when he is brought into their heresy. But some say that baptism does not profit little children, because they are never able actually to believe.'[11]

It may be that some of these writers did not intend these remarks to apply to the Waldensians alone, or if so, to all of them without exception. Some of the early members of the sect may have earnestly rejected infant baptism, while it is certain that many of the Dispersed did and practiced only the baptism of believers. Clearly those of the Romance class, who united with the Reformers in the sixteenth century, held few Baptist sentiments which made either party hesitate at the union. The embassy sent to Bucer and Œcolampadius, in 1531, shows how these communities stood with Rome on that subject. They really came to learn of the Reformers what their contest with Rome meant; for they did not understand the full difference between the contestants, and wished to be instructed. A great Council of the Waldensians was held at Angrogna, in Savoy, 1532, to which the Swiss Protestants sent Farel and Olivetan, and then a new departure was taken. Henceforth the Piedmontese Waldensians were joined to the Swiss Protestant Pedobaptists; although a minority of the Council refused to be bound by its decision, though not on purely Baptist grounds. One of the weaknesses of the Swiss Protestants has always been that they have spent their strength in asserting that Pedobaptism is valid; as if they had derived the first practical benefit from it in their struggle with Rome; and as if this hugging of a limb of popery were really necessary to an efficient protest against the other errors of that dark system. At the time that this union took place the Reformers were bitterly persecuting the so-called Anabaptists, even unto death, for rejecting infant baptism.

There was, however, a remarkable association between the Waldensians of the Dispersion and the Baptists in the sixteenth century, both in doctrine and practice. Mosheim and Limborch mark this likeness, the latter saying: 'To speak candidly what I think, of all the modern sects of Christians, the Dutch Baptists most resemble both the Albigenses and Waldenses.' [12] Indeed, in some cases, the Baptists evidently sprang from the Waldensians, and every-where in that century pushed resistance of infant baptism to the front; so that it was made the chief ground of their martyrdom by both Protestants and Catholics. Goebel, in his 'History of Christian Life in the Rhine Provinces,' says that wherever in Germany, before the Reformation, there were large bodies of Waldensians, there, during the Reformation, large bodies of 'Anabaptists' sprang up. At that time this people alarmed all Europe. Every Church and State stood in awe of their increase, and this panic united all their foes in the ignoble bonds of bloody persecution. While some Protestants denied the doctrine of baptismal regeneration, not believing that unbaptized children, dying, perished; yet they were as firmly resolved to burn all who cast infant baptism aside, as were those who lodged the salvation of babes in their baptism.

On one point more the Waldensians of the Dispersion were one with the Antipedobaptists. They insisted upon a regenerate Church membership marked by baptism upon their personal faith; while in later times, at least, most of the Romance Waldensians became Pedobaptists and semi-Romanists upon that point. The Baptists of to-day and the original Waldensians have much in common. They sought the restoration of Apostolic Church life in a true Christian character and in a holy Church membership; they followed the literal interpretation of Scripture; their priesthood was that of believers and not of a hierarchy, men renewed in heart and life; they rejected the error of regeneration by baptism; they believed in and practiced immersion only, even if their babes were baptized; and they made holiness of heart and life the point on which every thing turned concerning the living material of which the Church of Christ must be composed.

As to the Church government of the Waldensians, it is necessary to speak with great caution. The French Waldensians held to the Episcopal form by three orders, bishops, priests and deacons; but Reinerius says of the sect in general: 'They say, the bishops, clergy and other religious orders are no better than the scribes and Pharisees.' This relates to character, however, but they did not despise a true Christian ministry; for the same writer, who was a resident of Lombardy, says that there they had 'elders.' Yet there is nothing to show that they had any order of ministers amongst them as a universal thing; or even regularly located pastors, as we should deem them. They had 'barbs' or preachers, but on the principle of the seventy disciples whom Jesus sent forth two by two. These were not divided into orders, but into three moral classes, from which the mistake has arisen concerning an Episcopal form of government. They had the preaching class of celibates, the contemplative class of celibates, a sort of monks and nuns, and the preaching class of married men. Waldo and his preachers committed large portions of the Bible to memory, and going into the highways, hedges, streets and lanes of their cities and villages they repeated these passages, explaining and enforcing them. Whether men and women were learned or illiterate, they taught them the gospels by heart and, in turn, sent them out to teach the same. These went from house to house teaching and preaching wherever they could find hearers. They have 'No fixed dwelling place, but go about two by two, barefoot, clad in penitent's raiment, like the Apostles stripped of all, following the Christ who was stripped of all.' [13] Preger says that all 'Ecclesiastical authority was vested in the congregation, so that there was no room for bishops;' and, of course, it was their only court of discipline and appeal. [14] In this fraternity of preachers, in the absence of orders distinction was made between them as major and minor. This arose from the custom of sending them out in twos, a young man and an older, that the younger might learn from the elder. Reinerius represents them as holding that all men in Christ's Church stand on an exact parity, no one being greater than another, and that the sacrament of orders is a nullity. The account of the conference of the twelve delegates held at Bergamo shows as much. The first question which they were called to settle was occasioned by Waldo's wish that no one should be put over all the societies. They agreed to a sort of general superintendency as most conducive to peace and prosperity in all their communities. The superintendents were to be chosen for a definite period, or it might be for life.

It was further determined that either new converts or tried friends might be appointed as preachers. Waldo had prejudice against the co-operative communities to which the Lombardy brethren belonged, fearing the undue influence of prosperity upon them. The community system they laid aside, and after that, preachers and people alike were allowed to earn money. Their system of preaching shaped itself after the order of an itinerancy. Every year their barbs or preachers met to confer about the general interests of their people, much as the Society of Friends do now, and to 'station the preachers' as the Methodist call similar work. This they denominated 'changing the twos;' for except the infirm and old, they remained from but one to three years in a place. These preachers were poor and made poverty a virtue both of necessity and choice, and small sums of money were given to them for their support. But they had no regular salary, and at their annual meeting they divided money amongst the poor who were not preachers and amongst themselves, as each needed. If any of these traveling missionaries had fallen into grievous sins through the year, they were expelled. If any had committed lighter faults, they were admonished and forgiven. And when all had asked forgiveness of each other, they went out to do the work of another year.

George Morel, one of their preachers, details all this and more to Bucer and Œcolampadius, A. D. 1530, in these words: 'So also we go forth once a year, *to visit our people in their homes*, for they dwell in the mountains, in various hamlets and villages, and we hear one after another in secret confession. . . . Our people for the most part are a simple peasantry, gaining their livelihood by agriculture, scattered by the frequent persecutions in many places, and separated from each other by great spaces. For from one end to the other is eight hundred miles. They are every-where subject to the civil magistrates and the priests of the unbelievers. Yet, by the grace of God, it never or rarely happens that a Waldensian man or woman is arrested or punished by the said authorities, or that one visits houses of ill fame.' In this passage the word 'milli' (miles) has been mistaken for *mille* (thousands), and some unknown writer has put the figures 800,000 into the margin of the manuscript; from which blunder all sorts of fabulous numbers have been ascribed to the Romance Waldensians, while the valleys in which they lived could not be made to support 100,000 people at the most. When, therefore, we read in Reinerius and others of Waldensian 'churches,' we are obliged to take the phrase in a modified sense; for in truth they seem to have been less of a sect, in the modern sense of the term, than a disjointed series of congregations or societies of religious men. According to the showing of Herzog, these congregations were not all alike either amongst the Romance or the Dispersed. They appear to have had no fixed ecclesiastical organization, for which they each claimed Gospel authority; but they left their plans free to be modified by their trying circumstances to any required extent. It is tolerably evident that they were religious bodies without due constitutional form, serving only the ends of a godly brotherhood in brotherly love, rather than the purposes of strict supervision, watchcare and extension. All can see from the circumstances of the case that it would have been extremely difficult, if not impossible, to keep up regular and visible Church organizations with the laws of the State sternly against them. They could maintain amongst themselves an understood separation from the Catholic hierarchy, but they had not the civil right to avow an open rupture with Rome, and to perfect an open organized separation.

Indeed, it is questionable whether they did not consider themselves as a body of holy men still within the Church of Rome, rather than as separate churches, in the proper sense of the word, something after the Wesleyan order of societies within the Established Church of England during the life of Wesley and long afterward. That Church persecuted them bitterly, and yet Wesley and his immediate followers went to it regularly for the ordinances. There is a singular confusion in the statement of Reinerius and others on this point. They charge the Waldensians with arrogance for assuming that they were the only Church of Christ, and in the same breath they charge them with craft for remaining in the Catholic communion. For example, a Roman Inquisitor who claims that 'he had exact knowledge of the Waldensians,' says: 'They communicate and administer the sacraments in the vulgar tongue.' And again: 'They celebrate the Eucharist in their household cups and say that the *corporal*, or cloth on which the host is laid, is no holier than the cloth of their breeches.' Then, with marked inconsistency, Reinerius makes these two separate statements, namely: 'They do not believe the body and blood of Christ to be the true sacrament, but only blessed bread which, by a figure only, is called the body of Christ. . . . This sacrament they celebrate in their assemblies, repeating the words of the Gospel at their table, and participating together, in imitation of Christ's Supper.' Yet after that he adds, either truly or falsely: 'They frequent our churches, are present at divine service, offer at the altar, confess to the priests, observe the Church fasts, celebrate festivals, reverently bowing their heads, though in the meantime they scoff at all these institutions of the Church, looking upon them as profane and hurtful.' Last of all he makes this remarkable statement which seems to cover both the others, namely: that they hold 'a great show of truth, for that they live righteously before men, and believe all things well of God, and all the articles which are contained in the creed, only they blaspheme and hate the Church of Rome.'

We must either throw his testimony aside as one tissue of falsehood, or believe that some of the original Waldensians did accept such offices from the Romish priests, possibly from fear. But we cannot reject this evidence, for Morel himself states to the Reformers: 'We abominate the masses, but we attend them, and receive the host at the hands of the Roman priests.' This the priests would not object to, for they did not look upon them as an ecclesiastical body, but as religious guilds of weavers. Yet they cursed them again and again, for between A. D. 1307–1323 the Inquisition of France passed six hundred and seven sentences against heretics, and ninety-two of them were against the Waldensians under one name or another. Besides, David of Augsburg, A. D. 1256–1272, declares that in his day they attended the confessions, fasts, feasts and sacraments of the Catholic Church. And at the time of the Reformation, Œcolampadius lays the same charge at their door: 'We hear that you, through fear of persecution, have denied and concealed your faith to that degree, that you hold communion with the unbelievers, and go to those masses which are only worthy of abhorrence.' He then tells them that they had better suffer 'in the abyss of hell' than endure against their consciences the blasphemies of the godless. And, according to Gillies, their own historian, they only gave up all fellowship with the Catholics when at the synod of Angrogna, A. D. 1532, the Reformers refused to unite with them on any other condition. But the Bohemian Waldensians, as late as 1573, gave as the reason why they had never united with some of their own Waldensian people elsewhere, that 'for the sake of peace they attended the papal mass, which they knew to be idolatrous.' It is more reasonabl to apply this evidence as showing the Waldensians to be a Christian body without formal Church organization, than to regard them as hypocrites, as Reinerius did, or as members of two antagonist Churches at the same time for any reason whatever.

A word may be needful on their pre-eminent love of the Bible. Stephen of Borbone tells us of Waldo's care that it be translated into the peculiar Romance dialect. No characteristic was more marked in the Waldensians than their love for the sacred volume, and this love compelled them to share the treasure with others by translations into the Flemish, German and French. Neander says that their two characteristics, above all others in Germany, were their general distribution of the Scriptures and the common priesthood of believers.[15] Herzog finds no sect which was so zealous for the circulation of the Scriptures as they. Others built Church systems and sought to make the Bible support them, thus rendering it a secondary means; but, says Ochsenbein, the Waldensians laid down the Bible as the foundation and practically built upon its truths.[16] A Romish Inquisitor, in speaking of them, tells us: 'They can say a great part of the Old and New Testaments by heart. They despise the decretals and the sayings and expositions of holy men and cleave only to the text of Scripture. . . . They contend that the doctrine of Christ and his Apostles is sufficient to salvation without any Church statutes and ordinances, and affirm that the traditions of the Church are no better than the traditions of the Pharisees, insisting, moreover, that greater stress is laid on the observation of human tradition than on the keeping of the law of God.' Seisselius, Archbishop of Turin, also states: 'They receive only what is written in the Old and New Testaments.' Last of all, Reinerius reports that 'whatever is preached that is not substantiated by the text of the Bible they esteem fables;' for which reason Pope Pius II. complains of their holding that 'baptism ought to be administered without the addition of holy oil,' a fact which explains the further remark of Reinerius: 'They hold that none of the ordinances of the Church which have been introduced since Christ's ascension ought to be observed, as being of no value.'

It is not likely that the Catholics were first impelled to forbid the Bible to the people by the malignant purpose of shutting them up in darkness, but by that ultra conservatism which dares not put it into the hands of the unlettered to-day without an accompanying creed. The public mind is esteemed by many to be unbalanced, and its bent must be shaped carefully or it will be perverted. The Waldensians cast all such rubbish to the wind believing that the Bible never corrupted any man, while creeds have corrupted millions. Hence we find in one of their sermons on the Sower the following tribute to the Holy Oracles: 'The word of God is the salvation of the souls of the poor, the cordial of the languishing, the food of the hungry, the consolation of the afflicted, the excommunication of vice, the heir of virtue, the shame of devils, the light of hearts, the way of the traveler.'

At the Conference of Bergamo, the Lord's Supper was a subject of wide difference, but both sides appear to have interpreted the words: 'This is my body,' literally, as Luther did. The Lombards would not admit, however, with their Romance brethren, that any one could change the bread into the body of the Lord, but confined that power to holy men. They quoted many texts of Scripture to prove that the sacrifices of the wicked are an abomination to the Lord. Yet in order to provide for a faithful worshiper who was served by an unfaithful administrator, it was asserted that God himself would change the elements in such a case without the aid of man. The Lombards were further asked, 'Why they had given up their former practice of confession?' To which they replied: 'When I was a child I spake as a child, but when I became a man, I put away childish things.' With confession, the Dispersed Waldensians put away the childish practice of the mass, and abandoned the dogma of the real presence in the Supper. The great theologian, David, of Augsburg, who died A. D. 1272, declares unequivocally of the Bavarian Waldensians: 'They do not believe that it is really the body and blood of Christ, but only consecrated bread, which is called the body of Christ, figuratively, as Christ is also called the 'Rock.' Herzog gives the following description of the Supper as certain of the Waldensians celebrated that ordinance:

'Every year they met for the observance. The presiding officer called the assembly to order. A goblet of unmixed wine and a cake of unleavened bread were placed upon a cloth-covered table. The administrator exhorted the assembly to pray for the forgiveness of their sins, and repeat the Lord's Prayer seven times, to the honor of God and of the Holy Trinity, that he would himself prepare the sacrament. Then all fell on their knees, and prayed the Lord's Prayer seven times. After they had arisen, the presiding officer made a sign over the bread and wine, broke the bread, distributed it among them, all standing. In the same manner he served the cup.' [17]

Their views of Religious Liberty are easily gathered. So free did they hold themselves, that they contemned excommunication even from the true Church of Christ simply for the holding of any particular religious opinions, and treated expulsion from the Catholics with contempt. They silenced their ministers for immorality, but we know next to nothing of other punishments in their brotherhood. As to civil interference, Alanus says that 'They denied the right to persecute men for their religious views and practices.' In keeping with this statement, their 'Cantica' denounces the 'clergy of the Church of the malignants as evil hunters, who kill the hunted after the manner of hungry hounds. Pretending to be spiritual hunters they are become wicked foxes, that slay with evil teeth the poor chickens of Christ. Such are the homicidal monks. . . . Verily, as in the days of Christ, Annas and Caiaphas and the rest were Pharisees, so, now, Pope Innocent; they would not go into the house of Pilate lest they be defiled, they delivered up Christ to the secular arm, just as they do yet.'

Thus God raised up this noble people in the deep gloom of the ages to shine as a light in the dark places of the earth—a white lily in Alpine snows, to bloom amongst thorns, thistles and weeds. They give this account of themselves in the 'Noble Lesson:' 'The Scripture says, and we can see it, that if there is a good man who loves and fears Jesus Christ, who will not curse and swear and lie and commit adultery, and kill and rob, and avenge himself on his enemy; they say at once he is a Waldensian and worthy of punishment.' One of their smaller Catechisms teaches six commandments of Jesus: 'Thou shalt not be angry with thy brother, nor look upon a woman to lust after her, nor put away thy wife except for the cause of adultery, nor swear, nor resist evil, and thou shalt love thine enemy.' For the maintainance of these things they were hated and abused for centuries. In the Alps they were a simple and primitive community of shepherds and farmers, whose country was naturally inaccessible and barren. They passed through thirty-six persecutions which spared neither age nor sex.

The crusade of Simon of Montfort so utterly destroyed them that Sismondi says: 'Simon stamped out not only a people but a literature.' Dominic, the father of the Inquisition, persecuted them with a high hand. From A. D. 1160–1500 their fortunes varied from the greatest prosperity to the depths of misery; alternating from an ardent zeal against the Romish Church to a cowering dread and a wretched compromise on the part of many with the doctrines of Rome, very similar to the Old Catholic movement of our times. The most dreadful of all their persecutions began in 1560, when many of their villages were deserted. The old, the feeble, women and children, fled to the forests, the rocks, the highest peaks of the mountains. Untrained peasants were obliged to form themselves into small brigades. Tottering old men and boys organized themselves into guards and sentinels, and accomplished immortal exploits by their skill and fortitude against veteran invaders. Possibly it had been better had they earlier invoked the spirit of men, who, in defense of their holiest rights to serve God, must measure swords with the incarnate fiends and craven bigots who dared to oppress them, on the ground that to thrash a coward is to challenge his respect. The horrible Inquisition was formed for the express purpose of planting an iron foot upon the throat of the most hallowed rights of man.

It never was suppressed till organized force chastised it; and the same treatment might have cowed its devilishness much sooner, both to the honor of God and man. This tribunal of infernal origin clothed certain monks with limitless power to torture Waldensians and lead them to execution without legal forms or the rights of trial. And that power was plied upon these inoffensive people in those extremes which nothing can inflame but sanctimonious infernalism. Many of them were frozen to death, others were cast from high precipices and dashed to pieces. Some were driven into caverns, and by filling the mouths of their caves with fagots were suffocated. Others were hanged in cold blood, ripped open and disemboweled, pierced with prongs, drowned, racked limb from limb till death relieved them; were stabbed, worried by dogs, burned, or crucified with their heads downward. Fox relates one case in which four hundred mothers

CAVE OF CASTELLUZZO.

who had taken refuge in the Cave of Castelluzzo, some 2,000 feet above the valley, entered by a projecting crag, were smothered with their infants in their arms. And all the time that this gentle blood was flowing, that sanctified beauty known as Innocent III. drank it in like nectar of Paradise. Of the Waldensians and other murdered sheep of Christ, he said: 'They are like Samson's foxes. They appear to be different, but their tails are tied together.' The blood-thirst of the Dominicans earned for them the stigma of 'Domini Canes,' or the 'Lord's Dogs.' The very sentences which they pronounced in mockery of trial and justice were a Satanic compound of formality and heartlessness, sanctimony and avarice, obsequiousness and arrogance. At the conclusion of a session of the Inquisition, held in Switzerland, 1430, the following decree was published:

'In the name of God, Amen. We, Brother Ulrich of Torrente, of the Dominican order at Lausanne, and with full apostolic authority, Inquisitor of heretical iniquity, in the diocese of Lausanne; and John de Columpnis, Licentiate and especially appointed to this work by the venerable father in Christ, Lord William of Challant, Bishop of Lausanne, have directed by the pure process of the Inquisition that you, Peter Sager, born at Montrich, now sixty years old, thirty years and more ago forswore the Waldensian heresy in the city of Bern, but since then have returned to that perverse faith, as a dog to his vomit, and held and done many things detestable and vile against the most holy and venerable Roman Church. You have stubbornly asserted that there is no purgatory, but only heaven and hell; that masses, intercessions and alms for the souls of the departed are of no avail; and there are many other things proved against you in your trial, that show that you have fallen back into heresy. O grief! Therefore after consideration, and investigation, and mature consideration, and weighing of evidence; and after consulting the statutes, both of divine and human law, and arming ourselves with the revered sign of the Holy Cross, we declare: In the name of the Father, Son, and Holy Ghost, Amen;— That our decision may proceed from the presence of God and our eyes behold justice, turning neither to the right nor to the left, but fixed only on God and on the Holy Scriptures, we make known as our final sentence from this seat of judgment, that you, Peter Sager, are and have been a heretic, treacherously recreant to your oath of recantation. As a relapsed heretic, we commit you to the arm of the secular power. However, we entreat the secular authorities to execute the sentence of death more mildly than the canonical statutes require, particularly as to the mutilation of the members of the body. We further decree, that all and every property that belongs to you, Peter, is confiscated, and after being divided into three parts, the first part shall go to the government, the second to the officers of the Inquisition, and the third to pay the expenses of the trial.

Some of the town expenses attending the execution of Peter are found in the town records, as follows: 'Paid to Master Garnaucie for burning Peter Sager, 20 shillings; for cords and stake, 10 shillings; for the pains of the executioner, 28 shillings; special watchmen during the execution in the city, 17 shillings, 6 pfennigs; in the citadel, 9 sols; for the beadles, 14 shillings.' The fuel must have cost a large amount, as twelve wagon loads were used. Side by side with this fiendish record stand these two charges: 'Twenty-eight measures of wine for the dance at the court-house, in honor of the Count of Zil. —— cauldron, in which Caspar Antoine, of Milan, was boiled.'[18] Have Waldensian blood and purity ever been avenged?

CHAPTER XI.

THE BOHEMIAN BRETHREN AND THE LOLLARDS.

IN the thirteenth century and onward, a few seers read the signs of the coming Reformation. Men's souls felt the need of it, and hope lived on. They saw that the cause of Christ was not dead, its vitality was but suspended, and every-where prophetic aspiration looked for the end of shameless pretension and scandalous morals in the Church. Three classes are known as the Reformers before the Reformation: the Theologic school, chilled by farcical superstition; the Mystical, who groaned in spirit after God; and the Biblical, whose faith in the word of God never faltered. This last school longed to cast the Bible into the mass of torpid profligacy, as the prophet threw salt into the pot of death. John Tauler, A. D. 1290–1361, was the most noble and noted of the Mystics. He was the son of a wealthy farmer of Strasburg. For eight years he sought some one to lead him nearer to God, and at last found his tutor in a beggar at the gate of the cathedral. He allied himself with those known as 'Friends of God,' at Strasburg and Cologne, and deserves to be ranked with Fenelon for learning, piety and eloquence. Of his sermons Luther said to Spalatin: 'If you enjoy solid theology, just like the ancient, get Tauler's sermons; for I have found no theology, whether in Latin or in any other tongue, that is more sound and consonant with the Gospel.' He did little, however, to reform his times; he enjoyed inner fellowship with God and trampled upon his own selfishness, but had no power to work on the dead level of a reformer.

With the great revival of letters the learned began to appeal from the decrees of the Church to the text of the Fathers, from them to the Latin Vulgate, and then from that translation to the Greek parchments. But the Italian thinkers rested in the revived literature; chiefly in philosophy, the charms of verse and the golden measurement of prose. Some of them were kings amongst men; but the restored classic form, diction, elegance, imagination, were the scepter which they waved, and its motions made no stir of dry bones in the open valley of vice. Rome gloried in the beauties of Hellas rather than in the beauties of holiness, in the song and the drama rather than in the realities of saving truth. At times shame aroused her humanist mood and she had fierce fits of morality, when she thundered against her own wickedness, being careful always not to strike herself with lightning. She was like the acolyte, who all his life had been too close to the altar to feel any reverence for its mysteries. Old Greek thought was welcome, but not the Galilean. But when her learning went on pilgrimage into the Transalpine kingdoms and touched the less volatile and more robust races, it was felt at the foundations of humanity. German and Italian mind met at Constance and Basle; the souls of Dante, Medici and Piccolomini (Pius II.) clashed with the controversialists at Prague, Vienna, Cologne and Heidelberg; and while this seething mass was all alive, Guttenburg threw the first printed Bible into the vast ferment, and it has never been quiet since. From that day, 1455, the Reformation began to set in firmly. That very year Reuchlin, the father of Hebrew learning in Germany, was born, and twenty-two years later, Erasmus. These were called the 'Two eyes of Germany.' The first was the great forerunner of Luther, and fought against indulgences for a generation before that monk was born. He dared to compare the Vulgate with the Hebrew and to point out its errors. When rebuked for doing so he said: 'I revere St. Jerome as an angel; I respect De Lyra as a master; but I adore Truth as a God.' In that saying he uttered the great thought of the Reformation.

The first great master who had grasped it was the princely Yorkshireman and pure-hearted pastor of Lutterworth. He was the father of the greatest idea of three centuries, namely: The gift of the Bible to England in English, as the inheritance of all, from the king and queen down to the plow-boy and milk-maid. He read the charter of God to man traced on the parchment, and while his own heart burned he quietly vowed that it was the native right of every Englishman to warm his bosom by its reading. Men call this lowly, daring farmer's son the 'Morning Star of the Reformation.' More gracefully may Wickliff wear the trope of Augustine, when he compares some saints to the sun. He charmed by the luster of his rising, he strengthened by the reign of his light, he filled the heavens with the glow of his decline, and after five hundred years the moon and the stars of the Reformation make to him their obeisance. The inflow of French had corrupted the old vernacular, so that the Anglo-Saxon version had become obsolete. Besides, it had become a crime for those who could read the Scriptures in their mother tongue to do so. The clergy themselves were grossly illiterate, many curates knew not the Ten Commandments, nor could they understand one verse of the Psalter. The pope sent his bull to Beaumont for his consecration as Bishop of Durham; and Andrews, in his 'History of Britain,' tells us that he tried again and again to spell out its words in public, but was so puzzled that at last he cried out: 'By St. Louis! it could be no gentleman who wrote this stuff.' Edward III. entered his protest against this state of things, and Wickliff resolved to end it forever. At that time a manuscript copy of one page of Scripture was of immense cost and printing was not discovered. The annual allowance of a university scholar was but fifty shillings, the wages of a laboring man three half-pence a day, and two arches of London bridge only cost £25, in 1240; yet in 1274 the Abbot of Croxton paid for a fairly written Bible in nine volumes the sum of £33 6s. 8d.

In Wickliff's day the contest between the Church and the civil power was just growing severe, and he devoted his whole life to a struggle with the papacy. Newman well describes the conflict: 'The State said to the Church, "I am the only power that can reform you; you hold of me; your dignities and offices are in my gift." The Church said to the State, "She who wields the power of smiting kings cannot be a king's creature; and if you attempt to reform her you will be planting the root of corruption by the same hand which cuts off its branches.'" Bull after bull was thundered against Wickliff for one thing or another, five of them in one month; but he quietly persevered, preparing his Bible for the common people. He took the greatest pains to make it plain, casting aside all foreign terms and scholastic words, using the uncouth language of the people, so that the most lowly and unlettered could understand what they read or heard. Knighton, Canon of Leicester, his violent foe, saw his drift and said: 'Christ intrusted his Gospel to the clergy and doctors of the Church, to minister it to the laity and weaker sort. But this Master Wickliff, by translating it, has made it vulgar, and laid it more open to the laity, and even women who can read, than it used to be to the most learned of the clergy and those of the best understanding; and thus the gospel jewel, the evangelical pearl, is thrown about and trod underfoot of swine.'

Wickliff finished his work in 1380 and died at Lutterworth, his body sleeping there amongst his flock, in the chancel of the parish church. As his Bible aroused the English conscience, the pope felt a chill; he heard unearthly sounds rattle through the empty caverns of his soul, and he mistook Wickliff's bones for his Bible. The moldering skeleton of the sleeping translator polluted the consecrated ground where it slept. The Council of Constance condemned his Bible and his bones to be burnt together. The pope shivered all over, chilled to the marrow, and he needed a fire to thaw him withal. So after the godly preacher had slept quietly for over thirty years, Chicheley, Archbishop of Canterbury, went down in state to Lutterworth to give new life to the venerable rector and to set him preaching again. A great body of solemn clergy went with him to enforce the grim sentence, and somehow managed to keep straight faces while they went through the pious farce of dragging the ghastly Yorkshire frame from the tomb. The little sanctuary stood on a hill, and when they had sated their ghostly ire at the charnel-house they drew the skeleton to the tiny river Swift, consumed it with dry fagots and threw the ashes into the generous stream. Every atom of his dust rested on a softer, purer bosom that day than Chicheley had ever known. Such a treasure had never floated on the laughing brook before, so it divided his holy ashes with the Severn and the sea. Little Lutterworth was too small either for his Bible or his bones, and now they are welcomed by the wide world.

Froude finds a resemblance between some of Wickliff's views and those of the Baptists, and others have claimed him as a Baptist. But it were more accurate to say that many who carried his principles to their legitimate results became Baptists.

His foundation principles were: 'That all truth is contained in the Scriptures, and that Christ's law sufficeth by itself to rule Christ's Church; that we must receive nothing but what is in the Scripture; that whatever is added to it or taken from it is blasphemous; that no rite or ceremony ought to be received into the Church but that which is plainly confirmed by God's word; that wise men leave that as impertinent which is not plainly expressed; that we admit no conclusion that is not proved by Scripture testimony; and that whoever holds the contrary opinions is not a Christian, but flatly the devil's champion.' In his translation he uses the words '*wash*,' '*christen*' and '*baptize*' in regard to the initiatory ordinance. His rendering of Matt. iii, 5, 6, is, 'Thanne ierusalem wente out to hym and al iudee, and al the cuntre aboute iordan: and thei werun waischen of hym in iordan and knowlechiden her synnes.' Again, in verse 11: 'I waisch you in watyr.' Also Mark i, 5: 'and thei weren baptisid of hym in the flum Iordan.'¹ He always retains the preposition '*in*' and never '*with*,' '*in* water,' '*in* Jordan,' even when he speaks of Christ's figurative baptism, his overwhelming in grief he gives the same rendering, Mark x, 39: 'Ye schulen be waischun with the baptym, *in* whiche I am baptiside.' The natural force of the word *in* is made doubly emphatic by the use of the word '*wash*,' wash in; showing that he intended to convey the sense of dip; according to Greenfield, 'It is evident, that to wash the body or person, without specifying any particular part of the body, must necessarily denote *to bathe*, which clearly implies *immersion*,' washing being the mere consequence of immersion. This sense of the translator agrees exactly with his common practice and that of his times.

Wickliff's translation was to kindle the truth afresh through all Germany, and to light the way of John Huss and Jerome of Prague through the flames of Constance. The Bohemians came of the Sclavonic race, and were originally known as Czechs. They conquered Bohemia in the sixth century, and becoming Christians under the labors of Methodius, a Greek priest, long remained members of the Greek Church. They were brought under papal supremacy in 968, when their ritual was abolished, the Latin imposed upon them, and the cup taken from the laity. Their king was elective, and while bent on preserving their constitutional freedom against the pretensions of Austria, they were restive under the religious restrictions of the pope. Huss was of this Czech blood, and intensely national in spirit, therefore antipapal, as all Bohemian Catholics were. Insular England, also, had the ear of Bohemia through Anne, the English queen, wife of Richard II., and sister to their own king. She was the personal friend of Wickliff, who was one of her husband's chaplains. Huss made his writings his constant study, and when he not only defended them but demanded their free use amongst the Bohemians, two hundred volumes of them were publicly burnt at Prague. Some Waldensians in 1385 had brought Wickliff's works to Prague, and the Queen of Bohemia had helped Huss to circulate them. Various scandals helped to awake Bohemia; notably amongst them the discovery in an old church at Wilsnak, of three communion wafers impregnated with what seemed to be blood. The priests proclaimed that this was the blood of Christ, and pilgrims came flocking from all the adjacent countries, even as far as Norway, to be healed, before the whole transaction was exposed as a fraud. When Huss and Jerome were burned all Bohemia was aroused, and in 1415, four hundred and fifty-two nobles not only subscribed to their doctrines, but bound themselves to protect the preaching of God's word on their estates. For a long time these Reformers maintained the Bible as the supreme authority in all matters of doctrine and life, but when they came to its interpretation they were hampered by the popish idea of uniformity; for they could not tolerate each other's rights, and so split into two parties. One body rejected all that was not expressly commanded in Scripture, the other accepted all ecclesiastical practices which the Scriptures did not expressly forbid; which is in essence the position of the Baptists and Pedobaptists down to this day. The radicals were called Taborites, from the name of the fortified mount which they held; the conservatives were known as Calixtines, from *calix* (cup) which became their symbol, and the kingdom was thrown into civil war.

The Taborites followed Ziska, a most intrepid leader. He was far in advance of Huss in his doctrines, not only pushing aside the traditions of the Church and leaving every man to interpret the Bible for himself, but, in 1420 his party published fourteen articles, amongst which are these: That the faithful are not to receive the views of the learned, unless they are found in the Bible; that no decree of the Fathers, or ancient rite, or tradition of men is to be retained, but those which are found in the New Testament; that infants ought not to be baptized with exorcisms, and that the use of sponsors should be discontinued.[2] Some members of this body joined the 'Brethren of the Law of Christ,' or the 'Bohemian Brethren.'

Before speaking of these, a word may not be unacceptable concerning that marked character, Ziska. He was a Bohemian nobleman, and in 1410 lost an eye in the war between the Prussians and Lithuanians. Afterward, he became chamberlain to King Wenceslaus. He was a most daring chief, whether of loyal or insurgent forces. Sigismund laid claim to the Bohemian crown, but Ziska withstood him with desperation. At Kuttenberg, a Catholic city, where his Catholic enemy burned, hanged and beheaded sixteen hundred prisoners of war as heretics, he retaliated terribly upon the monks and priests; and no wonder. He lost his remaining eye by an arrow-shot in a great battle which defeated Sigismund, A. D. 1420. But this made no difference with him as a chieftain. When entirely blind, his hot blood made him the same indomitable victor. He would take his stand on an elevation in the center of the battle-field, with his best officers all around him. Then he borrowed their eyes, as he turned his empty sockets this way and that. His staff reported to him the progress of the fight, and he gave his imperious commands accordingly. Almost without fail, panic seized the Germans, who were utterly routed again and again. At last, the emperor finding that he could do nothing against him, offered him the government of Bohemia, the command of his own armies, and a yearly tribute, if he would acknowledge him as the King of Bohemia. He spurned the tender, and at that point died of the plague. He had been the perfect terror both of the pope and the emperor when he had but one eye, and when he lost the second their torment increased. This dauntless, blind, old semi-Baptist, must have been of the sturdy type after which the iron-boned Roundhead and the steel-nerved Covenanter and the adamantine Puritan took cast. For, it is said that before he died, he pledged his followers to tan his skin for a drum-head, that the very sound of his hardened hide might strike terror into these brazen foes of God and man. This may be legend, but it is as seriously said that they granted his request; if so, to the honor of his religious posterity, he that hath ears to hear, can catch the sound of that 'drum ecclesiastic' all round the globe in this nineteenth century.

The Bohemian Brethren became numerous, counting about one fourth of the people. Even a century before Huss, King Ottocar II. found so many heretics in his realm that he applied to the pope to extirpate them. Peregrinus, A. D. 1310, attempted to convert or destroy them. But John of Drasic released the prisoners from patriotic motives and abolished the inquisitor's court. The Waldensians abounded over the border in Austria, and kept up their union with those of Lombardy. They so developed in Bohemia that they supplied numbers of preachers for Northern Germany, for in the Acts of the Inquisition in Brandenburg and Pomerania, 1391, four hundred Waldensians are mentioned by name. In 1393–94 it brought one thousand Waldensians under its power in Thuringia, Brandenburg, Bohemia and Moravia. Endless numbers evaded the inquisitors, but in 1397 one hundred of them were burnt in Steyer, Austria; and in the opening of the fifteenth century they had great influence in Bohemia. Peter Chelcicky, named from the village of Chelcic in Southern Bohemia, was the forerunner of the 'Brethren.' He was an original and independent thinker, criticised John Huss freely, and would take sides with neither of the Hussite factions. He first appears in public life in the Bethlehem Chapel, Prague, 1420, in a dispute with Jacobellus, on the wrong of appealing to arms in questions of religion, nor did he believe in war at all, not even in self-defense. He insisted on the new birth, and thought it better to baptize believers only, who could show their faith by their works, but did not absolutely forbid infant baptism; still, he would confine it to the children of believing parents. He says that Christ 'Speaks of faith first, then of baptism. And as we find this doctrine in the Gospel we should keep it now. But the priests err in baptizing the great multitude, and no one is found, neither old nor young, who knows God and believes his Scriptures. Nevertheless, all without discrimination are baptized. But we should hold firmly that baptism belongs to those who know God and believe in his Scriptures.' He complains that the masters at Prague had made baptism as common 'As a huckster who sits in the market-place and sells plums.'[8]

Palacky ranks him next to Huss, as the greatest thinker of Bohemia in the fifteenth century, and says that he was familiar with Waldensian views as early as 1419. Goll believes that he was one of their body when he came to Prague from his home on the Austrian border; as, in his neighborhood great open-air meetings were held, with lay preachers and baptizers. A council held at Bourges, A. D. 1432 complains thus: 'In Dauphiné there is a certain district included between the mountains which adheres to the errors of the Bohemians, and has imposed and sent tribute to them.' The Waldensian prisoners before the Inquisition at Freiburg, 1430, acknowledged that some of their apostles came from Bohemia; and Æneas Silvius, afterward Pius II., wrote, July, 1451, that all sects had migrated to Tabor, the chief being Waldensians.⁴ When they organized in the north-east corner of Bohemia, they so feared to take any but Gospel steps that they sent delegates to search for the true Church in any part of the earth, but met their ideal nowhere; then they sent to Vienna, to confer with Stephen for a formal union with the Waldensians, but it failed.⁵ The followers of Peter became a separate society, known as the 'Brethren of Chelcic,' but persecution and division nearly extinguished them in about fifty years, when they revived under Lucas, a new leader, who was sent, with another delegate, to visit Italy. On their way to Rome they passed through Florence, and witnessed the burning of Savonarola, May 23, 1498. These brethren found a welcome amongst the hidden Waldensians at Rome and more openly in Piedmont, but it was especially warm at the latter place, where they had much conference on points of faith and practice. The two parties could not agree in all things, but some of them united in a famous protest against the Romish Church, in which they say: 'Antichrist has, by cunning, taken away from the Lord Jesus the grace and truth of true hope by Christ's merits, and ascribes this truth to saints, clergy, sacraments, words, yes, to hell-fire. Participation in the merit of Christ is gained by faith, poured in by the Holy Spirit. The deception consists in this: Antichrist awakens the faith that, if one is only baptized and receives the sacrament, he has received the sacrament and the truth. Antichrist attributes the reformation effected by the Holy Spirit to dead, external faith, and baptizes infants in that faith, and in the same gives its orders and other sacraments.' What Erasmus said of some of the Hussites, appears to have been true of the Brethren: 'They admit none until they are dipped in water.' So, Camerarius tells us that many who united with the Brethren renounced the baptism of infants which they had received in the State Church, and were baptized before they came into the new fellowship.

Herzog shows very fully that at the opening of the Reformation, the Waldensian communities were numerous, not only on the Cottian Alps, but in Naples and Provence, 'besides scattered congregations in Italy, Switzerland, France, and Germany.' He also says: 'At various times they appear to have been numerous at Bern, Strasburg and Passau. In the last-mentioned place they attracted attention by refusing to pay tithes, and by rejecting monasticism, *infant baptism*, exorcism, and the sacrament of confirmation. When the reformatory movement began in

Bohemia, they were naturally attracted by it, and their connection with the Bohemian Brethren became a turning-point in their history.'[6] Goll, in his 'History of the Bohemian Brethren' (i, p. 73), says that their Tract, 'Reasons for Separation from Rome,' 'rejects infant baptism.' There is scarcely ground for doubt that the Brethren baptized all who came to them from the Romanists, they also rejected infant baptism as such, and in its place substituted this singular process, which they called a 'Baptismal Agreement.' When the child was christened, they exacted a solemn promise of the sponsors to bring him up in the faith. But when the child was grown up, and was able to profess his own faith in Christ, he received a second baptism, entering into the real baptismal covenant; of which, Herzog says : 'Really, as Flaccius protested to Bodenstein, the second act damned the first.'[7] They would not allow the baptism of a dying child, but would pray for him instead. 'Doubt as to the value of infant baptism is a specific mark of the Brethren.'[8] Lucas defended the practice of repeating baptism, both in those who came from the Catholics and those amongst themselves who had not received it upon their personal faith, down to 1521; but after his death, under Luther's influence, the second baptism was dropped and confirmation took its place.

About A. D. 1500 the 'Brethren' of all sects in Bohemia were so numerous in city and country, that Pope Alexander VI. sent Dominican monks to preach amongst them and hold colloquies, to win them back to his fold. But this failing, King Ladislaus II. was persuaded, in 1503, to issue bloody edicts banishing their laymen, who refused to recant, and committing their preachers to the flames. This scattered them as the hoof of a beast separates the roots of a bed of camomiles, but it did not crush them. On the contrary, they used the most active measures for their own vindication and defense, especially through the press, and the growing intelligence of Europe listened to their manly story. This persecution continued long, its tortures, imprisonments, and burnings ending only with the king's death, March 13, 1516. Bohemia has well been called the 'Cradle of the Reformation.' It is difficult to ascertain exactly when the Scriptures were first rendered into its native tongue, or by whom they were translated from the Latin vulgate. But portions so translated were in circulation before Huss, and about the time that he began to preach these several parts were collected for the first time; after his martyrdom copies were greatly multiplied. The greater part of a Bohemian Bible was extant at the close of the fourteen century, as it is well-known that Queen Anne of England possessed a Bohemian Bible. Æneas Sylvius remarked that 'It was a shame to the Italian priests that many of them had never read the New Testament, while scarcely a woman could be found among the Bohemians (or Taborites) who could not answer any questions respecting either the Old or New Testaments.' From A. D. 1410 to 1488, four different recensions of the entire Scriptures can be traced, and many more of the New Testament, some being translated anew. It is an interesting fact, that Guttenberg, the inventor of cut metal types, used them in printing the earliest edition of the Latin Bible (the Mazarine), A. D. 1450–1455 ; and that the Bohemian Bible, published by the Brethren in 1488, was one of the first instances on record, where the newly-invented art of printing was applied to the use of the Bible in a living language. This was fifty years before England enjoyed Wickliff's Bible in print, and four years before the discovery of America by Columbus. The love of freedom and education went hand in hand in Bohemia, and were common to her whole people. Before A. D. 1519, six printing-presses were running, three of which were owned by the Brethren, whose authors issued sixty productions between A. D. 1500–1510, witnesses to their mental activity. They also produced those hymns which have made them immortal. While under fierce persecution, their families were compensated for the loss of sermons, by tracts, books of devotion and inspiring hymns.

This godly literature went on increasing and preparing the world for the Reformation. When Bohemian nationality was lost in the Thirty Years' War (1620), three fourths of her population were Protestant, and the cultivated people of the nation choosing to renounce their country rather than their religion, sought their homes where they could, to the number of seventy thousand men, including artists, clergy, nobility and scholars. Every Bohemian book was burnt on suspicion or brand of heresy, and some individuals boasted that they had burnt sixty thousand copies of this sacred literature. Such precious relics as escaped the flames were shut up in various places, guarded by bolts, chains, iron doors and gates, and labeled 'Hell.'

In all that related to love for the Bible and religious liberty, Savonarola, the confessor of Florence, was in sympathy with the Brethren of Bohemia. He was a Dominican monk, A. D. 1452–1498, earnest, devout, and so versed in the Scriptures that he could almost repeat them from memory. He was a Christian patriot, who vindicated the rights of the Florentine Republic, and a political leader in that cause. He demanded the removal of the pope and the recognition of Christ as King. In person he was small, awkward in his gestures, violent in his manner, and profuse of imagery ; hence the vehemence of his preaching against the Medicean court and the pope, whom he regarded as an atheist. Pope Alexander VI., of abominable memory, tried to silence him by the offer to make him a cardinal. This offer he spurned, with the remark that he wished no red hat but one dyed in his own blood, 'the hat given to the saints.' Long practice at public speaking and much study so removed or overcame his natural defects that he became a consummate orator, who swayed the people almost to fanaticism, so that they held regular burnings of elegant but licentious books and works of art. He was excommunicated and finally burnt, with two of his disciples.

The LOLLARDS form an important link in this chain of events. The followers of Wickliff were early known by this name ; but some trace their origin to Walter Lollard, who was burnt at Cologne about A. D. 1322. The term was applied at

Antwerp to a society formed there in 1300 for ministering to the sick—it is supposed from the Dutch *lullen*—to sing in a low tone, as at funerals, where they soothed by slowly sung dirges. But it soon became a term of reproach, by an ingenious twist, as if it were derived from *lolium* (darnel), tares amongst wheat. Wickliff was regarded as the father of the Lollards, but whether his followers assumed that name, or it was pinned to them in stigma, is uncertain. During his life-time Wickliff sent out great numbers of itinerant preachers, who preached in market-places, moors, commons, and wherever they could find hearers. They increased so rapidly that Pope Martin raved against them in the most vulgar manner, and Archbishop Courtenay spent five months in purging Oxford University of their presence. The underlying spirit of Lollardism sought the right of unfettered thought, the free interpretation of the Bible as the rule of faith, and the apostolic simplicity of the ordinances. During the reign of Richard II., the followers of Wickliff sent Twelve Articles to Parliament seeking certain social and politico-religious reforms, for they shared in the political dissatisfaction which swept over the continent in the fourteenth century. It had taken an exciting form in Italy, France and Germany; in England, it concerned ecclesiastical property and the right of the State to confiscate it; the Lollards taking the negative of that question, not believing in the union between the Church and the State.

In seeking a thorough reformation of religion, it was necessarily involved in political struggles, for religion was held at the caprice of political tyranny. The pontiffs made pretensions to all temporal as well as spiritual power, and kings were sworn to obey them in all things. Innocent III. coolly instructed John of England what to do in his kingdom, and when he disobeyed, deposed him, expelled him from the Church, put his kingdom under interdict, absolved his subjects from their allegiance and forbade them to obey him. Thus crushed, May 15, 1213, John publicly took his crown from his head and gave it to the pope's legate, who, by his master's command, returned it in five days. The nation wrung its great Bill of Rights, Magna Charta, from John A. D. 1215, but the pope had the impudence to annul all its provisions. His bull reprobated it as a conspiracy against himself, as dangerous to the cross of Christ and destructive to the regal rights of England. He prohibited and annulled it in the name of the Trinity and of the Apostles Peter and Paul, then laid 'the fetters of excommunication' on the barons, placed 'their possessions under the ecclesiastical interdict,' and required the bishops to proclaim his sentence with the ringing of bells and the burning of candles. Things went on from bad to worse, until, when Henry IV. was crowned, the pope bound him by oath to obey him as sovereign lord in all things. This insufferable impertinence kept England in a continual broil with Rome, and as true Englishmen the Lollards could brook such outrages no longer. Their resistance made them objects of pontifical hate. Walden and others charged Wickliff with being one of the seven heads from the bottomless pit, and the adherents of Rome generally indulged in the same black tirades; amongst them Arundel, Archbishop of Canterbury, who denounced them as 'malignants,' 'putrid' and 'rotten,' till he frothed at the mouth. The result was, that from the accession of Henry IV., 1399, their blood flowed in a stream for nearly two centuries with slight respite, chiefly while York and Lancaster fought the bloody battle of the roses. Fuller touchingly remarks: 'The very storm was their shelter.' Capital punishment for matters of opinion in religion was introduced into the laws of England, 1401, and William Sawtre was the first Lollard martyr under that savage provision.

Fuller says that Henry was more cruel to the Lollards 'than his predecessors,' and Fox states that he was the first English monarch who burnt heretics. But Camden alludes to a case, it is thought the one recorded in the Chronicle of London, of one of the Albigenses who was burnt in 1210; and Collier tells of a deacon who became a Jew, was degraded by a council at Oxford, 1222, and burnt under Henry III. This inhuman torture had long existed on the Continent, and Burnet attributes its late introduction into England to the high temper of the people, who would not submit to such severity. But this consideration is not satisfactory, while the fact stands that Parliament deliberately enacted the law for the burning of heretics, making the nation responsible for their murder, while in other lands the will of the prince was sufficient to burn heretics without statute law. The English sheriffs were forced to take an oath to persecute the Lollards, and the justices must deliver a relapsed heretic to be burned within ten days of his accusation.[9] The fact is, that the pope

MARTYRDOM OF JOHN BADLY, 1409.

dictated English law at the shrine, and Archbishop Chicheley says openly, in his Constitution, 1416, that the taking of heretics 'ought to be our principal care.' John Badly, a Lollard and a poor mechanic, was brought before Archbishop Arundel, March 1, 1409, on the charge of heresy touching 'The Sacrament.' He said that he believed in the omnipotent God in Trinity, but if every wafer used in the sacrament were Christ's veritable body, soul and divinity, there would be 20,000 gods in England. Being condemned to death March 16, he was bound with chains, put into an empty barrel and burnt in Smithfield, in the presence of the Prince of Wales, afterward Henry V., who at the stake offered him a yearly stipend from the treasury if he would recant. Even where the accused recanted the punishment was barbarous. John Florence, accused of heresy, renounced his views but was sentenced to be whipped for three Sundays before the congregation in the Norwich Cathedral, and for three Sundays more in his own parish church at Shelton, bearing a taper and clothed only in canvas undergarments. The English had become mere serfs to a religious despotism, which brought them to the climax of wickedness that murdered its best subjects for claiming the sacred immunity to worship God as they would. England made certain shades of opinion in the Church 'high treason to the crown,' simply constructive treason at the most; for so-called heresy was made disloyalty under the pretense that the 'King of Glory was contemned under the cover of bread.' In other words, the denial of the 'Real Presence in the sacrament of the altar' was made an overt act against the monarch of the realm. And so, the chief aim of king and Parliament was legally to grill to ashes the most patriotic people of England. The secular method of punishing treason was by hanging or beheading, but Bale says that at the Parliament at Leicester it was enacted (2 Henry V.) that the Lollards should be hanged for treason against the king and burnt for heresy against God.

THE WHIPPING OF JOHN FLORENCE.

It was in keeping with this double-handed tyranny that Lord Cobham (Sir John Oldcastle) was put to death. He was a Welshman of great ability and consecration to Christ, who had been imprisoned in the Tower, but had escaped and was recaptured after being hunted for four years, with a price upon his head. Bishop Bale says that: 'Upon the day appointed, he was brought out of the Tower with his arms bound behind him, having a very cheerful countenance. Then was he laid upon a hurdle, as though he had been a most heinous traitor to the crown, and so drawn forth into St. Giles's field, where they had set up a new pair of gallows. As he was come to the place of execution, and was taken from the hurdle, he fell down devoutly upon his knees, desiring Almighty God to forgive his enemies.

JOHN OLDCASTLE.

Then was he *hanged* up there by the middle in chains of iron, and so consumed alive in the fire.' That is, he was hanged over the fire as a traitor, and then burnt as a heretic, 1418. This state of things did not cease down to the time of

Henry VIII., when tyranny changed hands only from the pope to the monarch. When the head of Anne Boleyn fell upon the scaffold, no man dared to proclaim her innocent, even on religious grounds, and the king used the power which the law left in his hands to persecute either Catholic or Protestant as he would. Indeed, for three hundred years no great soul arose in England who was able to arrest the despotism of pope and sovereign. Religious freedom or bondage ebbed or flowed through the will of the monarch, and, in that matter, the nation counted for little as against imbecile pope or royal despot.

When a heretic was condemned the church bells tolled, the priest thundered and the sentence of excommunication was pronounced. The priest seized a lighted candle from the altar and cried: 'Just as this candle is deprived of its light, so let him be deprived of his soul in hell.' All the people were obliged to say 'So be it;' then came fine, imprisonment and death. Under Henry VIII. it was proposed to consolidate all the penal laws against religion, when he said: 'Leave that to me.' He and his bishops then framed the 'Six Article Act,' which decreed that if a man denied that the bread and wine in the Supper were the very Christ, he should suffer death by burning and forfeit all his possessions to the king, as in high treason.[10] No mercy was shown under any circumstances.

The views of the Lollards on infant baptism are not so easily stated, as their teachings on the Real Presence and their resistance to Church power. Possibly Dr. Williams states the case as carefully as any one. He says: 'There were also among the Lollards, or early English followers of Wickliff, some who followed out the results of Wickliff's principles, in the study of the vernacular Scriptures to the conclusion that baptism went with faith, and that infants, not capable of exercising the one, should not receive the other.' He also cites the fact which Rastell has preserved in his Entrees: 'A Latin writ, sending over to the bishop for judgment according to the canon law, three several groups of Lollards, who all reject infant baptism.'[11] Walden denounced Wickliff 'for denying infant baptism, that heresy of the Lollards, of whom he was so great a ring-leader;' but probably unjustly. Fox also complains that one error of the Lollards was that they denied that children are lost who die before baptism. Wickliff practiced infant baptism, but denied that babes were lost if they died unbaptized. Hence, when some of his followers came to separate their salvation from their baptism, they naturally held it in light esteem, after the order of John Frith, who said: 'Baptism bringeth not grace, but doth testify unto the congregation that he which is baptized had such grace given him before.' The testimony is too nearly unanimous to be contradicted, that many, if not most, of the Lollards did not practice infant baptism, while some did, amongst them Wickliff himself. Knighton informs us that in a few years after Wickliff's death more than half the people of England became Lollards, and sowed a free harvest for the Baptists, but their sufferings were intolerable.

The most monstrous barbarity attended the martyrdom of William Tylesworth and James Bainham. Tylesworth was burnt at Amersham, 1506, when his only daughter was compelled to take a brand and set fire to the pile which consumed her honored father. Proclamation was made at his burning that whoever brought a fagot or stake to consume him should have forty days' pardon. Crowds of ignorant people brought them, and caused their children to bring them. After his martyrdom that daughter, with twenty-four others bearing fagots on their necks, were taken to Aylesbury and other towns as a show, after which their cheeks were branded with red hot irons.

JAMES BAINHAM AT ST. PAUL'S.

James Bainham, a barrister of the Middle Temple and the son of a knight, was imprisoned by Sir Thomas More, who tied him to a tree and whipped him with his own hands. He was sent to the Tower, loaded with irons, and condemned to death by Bishop Stokesley on charges of heresy. Amongst other things, he said of baptism: 'We belong to God by adoption, not by water only, but by water and faith.' His sufferings overcame his flesh and he recanted. He was then sentenced to walk before a cross to St. Paul's barefoot, to stand before the preacher during the sermon with a fagot on his shoulder and a lighted taper in his hand. After paying a fine of twenty pounds he was released; but on publicly renouncing his recantation with deep sorrow, he was burnt in Smithfield, April 30, 1532, and joined the noble army of martyrs gathered from the ranks of the Lollards.

WALDSHUT ON THE RHINE.

THE ERA OF THE REFORMATION.

CHAPTER I.

THE SWISS BAPTISTS.

A WORD here may be necessary as to the proper name of this interesting people; were they Baptists or Anabaptists? They are commonly characterized as 'Anabaptists' by friends and foes; yet this name was especially offensive to them, as it charged them with *re*baptizing those whom they regarded as unbaptized and because it was intended as a stigma. By custom their most friendly historians call them 'Anabaptists,' yet many of their candid opponents speak of them as 'Baptists.' The Petrobrusians complained that Peter of Clugny 'slandered' them by calling them 'Anabaptists,' so did their Swiss and German brethren after them. The London Confession, 1646, protests that the English Baptists were 'commonly though unjustly called Anabaptists.' Knollys resented this name, calling it 'scandalous;' and Haggar, 1653, rebukes Baxter for its use. 'You do very wickedly to call them Anabaptists, thereby to cast odium upon us, . . . why, I pray you, are you so wicked and malicious as to call them Anabaptists?' Blackwood, 1645, complains of being 'nicknamed Anabaptists. We deny your title; Anabaptism signifies baptism again; our consciences are fully satisfied with one baptism, provided it be such as we judge to be the baptism of Christ; and if our consciences judge that sprinkling we had in our infancy to be none of Christ's baptism, I ask you whether can we, in good conscience, rest satisfied therewith? We are, if we must needs be new named, Antipedobaptists, or Catapedobaptists, but no Anabaptists.' Baptists now refuse to be called 'Anabaptists,' and for the same reasons. Respect for ourselves and our ancestry demands that the offensive title be thrown aside, and it is not used in this work excepting in quotations. Neither we nor our fathers can properly be named Anabaptists, and to use the term is simply to accept a misleading 'nickname' pinned upon us in contempt. Modern Baptists need the admonition of Keller, who says: 'Whenever, at the present time, the name "Anabaptist" is mentioned, the majority think only of the fanatical sect which, under the leadership of John of Leyden, established the kingdom of the New Jerusalem at Münster. . . . There were "Baptists" long before the Münster rebellion, and in all the centuries that have followed, in spite of the severest persecutions, there have been parties which, as Baptists or "Mennonites," have secured a permanent position in many lands. The extent of the Baptist movement in the first period of its growth, is at present very considerably undervalued in cultivated circles.' He calls the Münster doings a 'caricature' of Baptist ideas, and adds: 'With the majority at the present time, those views are the ruling ones which three hundred years ago were vanquished after a severe conflict. . . . A more correct understanding of the movements, which, at the beginning of the Reformation were thus in collision, would be of the greatest value for an understanding of much of the development of to-day; and, any way, it is unjust that the nation (Germany) should fail to recognize some of its most gifted men simply because they are known as Anabaptists. In the last decades, out of the ruins and rubbish left behind in the desolation wrought by the religious war, already many an old work of art of that day has again been brought to light.'[1] Let us at least respect our ancestry enough to join the latest and best continental writers in calling them Baptists.

Baptist Switzerland did not lie in the forest cantons, in the narrow valleys sheltered by pinnacles which rend the clouds and are crowned with eternal snow. It ran farther north through the belt of free cities on the Upper Rhineland, on both sides of the river and the frontier. On the Swiss side it included Berne, Basel, Zurich, St. Gall and Schaffhausen; and on the German side Strasburg, Ulm, Augsburg, with other great centers of wealth and high culture. This republic of letters contained the best schools and universities in the Republican Confederation. Democratic ideas took root amongst patriots who had won their independence over the body of Charles the Bold at the gate of Nantz. They first prized the political principles on which their republics bravely stood, but found religious bondage incompatible with free States. When neither bishop nor king linked them to Church life politically, they concluded logically enough that religion was no longer a governmental science. In mediæval and aristocratic Saxony and other monarchies the Church and State formed one body, and religious life was honey-combed by a legal membership in the Church of newborn babes. Many asked, therefore, why republicanism could not properly let the commonwealth of Israel alone? Hence, when republics claimed the right to bind the consciences of their citizens and counted all criminals who resisted their mandates, a dark shadow fell athwart the republican escutcheon, for that class. As Baptists, they discovered that the conscience of each man being free Godward, nations who had conquered the right to take care of themselves could never be cramped back into an enforced religious uniformity.

The great Baptist movement on the Continent originated with no particular man nor in any one place. It seems to have sprung up in many places at about the same time, and its general growth was wonderful, between 1520 and 1570—half a century. Keller says: 'A contemporary, who was not a Baptist, has this testimony concerning the beginning of the movement: "The Anabaptist movement was so rapid, that the presence of Baptist views was speedily discoverable in all parts of the land."' He mentions Switzerland, Moravia, the South and North German States and Holland, with many principalities, and writes: 'The more I examine the documents of that time, at my command (as archivist of Münster), the more I am astonished at the extent of the diffusion of Anabaptist views, an extent of which no other investigator has had any knowledge.' He speaks of their churches in Cologne, Aachen, Wesel and Essen, in East Friesland, the duchies of Bentheim, Linden, Oldenburg, Lippe and the city of Minden.² He cites Frederic of Saxony, the Duke of Lüneburg and the Reformer Rhegius, to show that from 1530 to 1568, Saxony and the Lutheran cities were filled with Baptists, also the Westphalian cities, Soest, Lippstadt, Lemgo, Unna, Blomberg, Osnabrück and others. He says: 'The number of Baptists was especially great both in Thuringia and in Hesse, as well as in the "Evangelical cities," Bremen, Hamburg, Lübeck, Brunswick, Hanover, etc.;' and that ' the coast cities of the North Sea and East Sea, from Flanders to Danzig, were filled with Anabaptist views.' Then he finds them every-where, from the duchy of Cleve on the Lower Rhine, up that river to the Alps. The sixteenth century opened with a general awakening throughout Europe to the need of religious reform, and this was specially marked in Switzerland, before Luther. In ideal, the Swiss reformers longed to get back to the Apostolic pattern, to a spiritual Church free from the control of human policy, and their aims took a Baptist bearing. It is sheer ignorance to represent the Swiss Baptists as merely urging reform in a defective baptism. This is a monstrous bugbear to frighten superstitious folk, who count the refusal of a spurious baptism to what they call 'covenanted babes,' as an affront to Christ, and all one with 'soul-killing.' They held infant baptism in discredit, not only as a human institution, but as a flagrant impiety palming itself off as an institution of God, and asking the State to enforce it on pain of death, while the Church claimed to administer it by the authority of the Trinity! This double claim rendered it an abominable thing which stepped in between them and their children, robbing both of their natural rights. Looking upon it in this light, it became an alarming perversion of the whole genius of a spiritual religion, and a piece of wild fanaticism which forestalled all right of choice in either parent or child, in order to smuggle the babe into the State-Church. To force its baptism under the magisterial domination of pains and penalties was to bind the infant to a clerical despotism, which, if repeated in England or the United States to-day, would shiver their governments to atoms. The scenic caricatures of these Swiss Baptists have been a simple mendacity answering the end of an historical trick to nullify real facts and render honest men hateful.

When Zwingli took lead in the Swiss Reformation, he demanded obedience to the word of God in all Christian matters, and resolved to reject what it did not enjoin. When debating with Dr. Faber, before six hundred Catholic dignitaries at Zurich, 1523, he laid down this foundation principle. Faber demanded who should judge between them on the matters in dispute, and Zwingli pointed to the Hebrew, Greek and Latin Scriptures, which lay before him. Instead, the doctor proposed that the issue should be decided by the universities of Paris, Cologne and Freiburg. Zwingli replied that the men in that room could tell better what the Scriptures taught than all the universities. 'Show me,' he demanded, 'the place in the Scripture where it is written that we are to invoke the saints.' When Faber defended that doctrine by the Councils, Zwingli showed that as these erred, nothing was binding but the Bible, and said that he would go to the universities if they accepted the Bible as the only judge. Dr. Blanche said: 'You understand the Scriptures in one way, and another in another. There must be judges in order to decide who has given the right interpretation.' But Zwingli refused to give any man a place above the Scriptures. Many of his hearers had strong Baptist tendencies and took in this radical doctrine. Educated by so skillful a general, they turned his own weapons upon him when they took issue with him on other subjects; and he was powerless, being obliged to appeal to the sword drawn from the Catholic armory. He was the most advanced of all the reformers biblically, but the moment that he fell into controversy with his own Baptist disciples, he broke with his fundamental principle and made the magistrates of Zurich the decisive judges in the dispute.

The Baptists said: On all such questions the Bible is autocratic; apply it honestly, under the divine right of private judgment, without trammel, and we will follow it; but we refuse to take the interpretations of it which the magistrates give us, for God has not made them our interpreters in such matters. This compelled Zwingli to fall back squarely on the Romish ground, and in turn to compel them to follow the Council. Then came the first break between him and them, on infant baptism. At that moment he was so nearly with them on that subject, that he was willing to delay the baptism of infants 'until they arrived at years of discretion.'[3] He said in 1525: 'The error that it would be better to baptize children when they had come to years of understanding, seized me too a few years ago;' giving as his reason that 'There is no clear utterance in the New Testament that commands the baptism of children.' Keller attests that, 'Luther at the outset designated Zwingli and his followers as the party associates of those who held views in reference to infant baptism, that were different from his own.'[4] 'We can easily see,' says Hase, 'why the Baptists were not satisfied with the excuses of the Swiss reformers;'[5] and as easily we can see why Zwingli complained: 'The Papists call us heretics, and the Anabaptists call us half-papists.' Sometimes he encouraged the practice, sometimes not, always denying the regenerating efficacy of baptism; but finally he concluded to continue infant baptism on the ground that if it ceased the people would clamor for circumcision, as they must have a bond of visible union. Œcolampadius had said: 'We have never dared to teach infant baptism as a command, but rather as an instinct of charity.'[6] Like him, Zwingli feared a division in the Reformed ranks and resorted to these expedients to prevent this, until Pedobaptist pressure forced him to turn over the question to the civil power. As Dr. Dorner says: 'He saw that the setting aside of infant baptism was the same as setting aside the national Church, exchanging a hitherto national reformation of the Church for one more or less Donatist. For, if infant baptism were given up, because faith was not yet, there only remained as the right time for it the moment when living faith and regeneration were certain. And then baptism would become the sign of fellowship of the regenerate, the saints, who bind themselves together as atoms out of the world.'[7]

The Baptists of Zurich began to assail infant baptism in 1523, one of their pastors calling it a useless thing. 'One might as well baptize a cow or a calf,' he said. Then Grebel writes: 'Those who understand the teaching of the Scriptures in reference to baptism refuse to allow their children to be baptized.' Reublin rejected the practice and held a public discussion with the pastors of Zurich, the only result of which was, that the Council arrested two men of his congregation and three from the village of Zollikon near by for refusing to bring their children for baptism, fining them each one silver mark and thrusting them into prison.[8] When the Council demanded why they refused, they answered that Christ required them to believe before they could be baptized; and they stood there firmly.[9] Zwingli had published a tract on the subject which fanned the excitement, and the Council had appointed a public discussion. Grebel asked that the debate be in writing, with the Bible as the only source of appeal, and Zwingli agreed to this, but the Council refused. Yet when they met in the Council Hall, January 17, 1525, and his disputants held him to this Bible restraint, he ungenerously charged them with dictating that he should preach nothing but what suited them; and he became so excited as to draw forth the counter-charge of violently stopping their mouths by interruption, screaming and long address.[10] Zwingli presented the current Pedobaptist arguments of his time, and the brave Council, as in duty bound, sagely declared him the victor. With equal gravity they decreed the next day that all should have their children baptized within a week or be banished, and that a christening font at Zollikon, which had been demolished, should be repaired. These forceful arguments were repeated almost daily, and on January 21 the Council came to New Testament example, after the Jewish order, and 'straitly charged' the Baptists to keep silent on this subject; which was about as hard a thing as they could ever do. Of course this made Zwingli's triumph good, and the Baptist preachers were ordered out of the country within a week, as a punishment for allowing him to become victorious and for the sin of rendering themselves harmless.

All left but Castelberger, who was ill and allowed to remain for a month, but they charged that he must not hold any meetings, and so put Zwingli to the needless trouble of vanquishing him over again. The Baptist babes, however, were not brought to baptism, and on February 1 the Council ordered the disobedient arrested and each child baptized as soon as it was born. Mantz and Blaurock, with twenty-four parents of Zollikon, were brought to trial within a week. After sentence to pay the cost of their imprisonment and a fine of 1,000 gulden, all were released except two. Mantz claimed the right to baptize all who came to him, but was threatened with the Tower if he repeated the crime, and Blaurock was to swear allegiance to the authorities in this matter. The fair conclusion is that they both flouted the magistrates; for soon after, at a great Baptist meeting at Zollikon, Blaurock spent the whole day in preaching and baptizing. When this sad news reached Zurich the Council fined those who had been baptized, and threatened with banishment all who should be thereafter. Some few recanted, but most of them refused to submit. Zwingli was not dictator in Zurich, but he cannot be relieved of responsibility in this matter. The Council, consisting of two hundred, had entire ecclesiastical power over the city and canton. He appealed to it again and again for religious decisions, and approved its doings; in fact he was its guide. Yet it organized itself into a Protestant Inquisition, robbed Christ's disciples of their freedom, tortured them, confiscated their property and put them to death, and he approved its acts. He believed that the officers of State were responsible for the religion of the people and helped them to make Swiss Protestantism as intolerant as Romanism. Hess puts this point clearly: 'Zwingli said public order demanded the severity he exercised, but his decrees were in the face of the proclamation which the Reformers had made of religious liberty.'[11] His theory was exactly that of the Catholics, and he invoked the edge of the sword as effectually as the pope. His dream was power, and under the pretext of removing what he called a canker of heresy, he wielded physical violence.[12] In his sixty-seven theses against Rome he said: 'No compulsion should be employed in the case of such as do not acknowledge their error, unless by their seditious conduct they disturb the peace of others.' But these Zurich Baptists were never in sedition. They simply worshiped Christ in their own houses or in the forests and gorges, and the nearest they came to sedition was to insist that the magistrates had no right from God to persecute them for doing so.

All sorts of lame and flimsy pleas have been created to cover these barbarities, but their blood stains 'will not out.' These Protestant Inquisitors well knew that when their own religious opinions subjected them to civil tribunals, they resented such interference. Their enthusiasm had only been fired and their convictions deepened by whippings, rackings and burnings. Yet they tried the same severity upon the Baptists which the Catholics had tried on them. And that, too, under the plea that while it was wicked for Catholics to torture them, it was but an act of saving love for Protestants to drown Baptists in murderous waters. Zealous republicans themselves, they comfortably forgot that their Baptist fellow-countrymen had a touch of William Tell and liberty about them; and so they proved their own love of freedom by treating their fellow-patriots as harshly as possible. The common hypocritical apology, that a charitable veil must be drawn over such murderous proceedings because of the darkness of the age in which they lived, is little better than a crime. They had the most thorough knowledge of the art of gentleness toward themselves, dark as was the age, and the gentleness of those whom they legally murdered stood in incarnate rebuke before them; hence it was but one step to the Golden Rule of Jesus, had they not been better pleased to use the iron rod. Common justice pushes this mendacious pretense aside, and finds a true verdict against them as narrow, fanatical and wicked. True, the brutal laws of Frederick II. were still in force, but they professed to be loving disciples of God's Lamb and not Thugs under the emperor; and no law of his could compel them to slaughter their fellow-disciples for Jesus' sake. We may hoodwink ourselves as we please, and gloss over their acts as we may, but this Reformed Inquisition has painted its own portrait black and it cannot be bleached white. Its Draconian holiness throws all honest forbearance into spasms. It is worthy of the Pharisaic and Sadducean Sanhedrin, but is a disgrace to the light and sweetness of the Son of Man, whom they slew.

In truth, Zwingli had his hands full. His opponents had as clear heads and stout hearts as himself, their education was as broad, and they stood serenely fortified by the word of God. When Hubmeyer raised the issue of infant baptism with him, 1523, he wavered, as we have seen; and afterward when his Baptist friend reminded him of this in his published work on baptism, and pressed him for scriptural authority, he replied: 'The New Testament does not command the baptism of infants, neither does it forbid it; therefore we must look to the Old Testament for an analogy which will clear up the matter.'[13] Dr. Rule, no lenient apologist of Baptists, says: 'The Council of Zurich had been called on by Zwingli to decide what the citizens should receive as true doctrine, and at once gave evidence of their incompetence by expelling a devoted Christian, who, being an unprotected outcast, was made the first martyr of the Reformation in these cantons.'[14] As far as appears, he approved all the cruelties of that tyrannical body without a word of remonstrance, although he brought every trivial subject to their notice—throwing the blame upon the Baptists themselves after the usual shift, 'they deserved what they got.' Playing fast and loose with the New Testament himself, and baptizing children in obedience to the 'silence' of the New Testament, still he demanded of the Baptists a positive injunction of Christ for baptizing on a confession of him those who had been christened as babes. So he could stand coolly by and see the Baptists drowned, but surely not because the New Testament was silent on the subject of drowning Baptists. If its silence gave consent to the baptism of infants, certainly it did not render the legal murder of Baptists holy. Well might he admit that 'nothing cost him so much sweat as his controversy with the Baptists.'[15]

Who were these Swiss Baptists, whom the Reformed Inquisition handled so savagely? One of them was CONRAD GREBEL, who early in the Reformation was Zwingli's most admired and admiring friend. Born about 1500, his father was a noted member of the Zurich Council. He educated Conrad in the universities of Vienna and Paris. Like Augustine, his son was proud, moved in high society and led a godless life when young. In 1521, Basel invited him to high literary work, and on returning to his native city Zwingli became his pastor, discovered his great intellectual power and became closely identified with him. In a letter to Myconius, August 26, 1522, he says of Grebel: 'He is a most candid and learned youth.' But the next year they began to draw apart on the true character of a Gospel Church and broke completely.[16] He told Zwingli: 'The Scriptures teach that all children, who have not arrived at the knowledge of good and evil, are saved by the sufferings of Christ.' He held infant baptism to be a sin, by attributing to itself what only belonged to the cross of Christ. Again he said: That by faith in the blood of Christ only can sin be washed away, 'So that the water does not confirm and increase the faith, as the Wittenberg theologians say, nor does it save. . . . Let us form a community of true believers, for it is to them alone that the promise belongs, and let us establish a Church without sin;' clearly meaning not an immaculate body, but a congregation of regenerate men, rejecting the practice which made all in the State members of the Church by infant baptism. This Zwingli did not want, but wanted a State-Church, and objected, that it was not possible 'to make a heaven upon earth, for Christ taught us to let the tares grow with the wheat till the harvest, when the angels would separate them.' Grebel cared less about keeping the angels busy than he did for obedience to Christ, but failed to bring Zwingli to his views. He had no political controversy with his countrymen, excepting on the question of religious liberty, but devoted himself to missionary work in the villages on Lake Zurich.[17] The peasants there were in revolt and the Pedobaptist pastors rose with them, but he kept aloof, preaching only the Gospel. The great Baptist Church at Hinwyl was established by him, with many others.[18]

FELIX MANTZ.

FELIX MANTZ was a noble Swiss Baptist leader, a native of Zurich. His father was a canon of the cathedral and gave him a liberal education. He was a thorough Hebrew scholar, was the firm friend of Zwingli, and had been with him from the first. He began to question the scriptural character of a State-Church and infant baptism in 1522. In a scholarly manner he endeavored to draw Zwingli to this Gospel ground, but he broke at once with Mantz, who began to preach in the fields, forests and his mother's house, translating his text from the Hebrew, and expounding his translations. For this 'and the rebaptism of adults' he was arrested at Chur and driven from the city, but returned under the threat of the authorities to take his life. As he was from Zurich, he was shortly after sent there for punishment, and lay in prison for a long time. There he went through all sorts of disputations and sufferings, for he lived on bread and water. His release was offered if he would stop baptizing, and finally he escaped with twenty others, hoping, as one expressed it, 'That they could safely reach the Red Jews across the ocean,'—the American Indians, then recently discovered, expecting more humanity from them than from the holy Swiss evangelicals. Mantz argued with Zwingli on baptism and asked him to write a book on the subject, which he did with great severity, but Mantz was not allowed to publish an answer. [19]

At last the Reformed Inquisition accused him of obstinately refusing ' to recede from his error and caprice,' for they said that he would ' Seek out those who wished to accept Christ and follow his word, and unite with them by baptism, but let the rest alone in their own unbelief,' and many other things in the same line. They then chose Jan. 5, 1527, as the black day for his judicial murder. His sentence gave him over to the executioner, who put him into a boat, bound his hands over his knees, put a block between his arms and legs, threw him into the water to drown, and then his property fell to the government. He denied before them that he opposed civil government, spoke of the love of Christ very sweetly and left one of the most pathetic letters, exhorting his brethren to a Christ-like spirit. He was led on the day of his slaughter from the Wellenburg, the heretics' tower, through the fish-market and shambles to a boat, preaching to the people as he went. A Reformed pastor at his side sought to silence him, but his faithful brother and his old mother brushed away their tears and exhorted him to suffer firmly for Jesus' sake. The executioner put the black cap on his head, bound him to a hurdle and threw him into Lake Zurich, as he cried, with Jesus, 'Into thy hands I commend my spirit!' [20]

The effect of his execution was electric, and Baptists sprang up all over the land. Capito wrote from Strasburg to Zwingli, Jan. 27, saying: 'It is reported here that your Felix Mantz has suffered punishment and died gloriously, on which account the cause of truth and piety, which you sustain, *is greatly depressed*.' He wrote again within a week to learn whether he died for ' violated public faith,' or on account of ' obstinacy ' in religion, 'and with what firmness he came to the end of life.' The crime of the Council haunted its members, after the manner of the Baptist and Herod, and they wrote in self-defense to Augsburg that they slew him 'as a warning to others.' Bullinger accounts for Mantz's fortitude thus: 'Malefactors are often stiff-necked when they are executed.' This poor 'malefactor' demonstrated his stiff-neckedness just before his death, in these words: 'The Gospel teaches divine love, leads us away from hatred and envy to love. According to the nature of his heavenly Father, Christ showed his love to all men. Love to God through Christ alone can stand. Like our heavenly Father, we should be merciful to all. Christ forces not one to his glory, but chooses the willing and prepared by faith and baptism.'[21] And this was one of those frightful Baptist fanatics, whose very name sends a chill through some Christian veins.

GEORGE JACOB BLAUROCK was another Swiss Baptist worthy. He was a monk who abandoned the monastery of Chur for the Gospel, a very simple-hearted man, who became an intrepid and eloquent disciple of Christ. When he reached Zurich he went at once to Zwingli to be instructed in the way of salvation, with but little satisfaction. He then sought the Baptists, and in great agony of soul obtained remission of sins from God while amongst them. At once he saw that his infant baptism was not of Christ, and begged to be baptized on a confession of his own faith in his Saviour. Falling on his knees, Grebel poured water on his head. Zwingli charged him with schism in becoming a Baptist. He replied that he had the same right to separate from Zwingli that Zwingli had to leave the pope. Then he held debates with the reformer, once in the cathedral, and Bullinger's account of them shows that he was a full match for Zwingli. As he must be answered, the old farce was repeated of chains, imprisonment, and finally death by drowning. On the day of Mantz's murder, the hands of Blaurock were bound, his body stripped to the waist; and he was led through the streets, where, by order of the Reformed Inquisition, he was beaten till his flesh quivered and his blood flowed in his tracks.[22] On reaching the gates of the city an oath was demanded of him, that if he was permitted to go free he would not return. This he refused for a time and was sent back to prison, but afterward he took it and left the city forever.[23] Then Zwingli was mean enough to reproach the Baptists for not excluding him from their fellowship for having taken an oath which, he said, was contrary to their principles. He was pursued from place to place until, according to Cornelius, he was burnt at the stake at Claussen, in the Tyrol, A. D. 1529, but not before he had moved the greater part of Northern Switzerland by his hallowed eloquence.

BALTHAZAR HUBMEYER was the noblest of the Swiss Baptists. He was born at Friedburg, Bavaria, A. D. 1480, and studied philosophy and theology under Eck, the great antagonist of Luther, graduating 1503. In 1512 he became preacher and professor of theology at Ingolstadt, but was cathedral preacher at Ratisbon in 1519. He embraced Luther's views in 1522, and leaving his preferments in the Catholic Church he settled at Waldshut, being in full communication with Zwingli. His power and eloquence moved that city; he assisted Zwingli in the great debate at Zurich with the Catholics, 1523, after which they became the closest and warmest friends. His powerful ministry almost destroyed Romanism in Waldshut, and Austria compelled him to seek refuge elsewhere. This he found in Schaffhausen, but soon discovered that the Reformation in Zurich had not gone back to the Apostolic model. He had laid his best thoughts before Zwingli and Œcolampadius, who at first

BALTHAZAR HUBMEYER, MARTYRED AT VIENNA, 1528.

saw their consistency, then rejected them. However, he followed his convictions, left the State Church and was baptized by Reublin, at Waldshut in 1525, with more than a hundred of his former congregation. He felt his way to Baptist principles very gradually and on thorough conviction. At first when children were brought to him as a Reformed pastor for baptism, he preached on the little ones being brought to Christ and blessed by him without the use of water (Matt. xix); but if their parents still demanded christening, he gratified them without yielding his own views. After forming a Baptist church, he baptized more than three hundred of his former hearers, and the population became largely Baptist. He preached in the open air to great multitudes at St. Gall also, and made a deep impression on the popular mind in the second disputation at Zurich. Being obliged to leave Waldshut the second time, he now found refuge amongst the Baptists of Zurich.

There he was soon arrested and cast into prison, where he lay four months, appealing to his old friend, to the emperor, to the Confederation and the Council, but in vain. His health was broken, his wife was in prison, and he lay in a dungeon with more than twenty others: 'Where no light of sun or moon penetrated, where bread and water were the only nourishment, and these could not be taken for days together, on account of the sickening odors of the place; where the living were shut up with the dead, with no hope of escape but in death or recantation.'[24] The Zurich Inquisition used all methods to compel him to recant, for he had written several powerful books which were stirring the public mind; amongst them one 'Concerning Heretics and those that burn them.' He showed that all butchery under the pretense of zeal for Christ was a fraud, and an open denial of him who came to save men and not to burn them. Another work of his on Baptism so aroused the Reformers of Berne, Basel and Strasburg, that Zwingli was forced to reply. Haller said: 'Many have been misled by Hubmeyer's book, but do not be alarmed too much, *the Council has banished every Anabaptist*.' Zwingli's reply was so bitter and vindictive, that Hosek says: 'He gave reins to his passions;' and Stern writes of Hubmeyer's production, that he 'Showed moderation, respect for his opponents, and force, not in coarse or violent language, but in thought.' Many of his positions were fresh and very forceful. In answer to the evasive and shallow pretensions of Zwingli, that the silence of the New Testament permitted infant baptism, he said that the spirit of our Lord's command to baptize the believing forbade its use to babes, thus: 'The command is to baptize those who believe. To baptize those who do not believe, therefore, is forbidden. For example, Christ commanded his Apostles to preach the Gospel; in so doing, the doctrines of men were forbidden.' Was he correct?

Zwingli, Jud, Myconius and others visited him in prison, and by one means or another wrung from him a recantation. Faber says that he was laid on the rack, and Cunitz, that he was compelled to recant, April 6, 1526. His own words imply the same. His appeal to the Council of Schaffhausen says:

'I pray you, for God's sake, and in view of the last judgment, do not press and force me or any other Christian teacher, but hear me, summon my calumniators to appear against me, have no respect for persons, great or small, but judge righteously, for judgment is the Lord's and the judges are his servants. But should this, my earnest and heart-felt request, not be heeded, though even the Turks would not refuse it, and I should be compelled by prison, torture, sword, fire or water, or permitted by the withdrawal of God's grace, to say or confess any thing different from the opinion by the enlightenment of God I now cherish; then I do hereby protest that nobody may be offended at my deed, whatever God may bring to pass, and testify before God, my heavenly Father, and before all men, that I will suffer and die as a Christian. May God lend me a brave, unflinching, princely spirit, that I may abide on his Holy Word, and in a real Christian faith commend my spirit into his hands.'

He also tells us that he offered to discuss these and other issues with Zwingli in public, and if convicted of error they might put him to death; but if Zwingli were shown to be wrong, all that he asked of him was to preach the truth. This Evangelical Inquisition, however, thought the rack their most conclusive answer to his holy convictions, and in a moment of weakness the great confessor fell into the relapse which met the noble Berengarius before him, and the learned Cranmer after him. And in the wail of a wounded and humiliated soul he exclaims: 'They compelled, or sought to compel, me, a sick man, just risen from a bed of death; hunted, exiled, and having lost all that I had, to teach another faith.' A great triumph, truly, for Christian men of their standing and pretensions!

The people were summoned to the great cathedral, which was crowded, to hear his recantation and the death-knell of the Baptists. Zwingli preached a great sermon on 'Christian steadfastness,' save the mark, and loud and long he declaimed against these heretics; then Hubmeyer was to mount the pulpit and renounce his firm faith, to the delectable edification of the Holy Inquisition of Zurich. Egli says that Zwingli warned the magistrates not to trust Hubmeyer to speak in the cathedral.[25] He had a lively memory of what many weeks of labor had failed to do in shaking his faith, till the rack summed up the whole Gospel case. As the inquisitors could not forego the show, all eyes now turned eagerly to the broken frame of the meek Baptist as he climbed the pulpit. He began to read his recantation in a broken, weak and quivering voice, until his heart choked his utterance and he broke down. He swayed to and fro before his audience like a bruised reed shaken by the wind; when suddenly the unseen hand of God was put forth to bind him up, and raising himself to his full height, he filled the sanctuary with the shout, that 'Infant baptism is not of God, and men must be baptized by faith in Christ!' The crowd surged like waves and burst into tumult. Some were seized with horror and some shouted applause, till the roof of the Minster rang. Zwingli screamed above the rest, the inquisitors were in a Pedobaptist panic, and the scene closed by dragging Hubmeyer from the pulpit, hustling him through the multitude, and thrusting him back into his dungeon. Once more in his cell, he rewrote his faith in Christ, which writing he closed in these words:

'O, immortal God, this is my faith. I confess it with heart and mouth, and have testified it publicly before the Church in baptism. I faithfully pray thee graciously keep me in it until my end, and should I be forced from it out of mortal fear and timidity, by tyranny, torture, sword, fire or water, I now appeal to thee. O, my compassionate Father, raise me up again by the grace of thy Holy Spirit, and suffer me not to depart without this faith. This, I pray thee from the bottom of my heart, through Jesus Christ, thy most beloved Son, our Lord and Saviour. Father, in thee do I put my trust, let me never be ashamed.'

After much more suffering he was permitted to leave the canton quietly, whence he made his way first to Constance and then to Moravia, where we shall meet with him again in his new home.

SCHAFFHAUSEN.

CHAPTER II.

THE SWISS BAPTISTS.—*Continued.*

IT was customary for the ancient Baptists to use private declarations of their principles drawn up by some member of their communion, as they had no official ruling body to issue such statements. Persecution obliged their private use, because documentary evidence of heresy was greatly desired by their enemies, in proof of treason to the State religion. Such a Confession, the first now known, existed in the form of 'Seven Articles,' drawn in the year 1527. On July 31st Zwingli issued his *Elenchus Contra Catabaptistas*, in which he says that he had two copies of this Confession. He also says that scarcely one of the Baptists was without a concealed copy and upbraids them with failure to give their Articles to the world. He professes to give a copy of them, translated into Latin, *ad verbum*, and publishes it for the purpose of sustaining his charges that they were 'fanatical, stolid, audacious and impious.' Virtually he charged the Baptists with failing to stand up to their Confession like men, pitting their manhood against their patriotism and the fear of death. They must have felt this accusation keenly, as they were ready to die for their principles. SCHLEITHEIM was a little village near the foot of the lofty hill Am Randen, seven miles north-west of Schaffhausen, at the eastern termination of the Jura range. From this quiet retreat, away from their foes, these venerable Baptists promulgated their Confession of Faith in the form of a circular letter addressed without limit to the congregation of their brethren, thus: 'Letter of the Brotherly Union of certain believing, baptized children of God, who have assembled at Schleitheim Am Randen, dated on Matthias' day (February 24th), 1527. To the congregations of believing, baptized Christians.'

This Confession is given in full in the Appendix, in a translation from a German copy now in the archives of the Canton of Schaffhausen, made from the original document for Dr. Osgood. It was probably first printed by Beck.[1] Of course, it is not accompanied by any statement as to who formed the assembly. Its value and bearing are determined not only by internal evidence, but it accords exactly with the copy of Zwingli, with such differences only as arise from his Latinized form. The number and order of its articles, with their subject-matter, expression and diction, are identical, allowing for his Latin transposition. Signature to it would only have courted death with Mantz, who had been drowned by order of the Council for the same sentiments, on the 5th of January of the same year. It is a clear and powerful document, evidently the work of one master-mind, as is shown not only by its unity but from the accidental retention of the personal pronoun 'me' (*mich*) in the Prologue. Its author is believed to have been Michael Sattler, an ex-monk, highly educated, quiet and amiable, who suffered martyrdom May 21st, 1527, at Rothenburg on the Neckar. Its substance and Christ-like spirit render it 'shocking,' as the 'Britannica' expresses it, that its adherents should have been treated with death.[2] We shall find this Confession a perfect defense against the slanders of the sixteenth century Baptists, and an interpreter of their principles and conduct throughout.

A long list of Swiss Baptist worthies must be passed in silence for want of space, as Hottinger, Stumpf, Reublin, Castelberg, Ockenfuss and others; but something must be said here of the life and labors of

LUDWIG HETZER. Where he was born and educated is not certainly known, but he was a thorough scholar and distinguished himself at Zurich as an adept in the learned languages. He acted as scribe and editor of the second discussion there, the debate relating to the use of images; on which subject he wrote a popular tract, in which he challenged the Catholics to show that images are good for any thing but fuel. He adopted as his motto, 'God redeem the captives.' He translated Bugenhagen's Commentary on Paul's Epistles, in the preface of which he laments the timid interpretations of the Reformers and their half-hearted work. In Zurich he associated with the Baptists and was obliged to leave with their leaders, January 21st, 1525. He made his way to Augsburg and fell in there with the same class of brethren, but does not appear to have united with them. In September of the same year Œcolampadius employed him in literary work at Basle. That great author had prepared a work on the Lord's Supper, which Hetzer translated into the German and put to press in Zurich. In his preface to this work he objected to infant baptism, because salvation was attached to the water, also because unbaptized children were believed to be lost and were buried in unconsecrated ground.[3]

Again being compelled to leave Zurich he went to Strasburg and became fully identified with the Baptists there. He remained with Denk, sometime at Strasburg and then at Worms, engaged in translating the Old Testament. Once more he was banished and made his way to Bishofszell and Constance, but was thrown into prison for four months at the latter place. One day a charge was framed against him and the next day he was beheaded February, A. D. 1529.

The records of Constance charge him with having two wives. There was no witness before the court, and it has been said that he confessed this immorality on his trial. He had married the widow of Regel, a high citizen of Augsburg, who loved Hetzer, and to whom Hetzer had dedicated a book on the conversion of the Jews. At Constance the falsehood was given out that he had married his wife's maid, but at Augsburg, where Hetzer was better known than most public men, this allegation was not made. Nor do Zwingli or Œcolampadius, who knew him a thousand times better than the fanatical court at Constance, hint at such a thing. Strasburg, Augsburg and Zurich had taken pains to banish this accomplished scholar, some of them twice, and yet no man in Germany or Switzerland knew of his two wives except his murderers at Constance, and this only came to their knowledge on the day before his murder, and on his own testimony at that, as they say! Alas, master! Happily does Keller resent this charge against Hetzer, as 'an unproved and unprovable statement.'⁴ How would a self-convicted polygamist conduct himself before magistrates to whom he had confessed his crime? And how did Hetzer behave? John Zwick, with Ambrose and Thomas Blaurer, say that they were eye-witnesses. Thomas Blaurer says that when Hetzer was sentenced to death he was filled with joy, and a throng of clergymen, councilmen and citizens of all ranks visited him all day long. Zwick and Metzler were Reformed pastors of Constance, and Zwick says that he 'conducted himself with great propriety, God be praised in his behalf.' His friends spent the night with him in singing and prayer; he rejoiced that he had translated the Scriptures for the common people, and was impatient to be with Christ.

THE BEHEADING BLOCK.

Zwick says that he saw him on the morning of his execution. And what did the adulterer say? 'He addressed us all as his dear brethren. He constrained us all to pray with him. The room was very full. He now prayed to God with a seriousness such as I have never seen or heard.' Then what? Did he confess his guilt to those kind pastors? O, no; instead, says the same witness, 'He gave an exhortation to us preachers, and mingled it with a few words on infant baptism, that we should not enforce it as if we must whether or no baptize the children, but suffer it to be quite free.' When led to execution, he called the names of

Mantz, Hubmeyer and others who had received the martyr's wreath, exhorted Constance to show God's word in its life, and offered prayer for all present, in which the people joined with tears. Hast reports, that when he laid his head upon the block he said to all: 'If I have offended any of you in my life, forgive me.' Then addressing the throne of grace, he cried: 'If I have offended thy majesty my God, I thank thee that thou hast extended my life, so that I can now, by my last confession, rescue many, many souls!'[5] After this manner he beautifully confessed Christ. Opening his Hebrew Bible at the Twenty-fifth Psalm, he asked the people to kneel with him and read in a loud voice, at the 15th verse: 'He shall pluck my feet out of the net,' like Paul with 'these chains;' he dropped his eyes on the cords that bound him, and the people repeated the words after him, as well as they could for sobbing. He then offered the Lord's Prayer, adding at the amen, 'Through Jesus Christ, the Saviour of the world, by his blood!' As the executioner approached with the ax he prayed that the Lord would not leave him, and a voice from the multitude cried, 'God will not forsake thee!' A slight flush tinged his cheek, he calmly laid his head on the block, the stroke fell and the learned translator was gone.

The court at Constance appears never to have read the false charge planned against Jesus for alleged blasphemy, and how the evidence destroyed itself by contradiction. If it believed that this good man was an adulterer, it should either have purified its records or put a padlock on the mouth of its city pastors. John Zwick, who knew the history of Constance and that Huss and Jerome were martyred there, says of Hetzer: 'A nobler and more manly death was never seen in Constance. He suffered with greater propriety than I had given him credit for. They who knew not that he was a heretic and an Anabaptist could have observed nothing in him. . . . We were all with him to his end, and may the Almighty, the eternal God, grant to me and to the servants of his word, like mercy in the day when he shall call us home.' So Thomas Blaurer, his fellow-pastor, says: 'No one has, with so much charity, so courageously laid down his life for Anabaptism as Hetzer. He was like one who spoke with God and died.'

After Hetzer's death, Zwingli said that he had suppressed a book of Hetzer's against the divinity of Christ. On this statement some have classed him with Anti-trinitarians, but it strikes us as remarkable that this alleged evidence of his heresy should have been destroyed by his accuser, and that not one line of this mysterious book has been produced, especially as there is no confirmatory proof that he held these views, excepting a passage violently forced into that service from one of his hymns. On the contrary Keller, quoting from Dr. Beck's recent history of the Austrian Baptists, affirms that the 'proof of this charge has not been found.'[6] Hetzer wrote many hymns, which were published in Zurich after his death and are now standard in Germany as spiritual hymns. This particular one commends itself to Spener, Freylinghausen, and Franke, of Halle, leaders of the Pietists, yet the sentiment complained of is not Hetzer's, but one which he puts into the mouth of the world concerning Christ. He wrote a tract against 'Revelry and the Abuse of the Tongue,' and dedicated it to Achatio, a citizen of Constance. In writing to this friend, he says of Christ, he 'Made the world by his word, became flesh and dwelt amongst us, whose glory shall be seen.' And who can believe that he rejected the vicarious atonement of Christ, who closed his last prayer with these words: 'Through Jesus Christ, who saved the world by his blood.' He was never suspected of being an Antitrinitarian till after his death, nor do the soundest Orthodox theologians so account him now.

There were many centers of Baptist influence in Switzerland besides Zurich and Waldshut, for in 1527, the year in which the Brotherly Union issued the 'Seven Articles' at Schleitheim to the 'Congregations of Believing, Baptized Christians,' there were assemblies of that character in thirty-eight places in the Canton of Zurich alone.

ST. GALL became a stronghold of Baptist principles. In 1523 a large crucifix, richly carved and ornamented, stood near the Upper Gate of Zurich. One night it was overturned and it was found that one of the trespassers was a Baptist, who, for his fault, was banished from the city. He made his way directly to St. Gall his native place, and one day when Kessler, the Reformed pastor there, was publicly expounding Rom. vi, the iconoclast interrupted him with the remark: 'I infer that you think children may be baptized.' Kessler asked, 'Why not?' to which the Baptist answered: 'He that believeth and is baptized, shall be saved.' Soon after this, Wolfgang Ulimann, son of a distinguished citizen of St. Gall, returned to the city. He had been immersed in the Rhine at Schaffhausen by Grebel, who met him on the way. Grebel told him that a change had taken place in his own mind on the method of baptism and he convinced Ulimann that he should be immersed. Kessler says that Ulimann 'Refused to be sprinkled out of a dish, and was drawn under and covered over with the waters of the Rhine.'

His return to St. Gall gave a great impulse to the new movement. Grebel soon followed him, and on April 9th, 1525, this evangelist took a large number of converts a distance of two or three miles and immersed them in the Sitter River. These Baptists worshiped in fields and woods where multitudes heard them, and soon their church numbered eight hundred. Crowds came in from the Canton of Appenzell to hear the new faith, some say as many as two thousand, who carried it back and scattered it through their Alpine hamlets and valleys. Reformed pastors and others of note embraced it, and Baptist congregations were gathered at Teufen, Herrisau and Brunnen. They went to rivers and streams as they could find them for immersion. Besides, they used a great wooden vat in the Butcher's Square, at St. Gall, until a building known as the 'Baptizing House,' came to be regularly used as a baptistery.[7] Baptists became so numerous in Teufen that the parish church dismissed its Reformed pastor and elected Hans Krusi, a Baptist, in his place. He was soon arrested by the Abbot of St. Gall, and would have suffered death had not the people rescued him. On his second arrest he was taken to Lucerne and bound to the stake, when he rushed out of the flames, and the Catholic crowd would not allow the sheriff to lay hands on him.[8] Two years later, Ulimann and two others were burned at the stake at Constance.

Vadian, perhaps the leading citizen of St. Gall, became alarmed at this state of things which threatened to destroy the State Church, admitted that infant baptism had become a shameful abuse and desired reform, but in a gradual manner. So, as a conservative measure, he asked the city Council to ply the old machine and grind this dissent to powder. Grebel warned him not to dye his hands in innocent blood, but the Council imposed a heavy fine on all who should be baptized, and forbade the Baptists either to baptize or break bread, on pain of imprisonment or banishment. A special police force of two hundred was sworn in to enforce the decree, and violence was let loose in the city.

The Baptist Church at St. Gall was noted for strict morality and deep piety, but soon it was put to a severer trial than persecution. Goaded by the suppression of all their religious rights, some of this flock became doubly zealous, and when their shepherds were driven away one man found his head so turned that he ran into wild fanaticism. Like many monks, friars and canonized saints, he went into visions, ecstasies and rapts, in which he said God commanded him to slay his own brother, as a test of his faith. He committed the terrible fratricide, and inflicted a staggering blow on the Church. The most honorable bodies of Christians have been disgraced by similar events in times of religious commotion. The Baptists of St. Gall were shocked at the horrible deed of this infatuated crank and promptly discarded the crazy murderer, as did also a general Council of their brethren, held the next year.[9] It is no small disgrace to many writers that they have taken special pains to lay the crime of this madman at the door of the Baptists of St. Gall, because they could blacken them in no other way.

Would that such writers knew more of the spirit of Chalmers when he says:

'A sect may be thrown into discredit by a few of its individual specimens, and the same association may be thrown upon all its members. . . . A system may be thrown into discredit by the fanaticism and folly of some of its advocates, and it may be long before it emerges from the contempt of a precipitate and unthinking public, ever ready to follow the impulses of her former recollections; it may be long before it is reclaimed from obscurity by the eloquence of future defenders; and there may be the struggle and perseverance of many years before the existing association, with all its train of obloquies, and disgusts, and prejudices shall be overcome.'

No reasonable man will brand all the Apostolate with the falsehood of Peter or the suicide of Judas, nor all the Presbyterians with the burning of Servetus, nor all the Swiss Reformers with the cruelties of Zurich; any more than a man with a fairly decent conscience can lay this man's sin at the door of all the Baptists of St. Gall.

Probably the simplest and most reliable account is given by the enemy of the Baptists, Vadian, a burgomaster and judge of that city, first published in 1877. He says that Thomas Schucker had taken too much wine, or in some other way had become unbalanced, and toward day-break on the 8th Feb. ('Foolish Thursday,' as it is called), he went and cut off his brother's head.

'Then without coat or shoes, in shirt and stockings, he came running to my house, and said he had drank vinegar and gall, but not a word about his deed. I saw he was not right, and had him locked up, and at the trial it was plain that Thomas was *non compos mentis*. Every body felt sorry for him, for Thomas's friends were a devout and honest set of people.'

Surely that fratricide cannot easily be misrepresented more to the injury of his Church than of his family.

BASLE ON THE RHINE.

BASLE was another center of Baptist influence. It had caught a liberal spirit from Erasmus, the genius of its University, and from Œcolampadius, who was much gentler than his compeers generally.

Not only was he a friend to Denk and Hubmeyer, but at one time his own doubts of infant baptism were so grave that he was half ranked with the Baptists His early bearing toward them as a people was worthy of high manhood, and in public and private he labored with them in a Christian and reasonable manner to win them to his views, at least for some years; after which he finally denied his humane impulses and followed Zwingli in the attempt to convert them behind prison bars. As early as June 2, 1526, they were banished from the city, but they filled the country districts, where Mantz preached with great success. In April, 1527, Œcolampadius became alarmed at the weakness of the cruel decree, and complained that the government was too lenient; and in May, 1528, the law was sharpened in vain, for the persecuted returned to their homes despite hate, insult and scourge, and were thrust into prison to be rid of them. They were required to stop preaching in the fields and forests and to attend the State Churches; but all to no purpose, for the city and country swarmed with them. In 1529 nine of their number were arrested and brought before the Senate. Œcolampadius expounded to them the Athanasian and Apostles' Creed, and tried, in his blandest manner, to win them, but this was all one with threats to the end of recantation. A simple-hearted miller replied to him: 'Since I heard the word of God, renounced my irregular life, and was baptized on confession of sins, I have been persecuted by every body, while before, when I was plunging into all manner of vice, nobody chastened me or put me in prision. I am confined in the Tower like a murderer, and what is my crime? What evil have I done? None. God be praised, in your conscience I know you are convinced of my innocence.' A wood-worker then took the laboring oar and said: 'Turn over the Old Testament and the New, and see if you can find you have a right to draw a pension. You have more time than I, for I must get bread by the toil of my hands, so as not to be a charge to any one.' This piece of nobility was more than the august Senate could stand, and it burst into laughter. Œcolampadius, ever manly, rebuked the court, saying: 'Gentlemen, this is no time to laugh. Rather pray for the glory of God, that the Lord would soften their hard hearts and give them enlightenment.' Another of the nine cried out: 'Why do you so blacken our doctrine of baptism? I pray you by the love of Jesus Christ, do not persecute good people.' And still another said: 'They can do nothing to us without the will of the Father, who counts the very hairs of our heads. Do not fear, God cares for you.' Three of them recanted and were released, and six were exiled with the threat of death if they returned.[10] Officers were sent to warn others to depart, but they refused to go. One simple rustic said: 'You are not lords of the earth to order us so haughtily to leave it. I am willing to obey the command of God. But he says in the Psalms, "inhabit the earth," and I will inhabit that part of it where I was born and educated, and no one shall expel me by any prescript or mandate, while I live.' On another occasion Blaurock took the same ground, saying: 'I would rather die than forswear the earth, the earth is the Lord's;' and Baumgartner said: 'God made the earth as much for me as for the magistrates.'

The only result of this and other measures was that Œcolampadius advised the Council to treat the obstinate with greater severity still; and on April 1st, 1529, it issued an edict to imprison all Baptists, and keep them there on bread and water till they publicly retracted; then, if they apostatized they should be put to death by the sword. Two prominent Baptists were scourged through the city, and as the blows fell they admonished the crowd that 'Our principles would not appear so odious if you left off your sins. We suffer these stripes cheerfully for the sake of Christ and his baptism, for that is the only charge they bring against us.'[11] A great number of peasants were brought into the city in chains, for traitors and informers were abundant. When asked what they had done, they answered: 'Nothing against Christ or his word, though perhaps against certain old customs and rites.' Then in turn they asked: 'Why can we not have a church of our own in which we can sow the true doctrine of Christ, confer baptism on penitents, celebrate the Lord's Supper, and practice excommunication? Why do you, Œcolampadius, forever attack us, and attempt to destroy us and annihilate our doctrine which is of God, and which in your conscience you approve? Were you ever injured by us in the least?' Sometimes they were branded in the forehead, had their fingers mutilated or the tongue cut out.[12] In 1530, five of them were drowned in the Rhine without a murmur, while the witnessing multitude wept, praised their pure lives, their simple manners and their bravery in dying; and many inquired if theirs was not the true doctrine.[13]

Gastius tells of one hero who was put upon the rack to force him to betray his brethren, especially the man who had baptized him, but he would not reveal a word. After long and full torture he cried at length:

'I am a citizen of the earth, my country is every-where, and my burial-place anywhere. Why do you not kill me? I will not betray my brethren even if you tear me to pieces. My body is yours, burn it, scathe it, lacerate, destroy it if you please. Increase your cruelty, you will gain nothing. Thus far my soul is free from torture but full of joy, from the consolations which God pours into my heart. I have received the true baptism. The testimony of sacred Scripture persuaded me to do it. I have left a life of sin, and put on the likeness of Christ. I have plotted no evil that I should receive such cruel treatment.' In response to the promise of liberation from the rack if he would betray his brethren, he spat in the face of his tormentor, saying: 'Get thee behind me, Satan, thou savorest not the things that be of God.' All that the man had done was to be baptized on his faith. They finally let him go.

There is scarcely an end to this record of barbarities, and this suffering was endured with a resignation of the most striking character. 'Nothing could exceed,' says Starck, 'the steadfastness with which they endured all this. They declared publicly that their sufferings had come upon them for the sake of the people, and on this account they were willingly endured.'

Schaffhausen shared largely in Baptist blessing, as well as Hallau, where a Church was formed by Brödli, who, together with Reublin, baptized the entire Reformed congregation—a fact which greatly disturbed the Zurich Inquisition, but it was powerless in the matter. In 1526 there was a good interest in Berne, but all Baptists were banished from the city and canton. As early as 1526 they were very strong in the Grüningen District, upon which the Council of Zurich turned all its power to crush them. In 1525, Blaurock was arrested by the bailiff of the district while preaching at Hinwyl. The officer demanded help from the people, and when they refused, he forced the preacher on a horse and took him away. In order to enlighten his understanding, they removed him to Zurich, had a great discussion on baptism, and then put him in irons and kept him on bread and water in prison till their logic took effect. They tried to prove to him that the children of Christians are not less God's children than those of Jews, and that those who are rebaptized crucify Christ afresh. But poor Blaurock was slow to see how these baptized children of God demonstrated their sonship in his case; while he readily saw how his rebaptism was crucifying him with Christ quite surely. So, in order to prove their sonship, the Council, by public proclamation on St. Andrew's day, 1525, prohibited 'rebaptism,' by punishment without further forgiveness. In this mandate they frankly say to the inhabitants of the district, that its wicked 'Anabaptists' have proclaimed their doctrines without the permission and consent of the Church, declaring :

'That infant baptism is not of God, but has sprung from the devil, and, therefore, ought not to be practiced. They have, also, invented a rebaptism, and many, even unlearned in the Holy Scriptures, taken with their vain talk and so far persuaded, have received this rebaptism, esteeming themselves better than other people. . . . Therefore, have we imprisoned, and punished for their good, some of the authors of Anabaptism and their disciples, and have twice, at their desire, ordained conferences, or discussions, on infant baptism and rebaptism. And notwithstanding that they were in all cases overcome, and some of them have been let go unpunished, because they promised to abstain from rebaptism ; and others have been banished from our jurisdiction and bounds ; yet have they, disregarding their promise, come again among you, and have sown their false doctrine against infant baptism among the simple people. Whence has arisen a new sect of Anabaptists. Therefore we have imprisoned these Baptists, and punished their followers for their own good.'

It is noteworthy that neither the Council of Zurich nor any other court in Switzerland brings the slightest charge of sedition or disloyalty to the State against the Baptists. Occasionally, some question of that sort crops out on the examination of an individual prisoner, and in every case he repels the charge and avows his civil loyalty. But in this historical document, the only antecedent of their 'Therefore,' relates to the subject of baptism and the ecclesiastical divisions which had grown out of this issue; the penalty enjoined clearly shows that they so understood the whole question. It is in these words, 'Therefore, we ordain, and it is our earnest purpose that henceforth all men, women, boys, and girls, abstain from Anabaptism, and practice it no longer, but baptize the young children. For whoever shall act contrary to this order, shall, as often as he disobeys, be punished by a fine of a silver mark ; and if he shall prove disobedient, we shall deal with him further and punish him according to his deserts without further forgiveness. Let each one act accordingly.' The Baptists of the district appealed to the people, explained at length their Bible views of baptism, and said, most reasonably, that they could not depart from their convictions, citing many passages from the New Testament to justify their faith and practice. Then they concluded with these words : 'If now the members of the Zurich Council designate the baptism of Christ as Anabaptism, the common people will be convinced that the reverse is the fact, and that infant baptism is really Anabaptism. Now, we desire that you will leave us alone with the truth; if, however, this may not be, we are ready, for the sake of the truth, to suffer through the grace and power of God.' But they could not let them alone. Falk and Rieman, two Baptist preachers, had been put in prison by the Grüningen magistrates; so the Inquisition was thirsting for their blood and trying to get them into its own hands. These authorities would neither execute them nor turn them over to the Inquisitors, and Zurich appealed to Berne for help. The question of jurisdiction being settled, they were delivered to the Inquisition and after long imprisonment, on August 11th, 1528, they were examined; when they refused to betray their brethren, or to refrain from baptizing on their faith in Jesus all who came to them. They were condemned to death, September 5th, and were taken to the middle of the river Limat and drowned.[14]

At first, Zwingli and the Council were content with the fine and imprisonment of their victims, but when this failed to cure them they were loaded with chains. On the 7th of March, 1526, the Council of Zurich decreed that those who baptized any person who had been previously christened, should, if condemned, be drowned without mercy. On this ordinance Füsslin makes these remarks: 'If any one asks with what kind of justice this was done, the Papists would have an answer. They would say, according to papal law heretics must die. There is no need to inquire further. The maxim is applicable here. What the papacy condemns is condemned. But those who hold to evangelical faith renounce the pope and papal authority, and the question now arises, with what propriety do they compel people to renounce their views or religion, and in case of their refusal inflict upon them capital punishment?' Upon the plea that Zwingli tried to induce the Council to be less severe, the attempt has been made to relieve him entirely of odium; and happy would it be for his memory if his name could be purged of this blot. He had opportunity enough to have sent his protest down to posterity had he desired to do so. But this is all he seems to have said on the subject, and without dissent: 'The most noble Senate determined to immerse in water, whoever shall have immersed in baptism, one who had previously emerged.' Hence, it soon passed into a sneering proverb: 'He that baptizes will be baptized himself.'[15] If Zwingli opposed this barbarity, we have scant means of explaining the fact that on November 19th, 1526, the Council confirmed this edict and afterward carried it into execution. Besides, the same infamy was practiced in other cantons; showing that it did not meet with the condemnation of the leading Swiss Reformers. In the Canton of Berne, a decree was passed requiring the Baptists to attend the regular State Churches, especially at the quarterly communion. If they refused, they were to be banished; on returning the first time they were to be ducked in water, the second time drowned without mercy; and all who had been baptized were to be fined ten pounds apiece.[16] In 1530 (January 20th), Conrad Winkler was drowned at Zurich, as the fourth of its murdered Baptists; and Weesen, who lived at Zurich at the time, says that he was martyred 'For having rebaptized, against express command, so many people that he did not know the number. He leaped up, struck his hands together, as if he rejoiced at his death; and immediately before he was thrust under, he sang with a clear voice one or two verses of a hymn.' The name of Appenzell should be held in special honor, for, when in 1532 her seven sister cantons ordered the drowning of Baptists, she declined to sign the decree and for a generation left them undisturbed.[17] Now and then, also, there was an individual protest against the general barbarity. There is an appeal in the Munich Library from a Reformed preacher, who, while he looks upon the Baptists as erratic, not only denounces their imprisonment and slaughter but invokes God's wrath on their persecutors, and gives as his reason that, 'They do not deserve punishment but need instruction.'[18]

Even at Basel, where all sorts of cruelties had been inflicted upon the brethren short of the death penalty, November 13, 1530, its Council decreed that all banished Anabaptists who returned should be dipped in water and sent away again; and should they return the second time they were to be drowned.[19] As if divine Providence had thrown a special shield over the heads of these poor harmless sheep of Christ, against the vile accusation that they were reckless seditionists and suffered as such in Switzerland, we not only have the voluntary testimony of their foes as to their purity, but we have evidence that some of the best of their enemies resented these monstrosities as unjustifiable. Haller writes to Bullinger that the 'Anabaptists avoid vices, are bound closely together, and impose on the simple by their strict behavior. Their pertinacious constancy in facing death has led so many into their ranks, that some of the Senate (Berne) are averse to any more executions and favor perpetual confinement. The question has come up, Whether the sword ought to be used *on those guilty of no crime?* We have sent to Strasburg to know what method they pursue.'[20] The result of these deliberations was a new edict in 1533, urging pastors to labor with the Baptists, who were not to be touched if they stopped their baptismal agitation; but if they continued preaching and baptizing they should be confined for life on bread and water, and not drowned. Whoever heard that the legal penalty in any land for sedition was drowning; and who can give an instance of a man in Switzerland being drowned for disloyalty to the government? Drowning was chosen to spite their faith as well as to kill their bodies; but within a month this relaxation of the law was interpreted to mean liberty. Nevertheless, the Senate breathed easier when they were no longer obliged by their own law to murder their fellow-religionists. If Zwingli was opposed to this terrible death penalty, why did Berne send to Strasburg for light and not to Zurich? But, on the contrary, Zurich now sought advice of Berne about killing Baptists, and in answer that city sent back its amended decree.[21] Toward the close of August, 1534, however, Haller wrote that they were increasing again rapidly, and that 'The Senate extorted from us our opinion as to the best way to get rid of them, hoping we would favor their slaughter. On the contrary, we showed the Senate that the cause of this disease and heresy was the vices and various scandals prevalent in the Church, and then we made known our project. Nov. 8th, the Senate, the Councils and the thirty-five bailiffs from the country met, read over the old decrees, and then agreed on a new one. In this they declare faith is a gift of God, and we have only to do with external affairs. The advice given was, for all to hear the ministers, have their children baptized, go to communion or give an excuse, and have their marriages celebrated in church.' The Baptists who would neither leave the canton voluntarily nor take the oath were to be reported to the Senate.

Four short months sufficed to tolerate this more humane edict. In March, 1535, the Senate issued a declaration supplementary thereto, providing that those who would not submit were to be imprisoned eight days, then, if they persisted, they were to be exiled, and the men who returned were to be put to death by the sword and the women drowned. Still the Baptists grew, and in 1537 they prepared for an open Conference, which, in March, 1538, was held in the capital, debating all the old points with their persecutors. So thoroughly were the authorities confounded, that in the autumn of the same year they decreed that every doctor, preacher and chief of the 'Anabaptists' was to be beheaded without mercy, even if he recanted. Before the execution he was to be put upon the rack to find out 'what his intention was, and what the Anabaptists would do if they became more powerful than the authorities.' All others of the sect who were arrested should first be labored with, and if persistent put to death, the men with torture added.

The Third Article adopted at Schleitheim says of the Supper: 'All who would break one bread for a memorial of the broken body of Christ, and all who would drink one cup as a memorial of the poured-out blood of Christ, should beforehand be united to the one body of Christ, to wit, by baptism.' Eachard said, in 1645, that the 'Anabaptists would not communicate with others . . . by strictness of order.' And as to the act of baptism, the First Article says that all who believe in Christ are 'To be buried with him in death, that with him they may rise.' At this time pouring and aspersion had become very common in most of the western countries, and the first question which arose amongst the Swiss Baptists related to the purging out of infant baptism rather than the restoration of immersion. When that question forced itself upon them they returned to the New Testament order. Dr. Rule, who speaks contemptuously of them, says that they took their converts 'and plunged them into the nearest streams;' which well accords with the First Article and with Hubmeyer's use of the word 'dipping' in his writings. He prepared a Catechism for those who were to be 'baptized *in* water,' and expresses his belief 'that Christianity will never truly prosper unless baptism is restored to its original purity.'

The fact that they built a baptistery at St. Gall, and that John Stumpf, a Lutheran pastor, who lived near Zurich from 1522 to 1543, and wrote of them in 1548 from personal knowledge of their practices, says that they 'Rebaptized in rivers and streams,' is good evidence that they immersed. As we have already seen, another Roman Catholic historian, August Neaf, Secretary to the Council of St. Gall, in his history of that city, published at Zurich (1859–1863), says that in 1525 the Baptists there 'Baptized those who believed with them, in rivers and lakes, and in a great wooden vat on the Butcher's Square, before a great crowd.' Simler says that 'Many came to St. Gall, inquired for the Taufhaus (Baptistery), and were baptized.' (*Collection*, i, p. 132.) Then Sicher, a Roman Catholic, gives this account of their baptisms at St. Gall: 'The number of the converted increased so, that the baptistery could not contain the crowd, and they were compelled to use the streams and the Sitter River, to which on Sundays those desirous of baptism went in so great numbers that they resembled a procession.' [22] At first Grebel poured water on the head of Blaurock, at Zurich, out of a 'dipper,' and called it baptism. Afterward, when he changed his mind on the subject, he immersed Ulimann in the Rhine, and Cornelius tells of the joyous procession which he led from St. Gall to be baptized in the Sitter, a distance of nearly three miles. Surely one 'dipper,' at least, must have been left in that city, April 9th, 1525, to have rendered this service had it been needed that day. Dr. Osgood tells us that he took the pains, in 1867, to walk from St. Gall to the Sitter, to inspect the country and reach the reasons for their long journey. He found that 'A mountain stream, sufficient for all sprinkling purposes, *flows through the city;* but in no place is it deep enough for the immersion of a person, while the Sitter River is between two and three miles away, and is gained by a difficult road. The only solution of this choice was, that Grebel sought the river, in order to immerse candidates.' [23]

All this shows us what Œcolampadius meant when he cried out: 'You are not Baptists but Catabaptists, that is, "perverters of baptism."' [24] Featley says: 'At Vienna the Anabaptists are tied together with ropes, and one draweth the other into the river to be drowned, as it should seem, the wise magistrates of that place had an eye to that old maxim of justice: let the punishment bear upon it the point of the sin, for as these sectaries drew one another into their error, so also into the gulf; and as they drowned men spiritually by rebaptizing, and so profaning the holy sacrament, so also they were drowned corporeally.' He clearly alludes to the drowning of Hubmeyer's wife and others in martyrdom at Vienna.

24

ZWICKAU.

CHAPTER III.

THE REFORMATION—ZWICKAU AND LUTHER.

AMONGST the so-called 'Anabaptists' there were three views as to civil government. A very small party, those of Münster, believed in establishing Christ's kingdom by the sword at the cost of sedition and revolution. We have seen that the party represented chiefly by Hubmeyer, believed in government, paid all taxes and obeyed all ordinances that did not interfere with the free exercise of religion. But, as a magistrate must bind himself by civil oaths and use the sword, they held that a Christian should not be a magistrate, because the Apostles knew nothing of Church taxes imposed by the State, held no civil office and took no part in war. They thought that civil government was necessary for the wicked; but their foes either could not or would not understand them. Their modern enemies evince the same state of mind. Hence, in one breath they tell us that they were perverse, enemies of civil government, and would not touch the sword either for war or capital punishment. And, without blushing, in the next breath they tell us as coolly that they drew the sword, established theocratic magistrates and deluged Germany with blood. That is, they deliberately did what their first principles would not allow them to do, and suffered martyrdom for doing that which, in conscience, they refused to do.

The Sixth Article in the SCHLEITHEIM CONFESSION contains a clear and distinct recognition of the divine sanction of civil government, its legitimate powers, duties, and obligations. It as fully defines the absolute separation of Christian discipline and polity from the civil power—denouncing the use of the sword by Christian people for any purpose. It enjoins abstention from lawsuits in worldly disputes, and is so careful of the sphere of Christian action, as to advise exclusive devotion to Christian duty and refusal to assume the responsibilities of civil office. Whether we approve their views or not, we cannot readily misunderstand what they were. They had never known a government which did not require magistrates to persecute others for their religion; and it was but natural that they should shrink from any civil service which demanded such persecution as a duty to God and man.

Hubmeyer represented a third class, who believed in all the usual forms of civil government, in which all citizens should participate in common, including the proper use of the sword outside of persecution. These were called 'Swordsmen' by the other parties, and in 1528 two hundred dissidents withdrew from Hubmeyer at Nicolsburg, calling themselves 'Staffsmen,' to designate their non-resistant principles, because they would not touch the sword either in revolt or warfare. When, therefore, the Zwinglian and Catholic peasants of Switzerland arose against the authorities, the non-resistant Baptists refused to unite their fortunes with them, and Grebel denied that he ever entertained a thought of subverting the government.[1] Hubmeyer complained that his enemies, of whom he said that he had as many 'as the old Dragon had scales,' misrepresented him on this subject, and to put himself right he dedicated a tract on 'The Sword' to the Chancellor of Moravia, in which he thus speaks of the passage, 'My kingdom is not of this world:' 'There must be judges, or the Scriptures will fall to pieces which speak of their duties. "The power of the keys;" yes, that power belongs to the Church, but it is distinct from civil tribunals. So long as men will not obey God there must be courts. Let us be thankful for a just government, though our sins deserve an unjust one. "An eye for an eye;" yes, that was old-time revenge, but now courts execute penalty. "Our weapons are not carnal;" no, not the weapons of the Church, but the weapons of the State are. The two swords should not be opposed to each other. A Christian judge will be most apt to be just. Satan, depart and no longer mislead simple people. "Love your enemies;" yes, that is for the individual, but the government does not punish from envy, from hatred, but from justice, and is not referred to in the text.' No Reformer of the sixteenth century holds the balance so exactly as this, in defining the relations of the State to its citizens and to the Church. He advocated civil government and the freedom of the Church from the State as clearly as any writer of our own day. Nor did Zwingli misunderstand the delicate distinction which this class of Baptists drew on that subject. Under the title of 'Who gives occasion to disturbance' he issued a challenge to them, in which he says: 'They want to have a Church, but no government is to protect the preaching of the Gospel by any violent measures or interfere with the freedom even of heretical preachers.'

Denk, whom Haller calls the 'Apollo of the Anabaptists,' held to the same principles. He says: 'The Apostles treat earnestly that Christians must be subject to government. But they do not teach that they may be governors, for Paul says,

"What have I to do to judge them that are without?" He would have Christians withdraw from politics, and leave unconverted men to wield the sword of the civil and military ruler as a thing entirely separate from the Church. Denk took the ground, that all government must be sustained as the Apostles sustained it, namely: That in the Church Christ was King and held the spiritual sword for excommunication. That was the only spiritual sword which he knew; but for the proper ends of civil government, the material sword was in the hands of the State, whose authority was from God. The other Reformers knew nothing about the distinction between civil and religious government on this broad and high plane. Keller draws this sharp distinction: 'While Denk, with energy, defended the proposition that it was not becoming in civil magistrates to proceed against their subjects with force in matters of faith; both Luther and Zwingli taught that it was the duty of the civil magistrates to establish the true faith within their territorial limits, and to maintain it with the severest penalties.' That discreet historian, Mosheim, recognizes these various classes of Baptists, and says: 'They are called Anabaptists because they all denied that infants are proper subjects of baptism, and solemnly baptized over again those who had been baptized in infancy; yet, from the very beginning, just as at the present day, they were split into various parties, which disagreed and disputed about points of no small importance.' He is too careful to make 'Anabaptism' and sedition convertible words, but says, that these Baptists

'Did not all suffer on account of their crimes, but many of them merely for the erroneous opinions which they maintained honestly, without fraud or crime. It is, indeed, true that many Anabaptists were put to death, not as being bad citizens or injurious members of civil society, but as being incurable heretics, who were condemned by the old canon laws, for the error concerning adult baptism. . . . I could wish there had been some discrimination made, and that all who believe that adults only are to be baptized, and that the ungodly are to be expelled the Church, had not been indiscriminately put to death.' [2]

But true history is bringing them its calm revenges of justification.

In the first quarter of the sixteenth century many Catholics were much stirred on the subject of Church reform, but the most earnest souls sought it mainly in the rise and growth of monastic orders, in which Saxony abounded. Their idea was, that withdrawal from the world was better than victory over it, that it were better to avoid temptation than to combat it, and to be a monk than to be a man. Pressed to this extreme, piety lapsed into senility on the one hand and into fanaticism on the other. In this atmosphere the mystics had sprung up amongst the pre-Reformers with much honor to Christianity. The forgotten doctrine of the Spirit, as an experimental fact, appeared in one direction and a sterner ritualistic system in another. The mystics threw aside the wild notion that baptism can cleanse the soul, and that the soul is sustained by a morsel of bread and a drop of wine, instead of by the indwelling Spirit. Tauler caught this doctrine from Eckart, his master, and while Luther was a monk, he embraced it from Tauler. But some mystics were deluded into that reflective method which associates the indwelling Spirit with direct revelations from God, and which lifts the soul above religious speculation or mistake.

The flourishing city of Zwickau was the home of many who held this view. It lay in Saxony near the borders of Bohemia. Silver mines were discovered there in 1491, the yield of which was so great that the ore could not be coined and fabulous fortunes were gathered. Many cloth-makers grew up under this wealth princely merchants, and in 1521, 300,000 pounds of wool were used and 10,000 pieces of cloth made. Amongst the well-to-do master-weavers was Nicholas Storck, probably a native of the city. He and his journeymen began to hold such meetings for prayer and praise as the Bohemian Brethren held.

Thomas Münzer was a friend of Luther's and pastor of the Lutheran Church in Zwickau. At Easter he pronounced from the pulpit that Storck understood the Bible better than the priests and was possessed of the Holy Spirit. Storck soon set apart twelve apostles and seventy-two disciples, rejected infant baptism, and baptized believers only. Münzer stood by him, but not as stoutly as Cellarius and Stübner, two young scholars, friends of Melancthon, who came to the city about that time. Dr. Sella, another Lutheran, a member of Münzer's congregation, was at the head of the city authorities as burgomaster and identified himself with the movement, which gained ground for about a year, without interference from the City Council. But he died April 10, 1521, and this opened a conflict.

On the 14th Wildenauer, another Lutheran pastor, of haughty manners and loose habits, being denounced by Storck, made a stir. On the 16th the Council deprived Münzer of his parish, as one of the parties to the quarrel, and he left for Prague. Great excitement followed; fifty-five weavers were imprisoned in the Tower, and the magistrates called Storck to account for many things, amongst others, for teaching that children are not benefited by baptism. Keller quotes an old chronicle, which says that Storck was brought before the Council for teaching heretical Bohemian sentiments.[3] In fact, he is charged with introducing the Bohemian heresy into Zwickau; thus connecting the Bohemian Brethren with the German Baptists. One, who met Storck soon after, says of his person: 'He was rather slim, wore a long gray coat without folds and a broad-brimmed hat. He conversed easily, pleasantly and humbly, and replied to answers in a manner as devout and holy, as if he had been an angel of God.'[4] Then he, with Stübner and Cellarius, went to Wittenberg to consult with Melancthon, while Luther was still at the Wartburg. Stübner spent six months with Melancthon, who said that Storck 'had the right understanding of the Bible.' He was charmed by their devout manner and spirit, for he thought that their views were agreeable to reason and deserved examination, and wrote to the Elector: 'I cannot tell how much I am moved by these men.' The Elector answered: 'We know not what God will accomplish through these plebeians; now and then he is wont to use obscure men in his service.' But he advised Melancthon not to hold a disputation with them on baptism. He had better wait for Luther, for they quoted St. Augustine to prove that nothing could be brought in favor of infant baptism, except ecclesiastical custom. Up to this point all these parties were Lutherans.

Carlstadt, a man of deep convictions, who sacrificed much for the truth, and was a superior scholar to Luther, espoused their cause at Wittenberg, and, all together, they greatly moved the city. In the ensuing April, however, Luther returned, and met them in sharp controversy, or, as he expresses it, began 'to rap these visionaries on the snout.' He denounced them in the cathedral, and they went to preach elsewhere. He also denounced Carlstadt as a 'fanatic' because he rejected the doctrine of the Real Presence and destroyed images. In September, 1522, Storck returned from a preaching tour through Thuringia, and labored with Luther to drop infant baptism and make the Reformation thorough. But while translating the Bible, at the Wartburg, Luther had determined to retain whatever practices it did not forbid. At first he had no light struggle on this subject of infant baptism. On other subjects he had been forced, against his will, step by step, to abandon the Fathers, the Councils and Catholic tradition, being driven to the authority of the Scriptures. But when he found no Bible authority for infant baptism, he assumed a new attitude. At that point he had a fiery contest with himself as to the true key of biblical interpretation, and he deliberately chose the negative turn. That is, he determined to abide by what the Scriptures did not forbid, instead of by what they enjoined, as the law of ordinances. He saw at a glance where his rule of interpretation on other subjects must inevitably lead him on this point; and he dared not venture one step further in free thought, for fear of invoking a complete moral revolution. To take one step more was to let infant baptism go and the State Church with it, so that a regenerate Church only would be left. But this was not the sort of Church that Luther wanted, and he said: 'Where they want to go I am not disposed to follow. God save me from a Church in which are none but the holy.' [5] Any man of discernment can see, with Plank, that Luther simply trifled with this truth. He says: 'Luther treated the objections to infant baptism very superficially, and dismissed the whole matter as a very inopportune question.' [6]

His embarrassment on this subject is clearly seen. Bellarmine, the great Catholic disputant, saw the utter insufficiency of Scripture to sustain infant baptism, and the absolute necessity of sustaining it as an unwritten tradition, which cannot be proved by Scripture. [7] Vilmar, also, reaches this conclusion: 'If baptism does not regenerate, but is a mere symbol, then the symbol and regeneration must come together. The Baptists are profoundly logical.' [8] Calvin takes the same ground, but goes a step further. He says:

'This principle must always be adhered to, That baptism is not conferred on infants that they may be made children of God. But because now, in this place and degree they are reckoned with God, the grace of adoption is sealed in their flesh.

Otherwise, the Anabaptists might justly exclude them from baptism. For unless the truth of the external sign applies to them, it will be mere profanation to call them into participation of the sign itself.'[9] But Luther stood with Augustine, and could not see that children could be 'reckoned with God' while they were in a state of original sin, and he christened them to wash it away, first baptizing them on the faith of others, and requiring them to be justified by their own personal faith afterward; and so, Strack's words are as true on this point as on others: 'Luther retracted some of his concessions to the people, out of fear of the Anabaptists.[10] And the 'Westminster Review,' of 1870, presents the exact truth when it says, that he was 'Terrified into inconsistency with his ultimate principles' by the 'Anabaptists.' Melancthon, also, was disturbed on this subject, and in order to remove his doubts, Luther said:

'What is not against the Scriptures is for the Scriptures, and the Scriptures for it,' and demands in his own dogmatic way: 'How can you prove that children cannot believe? Unless we insist on the presence in them of the faith of the Church, we cannot continue the fight, but must simply reject infant baptism. You say, the examples of such faith are weak. I find nothing stronger. The Church has power not to baptize children at all, because there is no place in Scripture that compels us to believe that, as we do other articles.'[11]

Thus, he would do as a positive duty to God whatever the Scriptures did not prohibit his doing; as in the Supper, Carlstadt asked: 'What Scripture have you for elevating the cup?' to which Luther indignantly replied: 'What Scripture is there against it?' By the same answer he might have justified the offering of masses for the dead, auricular confession, purgatory, the infallibility of the pope, or any other absurdity which the Catholics practiced, but which the Scriptures had not positively forbidden by name. The mere mention of such a shallow but dangerous position lays bare its fallacy, and its practical bearings involved Luther at last in shocking inconsistency, as his conduct in the bigamy of Philip of Hesse shows.

Christina, the daughter of George of Saxony, had been Philip's lawful wife for sixteen years, and was the mother of eight children. But her husband wished to add Margaret von der Saale as a second wife, and as if he desired to act on Luther's principle of interpreting the Bible, he wrote to the Wittenberg theologians, reminding them that the Scriptures did not forbid him to have two wives! This practical test of Luther's rule greatly troubled its author, yet, nothing daunted, on December 10th, 1539, he and Melancthon united in an answer, in which they boldly took the ground, that what Moses had allowed in regard to marriage the Gospel did not forbid: 'Therefore,' they say: 'Your highness has not only our approbation in this case of necessity, but also our reflections upon it.'[12] This bigamous marriage took place at Rothenburg, March 4th, 1540, without divorcing his first wife, and on the next day the Landgrave wrote Luther, 'with a cheerful conscience,' thanking him for his counsel in the case. In Luther's reply of April 12th, he says: 'I notice that your highness is in glee about the advice given, which we like to be kept silent, otherwise the rough peasants will follow your example, alleging still more grievous causes. This would create a great deal of trouble.'[13] And why should not Luther, on his negative system of interpreting the Bible, permit polygamy in the marriage of Margaret as readily as the baptism of Christina's children in the name of the Trinity, if the Scriptures did not forbid either? The one position is as consistent as the other.

This is the most vital point in connection with the Reformation, showing where Luther broke with the principle of absolute obedience to God's word; and as the ablest writers of modern times locate his weakness here, we must stop to look calmly at his mistake. Goebel says: 'As Luther, since 1522, so did Zwingli, in 1525, forsake the positive principle of depending on the Scriptures, for the negative stand-point, saying: "Infant baptism is nowhere forbidden in the Scriptures."'[14] The Romanists took advantage of his blunder at once. Fabri, their great doctor, asks: 'How can you convince an Anabaptist out of the Scriptures that infants should be baptized? In what Gospel is it commanded? The Donatists demanded Scripture of Augustine for infant baptism, but he referred them to the tradition of the Apostles.' He then says, that if the Lutherans would convert the Antipedobaptists 'from their error, you must ask help of the Catholic Church and her apostolic tradition, for she says with Augustine, ' That must be observed which the Church observes.' Möhler, another great Catholic authority, thinks that ' Luther having connected the efficacy of the sacraments with faith only, it is not possible to understand why infants should be baptized. From the Reformer's point of view, there was the utter want of an adequate ground for this ecclesiastical rite.'[15] And Bayle says, that the Reformers were obliged to refute the Antipedobaptists: 'By the arguments of the Papists against themselves.'[16] Jörg fully agrees with all this, saying: 'Infant baptism is the offspring and guide of an infallible Church. The Baptists, alone, carried out the idea of the Reformation. . . . Having abolished the authority of Rome, the Reformers proceeded to substitute for it their own.'[17] Cardinal Wiseman also teaches that infant baptism cannot be without an infallible Church to give it authority.

A few visionaries attempted to push Luther's partial Reformation to a one-sided revolution by new revelations of the Spirit, and Luther swung to the other extreme of rejecting the healthful results of Bible teaching. Hess shows that the Baptists wished to strike the happy medium between these extremes. 'Unable to rise to a higher stand-point, they wanted to restore the manner of life of the primitive Church.'[18] They demanded that each person should be baptized upon his own faith. Luther built a Church on sacraments and enforced its tests of discipleship by State legislation, just as the Catholics had done. He held the doctrines of a universal priesthood of believers and of justification by faith alone, but he could not make infant baptism harmonize with either of them. He denied that baptism could avail any thing without faith, and so was obliged to ascribe to the infant ' the faith of the Church,' whatever that might mean. Thus, he found in the faith of the sponsor a quasi magical virtue, of which the Bible knows nothing; but which, ratified by the State law, made the babe a member of the Church.

Beard, the able Oxford lecturer, puts this point thus:

'When this distinction is clearly seen, it helps to liberate the mind from the influence of ecclesiastical usage, and to reveal the Scriptural justification of infant baptism in its real weakness and insufficiency.'

Of the Baptists he says:

'Theirs were the truths which the Reformation neglected and cast out, but which it must again reconcile with itself, if it is ever to complete its work.'

And still again he says, of a baptized believer:

'Here the conditions of a true sacrament are fulfilled; the grace of God, the outward sign, the operative faith, are all present. . . . It was, therefore, no dogmatic accident which made the mysticism of the Reformation assume the Anabaptist form. The word Anabaptist, as I have already pointed out, is used to cover very various phases of religious belief. But this one peculiarity was common to all Anabaptists.' [19]

Luther could see the bearings of baptism on the justifying faith of a believer, for justification by faith was a mystical doctrine; but when he came to the faith of sponsors for christened babes, he was at sea. The Baptists pushed Luther's doctrine of a universal priesthood of believers to a wholesome application, by denying all Church authority to make, and all civil authority to say, without Bible direction, who were or were not believers. Luther said: 'I am governed in this matter by the silence of the New Testament;' the true Baptists replied: 'The case must be decided not by the silence of the New Testament, but by its positive instructions.' Here was the radical point of difference between them. Luther believed Scripture to be the word of God, but practically restricted its free interpretation by insisting on the binding force of its silence! Forsaking the direct instruction of Scripture to follow its silence, he landed in politico-ritualism; other extremists added to its positive instructions and landed in politico-fanaticism; the Baptists contented themselves with following its absolute requirements, and were branded by both the other parties as 'heretics,' fit only to be put to death for their obedience to Christ. Thus in the Reformation weak humanity swung from one extreme to another. The theological inconsistencies of Luther drove him to ultra-ritualistic ground; and belief in new revelations of the Spirit carried the Zwickau men into ultra-Quakerism on the doctrine of the Spirit. The true Baptists anchored themselves to the positive requirements of the word of God, and stood firmly there to their death. Dr. Keller, in his new book 'Die Waldenser' sums up the whole case thus: 'Two things characterize the Baptists: "The Lord has forbidden, and Christ meant what he said."' [20]

MÜNSTER.

CHAPTER IV.

THE REFORMATION—PEASANTS' WAR—MÜHLHAUSEN AND MÜNSTER.

THE Peasants' War of A. D. 1525-26 shook Southern and Central Germany. The age was in a fever of political excitement, and this war was not an affair of religious doctrine but of political liberty and the natural rights of man. The first German conqueror took possession and then gave lands in fee to his officers or lords, and in turn these bound their dependants to servile occupancy. The citizens took rank as nobles and 'villains,' and all others were serfs, the serfs going with the soil on which they were born. They could not leave their master's domain nor appeal from his authority, nor could he sell them. He took to himself the common pastures, the fish and game, exacting high rents or tithes, and they must submit or revolt. He also forced his religion upon them and made them act through the religious idea, their knowledge being narrowed down to a few notions on that subject. For ages Germany had boasted that liberty was the birthright of her people, boor and prince. Her primitive Teutonic population were farmers and graziers, who wandered without landmark or fixed habitation. Then, they formed themselves into little States under a kind of land ownership but with few conventional restrictions or claims to the perpetual right of property. In time, however, estates shaped themselves after the map of restricted society and revenue became hereditary. Thus feudal tenures sprang up, defense became necessary and authority grew. As wealth increased, military power and imperial rule followed, with all the exactions of blind obedience. Under this yoke the peasant was uneasy for ages, periodically waking up to his lost liberties, with new attempts to break the bond of 'villanage' and shake off his burdens.

As far back as A. D. 1073 the peasants of Thuringia and Saxony rebelled and Henry IV. shed torrents of their blood. In 1476 there was a rebellion at Würzburg; in 1491 another in Swabia; and in 1503 the peasants of Spire formed a confederacy, called the 'League-shoe,' from the device painted on their standard. The King of France stirred up a peasant outbreak in Belgium, and a rustic army 30,000 strong, with a loaf and a cheese on its banners, went forth to reduce the nobility to decency, but were themselves slain by Albert of Saxony. In 1514 'Poor Kuntze,' a farmer of Würtemberg, led a seditionary force which took several cities, threatening destruction to the clergy and nobility because of their avarice and tyranny; but the emperor and princes were alarmed and made concessions to avoid worse calamities. In Poland, Hungary and Transylvania there was another peasant revolt in 1515 against the oppressions of their rulers. Laurence, a Catholic presbyter, and Michael, a monk, were amongst their captains; 400 nobles perished, 13 bishops were impaled, only one escaping, and 70,000 people were slaughtered. In fact, the fiery waves of revolution seethed under the whole German Empire, discontent was universal and every peasant was ready to grasp the sword in revolt. But at this time, the people afterward called 'Anabaptists' were not known in Germany.

When rebellion burst forth in 1525–26, it was neither at Zwickau nor at Münster, but in the Black Forest. Church and State united to grind the faces of the poor peasants under the pretense of fighting the Turks, and they resolved to wear the iron collar no longer. John Müller, their chief, wore a red cap and cloak and carried the standard of revolt, a flag of black, white and red, through the forest region. Village after village was aroused, enthusiasm spread like wild-fire, new towns and cities threw open their gates and the people swelled the ranks from all quarters. They marched triumphantly everywhere. Nor was this uprising a mere blot upon the face of history, as is commonly represented. If it is right to rise in arms at all against tyrannical princes, this war was as holy as any that ever was waged. The peasants tell their story well in their immortal manifesto submitted to the reason and justice of mankind. They held public meetings everywhere, to express their grievances and petition for redress. They prayed for the Gospel of freedom, but no relief came, and at last they stated their case in Twelve Articles, of which instrument Voltaire said that 'Lycurgus would have signed it.' Luther declared to the princes that its several articles were 'So just and right, that all feelings of consideration toward you, before God and the world, are removed.' There has been much doubt as to the authorship of this noble State paper, but Prof. Pfleiderer attributes it to Hubmeyer.[1]

So honorable and patriotic was this document in its demands and so temperately worded that it is simply a picture of their exhausted long-suffering. They asked for the pure word of God and the right to choose their own pastors; for their exemption from all tithes, except that of wheat, of which they would pay a tenth for the support of their pastors and the poor; for relief from bondage and from such obedience to the magistrates as it is not lawful for Christians to render; for justice administered fairly and firmly according to plain, written laws; and for permission to fish in the rivers and hunt in the forests. They back each article with a forceful passage of Scripture, because, in some way, they had come to believe that Christ intended men to possess rights of conscience. They say: 'Christ bought and redeemed us by his precious blood, the shepherd as well as the noblest, none being excepted; wherefore, it accords with Scripture that we are and will be free.' They close by promising that if any of these demands be unjust they shall have no force. These articles were read publicly in every place and adopted by the people. They marched triumphantly into Würtzburg; and before long, Spires, the Palatinate, Alsace, Hesse and other great centers adopted the articles. Many of the upper classes, Catholics and Reformers, put themselves at the head of the peasants. The general uprising took place by concert, January 1st, 1525; as a signal, the Convent of Kempton was captured, and from that moment the country was in a blaze from the Rhine to the frontier of Bohemia. Monasteries, castles and cities were destroyed, and every kind of excess was committed by 300,000 men in arms maddened by intolerable oppression to the desperation of despair. All this took place ten years before the madness of Münster, showing it to be but an incident in the long German uproar.

We see here how religion entered the contests of the Peasants' War and by whom it was introduced. It is simply absurd to say that these peasants were 'Anabaptists.' Did they demand the right to choose their own pastors because their masters had forced unwelcome 'Anabaptist' shepherds upon them? The peasants were Catholics and Lutherans, and their enforced ministers were the same. Many of their masters were bishops and other clergy. The entire disturbance was simply the abnormal German mind forcing its way back in a crude manner to its native freedom, and the 'Anabaptists' cannot for any purpose be made a stalking-horse, in the face of historic truth, to force a false issue to the front. The chief actors in these scenes candidly lay before us the real facts. When the princes desired the Elector to aid them against the rebellion, he said to his brother, John: 'Cause has been given for the poor people to make this uproar. . . . They have been dealt hardly with in many ways by us rulers, both spiritual and temporal.' The deputies from Saxony and Hesse said in the Diet at Augsburg:

'The rising of the peasants was the effect of impolitic and harsh usage.' At first, Luther, being the son of a peasant, sympathized with his own race and said to the bishops: 'It is your guilty oppression of the poor of the flock which has driven the people to despair.' To the princes he said: 'My lords, it is not the peasants who have risen against you, it is God himself who is opposing your madness. Think not that you can escape the punishment reserved for you. For the love of God, calm your irritation; grant reasonable terms to these poor people, appease these commotions by gentle methods, lest they give birth to a conflagration which shall set all Germany in a flame.' In his 'Secular Magistracy' he uses this strong language: 'God Almighty has made our princes mad, so that they imagine they can act and command their subjects as they please. God delivers the princes to their reprobate senses. They wish even to govern souls, and thus they bring upon themselves, God's and all people's hatred, and in this way they perish, with the bishops, priests and monks; one rascal with the other. The people wearied of your tyranny and iniquity can no longer bear it.' He calls them 'Blockheads, who wish to be called Christian Princes.'

His work on 'Christian Liberty' drew the peasants to him as a leader, and then many of them declared for the Reformation; but up to 1525 possibly nine tenths of them were not allowed to hear the Reformation preached. For some reason, which is not clear, he suddenly turned his back on them and in that year published his infamous pamphlet 'Against the Rapacious, Murderous Peasants.' They then charged him with being a fawning sycophant to the nobles. 'From that day,' says Beard, 'he became harder, more dogmatic, less spiritual, less universal. He is no longer a leader of thought, but the builder up of a church, on conditions prescribed by the existing political constitution of Germany.' After the war the rebels returned almost as a body to the Catholics, and Luther did more to drive them back than any other man. His bitterness and cruelty toward them were appalling. He denounces them as 'faithless, treacherous, lying, disobedient, boobies and rascals, who deserved the death of soul and body.' He declared them under the ban of the God and Emperor, and 'he who strangles them first does right well.' He charged them with 'three horrible crimes against God and man: rebellion against rulers, robbery of castles and convents, and the pretense that they fight under the Gospel.' Yet, in 1524, when Erasmus wrote him that he feared 'a bloody insurrection,' he replied: 'A common destruction of all monasteries and convents would be the best reformation, because they are useless.' Many of the peasants destroyed these and he raved against them after this coarse fashion:

'A wise man gives to his ass food, a pack-saddle and the whip; to the peasant oat straw. If they are not content, give the cudgel and the carbine, it is their due. Let us pray that they may be obedient; if not, show them no mercy. Make the musket whistle against them, or else they will be a thousand times more wicked.'[2] He exhorted the princes to hunt them down like 'mad dogs.' 'Strike! slay front and rear! Nothing is more poisonous, pernicious, devilish than a rebel. . . . So wonderous are the times now, that a prince can win heaven with blood more easily than others can by prayer. . . . Beat, strangle, hang, burn, behead and mutilate them.'[3]

Certain writers never weary of attributing this bloody work to the 'Anabaptists.' But Bishop Jewel honestly lodges it where it belongs; while he would screen Luther, he says that the partners of this 'conspiracy had for their watch-word the name of Our Lady, and in honor of her were bound to say five Ave Marias every day.' Great concessions were made to the peasants for a time; during the war much church property was put to secular uses, many high privileges and taxes were abolished, all princes but the Emperor were brought down to the democratic level of citizens, free courts were established, the clergy were restricted to their individual churches, and uniformity was given to weights, measures and currency. But these were not secured until the war had cost possibly 150,000 lives, and the burning of several hundred castles, convents, hamlets and towns. Sometimes Luther attempted to wash his hands as innocent of the whole affair, and then again he was willing to bear the whole responsibility, but others laid the blame at his door. Erasmus said to him: 'You disclaim any connection with the insurgents, while they regard you as the author and expounder of their principles.'[4] A controversial writer of 1532 says: 'Luther first sounded the tocsin; he cannot clear himself from the rebellion, although he wrote that the common folks should not use force without the magistracy. The common people do not hear that, but they observe whatever part of Luther's sermons and writings they please.' Osiander writes: 'When Luther saw the peasants attacking not only the bishops and clergy, but also his teaching and the princes, he preached their slaughter like that of wild beasts;'[5] and the enemies of the peasants were as bitter toward him as the rebels themselves. In 1525 Amerbach received a letter from Zasius, in which the latter says: 'Luther this pest of peace, this most pernicious of all two-legged beings, has plunged the whole of Germany into such a fury that one must regard it as a sort of security if he be not killed at once.'[6] Sometimes, when looking round for a scape-goat, Luther attempted to throw the responsibility on 'the prophets of murder,' as he called the Zwickau men. But at other times he arrogated prerogatives to himself, for which, as Erasmus says, 'no parallel can be found, scarcely distinguishable from madness,' and for which no apology can be made, such as this: 'I, Martin Luther, have slain all the peasants in the insurrection because I commanded them to be killed; their blood is upon my head. But I put it upon the Lord God, by whose command I spoke.'[7]

These and many other facts sufficiently show why Gieseler says that 'no traces of Anabaptist fanaticism were seen' in the Peasants' War. Some individual 'Anabaptists' were drawn into the contest, as at Mühlhausen, under the lead of Münzer, who was not in any proper use of the term an 'Anabaptist' himself. On the contrary, Keller, in his late work on the 'Reformation' (p. 370), says that Cornelius has shown that in the chief points Münzer was opposed to the Baptists. It seemed an inevitable result that religious fanaticism should be thrown into a contest in which politico-religious questions formed the chief element, and especially where such a fiery spirit was allowed to come to the front. Yet it is questionable justice, whether even he ought to be blackened from head to foot. The true story of Thomas Münzer appears to be this. He was born in Stollberg, at the foot of the Hartz Mountains, A. D. 1490, and studied, some think at Wittenberg, others at Leipsic; that he took a degree as master of arts is clear, and that he had large knowledge of the Scriptures. After teaching in several places, he became a chaplain and confessor to the nuns at

Bentitz, near Weissenfels. There he rejected transubstantiation and united himself with the Lutherans. In the following year he became one of their pastors at Zwickau. But soon he broke with the Wittenberg reformers on account of what he called Luther's 'halfness;' for he demanded a pure Church on the mystic idea, yet, in direct contradiction therewith, that it should first be established by force, and then defended by divine and miraculous interposition. After leaving that city he fled from place to place and settled at Mühlhausen near the close of 1524. There he preached his gospel of the sword and of divine revelations, actually caring little about the true character of the gospel Church. His politics soon brought him into direct conflict with the city council, which he entirely overthrew. Here he diverged from the Baptists and drew from them a severe rebuke. Grebel, in the name of the Zurich Baptists, September 5th, 1524, addressed him as follows:

Is it true, as we hear, that you have preached in favor of an attack on the princes? If you defend war or any thing else not found in the clear word of God, I admonish you by our common salvation to abstain from these things now and hereafter.... Unless every thing is to be altered after the example of the Apostles it were better to alter nothing. If this radical and complete change cannot be made at once, teach, at least, what ought to be, for it is far better that a few should be rightly instructed by the word of God, than that many should believe through deception an adulterated doctrine.'[8]

In his youth certain mystical writings had given a false direction to Münzer's piety, which bent cleaved to him both as a Catholic and a Lutheran, and following only what he called the 'inner light' he fell into all sorts of vagaries. He was ambitious, eloquent, thirsted for fight and fame, and was ready to lead a faction whenever opportunity offered. At Alsted he headed a mob, broke into a church and destroyed its images; at Mühlhausen he put himself at the head of the city government, and when the Peasants' War commenced there he led its whole population in revolt. After a fierce and fantastical captaincy on his part and the slaughter of his followers, he was captured May 15th, 1525, was put to brutal torture and then beheaded. Most of the later writers agree with the author of Johnson's 'Cyclopædia' in saying that 'He entertained peculiar ideas of infant baptism, *similar* to those of the Anabaptists, with whom, however, he had no direct connection.' This point of similarity consisted in that he rejected infant baptism in theory, on the ground that the baptism of the Spirit, as he called it, was the only true baptism for any person, babe or adult. But, differing with the Baptists, he practiced infant baptism in form, twice a year christening all born in his congregation. In 1522 at Alstedt he threw aside the Latin liturgy and prepared one in German, in which he retained the formula for infant baptism. He also wrote against Luther's view of baptism, but not on Baptist grounds. The Swiss Baptist leaders, in the letter just cited, express the hope that as he had spoken against infant baptism he would go further and take their ground, that 'believers only are to be baptized' and that 'you decline to baptize infants,' a thing which he had not then done. He spent eight weeks in Switzerland in the autumn of 1524, and had a conference with some of these leaders at Klettgau; but they seem not to have agreed either on this subject or on the use of the sword, and he never became one of them. On this journey, according to Herzog, he met Œcolampadius at Basel and uttered views to him in no wise Baptist; this was in harmony with his whole life. The fact that he was a Roman Catholic priest and a Lutheran pastor shows that he had been christened as a babe; and there is no evidence that he was ever baptized upon his own faith or that he baptized others on their faith who had been christened as infants. It is, therefore, a singular perversity that so many writers should have attempted to palm him off as a Baptist and the father of them. Dr. Rule in his 'Spirit of the Reformation' says: 'He performed a ceremony on baptized persons which they mistook for baptism, and with his followers received the designation of Anabaptist.'[9] But Uhlhorn says that he 'did not practice rebaptism and did not form a congregation.'[10]

The barbarities which accompanied the Peasants' War so enraged the German princes that they followed the revolt with the most sanguinary and remorseless measures. They simply massacred their subjects with frigid callousness, as butchers would kill sheep. The atrocity of the imperial party was a perfect match for that of the peasants. These once crushed, the bishops and nobles found it their turn to glut themselves in the coarsest manner upon the tears and blood of these tillers of the soil. Their fury and brutal cruelties render it doubtful whether they were not superior to the rustics in the acts of bitter revenge. They shed blood wherever they could find a vein, and in the chill temper of steel they hanged their prisoners by companies on the roadside.

But when the peasants were beaten the spirit of revolt was not broken; they were more oppressed than ever and kept their rebellion smothered. The Catholic princes charged the Lutheran princes with fostering sedition, and they retorted that it was the result of Romish persecution. They all saw that if this violence was continued worse calamities must follow, and yet they dreamed that they could tear patriotism from the hearts of their subjects by main force. They sought to cure political revolution by religious strategy. But this drove the courage of the peasants into religious madness, under the delusion that they could now achieve a spiritual victory by the sword. Common sense would have prevented the sedition entirely, and then the religion of the peasants would have taken healthy care of itself; but this was not commanded. Catholic and Lutheran kept the outrages seething all over the land, and at last, ten years after Münzer, came Münster.

Few writers have treated this subject with greater care and clearness than Ypeig and Dermout in their 'History of the Netherland Church.' They say of the Münster men that while they are known in history as 'Anabaptists,' they ought by no means to be known as Baptists. 'Let the reader,' they request, 'keep this distinction constantly in mind in the statement which we now make respecting them. . . . Since the peculiar history of the Anabaptists and Baptists has exerted so powerful an influence on the Reformation of the Church in this country, the nature of our historical work requires that we present in its true light the whole matter from its origin.' After speaking at great length of the Münster men and their excesses, especially of their leaders, they say of Mathiesen: 'He laid as the foundation of his new system of doctrine that teaching respecting the holy ordinance of baptism which, in part, had long before been maintained by the Baptists. He considered infant baptism not to be of the least advantage to the religious interests of a Christian. In his opinion baptism should be delayed to years of discretion and after a profession of faith on the part of the baptized. Therefore every one who passed over to the community of which he was the head must first be baptized, *even if he had been baptized in another society at an adult age.* When he renounced his confession of faith he also renounced his baptism. . . . It can now be easily understood how the followers of the Münster leaders received the name of Anabaptists or *re-baptizers.* So far as their views of baptism are concerned, these could easily have been tolerated, and they need not have been hated by reasonable persons on account of these. But besides these they taught doctrines fraught with important errors, partly founded on old Pelagianism, partly on Unitarianism, partly on Mysticism and partly on other impure principles.

Yet, even with these opinions they could have been suffered to exist had they behaved themselves properly as members of society. But their peculiar notions of Christian freedom were extravagant in the highest degree, and with these were united all sorts of foolish ideas derived from an incorrect interpretation of the Apocalypse, ideas of a thousand years' kingdom at hand, in which the saints shall reign with Christ and enjoy every kind of physical and spiritual pleasure. The community imbibed these opinions from Mathiesen, and by these their sensual feelings were so greatly excited that they united themselves to him, for the promotion of a happy life here upon earth, with impetuous ardor and sanguinary violence to overthrow entirely the thrones of princes, if it were possible, and of this they had no doubt. Mathiesen, like another Mohammed, sought through fire and sword to effect the downfall of all governments which were within the reach of his foolhardy undertakings, and to found an everlasting kingdom, which, under his royal administration, should spread itself over the whole earth. He should conquer the world and triumph over all the enemies of the kingdom of God. Then Christ should appear in the clouds of heaven and confirm him in his regal dignity, depose the pope as Antichrist, and solemnly place himself in the same situation as the highest ruler over the Church. . . . Since the enlisting of the rebel Anabaptists happened in this manner, it is sufficiently evident that the great majority cannot be supposed to have been Baptists in heart or belief. *They were people of every variety of religious beliefs, and many of them of no religion at all in heart, although they aided the Protestant cause.*

From the nature of the case the majority of the Romanists knew no difference between the various Protestant parties and sects, and would make no distinction. Hence the abhorrence only deserved by some of the Anabaptists was bestowed upon all Protestants. The honest Baptists suffered the most severely from this prejudice, because they were considered by the people to be the same and were called by the same name. The fact that they agreed in their opinions in respect to the holy ordinance of baptism was the unfortunate occasion of this thing. On this account the Baptists in Flanders and in Friesland suffered the most terrible persecutions. In the next place the anger of the Romanists was excited against the Zwinglians, since these agreed most nearly with the Baptists in their simple religious rites, and had deviated most widely from the ancient Church. Besides these, the Lutherans also were compelled to undergo the most distressing persecutions on account of the indignation of the Romish government and priesthood at the wicked conduct of the Anabaptists. It is to these disturbances caused at Münster that we must ascribe the stringent measures against the Lutherans at Deventer in 1534–35. Lutheranism was considered the fruitful source of all manner of corruption in Church and State.'

Here is a most important point brought out clearly. If the Lutherans and Zwinglians were confounded with the 'wicked Anabaptists,' as our authors call the Münster men, how much more easily did both Catholics and Protestants come to confound the 'honest Baptists' with these madmen. The Dutch historians go on to state that:

'The Baptists suffered the most, yet the entire mass of the Protestants were more or less injured. This will appear if attention be directed to the edicts which since that time have been issued by the Emperor for the purpose of retarding the work of the Reformation. In these all Christians who separated from the Romish Church were called Anabaptists. . . . The Emperor and all his statesmen knew that the Baptists generally had, both by word and deed, testified that their peace-loving hearts abhorred the seditious conduct of the Anabaptists. . . . In this manner the attempt was made to throw sand in the eyes of the superficial thinkers among the Romanists. It was no very difficult task to do this. Since the government comprehended all the Protestants under the general name of Anabaptists, the short-sighted Romanists confiding in its superior discernment, could easily be brought to the same unfavorable point of view. . . . The Anabaptists seemed to them to be a lawless people, consisting partly of Baptists, partly of Zwinglians, partly of Lutherans —men who formerly adhered to the old Catholic faith, but who had now entirely renounced religion. . . . They would not see that which they might have seen. How evident it was that although the Baptists appeared to agree with the Anabaptists in respect to the baptismal question, the former entirely disapproved of the course pursued by the latter. For it had been, and continued to be, a doctrine of the Baptists, that the bearing of arms was very unbecoming to a Christian. Did not the Anabaptists pursue a course directly the opposite of this? . . . Who could have imagined that such a purpose prevailed among the Baptists, who were the meekest of Christians? And yet the Romanists, without dissent, agree in ascribing these things to all the Baptists. We have nowhere seen clearer evidences of the injurious influence of the prejudice, nowhere have we met with a more obstinate unwillingness to be correctly informed, and a more evident disposition to silence those who better understood the truth of the matter. Prejudice, when once deeply imbibed, blinds the eye, perplexes the understanding, silences the instincts of the heart and destroys the love of truth and rectitude.

We shall now proceed more at length to notice the defense of the worthy Baptists. The Baptists are Protestant Christians entirely different from the Anabaptists in character. They were descendants from the Ancient Waldenses, whose teachings were evangelical and tolerably pure, and who were scattered by severe persecutions in various lands, and long before the time of the Reformation of the Church were existing in the Netherlands. In their flight they came thither in the latter part of the twelfth century. In this country and in Flanders, in Holland and Zealand they lived as quiet inhabitants, not intermeddling with the affairs of Church and State, in the villages tilling the land, and in the cities working at some trade or engaged in traffic, by which means each one was well supplied and in no respect burdensome to society. Their manner of life was simple and exemplary. No great crime was known among them. Their religious teaching was simple and pure, and was exemplified in their daily conduct.' [11]

In 1524–25 Münster had risen and been subdued with the other cities of Southern and Central Germany, and things flowed once more in the old channel. Then, in 1532, Rothmann, a very powerful Lutheran pastor of Münster, stirred it so effectually that six entire parishes fell into the hands of the Lutherans, and nothing was left to the Catholics but the monastery and cathedral. The Lutherans took possession of the city government, drove away the Catholic bishop and clergy, and equipped troops to protect the Lutheran religion. The spirit of insurrection spread and the two prevailing sects were drawn into the movement, when, in 1532, Rothmann, whose influence was sweeping all before him, suddenly avowed himself an 'Anabaptist' and ran into every kind of wild vagary. He taught an illumination of the Spirit which superseded the need of the written word of God, and afforded new revelations by visions and dreams; that rank and station should be abolished; a community of goods established; that Christ was about to return to the earth; and that it must be conquered to him by force of arms, that he might reign here a thousand years.

Others flocked about him, amongst them Bockhold and Mathiesen. These soon outran Rothmann, and each in turn became prophet and king. They called Münster 'Mount Zion,' and proclaimed it the center of the world, for there Christ would right the wrongs of all the peasants, and establish the millennial kingdom of God. They proclaimed a theocratic government, put many to death and confiscated the estates of the citizens. The population soon became a rabble of all religious sects and none. Bockhold, the sham monarch, inaugurated a reign of terror, in which every vile passion was let loose and every crime was committed without decency or limit. The horrible violence which reigned for about a year threw common humanity to the winds, so frantic and sanguinary was the madness; and the cause of virtue is best served by avoiding the monstrous recital in detail. Münster fell completely under that general law of political, moral and fanatical epidemics which always works out such results, where superstition first makes men cruel, and then fiery passions sway their whole being. The town was taken June 24th 1535, and in the following January the ringleaders were put to death. Violence has ever been the natural consequence of soulless oppression, and yet any attempt to excuse the outrages of Münster is itself a crime. The wrongs of these people lived long after the Peasants' War, and could not die in their revengeful memories. Both the oppressors and the oppressed acted more like demons than men, and the result was seen in that desperation of all subject races when brought to bay after long degradation.

That ignorance is inexcusable which attributes the rise of Baptists to 'The period of the Münster kingdom; much rather can it be proved that in the lands mentioned Baptist Churches existed for many decades, and even centuries. [12] No greater injustice can be done to any people than has been done to the German Baptists, in the attempt to 'saddle them with the evils of the Peasants' War and the villainies of Münster. Not one of their old and acknowledged leaders was found in the uproar either at Mühlhausen or Münster, and but few of their people were mixed up with these proceedings. As to numbers, they were an insignificant sect in Germany proper at that time, and as a body on principle, they stood aloof from filling the magistracy, from oaths and the sword. In Switzerland, where the Peasants' War raged as violently as in Germany, they positively refused to unite their fortunes with the peasants, and their course there throws light upon their conduct in Germany. Grebel and Simon Stumpf, to their honor, sympathized with the down-trodden people, but their principles would not allow them to draw the sword. Grebel branded the oppressors as 'The tyrants of our forefathers,' but he denied that he had ever thought of subverting government.[13] When the Swiss peasantry revolted in the Grüningen district, they attacked the cloisters of Bubikon and Ruti with their Zwinglian pastors in their ranks. Their Baptist neighbors, meanwhile, gave them their moral support, but left the sword sheathed for conscience' sake. They relied upon the spirit and morals of the Gospel to enlighten the souls of the people, believing that this would work out their social liberties too. Hubmeyer aided the peasants at Waldshut much in the same way. Zimmerman, the historian of the Peasants' War, says: 'In Waldshut and the Evangelical Brotherhood there were heads capable of grasping the bold and great thought of uniting the forces of the peasants, split up as they were among countless leaders, in one purpose and aim: namely, the restoration of the old liberty of the empire, and the overthrow of existing un-Christian oppression. To this end brotherhoods were formed and armed throughout the entire German empire, and communication by means of correspondence and messengers was regularly sustained.' This 'Brotherhood' was entered by 138 cities, and by counts, knights and bishops innumerable, but by few Baptists. A branch was organized at Waldshut, which city Müller entered with 1,200 peasants; but when the persecuted Baptists there were charged with heresy and sedition, they uniformly denied the second charge, although they delighted in the doctrinal heresy charged upon them. Jacob Gross, a disciple of Hubmeyer, fled from Waldshut rather than bear arms. When Bruppacher was examined on the rack at Zurich, he said that he had never heard his brethren 'Teach that there should be no magistracy; or that in case they should be successful they would overthrow the State.' And they uniformly denied that they had any thing to do with sedition, while doctrine and not sedition was the burden of their oral discussions and literature.

Happily, in modern times, the calumny that the Baptists were responsible for the horrors of Münster has lost its edge and the truth has found its way to the surface. Brandt attributes them to some 'enthusiastical Anabaptists,' but is careful to add:

'Not to the well-meaning Baptists.' Schaff pronounces it 'The greatest injustice to make the Anabaptists, as such, responsible for the extravagances that led to the tragedy of Münster.'[14] Uhlhorn says that 'Sedition, or a call to sedition, is not chargeable against the Anabaptists of Southern Germany at this time; I have found no trace of any fellowship with the seditious peasants.' But their contemporaries, who knew them well, bear the same testimony. Capito, their stern opponent at Strasburg, says that he must 'openly confess' that most of them manifest 'godly fear and pure zeal. Before God I testify that I cannot say that their contempt for life springs from blindness rather than from a divine impulse.' Wetzel, the Catholic, declared that 'Whoever speaks of God and a Christian life, or earnestly strives after personal improvement, passes as an arch Anabaptist.' And Frank, who wrote in 1531, says of them: 'They teach love, faith and the cross. They are long-suffering and heroic in affliction. . . . The world feared they would cause an uproar, but they have proved innocent everywhere. If I were emperor, pope, or Turk, I would not fear revolt less from any people than this.' [15] . . . All the Baptists oppose those who would fight for the Gospel with the sword. Some object to war or any use of the sword, but the most favor self-defense and justifiable war.' [16]

The truth is out of joint somewhere when men charge them with enmity to civil government, with being revolutionary and the veriest butchers, because their faith forbade them to draw the sword. Bayle tells us that Turenne remonstrated with Van Benning for tolerating them, when he replied: 'They are good people, and the most commodious to a State in the world, because they do not aspire to places of dignity. We fear no rebellion from a sect that makes it an article of their faith never to bear arms. They edify the people by the simplicity of their manners, and apply themselves to arts and business, without dissipating their substance in luxury and debauchery.' Nay, Bayle himself says that their great enemy De Brés 'Says nothing to insinuate that the Anabaptist martyrs suffered death for taking up arms against the State, or for stirring up the subjects to rebel, but represents them as a harmless sort of people. . . . 'Tis certain that many of them who suffered death for their opinions had no thought of making any insurrection.' [17] A few madmen of Münster, with Rothmann at their head, aroused their new converts to their views, and so brought disgrace upon their name; but if any of the acknowledged leaders had to do with the vile conspiracy, who and where were they?

Melancthon says that he made particular inquiry whether Storch was with Münzer in his uprising, but he found nothing to justify his suspicions. And Hase adds: 'No one can prove that Storch was guilty of direct political aims. He went about seeking out the elect, who forsook home and their native land for the sake of the truth.' [18] Cornelius sums up the whole matter, covering the time from 1525 onward, when he says: 'Anabaptism and the Peasants' War had no conscious connection. The two movements were generally distinct.' [19]

So much has been said of these disgraceful transactions at Münster, and said so rashly, to the injury of Baptists, that one is tempted to add cumulative evidence on the subject, even to prolixity. The mean-spirited charges were flung in their faces by men who persecuted them at that time, and they repudiated them with deep feeling, as cruelly adding insult to injury. This side of the case must be noticed. Keller quotes an old chronicle to show that Greble and Mantz were called 'false prophets' by the fanatical libertines in Abbacell, whom they rejected and combated, keeping clear of them in entangling alliance because they were libertines.[20] The Schleitheim Articles as well as many private writings throw a strong light upon this subject. Not only does the sixth article, on 'The Sword,' relieve them from this odium, but they wash their hands of the revolutionary transactions at Zwickau and Mühlhausen, the first in 1521, the last in 1524, under Münzer. They say to the Baptist congregations:

'Scandal has been brought in amongst us by certain false brethren, so that some have turned from the faith, imagining to use for themselves the freedom of the Spirit and of Christ. But such have erred from the truth and have given themselves (to their condemnation) to the wantonness and freedom of the flesh; and have thought faith and love may do and suffer all things, and nothing would injure or condemn them because they believed.' They warn that 'faith' does 'not thus prove itself, does not bring forth and do such things, as these false brethren and sisters do and teach. . . . Beware of such, for they serve not our Father, but their father the devil. But ye are not so, for they who are in Christ have crucified the flesh, with all its lusts and longings.' After they have given the seven articles, they say: 'These are the points which some brethren have understood wrongly and not in accordance with the true meaning, and thereby have confused many weak consciences, so that the name of God has been grossly blasphemed. For which cause it was necessary that we should be united in the Lord, which, God be praised, has taken place. . . . Mark all those who walk not according to the simplicity of divine truth, which is contained in this letter, as it was apprehended by us in the assembly, in order that each one among us be governed by the rule of discipline, and henceforth the entrance among us of false brethren and sisters be guarded against. Separate the evil from you.'

One of the Baptist martyrs, Dryzinger, in 1538, only three years after the craze, was examined as to whether he and his brethren approved of these vile proceedings. He answered that 'They would not be Christians if they did.' Hans, of Overdam, another martyr, complained of these false accusations of violence. He said: 'We are daily belied by those who say that we would defend our faith with the sword, as they of Münster did. The Almighty God defend us from such abominations.' Young Dosie, a beautiful character, who was a prisoner to the Governor of Friesland, and endured cruel slaughter for his love to Christ, was asked by the governor's wife if he and his brethren were not of that disgraceful people who took up the sword against the magistrates. With the sweet innocence of a child he replied: 'No, madam, those persons greatly erred. We consider it a devilish doctrine to resist the magistrates by the outward sword and violence. We would much rather suffer persecution and death at their hands and whatever is appointed us to suffer.' All this is no more than Erasmus said of them in 1529: 'The Anabaptists have seized no churches, have not conspired against the authorities, nor deprived any man of his estate or goods.'[21] They had no sturdier foe than Bullinger, yet he renders this verdict: 'Say what we will of the Baptists, I see nothing in them but earnestness, and I hear nothing of them except that they will not take an oath, will not do any wrong and aim to treat every man justly. In this, it seems to me, there is nothing out of the way.'[22]

But Cornelius tells us plainly: 'All these excesses were condemned and opposed wherever a large assembly of the brethren afforded an opportunity to give expression to the religious consciousness of the Baptist membership.'[23] This was the case at Augsburg, where a formal convention of their leaders discountenanced all political measures. No one outside of their number has better described their advanced position as a people in all respects than Füsslin, in his preface to vol. ii of Beiträge:

'The Reformers rejected the superstitious abuses attached to the sacraments; the Anabaptists restored the sacraments themselves to memorials for believers. The Reformers preached against unnecessary bloodshed; the Anabaptists denounced war of *every kind*. The Reformers protested against Catholic tyranny; the Anabaptists denied to any civil power authority in matters of religion. The Reformers decried public vices; the Anabaptists excluded the immoral from their fellowship. The Reformers sought to limit usury and covetousness; the Anabaptists made them impossible by the practice of communism. The Reformers educated their preachers; the Anabaptists looked for the inner anointing. The Reformers condemned the priests for simony; the Anabaptists made every preacher depend on the labor of his own hands and the free gifts of the people.'

The Baptists of our day are the first and the freest to wash their hands of all the black deeds at Münster, not only because they are black, but also because their true brethren of the sixteenth century renounced them as honestly and earnestly. Several of the Münster men professed some things in common with the Baptists, but more that the Baptists detested. Füsslin, with characteristic impartiality, says: 'There was a great difference between Anabaptists and Anabaptists. There were those amongst them who held strange doctrines, but this cannot be said of the whole sect. If we should attribute to every sect whatever senseless doctrines two or three fanciful fellows have taught, there is no one in the world to whom we could not ascribe the most abominable errors.' He clearly alludes here to the Münster teachers. But, as clearly, he did not look upon them as the fathers of the Baptists in Germany. Without doubt a handful of Baptists in that city ran into polygamy, the only instance in all the centuries where a congregation of them has embraced that abomination. But even there the shocking practice was condemned and resisted at every step. Goebel tells us (i, p. 189) that two hundred moral and moderate Baptists in Münster heroically withstood the iniquity, and it was not established until forty-eight of this number had been put to a bloody slaughter for their resistance. So that in the struggle nearly fifty true Baptists fell martyrs to purity in that German Sodom; and at last, the ministers and most of the people yielded to the clamor for polygamy under this reign of terror.

While this handful of madmen had not been educated in visions, violence and indecency by the Baptist leaders of Switzerland and Germany, others had impregnated them with these doctrines from their cradle. For centuries these teachings and practices had filled the air. The doctrine of wild visions, both of God and the devil, was taught in the monastic institutions, and wonders of this sort were blazoned abroad by bishops, cardinals and popes everywhere. The Catholic communion believed then and still believes in new revelations from God. Saints innumerable are mentioned who heard voices from heaven, had visits from the Virgin, the Father, the Son and the angels—as Ignatius, Aquinas, Teresa, Felix and Anthony. Francis was not only inspired to read men's minds and consciences as well as their faces, but he received the rules of his new order of monks directly from God. Like John of Leyden he appointed twelve apostles, and one of them hanged himself to boot. He also 'prophesied' that he should become 'a great prince' and be adored over the whole earth. Bridget, Catharine and Rosa, with endless nuns, were prophetesses. Teresa took the crucified Christ by the hand, was espoused to him and went up to heaven in the shape of a white dove. The Münster men never had such dreams, raptures, apparitions, phantasms and ecstasies as the canonized saints of Rome. Neither did Luther help the lunatics to sounder doctrine when he saw the devil in the form of a 'dog,' 'a whisp of straw,' a 'wild boar' and 'a star;' nor when he threw the inkstand at his head. As to violence:

Catholics and Protestants taught them that tradition, reason and Scripture made it the pious duty of saints to torture and burn men as heretics out of pure love for their holiness and salvation. Protestants told them that it was sacred duty to slaughter those as schismatics, sectaries, malignants who corrupted the Church and would not live in peace with the Reformed. Who educated these fanatics in Christian love and gentleness? The law of their times was to repel force with force. When the Münster men came into power they applied the reasoning of their tutors in atrocity, saying: 'Our bounden duty is now to rid the earth of Christ's enemies and ours, as they would rid it of us.' And who will say that all these murderers did not stand on the same plane of outrage and barbarity in this respect? As to immoralities:

Every pure mind shrinks from the abhorrent indecencies of Münster. And who had set them this example? They practiced polygamy; but ten long years before this, 1524, Luther had written: 'The husband must be certified in his own conscience and by the word of God that polygamy is permitted to him. As for me, I avow that I cannot set myself in opposition to men marrying several wives, or assert that such a course is repugnant to the Holy Scripture.'[24] About the same time he preached his famous sermon on 'Marriage,' which chastity may well pass in silence, beyond this one expression: 'Provided one has faith, adultery is no sin.'[25] It was not the madmen of Münster but Martin Luther who said: 'Whatever is allowed in the law of Moses as to marriage is not forbidden by the Gospel.' His course in the shameful affair of Philip, Landgrave of Hesse, shows that although he 'did not wish to see this practice (polygamy) introduced among Christians,' yet he held to his old views. Hence, in 1539, four years after the Münster abomination, Philip told him, with what Michelet calls 'a daring frankness,' that he must marry another wife or continue his adulteries, saying: 'I have read with great attention the Old and New Testaments, and I can discover no other resource save that of taking another wife; for I neither can nor will change my course of life; I call God to witness my words.' Yet with that unblushing brow before him, Luther, with Melancthon, Bucer and four others, signed and sealed a document, attempting to dissuade the Landgrave, but failing of that, closed by saying: 'If, however, your highness is utterly determined upon marrying a second wife, we are of opinion that it ought to be done secretly.' Antony Corvinus, the fourth signer of this reply to Philip, gives an account of the examination of John of Leyden, at which he was present, in which John gave his seven articles of faith. He intrenched himself behind Luther's position, saying that they followed 'the example of the patriarchs,' declared marriage a 'political institution,' and then put in the same plea as Philip. In Philip's letter to the Wittenberg divines he said: 'Ever since my marriage I have lived constantly in a state of adultery and fornication, and as I will not forego this course of life, I am interdicted from taking the holy communion; for St. Paul expressly says, "The adulterer shall not see the kingdom of heaven."' John of Leyden adopted this plea, saying, in his seventh article: 'It is better to have a plurality of wives than a multitude of prostitutes. God be our judge.' Henry, the Duke of Brunswick, berated Luther for his approval of Philip's bigamy; when Luther replied, with his usual mildness, in his famous article, 'Against the Buffoon:' 'The duke has daily swallowed devils, and he is chained in hell with the chains of divine judgment.' He then exhorts the pastors to denounce the duke from the pulpit as one who 'has been damned by divine judgment.' But when he revised his pamphlet, he said to Melancthon that he had been altogether too moderate.[26]

And what better examples had the Catholics set the Münster men in the line of purity? From the ninth century down, as Bowden says, in his 'Life of Hildebrand:' 'The infamies prevalent among the clergy are to be alluded to, not detailed.' The open licentiousness of the popes was appalling. The popes of the fifteenth century were profligate and debased beyond belief. Innocent VIII. publicly boasted of the number of his illegitimate children. Alexander was a monster of iniquity, who gave dispensations for crimes that cannot be written. Baronius says that the vilest harlots domineered in the papal see, at their pleasure changed sees, appointed bishops, and actually thrust into St. Peter's chair their own gallants, false popes. Take simply the case of John XII. Bowden wrote: 'The Lateran palace was disgraced by becoming a receptacle for courtezans; and decent females were terrified from pilgrimages to the threshold of the Apostles, by the reports which were spread abroad of the lawless impurity and violence of the representative and successor' of two others equally vile.[27] But these were no worse than Sixtus IV., who erected a house of ill-fame in Rome, the inmates of which, according to Dr. Jortin, 'paid his holiness a weekly tax, which amounted sometimes to 20,000 ducats a year. The purest spirits in the hierarchy blush to tell the hard narrative of monastic life in the sixteenth century, although it made pretension to spotless virtue. Archbishop Morton, 1490, accused the Abbot of St. Albans with emptying the nunneries of Pray and Sapnell of modest women and filling them with vile females. The clergy kept concubines openly from the pope down. Ten priests addressed a letter to the Bishop of Constance, asking permission to marry, confessing that their wicked mistresses had been their 'scandal and ruin.' He absolved them and others on the payment of five gulden; and Hottinger writes that the revenue from this source was 7,000 gulden. This was a full match for the obscenities of Münster. Such transactions in sacred life led these madmen to throw away all license in civil life.

A word as to the nude indecencies of Münster must finish this chapter. People appeared naked at the baptistery and in public places. Where had they learned these revolting practices? For centuries the fanaticism of Rome had immersed all persons in a state of nudity. As far back as A. D. 347, the Ritual of Jerusalem required the candidates for baptism 'to put off the garments wherewith they are clothed.' Brenner, the great Catholic authority, says: 'For sixteen hundred years the candidate for immersion was completely undressed.' The Synod of Cologne, in 1280, carried this fanaticism to such an extent, that they decreed that an infant must have water poured upon its head in the name of the Trinity to save it from perdition, if dying, when but half-born. How like Lambecius, who blamed the Danes and Swedes for delaying baptism through 'bashfulness and shame. . . . Since, formerly men and women laying aside their bashfulness, their whole bodies being entirely nude, were baptized in the presence of all; and that not by sprinkling, indeed, but by immersion or sinking them.'[28] These are the men who now shudder at Münster! These are the men who formerly put hundreds of thousands upon the rack, of every rank, age and sex, to be tortured.[29]

Rome practiced the same indecencies in flagellation, borrowed from the heathen feast of Lupercale, in which, according to Virgil and Plutarch, young noblemen walked through the streets naked, cutting themselves with whips and rods, in austerity, while sacrifices were burning to the gods. The same barbarity was practiced by Christian women in France, Mezaray being authority. For two centuries this flagellant madness ran through Bavaria, Austria, the Upper Rhine and Italy, nay, through Saxony itself. These morbid fanatics practiced all stages of undress, formed a brotherhood, swept in thousands through these lands, singing hymns, having revelations from angels and the Virgin, and with a letter from Christ himself, which they exhibited in their pilgrimages. Motley calls the Münster men, 'Furious fanatics, who deserved the mad-house rather than the scaffold:' and how much better were Catholics or Protestants, in practicing the same things? It is hardly worth while sending the Münster fiends to perdition alone, *nolens volens*, for unbearable beastliness. There was this difference between their butchery and the legal murders of Protestant and Catholic, called martyrdoms, namely: that theirs were acts of violence perpetrated in a religious craze or frenzy, while the others were the result of deliberate legislation, put on the statute-book, in that icy sublimity which dresses itself in the guise of human and divine law. But history will mete out to all these parties that tardy justice which will be honestly accepted by all in due time.

CHAPTER V.

THE REFORMATION—THE GERMAN BAPTISTS.

THE German and Swiss Reformation preceded the English in point of date, all being due to the same causes, while each in a sense stood alone. When Wessel, the mystic, died Zwingli was a boy of five years, Luther of six, Erasmus was a man of twenty-two, Reuchlin of thirty-four and Melancthon was unborn. Luther did not nail his theses to the cathedral door at Wittenberg till 1517, but the Bohemian Reformers sent a delegation to Erasmus at Antwerp as early as 1511, asking him to point out any errors in their Confession of Faith, but he found none. Sebastian Frank, who published his history A. D. 1531, says: 'The Picards in Bohemia are divided into two, or as some say, into three parties, the large, small, and very small, who hold in all things with the Anabaptists, have all things common, baptize no children, and do not believe in the real presence.' So far from finding the origin of the so-called 'Anabaptist' movement in the lawless extravagance of Münster, 1534–35, it is seen that the Swiss history of the Baptists which has been given, preceded that date, and a similar history marks their movements in Bohemia. Addis and Arnold, in their Catholic Dictionary, say that various sects repudiated infant baptism in the Middle Ages, and they trace not only a genetic but an historical connection between these and the Baptists,—agreeing with the 'Encyclopedia Britannica,' that 'The continuity of a sect is to be traced in its principles, and not in its adherents.'

MORAVIA. After Hubmeyer fled from Zurich in 1526, he made his way to Nicholsburg in Moravia, where he established the Baptist cause. This became the field of his labor and the churches multiplied rapidly, partly from the banished of all lands and partly from new converts. They were no more welcome to the king and emperor there than elsewhere, but the rulers stood in fear of the Turks at the time; the Hussites were passive, yet welcomed the Baptists to their estates, so that they could preach and celebrate the ordinances, and they had peace. Ulimann had also fled from Switzerland to Moravia, but in 1530, he returned to persuade his Baptist brethren to leave their Alpine home and seek freedom there too. Full of hope, many gathered their little property and started on this long pilgrimage, but were waylaid at Waldsee, and because they would not renounce their principles, Ulimann and the men were beheaded, while the women were drowned. The question concerning the use of the sword soon divided the Moravian Baptists, Hubmeyer believing in its civil use, but a party of non-resistants withdrew to Austerlitz in 1528. That party subdivided in 1531, when Reublin, another Swiss Baptist, took a company of one hundred and fifty to Auspitz, on the plea that they had not sufficient freedom at Austerlitz in public speaking, that their brethren intermarried with unbelievers and that they were not treated with equality. This party soon fell into 'vain janglings,' and Reublin was excluded for withholding from the common funds.[1] Jacob Huter, however, soon restored harmony by means of a common constitution, and his followers were known as the Huterites.

The Baptists increased to sixty congregations in twenty years, each numbering several hundreds; besides, many settled in Hungary and Transylvania to avoid persecution.[2] By vote of the people, each congregation chose its pastor and deacons.[3] Their pastors were good Bible students, and their people were fond of sacred song, some of their hymns numbering forty-five verses each; for they put an exhortation, a Bible story or the history of a martyr into rhyme. They formed themselves into a community under the direction of one head, and divided into households; each with 'ministers of the word' and 'ministers of need,' and the whole fraternity labored. They taught their children in a common school, and when old enough put them to a trade. Marriage was restricted to their own sect, and their joint earnings went into a common treasury, out of which all were supported. De Schweinitz, a little later than the middle of the century, says of them:

'In Moravia there were many Anabaptists. . . . This sect, which numbered seventy communities in Moravia, was divided into three factions; the communists, who kept up a community of goods, the Gabrielites, and the Sabbatarians. It is said of the Anabaptists, that they were the best farmers, raised the best cattle, had the best vineyards, brewed the best beer, owned the best flour mills, and engaged on a large scale in almost every kind of trade known in their day.' He further says that in spite of frequent persecutions they prospered. 'Their industrial pursuits, for which they became celebrated, won the good-will of powerful families among the nobility; and when Maximilian expressed his surprise that they had not been extirpated in his father's time and casting his tolerance to the winds, proposed to drive them out of the country, the Upper House of the Diet protested against such a measure as destructive to the interests of the kingdom. Hence they were allowed to remain, but loaded with taxes.'[4] Keller says: 'In Moravia, where the Baptists for a long time found influential protectors, persecution begun in 1528. At Easter, in Brünn, Thomas Waldhausen, with two associates, was burned, and at Znaym and Olmutz several of the leaders were put to death. Also at Bruck, in Steinmark, nine men were beheaded and three women were drowned.'[5]

Erhard tells of a curious Catholic, who visited them and evidently 'cast a wishful eye' upon their full cheer.[6] He complained:

'They will not have any poor among them, the sisters dress like the nobility in silk and satin, though they are only waiters' and porters' wives. They have no lack of grain, but gather every year enough for seven. They have plenty of ducats and gold crowns, so that they paid one bill of twenty-two hundred gulden. Their tables are loaded with hare, fish, fowl, nor do they lack good Holland cheese. They ride in beautiful wagons and on fine horses. Their stalls are filled with fat cattle, swine and sheep. They monopolize all the trades, and it looks as though they would soon buy out the lords.'

Good for the 'Anabaptists,' for once they evinced grand common sense, and none the less for keeping that hungry monk out, even if his eyes did water. Still, they were kind, and when famine passed over the land they had enough and much to spare for their neighbors. Then their abundance made Moravia a sort of 'Promised Land' for their pinched brethren who came flocking to them from other countries, for bread and liberty. When these gaunt wretches arrived they said: 'Brother, it is ours by God's gift. In your poverty we will give you and your little ones food and clothes, shelter and schools.' And they had many such calls, as in one year sixteen hundred Baptist emigrants left Switzerland and Bavaria for Moravia. Their manner of life was very frugal, they used few words, were vehement in disputation, and willing to die, but not to yield.[7] They called themselves 'Apostolical;' and elected their general superintendent, who instructed them in the rules of faith and life, and prayed with them every morning before they went to work. A quarter of an hour before eating they covered their faces with their hands in meditation. Their dress was plain and dark, and they conversed much on the future.[8] Erhard, an eye-witness, wrote in Latin rhyme: 'Would that Diogenes might see your baptism and make sport of your washings. You will sometime be called Trito-Baptists, when you are immersed in the Stygian lake.' This evidently alludes to their method of baptizing believers, for they denounced infant baptism severely. When Zeiler visited them long afterwards, 1618, he reported them as still living after the same simple order, and says that they numbered seventy thousand. His account of their communion is very interesting.

'In summer, they would gather at some central point to "break bread," as they called the communion. Long tables were arranged with seats for the company. The day preceding, preparatory sermons were preached, with another early on the day of the celebration. After reading the words of the institution and a prayer, a slice of a large loaf of bread was handed to the presiding preacher, in this case one of the nobility, he broke off a piece and passed the rest to his neighbor, and so on from table to table. Slice after slice was broken until every one had taken a morsel. In like manner the wine was poured out of large vessels into smaller ones and passed around.'[9]

When we bear in mind the constantly recurring outbursts of persecution, their steady increase seems remarkable. They were deprived of Hubmeyer, their great leader, in 1528, seven years before the Münster uproar. The Austrians imprisoned him at Vienna, where Faber and Beck tried earnestly to lead him back into the fold of Rome, but he would not yield a hair's-breadth and was burnt, March 10th. Three days after, his wife was thrown from a bridge into the Danube with a heavy stone around her neck, and drowned. He was a great character and a prolific author of large literary ability. His motto, 'Truth is immortal,' gives the key-note to his high, bold and logical spirit. His full mind overflowed with original thought, delighting in that keen insight which eagerly hails the truth of God without gloss as supreme. His translations of the Gospels, Epistles to the Romans and Corinthians, with his twenty-four works, are prohibited in the Index at Rome, although he was one of the most pure and amiable men of his age. Herzog, in speaking of his great controversy with Œcolampadius, remarks: 'From what has come down to us concerning the discussion, the claim (of victory) is not a matter of surprise. The only direct consequence of the whole affair was to confirm the Anabaptists in their position.' [10] Here is a specimen of his ability, shown in his colloquy with the great professor at Basel:

Œcolampadius. 'It is ridiculous to say the Christian Church has been in the wrong so many centuries.' Hubmeyer. 'That is a loose argument, commonly used by the godless. You must be hard pushed to brandish this sword of straw. If it had been sharp it would have pierced you long ago, when handled by the papists.' Œ. 'It has been the custom of Mother Church to baptize infants.' H. 'Yes, of the papal, but not of the Christian Mother Church. Not of the Father of the Church, who is in heaven, or he would have his Son plant it.' Œ. 'What need is there of separation on account of water?' H. 'It is not a matter of water, but of the high command and baptism of Christ. *Water is not baptism!*' Œ. 'I will prove my statement out of Exodus.' H. Baptism is a ceremony of the New Testament. I demand a text with which you support infant baptism out of the New Testament.' Another asked, 'Whether Christ did not entitle those to baptism who were of the kingdom of heaven.' Hubmeyer answered: 'Tell me, were the infants our Lord loved, embraced, and blessed, *previously* baptized or not? If yes; you throw away your argument against those who keep them back from baptism. If no; am I to understand that Christ calls, embraces and loves unbaptized children? What need have they, then, of baptism?'

He had met Zwingli much in the same way, when the Reformer said: 'The child is born of Christian parents.' H. 'What is born of the flesh is flesh.' Z. 'All Judea came to John to be baptized, surely there were infants in Judea.' H. 'Then Annas, Caiaphas, Pilate and Herod came, too, I suppose.' Z. 'There are many things besides infant baptism, not expressly mentioned in the Bible, not against God.' H. 'Be still, Zwingli, or the Catholic, Faber, will hear you. That is what he said to you, but you demanded a plain passage from him.' Z. 'Paul says he baptized the household of Stephanus. Is it not credible that children were in that household?' H. 'That is credible which can be proved by the word of God. Paul was glad that he had baptized no more than this household, lest they should *boast*. Now infants would not trouble the Apostle in that way.' Zwingli might well 'be still.'

Hubmeyer's death scattered his flock to the forests and mountains, and they were scarcely settled again when a second storm burst upon them, in 1535. But Huter became a leader, and soon displayed great independence of mind, with large resources. He did not believe in the use of the sword, but was very forceful with the pen. His letter to the Governor of Moravia is a marvel of intelligence, manliness and reason, indicating one of those strong minds which rise above passion into the calm and broad penetration of right and honor. King Ferdinand had slaughtered the Baptists without mercy, destroyed their property and driven them into exile, and now the remnant were ordered to leave the land. But so faithful, fearless, kind and statesmanlike was Huter's demand for human rights that its scope and spirit commanded the conscience of the persecutor, who revoked his cruel decree to extirpate them, a thing scarcely known before in history. The result was that they returned to their homes and had rest for twelve years; then for seven years Ferdinand hounded them again, when their landlords were threatened with royal displeasure if one was found on their estates, and after a time they were obliged to fly to Hungary. Soon, however, the gallows were erected before their own doors; their new home together with Poland and Wallachia rejected them, and they sought refuge again in Moravia, but gave up the attempt to keep together and hid in woods and caves till 1554.

When the ferocity of their foes abated they prospered again in Moravia for nearly fifty years, and became very numerous, as we have seen. As early as 1528 two thousand had joined them from Silesia through the influence of Gabriel of Scherding, and Hast says that by 1526 infant baptism was almost obsolete in Silesia.[11] In 1530 there were about fifty Baptist churches, ranging from four to six hundred attendants each and stretching from the Eifel to Moravia.[12] After half a century's quiet Rudolph II. made another savage attempt to extirpate them. He was a descendant of Ferdinand, inherited his hatred of the Baptists, and fined any one of his subjects five hundred ducats who fostered them. In 1622 nearly forty congregations of them were driven out of Moravia into Hungary and Transylvania.[13] For what? In the height of their prosperity, 1589, Christopher Erhard, a Catholic, had spent some time with them and published his observations in a book. He says that the devil helped them to repeat long passages from the Bible, quoting chapter and verse; that they regarded baptism as the covenant of a good conscience and the Supper as a memorial of Christ's death. He thought, however, that they were armed, because some said that they shot rabbits and ducks, and Kelner, of Austerlitz, had swords hanging over his bed. Then he tells this story to prove their pugnacity:

'They say that they do not strike, but let any one try and see. He will prove by his own skin whether they smite or not. The holy David wrote concerning them: "He toucheth the hills and they smoke." One day I spoke to one of them, and called him an Anabaptist. He resented the name, and when I proceeded to justify the appellation, he proceeded suddenly to lay a stick five times, with all his might, upon my back, and might have seriously harmed me. When I met another and told him the insult I had received, he repeated the same thing. These are the men that never use the stick.'[14]

If Shakespear had called out this verdant gentleman in 'Much Ado about Nothing,' he would probably have introduced him as he did Dogberry: 'O that he were here to write me down an ass. But, masters, remember that I am an ass; though I be not written down, yet forget not that I am an ass.' He was unwise to call his Baptist brethren nicknames, when they carried sticks.

All kinds of evil reports concerning the Moravian Baptists were sent back to Bavaria, but despite these a constant stream of emigration flowed thither; and so absolute was the satisfaction afforded by the new faith that few were terrified into recantation.[15] By great judiciousness the many companies of women and children who crossed the borders completely eluded the officers of the law, traveling at night in disguise and in the by-ways; thus they foiled their enemies. Prince William V. offered a reward of forty gulden for every Baptist captured, with sixty extra for a missionary.[16] The missionaries lived in dens and caves, as did David when he was hunted by Saul, and the gatherings of the people were as secret as those of the Covenanters in the Highlands of Scotland. As early as 1547 the Huterites had published what they called a 'Reckoning of their Faith,' from the pen of Peter Reidemann. The Jesuits attempted to blot this book out of existence, and nearly succeeded. No copy is known to remain of the first edition, and but two of the second; one of which is in the Baptist Seminary at Morgan Park, Illinois. Their enemies distributed the so-called 'Nicholsburg Articles' through Europe as their doctrinal standard, which charged various heresies upon them. But this 'Reckoning,' as well as the investigations of Cornelius, shows that these 'Articles' are a forgery, most probably made up by an inquisitor.[17] Scultetus says that the Huterites were still in Moravia in 1718.

The pen was wielded against them as well as the sword, and in all its power. In 1528 Bishop Fabri published six sermons against them at Prague. He stoops to tantalize them with their forced wanderings, as evil spirits seeking rest and finding none; places them in company with Herod for shutting infants out of heaven by refusing baptism to them, which he calls the murder of the innocents. As to confessing Christ before baptism, he demanded with solemnity *ex cathedra*: 'What will you do with mutes? And where do the Scriptures say that a babe shall confess? You say that preaching goes before baptism; well, we always preach before we baptize an infant. If you are so literal you have no right to baptize any one until you have gone into all the world.' Dr. Leopold Dick published a tractate against them in 1531. He took ground that 'it is certain the Apostles always baptized infants,' because 'it cannot be shown that they did not baptize them,'—in substance Luther's argument. In the same way he could as easily have proved that they gave them the Supper after they were circumcised. 'Wolves, he says, 'ought to be killed, and the Anabaptists are wolves.' Bullinger, the successor of Zwingli, launched a volume against them full of hard words and weak arguments. He complains of them bitterly to this effect: They say such good and pious things of God, that they must be bad—they praise God when they are mistreated, and joyfully die for their religion, and there must be something wrong about such people,—the reason why they withdraw from others is that they will not tolerate wicked folk in their fellowship, and, in fact, say that it is vain to demand that people forsake sin and then draw no line between saint and sinner; then he insists that doctrine is more than baptism, although he confesses that baptism is doctrine. He is grieved because their traveling preachers will go to people and read the New Testament and keep up that practice, too, until they are baptized; that they always carry books with them, even when they labor at cutting spoons and twisting baskets—nay, they arm their converts with power to dispute out of the New Testament with the regular clergy, and meet in barns and forests instead of going where infant baptism is defended; and what is quite as bad, they actually refuse interest for loans of money, and think slavery as bad as usury. After calling them most of the harsh names which the liberal vocabulary of his day furnished, he appeals to them affectionately to desist. The essence of his appeal is this: Dearly beloved Anabaptist brethren, do not divide our State churches after this fashion. Let those remain Christians whom Christ has not positively rejected. You want to be called Christians, and are very devout Christians. Why do you act so? You ought to know better. And if you will not learn better, you deserve to be burnt. Light the fagots for them, brethren.

Returning now to the Rhine, we find there, that, when the Baptists were driven over the borders of Switzerland, they made their way into Baden, Bavaria and Austria, where, as Uhlhorn expresses it, they propagated their tenets 'by itinerant missionaries,' and great success attended them at Strasburg, Nürnberg and Augsburg.

STRASBURG. This free imperial city was the Wittenberg of the South and a Baptist stronghold. It was famous for its wealth, refinement and tolerance, so that persecution filled it with fugitives from every quarter, for its magistrates leaned toward liberty of conscience. Bucer, Zell and Capito were the three great Reformed preachers there. Bucer wished to adopt vigorous measures against heretics, but his coadjutors were reluctant, and for once suppression was the unpopular side. He preached to small audiences, his books were little read, the people favored the Baptists, and he demanded a disputation. Capito entertained them at his hospitable home, and spoke of their godliness in the highest terms, so highly, indeed, that Zwingli and Œcolampadius, in 1528, thought that he had become one of them.[18] He never rejected infant baptism, however, but in 1524 he wrote to Zwingli that he was undecided on the subject. He utterly rejected the notion that baptism was a channel of grace, for unless the condition of heart corresponded with the significance of the rite it becomes a false sign. He had published his 'Commentary on Hosea,' in 1528, in which he said of the Baptists:

'Great good comes to all the Churches by their appearance. The people are more prudent, the preachers more watchful, all offices are better filled. Those who, in the face of the hardest tyranny, defend Anabaptism in connection with the confession of Christ, err, if they err, without bad intention, for they make use of rebaptism not as a means of dividing the Churches, but as a sign that they believe the Word of the kingdom and are ready to lay down their lives for their Redeemer. We should, however, pray that the Lord would fill with the knowledge of his name these servants of God, witnesses of Christ, and our dearest brothers; though I do not think less of them if they are weak in this point.'

When the Austrian government went to butchering the Baptists at Rothenburg, in 1527, Capito plead their cause thus, with his pen:

'In regard to baptism, magistracy, and oaths, our dear brothers and brave confessors of the truth may have erred somewhat; but in other matters, they are glorious witnesses of the truth and vessels of honor, and this error does not affect their salvation, for God knows his own. Of the elect, surely are these prisoners, for they have the fear of God, and their very zeal for his honor has led them to this error. In chief matters of faith and essential points, they do not err. Do not, therefore, punish them, but rather instruct them.' [19]

The first so-called rebaptism at Strasburg was administered by Jacob Gross, a disciple of Hubmeyer, in 1526. He had fled from Waldshut in company with Reublin, the man who at Basel joined a Romish procession following a relic and holding up a Bible above his head, cried: 'This is the only true relic, the rest are dead men's bones.' Many were converted at Strasburg, and not a few of the most learned and distinguished citizens. Amongst them was Otto Brunfels, who was first a monk, then a teacher and a physician. He was the publisher of the works of Wickliff and Huss, and Linnæus himself calls him 'the father of botany.' [20] Lucas Hackfurt, the Superintendent of Charities; Fridolin Meyer, the Notary; John Schwebel, the teacher; Jacob Vielfeldt, a noted scholar, and Paul Volzius, to whom Erasmus dedicated his 'Enchiridion' and willed one hundred gulden, whose piety equalled his learning. But the most marked of them all was Pilgram Marbeck, a noted civil engineer from the Tyrol. He built aqueducts about the city and constructed a wood-slide, by which timber was brought to market from distant mountains, which timber long bore the name of 'Pilgram-wood.' He had been driven from the Catholic Tyrol for conscience' sake, to stand at the head of the Baptists in a Protestant city, and he boldly attacked the errors of the Reformers. He reached Strasburg in 1530, and in 1531 published two books advocating Baptist views. The sale and reading of these books were immediately forbidden, and he was summoned before the Council. Before that body, he said: 'This matter is subject to no human tribunal, though I gladly speak of it before all Christians.' He begged the Council not to regard the person of any one for his religion, but to judge impartially. He said: 'It is baptism, everywhere misused, that involves us in hate. I have received it as the sign of an obedient faith, looking not at the water but at God's command.' He charges the preachers with crying out against the Baptists without warrant of Scripture, for there is not one letter there in favor of infant baptism, and so, they sought to compel people through infant baptism to enter the kingdom of heaven. He denied that the magistrates had the right to interfere with the kingdom of God, for that in matters of faith there is no judge invoked but Jehovah. Bucer showed how the aid of the magistrate had been sought. Marbeck replied: 'He who will not be taught by the Word, let him go to the magistrate.' But, December 18th, 1531, the Council banished him. He said: 'I have always submitted to the ordinances of the magistrates, and will yield to this decision, but if in future the Spirit of God should lead me back, I will make no promises.' He then asked for three or four days to get ready. He thanked the magistrates that they had saved the city from the stain of his blood, and exhorted them not to oppress the consciences of those who had nowhere in the world to go for protection, and had fled to them for shelter. After wandering all through Germany, he died at Augsburg.

Nicholas Prugner, an able astronomer, was strongly suspected of being a Baptist, yet he never fully identified himself with them. Eckard Trubel, a grand old knight, sent out his ringing sentiments from his castle. To his brethren he said: 'Great is your reward if you are faithful, but all divine and human rights of heathen and Christians forbid the execution of any one, be he Jew, Turk, heathen or Christian, on account of his faith.' This sentiment is worthy of use as the text to the 'Bloody Tenet,' and the key-note to American Religious Liberty. This he backed by such advanced and statesmanlike utterances as these:

'He who has a good conscience, by the word of God, should not allow it to be broken by human reason and opinion, but remain steadfast. It is better and easier to go to prison or hang on a tree with a good conscience, than to live with a doubtful, restless conscience, even in the glory of King Solomon. Man's hands make short work of it, but God gives eternity. The government has no power to use force with consciences.'

Denk came to Strasburg in 1526, and rendered great service there. And in 1528, Jacob Kautz, who had been the chief Lutheran pastor at Worms, but had become a leading Baptist, was banished thence and came to Strasburg. In 1529 he was cast into prison for the bold advocacy of his principles and united with Reublin, his fellow-prisoner, in calling the Reformers: 'Unskilled carpenters, who tear down much, but are unable to put any thing together.' In the appeal of the sufferers from their dark prison, they say:

'We have told others of the way of salvation through Christ, and those who surrendered themselves to God we have at their own request baptized, not of ourselves, but according to the strict command of Christ. Baptism is the registering of believers in the eternal Church of God. It must not be refused to those who have heard the word of repentance and yielded to it in their heart. Faith confessed is wine, and baptism is the sign hung out to show that wine is within. What a thing is this, to hang out a sign while the wine is still in the grape on the vine, where it may be dried up.' They mean, as in the case of an infant baptized on another's faith for the future, that it may fail, as the promised wine may blight while in the grape on the vine. Then they say: 'Infant baptism is not according to the command of Christ, for no one can tell by it who is Esau and who is Jacob, a believer or an unbeliever.'

In process of time they were taken from the Tower and banished, and in 1532 Kautz asked permission to return to Strasburg, but was refused. Reublin went to Moravia. For a long time severity failed to dislodge the Baptists in Strasburg. Bucer, in writing to Blaurer, 1531, said: 'They cause me infinite trouble.' In the next year he vehemently congratulates him upon his bloody triumph over them at Constance, and expresses the hope that necessity may compel the Senate at Strasburg to move more heartily in this matter. And still, the following year, he complains: 'We will lose our Church and commonwealth, by preposterous and impious clemency to the sectaries. They say, Strasburg will cease to be a free city if violence is done to conscience. But the sects are so increasing, necessity will change the mind of the Senate. Meanwhile, popular hatred is concentrated on Hedio and me.' Again, he calls this clemency 'the sin of the Senate,' until it finally yielded to his entreaties and drove the Baptists from the city, after eight days' warning, in 1534. In 1535 the magistrates ordered that, 'For the sake of Christian unity and love,' nobody should thereafter shelter, feed or assist any 'Anabaptist,' but every one, old and young, who hears of one anywhere shall at once report the same to the authorities. Moreover, no child was to go more than six weeks without baptism, or punishment should follow. Yet, this did not work a perfect cure, and in 1538 the Senate said:

'We have not desired to take the lives of these sectaries, as we were authorized and commanded by imperial law to do; but hereafter, those who return after a second banishment shall lose a finger, be branded in the cheek, or put in the neck-iron; and if any return the third time, they shall be drowned. We do this, not to make men believe as we do. It is not a matter of faith, but to prevent division in the Church.'

Yet, the axe, the branding-iron, the river, did not daunt Baptist consciences, the heretics remained and increased in Strasburg, just as if they had not been forbidden.

AUGSBURG was the head-quarters of Baptists in Southern Germany. It was a rich city with a large laboring class, whose chief comfort sprang from the Gospel. Dr. Osgood writes that in 1527 the Baptist church there numbered 800 members.[21] When Hetzer was a young man he gathered the first company of Baptists there, 1524. After him John Denk became their leader.[22] Uhlhorn speaks of him as intellectual, of elegant manners, classical culture and profound nature. He was born in Bavaria, near the close of the fifteenth century, and studied at Basel. He graduated a first-class Latin, Greek and Hebrew scholar. For a time he acted as proof-reader to two publishers in Basel and attended the lectures of Œcolampadius, who procured for him the position of principal in St. Sebald's school, Nürnberg, the German center of printing if not of learning. According to Keller, when this school was formed Melancthon was selected for its principal and he accepted, but for some reason did not serve. The next best man for the place was Denk, who was installed in 1523. His high and independent views of God's word and of the Supper soon brought him into collision, however, with Osiander the Reformer, and after eighteen months' service he was banished, January, 1525, and forbidden to come within ten miles of this famous free city, on pain of death. Osiander was one of those harsh and unlovely spirits who anticipated the narrow Lutheranism of the next generation. Denk went to Augsburg and kept a private school. There he met Hubmeyer, who baptized him before he went to Moravia.

Wagenseil, in his 'History of Augsburg' (1820–'22, ii, p. 67), says of the Baptists of 1527, they held 'That baptism should be given to none who had not reached years of discretion, and the candidates must not be merely sprinkled with water, but wholly submerged.' Clement Sender, a Catholic contemporary, from 1518 to 1533, in his 'Rise and Progress of Heresy in Germany,' Ingoldstadt, 1649, p. 25, writes: 'In Augsburg, in three gardens attached to houses, there used to assemble more than eleven hundred men and women, rich, mediocre and poor, all of whom were rebaptized. The women, when they were rebaptized, put on trousers. . . . In the houses where a baptistery was these trousers were always kept.' [23]

Denk soon drew many noted merchants to the Baptists, including two members of the lower council and other citizens, to the number of eleven hundred in the city alone, besides forming many churches in adjacent villages. Hans Hut was one of his converts and became a strong leader. Denk's powerful pen was kept busy in defending his cause against attacks from Rome, Wittenberg and Zurich. Rhegius, the Lutheran, soon persecuted him out of the city, and he found refuge in Strasburg, where most sects were tolerated. Capito and Zell were the leading Reformed ministers there; both opposed police interference with the Baptists, whose ranks were full of public men and many first-class scholars. Denk stirred the whole city by a tract, and met Bucer in public disputation, winning great honor by his dignity and mental expertness. This was followed by violence, and he retired to Landau. Here Baader, the Lutheran pastor, drew him into debate, the result being that he and all his congregation abandoned the practice of infant baptism. We find Denk at Worms with Hetzer in 1527, translating the Old Testament prophets. Osiander had its sale prohibited at Nürnberg, but with little effect, as it soon passed through thirteen editions, and in all has numbered seventeen.

This was the first modern German translation of the prophets. Possibly Keller, the present archivist of Münster, has given this subject as full investigation as any one now living. He says that from 1466 to 1518 eighteen editions of the entire German Bible had been issued, besides twenty-five editions of the New Testament. Dr. Jostes and others claim Catholic origin for some of these, but he stoutly contends that all editions published down to 1518 were the work of the Waldensians; and this is likely, for the inquisitors at Strasburg found and destroyed German Bibles in 1404, and at Freiburg in 1430; and in 1468 the German primate, Berthold of Mayence, prohibited the use of the German Bible. The Bible of 1483 puts a print of the pope at the head of the host overthrown by the angels in the Apocalypse, which proves its anti-catholic origin. Dr. Keller also puts Denk and Hetzer amongst the standard translators of the German Bible; and Metzger thinks that the frequent agreement between the Zurich and Wittenberg versions is due to the fact that both used the 'Worms' translation. The translation made by Baptists in

1527 leaned to the ancient Waldensian version, and for a century the Mennonites preferred the Waldensian version to the Lutheran.

In August, 1527, there was a gathering of sixty Baptist leaders at Augsburg, over which Denk presided, which, amongst other things, declared that Christians should never take possession of government in an unlawful way. The result of that meeting unified their faith and enkindled their missionary zeal, so that the empire felt the pulsations which it sent out. For a time he sought rest in Basel, but just before his arrival Baptists had been forbidden there; to the honor of his old friend, Œcolampadius, however, he was made an exception, and the gentle wanderer was protected. Worn out with labor and persecution while yet young, he passed through a quiet illness, and died a natural death at Basel, in great peace of soul, 1527. Almost his last work was a series of articles setting forth his faith in the sweetest and most apostolic spirit. Arnold was so struck with these features that he remarks: 'From them it may be seen whether he can be regarded as godless and his followers as diabolical.' The following extract from Dr. Keller presents this beautiful character in his true light:

'John Denk, according to the opinion of competent judges, belonged to the most distinguished men of his time. Although by his position in reference to the Church he drew upon himself the opposition of the ruling powers, and in all places was surrounded by enemies, no one has been able to bring into doubt his masterly gifts, or to discover even the smallest spot in his character. Unstinted praise is accorded to him in the testimonies that have come down to us concerning him, a fact which is all the more important since we have only the testimony of his opponents. The well-known Strasburg reformer, Wolfgang Capito, praises Denk's most exemplary walk in life, his remarkable talent, and his outward bearing, qualities which, as Capito says, drew the people to him and held them in a wonderful manner. Vadian, the friend of Zwingli, made a brilliant sketch of the young man. "In Denk, that distinguished young man," he says, "were all talents so extraordinarily developed that he surpassed his years and appeared greater than himself." The pastor of St. Gall, John Kessler, who had the opportunity of making Denk's acquaintance, says concerning him: "This John Denk was exceedingly familiar with the letter of the Holy Scriptures, and had a good knowledge of the three leading languages. In person he was tall, of most agreeable manners, irreproachable in life, and highly indeed to be commended, had he not defiled his mind and doctrine with such fearful errors."' [24]

Another contemporary said of him: 'The world will not heed the dear man. Well, when the time of misfortune comes, it will have to say that it brought on itself its evil days.' A late biographer says of him: 'The prophecy came true in a more powerful manner than could have been anticipated. As long as Denk's words, "In matters of faith every thing must be left free, willing and unforced," were despised, an unlucky star ruled the destiny of Germany. Nearly three centuries were necessary to make room for Denk's ideas. The injustice which has been done the men of Denk's party cannot be made good by later times, but it is the duty of the historian to see that the property right in the ideas for which they suffered be not snatched from them, or ascribed to those who battled against their principles, as may be proved in the most decisive manner.' Beard says in his Oxford Lectures:

'There is a great concurrence of testimony both to the depth of the influence which he exerted, and the integrity and sweetness of the character which justified it.' Franck calls him 'a quiet, retiring, pious man, the leader and bishop of the Anabaptists. . . . He belonged to that age of Anabaptism when it was at once a deeply religious and a truly ethical movement, before the relentless rage of stupid persecution had deprived it of its natural leaders, and handed it over to extravagance and license. Men gathered eagerly about Denk, hung upon his lips, adopted his principles, and were afterwards not afraid to suffer for their faith. He showed himself, in the three years within which all his activity was comprised, a great religious leader, and he might, possibly, had his life been prolonged, have developed into a philosophical theologian too. In a quiet, singular way, he united the qualities which kindle religious enthusiasm in others with a sweet reasonableness, such as belongs to hardly any other theologian, orthodox or heretical, in the age of the Reformation. . . . In him, radical Protestantism lost a leader whose place no Spanish or Italian rationalist can supply.' [25]

This 'Apollo of Anabaptism,' as Haller calls him, died nearly eight years before the Münster outbreak. God enabled him to lay the foundations of Baptist truths very solidly in Southern Germany, and no wonder. His heart was brimful of child-like purity and simplicity, his thinking was elastic, forceful and versatile, and his literary compositions were finished and winsome, for his discussions laid open his entire heart. No man of his times commanded a fitter cast of mind or broader literary powers to lead men back to first principles and make himself the center of a great movement. His body was frail, but his whole being delighted in Christ's teachings, he had no suspicion of his own honesty and his heart never failed him or the truth.

In the year that Denk died, Langenmantel, a nobleman, became the Baptist pastor at Augsburg, and faithfully did his work in this powerful Church. [26] At first he received the Baptists to his house and then defended them. October 15th, 1527, he was arrested for complaining of the reformed preachers that they were avaricious, that they charged double fees for baptizing children, that they neither preached nor lived according to God's word, but that they taught this doctrine: 'He who is foreordained to sin must sin.' These he calls words of 'horrible blasphemy, the voice of Satan, not of Christ, as God gives no cause for sin,' and he exhorted his brethren to 'stand firm, for soon they will hang, burn and behead.' When brought into court, he was told that he deserved to be beheaded, but because his noble relatives pleaded for him, perpetual banishment should suffice. He wrote a hymn and four tracts, which are extant. One of the latter was on the 'Old and New Papists,' in which he defended the Gospel Supper as a simple memorial, in reply to Luther's absurdity that Christ is in the bread, as fire is in the red-hot iron. Another is a complete defense of the Baptists from the Scriptures. He rejects the term 'Anabaptist,' which means to baptize again, for he says: 'We are Co-baptists, but you are Anti-baptists.'

. . . You do not keep the commandments of Christ, especially that relating to baptism. Is it right, when Christ speaks four or five words, for one to take the last word and put it first and the first last? You turn it about and take the last word first, according to your will. Where is it said to baptize without preaching the Gospel and faith? Now, I demand testimony before the whole world, and give them all the Scriptures to show where God has so commanded.' He was finally put to death by the sword, although his family offered five thousand florins for his release.

Several other leaders were imprisoned and condemned at Augsburg, amongst whom were Gross, Hut and Snyder. The 'Martyrology' says, that many of the Baptists there were branded and one had his tongue cut out. Hans Koch and Leonard Meyster were put to death in 1524, and Leonard Snyder in 1527. Hut had refused to bring his babe to baptism in 1521. Early in his religious life he had tendencies to sedition and was always a strong millenarian. Hubmeyer contended with him on these points, and in his preaching he said much of the end of the world. The circular which called for his capture described him as 'a very learned man;' his conduct shows him to have been brave and even daring. In his prison he kindled straw to burn the beam and loosen the chain which bound him, and was suffocated in the effort. His corpse was brought out amid the ringing of the city bells and burnt on the public square, and his ashes thrown into the Wertach. In 1527 the Dukes of Bavaria issued decrees for the arrest and imprisonment of all Baptists. This document was posted in the market-places and read from all state pulpits. Duke William was very zealous, and wrote a full description of one poor offender to the Bishop of Passau: 'His name is Anthony, born at Salzburg, a lastmaker, a big, heavy fellow, thirty years old, lame in his right hand, wears a red cap, left Augsburg without a coat, will stop with Hermann Kheil, a brother, on the fishmarket.' Soon the prisons were crowded with Baptists, many died in prison, others were branded, burned or drowned in the Isar; but few left the Falcon Tower unpunished. At Augsburg it was made the duty of one of the city councilors to be present at the opening and closing of the gates, so that no Baptist should enter.[27] Sender, a monk of the city, kept an account of the daily outrages practiced upon them: January 12th, 1528, twelve were banished; 13th, thirty were imprisoned; 18th, ten perpetually exiled; 19th, twenty driven out of the city; 22d, seven scourged out of town; 23d, three men and five women driven out; 24th, one refusing to take the oath was branded on the cheek.[28] The barbarous crusade ran on till February, when a general sweep was made. At Easter two hundred were surprised at the house of Ducher, as they were holding a 'love-feast;' then Seebold preached and his sermon cost him his life, for he was slaughtered April 25th, his congregation being driven in all directions; a little later twelve were slain at Augsburg.

Rhegius, the reformed preacher, was at the bottom of this bloody work, and a lady of the nobility, a prisoner, said to him : 'There is a great difference between you and me. You sit on a soft cushion beside the Burgomasters and declaim as Apollo from his tripod, while I must speak here on the ground bound in chains.' He said that if the 'Anabaptists would keep their errors to themselves they would be let alone ; but if they proposed to gather a peculiar people to God and return from banishment, then the government must use the sword.' [29]

In February, 1527, George Wagner (Carpenter), was captured by dragoons and cast into prison at Munich, and every means was used to make him recant, even the duke visiting him to change his mind, but in vain. The fourth charge against him was, 'That he did not believe that the very element of the water itself in baptism doth give grace' (regeneration). He was asked why he esteemed baptism lightly, knowing that Christ was baptized in the Jordan. He then showed why Christ was baptized, but that our salvation stands in his atonement and not in his baptism. Then he opened the true use of baptism. Foxe, i, 402. When brought out for execution, the procession halted at the steps of the City Hall to hear the charges of heresy read, and a school-master asked him, 'George, are you not afraid to die, would you not be glad to go back to your wife and children?' He replied, 'To whom would I rather hasten?' 'Recant and you can go.' On his way to the stake his wife and children came, and kneeling before him, begged him to recant and save his life. [30] He said: 'My wife and children are so dear that the duke could not pay me for them with the revenue of the State, but I part with them for my inmost love to God.' 'Do you really believe in God as confidently as you say?' 'It would be hard for me to face a death so terrible if I did not.' He offered prayer, and a priest promised to say masses for his soul, when George said: 'Pray for me *now*, that God will give me patience, humility and faith. I shall need no prayer after death.' A brother asked him for a sign of perseverance in the flames, when he promised to confess Christ as long as he could speak. As he fell in the fire he cried, 'Jesus! Jesus!' and was with him.

Two letters from prisoners fell into the hands of Rhegius, 1528, in which they show most beautifully their reliance on the saving work of Christ. Amongst other things this is set forth:

'The only answer to give our enemies is faith and patience, for this is the hour and power of darkness. . . . If any one asks you why you were baptized, tell him to go and ask Jesus, the Son of God. He will tell you why he gave the command. If you reply out of the Holy Spirit you will not contradict the command of Christ, for the Holy Spirit gave the command through Christ. Christ, our Brother, was circumcised after the law when he was eight days old, but baptized to fulfill all righteousness, according to the New Testament, when he was thirty years old. The truth says that teaching is the principal and most needful thing, for the apostles made disciples before they baptized them. He who baptizes children confesses that baptism is more necessary than teaching.'

Another apostle amongst the Bavarian Baptists was Augustine Wurzelburger, a school-teacher who did a great work amongst them, but the dukes demanded his execution. The magistrates of Regensburg, however, reported that they found so much 'reason in his views,' that they counted him not worthy of death, he had simply been rebaptized. The dukes frankly declared this guilt enough, according to many princes and prelates. On a second demand he was promptly put to death. Also, at Salzburg, many were slain. Seventeen of them were discovered in the pastor's house, and all were burned, but those who recanted had the privilege of being beheaded beforehand. Many were locked in their place of worship and burned therewith. Also a beautiful child of sixteen was condemned to be burned, and the whole town interceded for her life. But she remained steadfast, and as an act of mercy the executioner carried her, like a lamb, in his arms, held her under water in a trough and drowned her, and then threw her body into the flames.[31] At Vienna one day a large number were drowned in the Danube, being bound together in such a manner that as one fell into the water he drew another after him. All met their fate with joy.[32] Martyrdoms took place also in many other cities, where Baptists were treated like reptiles and wild beasts. This was especially true at Rothenburg on the Neckar, where Michael Sattler, who had been a monk and had become a Baptist, was slaughtered. The fiendish sentence was carried out to the letter in 1527. His tongue was cut out, twice his flesh was torn with red-hot pincers, and then he was brought in a cart to the city gate, where his flesh was torn five times more before he was burned to ashes. His wife and several other women were drowned, several men were beheaded and about seventy more were murdered in one way or another.

CHAPTER VI.

THE REFORMATION—GERMAN BAPTISTS—*Continued.*

MOST interesting facts are connected with the Baptists of the Tyrol. Fugitives from other lands flocked to this Austrian province as early as 1525, and Ferdinand began to persecute them in 1527. Their places of worship were torn down and their ministers made to suffer by water, fire and sword. When Bishop George issued his command for their arrest, Ulrich Müller was forthwith burnt alive at Brixen, for the king had confiscated all Baptist property and ordered the burning of all their preachers. Sunday after Sunday his decrees were read from the State pulpits, and priests failing to publish them were to be punished. Despite all this activity, Baptists filled Innthal and the Brenner Pass. Schwatz, a town of twelve hundred people, had eight hundred of the new faith. A prisoner at Innsbrück, confessed that he had himself baptized four hundred. This sudden growth was due in part to the coming of Blaurock from Switzerland, whose eloquent enthusiasm ranked him, in the eyes of the people, as a second Paul. Many fled from this persecution to Moravia, and, angered by their escape, the king issued a a new order in 1529, inflicting death on all, regardless of recantation. Baptists were burnt in every village and city wherever found, and amongst them Blaurock, at Claussen. The town records say that sixty-seven perished at Kitzbuhel, sixty-six at Rattenburg, and twenty-two at Kuffstein. Down to 1531 one thousand had been put to death in the Tyrol, or two hundred and fifty a year; whereas only two hundred and sixty-four persons were martyred in the reign of 'bloody Mary.' No writer of the present day possesses such facilities for full and accurate statement on this subject as Dr. Keller, of Münster; and, on what he pronounces 'reliable statements,' the number of Baptists put to death was as follows: In 1531, 1,000 had been martyred in the Tyrol and Görtz, 600 at Enzisheim, 73 at Linz, from 150 to 200 in the Palatinate. In 1527, 12 had suffered death in Switzerland and about 20 at Rottenburg. He cites Hase, a stout opponent of the Baptists, who says: 'The energy, the capacity for suffering, the joy in believing, which characterized the Christians of the first centuries of the Church, reappeared in the Anabaptists.'

Under the edict of 1530 all houses were searched, to discover who refrained from mass, and what children had been held back from baptism; the houses of all who sheltered Baptists were to be destroyed, informers were rewarded from twenty to forty gulden and Baptist property was to meet the costs of the Inquisition. The trials were private, and the purpose of Ferdinand was to annihilate these homeless disciples. When the storm was at its height the Baptists of Moravia heard 'what a great work God was doing in the Tyrol,' and sent Jacob Huter, their leader, to assist them. He saved many of them from the blood-thirst of Ferdinand by sending them into Moravia; but on his second visit he was arrested and executed. A gag was put in his mouth, he was led to Innsbrück, where he was first thrown into cold water, then into hot, then his flesh was torn with pincers, the wounds filled with brandy and set on fire.

Sigmund von Wolkenstine, a young noble of seventeen, was another victim. After a year's imprisonment he was set free for a little time, to choose between recantation and new sufferings. He selected the latter, but his powerful family induced the king to permit him to enter the army. A price was put upon the head of Griessteller, now the Baptist leader. The officers of a dozen districts combined and found him in the mountains, between Bruneck and Rodeneck. After a long hunt, the king was delighted with his capture and he was speedily put to death at Brixen. The fagots had been soaked in rain the night before and would not burn, so the people begged for the sword as the easier death, but dry fuel was brought and he was burnt alive. Spies were hired to be baptized, to gain the confidence and find out the secrets of the sect, and after all other measures had failed to crush them it entered into somebody's head that possibly argument and exhortation might convert them! Hence, Cardinal Bernard ordered his priests to preach the word of God, according to the Scriptures—the best cure for 'Anabaptism' ever devised. But, in the eyes of Ferdinand, this made things worse and worse and he went back to the old weapons. Then he made his edicts cover all Austria and her dependencies, and thus, in 1545, Moravia became as perilous to the Baptists as the Tyrol. Yet, these Tyrolese brethren stood as firmly as their own mountains; when the king became emperor, State affairs so absorbed his attention that he forgot all about this hated people. When he returned to his task, however, every valley and ravine was scoured, and the old scenes were re-enacted. Baptists swarmed in Pusterthal, and in Au they were the ruling power in society.

In 1585 four Tyrolese Baptists ventured from Moravia to labor in their own country. Jacob Pauzer had left home when seventeen, but was now a man of forty, simple-hearted, active and strong in the faith. Ruprecht Sier, thirty years of age, Leonard Mareez, aged forty-two, and a fourth, whose name is not given, formed the heroic band. Each of them was rooted in the faith, and would stretch upon the rack rather than betray a brother. They met their friends in forests, by-ways and crags, as best they could, but some of their relatives were in prison and could not be reached. They were hunted at every point, two of them wavered and one fled, but Pauzer met martyrdom by the axe. These facts, with many others of equal interest, are found in Kripp's 'Contribution to the History of the Anabaptists in the Tyrol:' Innsbrück, 1857.

The first effect of the Reformation in Germany was to drive away the old

Catholic priests, often in disgust and angry controversy, long before Reformed pastors could fill their places, and when they did come the community was convulsed more than ever. At first the change was not for the better in the public morals, but the contrary. The newly-preached doctrine of Justification by Faith alone without the merit of works was not understood, and many acted as badly as they could, because good works could not save them. People paid absolute obedience to the old authority; but when that discipline was thrown aside the new clergy had little power over them, and were obliged to depend upon the secular arm to bring under moral restraint a multitude of nominal believers without the bond of heart-love for the Gospel. Blaurer, the Reformer at Constance, complained: 'Ourselves bear a great share of the blame. We want to hear so little of real penitence that our doctrine itself is open to suspicion. My labor and my life become distasteful to me when I regard the condition of many cities, evangelical to such a small degree that scarcely any trace of genuine conversion can be shown in them at all. Out of Christian liberty they make, by a godless interpretation, liberty to commit sin. It is agreeble to be justified, redeemed, saved for nothing; but there is not one who does not resist with hands and feet mortification of the flesh, crosses and sufferings and Christian devotion.'

Luther said, in 1526: 'Those who want to be Christians in earnest, and confess the Gospel by hand and mouth, ought to enlist themselves by name and assemble apart from all kinds of people in a house alone to pray, read, baptize, receive the sacrament and practice other Christian duties. In this manner we could know who were not Christians, punish, correct, exclude and excommunicate. Then we could expect general thanksgiving, giving willingly and distributing among the poor. I cannot yet found such a church, for I have not the people to do it with, and do not see many who are urgent for it.'

This frank utterance shows that at heart he shared the high and pure intentions of the Baptists for a thorough reform, and a return to a purely regenerated church, after the Gospel pattern. But his hands were tied, for the condition even of the German clergy was much like that of the Swiss, of whom Bullinger honestly confesses that only three deans in Switzerland could read the Old Testament, some did not know of the Bible at all, and not all of them could read the New Testament. After the general upbreaking, this was the material on which the Reformation was obliged to depend for its ministers in many places. Luther and several other leaders were more than half Baptists at that time. Early in his ministry he told certain Bohemian brethren that he did not like their views of infant baptism because they used it in hope of future faith when they came to years of responsibility. It either regenerated the children or it meant nothing. He said: 'If you receive the sacraments without faith, you bring yourselves into a great difficulty, for we oppose against your practice the saying of Christ: "He that believeth and is baptized shall be saved."'[1] At that time he also taught the practice of immersion. He said:

'The term baptism is Greek, and may be rendered dipping, as when we dip something in water, so that it is covered all over. And although the custom is now abolished amongst many, for they do not dip children, but only pour on a little water, yet they ought to be wholly immersed and immediately withdrawn. For this the etymology of the term seems to demand. And the Germans also call baptism *taufe*, from depth, which in their language they call *tiefe*, because it is fit that those who are baptized should be deeply immersed. And certainly, if you look at what baptism signifies, you will see that the same is required. For it signifies this, that the old man and our sinful nature, which consists of flesh and blood, are totally immersed by divine grace, which we will point out more fully. The mode of baptizing, therefore, necessarily corresponded with the signification of baptism, that it might set forth a certain and full sign of it.' [2]

Keller shows that most of the leaders stood on semi-Baptist ground at that time. Œcolampadius writes, February 6th, 1525: 'I have some letters to friends advocating infant baptism, but hardly any one will listen to me;' so general was the defection on that subject. And in 1528, William Farel, Calvin's patron, defended the Baptists against their foes. A year before, September 7th, 1527, he said: 'It is not understood by many what it is to give one's name to Christ and fight for Christ, to walk and persevere in newness of life by the infusion of the Spirit with whom Christ immerses his own, who, in this mind and by this grace wish to be immersed in water [*intingi aqua*] in the presence of the Christian congregation, that they may publicly protest what they believe in their hearts, that they may be dearer to the brethren and closer bound to Christ by this solemn profession, which is only rightly dispensed as that great John, and that greatest of all, Christ, commanded.' [3]

In this state of the public mind Baptist evangelists came preaching personal repentance, faith and a holy life, salvation finished, full and free through Christ's atonement; with a church sustained by pure love to him and not by the secular arm. They taught that 'The water of baptism does not save by its natural force, for it is no more than any other creature of God,' but that men are effectually saved from their sins by faith in Christ's sacrifice. 'But,' said they, 'if faith in Christ saves, wherefore baptism? Faith is a root of a faithful heart. If you believe, you do the works of a believer, as a good tree bears good fruit. Yet, these works do not merit salvation. The word that teaches me to believe teaches me to be baptized, for faith without works is dead.' This preaching threw new light upon the whole Gospel system, and so effectually turned men to holiness that a net of small Baptist churches was formed in all the districts of Germany, from Alsace to Breslau, from Hesse to Etschland.[4] In many places the commotions of the times had left the people without teachers, and these evangelists were plain men who supported themselves, preached in barns, woods, gardens, private houses, the poeple heard them and many were radically converted. These formed themselves into simple churches, with the Bible as their only guide, each choosing its own pastor and officers. They met for prayer (the prayer-meeting was commonly called 'the Heretics' School'), for fellowship, the breaking of bread, and the exercise of brotherly watch-care and discipline. Not believing in State support and receiving none, they voluntarily divided the results of their daily industry, without selfishness, as did the saints at Jerusalem under similar circumstances of persecution. They had 'all things common,' not in the sense of renouncing the right of property, but in the sense of sharing it freely one with another, in suffering.

It is needless to say that people living such lives have always been systematically traduced, as these men were in the heat of their adversaries; but as the world has had time to cool, every man now owes the naked justice to himself to read their history with open eyes, throwing aside the old trick of defaming those whom it is not convenient to understand. Historical aptitude should be quickened by the unveilings of three centuries to a sharper insight into this great movement, so that its length and breadth can be taken in, with that round compactness which the Germans themselves call *combinationsgabe*. The branding of men with ink who cannot be reached with iron should cease. Day by day their entire trend is becoming clearer and clearer, until the best investigators of passionless history accord to nineteen twentieths of them the honest aim of restoring apostolic Christianity by molding simple societies of godly men after the ideal of Christ. Their foundation idea was to develop all goodness, not by bringing the State into the Church as a part thereof but by taking each citizen into the Church on his individual consecration to Christ. This, of course, destroyed sacerdotalism, uprooted all political bases in religion and made the Bible, which embodies Christ's will, the touch-stone of all Christian truth. The State was to protect all its citizens as citizens, without regard to their religious opinions, so that the civil magistrates could control no man's conscience. Zwingli would have them do no injustice in exacting tithes, but the Baptists said that the civil authorities should levy no such tithes at all. Catholic and Protestant alike made it the duty of the magistrate to establish religion and enforce it by fine, imprisonment and death; but the Baptists said, 'No; this is a remnant of heathen usurpation, of which Christ's law knows nothing.' Few authorities have caught the broad view of the Baptists better than the 'Encyclopædia Britannica,' which says:

'The Anabaptists ot Germany were historically noteworthy, not because they insisted on rebaptism as a condition of admission into their communion, but because the enthusiasm of the Reformation manifested itself to them in a form and manner altogether peculiar. Their views as to the constitution of the Church and its relations to the State, and the efforts they made to realize these views, furnish a problem, partly theological, partly historical, of which the satisfactory solution is not easy. Anabaptism, as a system, may be defined as the Reformation doctrine, carried to its utmost limit; the Anabaptists were the extreme left of the army of the Reformation. It is true that they regarded each other as in different camps; but their mutual denunciations cannot conceal the fact that even the most peculiar doctrines of the Anabaptists were to them only corollaries illegitimately drawn, as the more orthodox Reformers thought, from the fundamental principle common to both, of the independence of the private judgment, and the supreme importance of the subjective element, personal faith in religion. The connection of this principle with this theory of the Church and its connection with the State, their doctrine of the sacraments, and even their political rising, is so obvious that it need not be dwelt upon.'5

Practically, the churches of the Reformation outside of the Baptist ranks were strangers to the highest doctrine in the scale of human rights, that of private judgment; they alone expounded, maintained and extended it to all. All persons were forced into the national churches by law. No matter how profane or skeptical they might be, the law made all members of the Church, and compelled the most licentious to go to the Lord's table, on pain of fine and torture. As clear and resolute thinkers, the Baptists saw that the Protest at Spire, in teaching personal justification by faith, touched the very essence of church-building and exploded the whole plan of National Church life. The Reformers saw the bearings of this fact, at a glance, and in order to guard the nascent system they fortified it with the sign which Rome had created, and practically threw the 'Protest' to the winds by punishing dissent with bloodshed throughout the continent. Out of that flow of blood sprang the eternal rights of conscience, which the Reformers claimed as their own right, and which they denied to those whose blood was shed. To them that right was a primary truth, to others unallowable. So, this was not a mere inconsistency either in logic or conduct, but a radical difference of principle between them and the Baptists. Let us examine this vital point closely.

In 1526 each German State had been left to manage its own religious affairs, as they might answer severally 'to their own conscience.' But it was not intended in this to recognize the right of the individual conscience in each man, but a State conscience, a nonentity, was created as a part of the Reformed system, so far seceding from a universal conscience located at Rome. Hence, at the second Diet of Spire, 1529, certain members began to feel their way back further, to a personal conscience, avowing that they could do nothing touching their salvation but what their own 'conscience directs and teaches.' They declared their willingness to obey the Diet in 'all dutiful and possible things,' but they must obey God, as they say, 'for our conscience' sake.' They stated that they could not 'hold and fulfill the imperial edict in all points' with a '*good* conscience,' it was 'against our conscience' to 'force them under the edict in question;' they based their dissent on the sanctity of Christian conscience, and the Diet was obliged to qualify its previous decree, and to tolerate religious differences amongst the Lutherans themselves within certain limits. Having admitted so much of the principle of soul liberty, right there the Baptist and anti-Baptist battle of the Reformation took its sternest quarters. Schenkel has caught the genius of the struggle, and says: 'The deepest source of that protestation is, the newly awakened consciousness of the eternal rights of conscience. . . . Protestantism is, therefore, a great deed of conscience. . . . In whatever confession or church institution this freedom is not recognized, that is anti-Protestant.'

But the famous Protest of Spire was defective, in that it attempted to make provision against what it considered the defects of conscience from ignorance and a wrong bent. It assumed what is true, namely, that personal conscience is no more infallible than the judgment or will; but it also assumed what is not true, namely, that the State conscience is more reliable, although its existence is a mere myth. Yet, for the relief of some parties who composed the Diet, it said that it would seek 'the honor of Almighty God, of his holy word, and the salvation of our individual souls,' by the dictates of conscience. Had it taken one step more the battle between it and the Baptists had been ended. It failed to lay down the doctrine that every Christian should be allowed to govern his own conscience by the absolute dictation of Scripture, under the divine right of its private interpretation; that the Christian conscience could not otherwise be free, and that conscience itself, as well as faith and life, should be left to the teaching of the Scriptures. This was the firm Baptist ground: that God demands the vital submission of the conscience itself to his infallible word, and that every disciple should be left free to follow that, as endowing him with a 'good conscience toward God.' The Baptists located the responsibility of conscience, as well as the exercise of intelligence, at the tribunal of inspired truth, as the last court of appeal in all soul life. The Reformers could not be made to see that point at all, but drifted further and further away from it, until as Hase says, 'The Protestant Church appears only like a purified form of Catholicism. In various ways it practically represented itself as infallible, and even expressly claimed that there was no salvation out of itself.'[6]

This blunder concerning the radical rule of faith led the Reformers into all sorts of absurdities, as the attempt to embody a whole nation in a church, in disregard of age or moral character, and it explains the principle on which they persecuted all whose consciences differed from their own. Their plea was, that all heresy is ruinous and must be crushed out, and that all consciences but ours are heretical. Looking at the Reformation from this point, Luther lamented that it was a failure. He wrote: 'Our evangelicals are seven times worse than they were before. For since we have learned the Gospel we steal, tell lies, deceive, gormandize, tipple and commit all kinds of vice.' Of course, it followed that he must set this to rights at the cost of any suffering to the wrong-doer, in 'all good conscience,' after the example of Saul, and he mistook his own imperiousness as zeal for God, for he confined not his interference to overt and immoral acts. This is his avowed claim: 'Whoever teaches differently from what I have taught, or whoever condemns, he condemns God and must remain a child of hell. . . . I will not have my doctrine judged by any one, not even by angels.'[7] This Lange confirms when he avows: 'Luther's imperious nature would allow no one else to have his own way.' He seemed at first to take the ground that the Scriptures were imperial, but fell back upon persecuting the consciences that yielded absolute submission to them. He granted that conscience is the eye of the soul, and there stopped; but the Baptists added, the Bible gives it light, and the conscience cannot be free unless guided by a free Bible. A free conscience governed by a free Bible forms the regnant, double franchise of God's sons.

Cardinal Hosius said truly that Luther did not intend to make all Christians as free as himself; thus, when they rejected his authority over their consciences, he treated them as the pope treated him; so Luther became a persecutor by slow degrees. He wrote to Spalatin, in 1522, concerning the Baptists: 'I would not have any who hold with us imprison them.'[8] In 1528 he also said: 'I am very sorry they treat the Anabaptists so cruelly, seeing it is only on account of belief, and not because of the transgression of the laws. A man ought to be allowed to believe as he pleases. We must oppose them with the Scriptures. With fire little can be accomplished.'[9] And still he sanctioned the decree of the Elector of Saxony, the same year, forbidding any but the regular ministers to preach or baptize, under penalty of imprisonment.[10] Charles V. issued the terrible edict of Spire in 1529, commanding the whole empire to a crusade against the Baptists. He ordered that: 'All Anabaptists, male or female, of mature age, shall be put to death, by fire, or sword, or otherwise, according to the person, without preceding trial. They who recant may be pardoned, provided they do not leave the country. All who neglect infant baptism will be treated as Anabaptists.' This was worse than any thing in mediæval persecution, for at least the *form* of a trial had been observed; but the Protestant princes who assented to this edict left no way of escape, 'The design' being, as Keller says, 'to hunt the Baptists with no more feeling than would be shown to wild beasts.'[11] The Peasants' War had only just closed when this ferocious edict was issued, yet it gives no hint that the Baptists were charged with sedition. The decree of 1529 was renewed in 1551, with this explanation: 'Although the obstinate Anabaptists are thrown into prison and treated with severity, nevertheless they persist in their damnable doctrine, from which they cannot be turned by any amount of instruction.'[12] If the remedy lay in 'severity' they ought to have been cured effectually, for everywhere they were treated much after the manner of serpents. A letter from a priest to his friend in Strasburg says: 'My gracious lord went hunting last Sunday, and in the forest near Epsig he caught twenty-five wild beasts. There were three hundred of them gathered together.'[13]

Wigandus breathes the same spirit when he asks: 'Do you patiently protect such terrible enemies of holy baptism? Where is your zeal for the house of God? Where such people as Jews and Anabaptists are tolerated there is neither grace nor blessing.'[14] Luther, Zwingli and Melancthon uttered the severest things possible against them, without once stopping to show that their faith was contrary to the teaching of Jesus. Leonard Kayser had been a learned and eminent Catholic priest in Bavaria. He became a Lutheran, was intimate with Luther and the Wittenberg doctors, but soon saw that the principles of the Reformation properly applied must lead him into the Baptist ranks. In less than two years after following his convictions, he was committed to the flames near Passau. When taken to the fire in a cart, he held up a flower, saying: 'My lord, if you can burn me and this flower I am rightly condemned; if not, reflect on what you have done and repent.' They piled on more fagots than usual, to burn him quickly. When the wood was consumed only his hair was burnt, and the flower was left unhurt in his hand. In giving an account of his martyrdom, Luther himself says that a larger fire being made, his head, hands and feet were burnt off, but the body was unconsumed. Braght tells us that the body was cut to pieces and thrown into the river Inn. Luther described the martyrdom of his old friend as wonderfully ecstatic and steadfast, yet he said of other Baptists that it was 'all of the Devil,' with whose councils he seems to have been uncommonly intimate. 'Holy martyrs,' he said, 'such as our Leonard Kayser, die with humility and meekness toward their enemies, but these go to their death strengthening themselves in their obstinacy.' Cornelius informs us that Kayser was an elder of the 'Anabaptist' Church in Scherding.

Zwingli shared Luther's views in the persecution of the Baptists. In his book against them he denounces them as 'bitter,' 'full of anger,' 'hypocrisy and slander,' and 'ought of all godly men to be suspected and hated.' He charges them with crying out against 'witnesses in baptism' (godfathers and godmothers), 'saying that the Scripture doth nowhere appoint them.' Zwingli, said they not that truly? do the Scriptures anywhere appoint them? Was he free from bitterness and anger when he and the magistrates convulsed the whole land with fire and sword, to enforce the senseless usage of godfathers and godmothers? Or did he think a few bundles of Swiss pine-knots threw the strongest possible light upon the words: 'Love thy neighbor as thyself?' Few of the Reformers possessed as many lovable traits of character as the Swiss Reformer, yet he could allow himself to say of these men who had never harmed him: 'Most of them find it easy to withold from the joys of the world, for they belong to the dregs of society. . . . But now out of their baseness they make a nobility to suit themselves,'—an unintentional tribute to their godly genius. Melancthon was, possibly, the most lamb-like spirit amongst the Reformers. Both Luther and Zwingli were excessively arbitrary and imperious, failing of that higher manhood which can brook contradiction with inquiring meekness. Their opinions differed on the Supper, and Zwingli said that 'Luther was not possessed by one pure spirit, but by a legion of devils.' When attempts were made to promote mutual good feeling between them, notwithstanding their differences, Luther replied: 'No, no; cursed be such alliance, which would endanger the cause of God and men's souls. Begone! You are possessed by another spirit than ours. . . . The Zwinglians are a set of diabolical fanatics, they have a legion of devils in their hearts, and are wholly in their power.' But who would expect Melancthon to belch out such rage as this against any human being? Yet even gentle Philip allowed himself to say: 'One Anabaptist is better than another, as much as one devil is better than another.'[15] 'It is the devil that makes them callous to death.'[16] In his letters to Myconius, 1530–31, he tells him that at the beginning of this movement he was 'foolishly merciful,' but now he looked upon them as a diabolical sect, not to be tolerated.'[17]

'Mild Melancthon' differed from other persecutors only in the deliberate manner in which he defended the slaughter of God's elect. The pope called their crime 'heresy,' he called it 'blasphemy,' but the victims knew only death, dealt out to them as to vipers. His mildness of manner made the pious homicide the more cruel, and he must have blushed when the three simple-hearted Baptists confronted him at Jena. He had fled thither from the pest, 1535, when a commission was examining certain poor imprisoned Baptist peasants, and the Council invited him to act with them. The Münster disgrace was at an end, and he asked the peasants whether they were there. They replied that they had never been at Münster, and that their consciences could not approve of sedition. When he examined them on the doctrine of the Trinity they answered that, not being learned, they could say little of that high article of faith. He demanded, Why they preached in secret? They replied: 'The divine word is relentlessly persecuted, we are not allowed to preach publicly, and now, we are forbidden not only to be hearers, but doers of the word.' As to the community of goods, they thought it their duty to share their property with their poor brethren who were suffering. They also denied the lawfulness of oaths and of infant baptism.[18] He reports, with a flavor of disgust, in his own narrative, that they said:

'Baptism of infants was not enjoined, and that all children are saved, whether of Christians, heathens or Turks. God was not such a God as would damn a little child for the sake of a drop of water, for all his creatures were good. And they denied original sin in children, for such have never covenanted to it; but when a man grows up and consents to sin, then, for the first time, original sin has power.'

He asked them of obedience to civil magistrates. They said that they needed none, they cleaved to God alone, but they did not condemn civil government for the world. If the magistrates would let them alone in their faith, they would cheerfully pay taxes and do as they were bidden. They were examined concerning the Supper, and said they did 'not believe in a Lord God made of bread.' Hase says that Melancthon found these unlettered peasants orthodox on the Trinity and the incarnation, but a little unsound on original sin.[19] Still, they denied infant baptism, and that was enough; so, on the 27th of January, 1536, they sealed their faith with their blood. Melancthon wrote what he thought a full refutation of their doctrines for John the Elector, but his real reply to the innocent peasants was the unanswerable anti-Baptist logic of ax and flame. Jobst Moller, the chief speaker of these helpless villagers, was purely illiterate, and yet he held his own against Melancthon with great strength. 'Since that time,' says Beard, 'the world has thrashed out many of the questions which were in dispute between Jobst Moller and the first scholar of Germany; and the result is not in all respects what the theologians of Wittenberg would have expected.'[20]

In what bold contrast the immortal words of John Denk stand to all this:

'There are certain brethren who think they have completely fathomed the Gospel, and whoever does not assent to their dictum must be a heretic above all heretics. If an account of faith is given, they call it sowing seeds of division and dissension among the people. If reproaches are passed by unnoticed, they say it shows fear of the light.' In his treatise on the 'Law of God,' published in 1526, a year before his death, are these words from this profoundly serene spirit: 'Love forgets itself, and the possessor of it minds no injury which he receives for the sake of the object of his love. The less love is recognized, the more it is pained, and yet it does not cease. Pure love stretches out to all, and seeks to be at one with all. But even if men and all things are withdrawn from her, she is so deep and rich she can get along without them, and would willingly perish herself if she could thereby make others happy. This love is God, who has made all things, but cannot make himself; who will break all things, but cannot break himself. Love cannot be understood except in Christ.'

Casper Schwenkfeld was far from being a Baptist, but he knew and loved Denk, and writes: 'The Anabaptists are all the dearer to me, that they care about divine truth somewhat more than many of the learned ones.' Then he candidly states what he understood the Baptists to believe, thus: 'The Old Covenant was a slavery, in so far as God, on account of man's perversity, constrained them to serve him. Hence, the sign of the covenant, circumcision, was put upon them before they desired it. They received the sign whether they were willing or not. But baptism, the sign of the New Covenant, is given only to those who, being brought by the power of God, through the knowledge of true love, desire it, and consent to follow true love. Unless love forces them they should not be compelled.' Melancthon fell into the mistake of all history, in compelling infant baptism. It was all right with him that the Council of Nice ordered the rebaptism of Novatians, whether they desired it or not; but when the Baptists baptized a man on his own request, because of his love to Christ, he became at once the worst of all men and must welter in his own blood for his crime.

Voltaire, the atheist, had the common sense to say that the Baptists 'laid open that dangerous truth, which is implanted in every breast, that mankind are all born equal.'[21] And Beard says that their sins can be easily counted: 'They did not baptize their children; they thought it sinful to take an oath; they refused military service.' The Anglican Gregory's sum of their tenets is this: 'Baptism ought to be administered only to persons grown up to years of understanding, and should be performed, not by sprinkling them with water, but by dipping them in it.'[22] Hozek, the Catholic, gives this summary: 'The Church was to be a perfect Christian people, living without reproach, observing the Gospel faithfully, possessing and governed by the Spirit of God.' Heppe, the Calvinist, gives this analysis of their doctrines: '1. Against all external churchism. 2. Against infant baptism. 3. Against any view of justification that does not involve sanctification, by the direct and essential indwelling of the Holy Spirit in the human heart.'[23] Hast, the critic, who resided at Münster, says that:

'To realize regeneration among men was the Anabaptist aim, and if they failed, the noble and exalted thought that animated them, and for which they strove, must not be deprecated. They have deserved in this particular the respect of an unprejudiced later age, before a thousand others; and they seem in the choice of means to attain this end, to have been generally equally worthy of respect. It is not so much the advocacy of the doctrine of regeneration that is so noticeable and characteristic of them, but the fact that they held on so hard for its realization. They stood in their consciousness much higher than the world about them, and, therefore, were not comprehended by it.'[24]

Whatever follies a few of them fell into, their high purpose and advanced thought put them as a people in the van of genuine reformers, whose standard the world is aiming to reach at the close of the nineteenth century.[25] Hence, to-day, we hear the impartial and philosophical Uhlhorn say of these German Baptists: 'The general character of this whole movement was peaceful, in spite of the prevailing excitement. Nobody thought of carrying out the new ideas by force. In striking contrast to the Münzer uproar, meekness and sufferings were here understood as the most essential elements of the Christian ideal.'[26] Thus, it came to pass, in the words of Ritschl, that 'The decision against the Anabaptists was effected by the power of the magistrates.'[27]

CHAPTER VII.

THE REFORMATION—BAPTISTS IN THE NETHERLANDS.

RECENT investigators, and especially Keller, have clearly shown that the principles of the Waldensians spread very early in Bohemia and influenced the Reformation under Huss, giving rise at last to the Bohemian Brethren. Tradition says that Waldo himself went thither, and that his followers abounded in Austria on the Bohemian border. It is equally clear that, as early as 1182, the views of Waldo had found their way into Holland, and when persecution raged against the Waldensians in Southern Europe, many of them found refuge in the Netherlands, so that by 1233 Flanders was full of them. Many of these were weavers (Tisserands), and the first Baptists found in Holland were of that trade. So numerous were they that Ten Kate says, All the weaving was in the hands of 'Anabaptists.' Van Braght records the martyrdom of hundreds of these refugees, who were known by different nicknames, and were living quietly in the Netherlands, long before Luther was born. Limborch describes them as 'men of simple life and judgment,' and thinks that if 'their dogmas and institutions are examined without prejudice, it must be said that of all Christian sects which exist to-day no one more nearly agrees with them than that called the Mennonite.' Ypeig and Dermout are of the same opinion. They say: 'The Waldensians scattered in the Netherlands might be called their salt, so correct were their views and devout their lives. The Mennonites sprang from them. It is indubitable that they rejected infant baptism, and used only adult baptism.'[1]

Further they say that their principal articles of faith were: The sole authority of the Scriptures; the headship of Christ; the rejection of Church authority; the accounting of the pope as a layman; confession to a priest as useless, as God alone can pardon sin; salvation only by Christ; good works in obedience to God, and confirmation of faith; no adoration of saints; and the observance of Baptism and the Lord's Supper. He declares that they cultivated religion of the heart, and regulated their lives by our Saviour's teachings, that they condemned the bearing of arms and self-defense against unrighteous power, and were known as the people who say 'Yea and Nay.' This is added: 'From this historical account of the ancient Waldenses of the Netherlands, as they were in the twelfth century, and of their doctrine as it then was and continued to be in the succeeding centuries, it can be seen how, in every respect, the ancient and modern Baptists of the Netherlands, whose condition and doctrine are generally known, resembled them. Yet we must notice, as an exception to this, the characteristic article of faith respecting baptism. In none of the Confessions of Faith of the Waldenses, it is true, is the article found, and yet it is certain that the Netherlands Waldenses always rejected infant baptism, and administered the ordinance only to adults. We may find this positively asserted respecting the Netherlands Waldenses by Hieronymus Verdussen, by the Abbot á Clugny, and other Romanist writers. Hence it is that they are better known in this country by the name of Anabaptists than by that of Waldenses.

It can easily be seen by a reference to their opinions respecting baptism how natural it was that, when in the sixteenth century some Anabaptists joined the seditious rabble, this evil was laid upon all Anabaptists, and all who afterwards preferred to be called Baptists were branded by their enemies with the same hated name. . . . They would, without doubt, quietly have done much good had they not made their doctrine respecting the baptism of adults too prominent. In this respect their religious zeal was not united with wisdom. They did not hesitate openly to entice many from the Romish Church to their community, and upon their initiation to rebaptize them. This greatly excited the anger of the people and the disapprobation of the government, which strictly forbade the practice. Before the name of Luther as a Reformer was known, it appears that the Anabaptists in this land carried on the work of Reformation originally undertaken by others, and drew many from the Church of Rome to them, and rebaptized them. . . . In the sight of the authorities they lived as peaceful citizens, obedient and noted for their upright honesty, conscientiousness, temperance and godliness. The earlier Roman writers who are willing to pay a proper respect to the truth admit this to have been the fact. From this narration it is not difficult to understand how greatly the Waldenses of the Netherlands, or so-called Anabaptists, were pleased when Luther and his followers so zealously commenced the Reformation. They immediately made known their approbation, they glorified God, who in their time had raised up brethren with whom they could so well unite, at least in the main points. Yet they adhered firmly to their own peculiar views, especially respecting the baptism of adults.'

These writers then go on to show that there was amongst them a mystical and fanatical element, known as the '*perfect;*' then there were the '*imperfect,*' who adorned their pure faith by a praiseworthy mode of life.

'These were, indeed, ornaments of the Christian Church, who, as lights placed upon a hill, sent forth a wide illumination in the midst of the surrounding darkness. Persons of both classes were scattered through Germany, Switzerland, the Netherlands, etc. Was it indeed surprising that the folly of many of the so-called *perfect* should, at the time of the Reformation, have affected the whole? This will appear the less astonishing if it be remembered that among the Lutherans and the Zwinglians might be found fanatical errorists who were learned instructors of the people. . . . By far the greater part of the Anabaptists of the first class, and absolutely all of the second sort, were the most pious Christians that the Church ever had, and the most valuable citizens of the State. These worthy Anabaptists, or, as they may more properly be called, Baptists, were to be found in great numbers in the Netherlands, in Friesland, Groningen and Flanders. In the provinces that we have not mentioned their ancestors, the Waldenses, were settled, as we have said, in the twelfth century.'

After giving a full account of their extensive internal influence upon all the Protestant Christians in the Netherlands, these authors add:

'Although there were among the Baptists few learned men, yet they were zealous students of the doctrines of the Christian religion, willingly reading moral, practical writings, but with greater eagerness studying the Bible and inciting each other to diligence in the understanding of this precious volume. What a beneficial influence this must have had on the other Protestants, both as regards a virtuous course of life and an inquiry into the truth of the faith. Even among the Protestant teachers, who, in other respects, were wholly Lutheran, there were found many who openly stated that, on account of the above-mentioned facts, they held the Baptists in the highest estimation and loved them as brothers.' Amongst these they mention the renowed John Anastatius: A 'very sensible, sedate, noble, thinking, upright Lutheran, who considered the Baptist brethren to be in error in some doctrinal points, but elevated above the other Protestants on account of their peace-loving disposition, strength of faith and godliness of life. This appears from a work which he wrote at Strasburg in 1550, in the Lower Rhine dialect, or Gelder language, entitled "The Guide of the Laity." '²

Here we see why the Baptists went by the name of 'Anabaptists' rather than by that of Waldensians. At the appearance of Luther they came out of their obscurity and hiding-places, and undertook to scatter the light of a more certain Gospel, and to break the power of Romish superstitions. Their zeal in pushing their doctrine of adult baptism aroused the opposition of government, which issued the sternest edicts against them. Nevertheless, they baptized many Catholics before Luther was heard of. The first question of Inquisitors was: 'Have you been re-baptized?' so wide-spread was this practice.

In the Reformation, according to De Hoop Scheffer, quite as many of the Waldensians in Holland identified themselves with the Baptists as with the Lutherans or Zwinglians, and those who fled from persecution in Germany proper and Switzerland made many converts. In 1523 a book appeared in Holland, without the name of the author, entitled 'The Sum of the Holy Scriptures.' It was soon translated into English, French and Italian, and so many editions were sold that it aided largely in spreading Baptist views throughout Europe. It has recently been reprinted. On baptism it says:

'So are we dipped under as a sign that we are, as it were, dead and buried, as Paul writes, Rom. vi, and Col. ii. The life of man is a battle upon earth, and in baptism we promise to strive like men. The pledge is given when we are plunged under the water. It is the same to God whether you are eighty years old when you are baptized, or twenty; for God does not consider how old you are, but with what purpose you receive baptism. He does not mind whether you are Jew or heathen, man or woman, nobleman or citizen, bishop or layman, but only he who, with perfect faith and confidence, comes to God, and struggles for eternal life, attains it as God has promised in the Gospel.'

One of the commonest errors classes the Baptists of Holland with the Münster insurrection, chiefly because John of Leyden and others from that country took part in that outbreak. Keller corrects this error thus: 'No one who impartially studies the history of Menno Simon and of John of Leyden can deny that the doctrines and the spirit of the two men were infinitely unlike, and much more unlike than, for example, the doctrines and spirit of the Lutheran and Catholic Churches.' The 'Encyclopædia Britannica' says: 'That after the Münster insurrection the very name "Anabaptist" was proscribed in Europe.' This of itself introduced confusion in tracing their history, because the name ceased to identify any specific sect, and classified immense numbers of men with the Münster uproar who were no more connected with it than the pope himself. But says this authority: 'It must be remembered that Menno and his followers expressly repudiated the distinctive doctrines of the Münster Anabaptists. . . . They never aimed at any social or political revolution, and have been as remarkable for sobriety of conduct as the Münster sect was for its fanaticism.' Menno himself says: 'I warned every man against the Münster abominations, in regard to a king, to polygamy, to a worldly kingdom, and to the use of the sword, most faithfully.' Ypeig and Dermout tell us that the Netherland Baptists were much scattered until 1536, when they obtained the position of a regular community separated from the German and Dutch Protestants; but at that time they had not been formed into one body by any band of union. This privilege was obtained for them by the sensible course of Menno Simon.

Menno Simon was born in Friesland, in 1492. He was thoroughly educated and possessed large native powers. He became a Catholic priest, but in due time went to Luther for counsel in seeking his soul's salvation. He tells us little of the result, but details fully the impression which the martyrdom of Snyder made upon his mind. Sicke Snyder, so called because he was a tailor by trade, was slaughtered at Leeuwarden in 1531, by the sword, his body laid on the wheel and his head set upon a stake, because he had been rebaptized. Menno says: 'I heard from some brethren that a God-fearing man had been beheaded because he had renewed his baptism. This sounded wonderfully in my ears, that any one should speak of another baptism. I searched the Scriptures with diligence, and reflected earnestly upon them, but could find no trace of infant baptism.'

MENNO SIMON.

He says that he consulted Luther's writings on that subject, who told him: 'We must baptize them on their own faith, because they are holy;' but he could not see that they were holy, or that they had any 'faith' if they were. He went to Bucer, who told him that: 'We should baptize them in order to bring them up in the ways of the Lord.' He went to Bullinger, who said that we should baptize all our children because the Jews circumcised their sons. Then, as none of them gave him scriptural authority in the case, he went to the Bible as his only guide, and finding it silent on the subject, he cast the doctrine aside as a human figment, united with a Baptist church and began to preach the Gospel. For a quarter of a century he did the work of an evangelist from country to country, enduring every sort of suffering for Jesus' sake, and established churches in Friesland, Holland, Brabant, Westphalia and the German provinces on the Baltic. One Reynerts sheltered Menno in his house, but this was a crime, and while the preacher escaped, his heroic host died a martyr rather than betray him. Blunt says that his followers became 'notorious for their deference to the Scripture, and, instead of claiming an inspiration superior to it, bowed down to the most literal interpretation of its precepts.' The Lord of Fresenburg, from admiration of the purity of his disciples, invited them to settle on his estate in Holstein and promised them protection. Many fled there, who established churches, and there Menno died in peace, 1559.

The two Dutch historians quoted so largely already say of him that he excluded from the community 'some of the so-called *perfect* who had either taken part in the riots or had not disapproved of them. He also excluded and gave over to the contempt of the brethren all the rest, who could not be checked in their wicked fanaticism by his sensible instructions. His abhorrence of these perverse men was so strong that he was not only ashamed of them, but he counted it a sin to eat and drink with them. As he also inspired others with the same abhorrence of their conduct, the whole community of Baptists was soon freed from the loathsome leaven of the riotous "Anabaptists." Through his instructions also the tolerably pure doctrines of some Baptists were made purer; much more nearly allied to the spirit of true Christianity. It was one of his fundamental principles that in the search for religious doctrines nothing should be embraced that is not found in the Holy Scriptures, and in the use and application of these mere human deductions should be avoided.'[8]

Whether he was ever immersed is a matter in dispute. Scheffer thinks that he was not, although he says that 'in Germany, until 1400, there was no other method than immersion.' It is clear that after that date the method changed, and that the Mennonites practiced pouring, at an advanced stage in their history. Menno's great testimony lodged against infant baptism, for which he and his people, in common with all the so-called 'Anabaptists' of the Netherlands, endured great persecution. The accounts given of their sufferings by such secular historians as Motley, as well as by the martyrologists, are horrible in the extreme. Christians of various sects were butchered in cold blood, so that, in five-and-twenty years, under Charles V., 50,000 persons are said to have been hanged, beheaded and buried or burnt alive in the Netherlands alone. A very large proportion of these were Baptists. June 10, 1535, a furious decree was fulminated at Brussels, calling for the death of this entire people. Even if they recanted they were to die by the sword instead of fire, the women were to be buried alive, and all persons were forbidden to petition for any grace, favor or forgiveness for them. Before suffering death in any of its sanguinary forms, these helpless victims were generally put to the rack. Motley thus describes this atrocity:

'The rack was the court of justice; the criminal's only advocate was his fortitude. . . . The victim, whether man, matron or tender virgin, was stripped naked and stretched upon the wooden bench. Water, weights, pullies, screws, all the apparatus by which the sinews could be strained without cracking, the bones crushed without breaking, and the body racked exquisitely without giving up the ghost, was now put in operation. The executioner, enveloped in a black robe from head to foot, with his eyes glaring at his victim through holes cut in the hood which muffled his face, practiced successively all the forms of torture which the devilish ingenuity of the monks had invented. The imagination sickens when striving to keep pace with these dreadful realities.' [4]

It was more common to bury the women alive than the men, and it was done generally in this manner. A coffin was made, so small that the poor wretch must be squeezed into it without room to struggle, with holes for iron bars to keep the body down. After laying it on a scaffold and forcing the body into it, a cord was run through the bottom of the coffin, tied round the neck and violently drawn tight. Then earth was thrown upon it, and the living burial was completed. Dr. Rule relates the case of a harmless woman at Leeuwarden, 1548, in whose house a Latin Testament was found. She was put on the rack and asked whether she 'expected to be saved by baptism?' She answered, 'No; all the water in the sea cannot save me, nor any thing else but that salvation which is in Christ, who has commanded me to love the Lord my God above all things, and my neighbor as myself.' A printer at Liesvelt was beheaded because he had put this note into one of the printed Bibles: 'The salvation of mankind springs from Christ alone.' About 1549, the Baptists were persecuted with great vigor. Twenty of them lay in prison at Amsterdam, when all but five men and three women made their escape. Elbert Jansen, a lame man, might have escaped but refused, and on the 20th of March he, with seven others, was burnt, on the charge 'that they had suffered themselves to be rebaptized and had wrong notions of the sacraments.' Rule mentions nine other men at Amsterdam who, for being Baptists, were taken out of their beds and removed to the Hague. There they were beheaded and their heads sent back to Amsterdam in a herring-barrel, where they were set upon stakes. Hans of Overdam was put to death at Ghent in 1550. He was a talented man, of gentle but indomitable spirit and of great spirituality. In the touching account of his sufferings it is said that he thus addressed his brethren:

'Dearly beloved, it is not enough that we have received baptism on the confession of our faith and by that faith have been engrafted into Christ, unless we hold fast the beginning of our confidence steadfast unto the end. The Council began to speak to us, why we were not satisfied with the faith of our parents and with our baptism. We said: We know of no infant baptism, but of a baptism upon faith, which God's word teacheth us.'

The account of his arrest is most interesting. One Sunday morning himself and a friend had met in the woods to worship God, with a company of their brethren. They sought other brethren in vain for near an hour, and were about to return, but began to sing softly, that if their friends were at hand they might hear them. They heard a rustling and stopped, when three armed men stood before them. Hans said pleasantly: 'Well, comrades, you have been seeking a hare and have not caught it.' The three bid them surrender as prisoners; and immediately their eyes fell upon a wagon load of their brethren, who were guarded by three justices and their officers. Hans and his friend were then bound together in irons and led to the castle, about a mile distant. Here they were kept for three days and then taken to Ghent, where they met their betrayer. They were charged with holding 'assemblies of this new doctrine,' contrary to the order of the emperor. Hans replied: 'It is not given him of God to make such laws; therein he exceeds the power granted him of God. In this matter we know him not as a ruler, for the salvation of our souls is dearer to us and we must give our obedience to God.' They went through various examinations and disputations, but were finally condemned to death. The Procurer-general said: 'The reason you are condemned as heretics is that various learned persons have disputed with you, and you have not suffered yourselves to be instructed.'

Motley, quoting at large from Brandt, records the noted case of Dirk Willemzoon, who was guilty of no crime but that of being a Baptist. Being sentenced to death, he made his escape over a frozen lake, late in the winter, when the ice had become weak. Three officers pursued him, and one of them breaking through, he cried for help, as he was drowning. The other two fled, but the tender-hearted Baptist left the shore at the peril of his life, flew across the cracking ice to his rescue, and the hero saved him. Having thus magnanimously rescued his enemy from death, he was himself burnt at the stake for his pains.[5] Time fails to enlarge upon these individual cases of suffering for Christ's sake, for Baptists were tolerated nowhere. Other dissenters fled to lands where they were safe, but no voice pleaded for them, and no arm was raised for their defense; hence Ten Kate says that in the Netherlands they furnished ten martyrs where other Reformed sects gave one. The following figures are appalling. The Dutch Martyrologies mention in Ghent, 103; in the Province of Holland, 111; at Antwerp, 229; and this ratio was kept up everywhere, except in the province of Groningen. Nor did it matter if they fled to other lands. The Martyrology relates the sufferings of 900 martyrs by name, and makes reference to 1,000 others. Liliencron collected the martyr hymns of Lutherans and Baptists. He found three Lutheran hymns, commemorating four martyrs, but sixty-two Baptist hymns, extolling the steadfastness of three hundred brethren. De Hoop Scheffer says:

'In 1635 the magistrates of Zurich undertook to compel the Mennonites by force to enter the Reformed Church. They were thrown into prison, and their property was confiscated. Schaffhausen, Berne and Basel joined hands with Zurich, and great cruelties were perpetrated. Berne sold a number of its Mennonites as slaves to the king of Sardinia, who used them on his galleys. In the course of about seventy years all Mennonites were expelled from Zurich, Schaffhausen and St. Gall.'[6]

The minor forms of persecution were numberless. Baptists met where they could to hear the Gospel, in darkness, in barn, and brake, and bush, through cold, and snow, and hail. Dragoons hunted them by the light of moon and stars, to detect their secret places of meeting, and tragedy commonly followed, in one form or another. Their first crime was to worship God and administer baptism at midnight; then came separation from home, wife, child, parent and other kindred. Flight or banishment followed; arrest, imprisonment, inquisitors and torture were only the beginning of the end. Said a simple-hearted prisoner:

'The chief reason for torturing me is to make me tell how many preachers there are, what their names and where they live, where I went to school, how many I have baptized, where I was ordained, and by whom. They wanted me to call the magistrates Christains, and say that infant baptism is right. Then I pressed my lips together, left it all with God and suffered patiently while I thought of the Lord's words: "No one has greater love than this, that a man should die for his friends."'

Nothing was left undone to terrify them into recantation, but they were strangers to fear. 'Let us not be frightened,' said they, 'though the hounds bay, and the lions roar; for God, who is with us, is a mighty God and will keep his own.' Ursula Werdum, a noble lady at Overyssel, was taken from her castle to the stake. Her mother and sister came from afar to change her mind, but their entreaties had no effect. On the way to execution she joined hands with one 'Mary,' who had been disowned by her family, and they sung the praises of God as they walked. They gave each other the kiss of peace and prayed for their persecutors. Mary begged the judges to shed no more innocent blood, but a priest drove Ursula from her and the burning pile. She turned back, saying that she wanted to go to the same glory, in the same way; and, turning to the stake, said: 'Our Father, who art in heaven.' 'Yes,' said the priest, 'that's where he is found.' She replied: 'Because I look for him there, I can face death here.' When she ascended the pile her foot slipped, and the judge thought that she yielded. 'No,' said she, 'the wood slipped; I will remain steadfast to Christ,' and died.

Buckle quotes from the official report of the Venetian embassador to the court of Charles V., made in 1546: 'That in Holland and in Friesland more than 30,000 persons have suffered death at the hands of justice for Anabaptist errors.' 'Hist. of Civilization,' i, p. 189. No chapter in history is more horrible than that which records the persecutions of the Netherland Baptists under Charles V. He ordained the amputation of a hand or the extraction of an eye on every author or printer of their books. All the accused were to be examined as to the baptism of their babes, midwives were sworn to baptize new-born children, mothers whose infants were born away from home must bring baptismal certificates, and all pastors were commanded to keep baptismal registers, that the parents of the unchristened might be brought to punishment. State baptismal records have figured largely in the persecution of Baptists. They appear to have been created for that purpose first by Zwingli:

'Because the Baptists have often said that they did not know whether they were baptized or not;' he requested the Council at Zurich to record the names of each child, with its father and godmother, 'as it will establish who are baptized, and Anabaptism will not be able to break in again overnight.' Hence, according to Höfling ('Sacrament of Baptism,' 2,245), on May 24, 1526, the keeping of registers was decreed, because 'many people would not have their children baptized.' Holland understood this way of entrapping Baptists as well as Switzerland.

The whole land was stricken with terror and the cries of the tortured were heard perpetually, gallows and trees on the highways were hung with dead bodies. Dr. Rule says: 'The very air was polluted with the stench, and the knell of death sounded heavily from every belfry. Alva gloated over the carnage.' This fiend invented many new methods of torture for the amusement of the soldiery, amongst them the screwing of iron to the tongue and the burning of the end till it dropped off, and when the sufferer screamed they mocked at his fine 'singing.'

Despite these persecutions they perpetually multiplied. Keller says that in 1530 there was scarcely a village or city in the Netherlands where Baptists were not found. Bullinger complains that the whole province of Belgium was infested with them; and Micronius wrote, that Menno's kingdom not only extends through Belgium, but from 'Flanders to Dantzic.' In 1550 the leading reformed element, according to Ten Kate, was Baptist, and in Friesland, in 1586, one inhabitant in every four was a Baptist. The magistrates of Deventer refused admission to the inquisitors, saying: 'We can make all the examination needful of the faith of our burghers. You have nothing to do in this matter, and we order you to leave without delay and never return on such an errand.' Baptist industry and frugality distinguished them in trade and commerce. Peter Lioren, one of them, introduced the cat-boat and extended the herring and whale fisheries, to the enrichment of the nation. Halbertsma asks:

'How was it possible to find better citizens? They brought into the treasury their thousands every year, and never took out a penny as officials. They set fire to no property, but dug wells to put out fires. They fired no musket, but they nursed the wounded. They were not soldiers, but they furnished the sinews of war.'

When men were martyred publicly a straw hut was built around the stake and the martyr consumed with it, so that he should neither be seen nor heard. Verbeck, a Baptist pastor, suffered in this way in Antwerp, 1561. The people could endure this diabolical work no longer, and the States of Holland declared the Prince of Orange Viceroy, in their determination to shake off at once the Spanish and Papal yoke.

William had been governor of Holland under the king of Spain from 1559. In 1556, while still a Catholic himself, he wrote to his subordinates: 'I have neither the will nor the means to help the Inquisition, or execute the placards. If peace is to be preserved in this land, liberty of worship must be guaranteed to every inhabitant. There must be a halt in persecution until an appeal can be made to the king.' When he was required to uproot heresy he determined to surrender his office, and then to take up arms against Alva. Possibly he did not at once comprehend all that his motto meant, but when his brother, Lewis, marched into Guelderland his new note was, 'Liberty of nation and conscience.'

A. D. 1572 the continent was still ablaze, however, with the fires of persecution, and human bodies were lighting men everywhere to a better day. Protestant raved against Catholic and Catholic against Protestant, and both against the Baptists. Philip of Hesse, the lone dissenter at the Diet of Spire, was the only prince of that day who was unwilling to dye his sword in innocent blood. He would imprison heretics and exile them to lands where they met with no mercy, but he would not slay them. And, possibly, inspired by his example, God was raising up a greater than he, who should defend every Christian against the blood-thirst of his brother Christian. No country was more thoroughly soaked with the blood of the saints than Holland, under Philip II. of Spain, Duke Alva and the Inquisition, but its bitterest trial came in the opening of 1572, in its contest with the Spaniard. As far back as 1559, the Prince of Orange was in Paris, when Henry II. told him that he and Philip had made a treaty to put all Netherland Protestants to the sword. At that time the young prince was but twenty-six, but he then and there mentally resolved to thwart that bloody policy by arousing the Protestant population of the Netherlands to throw off the Spanish yoke. In due time he appealed to them and to the courts of Northern Europe to aid him in rescuing Holland, but at first largely in vain. After several victories had awakened popular sympathy, his appeals for aid to the wealth of Holland were met with coldness and frowns. He had thrown all his own possessions into the contest, had even sold his plate and jewels and mortgaged his estates, to carry on the war against Spain, and was nearly obliged to abandon the attempt, when a trivial circumstance gave him new courage.

Early on an April morning, and oppressed with anxiety, he was walking near his head-quarters at Dillenburg, when two simple strangers approached him and, taking him to be one of the royal household, asked if they could have an audience with the prince. He led them into the castle and made himself known. On asking who they were and their business, he found that they were Jacob Fredericks and Dirk Jans Cortenbosch, two Holland Baptist preachers. They had been visiting their brethren on the Rhine, and on their return home came to see whether they could serve the prince. They explained to him their principles, and he told them his general purposes and needs, asked them to urge their friends to contribute money to the advancement of the common Christian cause, and thanked them heartily when they promised to do so. On the 20th of the same month he issued the following decree: 'Be it known to the magistrates and the officials in the North, that you are by no means to allow any one who preaches and observes the true word of God, according to the Gospel, to be hindered, injured or disturbed, or to have his conscience examined, or on that account to be persecuted by inquisition or placards.' A fortnight later, May 5th, he sent his secretary with a letter to his Baptist friends pleading: 'Let every one contribute. This is a time when even with small sums more can be effected than at other times with ampler funds. His lordship will ever be ready to reward them for such good and faithful service to the common cause and to their prince.'

With slight variations in minor things, Motley also touchingly details these circumstances. He says:

'These appeals had, however, but little effect. Of three hundred thousand crowns, promised on behalf of leading nobles and merchants of the Netherlands by Marcus Perez, but ten or twelve thousand came to hand. The appeals to the gentlemen who had signed the compromise, and to many others who had, in times past, been favorable to the liberal party, were powerless. A poor Anabaptist preacher collected a small sum from a refugee congregation on the outskirts of Holland, and brought it, at the peril of his life, into the prince's camp. It came from people, he said, whose will was better than the gift. They never wished to be repaid, he said, except by kindness, when the cause of reform should be triumphant in the Netherlands. The prince signed a receipt for the money, expressing himself touched by this sympathy from these poor outcasts. In the course of time, **other contributions from similar sources, principally collected by dissenting preachers, starving and persecuted church-communities, were received. The poverty-stricken exiles contributed far more, in proportion, for the establishment of civil and religious liberty, than the wealthy merchants or the haughty nobles.'** [7] The same author speaks of the prince, as conceiving 'the thought of religious toleration in an age of universal dogmatism,' for that 'he had long thought that emperors, kings and popes had taken altogether too much care of men's souls in times past, and had sent too many of them prematurely to their great account. He was equally indisposed to grant full powers for the same purpose to Calvinists, Lutherans or Anabaptists.' [8]

Immediately on giving their promise the Baptists made the collections, but, owing to the loss of one of their collectors in the perilous undertaking and the poverty of their churches, their returns were delayed. Fifty years of unrelenting persecution had left them but little besides their patriotism; yet, on July 29th, they brought their patriotic offering of a thousand florins to the prince at Remund. The prince had faithfully kept his word. At a meeting of the Estates of Holland, July 15th, he had been declared governor, in place of the Duke of Alva; and had proclaimed that 'the freedom of religion shall be guarded, every body shall exercise it freely in private or in public, in church or in chapel, without let or hinderance from any one.' And eight days later, in camp, he made proclamation to protect Catholics. 'No one, whether priest or layman, shall be wronged or injured in property or person;' and offenders against this order were to be put to death, as malcontents and disturbers of the general quiet and welfare. When the Baptists made their offering to him out of the penury of their confiscation, burdened by hosts of widows and orphans, left by thousands of their martyrs, he asked them: 'Do you make no demand?' They answered, 'Nothing but the friendship of your grace, if God grants to you the government of our Netherlands.' He assured them of his sympathy for them and for all men. And he kept faith with them to the letter, although his fidelity involved him in perpetual turmoil with his best friends. Motley says that:

'His intimate counselor, the accomplished Saint Aldegonde,' was 'in despair because the prince refused to exclude the Anabaptists of Holland from the rights of citizenship. At the very moment when William was straining every nerve to unite warring sects, and to persuade men's hearts into a system by which their consciences were to be laid open to God alone, at the moment when it was most necessary for the very existence of the fatherland that Catholic and Protestant should mingle their social and political relations, it was indeed a bitter disappointment for him to see wise statesmen of his own creed unable to rise to the idea of toleration. "The affair of the Anabaptists," wrote Saint Aldegonde, "has been renewed. The prince objects to exclude them from citizenship. He answered me sharply, that their yea was equal to our oath, and that we should not press this matter unless we were *willing to confess that it was just for the Papists to compel us* to a divine service which was against our conscience." It seems hardly credible that this sentence, containing so sublime a tribute to the character of the prince, should have been indicted as a bitter censure, and that, too, by an enlightened and accomplished Protestant. "In short," continued Saint Aldegonde, with increasing vexation, "I don't see how we can accomplish our wish in this matter. The prince has uttered reproaches to me that our clergy are striving to obtain a mastery over consciences. He praised lately the saying of a monk who was not long ago here, that our pot had not gone to the fire as often as that of our antagonists, but that when the time came it would be black enough. In short, the prince fears that after a few centuries the clerical tyranny on both sides will stand in this respect on the same footing."' [9]

Nor did it matter that his most intimate friends were offended with his broad toleration. Motley further says: 'No man understood him. Not even his nearest friends comprehended his views, nor saw that he strove to establish, not freedom for Calvinism, but freedom for conscience. Saint Aldegonde complained that the prince would not persecute the Anabaptists, Peter Dathenus denounced him as an atheist, while even Count John, the only one left of his valiant and generous brothers, opposed the religious peace—except where the advantage was on the side of the new religion.' [10] Again, he adds: 'Sincerely and deliberately himself a convert to the Reformed Church, he was ready to extend freedom of worship to Catholics on the one hand and to Anabaptists on the other, for no man ever felt more keenly than he that the Reformer who becomes in his turn a bigot is doubly odious.' [11] He moreover rebuked those who would interfere with his generous impulses and principles, as another remarkable passage from this distinguished writer will show:

'The Prince of Orange was more than ever disposed to rebuke his own church for practicing persecution in her turn. Again he lifted his commanding voice in behalf of the Anabaptists of Middleburg. He reminded the magistrates of that city that these peaceful burghers were always perfectly willing to bear their part in all the common burdens, that their word was as good as their oath, and that as to the matter of military service, although their principles forbade them to bear arms, they had ever been ready to provide and pay for substitutes. "We declare to you, therefore," said he, "that you have no right to trouble yourselves with any man's conscience, so long as nothing is done to cause private harm or public scandal. We therefore expressly ordain that you desist from molesting these Baptists, from offering hinderance to their handicraft and daily trade by which they can earn bread for their wives and children, and that you admit them henceforth to open their shops and to do their work, according to the custom of former days. Beware, therefore, of disobedience and of resistance to the ordinance which we now establish."' [12]

In William's letter to Middleburg, 1577, he praises the Baptists, who had brought their contributions at the peril of life, and had 'helped to win liberty.' In the previous year, when writing to induce Amsterdam to join the States, he had said: 'I am determined to oppress no man's conscience, and to force no one to adopt my religion.' When, therefore, in 1577, the Reformed preachers, headed by Vander Heiden and Jan Paffin, tried to persuade him to limit the liberty of the Baptists, he replied that 'the time is past for the clergy to assume control over consciences, and attempt to subject all men to their opinions.'

The result of this long, dark struggle of the Baptists was that through this 'silent' but sincere man their radical principle of soul liberty for Christians found its way into the first compact of States since the foundation of Christianity. While this instrument was not a constitution, but only a compact, yet Motley says that it became 'the foundation-stone of the Netherland Republic.' [13] And that republic, says Motley, 'became the refuge for the oppressed of all nations, whether Jews or Gentiles; Catholics, Calvinists, and Anabaptists prayed after their own manner to the same God and Father.' [14] In 1579, Article XIII of the Union of Utrecht declared: 'Every one shall be free in the practice of his religious belief, and that, in accordance with the peace of Ghent, no one shall be held or examined on account of matters of religion.' [15]

Many of the Reformed clergy were extremely restless under this provision, and some of them sought to turn the prince against the 'Anabaptists' in utter disregard thereof. But his answer was that, 'To persecute them would justify the Catholics in the persecution of the Protestants.' These transactions and especially the testimony of the prince to the true character of the 'Anabaptists,' serves to put them in their true light, despite all the conscienceless slanders of their enemies. He speaks of them as 'Peaceful burghers, always perfectly willing to bear their part in all the common burdens.' In governmental matters they held substantially to the views of the Society of Friends in Great Britain and the United States, but they were found amongst the most loyal and firm supporters of the government, in all that left their religious rights untouched. The thousand florins which they wrung from their poverty to speed the cause of civil and religious liberty are a thousand flat contradictions of the slanders which have been thrown in their faces, and the testimony of their prince should make any man blush to the ears who has the impudence to repeat them, and enter him on the list of false witnesses.

Prince Maurice, his son and successor, showed the same noble spirit. Zeeland went on, still treating the 'Anabaptists' with severity by insisting that they should take the oath, although they were as loyal to the government without the oath as others who swore. They were also refused permission to print a book or hold a meeting, without the consent of their zealous and petty tyrants. Maurice came to their rescue and demanded that they should be let alone; nothing should be exacted of them which injured their consciences. Even after the victory for religious liberty at Middleburg, and regardless of all honorable obligations which the authorities had given to maintain it, in 1591, when a scurrilous edict was issued against the Baptists, he wrote thus: 'Although the declaration of the Estates and of the prince, our father, of glorious memory, suffices to regulate your conduct toward the Anabaptists, nevertheless we have judged it necessary to write you to observe the statutes and to let the Anabaptists alone, until the Estates pass some other order.'

The noble spirit of William lived after him; for in 1582 the magistrates of Leyden dared to use these words to the Estates of Holland: 'We will tolerate no religious oppression whatever, in great or in small, nor receive any statutes or decrees that involve it. Our unanimous opinion is, not to trouble each other in matters of worship; and we will not be turned from this position by any synod's decree. We will, by God's grace, maintain this position to the death, for liberty ever consists in the freedom of every man to speak his opinion. We exhort the estates, therefore, to join hands with us, to bear in love each party in its peculiar beliefs, so far as they do not conflict with public security, and thus have a good-natured people united against the common enemy.'

Afterwards, the Articles of the Union of Utrecht were so interpreted and amended as to permit their persecution, but the names of William the Silent and his son will ever stand as the first amongst princes to advocate liberty of conscience. And all honor to Holland, which ever after remained a land of comparative safety, if not of comfort, for the men of all faiths. This was amongst the first of reasons which led to her speedy rise to a front rank amongst the nations, in commerce, wealth and learning, and opened her harbors to the noblest fugitives from all lands. For these blessings Baptists should give thanks to their simple preachers and their brethren, who cheered the grand prince in his darkest hours, and for whose sake he threw the shield of liberty over the heads of all hounded and hated men who love God. In addition to the pen of Motley, the above facts may be found in Doopsgezinde Bijdragen, J. G. De Hoop Scheffer, 1873; Ottii Annales, p. 158; Brandt, Hist. Reformation, i, p. 609; Schröck's Hist. Ch. on Anab. 'n Holland; and Hist. des Anabaptistes, pub. by Desbordes, 1599, p. 244.

The Baptists of the Netherlands fell into many divisions on church discipline, about marriage, dress and social relations; they laid great stress on managing the members of their own congregations. Menno lodged the true marks of a Christian congregation in: The faithful preaching of God's word, and obedience thereto; in the confession of Christ's name by the observance of baptism and the Supper; in love toward men, a holy life and the endurance of persecution, if need be, for Christ's sake. The following are some of their acts of discipline. In 1538, at a conference at Buchold, they separated from every seditious remnant of the Münster fanatics, who were led by Battenburg. In 1554, at a conference held at Wismar, Menno's home, they recommended the temporary exclusion of members who married outside the congregation and their restoration if they maintained their faith. But some insisted on the separation of husband and wife, in case of the exclusion of one of them. On these and other questions, they split up into numerous sects, disfellowshiping one another; some of them even required rebaptism of those coming to them from the other factions, and they called each other all the unlovely names that commonly disgrace quarreling Christians. Their divisions and subdivisions abounded in petty questions, such as the treatment of bankrupts, whether or not they should patronize the vessels of excluded members, and similar points, until, in the little city of Hoorn there were thirteen sorts of Baptist Churches. Their contentions became so perfectly disgraceful that Menno said: 'My sadness was as bitter as death, and I knew not for grief what to do. Yes, if the gracious breath of the Almighty had not preserved me, I should have lost my senses.' As to the question of immersion amongst the Netherland Baptists:

There is not conclusive evidence that they immersed as a rule, until after the middle of the sixteenth century. As sprinkling and pouring had commonly taken its place amongst all sects, they adopted the prevailing method, though often practicing immersion, as was still done by the Catholics. Yet that many of them clung to immersion is evinced by the fact that some of the followers of Menno pleaded that they could not immerse in prisons, nor always in their own houses, and so practiced pouring. Robinson says of Menno, that 'he was dipped himself, and he baptized others by dipping.' Dr. Angus, a critic in Mennonite lore, says that he 'always laid great stress on immersion.' Menno's own words imply this: 'After we have searched ever so diligently we shall find no other baptism besides dipping in water, which is acceptable to God, and maintained in his word. . . . Let who will oppose, this is the only mode of baptism that Jesus Christ instituted, and that the Apostles taught and practiced.' [16]

Most of the Church historians in Germany and the Netherlands accord to the Baptists of those countries a high antiquity, which they are able to trace by lines more or less distinct, but which they do not formulate into full and authentic record. For example, Mosheim says of the Dutch Baptists that their true origin 'is hid in the remote depths of antiquity, and is, consequently, extremely difficult to be ascertained.' Drs. Dermont and Ypeig, in reporting their historical investigations to the King of Holland, say that: 'The Baptists, who were formerly called Anabaptists, and in latter times Mennonites, were the original Waldenses, and have long in the history of the Church received the honor of that origin. On this account the Baptists may be considered the only Christian community which has stood since the Apostles, and as a Christian society, which has preserved pure the doctrines of the Gospel through all ages.' So Dr. Keller, in his recent work, which throws a flood of light upon the early history of the German Baptists, says, after describing their great numbers: 'It would be a great mistake if one should believe that all these remarks have reference only to the period of the Münster kingdom; much rather can it be proved that in the lands mentioned Baptist Churches existed for many decades and even centuries.' He also adds: 'The more I examine the documents of that time at my command, the more I am astonished at the extent of the diffusion of Anabaptist views, *an extent of which no other investigator has had any knowledge.* Even Zwingli, who died in 1531, said: 'The institution of Anabaptism is no novelty, but for thirteen hundred years has caused great disturbance in the Church.' Yet, in the main, these writers do not trace the line beyond the statement of the countries and cities where they existed, of which Keller, who is possibly the most learned investigator of the subject now living, gives a long list, but adds that a perfect list of 'Baptist Churches cannot be enumerated, for the reason that their existence was a profound secret.'

For the same reason it is difficult to trace the history of the Collegiants to their origin, but this, at least, is known, namely, that they were found in Holland as early as 1619, and can be traced down for about two hundred years, under the name of Collegiants, from their collegia, and Rheinsbergers, from the name of the village near Leyden, where they held their great assemblies. They are supposed to have received immersion from certain Baptists exiled from Poland. They laid out grounds and put up buildings at Rheinsberg, where they sunk a stone baptistry on their own premises and immersed their converts, the candidate kneeling in the water, his head being bowed forward and buried. Their Confession made the Bible their standard of faith and life, they required faith in Christ as the Son of God, before the reception of baptism and the Supper, they demanded a holy life, exercised the liberty of prophesying, defended the right of private judgment, and kept their piety active by prayer and conference meetings, when these were unknown elsewhere in Holland. They first organized into an Assembly, after the decree of the Synod of Dort, 1619, which removed two hundred Arminian pastors, for they were Arminian in doctrine, and were opposed to war and oaths. Their leaders were the brothers Van der Kodde, members of a devout family, which had suffered persecution for more than a hundred years, as Reformers. Their grandfather, William Jansoon, was a great Bible student, who kept the Scriptures hid for safety on his farm. His seven grandsons were good Latin scholars and one of them taught Hebrew in the high-school at Leyden. Prince Maurice said to D'Aubert, the French embassador, one day as they rode through the Collegiant lands: 'Our peasants can read Latin.' He then summoned these brothers from their work in the field, and, to the astonishment of the diplomat, talked with them in Latin and French.

They established an orphan asylum, for which the widow of the clerk of Rotterdam gave them 10,000 gulden; they frequently raised 60,000 gulden a year to take care of their own poor, and when the dykes burst, in 1740, they commenced a subscription for repairs which reached 60,000 gulden. They had meetings in eighteen different towns in 1740, but their meetings ceased at Rheinsberg in 1787. At the beginning of the present century Hefele still traced some remains of the

BAPTISM AT RHEINSBERG.

sect, but they divided into two parties, one of them running into Unitarian views. They built two places of worship at Rheinsberg, and continued the contest for thirty years; but at present the sect is about extinct, some of them being absorbed into the Mennonite and other bodies, from which originally they were entirely separate.

Dr. Angus kindly forwards the above picture of baptism as administered in Rheinsberg by the Collegiants, and as representing the Mennonite baptism of those times.

The history of the Netherland Baptists is a most exhilarating and sad one. As a body, they have largely faded away in their original testimony. Perhaps they did the great work which called them into existence and kept them alive so long, namely, the defense of Denk's great principle, 'That the civil magistrates should not use force in matters of faith.' For this they suffered all that men can suffer. In the language of Froude: 'On them the laws of the country might take their natural course, and no voice was raised to speak for them. For them no European agitated, no courts were ordered into mourning, no royal hearts trembled with indignation. At their death the world looked on complacently, indifferently, or exultingly. For them history has no word of praise.' Menno Simon said that while their murderers were 'saluted by all around as doctors, masters, lords, we are compelled to hear ourselves called Anabaptists;' and so are treated as the pests of society. 'What misery and anxiety have I felt in the deadly perils of persecution for my poor sick wife and little children! While others lie on soft beds and cushions, we must often creep away into secret corners. While others engage in festivities to the music of fife and trumpet, we must look around whenever a dog barks, fearing the spies are on our track. Yet those who suffered with Jesus then reign with him now.'

BAPTISTS OF GREAT BRITAIN.

CHAPTER I.

IMMERSION IN ENGLAND.

FROM the introduction of Christianity into Britain, its baptism was immersion. Simpson says, in the preface to his 'Ancient Baptismal Fonts,' of which he names 353 in England: 'As immersion was practiced in this Church until the Reformation, and perhaps occasionally later, as will afterwards appear, all fonts were up to that period sufficiently large for the purpose.' Grose also says of the baptisteries in the churches, that: 'The basins were very large. There was an anteroom where the ceremony of immersion was performed.'[1] So Lingard, in his 'History of the Early English Church' tells us: 'When an adult solicited baptism, he was called upon to profess his faith in the true God, by the repetition of the Lord's Prayer and the Apostles' Creed, and to declare his intention of leading a life of piety. . . . He then descended into the font, the priest depressed his head below the surface, saying, I baptize thee,' etc. The candidate 'was plunged into the

ANCIENT FONT AT ST. MARTIN'S, CANTERBURY.

water, the mysterious words were pronounced, and he emerged a member of the Church.' The same author says again, that when infant baptism had been introduced, 'The priest himself descended into the water, which reached to his knees.

Each child was successively delivered undressed into his hands, and he plunged it thrice into the water.'[2] Gregory the Great is the authority for the statement that in 597 Austin and his missionaries baptized ten thousand in one day, to which Gocelin, Bede and others add that this baptism was in the river Swale. This river is in Kent, running between the Isle of Sheppy and the main land, and is navigable for ships of 200 tons burden. Green speaks of this scene, saying: 'The Kentish men crowded to baptism in the river Swale.'[3] And Gocelin calls it 'the river of holy baptism,' adding: 'All entered the dangerous depth of the river, two and two together, as if it had been a solid plain; and in the true faith, confessing the exalted Trinity, they were baptized one by the other in turns, the apostolic leader blessing the water. . . . So great a progeny for heaven born out of a deep *whirlpool!*'[4]

After the Venerable Bede has given an account of a large wooden baptistery

THE VENERABLE BEDE.

hastily built at York, A. D. 627, for the baptism of Edwin, king of Northumberland, he describes the baptism of Paulinus in the Yorkshire river 'Swale, which flows past the village of Cateract (Carric); for as yet oratories or baptisteries, in the very beginning of the infant Church there, could not be built.' Alcuin, when speaking of the immersion of the king and his nobles 'in the sacred fountain,' says that York remained illustrious: 'Because in that sacred place King Edwin was washed in the water.' Theodore, Archbishop of Canterbury, 669, enjoined triple immersion. Canon Ladaius said: 'If any bishop or presbyter does not perform the one initiation with three immersions, but with giving one immersion only, into the death of the Lord, let him be deposed.' Brown's 'History of York Minster' marks the position of the wooden baptistery, 'inclosing a spring, still remaining, which, according to Dr. Giles, was discovered while making repairs of the present cathedral.' In gathering up these and other cases, Bede, who died A. D. 735, says: 'For he truly who is baptized is seen to descend into the fountain, he is seen to be dipped in the waters, he is seen to ascend from the waters.' The Council of Calichyth (Chelsea), held under Kenwolf, king of the Mercians, in 816, passed this canon: 'Let the presbyters know when they administer sacred baptism, not to pour holy water upon the heads of the infants, but always to immerse them in the laver, after the example given by the Son of God himself to every believer, when he was three times immersed in the waters of Jordan.' In the following century the baptism of Ethelred took place on this wise, according to William of Malmesbury: 'When the little boy was immersed in the font of baptism, the bishops standing around, the sacrament was marred by a sad accident.' Such immersion is in keeping with the 'Sarum Use' (Liturgy), which existed from 1087, and of which Dr. Wall remarks, that it did all along enjoin dipping, without any mention of pouring or sprinkling. Cardinal Pulis, a lecturer at Oxford and Paris, in a treatise published about 1150, writes: 'Whilst the candidate for baptism in water is immersed the death of Christ is suggested; whilst immersed and covered with water the burial of Christ is shown forth; whilst he is raised from the waters the resurrection of Christ is proclaimed. The immersion is repeated three times.'

In 1200, the Council of London enjoined immersion; that of Sarum in 1217, and that of Oxford in 1222, did the same: while the Synod of Worcester, 1240, decreed that 'In every church where baptism is performed, there shall be a font of stone of sufficient size and depth for the baptism of children. . . . And let the candidate for baptism always be immersed.' Two Councils held at Perth, 1242, 1296, by canon instructed the minister what to do before immersion, and in the days of Wallace and Bruce, a barbarous custom prevailed in the clanish feuds, amongst the border countries, which left the right hands of male children undipped in baptism, in order that they might with this unsanctified hand deal the more deadly blows upon their foes, as one of our great poets embodies the sentiment:

> 'And at the sacred font the priest
> Through ages left the master hand unblest,
> To urge with keener aim the blood-incrusted spear.'

Sir Walter Scott refers to this custom in his notes on the minstrelsy of the border, and says, that it existed in Ireland also. The Percy Society's poems of Wm. de Shorham, vicar of Seven Oaks, gives an exposition of baptism about 1313, in which he says, that men may dip in warm water 'in whaut' (winter) and in the 'salt sea.' But he forbids dipping at baptism in wine, 'sither' (*cyder*), 'ne in pereye,' also in ale and 'other liquor that changeth water's kind,' a practice which prevailed to some extent. Water only must be used, but he allowed ice to be melted, for the purpose of procuring water. Pope Stephen allowed baptism in wine, if death impended, and water could not be had, and several cases are on record, in the Irish Church, where children were immersed in milk. They had water enough at hand anywhere for the purpose of aspersion, but immersion in some fluid was indispensably necessary in the absence of water, even if rarer and more expensive than water.

Before this time, however, as these many injunctions show, aspersion was made an exceptional method of administering the rite, in consequence, no doubt, of the permissive decree of the Council of Ravenna, 1311, before which it had no sanction. But the exceptions were few for a long period. Arthur, the eldest brother of Henry VIII., and Margaret his sister, were immersed in the years 1486 and 1502 with elaborate ceremonies. Leland describes at length the new font made for the baptism of the prince at Winchester, lined with cloth to prevent the cold sides touching the child, and says, that 'the prince was put into the font.' The same writer describes the baptism of Margaret, grandmother to Mary Queen of Scots, at Westminster Abbey: 'As soon as she was put into the font all the torches were lighted.' He gives similar accounts of the dipping of Edward VI. and Queen Elizabeth, showing that the royal family was immersed as well as the common people, according to the ecclesiastical requirements of the times.

It is clear enough that dipping continued as the normal form of the rite all through Edward's reign (1547-52), but Walker says, 'Sprinkling was sometimes used.' Indeed, the first Church permission found in England for any thing but immersion is in the Prayer-Book of 1549, which says, that 'If the child be weak, it shall suffice to pour water upon it.' With this exception the rubric demanded that the priest shall 'take the child in his hands,' and 'shall dip it in the water thrice. First dipping the right side : second the left side : the third time dipping the face.' In 1552 the word 'thrice' was dropped from the book, together with the directions for the dipping to the right, left, etc., and the instruction was simply, 'shall dip it in water.' But this gradual change met with great resistance. Tyndale, in his Doctrinal Treatise, 1528, writes :

'Ask the people what they understand by their baptism or washing? And thou shalt see, that they believe, how that the very plunging into the water saveth them. . . . Behold how narrowly the people look on the ceremony! If aught be left out, or if the child be not altogether dipped in the water, or if, because the child is sick, the priest dare not plunge him into the water, but pour water on his head, how tremble they! how quake they! How say ye, "Sir John" [a common name for a priest], say they : "Is this child christened enough, hath it full christendom?" They believe verily that the child is not christened.' Again he says : 'Tribulation is our right baptism, and is signified by plunging into the water.' So the people were gradually robbed of the only symbol which gave the right import of their baptism, which was made what he quaintly calls : 'A turn-again lane unto them, which they cannot go through, nor make three lines agree together. . . . The sentences of the Scripture are nothing but very riddles unto them, at the which they guess as the blind man doth at the crow' and expound by guess, a hundred doctors by a hundred ways.' In his Obedience of a Christian Man he says, that 'The plunging into the water signifieth that we die and are buried with Christ, and the pulling out again sign¦fieth that we rise again with Christ in a new life.' And in his Prologue to John's I. Ep., he adds : 'Now, we be all baptized ; but, alas! not one, from the highest to the lowest, ever taught the profession or meaning thereof. And, therefore, we remain all blind generally, as well our great rabbins, for all their high learning which they seem to have, as the lay people. Yea, and so much the more blind are our great clerks (the learned), that where the lay people, for a great number of them are taught nothing at all, they be all wrong taught, and the doctrine of their baptism is all corrupt unto them with the leaven of false glosses, ere they come to read the Scripture ; so that the light which they bring with them, to understand the Scripture withal, is utter darkness, and as contrary unto the Scripture as the devil unto Christ.'

It was with all this and much more in view that Watson, Bishop of London, 1558, wrote : 'Though the old and ancient tradition of the Church hath been from the beginning to dip the child three times, etc., yet that is not of such necessity, but that he is but once dipped in the water, it is sufficient, yea, and in time of great peril and necessity, if the water be but poured on his head it will suffice.'[5] So stern was the resistance, however, to this innovation, that Middleton, Bishop of

St. David's, issued an 'injunction' in 1582, forbidding trine immersion in baptism. [6] The second Prayer-Book of Edward VI., 1552, enjoins only a single immersion, and that of Elizabeth, 1560, made no change in this rubric. This is still the law in the English Church. But, so far as appears, the word 'sprinkle' first took rank in an English ritual, in the Catechism of 1604. In answer to the question, 'What is the outward visible sign or form of baptism?' it replies, 'Water, wherein the person baptized is dipped or sprinkled with it.' This was followed by the Westminster Directory, 1644, which decided, that 'It is not only lawful, but also sufficient and most expedient, to be by pouring or sprinkling water on the face of the child.' Thus, in less than a century, what had been the general rule was reversed, and what had been the rare exception became the rule; yet, in 1660, dipping had not become entirely extinct, as it was common in 1644. Lord Brooke, in his 'Treatise on Episcopacy,' 1641, charges, that the 'Anabaptists' refuse baptism to their children till they come to years of discretion, 'but in other things they agree with the Church of England.' His subject is baptism, and his 'other things' must relate to this subject, for in doctrine and government they were wide apart. Blake, of Tamworth, says, in 1644: 'I have been an eye-witness of many infants dipped, and I know it to have been the constant practice of many ministers in their places for many years together. Those that dip not infants do not yet use to sprinkle them, there is a middle way between these two. I have seen several dipped; I never saw or heard of any sprinkled, or (as some of you use to speak) *rantized*. Our way is not by aspersion, but perfusion; not sprinkling drop by drop, but pouring on at once all that the bowl contains.' Dr. Wall attributes the change to the Puritan clergy, whose deference to Calvin's authority led them to adopt sprinkling in accordance with his own form, adopted 1545.

Walter Cradock, preacher at All Hallows, and one of the sweetest spirits of his day, preached before the House of Commons, at St. Margaret's, Westminster, July 21, 1646, in which sermon he exhorts Parliament not to establish 'any outward external' for a test of church-fellowship, as:

'Baptizing this way or that way, I mean by dipping or sprinkling, or by conjunction of opinion on some controverted point. . . . Therefore, when I have communion with a saint, I must not look so much whether he have taken the covenant, or have been baptized once or twice or ten times.' And in a marginal note he adds: 'I speak not this as if my opinion were for rebaptizing or against the baptizing of infants of believers, *the contrary appears by my practice*.' [7]

The value of his testimony is found in the fact that he gives no hint whatever that immersion was a new thing in England, but the implication runs all through his writings that it was very prevalent, and the public were as familiar with it as with the 'covenant' or any other 'controverted point' of that period. Besides, if immersion had been introduced amongst the 'Anabaptists' in 1641, it would have been simply preposterous for a learned clergyman to be exhorting Parliament, five short years after, not to make 'baptizing this way or that way, by dipping or sprinkling,' the foundation of church-fellowship. Nothing could be more far-fetched, or even impertinent, than such an appeal. Fortunately, he throws much light upon the general subject two years later, 1648, in his 'Gospel-libertie, its Extensions and Limitations,' from which the following passages are taken :

Page 23–4 : ' Saith Christ, Baptize all nations, that is, go and use water for their washing, for whatever men find in the word, I speak not of now. . . . If Christ had tied men to go into Jordan, as in that country it was so hot, they might go with a great deal of comfort ; but if Christ had made baptism such an ordinance as that in all climates and countries and regions they must go over head and ears in a river, we know in some climates it would have been present death. As with us in this climate, at some times of the year to be put over head and ears in the Thames, it would be death, at others not.'

It is refreshing in the bitterness of the seventeenth century, side by side with Featley, to find a man who had the candor to apply his own logic on this subject and stand by it to its legitimate conclusions. Thus, on the Supper he says, p. 24 :

' The Lord took bread and wine, and blessed, and broke and gave them ; and the drift of all the business is to show the breaking of his body, and the shedding of his blood. Now, he hath bound us that we should break bread and drink wine, that may represent the thing ; but he hath not bound us to *bread* so properly called, or to *wine* properly so called ; for there are some countries that have neither bread nor wine, but only roots that they call bread, and they have water for their drink. Now, if Christ had said it must be true bread, and true and real wine, that must do the deed, these people could never have the Supper of the Lord.'

Like Baxter, he was very nervous about the health of the English nation, and had little love for cold water to that end, but he never charges the Baptists with being the authors of a new style of homicide. He does think, however, that they laid too much stress on dipping, and says on p. 26 :

' Of dipping over head and ears, because the word *bapto* signifies over head and ears sometimes, and because the preposition *em* signifies to go into, from that they bind *all the saints all the world over*, to go into rivers, so that if a man be not *dipped*, but only sprinkled, because of the preposition *em*, that makes a nullity of the Church, that it is no church, and so, consequently, there shall be no church at all.'

Still, with a charity far in advance of his age, he cannot bear to have the Baptists abused, especially in nick-naming them, and several times he rebukes this sharply, as on page 40, thus :

' I see the devil gets much advantage by nick-names, by calling men Presbyterians, and Antinomians, and *Anabaptists*, and I know not what. Therefore, I beseech you, beware how you use those names, though I say not it is unlawful, yet there be mistakes, let us call them as gently as we can, that are generally among us.'

Here is no 'Gangræna' nor vulgar slang, but a Christian scholar, and more, a Christian gentleman, who understands the times in which he lives, and knows how to talk about decent people with whom he differs on serious questions. On p. 100 he says:

'There is now among good people a great deal of strife about baptism; as for divers things, so for the point of dipping, *though in some places in England they dip altogether*. How shall we end the controversy with those godly people, as many of them are. Look upon the Scriptures, and there you shall find that *bapto* (to baptize), it is an ordinance of God, and the use of water in way of washing for a spiritual end, to resemble some spiritual thing. It is an ordinance of God, but whether dipping or sprinkling, that we must bring the party to a river, or draw the river to him, or use water at home, whether he must be in head and foot, or be under the water, or the water under him, it is not proved that God hath laid down an absolute rule for it. Now, what shall we do? conclude on the absolute rule that God hath laid down in Scripture, and judge of the rest according to expediency. . . . Let us judge whether sprinkling or dipping be more *expedient*, and then there would be no strife. For there is scarce a man in this place that if he were persuaded that dipping were not an absolute rule, but it were to be judged according to expediency, he would rather have in a modest way the use of water, than to have men and women, and weak people, it may be in the winter time, over head and ears into the river; he would rather make use of water in a more civil and safe and less dangerous way.'

He neither charges upon the Baptists that their practice was unscriptural, new, nor a change from their former practice. On the contrary, he asks: 'How we shall baptize, whether by sprinkling or going into a river, because it is probable that some of them did;' as to the English practice he says: 'In some places in England they dip altogether. How shall we end the controversy with those godly people, as many of them are.' He then frankly intimates his honest opinion that the controversy was as old as Christ's command to baptize, for he says, on p. 16, that when Christ sent his disciples to baptize he gave the command. 'And there was an end. They might ask a hundred questions. Shall we do it in a river or in a brook? to young or to old? in winter or in summer? . . . But Christ lays down the sum of the doctrine, and the end of it, In the name of the Father, and of the Son, and of the Holy Ghost, and there is no more of it.' The only new thing that he hints at in this whole question of dipping, is his great concern for the life of the dipped. For centuries those opposed to them had been devising every conceivable method of getting rid of them, by fire and fagot, as in England and Holland, and by drowning outright, as in Switzerland and Austria. But now, one tender-hearted opponent springs up, who cannot bear the thought even of having their feet wet. Compassion was a new thing in their case, they were sickly and 'weak,' and to think of taking such 'feeble folk' into the 'Thames' and other rivers or brooks and wetting their 'ears,' and that in winter too, was a moving thought for kind-hearted Walter Cradock. Yet as the Baptists would not stop this old, uncivil, unsafe and 'dangerous way,' he says, page 108:

'I speak not that you may persecute godly people, or that it is altogether unlawful for the saints to meet in another place. . . . Or thus, suppose in this country or in a colder that people did go and baptize in rivers, whereas this is not an absolute command. But only the using of water, lay down that, and by that means divers subjects *die*, and lose their lives, suppose this were real, herein for aught I know the magistrate may determine a course, and take another way, because herein is prejudice to his subjects.'

This last is the passage referred to by Baxter in his 'Plain Scripture Proof,' pp. 134–137, in evidence that dipping is a violation of the Sixth Commandment, and should be stopped by the magistrate. His words are:

'As Mr. Cradock shows in his book of Gospel Liberty, the magistrate ought to restrain it, to save the lives of his subjects. That this is flat murder, and no better, being ordinarily and generally used, is undeniable to any understanding man.'

Certainly, Cradock's words will bear no such construction as Baxter put upon them, and that he meant no such thing is clear not only from the words themselves, but from the kind manner in which he uniformly treated those who had been 'dipped over head and ears in the river.' He saw a slight tendency to suicide in such conduct, and he thought such people were too good to 'die and lose their lives,' and for aught he knew to the contrary 'the magistrate *may* determine a course, and take another way.' He could not bear him to lose such 'subjects,' he had too few of them now, but he hardly knew how to prevent it, for he says: 'I speak not, that you may persecute godly people,' who are dipped as they were altogether, 'in some places in England.'

The reader may want to know somewhat more of this open-hearted, honest Walter Cradock, who, according to Baxter, thought Baptists guilty of murder. Joshua Thomas states that he was a Welshman of a reputable family in Monmouthshire, who, when a student at Oxford, visited his friends in Wales, and while there heard Mr. Wroth, the rector of Llanfaches, preach, and was converted. The next news we have of him is through Archbishop Laud, in 1634, to whom the Bishop of Landaff had reported that Walter was preaching as curate in St. Mary's in Cardiff; but that 'being a bold, ignorant young fellow, he had suspended him, and taken away his license.' Then Neal tells us that in 1634–35 he was cited to London and condemned as a schismatic, so that he was compelled to leave the Establishment and preached all through Wales with great power. One of Laud's most serious charges against him was that he said in the pulpit, 'that God so loved the world, that for it he sent his Son to live like a slave, and die like a beast.' Brooks tells us, that this earnest Puritan formed an Independent Church at Llanfaches in 1639, and Orme, in his Life of Baxter, writes that about 1635, Baxter and Cradock became acquainted in Shrewsbury, when a strong affection was formed between them. But the 'Broadmead Records' inform us that in 1643 he and his church were obliged to fly from Wales to Bristol before the king's army; they took refuge in Bristol, which was held by the 'Parliament's army.' Then Cradock was glad to find a home amongst those who had been dipped head over ears in the river Frome, and as they had no pastor he administered the Supper to them: 'First at ye Dolphin, in ye greate Roome, then afterwards sometime at a Baker's house, upon James' Back, who was a Member of ye Church.' When the king's army captured Bristol, these Welsh Independents and the Bristol Baptists fled together to London, and there 'Did commonly meet at Greate Allhallows for ye most parte. Only those professors that were Baptized before they went up, they did sitt downe with Mr. Kiffen and his Church in London, being likewise Baptized.'⁸ In 1646 we have his great sermon before Parliament, while preacher at All Hallows, and in 1648 his Gospel Liberty, which Baxter uses to such poor account; and not least of all his statement that in some parts of England dipping was used altogether; with his request, in 1646, that Parliament would not make this a test of Church fellowship. He died about 1660.

Amongst the opponents of the new practice of sprinkling, some of the Baptists were found in stout resistance; notably, as early as 1614, Leonard Busher, the author of 'Religions Peace,' wrote thus:

'It is well worthy consideration, that as in the time of the Old Testament the Lord would not have his offerings by constraint, but of every man whose heart gave it freely: so now, in the time of the Gospel, he will not have the people constrained, but as many as receive the word gladly, they are to be added to the Church by baptism. And therefore Christ commanded his disciples to teach all nations, and baptize them; that is, to preach the word of salvation to every creature of all sorts of nations, that are worthy and willing to receive it. And such as shall willingly and gladly receive it, he hath commanded to be baptized in the water; that is, *dipped for dead in the water.*'⁹

S. Fisher also, in his 'Baby Baptism mere Babyism,' resists the innovation bravely. On July 29, 1649, he held a controversy at Ashford, with several clergymen, and in 1653 published his book, in which he devotes 159 pages to show that sprinkling cannot be called baptism without perversion. He says:

'Having raised the rotten basis of your Babyism, I come now to reckon with your Rantism, and to examine whether our manner of baptizing, which is by dipping, is the baptism which was instituted by Christ.' He closes page 464 as follows: 'Thus have I done with both parts of that subject of rantizing, which partly at the motion of your Ashford disputants I was engaged in, and partly by that mere demi-reformation that is made on this point on a party of men in Lincolnshire and elsewhere (of whom I suppose there are several congregations), who having long since discovered the true way of baptism as to the subjects, namely: That professing believers only and not any infants are to be baptized, but remaining ignorant of the true way and form of administering the ordinance, are fallen into the frivolous way of *sprinkling believers;* which to do is as much no baptism at all as to dip infants is no baptism of Christ's ordaining. Which people, for whose sakes as well as others I write this, will be persuaded, I hope, in time, to be as to the outward form, not almost only, but altogether Christians, and rest no longer in that mere midway, mongrel Reformation.'

Baxter said in 1650: 'I may say, as Mr. Blake, that I never saw a child sprinkled, but all that I have seen baptized had water poured on them, and so were washed.' From that time onward, sprinkling pushed pouring out of the way so fast that Selden, who died in 1654, remarks sarcastically in his 'Table Talk:'

'The baptizing of children with us does only prepare a child, against he comes to be a man, what Christianity means. In the Church of Rome it has this effect, it frees children from hell. . . . In England, of late years, I ever thought the parson baptized his own fingers, rather than the child.' This is substantially what Featley had said in 1644: 'The minister dippeth his hand into the water, and plucketh it out when he baptizeth the infant.'¹⁰

So fast did the exception become the rule, that in the opening of the eighteenth century Dr. Wall tells us that he had heard of two persons then living who had been dipped in the font; also of one clergyman then living who had so baptized infants, and that at the requests of the parents he had himself administered baptism in the same way. He further states that during the reigns of James and Charles I. all christened children were carried to the font, which act said: 'The minister is ready to dip the child if the parents will venture the health of it.' Dean Comber, in his work on the Common Prayer, 1688, said of the baptismal rite: 'Because the way of immersion was the most ancient, our Church doth first prescribe that, and only permits the other where it is certified the child is weak, although custom has now prevailed to the laying of the first wholly aside.' To this day, however, as Dean Stanley says: 'In the Church of England immersion is still observed in theory. . . . The rubric in the public baptism for infants enjoins that unless for special causes they are to be dipped, not sprinkled, but in practice it gave way from the beginning of the seventeenth century.' Occasionally it is used now, but according to the annals of that Church the last recorded instances of immersion before the Restoration were in dipping three infant sons of Sir Robert Shirley, in the reign of Charles I. This agrees with Gale's answer to Wall, that dipping continued till Queen Elizabeth's time, 'and then fell into total disuse, within a little more than a hundred years, and sprinkling, the most opposite, was introduced in its stead.'

We fall into a mistake, however, if we suppose that the Baptists were the only people who resisted this change. Becon tells us that in the reign of Elizabeth there was contention on the subject in the Established Church. Wall treats of this at great length, and of the efforts made by many to restore dipping, not only, as Rogers expresses it to D'Anvers, 'in order to the peace of the Church,' but also to conciliate the Baptists, 'by your reunion with it, and the saving of your souls by rescuing you from under the guilt of schism, I could wish the practice of it retrieved into use again.' Indeed, Daniel Rogers went so far as to say: 'I believe the ministers of the nation would be heartily glad if the people would desire or be but willing to have their infants dipped, after the ancient manner, both in this and in other churches; and bring them to baptism in such a condition as that they might be totally dipped.' Walker, Towerson and other divines took the same ground. Sir Norton Knatchbull, one of the most learned men of his day, was of the opinion, 'That it would be more for the honor of the Church, and for the peace and security of religion, if the old custom could conveniently be restored.' And Sir John Floyer, whom Wall pronounces 'a learned physician,' wrote a 'History of Cold Bathing, Ancient and Modern,' in which he showed its healthiness and blessings, without regard to climate, adding, that he could not 'advise his countrymen to any better method for preservation of health, than the cold regimen, to dip all their children in baptism,' and 'to wash them often afterwards, till three quarters of a year old.' By 'wash' here he evidently means dip. He thought, also, that 'the approbation of physicians would bring in the old use of immersion in baptism.'[11] The strange medley into which Baxter fell on the subject may throw light upon Sir John Floyer's position. The Kidderminster divine had become deeply concerned on this matter of immersion as affecting the national health, and had said, in 1650, that it was 'A plain breach of the Sixth Commandment, "Thou shalt not kill."' So far then from being an ordinance of God, he denounced it 'as a most heinous sin,' and thought that 'the magistrate ought to restrain it, to save the lives of his subjects.'

This seemed to afford amusement for the ablest physicians of that period, but in the nineteenth century, when the bath is accounted a constant necessity to health, what an edification it must be to the bathers at Newport, Long Branch, and Cape May to hear the pious author of 'The Saint's Everlasting Rest' declaim thus, in depicting the terrible calamities which follow immersion. He says:

'Apoplexies, lethargies, palsies, and all other comatose diseases would be promoted by it. So would cephalalgies, hemicranies, phthises, debility of the stomach, crudities, and almost all fevers, dysenteries, diarrhœas, colics, iliac passions, convulsions, spasms, tremors, and so on. All hepatic, splenetic, and pulmonic persons, and hypochondriacs, would soon have enough of it. In a word, it is good for nothing but to dispatch men out of the world that are burdensome, and to ranken churchyards. I conclude, if murder be a sin, then dipping ordinarily over head in England is a sin; and if those who would make it men's religion to murder themselves, and urge it upon their consciences as their duty, are not to be suffered in a commonwealth, any more than highway murderers; then judge how these Anabaptists, that teach the necessity of such dipping, are to be suffered. ... If the minister must go into the water with the party, it will certainly tend to his death, though they may escape that go in but once. ... I am still more confirmed that a visible judgment of God doth still follow anabaptizing wherever it comes.'[12]

Baptists of our day ought not to be more severe on Baxter than to quote his own well-weighed words, for when he got over these occasional Anti-Baptist fits, he contended earnestly that he ought to take the Lord's Supper with his Baptist brethren, and then 'Richard was himself again.' We have room for gratitude that he lived not in this age, or not a man of us could have obtained a Life Insurance Policy. Perhaps all the suffering that he deserved was meted out to him by Dr. John Owen, in these words:

'I verily believe that if a man who had nothing else to do should gather into a heap all the expressions which, in his late books, confession and apologies, have a lovely aspect towards himself, as to ability, diligence, sincerity, on the one hand, with all those which are full of reproach and contempt toward others, on the other, the view of them could not but a little startle a man of so great modesty, and of such eminency in the mortification of pride, as Mr. Baxter is.'

With a change in the ordinance itself, there naturally came in a change of the name by which it was known, namely, a 'washing.' From the most ancient times, washing had been spoken of as the result or consequence of dipping, as in the case of Naaman, who washed in the Jordan seven times, having dipped himself that number of times. To wash does not necessarily now mean to dip, yet, as the less is contained in the greater, so he that is dipped is washed. After his seventh dipping, Naaman was 'clean.' So Meyer, on Mark vii, 4: 'Except they *wash* is not to be understood of washing the hands, but of immersion, which the word in classic Greek and in the New Testament everywhere means; here, according to the context, to take a bath.' Plumptre, on the same passage, says: 'The Greek verb (that to *wash*) differs from that in the previous verse, and implies the washing or immersion (the word is that from which our word *baptize* comes to us) of the whole body, as the former does of a part.' Beza, on the same text, says that '*baptizein* does not signify to *wash*, except by consequence. For it properly means to immerse.' Lightfoot describes unclean persons amongst the Jews as '*washed* in some confluence of waters, in which so much water ought to be as may serve to wash the whole body at one dipping.' For centuries the word wash was not used as a synonym for baptism, but was commonly used to express the cleansing effect of baptism, as an immersion. Cyprian says of clinics, that they were 'not *washed* but perfused by the saving water;' evincing that in his judgment perfusion was not to be accounted as washing in the same sense as immersion.[13]

Pouring and sprinkling having taken the place of immersion in England, baptism came to mean another thing from its former self; the words wash and washing naturally changed to adapt themselves to the new ordinance and to the theology by which it was interpreted. Hence, Baxter speaks of babes who had water poured upon them, and so were washed. In keeping with the change of the ordinance, P. de Witte asks: 'Ought we not again to bring in dipping as the Muscovites and others did?' and answers: 'It is not necessary, because washing is done with sprinkling as well as by dipping.' Until the Puritan divines returned from Geneva, they held the idea that tropical washing was the consequence of being overwhelmed, just as wetting is the consequence of immersion. Wickliff had so used the word in translating Mark x, 39: 'Ye shall be *washed* with the baptism in which I am baptized.' And it is specially interesting to note how reluctantly the English people received the new sense of the word wash, in association with sprinkling in baptism. Not being able to see how that act could express the thought of cleansing without the full dipping, some resorted to the absurd idea that rubbing the water in would supply the place of immersion, in efficacious washing, and so we have several accounts of the adoption of this practice. P. Barbour's 'Discourse,' 1642, records a striking example of this absurdity. He pronounces this sage opinion on the efficacy of 'rubbing, p. 14: 'All do or may know that a thing dipped in water is not, therefore, washed or made clean, neither is washing always intended in the dipping of a thing in water. Indeed, washing to make clean is by the way of dipping in many times, that by putting the thing into water and *rubbing* of it or the like it might be cleansed, which I conceive it was the way of their washing in those times and countries where Baptists first began.'

CHAPTER II.

IMMERSION IN ENGLAND (*Continued*).—PERSECUTION.

LET us now look at the practice of the people commonly known amongst the English as Baptists, *par excellence*. In the absence of definite information the inference would be warranted, that their administration of the rite corresponded to that which they saw in the State Church; for their chief controversy with their brethren at that time did not relate to the 'mode,' but to the subject of baptism. Their important word was not 'how,' but to 'whom' should baptism be administered? Their foes called them '*Ana*baptists,' those who baptize again. Their offense, as a general thing, was not that they administered this ordinance in a different way from other Christians, but that they baptized on a confession of faith those who had been 'baptized' in infancy. There was no sharp controversy in the earliest literature of the 'Anabaptists' on the method of baptism, although we have some clear definitions of baptism and some cases of immersion. But, as a rule, in the maintenance of baptism on personal trust in Christ, they said little of immersion until they saw it vanishing away before human authority, even in England, where it had maintained itself so long. Step by step, the Reformation in England was feeling its way first to the naked and radical question: Who shall compose the Church of Christ? The Roman yoke was broken, but in their efforts to rid the nation of superstition the Protestants were divided. The Puritans were still in the State Church, and many of them wished to stay there; but the Baptists took the ground that the pale of the Gospel Church could never be measured by the boundaries of the nation. The Church must be made up only of Christians, and the settlement of that question must radically change the British Constitution. The consequence was that they threw themselves first into the recovery of a purely spiritual Church, and then into the restoration of apostolic immersion. That the struggle was hard and hot is seen in the fact that about two hundred works, *pro* and *con*, were issued in the seventeenth century on the questions of infant baptism and dipping. Many of these are preserved amongst the 'King's pamphlets' in the British Museum, and others are lost. Public oral disputation on these subjects was rife also, in the hands of noted champions. One platform dispute was held in Southwark, 1642, between Dr. Featley and Mr. Kiffin; another in London, 1643, in which Knollys, Kiffin and Jessey took a part. T. Lamb and others held a third debate at Turling, in Essex, 1643; and a fourth was had in 1647, at Newport Pagnall, by J. Gibbs and R. Carpenter. S. Fisher and several clergymen held a fifth at Ashford, in

1649; and in the same year another took place at Bewdley, between Richard Baxter and John Tombes. Similar contests occurred between Dr. Chamberlain and Mr. Bakewell, in London, 1650; H. Vaughan, J. Craig and J. Tombes, at Abergavenny, in 1653; and still another at Portsmouth, in 1698, between Dr. Russell and Samuel Chandler, 'with his majesty's license.'

At the very time of these public disputations the Westminster Assembly met, by order of Parliament, and was in session from 1643 to 1649, and its discussions were sorely disturbed on this question of 'dipping.' Yet, according to Neal, there was not one Baptist in that body. Dr. Lightfoot,[1] one of its leading members, kept a journal of its proceedings, and his entry for August 7, 1644, tells us of 'a great heat' in the debate of that day, when they were framing the 'Directory' for baptism, as to whether dipping should be reserved or excluded, or whether 'it was lawful and sufficient to besprinkle.' Coleman, called 'Rabbi Coleman' because of his great Hebrew learning, contended with Lightfoot that *tauveleh*, the Hebrew word for dipping, demanded immersion 'over head;' and Marshall, a famous pulpit orator, stood firmly by him in the debate, both contending that dipping was essential 'in the first institution.' Lightfoot says that when they came to the vote, 'So many were unwilling to have dipping excluded that the vote came to an equality within one, for the one side was twenty-four, the other twenty-five; the twenty-four for the reserving of dipping, and the twenty-five against it.' 'The business was recommitted,' and the next day, after another warm dispute, it was voted that 'pouring or sprinkling water on the face' was sufficient and most expedient. How did this Presbyterian body, without a Baptist in it, come to such 'a great heat' on dipping if it were a novelty and an innovation amongst them in England?

It is a significant fact also that S. Fisher, in his 'Anti-Rantism,' complains that at Ashford and elsewhere the clergy would discuss only the 'subjects,' carefully avoiding all discussion of the method of baptism, a thing which they would have been slow to do if they had known that the 'so-called' new baptism or immersion was, as such, an innovation in England. This they were careful never to charge. Dr. Funk, Catholic professor at Tübingen, dates the rise of sprinkling and its first prevalence thus: 'Throughout the fifteenth century, in decrees of synods, immersion is referred to as the general and orderly form of baptism.' Of sprinkling he says: 'The first sure evidence of its practice is met with at the Synod of Florence, when the Archbishop of Ephesus made it a subject of complaint against the Western Church' (1439). When it was introduced immersion long resisted it as a new form, and this scholar says that when water was poured upon the head the rest of the body was still immersed. On the general subject, he quotes from the Synod of Passau, 1470; of Wurzburg, 1482; of Besancon, 1571; of Aix, 1585; and Caen, 1614.

These discussions had produced such a growing distrust in the public mind on the subject of infant baptism, as early as 1661, that for the first time a form of service was introduced into the Prayer-Book for the public baptism of those of riper years. The preface honestly states the reason : ' By the growth of Anabaptism through the licentiousness of the late times, crept in amongst us, is now become necessary, and may be always useful, for the baptizing of natives in our plantations and others, converted to the faith.' The Baptists were assailed for attempting to restore the ancient state of things as if they had committed an unheard-of crime, and but for the history and literature of many centuries the clamor might lead to the supposition that immersion had never been heard of until they sought to restore the normal English baptism. They were called a 'New-washed company,' were charged with bringing in a 'new dipping,' a 'novelty' and an 'invention,' with being 'led away of the devil,' with 'murdering the souls of babes,' and a few other things of the same gracious sort. Bigotry and hate could not have raised a greater howl if immersion had then been practiced on English soil for the first time. And yet even Dr. Featley is compelled to say in his ' Clavis Mystrica,' 1636 : ' Our font is always open, or ready to be opened, and the minister attends to receive the children of the faithful, and to *dip* them in the sacred laver.' Even in our day an attempt has been made to leave the onus of invention upon the English Baptists, in the matter of immersion, because simple-hearted Barbour happened to say, in 1642, that the Lord had raised him up to '*divulge* the true doctrine of dipping.' Yet, his entire treatise discusses the question, ' What is the true ordinance of the dipping of Christ, and wherein does it differ from children's dipping ? ' In the very sentence which speaks of *divulging* the doctrine he says that it ' was received by the apostles and primitive churches, and for a long time unavoidably kept and practiced by the ministry of the Gospel in the planting of the first churches.' The word 'divulge' was not confined at that time to the sense of disclosing or discovering a thing, as now, but it meant primarily to 'publish.' Henry Denne was immersed in 1643, and preached the Gospel from that time onward ; and yet, in sending him forth on a special mission, the Baptist Church at Fenstanton, October 28, 1653, says that, ' On that day' he ' was chosen and ordained, by imposition of hands, a messenger to *divulge* the Gospel of Jesus Christ ; '[2] surely not to make it public, as a new thing. Barbour speaks of the ' dipping of infants' more than a score of times, as a thing with which all were familiar, but he says : ' That dipping whereof we speak is burying or plunging a *believer* in water, he desiring of this ordinance.'

There is less clear and decisive evidence of the practice of immersion amongst the English Baptists from 1600 to 1641 than might be desired, but the passage cited from Leonard Busher, and other proofs, render it certain that they did not first practice it in 1641. It is quite clear that some of them practiced affusion up to that time, while some immersed, but after that date affusion seems to have ceased amongst them and only immersion obtained. The case of John Smyth, who baptized himself in 1608, may be conceded to have been an affusion, and yet this is by no means certain, neither has his immersion been proved. After all that Dr. Hoop Scheffer and others have said on the subject, passages from Smyth's three

Confessions of Faith are strangely in conflict with the thought that he practiced aspersion upon himself for baptism. Article XIV in his Latin Confession describes baptism as 'the external symbol of remission of sins, of death and resurrection.' Article XXX in his English Confession says: 'The whole dealing in the outward visible baptism of water setteth before the eyes, witnesseth and signifieth, the Lord Jesus doth inwardly baptize the repentant, faithful man in the laver of regeneration and renewing by the Holy Ghost, washing the soul from all pollution and sin, by the virtue and merit of his bloodshed.' The confession of himself and friends, published after his death, Article XXXVIII, says: 'That all men, in truth died, are also with Christ buried by baptism into death (Rom. vi, 4; Col. ii, 12), holding their Sabbath in the grave with Christ.' And Article XL, 'That those who have been planted with Christ together in the likeness of his death and burial shall be also in the likeness of his resurrection.' These utterances savor more of immersion than affusion, and yet they were probably written after his Se-Baptism, so that its form is left in doubt, with the probability that it was a dipping.

A feeble but strained attempt has been made to show that none of the English Baptists practiced immersion prior to 1641, from the document mentioned by Crosby in 1738, of which he remarks, that it was '*Said* to be written by Mr. William Kiffin.' Although this manuscript is signed by fifty-three persons, it is evident that its authorship was only guessed at from the beginning, it may or may not have been written by Kiffin. The church referred to was that of which Messrs. Jacob and Lathrop had been pastors, but the fact that a part of this congregation did not know that the immersion of believers had been practiced in England cannot be accepted as decisive proof that all the Baptists were strangers to that practice, still less that it had never been known in England before 1641. It can scarcely be supposed that Leonard Busher should have written in 1614 that Christ 'commanded' those who 'willingly and gladly' received 'the word of salvation to be baptized in the water, that is, dipped for dead in the water,' and that he neglected to obey that command himself. He calls himself 'a citizen of London,' and his style as an English writer, though somewhat unpolished, was equal to the average of his times; he appears to have been acquainted with the Greek Text of the New Testament; he addressed the king (James) and 'the High Court of Parliament' as a man who had the right to address them as a 'citizen,' and with a full knowledge of English affairs. He speaks of himself and his brethren as: 'We that have most truth are most persecuted, and therefore most poor,' and his work bears internal evidence that at some time he had been exiled from his native land for his religion. The 'Address to the Presbyterian Reader,' which forms the Introduction of his Treatise, is signed H. B., supposed to be Henry Burton, and it says of Busher that he was 'an honest and godly man.' What the Treatise itself says of Robinson and the Brownists, with these circumstances, all point to the supposition that he was a member of the Baptist Church, formed in London by Helwys in 1612-14. But, in any case, the fair inference from his own words is, that he was an immersed believer nearly thirty years before the MS. to which Crosby refers was written. The following is the text of that paper:

1640. 3d mo. The church became two by mutual consent, first half being wth. Mr. P. Barebone and ye. other half wth. Mr. H. Jessey. Mr. Richd. Blunt wth. him being convinced of Baptism yt. also it ought to be by diping ye Body into ye. Water, resembling Burial and riseing again, Col. ii : 12 ; Rom. vi ; 4 : had Sober Conference about it in ye. Church, and then wth. some of the forenamed, who also were so convinced. And after Prayer and Conference about their so enjoying it, none having so practiced in England to professed believers, and hearing that some in the Nether Lands had so practiced, they agreed and sent over Mr. Richd. Blunt (who understood Dutch) wth. Letters of Commendation, who was kindly accepted there, and Returned wth. Letters from them ; Jo. Batte a Teacher there ; and from that Church to such as sent him. 1641. They proceed on therein, viz.: Those persons yt. ware perswaded Baptism should be by diping ye. Body, had mett in two Companies and did intend so to meet after this : all these Agreed to proceed alike together : And then Manifesting (not by any formal Words) a Covenant (wch. Word was Scrupled by some of them) but by mutual desires and agreement each testified : These two Companyes did set apart one to Baptize the rest, so it was solemnly performed by them. Mr. Blunt Baptized Mr. Blacklock, yt. was a Teacher amongst them, and Mr. Blunt being Baptized, he and Mr. Blacklock Baptized ye. rest of their friends yt. ware so minded, and many being added to them they increased much.

Dr. Featley, author of 'The Dippers Dipt,' born 1582, died 1645, bears direct testimony to the practice of believer's immersion amongst the Baptists at a much earlier period than 1641. In that year he held a dispute with four Baptists at Southwark; and, as he says, in his dedication to the reader, Jan. 10, 1644, 'I could hardly dip my pen in any thing but gall,' we may not suspect him as stating facts within his knowledge to their special advantage. Yet on this subject he says of them: ' They flock in great multitudes to their *Jordans*, and both sexes enter into the river, and are dipt after their manner. And as they defile our rivers with their impure washings, and our pulpits with their false prophecies and fanatical enthusiasms, so the presses sweat and groan under the load of their blasphemies. . . . This venomous serpent (*verè Solifuga*) is the Anabaptist, who, in these latter times, first showed his shining head, and speckled skin, and thrust out his sting near the place of my residence, *for more than twenty years.*' He conveys the idea that they had defiled the ' rivers with their impure washings,' in being ' dipt after *their manner,*' quite as long as they had defiled '*our* pulpits' and 'presses,' and that near his own residence ' for more than TWENTY years.' To his knowledge, then, they had ' dipt ' ' both sexes,' in the English ' rivers ' from before A. D. 1624; his whole work treats of them as 'Dippers,' who in baptism always ' dipt,' and had he known that they had ever done any thing else, he would have been very happy to have charged them with now throwing aside the right method and with taking up the wrong.

When P. Barbour speaks of the way of 'new baptizing,' he also speaks of baptism having been ' in captivity in Babylon ;' which indicates, not that the Baptists had now originated dipping in England, but that they had restored the historical baptism which England had ever known till that time. This he calls 'God *returning* to build his tabernacle.' Smyth himself, in reply to Clifton, calls the baptism of the Baptists '*new*,' but in what sense? He says: 'They set up a *new or apostolic baptism which Antichrist had overthrown*. . . . When all Christ's visible ordinances are lost, either men must *recover* them again, or must let them alone.' The word 'new' was customarily applied to reforms in those days. Gov. Bradford calls Smyth's church at Amsterdam a 'new communion,' a term which Bishop Hall applied to the Brownist churches, but neither of them meant that a church was a new device in the earth. The Bishop complains that the Separatists classed the Church of England with the old Church of Rome, saying: 'The want of noting one poor distinction breeds all this confusion of doctrine and separation of men. For there is one case of a New Church to be called from heathenism to Christianity; *another*, of a former church to be reformed from errors to more sincere Christianity. . . . This is our case. We did not make a New Church, but mended an old. Your Clifton is driven to this old, by necessity of argument; otherwise he sees there is no avoiding of Anabaptism. . . . Neither is new baptism lawful (though some of *you* belike of old were in hand with a rebaptization; which, not then speeding, succeedeth now to your shame), nor a *new*, voluntary, and particular confession of faith besides that in baptism, though very commendable, will ever be proved simply necessary to the being of a church.'³

Even Baxter has been called to the stand for the purpose of saying that the Baptists 'do introduce a *new sort* of Christianity' . . . and 'a new sort of baptism, which the Church of Christ never knew to this day. . . . As if they were raised in the end of the world to reform the baptism and Christianity of all ages, and were not only wiser than the universal Church from Christ till now, but also at last must make the Church another thing.' When Baxter explains Baxter, whatever else he may mean, he does not mean that dipping was a new device either in England or in Christianity. In defining baptism he writes: 'The action of the minister on God's part is to wash the body of the baptized with the water, which, in hot countries, was by dipping them over head, and taking them up.'⁴ Again: 'It is commonly confessed by us to the Anabaptists, as our commentators declare, that in the Apostles' time the baptized were dipped over head in the water. . . . We have thought it lawful to *disuse* the manner of dipping, and to use less water.'⁵ Nor did he think that 'rebaptism,' as he calls it, was a 'new sort of Christianity and baptism,' for he declared that 'If any person discovered a minister who baptized him to be no minister' he might be baptized again; 'nor would I account it *morally* twice baptizing, but a physical repeating of that act which morally is but one.'⁶ Neither did he think that Baptist dipping had made 'the Church another thing' in such sense as to cut them off from Christian fellowship. He says: 'For the Anabaptists themselves, though I have written and said so much against them, as I found that most of them were persons of zeal in religion, so many of them were sober, godly people, who differed from others but in the point of infant baptism, or, at most, in the points of predestination, free-will and perseverance.'[7] He asks: 'May Anabaptists, that have no other error, be permitted in church communion? Ans. Yes, and tolerated in their practice also: For 1. They agree with us in all points absolutely necessary to communion. 2. The ancient Christians had liberty either to baptize, or let them stay till age, as they think best: and, therefore, Tertullian and Nazianzen speak against haste: and Augustine and many Christian parents were baptized at age.'[8] After yielding the whole ground to the Baptists in this way, it is hard to understand what he means by 'a new sort of baptism, which the Church of Christ never knew to this day,' unless it be the new line or succession of baptism which Smyth had introduced by baptizing himself.

This is clear enough from P. Barbour's discourse. After attempting to prove that the baptism of the Roman Catholic Church is valid, he speaks of Smyth's baptism, protesting that if pure baptism

'Is nowhere else to be found remaining in the world, there is no ground for this practice of *raising* baptism: by persons baptizing themselves.' Instead, there should be 'a seeking out of the Church where she were to be found, and there receiving the holy obedience of Christ's baptism as in *a right line*, and so be added to the Church, and from thence conveying the truth into these parts again where it had *ceased*.' He then tries to show at great length that if baptism be 'lost and fallen out of the world, and an idol and likeness were in the room of it,' no persons have the right to attempt a 'new beginning,' or 'go about the raising, erecting, or *setting up of it again*, without a special commission from God.' He then complains that those who reject Roman baptism insist on the practice of dipping; 'and that persons are to be dipped, all and every part to be under the water, for if all the whole person is not under the water, then they hold that they are not baptized with the baptism of Christ. . . . 'Truly they want a Dipper that hath authority from heaven as had John. . . . I hope when they have further considered this matter they may abate of the fierceness of their opinions, so as to think that baptism under or in the defection may be God's ordinance, so as there shall be no need of this new dipping,' which he admits to have been but a revival of the old practice.

Denne put the question of dipping in England in its true light in his public disputation at St. Clement Dane's church with Mr. Gunning in 1656. At p. 40 he says:

'Dipping of infants was not only commanded by the Church of England, but also generally practiced in the Church of England till the year 1600; yea, in some places it was practiced until the year 1641, until the fashion altered. . . . I can show Mr. Baxter an old man in London who has labored in the Lord's Pool many years; converted by his ministry more men and women than Mr. Baxter hath in his parish; yea, when he hath labored a great part of the day in preaching and reasoning, his reflection hath been (not a Sack-possit or a candle), but to go into the water and baptize converts. . . . I wonder that Mr. Baxter should forget that he hath read in authors, which he deems authentic, who write that Ethelbert King of Kent, with 10,000 men and women, were baptized in Canterbury, upon the 25th of December, in the year 597.'

And the same tone is maintained by 'R. W.' in his Declaration against Anabaptists in answer to Cornwall; he says, London, 1644, p. 1:

'You argue thus, "That which God hath joined together, no man ought to separate, (But faith and baptism, or more properly dipping,) God hath joined together; therefore, faith and baptism (or dipping as the original renders it) no man ought to separate."'

The fact is, that it was not the dipping of the Baptists which shocked their opponents so much as Smyth's act with some of its consequences. The Anti-Baptists possessed a certain church and ministerial succession, and under this idea they regarded his course as profanity. They considered Baptists as mere interlopers, having no right to administer the ordinances in any way, as they had renounced that succession. The Baptists were regarded as 'upstarts,' and their 'new dipping,' looked at in any light, was but an innovation. Backus caught this distinction with great clearness, and says: 'Being hardly accused with the want of *valid administrators,* moved seven Baptist churches, who met in London in 1643 to declare it as their faith that by Christ's communion every disciple who had a gift to preach the Gospel had a right to administer baptism, even before he was ordained in any Church;' much less that he should be required first to prove his regular descent by succession from the Apostles. (Backus, ii, p. 4.) Whoever the Baptists immersed had, in the opinion of their foes, been baptized as babes, and so their after-dipping was new and unauthorized, especially when had in unconsecrated places, as rivers and streams; such as Old Ford River, near Bromley, in Middlesex, which Wilson, in his 'Dissenting Churches,' says 'was much frequented' for this purpose. Nay, their foes even professed themselves shocked with the bodily exertion of such immersions. John Goodwin, in semi-comic style, says of 'the Baptist who dippeth' that he 'had need be a man of stout limbs, and of a very able and active body; otherwise the person to be baptized, especially if in any degree corpulent or unwieldly, runs a great hazard of meeting with Christ's later baptism instead of his former.'

Baxter affected to be shocked, for it was reported to him that they baptized in the rivers, naked. Featley and others report the same, but none of them pretended to have been eye-witnesses of these reported indecencies. On the contrary, Baxter adds: "I must confess I did not see the persons baptized naked, nor do I take it to be lawful to defame any upon doubtful reports,' words which imply honest doubt. But Richardson resented this imputation, saying: 'We abhor it, and deny that any of us ever did so;' then he challenged Featley 'to prove it against us if he can.' This the Doctor was careful never to attempt. Haggar declares that he had baptized and been at the baptizing of 'many hundreds if not thousands, and never saw any baptized naked in his life, neither is it allowed nor approved of amongst any that I know of.' Baxter lived near Tombes, his great Baptist disputant, and yet followed 'common fame' in this matter, instead of inquiring of him, thus allowing anonymous slanderers to fill his ears. He said that he was willing to commune with the Baptists, but he seems never to have taken one step to learn the truth of this charge against his dear brethren. Even had he found the charge true, he should not have been too much shocked that they copied the fanaticisms of the Fathers, whom he so much revered: Chrysostom, Augustine and Cyril, who stickled zealously for nude baptism. Besides, in England the children were baptized without clothing at that time. Dr. Wall says that 'the wealthy people began to object to the stripping of their children naked, and the affrighted screams with which they received immersion.' Bacon confirms this, saying that 'honesty and shamefacedness forbiddeth to uncover the body, and also the (weak) state of infants, for the most part, cannot away with dipping.' Wall coolly adds that the Baptists need not to have made so great an outcry against Baxter's charge of indecency, for that the primitive Christians baptized in entire undress. And for the same reason Baxter need not to have cried out against the Baptists, even if he could have proved that they followed this bad example of the primitive Christians; which, however, they seem to have avoided with all carefulness. Their confession of 1643 evinced their modesty, by requiring 'convenient garments, both upon the administrator and subject, with all propriety, when they immersed.'

This chapter can scarcely be closed better than by showing that the so-called 'Anabaptists' of the realm had long practiced according to these views. There are traditions of Baptist Churches in England from the fourteenth century, but they are not well sustained by historical records. Collier speaks of many infants who were left unbaptized in the middle of the twelfth century. Robinson says that there was a Baptist church at Chesterton in 1459; and others mention 'heretics' all over England, who refused baptism for infants in various reigns down to Henry VIII. The law of the land demanded the baptism of all, but as we have no reliable records of Baptist churches it is fair to infer that these objectors were either English Lollards or foreigners driven from the Continent. We do not find the name 'Anabaptist' applied to English 'heretics' until the reign of Henry, 1509, nearly a century after all trace of the Lollards is lost, their chief relic then being the Lollard's Tower, that of St. Gregory's Church, contiguous to St. Paul's Cathedral, which had been used as their prison. Fox records that in 1535, according to the registers of London, nineteen 'Anabaptists' were put to death in various parts of the realm, and that fourteen Hollanders were burnt in pairs in England. A 'History of the "Anabaptists" of High and Low Germany' was written in 1642, and is now amongst the 'King's Pamphlets.' Its bitter author writes (p. 55): 'All these are scions of that flock of Anabaptism that was transplanted out of Holland in the year 1535, when two ships laden with Anabaptists fled into England; . . . here it seemeth they have remained ever since' (p. 48). Barclay also reports that in 1536 'Anabaptist' societies in England sent a delegation to a great gathering of their brethren in Westphalia.[9] It appears, therefore, that the origin of the English Baptists, as a distinct sect, is to be found amongst the Baptist refugees who were driven from the Netherlands.

The Lollards had prepared the way for the rapid spread of the principles of these Dutch Christians, and since 1535 Baptist witnesses for the truth have stood firmly on British soil, either as individuals or as organized churches. By 1536 their doctrines had so spread amongst English folk that a Church Convocation denounced them by name, requiring the people to repudiate their principles and practices, 'as detestable heresies and utterly to be condemned.' Dr. Wall, in recording this proceeding, says: 'Some people in England began to speak very irreverently and mockingly about some of the ceremonies of baptism then in use;' and he gives a catalogue of 'profane sayings that began to be handed about among some people,' as follows: 'That it is as lawful to christen a child in a tub of water at home, or in a ditch by the way, as in a stone font in a church.' Custom then immersed the child in the consecrated 'font,' not in unhallowed streams. Another 'profane saying' was: 'That the hallowed oil is no better than the Bishop of Rome's grease or butter.' Again: 'That the holy-water is more savory to make sauce with than the other (water), because it is mixed with salt; which is also a very good medicine for a horse with a galled back; yea, if there be put an onion thereto, it is a good sauce for a giblet of mutton.' This kind-hearted divine resented such unreverential reflections of the English Anti-pedobaptists, and so did the king and Convocation. Still the good doctor thought that this threw no dishonor on infant baptism, but Henry and the Convocation saw disdain for the thing itself, in contempt for the ceremonies which attended it, and proceeded to read the nation a lecture, in six particulars. They declared baptism necessary to eternal life, that it belongs to infants, and makes them sons of God; that, being born in original sin, they cannot be saved but by the grace of baptism, etc. Then they discover the real *animus* of their action with their alarm for the mischief on the subject which the Baptists had already wrought in the public mind. They say to all Englishmen 'that they ought to refute and take all the Anabaptists' and Pelagians' opinions in this behalf for detestable heresies.' Then Wall cites Fuller out of Stow to prove that in 1538 six Dutch Anabaptists were punished in London, 'four bearing fagots at Paul's Cross, and two being burnt in Smithfield.' Again quoting from Fuller, he writes: 'This year the name of this sect first appears in our English chronicles,' and from Fox, that ten Dutch 'Anabaptists' were put to death in England in 1535, a year before these utterances of Convocation. The sixth article condemns this heresy in '*other men*,' who were not of these prescribed bodies, alluding to the English Baptist infection; for the lower house complained to the upper, in its 'catalogue of some errors that began to be handed about among some people,' and which the united body sharply rebuked. The king published a proclamation, 1538, condemning all Baptist books; an Act of Grace was passed the same year from the benefits of which the Baptists were excepted, and the

Bishops of the Southern Province issued a commission to seek out and punish them. Brand reports that in 1539 thirty-one 'Anabaptists' fled from England and were slaughtered at Delft, Holland; the men were beheaded and the women drowned.

Froude mentions a number who were put to death for 'being faithful to their conscience,' and Stow tells us of four being burnt in Smithfield. These facts indicate their growing strength at that time. In a royal proclamation, issued in 1540, some of their so-called errors are thus enumerated, namely: 'That infants ought not to be baptized, and that it is not lawful for a Christian man to bear office or rule in the commonwealth.' But persecution only promoted their increase. Strype tells us that about 1548 'Anabaptist' congregations had been gathered at Bocking and Feversham, amongst whom are many English names. Sixty of their members were arrested; and Hart, Middleton, Coal and Brodbridge, four of their ministers, were made prisoners. Middleton was martyred in the reign of Edward, and when Archbishop Cranmer threatened him with death he replied: 'Reverend sir, pass what sentence you think fit upon us. But that you may not say that you were not forewarned, I testify that your turn may be next;' and twenty years afterwards his expectation was realized. Hooper wrote to his friend, Bullinger, 1549, that he was lecturing twice a day to great crowds, but that the 'Anabaptists' flocked to the place and gave him much trouble, another indication that these hearers of his were English born. And last of all, Latimer, in preaching before Edward VI., March 29, 1549, told the king that he had heard of many of them in the realm, of five hundred in one town, and that in many places they had been burnt, dying cheerfully for their faith, coolly adding: 'Well, let them go.'

The literature of the times is in keeping with these statements. In 1548 John Vernon translated and published Bullinger's 'Holesome Antidote Against the Pestilent Sect of the Anabaptists.' William Turner, a physician, 1551, issued a treatise called a 'Triacle' (*remedy*) 'against the poyson lately stirred up agayn by the furious Secte of the Anabaptists.' Philpots, in his sixth examination before Lord Riche, 1555, told him that every heretic would have a church to himself, 'as Joan of Kent and the Anabaptists.' The phrase 'lately stirred up *agayn*,' in the title of Turner's book, must have reference in the past, to the Act of Convocation and to the Commission of 1538, when Cranmer and eight others were appointed to persecute them with all severity. Henry had required every English justice to enforce the laws against them, and thus to scour the whole realm. This stringency was not needed to hunt out a few exiled foreigners in London, Essex and Norfolk. Everywhere there was a growing neglect of infant baptism. One of Bishop Ridley's warrants of search, in 1550, demanded, 'whether any speaketh against baptism of infants.' Even Hooper was suspected on that question. Before he was nominated for the bishopric he held: 'We may not doubt of the salvation of the infants of Christians that die before they be christened;' showing that such opinions were no bar to public confidence. But Ridley had a mania for infant baptism, and in 1553 ordered that all the children in his diocese 'be christened by the priest;' and in his 'Declaration of the Lord's Supper' we find him talking such superstition as this: 'The bread indeed, sacramentally, is changed into the body of Christ, as the water in baptism is sacramentally changed into the fountain of regeneration, and yet the material substance thereof remaineth all one, as was before.' A congregation of Baptists was found in London in 1575, twenty-seven of whom were imprisoned, and two burnt in Smithfield; and the sect can be traced by their blood all through the century, aided by the light of Burnet, Fuller and Fox.

Tradition connects the name of ANNE ASKEW with the Baptists. She was a thorough Protestant, a firm friend of Joan Boucher, and a helper to her in circulating the Bible and other religious books privately in the palace. She was the youngest daughter of Sir William Askew, was thoroughly educated, being as delicate and gentle a spirit as ever ascended from Smithfield to paradise. She was intimate with Queen Catharine Parr, and so fell a victim to Bishop Gardiner's craft, he expecting to attaint her majesty of heresy through Anne, who was but four and twenty years of age. Much of her time, day and night, was spent in prayer; she reveled in the freshness of the Gospel, and her frank, meek, unsuspecting simplicity won the queen's heart. She was arrested and thrown into the Tower on the charge that she rejected the mass. There she was put to the rack, but her clear and calm mind would neither criminate herself nor Catharine. Hence, when Bishop Gardiner and Chancellor Wriothesley saw that their policy was to be thwarted, the chancellor demanded that Sir Anthony Knevett should torment her further. This the lieutenant of the Tower refused, when Wriothesley threw off his gown, and drew the rack so severely that he almost tore her body to pieces. She endured this with such firm trust in God and such lofty courage that she seems like an angel of light amongst her tormentors. She had various hearings, in which her harmless wit overpowered her foes. The lord mayor demanded of her: 'Sayest thou that the priests cannot make the body of Christ?' She answered: 'I say so, my lord; for I have read that God made man, but that man can make God I have never yet read.' *Qu.* 'What if a mouse eat of the bread after the consecration? What shall become of the mouse, thou foolish woman?' *Ans.* 'What shall become of her say you, my lord?' He replied: 'I say that that mouse is damned!' She artlessly rejoined, to his lordship's chagrin: 'Alack, poor mouse!' When condemned to be burnt, her torture forbade her to walk to the stake, and she was carried in a chair. There a written pardon was offered to her from the king if she would recant. She calmly turned her eyes away, and fell in the flames a sacrifice to Jesus, 1546, before she was five and twenty. Shaxton, the apostate, preached at her burning, and a disgusting scene followed. The chancellor, the Duke of Norfolk, the Earl of Bedford, the lord mayor, and other

BURNING OF ANNE ASKEW AND OTHERS AT SMITHFIELD.

dignitaries feasted their eyes on her and the three who perished with her, seated on a bench under the shadow of St. Bartholomew's church. A rumor spread that benevolent hands had put gun-powder about the martyrs to shorten their misery. These cravens were filled with terror for their own safety, lest the powder should cast the fagots where they sat. They could gloat upon the heroine, whose love for Christ was reducing her to ashes, but sat trembling lest the brands should touch them. Jesus, rising from his throne, welcomed her to a security which these selfish cowards could never disturb again.

Four years afterwards, under Edward VI., we have the fearful martyrdom of JOAN BOUCHER, of Kent, probably of Eythorne, near Canterbury, where there was a Baptist assembly. She was a lady of note, possessing large wealth, and was well known at the palace in the days of Henry and Edward. With her friend Anne Askew she was devoted to the study and circulation of Tyndale's translation, which had been printed at Cologne, 1534. Strype says that she carried copies of this prohibited book under her clothing on her visits to the court; and very likely to the prisons also, which she often visited, using her wealth to relieve those who suffered for Jesus' sake. She was charged with various heresies, and was arrested, May, 1549. Amongst other things, she denied that the Virgin Mary was sinless by nature, insisting that like other women she needed to rejoice 'in God her Saviour,' as she herself said. Joan neither denied the proper humanity of Jesus nor that he was Mary's son. But she held, with many others of her day, that he became man of her 'faith,' not of her flesh, lest he should inherit her sinful taint; yet, she believed in Christ's miraculous incarnation, and in him as 'that holy thing' born of Mary. Her idea was a mere speculation, or, as Vaughn expresses it, 'a subtle fancy,' not in itself half so weak as the notion of Mary's own immaculate conception, manufactured to meet the conclusion which Joan wished to avoid, namely, the peccability of Christ's humanity. On this frivolous quiddity was this noble woman kept a year and a half under the hair-splitting batteries of Cranmer, Ridley, Whitehead, Hutchinson, Cecil, Lord Chancellor Riche, and others of the Protestant Inquisition; more is the pity that they had no better business. She was examined and cross-examined, entreated and threatened, all to no purpose. Neal, Burnet and Philpot have affected to treat her as 'weak,' 'vain' and 'fanatic,' charges which their manliness had better have applied to her learned tormentors; for her recorded examinations show more of these infirmities in them than in her. They did not evince one thoroughly amiable trait in the whole transaction, while she displayed an acute and powerful mind, moved by a warm and impulsive heart.

True, she rejected their notion of Mary's sinlessness and demanded Scripture for their teaching, while they had none to give; then, she gave none for her own speculations, and that was about all of consequence between them, on this issue. The whole farce was a small and mean business for men of their cast and cloth, and if she were an empty-headed woman, as they pretended, they honored themselves but little in spending eighteen months of their time and labor on her figment, for she well held her own with the whole learned and malignant crowd of them. Lord Riche says, that he kept her at his own house for 'a fortnight,' and had Cranmer and Ridley visit and reason with her daily. Ridley bent all his eloquence upon her mind, but could not shake her convictions. Her judges called her every thing but the lady which her parentage, position and character demanded, and they felt terribly grieved when her insulted patience told them the plain truth, in more polite language than their own. 'Marry,' said she, 'it is a goodly matter to consider your ignorance. It is not long ago since you burned Anne Askew for a piece of bread, and yet you came yourselves soon after to believe and profess the same doctrine for which you burned her. And now, forsooth, you will burn me for a piece of flesh, and in the end you will come to believe this also.' Did Thomas Cranmer and Nicholas Ridley remember her true words in the flames, and did they help to light them through the fire? Fox tried hard to save her, and to induce John Rogers to help him. Rogers refused, thought that she ought to be burnt, and spoke lightly of death by burning, but then he did not dream of being chained to the stake himself. Fox, pitying her, seized the hand of his friend Rogers and replied: 'Well, it may so happen that you yourself will have your hands full of this mild burning.' Whether he had or not, his poor wife proved the force of Fox's prophetic apprehension when she stood with her eight children and saw her husband consumed to ashes, five years later.

Joan Boucher suffered amongst the fagots, May 2, 1550, to the eternal disgrace of all concerned. Common decency might have spared her the mockery of having Bishop Scorey preach to her while at the stake and vilify her there, under pretense of pious exhortation. Yet, possibly, her last act did him a service which he much needed, and which had never been done to him before. Her sermon to him is immortal, while his to her has long since been forgotten. Listening to him just as her soul ascended to heaven in the flame, she said in reply: 'You lie like a rogue. Go read the Scriptures!' Much needless ink has been shed on an attempt to show that Edward stained her death-warrant with tears when he signed it, because Cranmer clamored for her life. But Hallam long since said that this royal tear-scene should be dropped from history, though detailed by Burnet. And the young Tudor well sustains Hallam from his private journal, which is any thing but tearful. With his own hand he wrote: 'Joan Boucher, otherwise called Joan of Kent, was burnt for holding that Christ was not incarnate of the Virgin Mary, being condemned the year previous, but kept in hope of conversion; and the 30th of April the Bishop of London and the Bishop of Ely were to persuade her, but she withstood them and reviled the preacher that preached at her death.' So much for his Journal, but there is no proof that Edward signed her death-warrant at all. This was seldom done by the monarch, and in her case it was issued by the Council to the Lord Chancellor. On the authority of Bruce, editor of the works of Hutchinson, Parker Society edition, the following is taken from a minute of the Council itself, dated April 27, 1550. 'A warrant to the L. Chancellor to make out a writt to the shireff of London for the execuçon of Johan of Kent, condempned to be burned for certein detestable opinions of heresie.' [10]

HENDRICK TERWOORT, a Fleming by birth, and of a fine mind, another Baptist martyr of note, was burned in Smithfield, June 22, 1575. He was but five and twenty, had rejected infant baptism, and held that a Christian should not make oath or bear arms. While in prison he wrote a Confession of Faith, in which he said: 'We must abstain from willful sins if we would be saved, namely, from adultery, fornication, witchcraft, sedition, bloodshed, cursing and stealing, . . . hatred and envy. They who do such things shall not possess the kingdom of God.' He also set forth that the 'Anabaptists' 'believe and confess that magistrates are set and ordained of God, to punish the evil and protect the good,' that they pray for them and are subject to them in every good work, and that they revere the 'gracious queen' as a sovereign. He sent a copy to Elizabeth, but her heart was set against him and his people, as hard as the nether millstone, and this young son of God must die because he would not make his conscience her footstool. Bishops Laud and Whitgift hated him and the Baptists, the latter dealing in this heartless slander: 'They give honor and reverence to none in authority, they seek the overthrow of commonwealths and states of government, they are full of pride and contempt, their whole interest is schismatic and to be free from all laws, to live as they list; they feign an austerity of life and manners, and are great hypocrites.' When he comes to the dangerous method of specification, he virtually admits his slander. He berates them for complaining: 'That their mouths are stopped, not by God's word, but by the authority of the magistrate. They assert that the civil magistrate has no authority in ecclesiastical matters, and ought not to meddle in cases of religion and faith, and that no man ought to be compelled to faith and religion; and lastly, they complain much of persecution, and brag that they defend their cause not with words only, but by the shedding of their blood.' [11]

Terwoort was not an English subject, but, persecuted in his own land for his love to Christ, he fled and asked protection of a Protestant queen, the head of the English Church, and she roasted him alive for his misplaced confidence. Nor was his a singular case. Bishop Jewel complains of a 'large and unauspicious crop of Anabaptists' in Elizabeth's reign, and she not only ordered them out of her kingdom, but in good earnest kindled the fires to burn them. Sir James Mackintosh says that no Catholic was martyred in Edward's reign, and happy had it been could he have written that the virgin Queen also avoided a Baptist holocaust. Marsden thinks that the Baptists were the most numerous dissenters from the Established Church in her reign, and Camden affirms that she insisted on their leaving the kingdom on pain of imprisonment and confiscation of property. Yet even this did not satisfy her implacable hate, as a real Tudor. She pursued them more and more, until they were driven in all directions, some being put to death; but the large part of them fled to Holland, where at this time they enjoyed more toleration. Dr. Some, however, an English clergyman of note in his day, informs us that they had several secret 'conventicles' in London, and that several of their ministers had been educated at the universities. In 1589, he wrote a treatise, attacking them and their faith. His charges against the Baptists were: That they insisted on maintaining all ministers of the Gospel by the voluntary contributions of the people; that the civil power has no right to make and impose ecclesiastical laws; that the people have the right to choose their own pastors; that the High Commission Court was an anti-Christian usurpation; that those who are qualified to preach ought not to be hindered by the civil power; that though the Lord's Prayer is a rule and foundation of petition, it is not to be used as a form, for no form of prayer should be bound on the Church; that the baptism of the Church of Rome is invalid; that a Gospel constitution and discipline are essential to a true Church; and that the worship of God in 'the Church of England is, in many things, defective. For these views they were accounted 'heretics,' and suffered so severely that from 1590 to 1630 we find but slight trace of Baptists in England.

About 1579 Archbishop Sandys declared both of the Brownists and Baptists: 'It is the property of froward sectaries, whose inventions cannot abide the light, to make obscure conventicles,' and he would compel them to attend the Established Church. He was the more disturbed because so many 'heretical' exiles from Holland had sought refuge in England, for it is said that in 1571 there were nearly 4,000 Dutch and other foreigners in Norwich alone, many of them Dutch Baptists, from whom Weingarten thinks that Brown borrowed his best ideas of a Gospel Church. Robert Brown, chaplain to the Duke of Norfolk, and Robert Harrison, the master of a grammar school, were Puritans, and went to Norwich in 1580. There they mingled with these exiles, and formed an independent Church, but the bishops had no rest till Brown was banished. He, with Harrison and about fifty others, in 1581, fled to Middleburg, in Zealand, and formed a Church, which became extinct because of divisions, and Brown returned to the Church of England. Elizabeth was especially set against the Separatists, and in 1597, Francis Johnson, pastor of their Church in London, with some of his flock, escaped to Amsterdam. On the accession of James I., 1603, the four sects of England were, the Roman Catholic, the Church of England, divided into the Puritans, who conformed in some things, and others who conformed in all, the Brownists, afterwards known as Separatists and Independents, and a few Baptists, who were disowned of all. The Gospel seed sown by Brown in his own country took root, and notwithstanding his return to the English Church, Sir Walter Raleigh said, in 1592, that there were 20,000 Brownists in England. John Robinson, a firmer and more steady mind, went to Norwich, then to Scrooby, 1600–1604, cast the Brownists in a healthier mold, and they became known as Independents.

CHAPTER III.

BRITISH BAPTISTS—JOHN SMYTH—COMMONWEALTH.

REV. JOHN SMYTH, educated at Cambridge, became vicar of Gainsborough, Lincolnshire, and a determined foe of the Separatists. After examining their sentiments for 'nine months,' however, he renounced episcopacy as unscriptural and was cast into the Marshalsea Prison, Southwark, but being liberated, he became pastor of the Separatist Church at Gainsborough in 1602. William Brewster was a Separatist at Gainsborough, but removed to Scrooby near Bawtry, where Clifton became pastor, with Robinson as assistant. Both these little flocks, however, were driven from their homes, Smyth fleeing to Amsterdam, probably in 1606, where he joined Johnson. Clifton and Robinson followed in 1608, settling first at Amsterdam, then at Leyden. In 1620 a portion of the Church at Leyden migrated to Plymouth, New England, with Brewster as elder, and formed the first Congregational Church in America. On arriving in Amsterdam, Smyth at first united with the 'ancient' English Separatist Church there, in charge of Johnson, with Ainsworth as teacher. At that time the Separatists of Amsterdam were in warm controversy on the true nature of a visible Church. Smyth published a work on the fallen Church, entitled 'The Character of the Beast,' and a tractate of seventy-one pages, against infant baptism and in favor of believer's baptism. For this he was disfellowshiped by the first Church, his former friends charging him with open war against God's covenant, and the murder of the souls of babes and sucklings, by depriving them of the visible seal of salvation.

This led Smyth, Helwys, Morton and thirty-six others to form a new Church which should practice believer's baptism and reject infant baptism. Finding themselves unbaptized, they were in a strait. They were on good terms with the Dutch Baptists, but would not receive their baptism, lest this should recognize them as a true Church; for they believed that the true Churches of Christ had perished. Besides, Smyth did not believe with them in the unlawfulness of a Christian to serve as a magistrate, nor on the freedom of the will and the distinctive points of Calvinism, he being an Arminian, which points he considered vital. He believed that the Apostolical Church model was lost, and determined on its recovery. He renounced the figment of a historical, apostolic succession, insisting that where two or three organize according to the teachings of the New Testament, they form as true a Church of Christ as that of Jerusalem, though they stand alone in the earth. With the design of restoring this pattern, he baptized himself on his faith in Christ in 1608, then baptized Thomas Helwys with about forty others, and so formed a new Church in Amsterdam. In most things this body was Baptist, as that term is now used, with some difference. This is established by their four extant forms, of what is in substance, one confession of faith. Two of these were written by Smyth and are signed by others, and the other two came from the same company, probably under the lead of Helwys. Their theology is Arminian, they claim that the Church is composed of baptized believers only, that 'only the baptized are to taste of the Lord's Supper,' and that the magistrates shall not, by virtue of their office, meddle with matters of conscience in religion.

Smyth and his congregation met in a large bakery for a time, but he soon saw his mistake in his hasty Se-baptism, and offered to join the Dutch congregation of Baptists known as 'Waterlanders,' under the pastoral charge of Lubberts Gerrits. Part of his congregation, under the leadership of Helwys, would not unite with Smyth in this movement, but excluded him from their fellowship and warned the Dutch Church not to receive him. Soon after this Smyth died, August, 1612, and the Dutch body recognized his company. Meanwhile the question had arisen with Helwys and his followers whether they were doing right by remaining in Holland, to avoid persecution in England, and at the peril of their lives they had returned to London, in 1611, and formed the first general Baptist Church there, 1612–14. Little is known of its history beyond the general statement that the Dutch Baptists of London rallied around Helwys and John Morton, his successor, that it was located in Newgate, and that in 1626 it numbered one hundred and fifty persons. Helwys published a work defending their course in braving persecution, and probably translated a Dutch treatise on baptism in 1618. No account is given of his death, but Taylor dates it at 'about' 1623. Masson says, in his 'Life of Milton,' 'This obscure Baptist congregation seems to have become the depository for all England of the absolute principle of liberty of conscience expressed in the Amsterdam Confession as distinct from the more stinted principle advocated by the general body of the Independents. Not only did Helwisse's folks differ from the Independents generally on the subject of infant baptism and *dipping;* they differed also on the power of the magistrate in matters of belief and conscience. It was, in short, from this little dingy meeting-house, somewhere in Old London, that there flashed out first in England the absolute doctrine of religious liberty.'

So far as is known, the Amsterdam Confession of the Baptists is the first which laid down the full principle of religious freedom, after the Swiss Confession of 1527. It is absolutely the first now known to take positive ground in favor of the salvation of all infants who die in infancy, from the time that Augustine taught the detestable doctrine that unbaptized infants who die are not admitted into heaven. Wickliff held that they are saved without baptism, but his doctrine was not formulated by a Christian body. Also, in defining the limits of Church and State, they came down to those foundation principles which the Independents had not reached. Ainsworth's Confession said: 'The government should protect true believers, strengthen the proper administration of the true worship, punish transgressors, and uproot false worship.' Helwys understood things better. He sent a copy of his work on religious liberty with a letter to James I., in which he boldly says: 'The king is a mortal man and not God, therefore hath no power over the immortal souls of his subjects, to make laws and ordinances for them, and to set spiritual lords over them. If the king has authority to make spiritual lords and laws, then he is an immortal God, and not a mortal man.' No English king had heard such words before. The Independents were far in advance of the Puritans and the Presbyterians on this subject; but even Johnson said: 'Princes may and ought to abolish all false worship, and to establish the true worship and ministry appointed by God in his word, commanding and compelling their subjects to come into and practice none other than this.' The Amsterdam Baptist Confession bravely said: 'The magistrate is not, by virtue of his office, to meddle with religion or matters of conscience, to force and compel men to this or that form of religion or doctrine, but to leave the Christian religion free to every man's conscience, and to handle only civil transgressors, for Christ is the only King and Lawgiver of the Church and conscience.'

When the Brownists left the English State Church, they objected to its hierarchy, liturgy, constitution and government, as antichristian. Smyth, therefore, broke with them on the issue that if that Church was apostate, as a daughter of Rome, then its clergy were not qualified to administer Christ's ordinances. The Brownists, however, considered them valid, and called the English Church their 'mother,' while they denounced her as 'harlot' and 'Babylon;' but Smyth, having been christened in her pale, concluded that he was yet unbaptized. Bishop Hall caught this point keenly, and was severe on the Brownists when he opposed Smyth. He wrote:

'You that cannot abide a false Church, why do you content yourselves with a false sacrament? especially since our Church, not being yet gathered to Christ, is no Church, and therefore her baptism a nullity! . . . He (Smyth) tells you true; your station is unsafe; either you must forward to him, or back to us. . . . You must go forward to Anabaptism, or come back to us. All your rabbins cannot answer that charge of your rebaptized brother. . . . If our baptism be good, then is our constitution good. . . . What need you to surfeit of another man's trencher? . . . Show you me where the Apostles baptized in a *bason!*'

Smyth having rejected infant baptism also on its merits as a human institution, Ainsworth said, in 1609, that he had gone 'over to the abomination of the Anabaptists.' Bishop Hall wrote the above words in 1610, calling him then 'your rebaptized brother,' which indicates that he left the Brownists about 1608. His enemies have represented him as hair-brained, fickle and fond of novelty. But Schaff-Herzog does him the justice to say that: 'Seized by the time-spirit, he was restless, fervid, earnest and thoroughgoing. . . . A man of incorruptible simplicity, beautiful humility, glowing charity, a fair scholar and a good preacher.' His writings show that he thirsted for the truth; and several times he shifted his positions before he felt sure that he stood on solid ground, a fact creditable to his convictions and moral courage. As to his Se-baptism the following things seem clear, namely:

1. *That he did baptize himself when he cast aside his infant baptism.* He believed that no man had a pure baptism or could administer the same, not only because of the corruption of baptism, as then practiced, but because of moral defection in all the Churches. This was no new doctrine. The Donatists held that the validity of baptism was affected by the bad life of the administrator; and Cyprian asks: 'Who can consecrate water who is himself unholy, and has not the Holy Spirit?' But Smyth was feeling his way far back beyond this to the Gospel ground, that the validity of baptism has no regard to the administrator, as it is governed by the faith of the candidate. He denied the need of all visible succession in the ministry and ordinances, and yet his sincere but impulsive mind was held in secret thralldom to this subtility. He denied that the fable of antiquity is an attribute of a true Church, and yet he would found a new line of baptizers, to give purity to the ordinance in the future. He evidently reasoned and decided thus: 'Let the fallen Churches stand alone. They have turned Christ's ordinance out of doors and established their own, so I cut loose from them and throw myself directly into the hands of God. I take the last method left of honoring him, and he knows my singleness of heart. My infant baptism was meaningless, a pious fraud practiced upon me, and its alleged blessings are mere nursery pictures. They have thrown shame on the Gospel, blunted my conviction of truth, and put my personal faith in Christ to a deep blush. Hence I will cut the last thread that binds me to "the defection of Antichrist."' Logic took him to that point, but love to Christ carried him further, and he resolved to offer himself to Christ in baptism, come what might, and he baptized himself, in obedience to an imperative sense of duty. There is a legend of Thekla, the unbaptized martyr, that when led out to the wild beasts, she threw herself into a trench full of water, and shouted, with joy: 'In the name of Jesus Christ, I am baptized on my last day!' Without her lot, Smyth possessed the same spirit. He denied the arrogance that salvation is lodged in ordinances, that God has given them into the keeping of any body of men to dispense, rejecting whom they please. Baptism was to him a right and privilege from God, and because it had been forced upon him as a child, the extreme view of the Church now forced him, as he believed, to throw aside all human intervention in the matter. Yet in his Confession he explicitly expresses his faith in an accredited ministry, a regenerate body, but he could not trace it through one century, not to say sixteen. He concluded, therefore, that it made no matter whether he, being unbaptized, baptized himself, or another unbaptized man baptized him. This was his Puritan mode of cutting

himself adrift from the last tie of popery in Protestantism. The result was the same, so far as baptismal succession was concerned, whether he baptized himself or was baptized by an unbaptized person. His entire being was impelled by that sentiment, and the quicksilver no more changes the weather, than eccentricity led him to Se-baptism.

However mistaken he was in his reasoning, he knew, as a matter of fact, that nearly half the so-called countries of the world are unable to tell by record whether the Gospel was first preached to them by ministers or laymen, much less can their personal baptisms be traced. He could not tell whether the man who brought it to the British Isles was himself baptized, or if so, who baptized him, where, when or how. Smyth held his own consecration to Christ in baptism acceptable to Christ, and he was better satisfied with it himself, than he had ever been with his infant baptism, of which others had told him. These being his motives to Se-baptism, we may now notice that:

2. *Its proof is found in his own uncontradicted statements and those of his contemporaries.* He defended his act by claiming that when succession is broken off, men are not bound to join fallen Churches: 'But may, being as yet unbaptized, baptize themselves, AS WE DID, and proceed to build churches themselves.' When Clifton asked him by what right he baptized himself, he replied: 'As you, when there was not a true Church in the world, took upon you to set up a true Church. . . . Seeing, when all Christ's visible ordinances are lost, then two men joining together may make a Church, as you say, why may they not baptize, seeing they cannot enjoin unto Christ but by baptism? . . . Each of them unbaptized, hath power to assume baptism *each for himself*, with others in communion.' Barebone charges against the Baptists, 1642, that they baptized themselves by the 'Way of new baptizing lately begun;' they have no warrant from heaven, he argues, 'As had John the Baptist, to set up baptism themselves,' nor to baptize themselves and others. In Clifton's 'Plea for Infants,' 1610, he calls upon Smyth to bring 'Warrant from the Scripture, that you being unbaptized may baptize yourself. . . . Resolve me, that you can baptize yourself into the Church, being out of it, yea, and where there was no Church.' In the same year, 'J. H.' published a book against Smyth, in which he says: 'Tell me one thing, Maister Smyth, by what rule baptized you yourself? . . . It was wonder you would not receive your baptism from the Dutch Anabaptists, but you will be holier than all.' Ainsworth, Robinson, Bernard and others, charge Smyth with being a Se-Baptist (self-Baptist), and he took the greatest pains to defend his own act as absolutely necessary.

3. *Whether he dipped himself is not so clear, but all the circumstances, with a few statements of that day, imply that he did.* Those who wrote against the Baptists after 1640 make no distinction on the matter of immersion between the Baptists of that period and those who had continued down from 1610, nor report any change amongst them, from affusion or perfusion to dipping. On the contrary,

they speak of them as one stock from Smyth downward. Sometimes they speak of him as the father of English 'Anabaptism,' and uniformly, in contempt, they call them 'Dippers.' Barebone says in his Discourse: 'They want a Dipper, that had authority from heaven as had John, whom they please to call a Dipper.' Bishop Hall's remark, 1610, when speaking of Smyth as 'your rebaptized brother,' is very significant. In scornful sarcasm he demands of the Brownists, who used affusion: 'Show me where the Apostles baptized in a *bason!*' 'What need you to surfeit of another man's trencher?' The very point of his thrust implies that Smyth had dipped himself, contrary to their practice, and that he had Apostolic authority for dipping as baptism. It further implies that the meat on Smyth's 'trencher' had nauseated them, because, like the Apostles, he had discarded the 'bason.' Featley, in what Orme calls his 'ridiculous book,' 'The Dippers Dipt over Head and Ears,' complains of the 'new leaven,' because they dipped, and says: 'It cannot be proved that any of the ancient Anabaptists maintained any such position, there being three ways of baptizing, either by dipping, or washing, or sprinkling.'[1] But in this declaration he contradicts himself several times, as we shall see. He clearly states their then current practice when he says, that the sick cannot, 'After the manner of the Anabaptists, be carried to rivers or wells, and there be dipt and plunged in them.' He adds, that they held 'Weekly Conventicles, rebaptized hundreds of men and women together in the twilight in rivulets, and some arms of the Thames and elsewhere, dipping them over head and ears.' He bitterly complains that they 'Flock in great multitudes to their Jordans, and both sexes enter the river, and are dipped after *their manner*;' and that they had followed these terrible practices 'neere the place of my residence for more than twenty years.' He wrote this Jan. 10, 1644, which would carry him back to 1624, at least. But he never accuses the English Baptists of substituting dipping for some other practice which they had previously followed. He gives not one hint that in England they had ever been any thing else but 'Dippers,' an unaccountable silence, if they had practiced something else there within the previous fifty years.

Directly to the contrary, his whole book assumes that the Baptists of his day were the veritable descendants of the Münster men. He calls Storke 'The father of the Anabaptists of *our age*,' and a 'blockhead' from whom 'the chiefs flew into England,' when he was hewn down in Germany; and makes Knipperdolling their 'Patriarch.' He alleges that they 'stript themselves stark naked when they flock to their Jordans to be dipt,' and is delighted to tell us, on the authority of Gastius, that at Vienna 'Many Anabaptists were so tied together in chains, that they drew the other after them into the river, wherein they were suffocated.' This, he thought, the proper punishment for their sin, and bewails that their successors were treated more leniently in England. His words are: 'They who drew others into the whirlpool of error, by constraint drew one another into the river to be drowned; and they who profaned baptism by a *second dipping*, rue it by a third immersion. But the punishment of these Catabaptists we leave to them who have the legislative power in their hands; who, though by present connivance they may seem to give them line, yet no doubt it is that they may more entangle themselves, and more easily be caught.' He clearly intends us to understand that these Continental Baptists had been immersed first as children, second on their faith, which 'profaned' the first, and entitled them to drowning in a 'third immersion.' He says that this 'Anabaptist' fire was subdued under the reigns of James and Elizabeth, but it had revived again from 'the ashes.' Amongst the 'six things' which he charges as peculiar to the sect, the first is: 'That none are rightly baptized' but those who are dipped, or as he loves to express it, those who 'Go into the water, and there be dipt over head and ears;' and he fails to hint that the English Baptists had ever done otherwise, when baptizing. Wilson's 'History of Dissenting Churches' (i. p. 29, 30) says of Smyth:

'He saw grounds to consider immersion as the true and only meaning of the word baptism, and that it should be administered to those alone who were capable of professing their faith in Christ. The absurdity of Smyth's conduct appeared in nothing more conspicuously than in this: That not choosing to apply to the German Baptists, and wanting a proper administrator, he baptized himself, which procured him to be called a Se-baptist. Crosby, indeed, has taken great pains to vindicate him from this charge, though it seems with little success. His principles and conduct soon drew upon him an host of opponents, the chief of whom were Johnson, Ainsworth, Robinson, Jessop and Clifton. The controversy begun in 1606, about the time Smyth settled in Amsterdam. Soon afterward he removed with his followers to Leyden, where he continued to publish various books in defense of his opinions.'

Neal says that he 'Settled with his disciples at Ley, where being at a loss for a proper administrator of the ordinance of baptism, he *plunged* himself, and then performed the ceremony upon others.'[2] In Smyth's case, it is nothing to the purpose whether the Mennonites, Waterlanders, or those 'Anabaptists' called 'Aspersi' used affusion or not, as he repudiated them all. There is not a particle of evidence that he affused himself, and it is a cheap caricature to imagine that he disrobed himself, walked into a stream, then lifted handfuls of water, pouring then liberally upon his own head, shoulders and chest. We have the same reason for believing that he immersed Helwys, as that he dipped himself. Masson writes: 'Helwisse's folk differed from the Independents generally on the subject of infant baptism and dipping.' And as he thinks that Busher was a member of that 'congregation' in 1614, the man who described a baptized person as one 'dipped for dead in the water,' the fair inference is carried that the first General Baptist Church of London was composed of immersed 'folk.'

Notwithstanding that Edward Wightman, a Baptist of Burton-on-Trent, had been burnt at Lichfield, April 11th, 1611, and that persecution of his brethren continued without martyrdom, they had so increased in 1626 that they had eleven General Baptist Churches in England: which, as Featley sourly says, had increased to forty-seven of various sorts in 1644. Some claim that a Particular Baptist

Church was formed at Shrewsbury in 1627, and another at Bickenhall, near Taunton, in 1630; but it is more likely that the first of this order was established by John Spilsbury at Wapping in 1633. These terms originated in the fact that the Arminian Baptists held to a general and the Calvinistic Baptists to a particular atonement; hence they adopted these titles.

Spilsbury's Church came into existence on this wise. In 1616 the first congregation of Independents had been gathered in London, under the pastoral care of Henry Jacob, who was succeeded by John Lathrop. A number of this society came to reject infant baptism and were permitted to form a distinct Church, September 12, 1633, with Spilsbury for their pastor; and, according to Lord Selborn, in the St. Mary's Chapel case, Norwich, for a number of years after its formation it was a Strict Communion body, so far as the Supper was concerned. Crosby says that 'most or all of these received a new baptism.' In 1638 William Kiffin, Thomas Wilson and others, left Lathrop's Independent Church, then under charge of Mr. Jessey, and united with Spilsbury's Church. Wilson, in his 'History of Dissenting Churches,' says that some time after this, disputes arose in Spilsbury's Church on the subject of 'mixed communion,' and Kiffin with others withdrew to form a new Church, Devonshire Square. At page 410 he explains what he means by 'mixed communion;' it was not the reception of unbaptized persons either to membership or the Supper, but 'mixed communion' with unimmersed ministers. His words are: 'In a course of time a controversy arose in that Church on the propriety of admitting persons *to preach* who had not been baptized by immersion. This produced an amicable separation, headed by Mr. Kiffin, who seems to have been averse to the plan of mixed communion, but the two societies kept up a friendly correspondence.' Not only that, but they coöperated in resisting the contumely of their enemies and in building up each other in the faith. By 1643 the Calvinistic Baptist Churches in and about London had increased to seven, while the non-Calvinistic Churches numbered thirty-nine, forty-six in all. The English Calvinistic Churches, together with a French Church of the same faith, eight in all, issued a Confession of Faith in 1643, of fifty articles; not to erect a standard of faith, but to close the mouths of slanderers. Its preface says of their enemies:

'They, finding us out of that common road-way themselves walk, have smote us and taken away our veil, that so we may by them be odious in the eyes of all that behold us, and in the hearts of all that think upon us, which they have done both in pulpit and print, charging us with holding free-will, falling away from grace, denying original sin, disclaiming a magistracy, denying to assist them either in persons or purse in any of their lawful commands, doing acts unseemly in the dispensing the ordinance of baptism, not to be named amongst Christians. All which charges we disclaim as notoriously untrue, though by reason of these calumnies cast upon us, many that fear God are discouraged and forestalled in harboring a good thought, either of us or what we profess, and many that know not God (*are*) encouraged, if they can find the place of our meeting, to get together in clusters to stone us, as looking upon us as a people holding such things as that we are not worthy to live.'

This Confession was signed by sixteen ministers, two from each Church; and amongst them both John Spilsbury and William Kiffin, a significant fact in its bearings on the ground of their after separation. A second edition was published in 1644, and a third in 1646, the last with an appendix by Benjamin Coxe. Edward Barber, the minister of the Church meeting in Bishopsgate Street, had published a treatise in 1641, to prove that 'our Lord Christ ordained dipping.' Now, in this 'Confession,' Art. XXXIII says, that a Church is 'a company of visible saints . . . being baptized into the faith of the Gospel;' and Art. XXXIX, that baptism is 'to be dispensed upon persons professing faith, or that are made disciples, who, upon profession of faith, ought to be baptized, and after to partake of the Lord's Supper.' Article XL defines the manner of baptizing 'to be dipping or plunging the whole body under water.' These articles, signed by Spilsbury as the fifth name and Kiffin as the eleventh, show that these two worthies were entirely agreed as to the question of immersion on a confession of faith in Christ as a prerequisite to the Supper, and that Wilson was right in stating that the disturbing element between them related to 'mixed communion,' but not amongst members of the same Church. They must all be 'dipped under water' on entering the 'company of saints' made 'visible' by this expression of their faith as 'disciples,' and 'after' that 'partake of the Lord's Supper.' Spilsbury and Kiffin being agreed here, as their signatures show, the controversy between them was 'on the propriety of admitting persons to *preach* who had not been baptized by immersion.' Wilson says that Kiffin 'seemed averse' to mixed communion after that stamp, and left amicably, so that their fellowship was not disturbed at all on the subject treated of in the 'Confession,' namely, communion at the Lord's Supper.

A most interesting branch of this history connects the name of Henry Jessey with this period. Henry Jacob continued to serve the Independent Church which he founded in 1616, until 1624, when he removed to America, and was succeeded as pastor by John Lathrop, who also went to America in 1634, and settled first at Scituate and then at Barnstable, Mass. Then Jessey became its supply in 1635, and its pastor in 1637. At one time or another this Church was seriously disturbed on the subject of baptism. Wilson tells us that under Mr. Lathrop's ministry 'some of the society entertained doubts as to the validity of baptism performed by their own minister; and one person who indulged these scruples carried his child to be *re*baptized in the parish church.' This giving offense to several persons, the subject was discussed at a general meeting of the society; when the question was put it was carried in the negative, and resolved by the majority not to make any declaration at present, '*whether or no parish Churches were true Churches.*' This action led to the withdrawal of those 'who were dissatisfied about the lawfulness of infant baptism,' and to the formation of the Calvinistic Baptist Church of 1633, under Spilsbury's ministry. Under the ministry of Jessey others left and united with the Baptists; six persons in 1638, a larger number in 1641, and a greater number still in 1643. These movements created frequent debates in the Independent Church. 'This,' says Wilson, 'put Mr. Jessey upon studying the controversy. The result was that he himself also changed his sentiments. . . . His first conviction was about the *mode* of baptism; and though he continued for two or three years to baptize children, he did it by *immersion*. About the year 1644 the controversy with respect to the *subjects* of baptism was revived in his Church, when several gave up *infant* baptism, and among the rest Mr. Jessey. . . . 1645 he submitted to immersion, which was performed by Mr. Hanserd Knollys.'[3]

It seems that Jessey's Church had become large by 1640, and by 'mutual consent' had divided, 'just half being with Praise-God Barebone, and the other half with Mr. Jessey.' They were in controversy on the subjects and method of baptism, Blunt and Jessey being the leaders of those who had embraced Baptist views, numbering fifty-three, and Barebone the leader of those who remained Pedobaptists. The fact that the eight Churches formulated baptism as a 'dipping or plunging of the whole body under water,' is sufficient to show that they themselves had been organized and had grown up in that order; as well as the declaration in the preface, that they had been accused of 'unseemly acts in dispensing the ordinance of baptism,' namely, by immersing nude persons. If they had not immersed from their origin, they were slandered in the statement that they immersed at all, to say nothing of alleged indecencies, 'not to be named by Christians,' in connection with their immersions. To say that Spilsbury's Church immersed in 1643, but had not practiced dipping from 1633, is to charge that Church with changing the form of its ordinance, and with repelling a slander to which it had never been subjected; for the accusation that it immersed naked persons carried with it the charge of dipping, whether the alleged nudity were true or false. Here, then, we have fifty-three persons, with Jessey at their head, seeking immersion; but they will not go for it to Spilsbury's Church, though, clearly, he had practiced it since 1633. And why? According to the anonymous account attributed to Kiffin, because none had then, May, 1640, 'so practiced in England to professed believers!' and so they must send to Holland to import dipping! What do they mean by this?

We have already seen that the members of Jessey's Independent Church were great sticklers for ministerial regularity, and lodged the validity of baptism very largely in the administrator. Nay, some of his own congregation had refused to acknowledge the authority of John Lathrop to baptize, and one member who believed in infant baptism, whose child Lathrop had baptized, would not accept it as properly done and took his babe to the parish Church to have it baptized over again on the ground of this irregularity; and so sensitive were 'the majority' on the subject that they refused to say whether or not the parish Churches were true Churches. Lathrop had been trained for the Church of England at Cambridge, had received Episcopal ordination, and served in that ministry in Kent; but no matter, having gone over to dissent, some of his own people doubted whether his baptisms were valid! And there are many reasons for believing that this is a similar case, and that these fifty-three members of the same congregation declined to accept immersion from what they considered an unauthorized administrator. They intended to be immersed, but the English Baptists at that time were universally accused of self-baptism, some of them having received their baptism from John Smyth; and while the Baptists denied this with spirit, none of them thought of insisting on a baptismal succession, but argued that any unbaptized Christian could baptize if needful. This point was in hot dispute at the time. The author of 'Persecution for Religion Judged and Condemned,' 1615, labors hard to show that it is not necessary that he who baptizes should be a baptized person. Barclay and others suppose that John Morton, who was with Smyth and Helwys in Amsterdam, was the author of this book. Whether Smyth immersed them or not, it is quite clear that they received no baptism after that which he administered to them. Some time before Smyth's death he frankly retracted his error in baptizing himself and them; therefore Helwys charged him as guilty of 'the sin against the Holy Ghost.' In his 'last book' he shows that Helwys still held that baptism to be valid, and accuses him of unchristianizing all who did not walk to his 'line and level,' even 'upon pain of damnation.' He says: 'If Master Helwys's position be true, that every two or three that see the truth of baptism may begin to baptize, and need not join to former true Churches, where they may have their baptism orderly from ordained ministers, then the order of the primitive Church was order for them and those times only, and this disorder will establish baptism of private persons.' But although Smyth had repudiated this doctrine which he himself had introduced, yet the English Baptists clearly held it at that time, and as clearly the fifty-three refused baptism at their hands because they held them to be irregularly baptized. Evidently Neal regarded the matter in this light. He pronounces Blunt's conduct in going over to Holland to be immersed ' strange and unaccountable;' but suggests this solution of the matter: 'Unless the Dutch Anabaptists could derive this pedigree in an uninterrupted line from the Apostles, the first reviver of this usage must have been unbaptized, and, consequently, not capable of communicating the ordinance to others.'[4] He understood immersion to have been revived in England at that time, but as the 'reviver' was not in the immersionist succession, Jessey's people thought his followers incapable of immersing them. Perkins and others held that if a Turk should be converted, and led others to Christ, he might baptize them, being unbaptized himself. John Robinson had charged that the Baptists of England were unbaptized on the ground that they had not received baptism from any authorized source, having rejected the Church of England as an apostasy. Even the Confession of the Eight Churches seemed to aim at covering the case by that article which says, the 'person designed by Christ to dispense baptism the Scripture holds forth to be a disciple; it being nowhere tied to a particular office or person extraordinarily sent.' How natural it was, then, for these brethren from an Independent Church to conclude that the immersion of the English Baptists being irregular, they not being properly immersed, therefore, that they must send to Holland for a pure baptism through a qualified administrator.

This charge was reiterated with great asperity. In 1691 Collins denies that they received their baptism from John Smyth, pronouncing the allegation 'absolutely untrue.' Yet, even later than that, John Wall persisted in declaring that their baptism was 'Abhorred of all Christians; for they received their baptism from one Mr. Smyth, who baptized himself; one who was cast out of a Church.' Edward Hutchinson, however, 1676, referring to this very case says, that after this godly band of men had resolved to lay aside infant baptism, 'Fears, tremblings and temptations did attend them, lest they should be mistaken. . . . The great objection was the want of an *administrator;* which, as I have heard, was removed by sending certain messengers to Holland, whence they were supplied.'[5] The greater part of the English Baptists looked upon this act as savoring of popery, it looked like seeking a baptismal succession. And the fact, that it ignored their baptism, may account for the use of the above article in the Confession. It was held that the Collegiants of Holland had received their immersion from the Polish Baptists, and when Batte, one of their teachers, had immersed Blunt there, he returned to England in 1641, and immersed Blacklock, one of the fifty-three, and they the rest of that company. But they never immersed the eight Churches; they having been dipped before the fifty-three became Baptists at all; they and their descendants have continued that practice ever since.

The rapid growth of the English Baptists at this time, in influence and numbers, aroused such fiery but strong minds as Thomas Edwards and Dr. Featley amazingly. In the Dedicatory Epistle to his 'Gangræna,' published 1646, he tells Parliament that 'The sects have been growing upon us, even from the first year of your sitting, and have every year increased more and more, things have been bad a great while, but this last year they have grown intolerable.' He speaks of an order of February 16th, 1643, in which Parliament had 'hindered' unordained ministers 'from preaching and dipping,' but says that they were 'bought off and released by some above.' On p. 16 he combats the opinion that the 'army commanders and common soldiers' were Independents. No; 'there would not be found one in six of that way,' for the army was 'made up and commanded of Anabaptism.' He says, on p. 58, that the 'Anabaptists' have 'stirred up the people to embody themselves, and to join in church fellowship, setting up independent government, rebaptizing and dipping many hundreds.' He denounces them on pp. 65, 66 because 'They send forth into several counties in this kingdom, from their Churches in London, as church acts, several emissaries members of their Churches, to preach and spread their errors, to dip, to gather and settle Churches;' yea, 'some of them went into the North as far as York,' where some were rebaptized 'in the river Ouse,' and the water was so hot as if it had been in the middle of summer.' On p. 95, part ii, he declares that Independents in armies, county, city, (were) falling daily to Anabaptists.' On p. 149 he says that they abounded at Hull, Beverley, York and Halifax. On p. 146, he tells Parliament that Oats went into the country from town to town 'dipping many in rivers,' the rich at ten shillings a head, and the poor at two shillings and six pence. Part iii, p. 139, shows him cut to the heart, because the Baptists 'kill tender young persons and ancient, with dipping them all over in rivers, in the depth of winter.' His heart is comforted, however, on p. 194, to be able to say that ' We shall find no Church sounder for doctrine than the Church of Scotland, nor greater enemies, not only against papacy and prelacy, but against Anabaptists.' But as he could not help himself, he nobly proposes, on p. 108, to prove a certain story which he has told, if his opponent will join the Presbyterians in a petition to Parliament for the forbidding of all dipping and rebaptization, and exemplary punishment of all such dippers as Brother Kiffin.' Yet he tells us frankly, on p. 178, that he never saw Denne, Clarkson, Paul Hobson, Lamb, Web, Marshal and many others : 'I know them not so much as by face, having never so much to my knowledge as seen them.'

The Confession of the Eight Churches was issued in the midst of the revolution, which, for the time, overthrew the Stuart monarchy. The issue between king and Parliament was still doubtful, as Marston Moor and Naseby were not yet fought. With great unanimity the Baptists enrolled themselves on the side of the people, and fought bravely for liberty, civil and religious. It has been inferred that Bunyan fought with the Cavaliers; mainly, from his silence on the subject. But at this time he was not a Baptist, and so there is no clear case that any Baptist drew his sword for the king. Their choice is easily explained. They had suffered tyranny too long and hated it too much to fight for a prince who was a tyrant on principle, who had Laud, the bigot and persecutor, for his spiritual adviser. Their patriotism soon won them high honor. Cromwell's son-in-law, Charles Fleetwood, Colonel and Lord-Deputy of Ireland, was a Baptist; as well as Major-General Harrison, who held the confidence of the Protector for so many years, and who owed his advancement to real merit. Lord Clarendon speaks of him as having 'an understanding capable of being trusted in any business,' a man who was ' looked upon as inferior to few after Cromwell and Ireton in the councils of the officers and in the government of the agitators; and there were few men with whom Cromwell more communicated, or upon whom he more depended for the conduct of any thing committed to him.' When the Protector dissolved the Long Parliament, an act which brought odium upon him, above all others he intrusted Harrison with that delicate duty, because of his prudence and integrity. Harrison was also appointed one of the judges to try Charles I. for treason to his people, and he signed the death-warrant. At the time of the trial he held Baptist views, but he and his wife were not baptized until 1657.

A contemporary chronicle informs us that his baptism occurred in the depth of winter, but we know not with what congregation he united.

Harrison became estranged from Cromwell in later years, because he regarded him as too ambitious. Cromwell fearing his military ability and popular influence threw him into prison; and having embraced enthusiastic views concerning the Fifth Monarchy, which Christ was about to set up on earth, he lost caste with the more sober Baptists, although they sympathized with him largely in his estimate of the Protector. Under Charles II., Harrison was executed at Charing Cross for the part he had taken in the death of Charles I., but to the last he justified that act. His execution was a piece of the most vulgar butchery. It occurred November 13th, 1660, and Pepys writes, that he went 'To see Major-General Harrison hanged, drawn and quartered: which was done, he looking as cheerful as any man could be in that condition. He was presently cut down, and his head and heart shown to the people;' and Ludlow adds, that his head was carried on the front of the sled upon which Chief-Justice Coke was drawn to execution. Harrison told his judges that he had no reason to be ashamed of the cause in which he was engaged, nor do his Baptist successors under Victoria blush for him.

MRS. LUCY HUTCHINSON.

Another prominent officer who cherished Baptist sentiments was COLONEL JOHN HUTCHINSON, who must be reckoned amongst the choicest spirits of his times. Lucy, his wife, was in every way worthy of him. She wrote a Memoir of him, which is one of the most charming biographies in English literature, for in point of learning she had scarcely an equal amongst the women of England, and not a superior. Her husband was born in 1616, was the son of a baronet and received his education at Cambridge. He loved God, prayer, meditation and the study of the Scriptures, and having ample property, settled in quiet retirement after his marriage. But when the civil war broke out he threw himself into the cause of the people with great patriotism, and after the death of Charles became famous as the governor of

Nottingham and its castle. There he exerted immense influence for English liberty, and became a great favorite with his countrymen. He and his wife were first Presbyterians, and she tells the interesting story of their conversion to Baptist principles. Her own mind became deeply interested in the question of infant baptism, from the fact that she looked for the birth of a babe; and having examined the Scriptures with her husband, doubts arose in their minds on that subject.

After the birth of their child they consulted a number of Presbyterian divines at their home, but concluded that the word of God gave no warrant for its baptism. This laid them open to much calumny and blame, but they stood firmly in their integrity. Lucy was the daughter of Sir Allen Apsley, governor of the Tower, while her husband's mother was a Byron, of which family the great poet came; and their influence for patriotism, consecration to Christ and family virtue, was their great shield against molestation.

As Colonel Hutchinson had been one of the judges who condemned Charles to death, he was imprisoned first in the Tower and then in Sandown Castle, where he died in Christian triumph in 1644. He was eloquent, fearless and powerful in the House of Commons, and so firm a defender of religious liberty, that Fox, the founder of the Friends, found him his chief protector when a prisoner at Nottingham.

WILLIAM KIFFIN.

We have already seen that John Spilsbury was a man of high repute in the Baptist ministry in those days, yet not much more than this has come down to us concerning him. His name, however, is mentioned for the last time as standing side by side with that of Kiffin in the Declaration against Venner's Rebellion, 1662. His colleagues now best known to us are Kiffin and Knollys.

WILLIAM KIFFIN was born in 1616, and lost both his parents in the Plague when but nine years old. William but just escaped death, having nine plague-boils on his body. At thirteen he became an apprentice to John Lilburn, the noted brewer, but at fifteen he left his master, and wandering about the streets of London in a melancholy manner, he passed with the crowd into St. Antholius's Church, where Mr. Foxley preached on the Fifth Commandment. He thought the preacher knew his case, so exactly did he describe his duty to his master, and he quietly returned home. After that, he heard Norton, the Puritan, preach from 'There is no peace to the wicked,' and was deeply stirred, but on hearing Davenport, in Coleman Street, from 'The blood of Jesus Christ his Son cleanseth us from all sin,' he says: 'I found my fears to vanish, and my heart filled with love to Jesus.' After the manner of Bunyan he alternated for months between hope and fear, temptation and triumph, until he joined the Church of which Lathrop was pastor. After enduring much persecution for holding religious meetings in Southwark, and being imprisoned, in 1643, he went to Holland for a time, and made a considerable sum of money in business before he returned. He went to Holland again in 1645, and returned worth several thousand pounds, on which he entered the shipping business, meanwhile preaching the Gospel without charge.

The government made him an assessor of taxes for Middlesex, and he reached great influence in the community, although he had become a Baptist in 1638. When the controversy arose in Spilsbury's Church on the propriety of admitting unimmersed persons to preach, he established the Devonshire Square Church, 1640, and became its pastor. Soon after he was arrested and committed to prison. On a Sunday afternoon between sixty and seventy Baptists were met for worship, when six of them were arrested, brought before Parliament, admonished and discharged, and on the next Sunday four peers attended their worship, one of them probably being Lord Brooke, who favored dissenters. It is quite likely that this led Featley to challenge them to a disputation before Sir John Lenthal, the justice who brought them before the lords, and who called Featley's book, 'Kiffin's Coffin.' Featley and Edwards, the author of 'Gangræna,' assailed him bitterly. Kiffin's wealth exposed him to wanton persecution, in which his foes expected fines or bribes. In 1655 he was brought before the lord mayor at Guildhall, charged with preaching 'that the baptism of infants is unlawful,' and Monk afterward annoyed him greatly, by sending him to the guard at St. Paul's. His life was long, for he served the Devonshire Square Church over half a century; which spread through the reign of five monarchs, James I., the two Charles, James II. and William III., besides the Protectorate of the two Cromwells. And it was full of trouble, for he was charged again and again with almost every conceivable plot against the government. Yet nothing was ever proved against him; and in 1701, he died at the age of 86, also full of honors. In sagacity, manners, godliness, labors and wisdom, he ranked as the leader of his denomination. Thurlow, Strype, Burnet and many others have honored his name with a high place in history, and Macaulay says of him: 'Great as was the authority of Bunyan with the Baptists, William Kiffin's was greater still.' The same may be said to-day of his molding influence upon American Baptists more than a century and two thirds after his death. Kiffin was the great champion of the Baptists in his day. Robert Pool, one of the sharpest Presbyterian controversialists of that period, made a savage attack upon the Baptists, and Kiffin came to their rescue in his reply, London, 1645. Pool demanded:

By what Scripture warrant Baptists separated from congregations where the Word and Sacraments were truly dispensed. Kiffin denied that they were so dispensed in the congregations from which they separated, otherwise they would be guilty of schism; then demanded: 'What Gospel institution have you for the baptizing of children, which was a pure invention of men and not an institution of Jesus Christ? When you have dispensed the word and power of Christ for the cutting off all drunkards, fornicators, covetous, swearers, liars, and all abominable and filthy persons, and stand together in the faith, a pure lump of believers, gathered and united according to the institution of Christ; we, I hope, shall join with you in the same congregation and fellowship, and nothing shall separate us but death.' Pool asked on what Scripture authority they separated from other *Reformers* and framed new congregations of their own? Kiffin replied: That Baptist churches existed before episcopacy, but Pool had withdrawn from Reformed Episcopacy. 'Whereas you tell us of a great work of reformation, we entreat you to show us wherein the greatness of it doth consist, for as yet we see no greatness unless it be in the vast expense of money and time. For what great thing is it to change Episcopacy into Presbytery, and a Book of Common Prayer into a Directory, and to exalt men from livings of £100 a year to places of £400 per annum? But where have they yet framed their State Church according to the pattern of Christ and his Apostles?' And when Pool pressed his point: On what Scripture ground the Baptists vindicated themselves from the sin of schism in defection from the Reformed Churches? Kiffin gave this home-thrust: The Presbyterians held that the baptism and ordination of Rome were valid, and that she was right in exacting tithes and state-pay, and yet held themselves guiltless of schism in leaving Rome. But when they shall return, 'as dutiful sons to their mother, we will return to you or hold ourselves bound to show just grounds to the contrary.'

At this time the Baptists of England generally distinguished themselves from the Pedobaptists as those of '*the baptized way*,' because they held that sprinkled folk were not baptized at all. But those of this '*way*' divided on the subject of communion, part of them being open communion, led by Bunyan, Jessey and others, while the great majority of them were strict in their communion. Kiffin led this wing of 'the baptized way,' being followed by Denny, Thomas Paul, Henry D'Anvers and others. The controversy was hot, and in his 'Right to Church Communion,' Kiffin says in reply to Bunyan:

'If unbaptized persons may be admitted to all church privileges, does not such a practice plainly suppose that it [baptism] is unnecessary? For to what purpose is it to be baptized, may one reason with himself, if he may enjoy all church privileges without it? The Baptists, if once such a belief prevails, would be easily tempted to lay aside that reproached practice, which envious men have unjustly derided and aspersed, of being *dipt*, that is, baptized, and challenge their church communion by virtue of their faith only. And such as baptized infants would be satisfied to discontinue the practice when once they are persuaded that their children may be regular church members without it, for if it be superfluous. discreet and thrifty people would willingly be rid of the trouble of christening-feasts, as they call them, and all the appurtenances thereto belonging. So that in a short time we should have neither old nor young baptized, and by consequence, be in a like condition to lose one of the sacraments, which would easily make way for the loss of the other, both having an equal sanction in Scripture. And the arguments that disarmed the one would destroy the other, and consequently all ordinances, and modes of worship, and lastly religion itself.'

No morsel of reasoning in the English language has ever disposed of the essence of the Communion question so fully as this; and if his proposition had been intended as a prophecy concerning Bunyan's Church itself, it could not have been more strictly fulfilled to the letter, in that it now discards baptism entirely as necessary to the right of church fellowship.

HANSERD KNOLLYS was born in Lincolnshire, 1598, was educated at Cambridge and ordained in the Church of England by the Bishop of Peterborough. He was a thorough scholar, and published many works, amongst which were grammars of the Greek, Latin and Hebrew languages. After holding a living at Humberstone, in Leicestershire, for three years, he resigned it on account of objections affecting the principles and practices of the Established Church.

In 1638 he left England to escape persecution, and arrived in New England, becoming pastor of a Church in Dover, then known as Piscataqua, New Hampshire. He returned to England in 1641, and became a very popular preacher in the various Churches of London. But one day, preaching in Bow Church, Cheapside, he spoke against infant baptism, which gave such offense that he was thrown into prison. On his release he went into Suffolk, where he was mobbed as an 'Anabaptist,' and after being stoned was sent to London on a warrant to answer to Parliament. Last of all he established a Baptist Church, meeting in Great St. Helen's, London, where he seldom preached to less than a thousand people. There, says Wilson, he gave great offense to his Presbyterian brethren, 'and the landlord was prevailed upon to warn him out of the place.' After this he preached to large congregations in Finsbury Fields, till he was 'summoned before a committee of divines in the Queen's Court, Westminster.' He had written a letter on the intolerance of the Presbyterian divines in London, to a friend in Norwich, which found its way to London and appeared against him. Again and again he was forbidden to preach, and as often he disregarded the charge and was pursued or imprisoned. At times he fled to Wales, Holland and Germany, to escape his foes. But his life was spared to the ripe age of ninety-three, and he preached the word in all parts of the kingdom; on Sundays generally delivering three or four sermons, and as many during the week, for a period of forty years. When in prison he had to content himself with one a day. Because of his great meekness and learning he won many distinguished persons to Baptist views. Amongst these was Dr. De Veil, a foreign divine, of the Gallican Church, and professor of divinity in the University of Anjou. On abjuring Rome he fled to Holland first and then to London, where he became intimate with Bishops Stillingfleet, Compton Lloyd, Tillotson, Sharp and Patrick. While passing his Minor Prophets, Solomon's Song, Matthew and Mark, through the press, he found some Baptist writings in the library of Compton, the Bishop of London, the examination of which led him to seek the counsel of Knollys, and he united with the Baptists, to the great shock of the bishops, all except Tillotson, who had been brought up a Baptist himself and knew how to value men of convictions. Knollys also immersed that great Oriental scholar, Henry Jessey, who spent his life upon a new translation of the Bible, a translation which, though not completed, was of great value to other scholars.

Those mentioned above were all Calvinistic Baptists, who were in a minority in and about London, but the General Baptists had men of equal piety, learning, and force of character amongst them. One of these was John Tombes, educated at Oxford, where he became a lecturer at the age of twenty-one. Leaving the university, he became famous as a Puritan preacher; and being satisfied at Oxford that infant baptism was an invention of men, his convictions were deepened at Bristol. In 1643 he went to London to consult the most famous of the Presbyterian divines assembled there; they rehearsed to him their stock arguments, and rejecting them as hollow, he was baptized upon a confession of Christ and became a Baptist pastor at Bewdly, near Kidderminster. He had severe controversies with Baxter and others on Baptist positions, and was pronounced by Baxter 'the most learned writer against infant baptism.' He wrote also more than a score of volumes on other subjects. Although a Baptist, such was his scholarship and intellectual power that in 1653 Parliament appointed him one of the 'triers,' or commissioners, to examine and approve those who were to exercise the public ministry in the national Church. After the Restoration he left the ministry and conformed to the Church as a lay member, claiming the right to do so without altering his opinions, and that after he had kept poor Baxter's hands so full for many years.

HENRY DENNE was educated at Cambridge, and became a minister in the Established Church, about the year 1630. He was a stout Puritan, but his convictions led him to unite with the Baptists, and he was immersed into the fellowship of the Bell Alley Church, London, by Mr. Lamb, in 1643, and entered the Baptist ministry at once. He attained great fame as a disputant and as a 'very affectionate' preacher. He not only met Dr. Gunning in debate, but answered Featley's ridiculous book. Persecution followed him everywhere, and he suffered much for Christ, but planted many Churches, chiefly in the eastern counties. He was heroic in following his convictions of duty wherever they led him, and withal he entered Cromwell's army in obedience to the demands of his patriotism. There he served as a 'cornet,' or cavalry officer, meanwhile preaching to the soldiers; but mutinied with the twelve regiments in Oxfordshire, who demanded a free government, after the death of Charles. Some of his companions were punished with death, but he was pardoned. He wept bitterly when his life was spared, and afterward gave a history of the whole transaction. His death soon followed the Restoration and his memory was greatly honored.

HENRY JESSEY was a famous Baptist of those times. He was a Yorkshireman, educated at Cambridge and ordained in the Established Church in 1627. He refused to conform to all the Romish notions which Laud set up as the standard of clerical orthodoxy. In 1637 he became pastor of the Independent Church which Henry Jacob had formed in 1616. From time to time members of this Church adopted Baptist views and separated from it, as we have seen in the cases of Spilsbury and Kiffin. These events turned his attention to the subject of infant baptism, which, after consultation with many leading Pedobaptist divines, he concluded was unscriptural, and in 1645 he was immersed by Knollys. He differed with the Confession of the Eight Churches on the question of communion, and published the first work known in England in favor of open communion. He was endowed with noble abilities and enriched with high Christian graces. After the Restoration he endured great persecution with holy fortitude, and died in prison in 1663. A letter of his informs us that one of the London Churches, meeting in Great Allhallows, received two hundred members by baptism between the years 1650-53; a fact which illustrates the rapid increase of Baptists not only in London and Kent, but also in the middle and northern counties.

HENRY JESSEY.

The Fifth Monarchy men waxed bold and numerous during the latter years of the Commonwealth. It was but natural that the somber and fiery religious spirit of those times should betray ill-balanced intellects into fanaticism. New sects sprang up in a day and disappeard as quickly, and amongst them the Fifth Monarchy men. They were Premillenarians, with this modification of the chiliastic views which have been held by some in various ages, namely: they believed that Christ was about to come and begin his millennial reign at once, and that they were divinely commissioned to set up his kingdom on earth. A few of them were disposed to effect this revolution by the sword, but the greater part favored peaceful measures. A meeting was called in London for debate concerning 'the laws, subjects, extent, rise, time, place, offices and officers of the Fifth Monarchy;' but probably the authorities suppressed it as mischievous, for it does not appear that it was held. The proposal to make it 'public' and to hear 'debate' indicate the pacific ideas of the leaders, and General Harrison was reported to be in sympathy with the movement, with a few other Baptists. But the Calvinistic Baptists were prompt to protest against the measure; they, with their brethren, the General Baptists, believing that the Prince of Peace will establish his kingdom without the sword. Just as the Protector's life was drawing to a close these misguided men chose Thomas Venner as their leader. He was a wine-cooper, and created an insurrection. He became nearly insane at the thought of monarchy restored in Charles II., and determined to destroy royalty as opposed to Christ. He rallied followers and armed them, adopted a banner on which was the lion of the tribe of Judah, with the motto, 'Who shall rouse him up?' and then proclaimed Jesus as King. The military were called out, and in a fight these men were slain or taken prisoners; Venner and fourteen others being hanged and quartered for treason. The fact that Venner and fifty men issued out of the Baptist meeting-house in Coleman Street has associated this mad proceeding with the General Baptists as a people, but very unjustly. Venner was not a Baptist; on the contrary, he threatened them that if he succeeded he would show them whether infant baptism were in the Bible, possibly as they had found it there so often, by the light of fagots. Mr. Lamb, the pastor of the Coleman Street Church, at once united with the London Baptists in issuing a strong appeal to the world, showing that they were bound in conscience to render to Cæsar his right, and had no sympathy with Venner's doings. This is clear enough from the fact that only fifty men issued out of the meeting-house with Venner, and yet Lamb's Church was 'by far the largest' Baptist Church in London. The British public believed the disclaimer of the Baptists, but not so the perfidious monarch; urged by his minister, Edward Hyde, Lord Clarendon, who hated the Baptists for their espousal of the Parliamentary cause, he made this insignificant piece of rant the pretext for a series of abuses upon the Independents, Quakers and Baptists, which will disgrace his name for ever. While some few Baptists believed in the doctrine of Christ's millennial reign, there is no satisfactory evidence that one of the fifty men were of their number, or that a single Baptist took part in the plot. Harrison was committed to the Tower for supposed complicity with it, but Carlyle, who studied this period with great thoroughness, gives it as his opinion that 'Harrison (was) hardly connected with the thing except as a well-wisher.' Froude sees the matter in much the same light, for he says: 'With the Fifth Monarchy men abroad, every chapel, except those of the Baptists, would have been a magazine of explosives. The Baptists and Quakers might have been trusted to discourage violence, but it was impossible to distinguish among the various sects.'[6]

CHAPTER IV.

BRITISH BAPTISTS.—JOHN BUNYAN.

WE must now look at the Baptists after the Restoration, the most noted of whom is JOHN BUNYAN. He was born at Elstow, near Bedford, in 1628, the famous year in which Charles I. was forced to yield the Petition of Right.

JOHN BUNYAN.

His education was next to nothing, yet he was favored above the boys of his village, for he attended the grammar school founded by Sir William Harper at Bedford; how long is not known, but at the best his educational attainments were quite scanty. Nature had given him a warm, light, frolicsome heart, which held him ready for any sort of glee and mischief, and under reversed circumstances subjected him not only to the pensive, but the desponding. He early feared God and longed to love him, but his giddiness and love of fun drew him into sin, until he became addicted to wrong-doing, principally lying and swearing. Because his father and himself were tinkers, and Gipsies in England have been tinkers from time immemorial, he was long supposed to be of this alien blood. But the records of his family are now traceable to about A. D. 1200, and the name itself, as then known, Buignon, indicates that the family was of Norman origin. This great descendant of that house was a man of intense feeling on all subjects. The religion of his times was of the most earnest nature, emotional, deep, almost fanatical, and when Bunyan's heart began to yearn after the Lord Jesus, his whole nature was inflamed. If we should take his own version of his case literally, he would compel us to believe that he was a sad scamp in youth and a desperate villain in early manhood. He tells us, however, that he was never drunk nor unchaste, and certainly he was never a thief nor a highwayman. He broke the Sabbath, loved dancing, ball-playing, bell-ringing and rough sports generally, and for these, with lying and profanity, his passionate self-accusings threw him into a deep and terrible sense of guilt. His agonies and conflicts continued for months; he dreamed frightful dreams and saw alarming day visions, heard warning voices and read his doom written in letters of fire. Meanwhile, he was a soldier in the civil war, and at its close married a poor, but godly, orphan girl. Froude says that his marriage speaks much for his character, for 'had he been a dissolute, idle scamp, it is unlikely that a respectable woman would have become his wife when he was a mere boy.' At any rate, his soul-conflict not only continued, but deepened, until his sufferings became unbearable, and he concluded that he was too wicked to be saved and must be lost. One day, when walking alone in the country, a flood of light broke upon his mind with these words: 'He hath made peace through the blood of his cross;' when, he says: 'I saw that the justice of God and my sinful soul could embrace and kiss each other. I was ready to swoon, not with grief and trouble, but with solid joy and peace.' Soon after this, 1653, Mr. Gifford immersed him in the river Ouse, when he became a member of the Baptist Church at Bedford, as we shall see more fully in the next chapters; and in 1655 he entered the ministry of the Gospel.

Lord Macaulay speaks thus: 'The history of Bunyan is the history of a most excitable mind in an age of excitement.' While this consideration does not throw light upon the source and sweep of Bunyan's genius, it may and does suggest a weighty reason why it took the hue and channel that it selected for its expression, both in his personal history and in the sixty works of his pen. The sixty years of his natural life ran through a long list of the most remarkable events in English annals. In his day the High Commission and the Star Chamber brought before his mind the most vital question of human rights. This Court was empowered on mere suspicion to administer an oath, by which the prisoner was bound to reveal his inward thoughts, opinions and convictions, and thus accuse himself on pain of death. Every day filled Bunyan's ears with some new, romantic and blood-stirring event. He held his breath and turned pale when he heard that Charles lost not only his crown but his head as a traitor, when Cromwell drew the sword for British liberties and progress, when Cavaliers and Roundheads flew in every direction, when the Commonwealth was nourished with the blood of his brethren, and when Naseby, Edgewood and Marston Moor decreed, that no irresponsible tyrant should ever mount the throne again. He was familiar with the mad plots of Oates, Dangerfield and Venner, with the Conventicle Act, the ejection of two thousand men of God from their pulpits in a day, the faithlessness of the second Charles, the hypocrisies of James, the butcheries of Claverhouse, the infamous mockery of justice in Jeffreys, and the fall of the perfidious Stuarts. The smoke of burning martyrs filled the air over his head, and he saw the blows for freedom which were struck by Hampden and Pym, Sidney and Russell. Howard, the great philanthropist, a hundred years afterward, walked the same streets and country roads that Bunyan trod, and, it is said, caught his spirit of prison reform largely from the 'Den' in which Bunyan had lain. The great singers of his day were Herbert and Milton, Dryden and Shakespeare. And the mighty preachers were Howe and Henry, Charnock and Owen, Tillotson and South, Sherlock and Stillingfleet. Bunyan's observation was keen and extensive; he lived in the very heart of England, was an actor in some of its most exciting scenes, and it is impossible but that the spirit of the times moved him at every step. In his day, English literature had become thoroughly imbued with all the elements of poetry and fiction; nay, even of romance. These had come down through high Italian authorship. Not only had the colloquial English descended through Wyckliff, and its higher literature through Chaucer, but they had been largely blended in the Bible, with which Bunyan was most familiar; so that simple, idiomatic Saxon English was prepared to his hand; being full of image and awe, of wonder and grandeur, which he could express to the popular mind in a very racy style. Unconsciously he felt the force of his mother-tongue; it stimulated his genius, became the groundwork of his thought and the model of his utterance; a choice which places him side by side with Shakespeare and the English Bible, as one of the great conservators of our powerful language.

In a burst of unreasoning loyalty the English people, in 1660, placed Charles II. on the throne, without exacting proper guarantees for that liberty which they had bought with their own blood. He had given his word on honor to protect all his subjects in their religious freedom; and then, like a true Stuart, he sold that honor to his lust of power. Hardly was he seated on the throne when Venner's petty insurrection furnished a pretext for vengeance upon all his opponents, and especially those in the dissenting sects, no matter how much they proved their loyalty. Amongst the first victims of his tyranny we find Bunyan, charged with 'devilishly' and 'perniciously' abstaining from going to church, 'as a common upholder of meetings contrary to the laws of the king,' and with 'teaching men to worship contrary to law.' He was sentenced to Bedford jail for three months, and at the end of that time to be transported if he refused to conform. But his judges kept him in prison for six years: and when released he instantly began to preach again, whereupon he was imprisoned for another six years. Being released still again, he began to preach at once, and was arrested for the third time, but was detained only a few months. His judges were harsh with him, but his real oppressors for these twelve weary years were the king and Parliament, who made it a crime for any one to preach but a priest of the Church of England. It was long supposed that he was imprisoned mostly in the town jail of Bedford, on the bridge over the river Ouse, but it is now clear that his long imprisonment was in the county jail, where his anonymous biographer of 1700 says, that he heard him preach to sixty dissenters and three ministers. There is good ground for believing, however, that he passed a considerable period in the jail on the bridge, and that he wrote his 'Pilgrim's Progress' there.

While we are obliged to reprehend the base injustice which kept this grand preacher pining in a prison, however leniently treated, the fact is forced upon us, that the wrath of man was made to praise God; for had not his zealous servant been compelled to this solitude, we should not have had that masterpiece of literature. His 'Holy War' and other productions would have brought down to us a literary name for him of no mean order, but his 'Pilgrim' is a book for all people and all time. Bunyan's great power is in allegory and this form of it is unique, because its facts and dress are not fantastic, but are inherent in man's common sense and moral nature. His 'Pilgrim' is full of truth—this he drew from the Bible; of

THE PRISON ON BEDFORD BRIDGE.

history, which he took from Foxe's 'Book of Martyrs;' of terse English, which he learned from Spenser and Chaucer; of human nature, which he borrowed from himself and his circumstances; of hallowed conviction, which he caught from the Holy Spirit; and of uncrippled boldness, which was inspired by his love of soul-liberty. In earlier times some treated this great book with sneer and scorn, but in later days the first critics have vied with each other to exhaust upon it the language of eulogy. Dr. Johnson, Coleridge, Arnold, Macaulay and Froude have pronounced it equally fit for the plowman and the philosopher, the peer and the peasant; and the Queen of England thinks 'Christian,' its great character, a pattern for her grandchildren to copy in the palace. The glorious truth which made the heart of Bunyan beat quicker under the tinker's doublet has since given 'heart's-ease' to many a throbbing bosom which heaves under the purple. And the humbler walks of life, from old age to childhood, have made it next to the Bible, the story of their lives. In all souls it has created visions, interpreted dreams, and awakened 'the joy that made me write.' The eight editions through which it passed in thirty years gave but small promise of the progress of its pilgrimage since. No book has been rendered into so many languages, except the word of God itself. To many who are now 'high in bliss upon the hills of God,' it first set 'the joy-bells ringing in the city of habitation.' The pauper and beggar of London have read it in thoroughfares and squares, and threaded their way by its guidance through Vanity Fair. The Italian has crouched beneath the shade of the Vatican, and trembled to look up lest he should see Giant Pope. The dusky Burman has taken it into the deep jungle, to show him stepping-stones through the Slough of Despond. The darker African has stolen with it into a by-path of the wild woods, and, under the palm-tree, has dreamed of the white man's heaven. The son of Abraham and the daughter of Jerusalem have read its pages to the sigh of the wind amongst the olives and the ripple of Kedron; and the Hindoo, with Bunyan in his hand, has resolved on courage when he crossed the 'deep river;' for angels, such as do not wait upon the banks of his sacred Ganges, beckon him over.

No wonder that when Mr. Brown, the minister of Bunyan's meeting, lately visited Scotland, a worthy Highlander was startled when introduced to him as 'Bunyan's successor.' Starting back and measuring him from head to foot, he exclaimed: 'Eh, mon! but ye'll ha hard work to fill *his shoon!*' Dean Stanley says: 'When in early life I lighted on the passage where the Pilgrim is taken into the House Beautiful to see " the pedigree of the Ancient of Days, and the varieties and histories of that place, both ancient and modern," I determined that if ever the time should arrive when I should become a professor of ecclesiastical history, these should become the opening words in which I would describe the treasures of that magnificent store-house. Accordingly, when, many years after, it so fell out, I could find no better mode of beginning my course at Oxford than by redeeming that early pledge; and when the course came to an end, and I wished to draw a picture of the prospects still reserved for the future of Christendom, I found again that the best words I could supply were those in which, on leaving the Beautiful House, Christian was shown in the distance the view of the Delectable Mountains, " which they said, would add to his comfort because they were nearer to the desired haven." ' This was a worthy and heart-felt tribute from Westminster to the dreaming tinker whose effigy now adorns the House of Commons, side by side with those of orators, heroes and statesmen in honor of the man, who, though he 'devilishly' abstained from attending the church 'contrary to the laws of the king,' has preached in all pulpits and palaces ever since.

After Bunyan's final release in 1672, he became pastor of the Church at Bedford, and so threw his life into Gospel labor, that his fame as a preacher increased until he was, perhaps, the most famous minister of his day. The few sermons which have come down to us, show that he spoke as he wrote. As in his Pilgrim he embodies more of the Bible than does Milton in his Paradise Lost, so in his sermons we find more true human nature than in Shakespeare. His sentences burn with sacred touches of divine experience and move us with sympathy, so that they must have melted his hearers to tears. They also abound in personification and figure, touched by a little quiet but keen satire, and are rich in reality, tenderness and life. So great was his success as a preacher, that the largest buildings to which he had access in London would not contain the multitudes who flocked to hear him. One of his early biographers says: 'I have seen about twelve hundred at a morning lecture, by seven o'clock, on a working day, in the dark winter time.

ZOAR STREET CHAPEL, SOUTHWARK.

I have computed about three thousand that came to hear him one Lord's-day at the town's end meeting-house, so that half were fain to go back again for want of room, and then himself was fain, at a back door, to be pulled almost over people to get up stairs to his pulpit.' John Owen heard him preach, probably at Zoar Chapel, and when King Charles expressed wonder that a man of his learning could bear to listen to the 'prate' of a tinker, he answered, that he would gladly give all his learning for this tinker's power. In the doctrinal controversies of the times, he gave and took many a hard blow, but his writings leave slight traces of personal bitterness toward his opponents. Indeed, hard feeling seems to have been a stranger both in him and his house. His wife was gentle to a proverb. When he was in prison she went to London to pray for his release, and induced a peer of the realm to present a petition to the House of Lords in his behalf; so the judges were directed to look into the matter afresh. She, therefore, appeared before Sir

Matthew Hale, Chester and Twisden. With all the simplicity of a woman's love she told her artless story. She said that her husband 'was a peaceable person,' and wished to support his family. They had four helpless children, one of them blind, and while he was in prison they must live on charity. Hale treated her kindly, Twisden harshly, and demanded whether he would leave off preaching if released. In child-like honesty she replied, that 'he dare not leave off preaching so long as he could speak.' Her request was denied and she left the Court in tears, not so much, she said, 'because they were so hard-hearted against me and my husband, but to think what a sad account such poor creatures would have to give at the coming of the Lord.' Jesus wept because Jerusalem stoned the prophets, and Bunyan's wife was much like him. But, this giant in genius was just as tender-hearted as his wife. Where do we find such pathos in any passage as this, which he wrote in prison:

'The parting with my wife and poor children hath often been to me in this place as the pulling off my flesh from my bones; and that not only because I am too, too fond of those great mercies, but also because I should have often brought to my mind the hardships, miseries and wants my poor family was like to meet with should I be taken from them; especially my poor blind child, who lay nearer my heart than all I had besides. Poor child, thought I, what sorrow art thou like to have for thy portion in this world! Thou must be beaten, suffer hunger, cold, nakedness and a thousand calamities, though I cannot now endure the wind should blow on thee. But yet, thought I, I must venture all with God, though it goeth to the quick to leave you. I was as a man who was pulling down his house upon the head of his wife and children. Yet, thought I, I must do it, I must do it.'

So loving was Bunyan's disposition, that he kept the heart of the jailer soft all the time. He not only allowed him to visit his church frequently, unattended, and to preach the Gospel, too; but his blind Mary constantly visited him, with such little gifts as she could gather for his solace. She had great concern for him, lest he sorrowed beyond all hope, and often when parting with him, would put her delicate fingers to his eyes and cheeks, to feel if the tears flowed that she might kiss them away. His blind babe died and left him in prison; with O, how many fatherly benedictions upon her sweet memory. It was meet that little, blind Mary Bunyan should enter the Celestial Gate before the hero of the 'DEN,' a true 'shining one' to watch and wait for his coming. Nor did she wait long. In 1688 he went to London to reconcile an alienated father and son, and succeeded. But on the journey a violent storm overtook him, and he contracted a fatal illness which after ten days took him to Jesus, the King in his beauty, and to blind Mary, when he first saw her sweet eyes blaze with light. She raised not a hand to his cheek then, as was her old wont in Bedford, for God had wiped away all tears from his eyes; and since then the old and young pilgrim have dwelt together in the golden city.

Bunyan died just as the day dawned on England when the second great Revolution was to make her a free nation, in which Baptists could breathe freely. Mr. Froude couples him thus with them, in his biography of Bunyan: 'In the language of the time, he became convinced of sin and joined the Baptists, the most thoroughgoing and consistent of all the Protestant sects. If the sacrament of baptism is not a magical form, but is a personal act in which the baptized person devotes himself to Christ's service, to baptize children at any age when they cannot understand what they are doing may seem irrational and even impious.'[1] Bunyan's ashes rest in Bunhill Fields, marked by a neat tomb, bearing simply his name. But in 1874 the Duke of Bedford, a descendant of Lord William Russell, the martyr to liberty, presented a most costly and beautiful statue to that city, in Bunyan's memory. The 10th of June in that year was one of the greatest days that Bedford ever knew. The corporation, with many thousands of distinguished persons from all parts of the kingdom, assembled on St. Peter's green, to unveil this work of art. This was done by Lady Augusta Stanley, sister of the Earl of Elgin and wife of the Dean of Westminster. Although Bunyan's back is still turned toward St. Peter's Church, the bells rang a merry peal, and immense crowds assembled in the Corn Exchange and on the green, to listen to addresses from the Mayor, Dean Stanley, Earl Cowper and many others of great note; and a banquet at the Swan Hotel crowned the day. As was fitting, 4,000 Sunday-school children of Bedford and Elstow consumed a ton and a quarter of cake and six hundred gallons of tea, in honor of the occasion; and with bands of music made a pilgrimage to Elstow, the birthplace of their enchanting dreamer; and the press of the United Kingdom that day called Bunyan blessed. The statue is of bronze, cast of cannon and bells brought from China, weighing two and a half tons. The figure of Bunyan is taken from a painting by Sadler, and is ten feet high. The idea which Boehm, the sculptor, has striven to give, is expressed in an inscription on the pedestal, and is taken from the picture of 'a very grave person,' which Bunyan saw hung in the Interpreter's house:

BUNYAN'S TOMB.

> 'It had eyes uplifted to heaven;
> The best of books in his hand;
> The law of truth was written
> Upon his lips. . . .
> It stood as if it pleaded
> With men.'

A broken fetter at his feet represents his long imprisonment, and on a tablet beneath is a *fac-simile* of his autograph in his will, 'John Bunyan.' Three sides of the pedestal contain scenes from ' Pilgrim's Progress,' in bold relief: Evangelist pointing Christian to the wicket gate; Christian's fight with Apollyon; Pilgrim released from his load and the three shining ones pointing him to the Celestial

City. The monument stands where four roads meet, but, like its original, it only faces one way and is full of repose, the ideal of that lofty spirituality, which claims

BUNYAN'S MONUMENT.

the right to look to heaven without a license from the established Church. Bunyan's figure is thus described: 'He was tall of stature, strong-browed, with sparkling eyes, wearing his hair on his upper lip after the old British fashion; his hair reddish, but in his latter days sprinkled with gray; his nose well cut, his mouth moderately large, his forehead something high, and his habit always plain and modest.'

That Bunyan was an open communion Baptist has never been seriously doubted until the recent publication of his life, by Rev. John Brown, A.M., minister of the Bunyan meeting at Bedford. This work throws new light on many points in his history and is ably written, but because of certain parish records which it publishes, and which seem to imply that Bunyan's children were christened, after he had united with the Bedford Church, it is needful to examine that subject candidly and carefully. Whether Mr. Brown intended to convey this impression or not, his book is well adapted to place Bunyan's practice in direct contradiction with many of his own utterances, and to render his conduct irreconcilable with the universal testimony of history as to his union with the Baptists. Yet Mr. Brown carefully avoids saying that he was not a Baptist. He quotes Bunyan's words: 'Do not have too much company with some Anabaptists, *though I go under that name myself*,' and then adds: 'This is plain enough. The only difficulty is how to reconcile his practice with his declaration; for he seems to have had three of his children baptized at church in their infancy, as we gather from the register of the parishes of Elstow and St. Cuthbert's.'

These words cannot be misunderstood, and their sense is re-affirmed thus: 'There can be little doubt, therefore, that the year after John Bunyan joined the Bedford brotherhood his second daughter, like his first, was baptized at Elstow Church. The third case, that of his son Joseph, is the most remarkable of all, for this child, according to the register, was baptized at St. Cuthbert's Church after Bunyan's twelve years' imprisonment for conscience' sake, and during the time he was conducting the c ⌄roversy on open communion with D'Anvers and Paul. The fact is curious, and an only be accounted for on the supposition that upon the question of baptism he had no very strong feeling any way.'[2]

On this question and others growing out of it, the writer opened a respectful correspondence with Mr. Brown, to which he responded in that manner and spirit which always prompt the high-minded investigator. Under date of May 1st, 1886, Mr. Brown writes concerning Bunyan's own baptism: 'There is no evidence that Bunyan was not immersed. Looking at what he says of himself (*vide* my 'Life of Bunyan,' p. 238, line 6), I should say he was immersed though there is no record of the fact.' These quotations are sufficient to show that Mr. Brown is not to be considered as saying that Bunyan was not a Baptist, but simply that he could not reconcile his position as a Baptist with the christening of his children. Before examining these records it may be a favor to the American reader, who is not familiar with the vicinity of Bedford in England, to say, that Elstow, Bunyan's birthplace, is a village about a mile and a half from Bedford, and that he continued to reside there probably till about A. D. 1655–56, when he removed to Bedford. At that time this town numbered less than 2,000 inhabitants, and for ecclesiastical purposes, was then and is now divided into four parishes, known respectively as St. John's, St. Peter's, St. Paul's and St. Cuthbert's. The first record to be examined is that of Elstow, which reads thus:

Elstow: 'Mary, the daughter of John Bonion, baptized July 20th, 1650.' As Bunyan did not unite with Gifford's Church till 1653, three years after this record was made, it has no bearing on the question whether he was a Baptist or not. When Mary was christened, he was, as he tells us himself, leading a wicked life, having no church connection aside from a nominal one in the Church of England. It may, therefore, be dismissed with the remark, that as it leaves nothing to 'reconcile' in his practice, it needs no further consideration. The second entry was made at Elstow, the year after his union with Gifford's Church, and reads as follows: 'Elizabeth, the daughter of John Bonyon, was borne 14th day of April, 1654.' Taking all things into the account and in the order of their dates, with a full knowledge of the circumstances of the case, we shall find this record Bunyan's second public protest against infant baptism, which he pronounced an infirmity of the weak. In his controversy with his strict communion brethren, they charged him with indulging Baptists, in disobedience to the requirements of truth, when he communed with those who had never been baptized upon their faith in Christ. To this he replied: 'But what acts of disobedience do we indulge in? "In the *sin* of infant baptism?" We indulge them not, but being commanded to bear with the infirmities of the weak, suffer it; *it being in our eyes such*, but in theirs, they say, a duty, till God persuade them.'[3] It matters not at this point whether, when Bunyan went with Gifford into the river Ouse, he was immersed or not, though Mr. Brown, judging by what Bunyan writes, '*though I go under that name myself*' ('Anabaptist'), says, 'I should say he was immersed.' This much, however, is clear, that whatever was done to Bunyan in the Ouse, he did there publicly repudiate his own infant baptism. Mr. Brown tells us (page 36) that he finds John Bunyan's name 'in the list of nineteen christenings at Elstow Church in the following form: "1628. John the sonne of Thomas Bounionn, Junr. the 30th of Novemb."' But as Bunyan could not go under the name of 'Anabaptist' on that christening, it follows that when he went with Gifford into the river he deliberately repudiated the infant baptism which his father had imposed upon him in 1628, in the discharge of what he regarded as his parental 'duty,' as a member of the Church of England. It remains to be seen whether or not, a year after this repudiation, he fell into what he calls the weakness of infant baptism, and which he said was such in his eyes, by taking his own daughter to that same Church of England to christen her, in 'duty, till God persuaded' him otherwise. This, of course, would imply that he recalled his protest against his own infant baptism made a year earlier, and in turn repudiated his believer's baptism, after he had solemnly taken it upon himself as an 'Anabaptist.' This conduct would show any thing but that he had no strong feeling on the question of baptism, for with his very tender conscience he must have had terrible feelings on the subject, if he backed and filled in that way. No; this entry evinces the deepest feeling on the question of infant baptism and is his second public protest against its practice, the first being in himself by his own baptism as a believer, the second in his beloved daughter and her simple birth record.

The difference between these two entries, the baptismal record of Mary and the birth record of Elizabeth, shows that between the years 1650 and 1654 a well-defined change had taken place in their father's mind on the subject of christening. Had he chosen he could have had Elizabeth christened and her christening entered in the same form as that of Mary, but he chose not to do that; and limiting the record to her birth, it simply says that Elizabeth was '*borne*' on the 14th day of April, 1654. The following facts throw a flood of light upon this record, as they prove, that in 1645 Parliament put the recording of births into the hands of the clergy, that in 1653 this registration was taken out of their hands, and that under William and Mary it was restored to them again, and all this for the best of reasons.

1. In 1645 Parliament had banished the use of the Prayer-book in every place of worship in England and Wales, and had substituted a form of worship called the Directory. This law required all Prayer-books to be given up, and fined any who used one in any place of worship, church or chapel, £5 for the first offense, £10 for

the second, 'and for the third offense one whole year's imprisonment without bail or mainprise.' It had also enacted, that

'There shall be provided at the charge of every parish or chapelry in the realm of England and dominion of Wales, a fair register book of vellum, to be kept by the *minister* and officers of the church, and that the names of all children baptized, and of their parents and of the time of their *birth and baptizing*, shall be written and set down by the minister therein.'

This act provided for the registration of *both* births and baptisms, and was careful not to confound the two as one.[4]

2. Down to A. D. 1653, the year in which Bunyan united with Gifford's Church, Quakers, Baptists and all who rejected infant baptism, were subjected to every sort of annoyance for neglecting to go to the recording clergy as thus required, to have their children christened and a record of their birth *and* baptism made in the 'book of vellum' at the parish church, the Church of England. The same was true also of their marriages and burials.

3. Having in view their relief, not only in the matter of baptism, but also in that of marriages and burials, Cromwell's short Parliament took this whole matter out of the hands of the clergy, making marriage a purely secular act, stripping birth, marriage and burial of subjection to all ecclesiastical usages, and put the entire keeping of the parish records into secular hands for civil purposes alone. Of course, Baptists, Quakers and all other such subjects loyal to the civil power were delighted to be freed from ecclesiastical contempt in this way, and to comply with a mere civil provision, which in no way conflicted with their convictions of right; and they cheerfully complied with a law which simply required them to record the *birth* of their children as in duty to the State.

4. It is of this Act that Cobbet speaks in his 'Parliamentary History,' under date of August 25th, 1653. He writes: 'Great part of this month had been taken up in canvassing a bill concerning marriages and the registering thereof, and also of *births* and burials. This day it passed the house on this question, and was ordered to be printed and published. This extraordinary Act entirely took marriages out of the hands of the clergy, and put them into those of the Justices of the Peace.'[5]

The writer has carefully examined this Act and would copy it entire, but as it covers many folios it is too long. It is found in the

'Acts and Ordinances of Parliament, examined by the original record and printed by special order of Parliament, by Henry Hills and John Field, printers to his Highness the Lord Protector, 1658; by Henry Scobell, the clerk of Parliament.'

For some reason, the Acts of the Commonwealth are not printed with the continuous laws of the realm, but are put in this special collection by themselves, and at the risk of a little tediousness, as this book is very scarce, a brief analysis of the Act may here be given. It directs 'how marriages shall be solemnized and registered, as also a register for births and burials,' but says nothing of baptisms.

It was extended to Ireland 'from and after December 1st, 1653.' It specially provides for the election of a Registrar by popular suffrage in the parish thus:

I. 'The Inhabitants and Householders of every Parish chargeable to the relief of the poor, or the greater part of them present, shall on or before the 22d day of September, 1653, make choice of some able and honest person (such as shall be sworn and approved by one Justice of the Peace in that Parish, Division or County, and so signified under his hand in the said Register-book), to have the keeping of said book, who shall therein fully enter in writing all such Publications, Marriages, *Births* of children and Burials of all sorts of persons, and the names of every of them, and the days of the month and year of Publications, Marriages, Births and Burials. And the Register in each Parish shall attend the said Justice of the Peace to subscribe the entry of each such Marriage; and the person so selected, approved and sworn, shall be called the Parish-Register and shall continue three years in such place of Register.'

II. This Act further provides, that 'All Register-books for Marriages, Births and Burials shall be delivered into the hands of the respective Registers appointed by this Act to be kept as Records.' Thus the clergy were not only stripped of the recorder's office, but the old books of register made previous to 1653 were taken out of their custody and put into secular hands: 'Any law, statute, custom or usuage to the contrary notwithstanding,' as the Act states.

III. The use of the Prayer-book and all religious services at marriages and burials was done away with, and as the Act knew nothing of christenings, of course, the registration of births called for no provision against such services. The parties to be married were to choose whether the Register should publish their intended marriage three Sundays in the church or chapel, or in the 'market-place next to the said church or chapel, on three market-days in the three several weeks next following.' On the day of marriage, in the presence of the Justice, the man was to take the woman by the hand and distinctly pronounce the following words: 'I, A. B., do here in the presence of God, the searcher of all hearts, take thee, C. D., for my wedded wife. I do, also, in the presence of God and before these witnesses, promise to be unto thee a loving and faithful husband.' When the woman had gone through the same form, the Justice declared them husband and wife. The Act then strips the clergy of all power to marry in these sweeping words:

'From and after such consent so expressed and such declaration made, the same, as to the form of marriage, shall be good and effectual in law. *And no other marriage whatever within the Commonwealth of England, after the twenty-ninth of September, shall be held or accounted a marriage according to the laws of England.*'

IV. The Act made a number of curious minor provisions which may be named, simply for the gratification of the reader, such as these:

The 'fee for Publications and certificates thereof 1s.; for marriages 1s.' 'From those who live upon alms nothing shall be taken.' The Justice 'in case of dumb persons may dispense with pronouncing the words; and with joining hands in case of persons that have no hands.' 'After the 29th of Sep. 1653, the age of a man to consent to marriage shall be sixteen years, and the age of the woman fourteen years.' All disputes as to the lawfulness of marriage were referred to Justices at the Quarter Sessions.

Under the well-settled rule in law, that the legislative intent can best be reached by examining all Acts on the same subject-matter and weighing them together, these Acts have been here presented, and so we cannot miss the intent of this particular Act of 1653. As the Act of 1645 had expressly put registration of births and baptisms into the hands of the clergy, and the Act of 1653 had put the registration of births into secular hands and said nothing about records for baptism or christening, taking all public registration out of clerical hands, the entry of baptisms was legally dropped from the public records, under the provisions of the last Act. That this was both the intention and practice under that law is more clearly seen in the further fact, that Acts VI and VII under William and Mary restored registration to the clergy, and made special provision for the record of christenings by those in Holy Orders.' This legislation was known as

'An Act for granting his Majesty certain rates and duties upon Marriages, Births and Burials, and upon Batchelors and Widowers, for the term of five years, for carrying on the war against France with vigor.' This Act once more made it the duty of those in Holy Orders: 'Deans, Parsons, Deacons, Vicars, Curates,' to keep 'a true and exact register in writing of all and every person or persons married, buried, *christened or born* in their respective parishes or precincts.'

These Acts taken together show how thoroughly discriminating and secularizing the Act of August 25th, 1653, was intended to be, and what a radical change it made both in the public practices and their records. Of course, it aroused the wrath of the State clergy to the hottest indignation. They treated it with every form of contempt which they could devise. When the Directory had pushed the Prayer-book out of use, many hundreds of them, some say thousands, either resigned their livings or were ejected for setting the law at defiance. It absolutely forbade them to use the Prayer-book for the burial of the dead, as well as in their churches. It enjoined that,

'When any person departed this life, let the dead body upon the day of burial be decently attended from the house to the place appointed for public burial, and then interred *without any ceremony*. . . . For that praying, reading and singing, both in going to and at the grave, have been grossly abused, and are no more beneficial to the dead and have proved hurtful to the living; therefore, let all such things be laid aside.'

Surely, this was all that the clerical flesh and blood of that day could bear. But now, to follow up that revolution with another, which eight years later not only took marriage entirely out of their hands, but denied them the right to record the births which honored those secular marriages, was unendurable to them. If any body wanted them to christen their infants, the law did not forbid their doing so, in the exercise of their religious rights. But the law would not have their christenings entered on the public records as acts of any civil interest or concern. Then, the way in which their former prerogatives were taken from them, was more exasperating still. The new Registrars were to be selected by the popular vote of their own parishioners, over whom they had so unconscionably domineered, and that without regard to the religion of either candidate or voter. Besides, his record of the marriages entered was to be purely secular and to be attested before a Justice of the Peace and not by a priest. And, worse than all, in the eyes of the priest, this Act of August 25th, 1653, left all who rejected the superstition of christening at liberty to enjoy the full rights of Englishmen by recording the 'birth' of their children, and of securing to them all the legal advantages which such a civil entry secured in property rights and courts of justice, without compromising their principles by a forced submission to infant baptism. Their children could now prove their lineage and derive all the political rights which such entry entitled them to while they lived, and when they died they could be buried decently in ground either 'consecrated' or unconsecrated without anyhow consulting the whimsical dictations of an arrogant priesthood. Such a state of things would suit Bunyan's ideas of liberty exactly.

Such a right had never been enjoyed by dissenting Englishmen before, and Cobbet well characterizes the Act as 'extraordinary.' Its passage was stubbornly resisted as a bold innovation; and he says that it held Parliament to discussion for a great part of the entire month, which 'canvassing' must have stirred the feeling of the entire realm. Especially must all Baptists and Quakers have been interested, as it took their marriages and burials out of the hands of an oppressive and offensive clergy, and left them at liberty to record the '*birth*' of their children and to stop there, as far as christening was concerned; so that they now stood before the law on an equality with their neighbors, free from all ecclesiastical proscription because they refused to have their children baptized. With this legal shield thrown over his head, we can easily understand why honest John Bunyan, who spoke so freely in his writings against infant baptism, as we shall see, felt it his duty as an English freeman to obey the law by entering the *birth* of his babe on the public records, when English law at last stepped forth sacredly to guard the rights of his conscience while discharging his duty as a citizen. Thus the entry of his child's *birth* without any entry of her christening stands to the end of time on the Elstow parish Register with the force of his public protest against the superstition of infant baptism enforced by the State. Then was Elizabeth Bunyan christened as a matter of fact? Certainly not. Mr. Brown quotes the entry in the Elstow parish Register and concedes that it certifies only to her birth. He also refers to the law of 1653 in the following words:

'It will be pointed out, perhaps, that the register notes that Elizabeth Bunyan was *born* on the 14th day of April, and says nothing about her baptism. But it must be remembered that the previous year an Act of Parliament had been passed requiring the date of birth to be inserted in the register instead of that of baptism.'

It is a matter of some surprise that the learned biographer has cited this Act in support of his theory. According to his idea, the object of Parliament in passing it was merely to change the form of words to be entered on the register. Upon analysis it is apparent that his claim must be that, although the record says *born*, she was in reality *christened* on that day, and that the fact was misstated in order that the law might be technically complied with. The improbability of this supposition is clear from its simple statement, and it, moreover, betrays an entire misconception of the purpose of the statute. It was not enacted simply to alter the verbal formulary used in the records, but to entirely secularize the department of vital statistics, and to allow marriages and births to be publicly recorded, though the clergy had not solemnized the nuptials or christened the children or buried the dead.

Mr. Brown in furtherance of his argument proceeds as follows:

'To show further that this Act of 1653 sufficiently accounts for the form of entry in 1654, it may be mentioned that in the Transcript Register from Elstow parish that year the name of Elizabeth Bunyan occurs in a list of twenty-three children, all returned under the head of "Christenings," and that the word "borne" and not "baptized" is used in every case.'

Of course, the writer, on this side of the Atlantic, not being able to inspect and compare these documents must rely on an inspection and comparison made by others. Hence he requested a gentleman of known accuracy in the employ of Her Majesty's government to examine both the original and the transcript registers. He writes July 29th, 1886:

'In the Parish Register at Elstow for April 14th, 1654, I find Elizabeth Bunyan recorded as "*borne*" without any mention of her christening. In all the entries down to the year 1662 each child is so entered. After 1662 the word "christened" is substituted and the word "borne" drops out. The Register is without headings, only the year and day of the month are entered, then the entries follow to the end of the year, when the same process is repeated. In the archives of the Archdeanery at Bedford, I find the Transcript Registers, and they give Elizabeth Bunyan, daughter of John, as "christened" April 14th, 1654. This stands along with 23 others, total 24. From that date the word "borne" does not occur again. Then as to the headings: as I said, the Elstow Register is without headings, and this order is continued in the Transcripts, which for the whole ten years are not only *without headings* but *without signatures*. I had omitted to count the number of entries at Elstow for 1653-54, and was obliged to write the vicar for the information which he kindly supplied in the enclosed letter:

'"Bedford, July 26th, 1886: Dear Sir: You ask how many were entered on the Register as "borne" during the years 1653 and 1654. In the former year only six were entered as born and in the latter twenty-four. The discrepancy between the original Register and the Transcript is curious. The Canons of 1604 ordered that copies of the Register should be sent annually to the Registry of the Diocese. I suspect this was discontinued during the Commonwealth, and that copies were not made again until after the time of the Restoration, when christenings were inserted and not births. Yours faithfully, James Copner."'

The discrepancy referred to by Mr. Copner (whose own valuable work on Bunyan is elsewhere cited in these pages) is simply that of the use of "borne" in the original and "christened" in the transcript. Otherwise it appears that the documents correspond. The investigation reduces itself to the inquiry, which shall be believed, the original register which says that Elizabeth was born on April 14th, 1654, or the transcript which states that she was christened on that day? It is to the last degree improbable that she was both born and christened on the same day, and therefore both records cannot be true. Born in her father's house on the 14th of April, even if he had wished her christened, she could not be taken to the parish church on the day of her birth. But if she was christened on the 14th of April and born at some other time, then the original entry is made a piece of confusion. It was never the custom of the English, or even of the Romish Church, to christen children on the very day of their birth, unless it was feared that the child would die immediately after coming into the world, and so its body was sprinkled to save its soul. Furthermore, it is not claimed that these transcript registers were independent records of facts outside of those contained in the originals. The transcripts were annual copies of the Parish Register sent up on parchment to the Archdeacon by the vicar or rector of the parish in compliance with the canons of 1603. They gave the names of all persons married, baptized, or buried the previous year copied from the Register, and forwarded each Easter. This was to provide for the existence of a duplicate copy in case the parish register should be lost. The transcripts, therefore, always purported to be exact copies of the originals and, in case of discrepancy, the originals would of course govern. We are thus brought to the question, which is entitled to credence: a public record kept and prepared under direction of the law of the land, with prescribed formalities by a duly elected civil officer, or the inconsistent statement contained in an extra-official document, without date or signature, which purports to be a copy of the original and is not a true copy thereof? Here again the mere statement of the proposition makes only one answer possible. It is a trite rule of the law that, for the purpose of evidence, a copy is not allowable in the presence of the original, and it is not easy to see why Mr. Brown should have brought in a professed copy with the original, especially as the original says one thing and the so-called copy another. In a letter dated May 21st, 1886, he says:

'This Transcript for 1654 is at Bedford in the Archives of the Archdeanery along with those from all the parishes of Bedfordshire. Those for the Commonweath Period were sent up for the whole ten years at once [1650–1660] after the Restoration by the vicar, Christopher Hall, and are complete.'

It is difficult to imagine any motive for the continuation of the custom of sending an annual transcript during the Commonwealth. The whole department of public records was taken out of the hands of the clergy and made secular, and they could have no reason for adding purely secular records to their canonical archives.

But with the Restoration the Church was re-established, and the civil functions of the priests as registrars restored. Then in the nature of things a new motive would arise —the desire to obliterate as far as possible all traces of the interregnum, and to have the ancient order of things go on apparently as if it had not been interrupted. This statement of Mr. Brown is fortified by the fact that these transcripts are not signed, or in any other manner formally authenticated. All that seems to have been done was to make copies of the Parish Registers, carefully substituting, however, the word 'christened' for 'born' in every case, and file them at the Archdeanery to fill the hiatus in the ecclesiastical records. The ecclesiastical motive for this substitution is apparent, but the civil record must stand unquestioned.

More than enough has been said to dismiss the entry in this transcript register from further consideration, but fortunately Mr. Brown has furnished us with a unique entry which throws additional light upon the general subject and the temper of the clergy in regard to this Act. Nothing better illustrates the peevish resentment of the priests to the Act of August, 1653, than the following note, taken from the Register of Maid's Moreton Parish, in Buckinghamshire:

'A. D. 1653. Now came in force a goodly Act made by the Usurper Cromwell's little Parliament, who ordered not the baptism, but the birth of children, to be recorded in the Parish Register. And though the baptism of some be not expressed here, yet these are to certify all whom it may concern, and that on the word of a priest, that there is no person hereafter mentioned by the then Register of the parish, but was duly and orderly baptized!'

The *animus* of the man who boldly foisted this extra-judicial note of interpretation into this Register, is evinced on its face. The legally appointed Register did not write it in 1653; it was smuggled in at a much later date, and for a purpose. It speaks of him as 'the *then*' Register of the parish, and of Cromwell as the 'Usurper,' forms of expression which the lawful Registrar of 1653 could not have used. The writer of this note understood the Act of 1653 to make a broad distinction between birth and baptism, and says that it 'ordered not the *baptism*, but the *birth* of children, to be recorded in the Parish Register,' and this distinction the interpolator of the note did not relish. Hence the record at Maid's Moreton expressed just what the Act honestly required: the record of the birth of the children and not of their baptism. He says that the baptism of 'some' was not expressed in the record. And why? Simply because the law did not allow the word baptism in the Register. But as he dared not to alter the record itself, and yet wanted to spite the memory of the 'Usurper,' he must needs bring outside testimony to corrupt the sense of the document. However, he could find no one in Maid's Moreton to serve as his witness but a priest, who was sadly disgruntled because marriage, the registration in parish records, and the right to force christening on all babes, whether their parents wanted it or not, had been taken from him. So, without giving his name or permitting his cross-examination, he is called in to give his 'word.' Contrary to the letter and spirit of the Act of 1653, a gloss must be introduced into an official register, and the 'word of a priest' must certify that at Maid's Moreton the 'Usurper' had been cheated, and that, in exact harmony with the priestly wishes of the witness, and to his great delectation these particular children had been 'duly and orderly baptized,' law or no law. This absurd note awakens the suspicion that it might possibly have been written by the 'priest' himself. Yet it serves to show with what accuracy all the provisions of the Act had been enforced, and that, for this reason, the 'priest' wanted to take off the sharp edge of the record itself.

In plain English, this 'priest' was piqued by the provisions of the Act, and intended to falsify the record, and so far as he could, in his helplessness, to nullify its effect. However, as this is not the record at Elstow, and that attempts no such shameless perversion of the law, the exact truth stands with the Elstow entry, as Bunyan intended it to stand, when it affirms that his daughter, Elizabeth, was 'borne' April 14th, 1654. John Bunyan himself is responsible for this entry, and not a 'priest.' Whoever foisted the word 'christened' into the transcript at Bedford, made at least six years afterward, might have strongly desired that she had been christened, but her father had no hand in making the copy, and, having good reasons for not christening her, simply certifies to the birth of his babe, in the form provided by the then existing law. In view of this original entry at Elstow, Bunyan may consistently ask, 'What acts of disobedience do we indulge in? "In the sin of infant baptism?"' The record that he made leaves nothing in his conduct to 'reconcile' with his professions as a Baptist, nor can he be held responsible for the substitution of a word in the professed copy which he never put into the original.

This record leaves the great writer where he put himself and where his brethren have always put him. Douglas says of the English Baptists: 'As to the ordinances of Baptism and the Lord's Supper, they confined these to persons who had made a scriptural and credible profession of their faith in Christ; and with reference to the former. they regarded it as the great line of demarkation between the Church and the world. Such were the views of Bunyan and the generality of the Baptists in former days.' [6]

General Index
to both Volumes 1 and 2
are in the back of
Volume 2.

THE BAPTIST STANDARD BEARER, INC.
A non-profit, tax-exempt corporation
committed to the Publication & Preservation
of The Baptist Heritage.

SAMPLE TITLES FOR PUBLICATIONS AVAILABLE IN OUR VARIOUS SERIES:

THE BAPTIST *COMMENTARY* SERIES
Sample of authors/works in or near republication:
John Gill - *Exposition of the Old & New Testaments (9 & 18 Vol. Sets)*
   (Volumes from the 18 vol. set can be purchased individually)

THE BAPTIST *FAITH* SERIES:
Sample of authors/works in or near republication:
Abraham Booth - *The Reign of Grace*
Abraham Booth - *Paedobaptism Examined (3 Vols.)*
John Gill - *A Complete Body of Doctrinal Divinity*

THE BAPTIST *HISTORY* SERIES:
Sample of authors/works in or near republication:
Thomas Armitage - *A History of the Baptists (2 Vols.)*
Isaac Backus - *History of the New England Baptists (2 Vols.)*
William Cathcart - *The Baptist Encyclopaedia (3 Vols.)*
J. M. Cramp - *Baptist History*

THE BAPTIST *DISTINCTIVES* SERIES:
Sample of authors/works in or near republication:
Alexander Carson - *Ecclesiastical Polity of the New Testament Churches*
E.C. Dargan - *Ecclesiology: A Study of the Churches*
J. M. Frost - *Paedobaptism: Is It From Heaven?*
R. B. C. Howell - *The Evils of Infant Baptism*

THE *DISSENT & NONCONFORMITY* SERIES:
Sample of authors/works in or near republication:
Champlin Burrage - *The Early English Dissenters (2 Vols.)*
Franklin H. Littell - *The Anabaptist View of the Church*
Albert H. Newman - *History of Anti-Paedobaptism*
Walter Wilson - *History & Antiquities of the Dissenting Churches (4 Vols.)*

For a complete list of current authors/titles, visit our internet site at
www.standardbearer.com or write us at:

he Baptist Standard Bearer, Inc.
No. 1 Iron Oaks Drive • Paris, Arkansas 72855

Telephone: (501) 963-3831   Fax: (501) 963-8083
E-mail: baptist@arkansas.net
Internet: http://www.standardbearer.com

www.ingramcontent.com/pod-product-compliance
Lightning Source LLC
Chambersburg PA
CBHW031957220426
43664CB00005B/52